MW00813264

THE ROYAL CANADIAN ARMOURED CORPS:

AN ILLUSTRATED HISTORY

**Badge of the Royal Canadian
Armoured Corps**

The Royal Canadian Armoured Corps

AN ILLUSTRATED HISTORY

John Marteinson

& Michael R. McNorgan

with

Sean Maloney

Foreword by

Desmond Morton

Maps and drawings by

Christopher Johnson

Published by

The Royal Canadian Armoured Corps Association

in cooperation with the

Canadian War Museum

to mark the 60th anniversary of the formation of the Corps

PRODUCED AND DISTRIBUTED BY ROBIN BRASS STUDIO

Produced and distributed for
The Royal Canadian Armoured Corps Association
92 – 51 Paulander Drive, Kitchener, Ontario N2M 5E5
by Robin Brass Studio Inc.
10 Blantyre Avenue, Toronto, Ontario M1N 2R4, Canada
Fax: 416-698-2120 / e-mail: rbrass@total.net / www.rbstudiobooks.com

Printed and bound in Canada by Friesens, Altona, Manitoba

Canadian Cataloguing in Publication Data

Marteinson, J. K. (John Kristjan), 1939–
    The Royal Canadian Armoured Corps : an illustrated history

Includes index
ISBN 1-896941-17-6

1. Canada. Canadian Armed Forces. Royal Canadian Armoured Corps – History.
I. McNorgan, Michael R. II. Title.

UA602.R52M37 2000   358.18'0971   C00-931980-8

Complimentary copies of this book have been distributed to Canadian libraries by

The Department of National Defence Millennium Fund

Contents

LIST OF MAPS

Foreword

This book was commissioned by the Royal Canadian Armoured Corps Association to commemorate the 60th anniversary of the formation of the Canadian Armoured Corps in August 1940. The Association is to be commended for filling a significant gap in Canadian military history, as the full story of armour in the Canadian Army has never before been told.

Marshal Ferdinand Foch, a brilliant French staff officer and ultimately the Allied generalissimo in the last year of the First World War, commended a quality in commanders he described as *coup d'oeil* – the ability to grasp the state of affairs in a single glance. It has always been the supreme talent in a cavalryman and, even more, of armoured leaders. As an arm that is characterized by speed and striking power – even while still being vulnerable – armour is the supreme weapon of opportunity, and it takes both brilliance and experience to grasp those opportunities.

A history of Canadian armour is, itself, a weapon of opportunity, at a time when the case for armour must again be argued. Does Canada really need large, lumbering vehicles that few of us have even seen, apart from the movies? Three generations have passed since the end of the Second World War, and apart from Israel and its Arab neighbours, how many real tank battles have been fought? Do Canadians really need something as brutal and costly as a Main Battle Tank? With its dual hint of smaller price and minimal harm, 'light' armour sounds more appealing to citizens, civil servants and politicians, and even to many generals. Because the future of armour in the Canadian Forces is still in question, as it has been for a generation, all Canadians need to understand the arguments. And here, set out in considerable and careful detail, is the record of Canada's experience with armour so far.

There is respectful attention to armour's roots in the cavalry, though eastern Canada, the authors remind us, was not 'cavalry country' until it had been well and truly settled. The West was different: prairie horsemen gave Canada a starring role in the South African War and two-thirds of the units in the Canadian Cavalry Brigade in the First World War, not to mention the North West Mounted Police and its descendants.

Sadly for its future soldiers, Canada missed out on tanks in the First World War except for a few units formed too late in the war to serve. The inter-war army was equipped, trained and led by officers as though the Great War was also the war to end all wars. Yet Canada became a mechanized society: for a time in the 1920s we were the world's second largest automobile manufacturer. Even the army, hidebound in old conceptions, sustained a cantankerous, insubordinate, endlessly inventive captain named Frank Worthington who literally earned his right to the title of Father of Canadian Armour and to make his nickname, 'Worthy', its private motto.

Worthington gave Canada an armoured corps for the Second World War. Perhaps an ordinary book for ordinary readers might be content to celebrate its achievements, praise the sacrificial valour of its members, and pass over the serious defects which cost lives and denied the Canadian Army some of the glory it had achieved in the earlier war. Italy and North West Europe were brutally expensive places for Canada's armoured regiments and brigades to learn basic tactical procedures, much less the tactical principles that divisional and corps commanders desperately needed to master. The authors of this book have explored history not to make us feel good but to show what happens when an army and its country ignore the consequences of sending unprepared, ill-equipped young men to war under commanders who don't even know their ignorance.

Long years of training in England between 1939 and 1943 produced skilled tank crews and competent troop and squadron commanders. Given faulty British tank doctrine, severely limited manoeuvring space and frequent rotations, promotions and dismissals, most senior commanders had neither an opportunity nor much encouragement to master their jobs. And no one worried much about battlefield teamwork, even when it had become the special job of the two independent armoured brigades. This book records that armour-infantry cooperation training for troops landing on D-Day was the subject of a single three-day exercise in mutual familiarization. The next lessons came under German fire in Italy and Normandy. As heavy losses brought inexperienced crews and commanders to the front, the lessons had to be repeated, in similar circumstances.

Senior commanders shouting "Get cracking" down the wireless net or scolding colonels of decimated regiments for being "yellow" seem as brutal as any of their First World War counterparts, but the army that trained them and the country that formed them share the responsibility. The competence to command an all-arms force is not learned overnight from promotion exam material. It comes from training and experience that Canadian commanders could not acquire in their own country or in England's cramped countryside. Many Canadians paid the price of tactical incompetence or confusion with their own lives or with terrible disabilities. In Canada's post-war forces, the survivors did their best to ensure that we would never again have to learn under fire. Their time has passed. Do we still remember?

This book is very personal for me. My father made his peacetime career with Lord Strathcona's Horse; by 1939, he was the senior captain in the Permanent Force and a natural to command his regiment's squadron when Canada decided to send a cavalry regiment overseas in 1940. My mother had to teach him the skills NDHQ gradually decided a cavalry officer needed: to ride a bicycle, a motor bike and finally to drive a car – who could afford a car on a pre-war captain's pay? In October 1941, he took command of the Fort Garry Horse at Camp Borden. The regiment became the centre of his being until at the end of August 1944, near Elbeuf on the Seine, he handed over the Garrys to an able and well-trained second-in-command. With a heavy heart, he left what, like any good CO, he believed was the best unit in the Canadian Army. Though he was shot out of several tanks and was close enough to German infantry to recall their smell of *eau de cologne*, he would have been delighted that the authors have preferred to cite able younger Garrys like Alec Christian, Bill Little and 'Benny'

Goodman, who knew pretty well what would happen to a Jew in Nazi hands, and still ventured often behind German lines. Most regiments have a similar share of a very complex story.

This history appears too late for my father and many other veterans. Chances are that many of its readers will find themselves at home only in the post-war chapters of the book, perhaps in the exciting days when Canada's troops and tanks were among the best in what may have been the best land force in the world, NATO's Northern Army Group. More probably, they have been part of the long, weary, dispiriting struggle to keep obsolete Centurions and then Leopard C1s running and to preserve tank training and the armoured spirit in a Militia that often feels like the army's despised stepson. However, we can take heart from the performance of the Canadian Coyote and the workmanlike Leopard C2 in NATO's continuing saga in Kosovo.

Whether they have direct armoured experience or a commitment to understanding the past, readers will find in this book the enduring lessons of Armour history. Whatever the movies tell you, war always involves teamwork. Yesterday in Italy, today in the Balkans, and who knows where tomorrow, no single arm or branch can deliver success; only teams can bring an enemy to yield its power. Teamwork comes from exercises and experience, not from memorizing the playbook. Armour in almost any imaginable combat setting will be part of the scene. Pleading with other countries' armies to provide part of the team because Canada cannot afford the cost is a guarantee that Canada's soldiers will lose their identity and most of their power to secure both success and survival. We should be ashamed of even the thought of it.

History isn't very respectful of mere tradition. Horses are magnificent animals but it was no tragedy when, except for the Polish and Indian Armies, most cavalry had converted to armour by 1939. History is very clear that modern armies need armoured fighting vehicles, be they heavy or light, tracked or wheeled, designed to deliver firepower or to carry it. History also insists that modern armies need teamwork and commanders with the knowledge to achieve it and the *coup d'oeil* to win victories. This book says why.

DESMOND MORTON
Director of the McGill Institute for the Study of Canada,
author of *A Military History of Canada*, and
a member of the Senate of the Fort Garry Horse.
16 July 2000

Acknowledgements

The Royal Canadian Armoured Corps, founded officially on 13 August 1940, has a proud and illustrious history in which all who served in its regiments, in war and in peace, can take enormous pride. Indeed, all Canadians should be justly proud of this story of dedication, selfless service and often great bravery in combat. This is also a story of inspired leadership, of perseverance in the face of adversity, and of a bond of comradeship that transcends time and place.

Other than a thin booklet published at the end of the Second World War, the history of the Canadian Armoured Corps as a whole has never before been written. The Corps, of course, has a wonderful legacy of superb regimental histories, but they rightly focus on the activities and accomplishments of their own unit and thus relate only a part of the overall story. (Many of them are long out of print and often are no longer readily available.) The need for a history of the Corps as a whole was first expressed in 1946, and it is unfortunate that it was not written while all the veterans who played the key roles could have contributed their part of the story. The 60th anniversary of the formation of the Corps has, however, provided both the incentive and the grand occasion to produce this volume. While the authors recognize its limitations and inadequacies, it is our hope that this book will highlight the glorious legacy bequeathed by all those who came before, even noting some of their failings, and will thus serve to inspire the upcoming generations of armour soldiers to meet and indeed better the great accomplishments of their forebears.

As is every task undertaken by armour soldiers, the production of this history of the Royal Canadian Armoured Corps has very much been a collaborative effort involving many hundreds of our members and friends who have contributed information, expertise, and indeed the funds to bring it to fruition.

Tribute must first of all be paid to Brigadier-General George Bell who, while Colonel Commandant, provided the impetus to begin the project, and gave advice, encouragement and wise counsel throughout the research and writing of the book.

If there is a single individual to whom this book owes its very existence, it is Major-General Robert LaRose. While serving as Colonel Commandant, in addition to his advisory and ceremonial duties, he singlehandedly undertook to implement the fundraising campaign which made the publication of this book possible. He has also given the authors his continuous support and advice, and we and the Corps as a whole owe him an enormous debt of gratitude for the exceptional work he has done.

Lieutenant-Colonel Jeffrey Dorfman, President of the Royal Canadian Armoured Corps Association and former chairman of the Association's History and Heritage Committee, must also be given profound thanks for his dedicated work and skilful coordination of so many aspects of the project. The other members of the History and Heritage Committee merit the gratitude of all members of the Corps for their continuing interest in the success of the project and their many hours of work.

Slightly more than 240 veterans and serving members of the Armoured Corps gave of their time to be interviewed by the authors, and we are especially grateful for the information they provided about their service. Space has, unfortunately, not allowed each one of them to be quoted directly in the book, but we would assure each of them that the information they provided has been used to make the contents of the book more accurate and balanced than it could otherwise have been. We would like to single out a number of the great men of the Corps who read all or parts of the manuscript and gave sound advice on ways to correct errors of fact or interpretation: Brigadier-General Ned Amy, Brigadier-General George Bell, Lieutenant-General Jack Dangerfield, Major Hunter Dunn, Colonel Bernard Finestone, Brigadier-General Pat Grieve, Colonel David Kinloch, Lieutenant-Colonel W.R.C. (Bill) Little, Lieutenant-

General Bill Milroy, Brigadier-General S.V. 'Rad' Radley-Walters, Major-General Jim Tedlie, and Brigadier-General George Wattsford.

A number of noted military historians read the manuscript in whole or in part and offered excellent advice on content and style, including Robert Caldwell, Dr. Gilbert Drolet, Donald Graves, Brereton Greenhous, Dr. Stephen Harris and Dr. Bill McAndrew. Captain John Grodzinski gave valuable assistance on the organization and structure of the Corps in the Second World War and on the post-war period. Jean Portugal generously gave permission to quote extensively from her seven-volume *We Were There* anthology of interviews with veterans. Stewart Bull, historian of the Queen's York Rangers, and Bruce Tascona, historian of the 12th Manitoba Dragoons, provided valuable reference material. Charles Prieur, editor of the Three Rivers Regiment *Chronicles,* was exceptionally helpful.

The book has made extensive use of the Canadian War Museum's magnificent collection of war art. We are especially grateful for the cooperation, support and advice of Dr. Dean Oliver, Senior Historian at the CWM, and of Leslie Redman, Curator of the War Art Collection, who assisted in the selection of paintings depicted in the book. The War Museum has generously permitted the reproduction of the paintings without cost to the Association, and has lent the cachet of its name as a co-publisher of this book.

We are deeply grateful to Cathy Murphy, Chief Librarian of the Keith Hodson Memorial Library at the Canadian Forces Command and Staff College, for her beyond-the-call-of-duty help in the course of the research, and to Dace Siefers, Assistant Librarian at the College. Ann Melvin, Librarian of the Royal Canadian Military Institute, also was of invaluable assistance in locating essential research material.

Military museums across the country were an essential source of information and illustrations for this book. As would be expected in a history of Canadian armour, the CFB Borden Museum, which houses the former Royal Canadian Armoured Corps Museum, was a prime source of reference material and of photographs of the early years of the Corps, and we would like to express sincere thanks to the staff for their outstanding support. Chief Warrant Officer Gordon Crossley and LCol Larry Lajeunesse of The Fort Garry Horse Museum deserve special mention for their exceptional assistance and cooperation; the Fort Garry Museum is undoubtedly the best source of armour reference material in the country. We would also like to express our thanks to LCol Dick Roach of the King's Own Calgary Regiment Museum, Col Ian Barnes of the Museum of the Regiments in Calgary, LCol Ciarroni and CWO Green of the Royal Canadian Hussars Museum, the British Columbia Dragoons Museum, the staff of the 1st Hussars Museum, Capt Scott Duncan of the Governor General's Horse Guards, Capt John Drygala of the Ontario Regiment Museum, the staff of Lord Strathcona's Horse Museum, Sgt Zoltan Szylvasi of the British Columbia Regiment and the Regimental Association of the Windsor Regiment (RCAC). We are also grateful to the many individuals who loaned photographs from personal collections.

Maps for the book and line drawings of the main vehicles used by the Corps over the course of its service were drawn by Christopher Johnson. Many of the regimental badges shown in the book were loaned by Major Lew Grimshaw. The DND paintings of uniforms are used with the kind permission of Dr. Serge Bernier, Director of History and Heritage in DND. Major Paul Lansey of the Directorate of History and Heritage advised on many ceremonial issues. Dianne Graves prepared the index.

Despite all the advice and assistance they have received, the authors acknowledge responsibility for any errors of fact or interpretation that remain. They would like to express their profound appreciation to Brereton Greenhous for his excellent copy editing, and especially to Robin Brass, the designer of this book, for translating their hopes into a reality of which they are very proud.

* * *

This work is dedicated, with great humility, to all who have served in the regiments of the Royal Canadian Armoured Corps throughout the years.

JOHN MARTEINSON
MICHAEL R. McNORGAN

CHAPTER 1

The Cavalry Heritage

The eastern part of Canada in the early years of settlement was not good cavalry country. Densely wooded countryside, broken only by rivers, lakes and a few primitive, rutted roads, made mounted troops somewhat of a military luxury. They were much more costly to raise and maintain than infantry, and could be used *en masse* only on rare occasions. Restrictions of terrain precluded any *arme blanche* tactics, that is attacking the enemy's main body with sword or lance. However, horsemen could sometimes prove useful in small numbers. In May 1759, it is recorded that two hundred men were recruited for mounted service in the defence of New France. Led by five French officers, the otherwise completely *Canadien 'Corps de cavalerie'* was employed in carrying dispatches and scouting, as well as screening the main French forces from the attentions of enemy scouts. This unit was disbanded in September 1760 following the surrender of Montreal.

Over the next half-century several short-lived cavalry units were raised in the Maritimes, but the first relatively stable units to be formed in what is now Canada were those created under the Upper Canada Militia Act of 1808 which authorized the formation of cavalry troops attached to county Militia regiments. Within four years there were ten troops of mounted men, many with titles such as 'Dragoons' and 'Light Dragoons'. The first of the cavalry troops thus raised was in the York Regiment of Militia in Markham, in what is now Ontario, commanded by Captain John Button.

The term 'dragoon' requires some explanation. For almost two hundred years there had been two types of mounted soldier in British service. Units of horse fought on horseback using edged weapons, the horse itself being a weapon used to ride down the enemy in a charge or in the pursuit. Dragoons were originally infantrymen, equipped with firearms, who fought on foot but were transported by horse, although over the years they were used less and less in the dismounted role until the distinction between them and the regiments of horse became

The *Corps de Cavalerie* (June 1759 to September 1760), the only cavalry raised in Canada during the French regime, was the first mounted unit in Canada. Painting by Eugène Lelièpvre. (Directorate of History and Heritage)

purely academic. During the Napoleonic wars units of light dragoons were formed. These soldiers were less heavily equipped and mounted on faster horses to facilitate their use in reconnaissance and screening operations. Within a few years most British light dragoon regiments would be retitled as regiments of hussars or lancers.

'Officer of the Upper Canada Militia'. Painting by G.A. Embleton. This uniform was worn by the earliest cavalry in Upper Canada, such as Button's Troop and Denison's Troop, as they were initially affiliated with county infantry regiments. (Directorate of History and Heritage)

THE WAR OF 1812

On the outbreak of war in June 1812, mounted units termed 'Provincial Corps' were raised in Upper Canada. Intended only for wartime service, several of them gained impressive reputations, among them the Niagara Light Dragoons. Major Thomas Merritt, a veteran of John Graves Simcoe's Queen's Rangers of the American Revolution, raised this unit on 24 April 1812. Merritt appointed his son, William Hamilton Merritt, to be a lieutenant, as well as Charles Ingersoll, brother of the somewhat more famous Laura Ingersoll Secord, as quartermaster. There were 58 other ranks, paid at the rate of nine pence per day, plus rations. The Niagara Light Dragoons saw action at Detroit in August 1812, then again at Queenston Heights in October of

the same year, where, after the death of Major-General Isaac Brock, his successor, Roger Sheaffe, delegated Merritt to receive the swords of the surrendering American officers.

Following the 1812 campaign, the enlistments of Merritt's men expired and the unit was disbanded. In the spring of 1813 a new unit, the Niagara Provincial Light Dragoons, was raised under the command of the younger Merritt, with Charles Ingersoll as second-in-command. The pay in this troop was fifteen pence per day for man and horse, and it saw hard service through the next two years, including the engagement at Lundy's Lane where its commanding officer was taken prisoner. In his post-war career Merritt became a member of the Legislative Assembly of Upper Canada, a member of the governing council, and an entrepreneur. He is now best remembered as the major promoter of the Welland Canal, joining Lakes Erie and Ontario. The troop finally stood down on 24 March 1815, two years to the day after it was first raised. A senior British cavalry officer wrote of Merritt that his unit was at "all times of the most essential service from their perfect knowledge of the country and the zeal and bravery they always displayed in its defence."

Mounted troops were also raised in the eastern district of Upper Canada. The Incorporated Provincial Light Dragoons,

'Trooper of the Canadian Light Dragoons'. Painting by G.A. Embleton. (Directorate of History and Heritage)

19th Light Dragoons, Full Dress, 1814. **Painting by Charles Stadden. Their smart uniform was impractical for the rough conditions in Canada. (Parks Canada)**

under Captain Richard Fraser, were mainly employed in carrying dispatches between Kingston and Montreal. In Lower Canada the Canadian Light Dragoons performed similar functions. This latter unit also served in Upper Canada in the actions at Beaver Dam, Black Rock and the Battle of the Thames in 1813. Both units were disbanded at the end of the conflict.

The single traditional-style cavalry charge of the war was made by the American Second Dragoon Regiment at Crysler's Farm on 11 November 1813. Just one British regular cavalry regiment served in Canada during the war – the 19th Light Dragoons. Arriving in May 1813, they fought at Lundy's Lane, gaining the battle honour 'Niagara', which was also granted to a very few of the county Militia regiments. None of the Provincial Corps of cavalry was honoured in this way, but in 1820 their veterans received something a little more tangible – special land grants.

The war did, however, stimulate recruiting for the Militia, which resulted in the raising of many new units in the immediate post-war period. Among these was the West York Troop of Cavalry, organized in 1822 by Captain George Taylor Denison, a veteran of 1812. It was a volunteer force in every sense, supplying its own uniforms and arms. It was not until 1837, upon the outbreak of rebellion in the Canadas, that the government

undertook to arm, equip and pay Denison's men. The West York Troop was on active service for six months in early 1838 during the rebellion in Upper Canada, and it was called out again from 31 October 1838 until 30 April the following year. With the rebellions suppressed, the various corps were again disbanded. The Denison family at that time made arrangements to buy their unit's uniforms and weapons from the government so that they could lend them to the men and carry on training.

A similar story can be told of Montreal. Here too a number of veterans of 1812 who had served with the locally-raised cavalry troop struggled to keep alive the memory of their unit. When the Rebellion of 1837 broke out, a volunteer unit was quickly raised and the unit gave good service during the three years of its embodiment.

A new Militia Act was passed in 1846 by the Province of Canada (present-day Ontario and Quebec), authorizing eighteen troops of cavalry. In keeping with the spirit of the times the troops were not paid. It was the legal duty of all able-bodied men between the ages of sixteen and sixty to serve in the Militia without remuneration.

Volunteer cavalry was also thriving in New Brunswick at this time. In April 1848, eleven existing troops, some having been formed as early as 1825, were amalgamated to form a regiment

Officer of the Queen's Light Dragoons, 1837. **It is a strange matter that two Canadian units at the time bore this same title, one in Toronto which became the Governor General's Body Guard, the other in Montreal which later vanished. This painting depicts the Montreal unit, but both wore the same uniform. (Courtesy of René Chartrand)**

entitled the New Brunswick Yeomanry Cavalry, under the command of Major Robert James, who had come to Canada with the British 7th Hussars. The New Brunswick Yeomanry Cavalry was the first volunteer cavalry unit of regimental size to be formed in British North America, and it continued to serve under that title until it was redesignated as the 8th Regiment of Cavalry in 1872.

THE MILITIA ACT OF 1855

The Crimean War of 1854-56 called away the better part of the British military garrison from North America, an action that raised concerns in the colonial legislatures. In the Province of Canada, a board of commissioners was appointed in October 1854 to review the situation. They found that the existing Militia could not react quickly to emergencies, in particular to calls for aid to the civil power which had been one of the more important and frequent duties of the British regulars. To overcome this difficulty the commissioners proposed that voluntary units, to be called the Active Militia, be armed, trained and paid, even in peacetime. The existing compulsory-service structure was retained at least nominally, termed the Sedentary Militia, but it was never again called into use. These recommendations resulted in the Militia Act of 1855, the legislation which laid the foundations for the Canadian Army of today.

Many of today's regiments claim a lineage that extends back to the War of 1812 and even to the American Revolution. These claims are legitimate and made in good faith. Official recognition of unit lineage extending back before the 1855 Militia Act has, however, been given only very rarely since the units existing before 1855 were, for all practical purposes, private organizations. Units were embodied only in time of war and disturbance, but were just as quickly disembodied when peace returned. There is thus no unbroken thread of official government service prior to 1855, even though the unbounded dedication of generations of Canadians and, indeed, the financial support of the officers, kept these units in existence for many years.

The significant difference made in 1855 was that, for the first time, members of the Militia would be paid, at a rate of five shillings a day for a trooper, and up to ten shillings a day for his captain. Training was to occupy ten days a year for cavalry and rifles, twenty days for artillery units. Additionally, each man, upon enrolment, received a grant of £2 for accoutrements, a further £2 after two years service and £2 more after seven years.

The establishment for each troop consisted of a captain, a lieutenant, a cornet (the equivalent today to a second lieutenant), three sergeants, three corporals, a trumpeter and 45 privates. Officers and men had to provide their own uniforms and saddlery, but the government usually supplied swords and pistols. The rank of the junior members of the troop was 'private',

Quebec Volunteer Cavalry (circa 1843). Between the War of 1812 and the re-organization of the Militia in 1855, the mounted arm consisted of volunteer units such as this. (RCH Museum)

but in Canada, as in Britain, cavalry privates were commonly referred to as 'troopers', a name originally given to the men's horses, 'the troop horses', while an officer's horse was called a 'charger'. Only at the time of the South African War did the term 'trooper' become an official rank, and then only in the British Household Cavalry. Not until the 1920s did Britain, and then Canada, officially apply the rank of trooper to all junior cavalry soldiers.

The senior of the sixteen cavalry troops raised in the Province of Canada under the new system, with an organization order dated 20 September 1855, was Kingston's 1st Volunteer Militia Troop of Cavalry of the County of Frontenac. Through a process of evolution this unit eventually became 'A' Squadron of the IV Princess Louise Dragoon Guards. Other troops were formed in Prescott, Cobourg, Toronto, Hamilton, St. Catharines, London, Chatham, Woodstock, Picton, Sandwich, Quebec City, Sherbrooke, Saint John (now St Jean, Quebec), Montreal and Ste. Marie.

Ontario cavalrymen in camp during the Fenian Raid of 1866. (National Archives of Canada C48845)

THE FENIAN RAIDS

Armed bodies of the Irish-American Fenian Brotherhood invaded Canada West on 1 June 1866 with the strange notion that if British North America could be held hostage, their dream of an independent Ireland would somehow be helped. On 2 June the Governor General's Body Guard of Upper Canada, from Toronto, was mobilized for active service. The regiment had adopted this name the previous April to replace the more cumbersome title of 1st Troop of Volunteer Militia Cavalry of the County of York. Under the command of Lieutenant Colonel George Taylor Denison III, its four officers and 55 men performed outpost duties and patrolled in the Niagara peninsula without coming into contact with the enemy. The men served for a pay of 50 cents a day, while their horses received 75 cents, thus inaugurating an unusual practice that would last for the next seventy years, whereby a horse was considered more valuable than its rider!

The failure to mobilize and use additional cavalry was a major failing of the campaign. Lack of information on the enemy's movements was a serious handicap, as was the inability to react swiftly to opportunities to harass or pursue the Fenian forces. At the one set-piece encounter of the campaign – Ridgeway, fought on 2 June 1866 – the Canadian force, which had no cavalry with it, blundered onto the Fenian position and found itself committed to an unanticipated battle. A cry of "cavalry," raised when someone saw a few mounted Fenian scouts, riding horses 'borrowed' from local farmers, led to an order for the militiamen to form a square. When the error was realized, a counter-order to re-form into line led to confusion and then to the disintegration of the Canadian force. Although not even present, cavalry decided the course of the battle.

On the Quebec–U.S. frontier cavalry was used to better effect. On 9 June 1866 at Pigeon Hill, Canadian forces encountered some two hundred Fenians. Seeing that they were outnumbered and out-gunned (the Canadians had light artillery while their opponents did not), the Fenians started a withdrawal. The officer commanding a Montreal unit with the ponderous title of The Royal Guides, Governor General's Body Guard For Lower Canada, ordered a charge. In the words of a trooper:

As we neared them our Captain ordered a charge, telling us to use only the flat of our swords and in a minute or two we were among them, slashing right and left. I saw fellows tumbling head over heels as they were struck. Quite a number of the Fenians emptied their guns, and I heard the zip, zip of bullets about my head. In this running fight we reached the boundary line. There a company of U.S. regulars was stationed and as fast as a Fenian tumbled over the line he was seized and disarmed.

Why the Guides should have been ordered to use "only the flat of our swords" when the Fenians were using real bullets was never explained.

One result of these raids was the confederation of four of the British North American colonies – Prince Edward Island, New Brunswick, and Upper and Lower Canada. Units of cavalry also began to amalgamate as some of the independent cavalry troops joined to form squadrons and then combined into regiments. A third result was the re-equipping of cavalry with Spencer repeating carbines, replaced in 1872 with Sniders.

In spite of the more modern weaponry, the trooper was still faced with a considerable problem. The government neglected to issue either an arm-sling or a rifle bucket for him to carry his firearm. The soldier, already bedecked with sword and bandolier, now had to use one hand to control his horse and the other to carry his carbine. Wearing a sword attached to him by a waist-belt while holding his carbine made dismounting to fight an awkward business. These equipment problems would not be solved until the South African War, when the sword was attached to the saddle and the saddlery augmented to include a rifle bucket, thus permitting two-handed control of the horse.

Only four British regular cavalry regiments ever served in what is now Canada. The first, the 19th Light Dragoons, has already been mentioned. The second and third were the 1st Dragoon Guards (later renamed the King's Dragoon Guards) and the 7th Light Dragoons (later the 7th Hussars). These units arrived in Canada in June 1838 and both assisted in the final suppression of the rebellion and the rounding up of the remnants of the rebel forces in Lower Canada. The first

The Canada General Service Medal with Fenian Raid 1866 bar. This was the first distinctively Canadian service medal.

FENIAN RAID 1866

CANADA

Militia cavalry school in Canada was conducted in 1838 at Fort George by a troop of the Dragoon Guards. Several weeks of instruction were offered to cavalry units in the Niagara, Hamilton and York (Toronto) areas, each being detailed to supply an officer, a sergeant, a corporal and a private, with their horses. The 7th Hussars were sent back to England in 1842, and the 1st Dragoon Guards in 1843.

The fourth British unit, one which was to have a notable impact on the Canadian cavalry, was the 13th Hussars. Brought to Toronto in the summer of 1866 as a counter to the Fenian threat, they stayed three years in Canada. As the only regular cavalry to serve in the post-Confederation era, their uniform, a blue tunic with buff facings, yellow hussar braiding, and busbies of dark brown fur with a buff bag and white plume, was widely copied, even by the mounted infantry units. The Hussars, like the King's Dragoon Guards before them, ran cavalry schools for the reserve units. At the end of the first course, held in Toronto in 1867, the Hussars' commanding officer reported on the "great zeal" displayed by the Canadian militiamen and expressed his surprise at how much they had learned in a short period "owing to their unremitting attention to their work."

Canada at this time produced its first military author of international repute. In 1868 George Taylor Denison III, of the Governor General's Body Guard, published *Modern Cavalry,* based on his observations of the U.S. Civil War. Using the widely successful Confederate cavalry as his model, he proposed that all cavalry be trained as mounted infantry. Ten years later, Denison produced *A History of Cavalry* that won the Russian Tsar's Prize of 5,000 rubles. Both books were translated into several languages and were highly regarded in Germany and Russia. British cavalry circles were less impressed. The *arme blanche* (units equipped with swords or lances) had no desire to revert to the traditional role of dragoons. Nevertheless, Denison's proposals were sound, and eventually all cavalry units did become mounted rifles, in practice if not in name.

The Fenian Raids provided the impetus for a further reorganization of the Militia, which, in effect, extended the Province of Canada's 1855 Militia Act to the rest of the country. The Militia Act of 1868 provided for an Active Militia of 40,000, (by contrast, only 5,000 had been authorized in 1855), in nine military districts – four in Ontario, three in Quebec and one each in New Brunswick and Nova Scotia. The structure had at its heart the idea that Canadian military units were an adjunct to the British troops upon whom the actual defence of the country rested. This comforting idea was quickly extinguished as Britain proceeded to remove its garrisons from British North America, the last troops leaving on 11 November 1871. Even so, the Canadian government did little to fill the void left by the departure of the British regulars. Militia strengths fell as many

The New Brunswick Regiment of Yeomanry Cavalry on parade in Fredericton, August 1871. (NAC C 56415)

units just dried up and withered away. The authorized manpower dropped from 45,000 in 1872, to 37,000 in 1880, seven cavalry troops being disbanded as a result of this measure. The Militia structure now became as much a social institution as one designed for active operations. Patronage and political interference, unfortunately, were rife.

THE CAVALRY SCHOOL CORPS

The first turn-around in this deteriorating situation was the creation of the Cavalry School Corps in December 1883, the officers and men of the Corps becoming Canada's first regular cavalrymen. The first commanding officer was Lieutenant-Colonel James F. Turnbull. The 48-year-old Turnbull had enrolled as a private in Quebec City's Queen's Own Canadian Hussars in 1861, and was soon commissioned. In 1865, then a captain, he visited the U.S. Army's cavalry remount depots before going on to the cavalry depot in the United Kingdom for a course of instruction. Still in Europe two years later, he was attached to the French Army's *Les Dragons de l'Imperatrice*. This was followed, in 1875, by an attachment to the British Army's 7th (Queen's Own) Hussars in Aldershot. This well-travelled, widely experienced officer was thus a natural selection for his new post. The role of the Cavalry School was to train the Active Militia units.

The training syllabus called for a 'short course' of three months duration broken down as follows: 5 days – squad drill; 20 days – mounted military equitation and stable duties; 3 days – marching; 5 days – carbine exercises; 5 days – sword drill; 7 days – troop drill and formations; 5 days – signalling; 5 days – formation and movement of troops and squadrons; 8 days – outposts, reconnaissance patrolling and scouting duties; and 12 days – regimental duties. Total – 75 training days.

The detailed syllabus for each month called for 25 hours of practical and 3 hours of theoretical instruction. The Short Course Certificate (the formal qualification for a commission which was often ignored in practice) required a grade of either 'A' or 'B'. The candidate had to pass a practical examination, conducted personally by the com-

The helmet plate badge of the Cavalry School Corps. (DHH)

The uniform of the British 13th Hussars, shown in this period painting, was widely adopted by Canadian Militia units. (Courtesy of René Chartrand)

bles, veterinary training and the employment of cavalry with artillery.

Reserve units also received sixteen days of drill per man per year at annual camps. Pay for camp was $16 for officers and $8 for other ranks. Travel allowances of six cents a mile for officers and three cents a mile for other ranks were permitted, and officers received an allowance of $12 for their horses.

In 1887 the School was redesignated the Royal School of Cavalry and in 1892, as part of a reform designed to improve Permanent Force morale, and improve the standard of care taken by officers of their men and horses, it became the Canadian Dragoons. The unit gained the title Royal Canadian Dragoons (RCD) the following year.

THE NORTH-WEST REBELLION

mandant, as well as a three-hour written examination of not less than 24 questions which was prepared and marked by the commandant. Following the short course, officers showing sufficient aptitude could attend a special course in military law, Queen's Regulations and Orders, interior economy, military topography, and reports and reconnaissance. Of the 36 one-hour lectures, three per week were to be delivered by the School commandant, or in his unavoidable absence, by one of the troop officers. Lecture subjects included discipline, the line of march, reconnoitring, outpost duties and patrolling, scouting, tactics, the management and care of horses and sta-

When the *métis* (and a few Indians) of the North-West Territories rebelled in March 1885, three cavalry units were mobilized for active service: the Governor General's Body Guard, with a strength of 81, under Lieutenant-Colonel G.T. Denison III, 'A' Troop of the Cavalry School Corps, 48 officers and men under Colonel Turnbull, and the Winnipeg Troop of Cavalry, 36 strong, under Captain Cornelius Knight. In the course of the campaign other mounted volunteer units were raised, primarily in the west, including Boulton's Scouts (also known as Boulton's Mounted Corps) with a strength of 113, French's Scouts numbering 35, Stewart's Rangers with 54 and the Alberta Mounted Infantry with 53 all ranks. In addition

Lieutenant-Colonel James Turnbull (standing in the centre), commanding officer of the Cavalry School Corps, with a group of Militia cavalry officers attending a course, ca 1884. RCD Archives.

Lieutenant-Colonel George Taylor Denison III, commanding officer of the Governor General's Body Guard (photograph ca 1885). Denison's belief that cavalry should be trained and equipped as mounted rifles had a far-reaching effect on the organization and training of the Canadian cavalry, and his ideas were influential in Russia and in Germany. (GGHG)

caches of provisions at staging posts along the route, which kept men and horses fed and offered some slight respite from the rigours of the march.

On the morning of 10 April 1885 the Body Guard set out across the second gap in the track, travelling a distance of nearly sixty kilometres across the ice of Lake Superior from Port Monroe to Jackfish Bay. There was a strong, biting wind, blowing snow and a temperature of minus 20 degrees. A.H. Hider would later capture the rigours of this trek in his famous painting. Here they paused the following day, resuming their journey on the 13th with another forty-kilometre march across the ice to Winston's Landing. From there it was on to Winnipeg by rail, reached eight days after leaving Toronto.

The Cavalry School Corps followed four days behind the Body Guard. After a rest at Winnipeg – if living in tents on a mud flat could be considered rest – on 23 April the two eastern units and the Winnipeg Troop departed by rail for Qu'Appelle, which had been selected by the force commander, Major-General Frederick Middleton, as the base for future operations. It lay at the start of the Carlton Trail, the most direct route to Riel's headquarters at Batoche. The trail led through the Touchwood Hills, location of a major concentration of Indians whose intentions were unclear, and through Humboldt, one hundred kilometres south of Batoche, which would become Middleton's advanced base of operations.

to these, the North-West Mounted Police were also placed on active service.

The Body Guard's march west in the spring of 1885 is the first epic feat of Canadian cavalry. Simply getting to the north-west was to prove half the battle. Four significant gaps still existed in the uncompleted Canadian Pacific rail line across northern Ontario and the regiment had to make its own way across the gaps between completed sections of track, contending with deep snow and bitterly cold temperatures along the way. On 9 April they reached the end of the most easterly section of track at Dog Lake and began a 600-kilometre trek along the north shore of Lake Superior, riding from one section of railway to the next. Loading and unloading the horses from the trains was a daunting and constantly recurring challenge since there were no gangways available for this purpose, and time and again snow ramps overlaid with railway ties had to be constructed. The CPR, and the preceding infantry units, had left

---

Order of Battle of the Canadian Cavalry in 1885

Military District No. 1, South-Western Ontario
    1st Regiment of Cavalry – London

Military District No. 2, Central Ontario
    Governor General's Body Guard – Toronto
    2nd Regiment of Cavalry – St. Catharines

Military District No. 3, Central Ontario
    3rd Provisional Regiment of Cavalry – Peterborough
    4th Provisional Regiment of Cavalry – Kingston

Military District No. 4, Eastern Ontario
    The Prescott Troop of Cavalry – Prescott
    The Princess Louise Dragoon Guards – Ottawa

Military District No. 5, Western Quebec
    5th Provisional Regiment of Cavalry – Cookshire
    6th Provisional Regiment of Cavalry – Montreal

Military District No. 7, Eastern Quebec
    The Queen's Own Canadian Hussars – Quebec City

Military District No. 8, New Brunswick
    8th Regiment of Cavalry – Sussex

Military District No. 9, Nova Scotia
    The King's Troop of Cavalry – Kentville

Military District No. 10, Manitoba
    Winnipeg Troop of Cavalry – Winnipeg

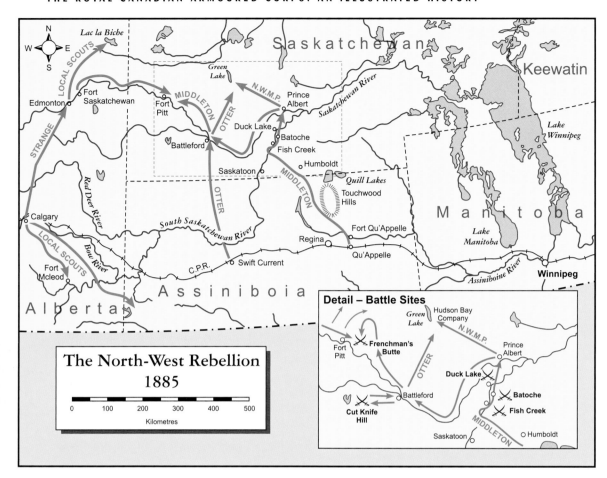

their first action at Fish Creek. Major Boulton described the fight:

> The leading section had not been gone many minutes … when a volley was fired at us, which, however, struck the trees in front. I gave the command "Left wheel, gallop!" and we charged down upon thirty or forty mounted men who were standing in the shelter of a bluff. When we came upon them, they at once turned their horses and bolted for a ravine about a hundred and fifty yards distant, dismounting as they galloped. I instantly gave the word to my men "Halt and dismount! Extend in skirmishing order and lie down!" Simultaneously the enemy opened a murderous fire upon us. I said "Fire away boys…", my object being to keep the enemy down in the gully and hold them in check until supports came up. We here sustained the whole of the enemy's fire, which was very hot and unfortunately fatal. … The main body soon came up and the fight began in earnest at the mouth of the ravine. Gradually the ravine was forced and the flanks clear, … and the hotly contested action was brought to an end….

The eastern cavalry units were destined to play only a subsidiary role in the campaign. It was the irregular units, the most prominent of which was Boulton's Mounted Corps, which got involved in the main actions. Charles Boulton was born and raised in Cobourg, Ontario. In 1858 he had been appointed an ensign in the Canadian-raised British Army unit, the 100th Regiment of Foot. When the 100th were serving in Gibraltar in the 1860s, Boulton had come to know Captain Frederick Middleton, another officer in the garrison.

Some twenty years later, on 27 March 1885, Boulton was standing on the station platform in Winnipeg awaiting General Middleton's arrival, and during Middleton's short stop-over Boulton persuaded him to authorise a force of mounted irregulars for service in the field. Although he was an infantryman, Middleton had commanded a cavalry troop in India in 1855 during the suppression of a local rising, and it was perhaps that experience that encouraged him to accept Boulton's offer. Agreement reached, Boulton rode home to Russell, Manitoba, a journey of some 350 kilometres, and set about recruiting his friends and neighbours. Within days, his force, organized in two troops each of roughly 65 men, was on its way west to join Middleton's column for the advance on Batoche. On 8 April they linked up at Qu'Appelle, and by the 25th they were engaged in

The battle itself was inconclusive, but Boulton's Scouts, armed with Winchester rifles and mounted on wiry, western horses, had prevented the *métis* from ambushing the marching infantry. The action confirmed in Middleton's mind the superiority of these irregulars over his eastern cavalry. Earlier, in his preparations for the expedition, concern had been raised over the ability of the eastern horses to adapt to the tougher climate and poorer grass of the west. The eastern units thus found themselves guarding Middleton's lines of communications, while the irregulars were involved in active operations. The Cavalry School Corps and the Winnipeg Troop of Cavalry maintained a military presence in the Touchwood Hills, while the Body Guard was tasked with guarding a one-key telegraph sta-

The Governor General's Body Guard Crossing Lake Superior on the Ice. Painting by A.H. Hider. In April 1885, en route to the West, the Body Guard made a 60-kilometre march across the frozen vastness of the lake. (Governor General's Horse Guards Officers' Mess)

tion and supply centre at Humboldt. These were necessary duties to be sure, but they were certainly not what they had expected to be doing. It might be argued that the Cavalry School Corps was performing a function that no one other than the NWMP could have done. The Body Guard, however, was utterly misused for a task that ignored their primary attribute – mobility. Capabilities aside, the most likely reason for Denison's unprepossessing role was political: he had been a loud and persistent critic of several British generals who had commanded the Canadian Militia in the past.

There were no real cavalry actions during the campaign. Both sides used their mounted men only for reconnaissance, and what fighting there was, was done dismounted. The *métis* sacrificed their inherent tactical mobility and this contributed greatly to their own defeat, since they could not hope to match the firepower of Middleton's marching infantry. Louis Riel, the leader of the rebellion, imposed this limitation on his field commander, Gabriel Dumont. Had he not done so, the Canadian cavalry might indeed have seen more action and the campaign undoubtedly would have been bloodier and longer than it proved to be.

Despite seeing such limited action in the North-West Rebellion, in its aftermath the Cavalry School Corps was augmented, in part to establish a School of Mounted Infantry at Winnipeg

which was formed on 20 July 1885. This School was a direct result of one of the main lessons learned: the utility of mounted rifles. Unfortunately, pay and morale were both low in the Permanent Force, and desertion was rife. Life for the regulars did not really improve until the reforms of 1894, when the Cavalry School Corps and the School of Mounted Infantry were transformed into the RCD and the designation 'troop' was changed to 'squadron'. The Permanent Force gunner and infantry components underwent similar metamorphoses to become the Royal Canadian Artillery and the Royal Canadian Regiment.

The RCD was soon to see more service in the west. The discovery of gold in the Yukon Territory led to a

The North-West Canada medal, awarded to all troops who participated in the operations in the North-West Territories in 1885.

(Above) The Winnipeg Troop of Cavalry leading a column of infantry through the Touchwood Hills, 1885. (NAC)

(Right) Two members of Boulton's Mounted Corps near Batoche, 1885. Photo by James Peters. The irregular cavalry employed in this campaign had no uniforms. (NAC C17611)

Fort Denison at Humboldt, May 1885, the base of the Governor General's Body Guard. Drawing by Trooper E. Kershaw, GGBG. (*Canadian Illustrated War News*)

Mounted troops in winter uniform, School of Mounted Infantry, Winnipeg, 1891. (NAC PA16007)

major gold rush and, fearing both a breakdown in public order and a move by the Americans to annex the Yukon, a military force was dispatched under the command of Lieutenant-Colonel Thomas B.D. Evans of the RCD. Evans was an excellent officer who had begun his military career as a Militia infantryman. A veteran of the Riel Rebellion (and later, the South African War, where he commanded the 2nd Canadian Mounted Rifles), some historians believe he would have achieved high command in the First World War had he not died at the relatively early age of 48.

After journeying by train from Ottawa to Vancouver and by ship and boat to Glenora in northern British Columbia, the Field Force, which included sixteen Dragoons from Winnipeg's 'B' Squadron (most of the Force were infantrymen), marched north from Telegraph Creek to Teslin Lake and then built their own boats and sailed down the Yukon River to Dawson. Here, for a year, they kept the peace, while far away, across the South Atlantic, the clouds of war were gathering.

THE SOUTH AFRICAN WAR, 1899–1902

Canada's first contingent in the South African War, more often termed the Boer War, consisted of a single infantry unit, a 2nd Battalion of the RCR. Following a series of reverses at the front, the Canadian government offered a second contingent which, in accordance with British wishes, consisted of mounted rifles. This force was to be made up of three squadrons, each of 116 men carefully chosen for their ability to ride and shoot. A fourth squadron would consist of scouts recruited in the North-West Territories. Supplementing the mounted rifles would be three batteries of field artillery, totalling 18 guns.

When the mobilization orders were issued the mounted rifle regiment totalled 25 officers and 417 other ranks. The orders were then amended to provide for a regiment of two battalions, to be called the 1st and 2nd Battalions, Canadian Mounted Rifles (CMR). The 1st Battalion was raised in the eastern provinces and Manitoba, and was placed under the command of Lieutenant-Colonel François Lessard of the RCD. Commissioner Lawrence Herchmer of the North-West Mounted Police initially commanded the 2nd Battalion, recruited in the North-West Territories, but once in South Africa the unit was taken over by Lieutenant-Colonel T.B.D. Evans.

The CMR regiment had four squadrons, lettered 'A' through 'D', two squadrons to a battalion. A major commanded each squadron, with a captain as second-in-command, and each of the four troops, forty strong, was commanded by a lieutenant. In action one man would hold four horses while the remaining three were fighting dismounted. Their principal weapons were the Lee Enfield rifle, with bayonet, and the .45 calibre Colt revolver. Each battalion also boasted two horse-drawn, water-cooled, Maxim machine-guns, later replaced by air-cooled Colts.

Canadian Mounted Rifles, South Africa. **Painting by Ron Volstad depicting the khaki uniform of strong duck cloth worn by Canadian troops in South Africa. (Directorate of History and Heritage)**

Lieutenant-Colonel François Lessard (left), commanding officer of the Royal Canadian Dragoons, with Lieutenants Young and Van Straubenzee during a pause on the march to Belfast in Transvaal, 1900. (RCD Archives)

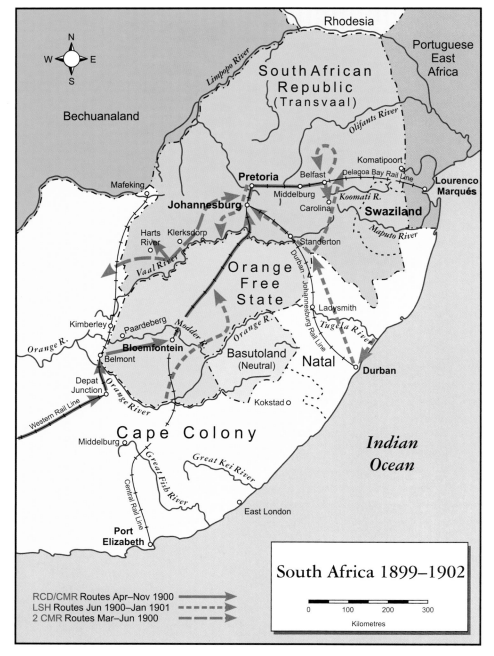

South Africa 1899–1902

RCD/CMR Routes Apr–Nov 1900
LSH Routes Jun 1900–Jan 1901
2 CMR Routes Mar–Jun 1900

0   100   200   300
Kilometres

mand the 2nd Canadian Division in the Great War. Although Lord Strathcona's Horse was Canadian in every respect, it was officially on the establishment of the British Army. It would not be the only mounted unit from Canada with that distinction.

The South African War had three distinct phases. The first phase, the Boer offensive into Cape Colony between October 1899 and January 1900, was the impetus for the raising of the first two Canadian contingents. The second phase, the British counter-offensive into the Transvaal, ended with the capture of Pretoria, the last Boer capital. However, instead of ending the war, Pretoria's fall initiated a third phase, guerrilla warfare.

Canadians did not reached South Africa in time to be involved in the disastrous first phase. During the second phase, the two CMR battalions were initially employed in escort duties for convoys and guarding lines of communications (shades of the North-West Rebellion). The CMR, along with the British 1st Battalion Mounted Infantry, served in the 1st Corps (brigade is the modern terminology) Mounted Infantry, under Lieutenant-Colonel E.A.H. Alderson, a future commander of the Canadian Corps in the First World War. Along with the 3rd Corps Mounted Infantry, they formed Major-General Edward Hutton's 1st Mounted Infantry Corps (division in modern terms).

Hutton had been General Officer Commanding the Canadian Militia up to the outbreak of war, and the plan for a Canadian contingent of mounted rifles had been his, but Colonel Lessard, unhappy with the nomenclature assigned to his battalion, risked Hutton's displeasure by going over his head and applying directly to the Queen to have the title Royal Canadian Dragoons restored. This was done officially in August 1900. With 1 CMR now the RCD, 2 CMR became simply the CMR.

The plan of campaign had several columns advancing on Pretoria. Field Marshal Lord Roberts' column was the central one, flanked on his right by Sir Ian Hamilton's primarily infantry force, which included 2 RCR, and on his left the cavalry column of Sir John French, which included the RCD and CMR. Advancing from Natal was a column under Sir Redvers Buller, to whom we shall return later.

The second contingent was not the sum total of Canada's commitment to the Boer War. In January 1900 the War Office in London accepted a proposal from Lord Strathcona to personally finance a mounted regiment for active service. The arrangement stipulated that Lord Strathcona would pay the difference between the imperial cavalry pay and the higher rate paid to the NWMP, since many of its recruits were policemen. The unit was to consist of three squadrons, organized like those of the CMR. The commanding officer was Lieutenant-Colonel Sam Steele, NWMP, formerly second-in-command of the 2nd CMR. Steele had served in the North-West Rebellion as a non-commissioned officer, and in later years he would briefly com-

After both RCD squadrons had performed detached duties that bore them forward toward the fighting, the regiment was reunited. It went into action as a regiment for the first time on 3 May 1900 at Boschman's Kop. 'B' Squadron RCD was acting as advance guard, preceding the main body in open order, in an attempt to draw enemy fire. When the squadron came under fire, the advance guard wheeled about and retired on the main body. The RCD were then ordered to dismount and engage the enemy, along with the 1st Mounted Infantry, the artillery and the machine guns. After a firefight lasting some two hours the enemy withdrew and the advance continued. What had happened, of course, was that during the two-hour-long firefight the enemy main body had steadily gained ground on the pursuing British. This scenario would be played out again and again as the fighting moved steadily north toward the Boer capital.

With the capture of Pretoria in June 1900 the war entered its final stage. The Boer commandos refused to surrender, so the British forces set about destroying their ability to continue resistance. This meant the burning of farms and crops, and removing the civilian population to 'concentration camps' where they could be guarded and prevented from aiding the commandos still in the field. The countryside was swept, again and again, by British troops in an effort to bring the commandos to battle.

The RCD and CMR were now employed in both these aspects of the fighting. At the beginning of November 1900 they participated in two operations that were intended to flush out the enemy. The first, which involved sending a mixed column of infantry, artillery and mounted rifles south into a Boer-held region, ended in failure. The weather conditions were appalling and the enemy proved adroit at eluding the British column. When the force commander, Major-General Horace Smith-Dorrien, ordered the column back to its base, the enemy hovered off the flanks looking for an opportunity to strike. The good work of the RCD kept the withdrawal from turning into a rout, but nonetheless the British had been chastened and the Boers encouraged by the outcome of the British offensive. Smith-Dorrien was determined to redress the balance and another operation was set up within a matter of days.

On 6 November 1900, Smith-Dorrien led his troops out of Belfast and south to the Komati River. They spent the night near a farm called Leliefontein. Once again the enemy proved elusive and on 7 November the order was given to withdraw back to the base camp at Belfast. The Boers had, however, gathered in significant numbers and now, with the British again withdrawing, they decided to strike.

The Dragoons, supplemented with the left section of 'D' Battery, Royal Canadian Field Artillery, were detailed to form a rear guard to protect the withdrawal of the main body and their slow-moving ox-drawn supply train. Colonel Lessard, the Dra-

goons' commanding officer, gave orders to his three remaining troops to deploy in six 15-man sections, each about 500 metres apart, with the two field guns and Sergeant Edward Holland's carriage-mounted Colt machine-gun just in rear of the centre troop. As the Dragoons were taking up their positions at about 0900 hours, Boer commandos several kilometres away were seen advancing both on the left flank and from the front.

By 1000 hours Boer horsemen had reached the forward edge of the Dragoon screen but it was still too early for any thought of a withdrawal as the slow-moving transport column had not

RCD soldiers taking a break from their trek in front of a typical 'kopje' on the South African veldt. (RCD Archives)

yet pulled back far enough to be safe. At about that time Lieutenant H.Z.C. Cockburn's troop, on the extreme left of the screen, came under heavy attack. As soon as Colonel Lessard became aware of this he ordered the artillery commander, Lieutenant E.W.B. Morrison, to take one of his guns to help Cockburn. The gunners quickly limbered up and galloped a thousand metres eastward to Cockburn's position, which was still holding out when the gun arrived. Barely twelve shots had been fired at the advancing Boers, however, when Colonel Lessard rode up, shouting "For God's sake, Morrison, save your gun!"

Another large party of Boers were at that very moment coming in on the left rear, and threatening to encircle the entire Dragoon position. As the gun was again limbered up and raced to the rear, Cockburn extended and dismounted his already depleted troop: the men all knew it was their duty to ensure that the gun was not captured.

Nearby, Sergeant Holland had been providing covering fire with his Colt machine-gun. The gun jammed and Holland knew that he had no time to clear the jam before the Boer horsemen would be on top of him, so he detached it from its carriage, grabbed a horse from one of Lieutenant Cockburn's

The Action at Leliefontein. **Painting by Peter Archer depicting the rearguard action which resulted in the award of three Victoria Crosses. (Royal Canadian Dragoons)**

horse-holders, and galloped to the rear. Cockburn was slightly wounded and his troop was then overrun by the Boers. His horse was killed and he was trapped under it. There was no choice but to surrender.

The Boers continued to press their attack for another hour or so, and the Dragoon rearguard, along with the two guns, delayed as best they could, often engaging in a mounted *mêlée* while gradually closing in on the retreating main body of the force. By this time the horses pulling the 12-pounder guns were so exhausted that they could barely move at a walking pace and, once again, the Boers were closing in. One last time the Dragoons had to come to the rescue; Lieutenant R.E.W. Turner, already wounded in the neck and arm, rushed in with about a dozen men, dismounted, and poured heavy fire into the Boer line. Turner and his men held out long enough for the guns to reach the rearmost of the main body.

While the operation had ended in failure, the gallantry that had been shown by many Dragoons was quickly recognized. General Smith-Dorien noted that the Dragoon action was "an event unprecedented in this war" and that he had "no praise too

high for the devoted gallantry" that had been shown. In April 1901 three awards of the Victoria Cross were announced in the London Gazette – to Holland, Turner and Cockburn. This was the largest number of VCs ever awarded to a Canadian unit for a single action, although still a far cry from the 'eleven before breakfast' awarded to British soldiers after the fight at Rorke's Drift, another South African battle fought on 22 January 1879.

In April 1900 a third Canadian contingent, Lord Strathcona's Horse (LSH), arrived in Table Bay. Their first assignment was the destruction of a bridge at Komati Poort, in Natal, on the other side of the country, but although the regiment deployed the operation was cancelled when it was learned that the enemy knew of the plan. They were then ordered to join Sir Redvers Buller's force, where they were attached to the Earl of Dundonald's 3rd Mounted Brigade.

The Strathconas saw almost continuous action with this force, skirmishing daily with the enemy as Buller pushed northward, marching on Pretoria from Ladysmith, in Natal. On 5 July 1900 a reinforcement party, *en route* to join the LSH, were involved in a firefight with a Boer commando. In the course of

Lieutenant Hampden Zane Churchill Cockburn, VC.

Lieutenant Richard Ernest William Turner, VC.

Sergeant Edward James Gibson Holland, VC.

Sergeant Arthur Herbert Lindsay Richardson, VC

the engagement, while under heavy fire, Sergeant Arthur Richardson rescued a fellow soldier whose horse had been killed. Richardson was awarded the Victoria Cross for his courage and presence of mind.

After Buller's column reached Pretoria, on 14 October 1900, the Strathconas were transferred to another column, this one under Major-General Barton, and returned to the field. When their year-long tour of duty ended in January 1901, the Strathconas sailed to England where all ranks were presented with their South Africa medals, the first issued to any troops. The unit also received a King's Colour from the new sovereign, King Edward VII. In March, the regiment reached Montreal, having suffered 26 fatalities (some from disease) and another 24 wounded in action.

In November 1901 Britain asked Canada for a third contingent, offering to pay all of the expenses. In this way the 2nd Regiment, Canadian Mounted Rifles (a *second* 2 CMR) was quickly recruited. It was the largest contingent yet, nine hundred all ranks, organized in six squadrons. The commanding officer was the same Colonel Thomas Evans, who had commanded the previous CMR unit. The new regiment included many veterans of the earlier contingents and proved to be a formidable force in the field. What was probably its finest hour came on 31 March 1902 at Boschbult, which is sometimes better known as Harts River. A British column that included 2 CMR, in chasing a party of Boers, found itself being ambushed. The British and Canadians, temporarily outnumbered, decided to hold in a defensive position until help could arrive. The site of

The Victoria Cross, the Empire's highest decoration for gallantry in action. This is the VC awarded to Captain H.Z.C. Cockburn of the Governor General's Body Guard who won it while serving with the Royal Canadian Dragoons. (Upper Canada College)

their stand was a farm called Boschbult, located on the Harts River.

When Lieutenant Bruce Carruthers, with two troops of 'E' Squadron, found himself cut off from the main body in the farm complex, he decided to dismount and fight outside the defensive perimeter. The Boers attacked his position in a fierce and prolonged action that killed or wounded 17 of the 21 Canadians. Although the position was overrun, the Boer attack ended here, and relief arrived the following day.

While Carruthers' men were fighting for their lives, a party of six other Canadians, under Corporal William A. Knisley, DCM, also found themselves cut off behind enemy lines. Knisley and his men could not get through to the farm at Boschbult, so decided to make for Klerksdorp, the British base camp. The second day on the trail they were overtaken by a group of some fifty Boers. The Canadians built a stone sangar on top of a rocky *kopje* (hill), and here they fought off repeated attacks for five hours. Corporal Knisley was killed, as was another soldier. Out of ammunition, the four survivors surrendered. Knisley had been nominated for a Victoria Cross at Leliefontein but had received the Distinguished Conduct Medal. His last stand against overwhelming odds was perhaps equally deserving of a Victoria Cross, but it was not to be. He is, nonetheless, one of the notable heroes of the Canadian cavalry.

In March 1902, Canada made additional offers of troops, and the 3rd, 4th, 5th and 6th regiments of Canadian Mounted Rifles were raised. They arrived in theatre just as the war ended in the spring of 1902.

(Above) The 2nd Canadian Mounted Rifles riding through the veldt while chasing down small bands of Boers in Transvaal, March 1902. (NAC PA173029)

(Right) The Queen's South Africa medal, awarded to all who served in the campaign in South Africa between 1899 and 1901. Lord Strathcona's Horse was the only unit in the Empire to receive this medal with the dates 1899-1900 on the reverse. Bars awarded with the medal indicated the territory or battles in which units served.

THE EXPANSION OF THE CAVALRY

At home there had already been a major expansion of the cavalry arm with the creation of the Canadian Mounted Rifles on 1 January 1901. It was initially comprised of a number of independent squadrons, lettered 'A' through 'L', spread across the country. Within a short period many of these squadrons segued or coalesced into separate regiments. 'A' Squadron became a Permanent Force unit titled the Canadian Mounted Rifles on 1 July 1901, and later the Royal Canadian Mounted Rifles in 1903. It was subsequently renamed Strathcona's Horse (Royal Canadians) in 1909 to perpetuate the name of the South African War unit, changing to Lord Strathcona's Horse (Royal Canadians) in 1911.

Squadrons 'B' through 'F' joined to create the 12th Manitoba Dragoons, with headquarters initially located at Brandon, out of which grew the 18th Mounted Rifles and later the 32nd Manitoba Horse and the 34th Fort Garry Horse. 'G' and 'H' Squadrons were disbanded in 1905 and 1904 respectively. 'I' Squadron evolved into the 23rd Mounted Rifles, later the 21st Alberta Hussars. 'J' and 'K' Squadrons combined to become the Toronto Mounted Rifles, later renamed the 9th Mississauga Horse. Finally, 'L' Squadron became the Prince Edward

Island Mounted Rifles, renamed the Prince Edward Island Light Horse in 1903.

In the years leading up to the Great War there was a virtual explosion of cavalry regiments as the 15th through 36th regiments were raised, mainly in western Canada. As well as new units, new formations were created – the 1st and 2nd Mounted Brigades in Ontario, the 3rd and 4th in Quebec and New Brunswick, the 5th in Alberta, the 6th in Manitoba and the 7th in Saskatchewan. These brigades never reached their authorized establishments, since they often lacked their engineer field troops, field ambulances and service corps companies. The Canadian cavalry arm was nevertheless steadily growing in sophistication and capability.

In the decade after the South African War the Militia gradually adopted khaki-coloured uniforms. By 1910 the traditional blue tunics and trousers of the cavalry, where they were still in use, were being condemned by inspecting officers as "worn out and in deplorable condition." 'Blues' or in some regiments even scarlet full-dress uniforms, were by then brought out for most formal occasions such as parades. Also in 1907 the venerable Snider carbine finally gave way to the short Ross Rifle.

Even so, not everything went the cavalry's way, and there were perennial problems to overcome. For many years, for example, there had been no horse shelters available at the large summer training camps, and the animals suffered dreadfully from exposure, particularly in wet weather. Consequently, soldiers stopped bringing their best horses to camp and training standards declined accordingly. Another factor in the decline of mounts at camp was the fact that government compensation for a lost or injured animal was, for many years, limited to $125, far below the market value of a good horse. In the early 1900s the government at last began the construction of horse shelters in the training camps, although there were never enough. For a few years this brought about an improvement in the quality of animals brought to camp. However, by this time the nature of the typical cavalry soldier had changed from that of a rural man who had trained his own horse, to a town-bred trooper who rented his horse, usually of inferior quality, from a contractor.

One of the more significant developments of this period was

the creation, on 6 May 1910, of the Canadian Cavalry Association. The idea for an organization "… to further the interests of, and obtain the greatest possible efficiency in the Cavalry branch of the Service" came about during a course of refresher training for field officers and adjutants of the Cavalry militia of Eastern Canada held at Stanley Barracks in Toronto.

From the beginning the Cavalry Association was an important component of the military scene. Its lists of resolutions, drafted at the annual general meetings, were forwarded to Militia Headquarters, and the Minister. Naturally, the emphasis was on problems requiring the attention of senior authorities, but the Association was also careful to praise and thank those in authority for their work, support and encouragement, even when the resolutions did not result in the action the Association sought.

(Left) A mounted rifles troop on parade near Calgary, 1901. Note the variety of uniforms, weapons and saddlery. (Glenbow Museum)

(Below) Brigadier-General Otter at the inspection of the 16th Light Horse at Fort Qu'Appelle during Militia manoeuvres in Saskatchewan, June 1909. (NAC C36346)

The first meeting of the Canadian Cavalry Association, Toronto, May 1910. Created to further the interests of the Cavalry corps, it evolved into the modern-day Armoured Corps Association.

* * *

After a century of existence, the predominant theme in the story of the Canadian cavalry was how mounted infantry concepts and practice proved repeatedly to be more relevant and useful than the *arme blanche* notions of cavalry charging with sword and lance. Canadian experience emphasized the value of reconnaissance and screening. This was true in the Niagara peninsula in 1813, on the western plains in 1885, and in South Africa in 1900. These circumstances bred a force that valued initiative and independent thought, and that was impatient with the more formal methods of soldiering and warfare practised by the British Army. The South African experience in particular gave the Canadian cavalry a well-deserved sense of self-confidence, something that they would need in the coming conflict.

The 19th Alberta Dragoons. Painting by Ron Volstad. (Directorate of History and Heritage)

Order of Battle of the Canadian Cavalry in 1914

PERMANENT FORCE

Royal Canadian Dragoons
[Toronto, Ontario, and St. Jean,
Quebec]

Lord Strathcona's Horse
(Royal Canadians)
[Winnipeg]

ACTIVE MILITIA

Governor General's Body
Guard [Toronto],
1st Mounted Brigade

5th (The Princess Louise)
Dragoon Guards [Ottawa],
2nd Mounted Brigade

1st Hussars
[London, Ontario],
Divisional Troops

2nd Dragoons
[St. Catharines, Ontario],
1st Mounted Brigade

3rd The Prince of Wales'
Canadian Dragoons
[Peterborough, Ontario],
2nd Mounted Brigade

4th Hussars [Prescott and
Kingston, Ontario],
2nd Mounted Brigade

6th Duke of Connaught's
Royal Canadian Hussars
[Montreal], 4th Mounted
Brigade

7th Hussars [Bishop's
Crossing, Quebec],
3rd Mounted Brigade

8th Princess Louise's New
Brunswick Hussars
[Sussex, New Brunswick],
Divisional Troops

9th Mississauga Horse
(Toronto), 1st Mounted
Brigade

11th Hussars [Richmond,
Québec], 3rd Mounted
Brigade

12th Manitoba Dragoons
[Brandon and Virden,
Manitoba], 6th Mounted
Brigade

13th Scottish Light
Dragoons [Waterloo and
Cowansville, Quebec],
4th Mounted Brigade

14th King's Canadian
Hussars [Middleton and
Kentville, Nova Scotia],
Unbrigaded

15th Light Horse
(Calgary), 5th Mounted
Brigade

16th Light Horse [Regina and Yorkton, Saskatchewan], 7th Mounted Brigade

17th Duke of York's Royal Canadian Hussars (Argenteuil Rangers) [Montreal], Div. Troops

18th Mounted Rifles [Portage la Prairie, Manitoba], 6th Mounted Brigade

19th Alberta Dragoons [Edmonton], 5th Mounted Brigade

20th Border Horse [Pipestone, Manitoba, and Estevan, Saskatchewan], 6th Mounted Brigade

21st Alberta Hussars [Medicine Hat, Alberta], Unbrigaded

22nd Saskatchewan Light Horse [Lloydminster and North Battleford, Sask.], Unbrigaded

23rd Alberta Rangers [Pincher Creek, Alberta], 5th Mounted Brigade

24th Regiment (Grey's Horse) [Ingersoll, Ontario], Divisional Troops

25th Brant Dragoons [Brantford, Ontario], Divisional Troops, 2nd Divisional Area

26th Stanstead Dragoons [Stanstead and Coaticook, Quebec], 4th Mounted Brigade

27th Light Horse [Moose Jaw and Swift Current, Saskatchewan], 7th Mounted Brigade

28th New Brunswick Dragoons [Saint John and Fredericton, N.B.], 3rd Mounted Brigade

29th Light Horse [Saskatoon and Prince Albert, Saskatchewan], 7th Mounted Brigade

30th Regiment (British Columbia Horse) [Vernon and Kelowna, B.C.] Unbrigaded

31st Regiment (British Columbia Horse) (Merritt and Kamloops, B.C.) Unbrigaded

32nd Manitoba Horse [Roblin and Russell, Manitoba], Unbrigaded

No badge was ever authorized.

33rd Vaudreuil and Soulanges Hussars [Rigaud, Quebec], Divisional Troops

34th Fort Garry Horse [Winnipeg], Unbrigaded

35th Central Alberta Horse [Red Deer, Alberta], Unbrigaded

36th Prince Edward Island Light Horse [Charlottetown, P.E.I.], Unbrigaded

CHAPTER 2

Canada's Mounted Troops in the First World War

What came to be known as the First World War was, for the most part, marked by hopeless immobility – trenches and barbed wire, hundreds of thousands of young men literally mowed down by machine-guns; walls of bursting artillery shells in grand attacks that got nowhere; and endless mud and filth and rats and lice. But there was always a glimmer of hope that a breakthrough would be won, mobility restored, and victory achieved, and eventually that did indeed happen on a limited scale. The day of the cavalry came to an end in this conflict, but there was a new vision born – of mechanized mobility that would significantly change warfare in the twentieth century. This is the story of Canadian mounted troops in this vicious war, of the cavalry, of the motorized machine-guns, of the cyclists, and of the first Canadian tank soldiers.

* * *

In the hot, cloudless days of the early summer of 1914, not many Canadians paid much attention to reports of the growing crisis in Europe. The old continent was, after all, far away, and there always were crises in strange places like the Balkans. But the assassination of the Austrian Archduke, Franz Ferdinand, in Sarajevo, the capital of the Austro-Hungarian province of Bosnia, on 28 June, set in motion a seemingly uncontrollable drive toward war between two rival alliances that had grown up in the early years of the century. One after another, the major nations of Europe began to mobilize their massive armies, mainly to ensure that they would not be beaten to the draw and thus risk defeat by a country that had reacted more quickly. Mobilization set in train the actual implementation of national war plans and, once begun, there seemed to be no way that those plans could be turned off.

Germany's plan was based on the need to avoid having to fight simultaneously against both the Russians and the French. Their first move was to be a pre-emptive strike against France, through neutral Belgium. With France out of the war, Germany could then turn eastward to deal with the Russians. Thus in the early morning of 4 August 1914 four German armies invaded Belgium, *en route* to northern France. Great Britain, who years earlier had guaranteed Belgium's neutrality, issued an ultimatum to Germany to withdraw from Belgium by midnight or a state of war would exist. There was no reply and Britain thus found herself at war.

As a British colony, Canada was also at war. There was no choice in the matter. But the Canadian government did retain the authority to decide what sort of contribution Canada

Recruits enlisted by the Governor General's Body Guard are introduced to customary military accommodation, Toronto, August 1914. Bell tents were still being used by the Canadian Army a half century later. (City of Toronto Archives)

Armoured cars of Brutinel's Canadian Automobile Machine Gun Brigade No. 1 preparing for an inspection by the Governor General, Ottawa, 23 September 1914. (NAC C11272)

Dragoons, which was to form the divisional cavalry squadron.

The patriotic fervour accompanying the mobilization prompted offers by several prominent citizens to raise units such as the Princess Patricia's Canadian Light Infantry at their own expense. Another such proposal came from a group which included Sir Clifford Sifton, a former Cabinet minister under Sir Wilfrid Laurier, and Raymond Brutinel, a French citizen resident in Montreal and self-made millionaire, who offered to raise and equip a unit of armoured vehicles carrying machine-guns. A parsimonious government, already facing enormous expenses, was only too eager to accept. Brutinel's new unit, called the Canadian Automobile Machine Gun Brigade No.1, was formed on 2 September 1914. When it was inspected by the Governor General only twenty days later, the unit consisted of two batteries totaling 135 all ranks, eight armoured cars, eight trucks, four automobiles, twenty Colt machine-guns, seventeen motorcycles and sixteen bicycles. The brigade – because it was equipped with 'guns' it used artillery nomenclature – sailed for Britain on 29 September.

In early October, after a month of rudimentary training in Valcartier organized by the Permanent Force units, the Canadian Expeditionary Force sailed for England. The Canadian regular units – the Royal Canadian Horse Artillery, the Royal Canadian Dragoons and Lord Strathcona's Horse – were added to the contingent only at the last moment. The Minister, a partisan supporter of the Active Militia, did not wanted any Permanent Force units included (he succeeded in barring the RCR, who were subsequently sent off to Bermuda on garrison duties for eighteen months) and it took the personal intervention of

would make to the war effort, and offered a contingent of 25,000 men. On 6 August the British accepted this offer, stipulating that infantry was what was wanted.

While there was a detailed plan for the mobilization of an overseas force of an infantry division and a cavalry brigade already in the files in Ottawa, the overbearing Minister of Militia and Defence, Sam Hughes, deliberately chose to ignore it. Instead, he decided to improvise. Hughes sent telegrams directly to each of the 226 Militia units with orders for them to begin recruiting volunteers for the Canadian Expeditionary Force (CEF). For reasons that have never been adequately explained, the Minister had decided not to mobilize any of the existing units, with their geographical connections, but rather to raise a force of numbered battalions which had no connection to anything. The next weeks were a time of utter chaos, with orders and counter-orders flowing from Ottawa. It was especially confusing to the cavalry units, who were not certain whether cavalrymen were wanted or not.

The declaration of war was greeted with enormous popular enthusiasm over much of the country, and young men flocked to recruiting centres. It was generally assumed that the war would be over by Christmas, and many did not want to miss this opportunity for adventure. Most cavalry regiments did, in fact, recruit large numbers of men, and it was not until they arrived at the newly constructed camp at Valcartier, near Quebec City, the concentration point for the CEF, that they learned there would be no cavalry in the overseas contingent. Those who wanted to serve would have to do so as infantrymen. Both the 5th and 6th Battalions thus came to consist of cavalrymen from western Canada. The only mounted unit mobilized specifically as cavalry was a squadron of Edmonton's 19th Alberta

Cavalry horses boarding a ship in Quebec harbour, October 1914.

the Governor General to have the cavalry regiments sent overseas. After spending an uncomfortably cold and wet winter in tents on Salisbury Plain, they became part of a newly-created 1st Canadian Mounted Brigade in late January 1915.

The Militia cavalry regiments were unhappy about being excluded from the war and influential officers began applying political pressure on the government. The result of this lobbying was that in November 1914 the Minister announced that four (later increased to thirteen) regiments of mounted rifles would be raised. The rationale for their creation was the possibility of service in the Middle East. However, the Australians and New Zealanders arrived there first, so the first six regiments were converted into infantry units and sent to Britain in the summer of 1915.

By early 1915 Canada's contribution to the war effort included four different categories of mounted soldiers: the cavalry, the mounted rifles, the motor machine-gun brigade and a cyclist company in the infantry division. Within the cavalry there were two variants: the Canadian Mounted (later Cavalry) Brigade, which served most of the war with Indian and British cavalry divisions; and the divisional (later corps) cavalry which served with the CEF. The other mounted units, the cyclists and the 'Motors', as the motor machine-gun units were popularly known, saw a great deal of fighting but little of this involved the kind of action for which mounted units traditionally existed. In the late summer of 1918 yet another type of mounted unit, three tank battalions, were added to this roster, but the war ended before any of them was sent into action.

THE CANADIAN CAVALRY 1915–1916

The Permanent Force cavalry in England posed a bit of a problem: no one quite knew what to do with them as they could hardly be part of what would become 1 Canadian Division and the British really did not want more cavalry than they already had. Nonetheless, the Royal Canadian Dragoons, Lord Strathcona's Horse and the Royal Canadian Horse Artillery were brigaded in what was called, at first, 1 Canadian Mounted Brigade on 28 January 1915. To fill out the establishment of three cavalry regiments, a British unit, the 2nd King Edward's Horse (2 KEH), raised in the summer of 1914 and containing a large number of expatriate Canadians in its ranks, was included. It was called 2 KEH because another reserve unit named King Edward's Horse had been in existence since 1901. Both units recruited men from the colonies who were living in London.

The next problem was to find a suitable brigade commander, but that was resolved when Field Marshal Lord Kitchener personally nominated Colonel The Right Honourable J.E.B. Seely, DSO, who, until shortly before the war, had been Britain's Secretary of State for War. Seely was a legendary character who had won his DSO in South Africa. A contemporary and close friend of Winston Churchill, both men had been

Brigadier-General The Right Honourable J.E.B. Seely, Commander of the Canadian Cavalry Brigade, 1915-1918.

Watering on the March. **Painting by Sir Alfred Munnings. (Canadian War Museum 8580)**

members of the British Cabinet in March 1914. In that month trouble had arisen in Ireland as Catholics and Protestants armed themselves for civil war over the issue of Home Rule, or local autonomy for Ireland. The predominately Protestant population of Ulster prepared to resist to the point of armed rebellion and any British intervention seemed likely to take the form of military action against the Protestant faction, but Anglo-Irish Protestants from Ulster formed a large and influential segment of the officer corps of the British Army and this group felt the pain of divided loyalties.

Seely, in a well-meaning but clumsy effort to appease them, offered to excuse any officers domiciled in Ulster from participating in active operations conducted in that province – a clear indication that strong measures were likely to be taken. His initiative led to the officers of an entire cavalry brigade tendering their resignations. Brigadier-General Hubert Gough led this protest, termed a mutiny by many. The government was acutely embarrassed, all contemplated military action against Ulster was shelved, and Seely was forced to resign from the Cabinet.

When war broke out, Seely asked for employment with the Army in the field. His handling of the March crisis had alienated many influential high-ranking officers (including corps commander Sir Douglas Haig) but he was too politically pow-

erful to ignore and so went to France as a senior liaison officer attached to the French Army.

When 1 Canadian Division deployed to France in February 1915, the Permanent Force cavalry was left behind, in England. By that time a continuous line of trenches had been dug from the North Sea coast in Belgium all the way to the Swiss border, and the war was degenerating into an immobile conflict dominated by barbed wire and machine-guns. This onset of trench warfare had reduced the requirement for liaison officers, so Seely was given command of 1 Canadian Mounted Brigade in Britain. Placing him with the Canadians neatly solved administrative problems for both the British and Canadians: what to do with Seely and what to do with the horsemen? It also inadvertently gave the brigade a high degree of political influence, something that it could never have achieved on its own.

By late April, after having suffered extremely heavy casualties in its first major battle, at Second Ypres, the division was desperately short of reinforcements. Seely, after consulting the unit commanding officers, agreed to a request from the War Office that his brigade go to France to serve temporarily in a dismounted role. This was not a popular decision with many of the officers and men of the brigade. Lieutenant Roy Nordheimer of the RCD later wrote:

> To the layman, this offer would seem to be the natural sequence of events. To the cavalryman, it was a supreme sacrifice, and a lowering of morale and efficiency. Years of training for horse and man were thrown away, and all the visions of 'shock action' with German cavalry disappeared in smoke. To place a cavalryman on foot, take away his sword or lance and give him a bayonet and a bomb [grenade], is like taking a skilled aviator, giving him a taxi, and telling him to drive according to the recognized rules of traffic.

Nordheimer expressed a typical view but 'Seely's Detachment', 1,486 men strong when it arrived in France in early May 1915, served with great distinction as infantry in the trenches, at Festubert, Givenchy and Ploegsteert, until the end of the year. Because they had performed so well in operations in the trenches, they were then selected to train the newly-arrived dismounted units of the Canadian Mounted Rifles (CMR).

Seely was a popular officer, especially with the men. He was also wise enough to realize that he was not a brilliant commander, so he made sure that he had clever officers in all key staff functions. He gave them a free hand and backed them to the hilt. When things went well he took the credit, but, more importantly, when things went wrong he took the blame. The result of this system was a confident, utterly loyal staff.

With the arrival in France of 2 Canadian Division, a Canadian Corps was formed. In mid-January 1916, after nearly a year in the trenches, Seely's Detachment was remounted and renamed the 1st Canadian Cavalry Brigade (CCB) – since there never was another Canadian cavalry brigade formed, the number was seldom used. At the same time 2 KEH was replaced by The Fort Garry Horse and the CCB was sent to join an Indian Army cavalry division serving in France.

Artist's depiction of a Cavalry Brigade attack on the German strongpoint known as 'L8', near Festubert, on 25 May 1915, while the cavalry were serving as infantry. *(Canada in Flanders)*

Another addition to the remounted brigade in early 1916 was the Canadian Cavalry Brigade Machine Gun Squadron. The pre-war establishment for a cavalry regiment called for a machine-gun section in its ranks. In the Canadian brigade, 2 KEH had had the standard two Maxim guns, while the Dragoons and Strathconas each had four Colts. To give the brigade more concentrated firepower these sections were amalgamated into an *ad hoc* squadron, a process that was carried out throughout the British Cavalry Corps.

While the Cavalry Brigade, primarily because of Seely's political connections, was remounted, there was no such reprieve for the Mounted Rifles The Cavalry Corps now had five divisions in France, and that was deemed sufficient. In December 1915 they were formally converted to infantry. The six regi-

The Organization of 1 Canadian Cavalry Brigade, 1916

Royal Canadian Dragoons

Lord Strathcona's Horse (Royal Canadians)

Fort Garry Horse

Royal Canadian Horse Artillery Brigade ['A' and 'B' Batteries]

Canadian Cavalry Brigade Machine Gun Squadron

7th (Cavalry) Field Ambulance

ments then in France were combined into four battalions to form 8 (CMR) Infantry Brigade in 3 Canadian Division.

Only two units escaped the fate of conversion to infantry. The 7th CMR, formed in south-western Ontario, had been tasked to supply the divisional cavalry squadron for 2 Division.

Badges of the Royal Canadian Dragoons, Lord Strathcona's Horse, Fort Garry Horse and 2nd King Edward's Horse.

Badge of the 7th Canadian Mounted Rifles.

Its commanding officer, Lieutenant-Colonel Ibbotson Leonard, a 1st Hussar from a prominent London, Ontario, family, convinced Ottawa to leave him in command of the squadron, still carrying the rank of lieutenant-colonel even though the unit should have been commanded by a major. (In selecting his officers, Leonard chose, as a troop leader, a personable young man who had recently left Leonard's old school, the Royal Military College at Kingston. Lieutenant William Avery Bishop accompanied the squadron to Britain, where he applied for a transfer to the Royal Flying Corps and went on to a spectacular career as a fighter pilot, including the award of a Victoria

Cross.) Shortly after arriving in France, Leonard, pulling more political strings, succeeded in having his squadron rebadged as 1st Hussars, the Militia regiment primarily responsible for raising the 7th CMR. The other two squadrons of the 7th CMR eventually formed the CCB depot in England.

The other mounted rifle regiment which avoided becoming infantry was Saskatchewan's 10th CMR. It was tasked with supplying the divisional cavalry squadrons for 3 and 4 Canadian Divisions. These squadrons, too, would eventually rebadge back to their parent regiment, the 16th Light Horse.

THE CYCLISTS, 1914–1916

During the first two years of the war the organization of a Canadian infantry division included a cavalry squadron and a cyclist company. Both organizations were similar in size and in role. Their duties included reconnaissance (which was virtually impossible because of the continuous lines of trenches), checking routes, locating billets, as well as the carrying of messages, traffic control, prisoner of war escort and the provision of stretcher parties, burial parties and labour gangs. The cyclists in pre-war years had specialized in intelligence matters, the location and identification of enemy units, the preparation of operations maps and the carriage of dispatches. This work appealed to the university students who filled the ranks of the cyclists companies in 1914 and 1915 and they were not pleased to find themselves filling and carrying sandbags behind the lines. With so many bright, young and disillusioned scholars in their ranks, the cyclists were a ready pool of potential officers for other arms and services.

THE MOTOR MACHINE GUNS 1915–1916

One group that might also have been disillusioned with the conditions of trench warfare was the Motor Machine Gun Batteries. Like the regular cavalry and horse gunners, Brutinel's Motor Machine Gun Brigade had been left behind in England when 1 Division deployed to France in February 1915, but it was sent to join the division after the battle of Givenchy in June.

Back in Canada three additional motor machine-gun units had been formed. A well-known Toronto merchant family financed the first of them, the Eaton Motor Machine Gun Battery. The legendary mining millionaire, 'Klondike Joe' Boyle, initially led his Yukon Motor Machine Gun Battery, raised in Dawson as a mounted machine-gun detachment. Their cap badge was reputed to contain a genuine gold nugget. The third unit was the Borden Machine Gun Battery, which was named for prime minister Sir Robert Borden by Sam Hughes. The

Trooper of Lord Strathcona's Horse. **Painting by Ron Volstad. By 1918 cavalry equipment and weaponry had evolved into its finest and final form. (Directorate of History and Heritage)**

Prototype armoured car of the Borden Machine Gun Battery, 1915. This battery was commanded by Major Edward Holland, VC, who won his decoration while serving with the RCD in South Africa. (NAC C2654)

Borden Battery, which was also sometimes referred to as the Holland Battery, was commanded by Victoria Cross holder, Major (formerly Sergeant) Edward Holland.

More by coincidence than by design, each battery eventually found itself attached to one of the four Canadian divisions. Brutinel, with the 1st Division, quickly showed his superior abilities in the way he used his unit. In the other divisions the machine-gunners were looked upon simply as being reinforcements with machine-guns, and they were usually employed to plug gaps in the line, the men and their weapons being spread along the trenches. By contrast, Brutinel kept his guns together and brought down masses of fire in specific areas, thus directly influencing the battle. Among other innovations, he developed the technique of creating a curtain of fire that could isolate sections of the enemy trenches that were under attack, and the machine-gun barrage, a concept that soon became a signature of the Canadian Corps and was adopted throughout the British Army.

Of equal or greater importance than Brutinel's innovative ideas was his ability as a trainer. From the training of his own unit, he went on to train all of the machine-gunners of the division, and later those of the entire Canadian Corps.

THE AMALGAMATIONS OF 1916
In July 1916, Brutinel was placed in command of all four of the motor machine-gun units, which were joined together to form the 1st Canadian Motor Machine Gun Brigade (1 CMMGB). The 'Motors', as they were known, fought at Vimy Ridge, Hill 70, and Passchendaele, growing steadily in capability and confidence. Even so, these battles were primarily tests of their gunnery skills and physical endurance as their vehicles were never brought into action at this time. At Vimy, for example, the batteries had to carry their machine-guns and ammunition forward by hand, since the shell-beaten, waterlogged ground was impassable to any form of mechanized transport. (Four British tanks assigned to support the assault all bogged down.)

Lieutenant-Colonel (later Brigadier-General) Raymond Brutinel, commanding officer of the 1st Motor Machine Gun Brigade. (Directorate of History and Heritage)

Organization of the 1st Canadian Motor Machine Gun Brigade, July 1916

'A' Battery [Brutinel's 1st Battery]

'B' Battery [Brutinel's 2nd Battery]

'C' Battery [Borden Battery]

'D' Battery [Eaton Battery]

'E' Battery [Yukon Battery]

Badge of the 1st Motor Machine Gun Brigade.

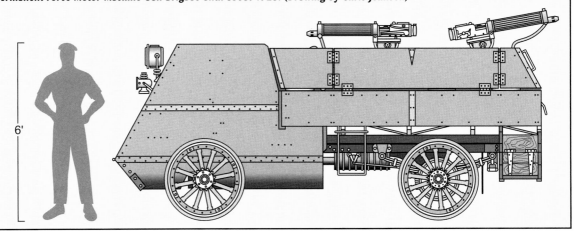

Armoured Autocar. Developed in 1914, the Autocar was in service with the 1st Motor Machine Gun Brigade throughout the First World War. In 1916 the original Colt machine-guns were replaced with Vickers .303 weapons. A few of the cars were brought back to Canada at the end of the war and were used by the Permanent Force Motor Machine Gun Brigade until about 1923. (Drawing by Chris Johnson)

Armoured Autocar
Country of Origin: Canada
Crew: 8 (Commander, Driver, 2 x
    Vickers .303 inch MG Gun Crews)
Length: 14 feet 9 inches
Width: 3 feet 7 inches
Height: 6 feet
Weight: 6,000 pounds
Engine: 2 cylinder, gasoline
Maximum Speed: 25 mph
Range: Unknown
Armour – Maximum: 9.5 mm
Armament: 2 x .303 inch Vickers MGs
    .303 inch Lewis MG (optional)

6'

Troops of the Canadian Light Horse advancing from Vimy Ridge after it was captured by the Canadian Corps, 9 April 1917. (NAC PA1111)

THE CANADIAN LIGHT HORSE

In May 1916, the four separate divisional cavalry squadrons were amalgamated into an *ad hoc* cavalry regiment under control of the newly formed Canadian Corps. Because each of the squadrons represented a different unit, there was considerable concern over the identity of the new regiment. In the end the squadrons retained their own identities. The Canadian Corps Cavalry Regiment – the cumbersome title was changed in February 1917 to The Canadian Light Horse (CLH) – was made up of three squadrons: 'A' Squadron from the 19th Alberta Dragoons, 'B' from the 1st Hussars, and 'C' from the 16th Light Horse. 4 Division's squadron, like that of the 3rd, had come from Saskatchewan's 10th CMR before it was converted to infantry, so it was easily absorbed into the 16th Light Horse Squadron.

At Vimy Ridge the troopers of the CLH toiled for months digging tunnels through the chalk for the

Badges of the units which made up the Canadian Light Horse: 1st Hussars, 19th Alberta Dragoons, and 16th Light Horse.

assaulting infantry. On the day of the attack, 9 April 1917, the regiment was tasked with sending patrols forward to maintain contact with the retreating Germans. However, the horsemen were quickly stopped by machine-gun fire and this brief foray into mounted operations came to a sudden end.

In May 1916, the Cyclists also found their four separate divisional companies amalgamated into a three-company-strong Canadian Corps Cyclists Battalion. Their tasks and experiences exactly paralleled those of the CLH with whom they served as corps troops in the Canadian Corps Headquarters. The battalion numbered 8 officers, 195 other ranks and 2 horses. The principal mount of the 'gas pipe cavalry', as they were called, was a Planet bicycle, which, fully loaded, weighted some forty kilograms. At Vimy Ridge the Cyclists, like the CLH, dug tunnels. Following the assault they had one company on standby for exploitation, but the setback suffered by the CLH brought plans for its use to an end.

THE 1917 CAMPAIGN

The 1917 campaign began in March with a general German withdrawal to a shorter, well-entrenched line known to the Allies as the Hindenburg Line. During their withdrawal, the Germans laid waste to the countryside they were abandoning, cutting down every tree and poisoning every well. The Allies had been caught off guard by this unexpected move, the infantry were unable to respond quickly enough, and the cavalry, including the CCB, in a brief return to mobile operations were sent forward to regain contact. On 26 March, the Canadians caught up to the German rearguard and captured a couple of hamlets, the first French communities retaken by the Allies in nearly two years. This resulted in extensive press coverage for the cavalry in general and Seely in particular. Sir Douglas Haig, now a field marshal and commander of the BEF, was sufficiently impressed to order Seely to repeat this performance the next day and capture two villages named Guyencourt and Saulcourt.

Cavalrymen pause in a sunken road during their advance to the Hindenburg Line, 16 March 1917. (NAC PA910)

Lieutenant Frederick Harvey, VC

On 27 March, Seely's brigade executed a pincer movement on the two villages, sending the Strathconas around to the north while the Garrys came up from the south. The Strathconas' way was blocked by machine-guns and a strongly wired position. The action taken by Lieutenant Frederick Harvey is described in *Thirty Canadian V.C.'s:*

He was in command of the leading troop of the charging Strathconas and rode well in front of his men. He was close to the edge of the village, when, by the failing light, he discovered a deadly menace to his command set fairly across his course – a wired trench containing a machine-gun and a strong garrison. He swung from his saddle and sprinted straight at the gun, firing his revolver as he ran. He reached the triple entanglement and hurdled it, shot the machine-gunner and jumped on to the gun.

With the way opened for them the Strathconas stormed into Guyencourt. Lieutenant Harvey, initially told that he had been awarded the Distinguished Service Order, later learned that the King himself changed the award to the Victoria Cross.

The great Canadian triumph at Vimy Ridge in April 1917 was followed in August by the battle for Hill 70, another outstanding Canadian success, and then in October by Passchendaele. In this most futile of Great War battles Canadian arms were again victorious in a murderous slogging match fought in the morass

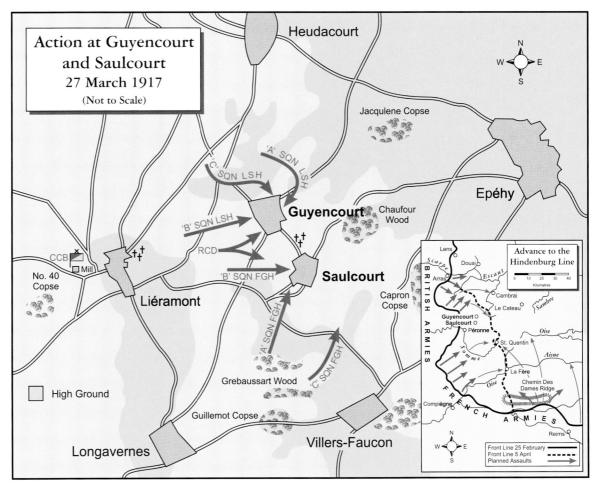

and rain of Flanders. Some 16,000 Canadian casualties were suffered in the capture of a relatively insignificant ridge. The horrors of Passchendaele, where the wounded often drowned in the mud, underlined the need for the restoration of mobile warfare, in which advances might be measured in kilometres rather than metres. On 20 November 1917 the British undertook just such an operation at Cambrai.

THE BATTLE OF CAMBRAI, 20 NOVEMBER 1917

Cambrai was intended to be a giant cavalry raid. The opening in the German lines would be made with large numbers of tanks, which were still an experimental weapon, and exploited by massed cavalry – no less than three divisions' worth! The tank attack proved to be a great success and their future as a new arm was virtually assured, but the cavalry were unable to take advantage of the opportunity created. Out of the three divisions deployed, only three squadrons, one of which was Canadian, managed to get past the German trench lines. Lieutenant Harcus Strachan of the Fort Garry Horse took command of 'B' Squadron when his squadron leader was killed. Under his leadership this single squadron, who were under the

Cambrai
20 November 1917

0 — 200 — 400 — 600 — 800
Metres

'B' SQUADRON FORT GARRY HORSE ROUTE

STRACHAN'S PARTY: ROUTE BACK

COWEN'S PARTY: ROUTE BACK

To Cambrai

Rumilly

Sunken Road

GERMAN ATTACKING POSITION

GERMAN INF AND MGs AWAITING SURRENDER

'B' SQN FGH

MASNIÈRES LINE

Masnières

GERMAN BATTERY

Spitlocked Ground

CAMOUFLAGE SCREEN

Mon Plaisir Farm

NFLD REGT

STRACHAN'S PARTY

Bridge smashed by tank

"Walker's Bridge"

COWEN'S PARTY

CANADIAN CAVALRY BRIGADE HQ

St-Quentin Canal

L'escaut River

'B' SQN FORT GARRY HORSE

impression that they were the spearhead of a divisional attack, were, in fact, on their own and cut off behind the enemy lines. The grand cavalry exploitation had been called off after they went in. Strachan later wrote an account of this exploit.

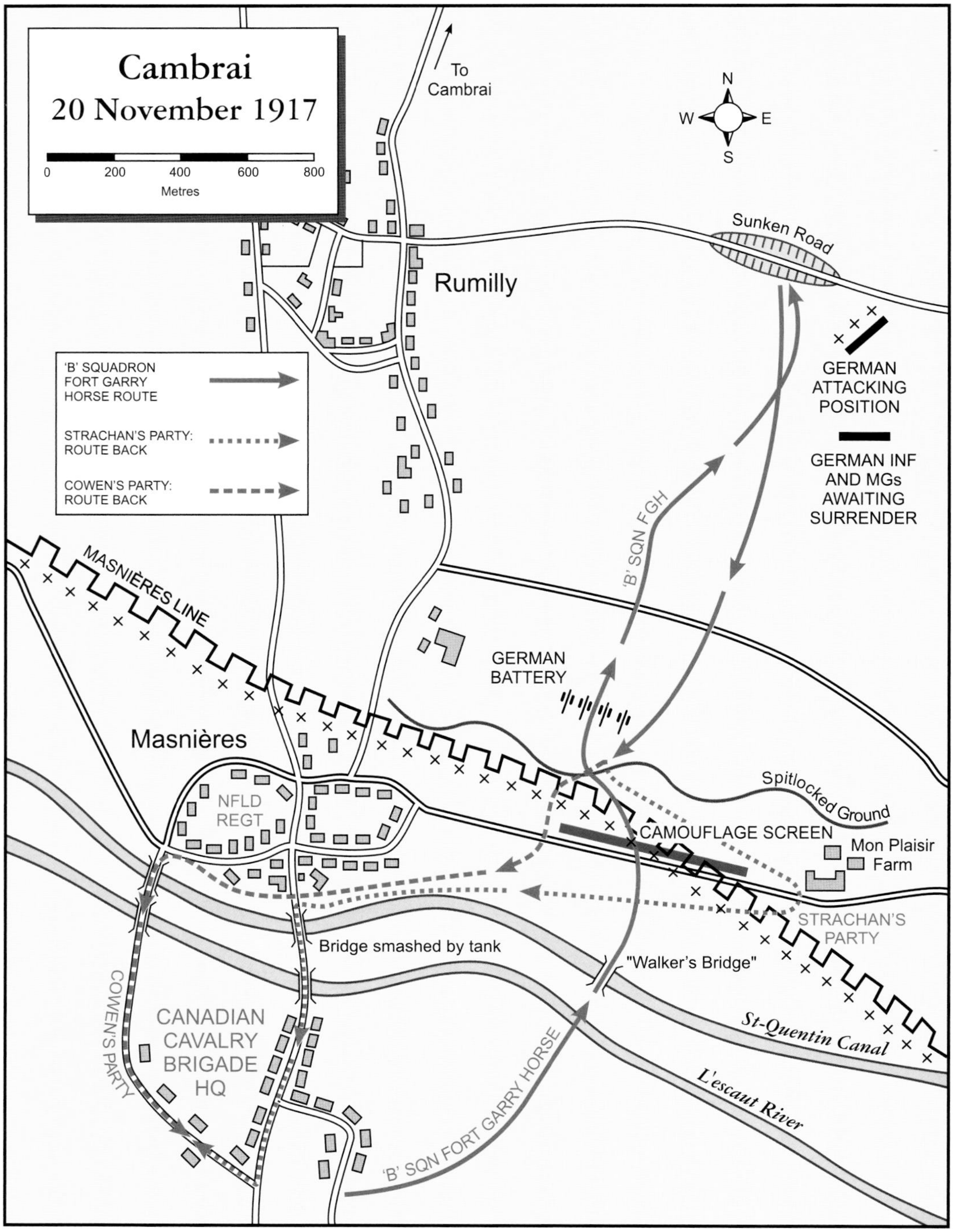

… On gaining the ridge, [we] came face to face with a German battery of four guns about 300 yards away. Fortunately swords had been drawn before crossing the [makeshift] bridge [over the Canal de l'Escaut] and the squadron charged the guns, each troop column converging on them. … One gun continued to fire until the last and those gun-

ners probably escaped over the difficulty of reaching them [with our swords], whereas the remaining gunners, who ran away as soon as we appeared, were accounted for almost to a man. … Whilst charging the guns we were fired on by machine-guns, but these ceased fire when the guns were taken.

Strachan's plainly worded report simply does not do justice to the vicious fighting that marked this action. Nearly half his men and their horses were killed or wounded. Galloping deeper into enemy territory, it was close to nightfall when the survivors realized that no one was following behind, and what was left of

British tank which frustrated the planned advance of the Canadian Cavalry Brigade by collapsing the bridge at Masnières. (Fort Garry Horse Museum)

the squadron took cover in a sunken road. The horses were utterly exhausted, some of them literally dropping dead while they were being inspected. Under the cover of darkness, the dismounted survivors then made their way back to the Allied lines, bringing in many prisoners and useful information on the German positions they had encountered. For his leadership and initiative, Strachan was awarded the Victoria Cross.

While Cambrai was a triumph for the tanks, it was a humiliation for the cavalry and the British prime minister, David Lloyd George, exploited the failure of the operation to pursue his political vendetta against the BEF's commander. Haig, hoping for a breakthrough and thus clinging to his cavalry, but bent on fighting a war of attrition that was proving unbearably expensive in manpower, was too well entrenched for Lloyd George to replace him. Instead, the prime minister worked to restrict Sir Douglas's ability to squander resources by limiting the reinforcements allotted to him and shifting emphasis from the Western Front to other, perhaps more fruitful and certainly less expensive, theatres of war. Early in 1918 the prime minister ordered a major reorganization of the Cavalry Corps with the expressed aim of reinforcing the cavalry in Palestine.

Out of the total of five divisions in France, two were broken up, including the

Lieutenant Harcus Strachan, VC. (Fort Garry Horse Museum)

5th in which the CCB was serving. At first, BEF headquarters had assumed that the Canadians, too, would be leaving, perhaps to be turned into infantry, but Seely once again used his political influence to ensure that his men remained employed as a cavalry brigade. The remaining three divisions were reorganized, with the CCB going to 3 Division.

1918 – BREAKING THE TRENCH DEADLOCK

The German-Russian armistice of December 1917, followed by the Treaty of Brest Litovsk in March 1918, meant that many German divisions could be transferred to the west and placed to strike a decisive blow before the Americans (who had joined the Allies in April 1917) could arrive in sufficient strength to influence the outcome of the war. A million-man German force struck the Allied line on 21 March 1918, their attack aimed at the junction point of the British and French armies. With the help of a heavy early morning mist, storm troopers specially trained in new infiltration tactics broke through the British line.

It was the British Fifth Army, under General Sir Hubert Gough, that felt the weight of the blow. This was the same Hubert Gough who had been involved in the March 1914 'mutiny' in Ireland that had led to Seely's resignation from the Cabinet. Gough's army was driven back, leaving him no choice but to commit his reserves, two of the three remaining divisions of the Cavalry Corps. 'Exigencies of the service' led to the CCB being temporarily transferred to 2 Cavalry Division, and it was as a part of the latter formation that it fought a week-long series of rearguard actions in support of the Fifth Army. Seely, no doubt, was delighted to be offered so instrumental a part in saving Hubert Gough's army from destruction. The irony of the situation, the fact that the very man who had brought about his fall from Cabinet in 1914 was now (to a degree) dependent on him in 1918, was positively delicious.

THE BATTLE OF MOREUIL WOOD, 30 MARCH 1918

At first light on Easter Saturday, 30 March 1918, the German offensive was nearing Amiens. Only one significant obstacle, the River Avre, stood between the Germans and this vital rail centre. The CCB was tired and understrength after nine days of unceasing operations during which they had mounted one delaying action after another in an effort to stem the German flood further north. In spite

Fort Garrys on the March II. Painting by Sir Alfred Munnings. Munnings, perhaps the foremost British equestrian artist, painted a number of notable works depicting Canadian cavalry units during the war. (Canadian War Museum 8585)

The Charge of Flowerdew's Squadron. Painting by Sir Alfred Munnings depicting the gallant charge of 'C' Squadron of Lord Strathcona's Horse at Moreuil Wood on 30 March, 1918. Casualties were extremely heavy but the action earned Flowerdew the posthumous award of the Victoria Cross. (Canadian War Museum 8571)

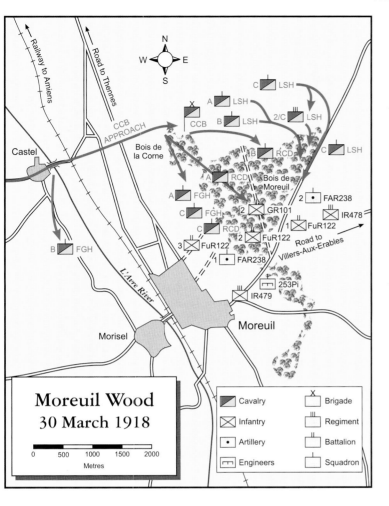

Moreuil Wood
30 March 1918

0   500   1000   1500   2000
Metres

◪	Cavalry	⊠	Brigade
⊠	Infantry	⫿⫿⫿	Regiment
•	Artillery	⫿⫿	Battalion
⫿⫿⫿	Engineers	⫿	Squadron

Lieutenant Gordon Flowerdew, VC. (Lord Strathcona's Horse Museum)

mated three hundred German soldiers were ejected from the far side of the wood as a result. The second squadron to arrive, 'C', was sent south along the west side of the wood. Topping a crest, it encountered a German infantry column and its supporting artillery battery and, unable to penetrate further south, turned east into the wood proper. Here it encountered stiff opposition. The attack of the third RCD squadron, 'B', miscarried. The half-strength squadron, instead of continuing on to the far side of the wood, turned into the trees too early and was stopped in its tracks.

To revive the plan, the Strathcona reserve, 'C' Squadron under Lieutenant Gordon Flowerdew, was ordered to complete the pincer movement by riding around the far side of the wood and down its eastern face. Rounding the corner of the wood the squadron encountered a steep bank, and, on reaching the top, found itself in a perilous situation. Flowerdew's Victoria Cross citation recounts what happened.

[Lieutenant] Flowerdew saw two lines of enemy, each about sixty strong, with machine-guns in the centre and on the flanks; one line being about two hundred yards behind the other. Realising the critical nature of the operation and how much depended on it, Lieut. Flowerdew ordered a troop under Lieut. Harvey, V.C., to dismount [and move through the woodline], while he led the remaining three troops to the charge. The squadron (less one troop) passed over both lines, killing many of the enemy with the sword; and wheeling about galloped on them again. Although the squadron had then lost about 70 per cent of its members, killed and wounded …, the enemy broke and retired.

Trooper James Bryant, who was with the Strathcona dismounted squadron just inside the edge of the wood, remembered the wounded horses.

They took an awful cutting up…. The men were shot out of their saddles, and the horses, most of them were wounded, hit. They all came back around and joined our horses beneath the wood. And they'd stand there and bleed to death. They'd put one foot out a little to one side, and then another, just trying to hold their weight up and then they'd finally just sag.

of this, however, its morale was unshaken. When Seely got orders to proceed to Moreuil, where the enemy was preparing for an assault crossing of the Avre, his men reacted as the seasoned professionals they had become.

Seely's intention was to recapture Moreuil Wood, which sat on a crest of land overlooking the Avre. Fortunately, a thin line of skirmishers were still holding out on the enemy (eastern) bank. Crossing the river on a small bridge at Castel, the CCB rode toward the wood. His quickly conceived plan called for the RCD to send a squadron around each side of the wood and one through the centre. The Strathconas would form up on the northern face of the wood, dismount, and, using two of their three squadrons, clear the wood on foot moving north to south. The Machine Gun Squadron would provide covering fire on both flanks, while the Fort Garrys and the third Strathcona squadron were held in reserve.

The first to arrive, 'A' Squadron, RCD, was sent into the wood near the location of Seely's headquarters. Fighting dismounted, the Dragoons struck the defending German infantry battalion on their left flank and started to roll up their line, and an esti-

45

The horses of Flowerdew's squadron which did not survive the charge.
(Imperial War Museum Q10858)

Flowerdew himself was mortally wounded. Nevertheless, his attack turned the tide inside the wood, where the enemy, confounded by the noise of battle in his rear, began to fall back.

The Canadians were barely holding their own at this point as Seely committed his last reserves. 'B' Squadron of the Garrys was dispatched back across the Avre to occupy a hill that overlooked the southern portion of the battlefield. From there they engaged the Germans with long-range rifle fire while the other two Garry squadrons were sent in to reinforce the Dragoons.

More assistance was needed and Seely appealed to the divisional commander for help. In response, 3 Cavalry Brigade was dispatched and Seely employed them to reinforce the 'C' Squadron, RCD, action. Sweeping through the wood with a dismounted firing line composed of British and Canadian troopers, the on-scene commander, Lieutenant-Colonel Geoffrey Brooke (who had, until recently, been the CCB's brigade major) drove the Germans back to its eastern edge. At nightfall the horse soldiers still held most of the wood and two days later they recaptured Rifle Wood, just to the north. The German assault was stalled, never to be resumed.

THE MOTOR MACHINE GUN BRIGADE

When the great German offensive opened on 21 March, the Canadian Motor Machine Gun Brigade was with the Canadian Corps on Vimy Ridge, but General Gough needed every reinforcement he could lay his hands on. Since most of the Cavalry Corps was already committed to his support, the one organization left that could reach the scene quickly enough to be effective was the CMMGB.

Armoured Autocar of the Motor Machine Gun Brigade preparing for action. (NAC PA2614)

There is some evidence that it was Seely who recommended the unusual Canadian motorized unit to Gough. Warned for action on the afternoon of 22 March, by 0530 hours the next day the Motors were driving south. 'A' and 'B' Batteries, Brutinel's originals, each had eight Vickers guns mounted on four armoured cars, while the other three Batteries, 'C', 'D' and 'E', each had eight guns carried in light trucks. The unit strength at this time was about 350 all ranks. The Motors arrived at Amiens after a six-hour drive and from there they were directed forward to Fifth Army headquarters at Villers Brettonneux, sixteen kilometres to the east, where a grateful 'Goughie' was on hand to greet them.

The vehicles with which 'A' and 'B' Batteries were equipped were products of the Autocar Company of Ardmore, Pennsylvania. Each vehicle carried two machine-guns and 12,000 rounds of ammunition and a searchlight was mounted on the front of each for night action. The machine-guns could be dismounted for firing, or they could be fired from the vehicle over the top of steel-plated sides, although that left the gunner's head and shoulders exposed. The original concept for their employment was to treat the vehicles more as mobile machine-gun posts rather than as fighting vehicles. However, in the March 1918 crisis they were to play the role of armoured cars. In an interview recorded years later by the CBC, Major-General Frank Worthington described how they operated.

The situation was confused and very fluid. The Germans had overcome the British defences and were now coming forward in their proper battle formations. The methods used by the Motor Machine Guns was very simple. We would take four or eight guns and open fire as the enemy was advancing, and bring him to a halt. Then the enemy would get ready to shell us out. We would move half our guns back to a rear position – maybe five hundred or a thousand yards back – and as the enemy would come on with their artillery support and advance closer we would pull out the forward guns. The battle line would be cleared and the enemy would sort of collect themselves and start moving

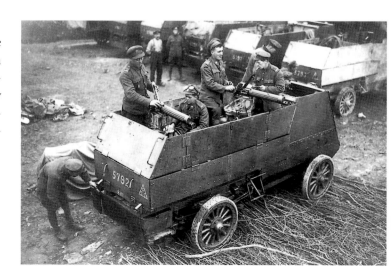

forward. Then you'd give it to them again. Day after day it was the same thing.

The greatest threat facing Fifth Army was being separated from the French on their right, that being one of the main objectives of the German offensive. A detachment of two batteries, 'D' and 'E', maintained the vital link with the French very effectively, while, on the other flank, 'B' and 'C' Batteries maintained ties with the neighbouring British Third Army. In the period 24 March through 3 April, the Motors lost almost half their strength in casualties, mainly because they were being used as armoured cars instead of as mobile machine-guns. The price was stiff, but the results of failure might have been catastrophic.

The sterling performance and great utility of the CMMGB during the March crisis did not to go unnoticed, for on 2 June 1918 a second such unit was created. This was done by amalgamating the CMMGB with three machine-gun companies belonging to 5 Division, which was being broken up for reinforcements. The new organization was commanded by now Brigadier-General Brutinel, who had become General Officer Commanding (GOC), Canadian Machine Gun Corps.

One of the officers in 1 CMMGB's 'E' Battery was the newly commissioned Second Lieutenant F. F. Worthington, MM and Bar, who would quickly rise to command it.

THE BATTLE OF AMIENS

On 5 August 1918, a newly-promoted Captain Worthington and the rest of 1 CMMGB received orders to move after dark. At daybreak they laid-up in a wood where each vehicle was camouflaged and the tire tracks were obliterated – measures never before employed by Canadian armoured vehicles and also a measure of the growing importance of aerial reconnaissance. The troops had no idea of where they were, a mystery they shared with the enemy who was quite unaware of their presence. The Motors were preparing to participate in the opening battle of the Allies' summer offensive at Amiens on 8 August 1918. In the future this series of operations, that ended

Organization of the Motor Machine Gun Brigades – June 1918

1st Canadian Motor Machine Gun Brigade:
'A' Battery – (Brutinel's former 1st Battery)
'B' Battery – (Brutinel's former 2nd Battery)
'C' Battery – (Borden Battery)
'D' Battery – (from the 18th Machine Gun Company)
'E' Battery – (from the 18th Machine Gun Company)

2nd Canadian Motor Machine Gun Brigade:
'A' Battery – (Yukon Battery)
'B' Battery – (Eaton Battery)
'C' Battery – (from the 19th Machine Gun Company)
'D' Battery – (from the 17th Machine Gun Company)
'E' Battery – (from the 17th and 18th Machine Gun Companies)

with the Armistice on 11 November, would come to be known as the Hundred Days.

As Worthy's 'E' Battery crossed the start line a protective mist covered its advance. By the time the mist had cleared, two and one-half hours later, the battery was heavily engaged in supporting French infantry in an attack on Mézières. In the midst of the fire fight, a dispatch rider arrived at battery headquarters with orders to withdraw and report to brigade. Protests against the order failed to have it cancelled, and so Worthy reported to headquarters in person, only to be told that he was to support a French attack on Mézières! Worthington, the novice commander, had been guilty of neglecting to give his higher headquarters a comprehensive picture of his battery's actions. It was a lesson he would not forget.

Amiens was the one and only battle during the war where all the components of Canada's mounted forces fought together. Worthy's battery was part of the Independent Force, a brigade-sized organization commanded by Brutinel and comprising three battle groups.

The main task of the Independent Force was to maintain contact with the French troops operating on the southern side of the inter-army boundary. The boundary itself was the Amiens–Roye road, a tree-lined, arrow-straight highway that the Motors were able to use to advantage, and just north of the road the CCB was operating, along with the rest of its parent division. The cavalry were intended to work with a newly-developed fast tank called the Whippet, which could cover a dazzling thirteen kilometres in one hour, but this experimental grouping proved to be unsuccessful. Cavalry in open country quickly out-galloped the tanks but once barbed wire or machine-guns

CMMG Brigade car in action along the Amiens–Roye road, August 1918. Combining firepower with mobility, the armoured cars proved very useful during the last months of the war. (NAC PA3016)

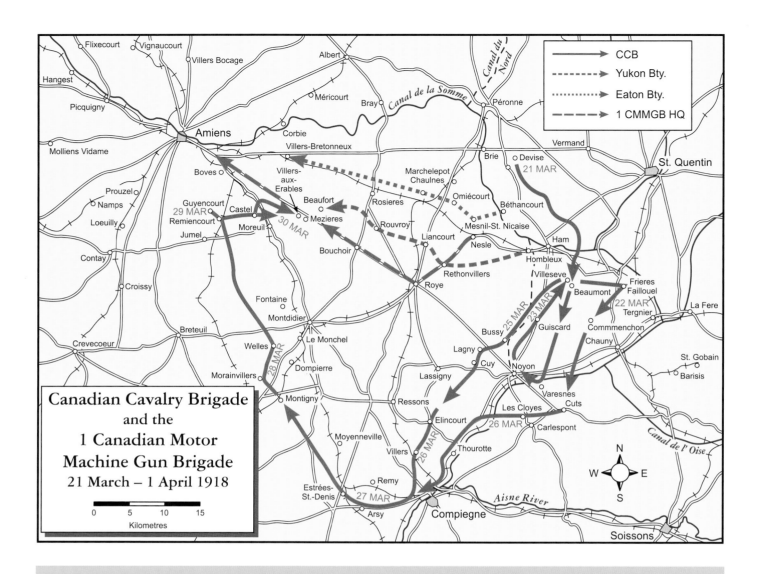

Canadian Cavalry Brigade and the 1 Canadian Motor Machine Gun Brigade 21 March – 1 April 1918

→	CCB
⇢	Yukon Bty.
⋯▸	Eaton Bty.
– –▸	1 CMMGB HQ

0   5   10   15
Kilometres

The Independent Force (Brigadier-General R. Brutinel) – 8 August 1918

Force Headquarters Armoured Car Detachment (Captain R.C. Clarke)
- 4 armoured cars,
- 10 motorcycles
- 1 platoon of cyclists

1st Group (Lieutenant-Colonel W.K. Walker)
- 1 CMMGB
- 20 motorcycles
- 2 platoons of cyclists

2nd Group (Lieutenant-Colonel H.M.V. Meurling)
- 2 CMMGB
- 20 motorcycles
- 1 platoon of cyclists

3rd Group (Lieutenant-Colonel I. Leonard)
- CLH Hotchkiss Detachment
- 2 armoured cars
- 10 motorcycles
- 4 platoons of cyclists

Trench Mortar Section (Captain J.N. McEachern)
- 2 6-inch trench mortars mounted on 3-ton trucks

Supply Column (Lieutenant G.H. May)
- 4 supply lorries
- 4 First Aid lorries
- 5 motorcycles

One of three Autocars that were destroyed in action. The damage to the rear plate, the corpse at the extreme right and the equipment strewn around indicate that this Autocar fell victim to shellfire. (Canadian Army Photograph)

The Independent Force (Brigadier-General R. Brutinel) – 2 September 1918

10th Royal Hussars

Canadian Light Horse

1st and 2nd Canadian Motor Machine Gun Brigades

Canadian Corps Cyclist Battalion

30th Field Battery, Canadian Field Artillery

2 Sections of Medium Trench Mortars

6 Heavy Armoured Cars (from the 17th Armoured Car Battalion, Tank Corps)

2 Light Armoured Cars (from the 2nd CMMGB)

1 Wireless Section

1 Supply Column

Canadian cavalrymen escorting prisoners captured during the Battle of Amiens, August 1918. (NAC PA2853)

were encountered the tanks could make headway where the cavalry could not.

In the fighting at Amiens, the CCB served under a new commander, Brigadier-General Walter Paterson, CMG, DSO. Seely had been slightly gassed in the fighting at Rifle Wood and that provided the official reason for his departure, although there was also a desire on the part of an increasingly nationalistic Cabinet in Ottawa to see the brigade in all-Canadian hands. Paterson had founded The Fort Garry Horse in 1912. A Winnipeg businessman in peacetime, he was Seely's handpicked successor in spite of the fact that the brigade was employing the best regular officers that the Canadian cavalry had to offer.

Cavalry reinforcements were no longer forthcoming, as recruiting into the cavalry had ceased altogether in June, and Haig was forced to husband his horsemen carefully, waiting for the appropriate moment to turn them loose on a beaten German army. The cavalry was not in action between 12 August and 9 October, when they next rode into battle at Le Cateau.

THE DROCOURT–QUEANT LINE

There was to be no such rest for the Motors. On 2 September the Canadian Corps undertook the breaching of the Drocourt–Quéant or D-Q Line. The Independent Force, disbanded after Amiens, was reconstituted in a slightly different form. Its task was the capture of a bridge at Marquion, which spanned the Canal du Nord, and the creation of a bridgehead on the far side of the canal. During the Battle of Amiens the Motors' progress had been stopped on the Amiens–Roye road by fallen trees

Brigadier-General Walter Paterson, Commander of the Canadian Cavalry Brigade March 1918-1919. (NAC PA4138)

blocking their path. In an attempt to ensure continued mobility in the event of a similar situation at Marquion, a second cavalry regiment was now added to the Independent Force.

As it had been at Amiens, the Force was divided into three battle groups, each containing a mixture of the troops available. One group, led by eight armoured cars and followed by the British 10th Royal Hussars, was soon halted by intense machine-gun fire, the cavalry finding themselves unable to deploy because of the terrain. To neutralize the machine-guns, the trench mortars were brought forward and came into action firing from the backs of their vehicles, while Worthy took his 'E' Battery around to the left in a successful effort to engage some German artillery. His courage and skill here resulted in the award of a Military Cross. Perhaps fortunately for the Motors, the pressures created by advancing infantry divisions on both flanks caused the Germans to abandon the defence of the bridge before the rest of the Independent Force reached it. The mixing of cavalry and armour was once again shown to be unworkable.

THE BATTLE OF LE CATEAU, 8–10 OCTOBER 1918

In 1914 the BEF had fought a successful delaying action at Le Cateau during the retreat from Mons. Now, four years later, a second battle of Le Cateau was fought by 3 Cavalry Division against the retreating Germans. The scene of the engagement was the old Roman road leading into the town from the west. The CCB, operating on the north side of the road, was parallel-

Armoured trucks of the Motor Machine Gun Brigade during the advance from Arras, September 1918. (NAC PA3399)

led in its advance by the British 6 Cavalry Brigade on the south, with the 7th in reserve.

The battle opened with an attack by the Strathconas against the village of Clary, while the Fort Garrys moved on Gattigny Wood. To divert the enemy's attention from the flanking attack, a troop of the Garrys' 'B' Squadron under Lieutenant James Dunwoody, DCM, was ordered to charge toward the centre of the enemy position. Lieutenant (later Colonel) Dunwoody wrote his own account of the action.

I rode back to my troop and surveyed the situation. A wide plain in front of the wood, no cover of any kind, bursts of machine-gun fire from the German position, a line of infantry (South African Scottish) halfway toward the wood and apparently pinned down by enemy fire. … I spotted a farm house about halfway between us and the wood…. I hastily figured that if my troop could make it to the farm buildings without loss it would reduce our casualties substantially.

I gave the order to advance and we galloped for the farm. Unfortunately for my dignity as a troop commander, my horse tripped on a sunken wire, fell and somersaulted me out of the saddle. The horse then followed the rest of the troop without waiting for me. I was so mad at myself when I got to my feet, about 200 yards from the farm buildings that, although machine-gun bullets were spattering around me, I

shook my fist at the Huns and walked to the farm. The troopers, of course, were still chuckling over an officer falling off his horse, an unforgivable sin in the cavalry. When I reached the farm I lined up the troop, explained the mode of attack – drawn swords, extended order, every man for himself – and Charge!

The Germans had never seen horsed cavalry. Their machine-gunners shot high, shot low, everywhere but in the right direction. We galloped past the amazed South Africans and hit the wood amidst a shower of machine-gun bullets. As we ascended the slope of the wood I was hit twice … and my horse was riddled. We had about fifty percent casualties, mostly wounded, and as fast as a man was hit, or his horse shot under him, he crawled up the sloping embankment towards the wood, dragging his rifle with him.

Lieutenant James Dunwoody, DSO, DCM. (Fort Garry Horse Museum)

The squadron closed with the enemy in the wood line and in a hand-to-hand struggle, backed up by South African infantry, succeeded in capturing forty machine-guns and some two hundred prisoners. Dunwoody, nominated for a Victoria Cross, was

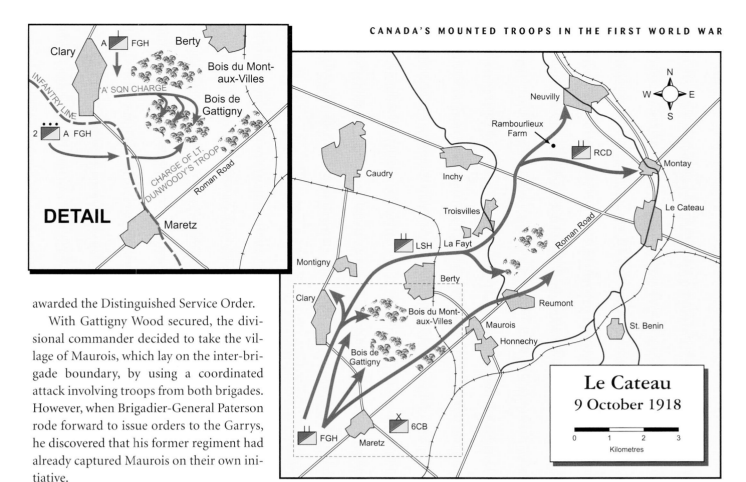

DETAIL

Clary · A FGH · Berty · Bois du Mont-aux-Villes · Bois de Gattigny · INFANTRY LINE · 'A' SQN CHARGE · CHARGE OF LT. DUNWOODY'S TROOP · 2 A FGH · Roman Road · Maretz

Neuvilly · Rambourlieux Farm · RCD · Montay · Le Cateau · Caudry · Inchy · Troisvilles · La Fayt · Roman Road · LSH · Montigny · Berty · Reumont · Clary · Bois du Mont-aux-Villes · Maurois · St. Benin · Honnechy · Bois de Gattigny · FGH · Maretz · 6CB

Le Cateau
9 October 1918

0   1   2   3
Kilometres

awarded the Distinguished Service Order.

With Gattigny Wood secured, the divisional commander decided to take the village of Maurois, which lay on the inter-brigade boundary, by using a coordinated attack involving troops from both brigades. However, when Brigadier-General Paterson rode forward to issue orders to the Garrys, he discovered that his former regiment had already captured Maurois on their own initiative.

The advance toward Le Cateau continued until nightfall, covering a distance of thirteen kilometres and yielding four hundred prisoners, one hundred machine-guns, several field guns and much other booty. This final action of the war for the CCB earned them high praise, including a comment from the Cavalry Corps commander that Dunwoody's charge at Bois de Gattigny was "the best cavalry action carried out by any cavalry unit on any front during the war."

During the First World War, members of the Canadian Cavalry Brigade won a total of three Victoria Crosses, as well as 394 other gallantry awards. One of the more unusual of the decorations was the Albert Medal awarded to Sergeant Victor Brookes of the 7th (Cavalry) Field Ambulance. The incident in question took place on 30 June 1918 at a base camp behind the lines. An enemy air raid had created a large bomb crater and for some unknown reason an airman was lowered into it, where he was overcome by carbon monoxide

gases. He could not be hauled to the surface because his head was caught in some way, and when two other people attempted to rescue him they, too, were overcome by the gas and had to be hauled out, unconscious. Sergeant Brookes met the same fate on a first attempt but insisted on making a second effort that proved successful. Brookes and the airman survived, but the other two would-be rescuers died. (After the Second World War the Albert Medal was replaced by the George Cross, second only to the Victoria Cross in the Imperial honours system.)

Canadian cavalry resting after coming out of action during the Allied advance, September 1918. (Canadian Army Photograph O.3236)

Horses and Chargers. **Painting by Sir Alfred Munnings. In this period, officers' horses were called 'chargers' while all other ranks rode 'troop horses.' (Canadian War Museum 8576)**

THE BATTLE OF NAVES, 9–10 OCTOBER 1918

The final Canadian cavalry action of the war took place at Naves, on the Erclin River, on 10 October. Naves, which would prove to be the last Canadian cavalry charge of all time, was as disastrous to the cavalry as Le Cateau had been successful. The action was fought by the Canadian Light Horse, aided by the Canadian Corps Cyclist Battalion, both part of Brutinel's Independent Force.

The Canadian Corps had completed the capture of Cambrai and was advancing toward the city of Valenciennes, in north-eastern France. The Independent Force led the advance across the Canal de l'Escaut, with the Canadian Light Horse, now commanded by Colonel Ibbotson Leonard, capturing the only remaining bridge over the obstacle. The following day, 10 October 1918, the 19th Battalion, CEF captured the village of Naves. It was to be used as a firm base for a further advance intended to secure a ridgeline that ran across the Corps front. In front of the ridge was the shallow Erclin River. Behind the crest was a sunken road that provided the defenders with a covered means of lateral movement. In all it was a formidable obstacle.

The infantry captured the village of Iwuy on the ridge's northern end. With the enemy's position flanked, 'A' and 'C' Squadrons of the Light Horse were told to secure the ridgeline.

'C' Squadron led off, coming under shell fire as it forded the Erclin. The rate of advance was increased and the squadron galloped up the hill into the fire of German machine-guns. Trooper Stewart Thornton, the sole survivor of his section of eight men, won a Distinguished Conduct Medal when he rode down a machine-gun nest, killing the crew and capturing the gun. 'B' Squadron followed 'A' up the bloody slope before Colonel Leonard halted the operation. The hillside was by then littered with the bodies of 66 horses and 23 men.

It was now the turn of the Cyclists. While the enemy was concentrating on the unfortunate troopers of the CLH and two vehicles of the 2nd Motor Machine Gun Brigade that had been halted by the blown bridge over the Erclin, a platoon of cyclists had crossed the river on foot and secured the southern end of the ridge. They were unable to capture more than thirty metres of the road behind the ridge line, but they maintained their toe-hold there until infantry came forward to relieve them after dark. The enemy's shellfire was so intense that the casualties, wounded and dead, lay out for two days.

In the last month of the war mounted troops were finally performing the duties that they had been organized and trained to discharge. The Canadian Corps advanced with two divisions forward, screened by composite battle groups. On 17 October, 1 and 4 Divisions were leading the pursuit, each with a Light Horse squadron, a company of cyclists, two medium machine-gun batteries and two armoured cars. The marches were long, and the weather wet and chilly. Each mounted squadron cleared an area about two kilometres wide on either side of a centre line. The object was to locate the enemy positions before the infantry came up, so that they could be by-passed, masked, or taken out by the main body.

2 and 3 Divisions took over the advance on 21 October. The officer commanding 'B' Squadron, CLH, Captain George Stirrett, MC, DCM, later recalled:

As we rode into a village, we trotted down the cobblestone streets. All windows for 300 yards to the village square were drawn and covered. As we reached the village square at the Catholic church, we looked to see the road full of women, older men, and children, filling the road with anything they could wave. We dismounted and the old priest took me by the ears and kissed me. This started things. The priest kissed the three men with me. Then they all seemed to go crazy at once. They even kissed our horses. Then the priest called for prayer and the entire village went to their knees at once, including my men and myself. We had a very similar experience in every village from then on. We were first into at least twenty villages with the infantry about a mile behind following us in column of route. As soon as we were fired on, we would retire and the infantry would take charge.

The advance continued relentlessly. The last two Canadian mounted soldiers killed in the war died on 10 November. Sergeant Patrick Quinn, DCM, and Corporal Delbert Bean, MM, were both from the Canadian Corps Cyclist Battalion. When the Armistice came into effect at 1100 hours on 11 November 1918, the lead infantry brigade was securing the city of Mons, while the Cyclist patrols were some five kilometres further east. Out of touch with their own headquarters, they learned of the Armistice from Germans coming forward to arrange terms.

THE CANADIAN TANK BATTALIONS

The idea of creating Canadian tank battalions had arisen in January 1918 in a conversation between Major-General H.J. Elles, General Officer Commanding the Tank Corps, and a Canadian gunner on his staff, Lieutenant-Colonel James Edgar Mills. Mills, who had won a DSO at Gallipoli, had run afoul of Canadian officialdom in England who disapproved of his methods in running artillery training. The result was his banishment to the Tank Corps. When Mills suggested to Elles, who was already short of manpower for his battalions, that Canada should be involved in this new form of warfare, Elles seized on the idea and immediately wrote to the War Office recommend-

(Right) Canadian Cyclists after having captured a trench. (Canadian Army Photograph O.3195)

(Below) Canadian Light Horse advancing during the last days of the war. (Canadian Army photograph O.3230)

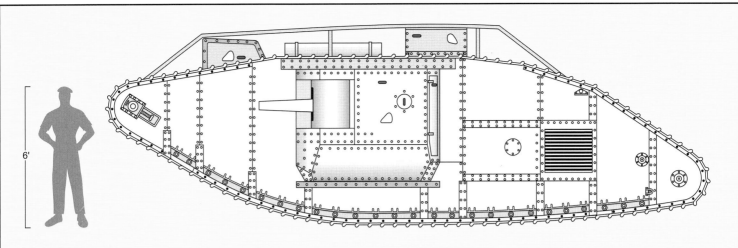

Mark V Male Tank. The Mark V was the fifth model in the British rhomboid series of tanks developed during the First World War, appearing in 1918. It was the main vehicle used for training by the 1st Canadian Tank Battalion. (Drawing by Chris Johnson)

Mark V
Country of Origin: Great Britain
Crew: 8 (Commander, 2 x 6 pdr Gunners, 2 x MG Gunners, Driver, 2 x Gearsmen)
Length: 23 feet 6 inches
Width: 12 feet 10 inches
Height: 8 feet 8 inches
Weight: 58,000 pounds

Engine: Ricardo 6 cylinder, gasoline
Maximum Speed: 4.6 mph
Range: 45 miles
Armour – Maximum: 16 mm
Minimum: 8 mm
Armament: 2 x 6 pdr Quick Firing in sponsons
4 x Hotchkiss MGs

Badge of the 1st Canadian Tank Battalion. (RCAC Association Archives)

ing that Canada be approached to recruit a battalion.

Ottawa was receptive to the suggestion and appointed Lieutenant-Colonel Richard Denison of the Winnipeg Rifles to raise and command the new battalion, which would form a part of the Canadian Machine Gun Corps. Within two months Denison recruited a complete complement of 688 all ranks from universities across the Dominion. As a new form of warfare, driven by technology, tanks held a fascination for men with an intellectual bent. 'A' Company of the 1st Canadian Tank Battalion was recruited from the University of Toronto, 'B' Company from McGill, 'C' from other universities, and each company was to consist of four sections, each of five tanks.

First brought together in Ottawa, the men were shipped to Britain in June 1918 and quartered in Frensham Camp, in Surrey, where they underwent basic training. Meanwhile, the officers were posted to Bovington Camp, in Dorset, where they were introduced into the mysteries of armoured warfare.

A tank crew of the Great War era comprised eight men. The earliest crews were made up of four drivers and four gunners. However, the Mark V, which the Canadians were to use needed only one driver. The other seven men were the crew commander (an innovation in that he did not also have to help to drive or man a gun) and six gunners. Weighing 29 tons, the Mark V was propelled by a 150-hp engine producing a speed of 8 kph. Its armament comprised two 57mm cannon and four

.303 machine-guns. Ergonomically, these tanks were a disaster. They had no suspension whatever, with the result that the crews were constantly – and often violently – shaken about. With the engine running, the interior of the vehicle quickly reached very high temperatures in an atmosphere saturated in gasoline fumes. Motion sickness, carbon monoxide poisoning and heat exhaustion were ever-present features of a tank crewman's working day. Crew fatigue was thus a major limiting factor in operations planning. Eight hours was considered to be the longest period a crewman could remain effective, but only a few very hardy souls could manage that.

When the officers and men were reunited in Bovington, tank training began in earnest in August 1918. The men divided into two groups: drivers and gunners. The courses for both trades lasted four weeks. As well as driving and gunnery, they were given instruction in camouflage, reconnaissance, gas defence, signalling (including the use of carrier pigeons), the compass and revolver training.

Just before they were scheduled to leave for France there was a change of command with Lieutenant-Colonel Mills replacing Denison. But the battalion never saw France. News of the Armistice arrived just as the 'Kantanks', as they had dubbed themselves, started their embarkation leave. Being one of the very last Canadian units sent to Britain, the battalion was at the end of the queue for repatriation and the unit marked time in Britain until 18 May 1919, when it embarked at Southampton for the journey home.

The 2nd Canadian Tank Battalion came from two separate locales. In France a large contingent from the Royal North-West Mounted Police had arrived for service with the cavalry. An ad-

Troops of the 1st Canadian Tank Battalion repairing a track on a Mark V* during training at Bovington Camp, England, October 1918. Tracks were among the most vulnerable parts of the tanks of this era. (RCAC Collection, CFB Borden Museum)

'Unditching' a Mark V* tank, Bovington, October 1918. While designed to cross trenches, tanks were very limited in the type of terrain they could negotiate. (RCAC Collection, CFB Borden Museum)

(Below) Tank park of the 1st Canadian Tank Battalion in the training area at Bovington, England, October 1918. (RCAC Collection, CFB Borden Museum)

ditional squadron, 'D' Squadron, was added to the CLH in October 1918 to accommodate them. Even so, there were men left over. Offered the opportunity to transfer to the tanks, a total of 226 policemen accepted and were posted to Bovington for armour training. Meanwhile, in Canada, a number of artillerymen in Petawawa were offered a choice between service in Siberia or service with the tanks, and most opted for the latter. The high quality of these men can be seen in their subsequent careers. One of them was the future Canadian diplomat Hugh Keenleyside. Another was the future co-discover of insulin, Dr. Charles Best, and a third was reporter, publisher and entrepreneur Floyd Sherman Chalmers.

The 2nd Battalion entrained in Petawawa on 3 October 1918, heading for Quebec City. With them travelled the influenza virus that was circling the world – destined to kill three times as many people as the war. At Quebec they boarded the *Victoria,* a converted cattle boat, some having to be carried aboard on stretchers. Only two days out, the first victim was buried at sea, and funerals then continued every day of the crossing. In four days the ship had exhausted its medical stores, but the convoy was unable to stop to replenish the supply from other ships. By the time the *Victoria* docked in Bristol, on 18 October, 27 lives had been lost.

Like the 1st Battalion before it, the 2nd underwent a period of isolation in Britain. In their case the 40 officers and 665 other ranks settled down in Kinmel Park Segregation Camp near Rhyl, north Wales. They were still at Kinmel Park when news of the Armistice arrived but ten days later they were on a ship heading home. By a happy coincidence they were conveniently to hand when space on the passenger liner *Aquitania* became unexpectedly available, and so they returned promptly and in some luxury.

The 3rd Canadian Tank Battalion, or, more correctly, *le 3e Bataillon de chars d'assaut,* was intended to be a French-Canadian unit. The commanding officer, Major Paul Emile Ostiguy, began recruiting at the Université de Montréal and had enrolled 57 men when recruiting was stopped on 19 November. The battalion was disbanded on 26 November.

Collar badge of the 2nd Canadian Tank Battalion. The cap badge was of the same design as that of the 1st Battalion, but only one example is known to exist, in the collection of the Royal Canadian Military Institute. (RCAC Association Archives)

Drawing of the badge of the *3e Bataillon de chars d'assaut,* based on a scan of a badge recently sold at auction.

Badge of the Canadian Tank Corps, 1918. (RCAC Association Archives)

Meanwhile, following on the quick success in raising the 1st Battalion, Canada had decided to create an armoured corps. A Canadian Tank Corps was authorized on 13 November 1918, an action which caused the two existing tank battalions to be transferred from the Canadian Machine Gun Corps to this new formation.

This first Canadian armoured corps suffered a total of 36 fatal casualties during its short existence. A few were the results of accidents; most were due to influenza.

* * *

If there is a theme that emerges from this examination of Canada's mounted units over the course of the First World War, it is the constant search for battlefield mobility. One might say that this was an underlying theme of the war, where immobility created by machine-guns and barbed wire confined operations to trench warfare for nearly three years. The mounted arms constantly worried and worked on this problem of mobility. Each of the different mounted organizations had its limitations. Horses could not get through barbed wire, cyclists could not overcome machine-gun fire, armoured cars were confined to roads and tracks, tanks were restricted in terms of speed, range and crew endurance. Experiments involving the mixing of the various components of the mounted arms in an effort to minimize their weaknesses and maximize their strengths proved fruitless.

However, the concept of the combined arms team was first developed by mounted forces on the Western Front. Examples of this include the experiment at Amiens in August 1918, where the cavalry divisions operated with tanks, and again in that most interesting of formations, Brutinel's Independent Force at the breaching of the Drocourt–Quéant Line in September 1918. The evolution of the Independent Force reflected Brutinel's inquiring mind as he searched for the right mix of mobility and firepower. Although the experiment of joining horsed cavalry to mechanized units failed in action, it showed a willingness to innovate and a desire to search for solutions to the problems of the day. That in turn reflected the inquiring and audacious character of the Canadian mounted soldier.

Canadian Cavalry, November 1918. **Drawing by Sir Alfred Munnings. (RCAC Association Archives)**

The experience of this terrible war also demonstrated that the long era of horsed cavalry had come to an end. Horses were simply too vulnerable to machine-gun bullets and massed artillery, and the widespread use of barbed wire brought an end to their battlefield mobility. While it would take some years for this reality to be felt in military organizations, armoured vehicles had come to be essential components of every modern army.

The mounted soldiers of the First World War were in many respects the spiritual founders of the Royal Canadian Armoured Corps. Although the RCAC would not come into existence for another twenty-two years, when it did appear its foundations were already firm. Its remarkable growth may be explained by the rich soil in which it was planted.

CAMPAIGN MEDALS OF THE CANADIAN AND BRITISH ARMIES

The 1914-15 Star, awarded to all members of the Canadian and British armies who were in action in France or Belgium prior to the end of 1915.

The British War Medal 1914-18, awarded to all with more than 90 days service during the First World War.

The Victory Medal, awarded to all who served during the First World War. All Allied nations issued a medal with a similar design and ribbon.

DECORATIONS FOR BRAVERY INSTITUTED DURING THE FIRST WORLD WAR

The Distinguished Service Order, usually awarded to senior officers for commendable wartime service. It was, however, sometimes awarded to junior officers as a gallantry decoration.

The Military Cross, instituted at the end of 1914 as a bravery decoration for junior officers.

The Military Medal, instituted in March 1916 for award to non-commissioned officers and men for acts of bravery in the field. The MM ranks just below the Distinguished Conduct Medal.

CHAPTER 3

Between the Wars,
1919–1939

With the return of peace in 1919, the Canadian military was faced with a dilemma. The Canadian Corps had created an international reputation for itself, one that its veterans were anxious to see perpetuated in the structure of the post-war army. The old Canadian Militia, however, was not willing to disappear in order to make room for units of the Canadian Expeditionary Force (CEF). To resolve the problem, and to establish a guide for a post-war military structure, the government formed a committee under General Sir William Otter, a pre-war Chief of the General Staff, and when the Otter Committee produced its conclusions at the end of 1919 the outcome was a compromise. The pre-war structure would remain but the Militia would perpetuate the CEF regiments and battalions. In that way the traditions forged and the battle honours won on the battlefields of Europe would be preserved, along with the historic and politically powerful pre-war units. This decision had its greatest impact on the infantry but there was some effect in cavalry circles as well.

Only three cavalry regiments had fought in Europe under their own names and badges: the Royal Canadian Dragoons (RCD), Lord Strathcona's Horse (LSH) and the Fort Garry Horse (FGH). Their situation was the simplest of all, for they simply kept the battle honours they had earned. Three other cavalry regiments had fought in France and Flanders wearing their own badges, although not as complete regiments, and the 1st Hussars, 16th Saskatchewan Light Horse and 19th Alberta Dragoons were granted the honours their squadrons had won serving with the Canadian Light Horse. Other Militia cavalry regiments perpetuated mounted rifles battalions, infantry battalions or motor machine-gun units.

In 1920 all existing units were "disbanded for the purposes of re-organization," and when that process was completed a new order of battle appeared. Both cavalry and infantry dropped the traditional numbering system in favour of territorial designations, but tradition died harder in the cavalry and many regiments insisted on retaining their numeral, even though that was often not an indication of seniority.

The Otter Committee, hoping that conscription would continue after the war and in an attempt to perpetuate as many units as possible, proposed an army structure of eleven infantry and four cavalry divisions, so that the total number of cavalry units was virtually the same as in 1914, even if some of the names had changed. The rationale for this huge force was the possibility of war with the United States, when Canadian troops would attempt to hold the Americans until reinforcements could arrive from elsewhere in the Empire. That scenario

The British Columbia Mounted Rifles breaking horses at the beginning of a summer camp in Vernon, B.C., 1922. (NAC PA116565)

The Order of Battle of the Canadian Cavalry in 1921

The Royal Canadian Dragoons

Lord Strathcona's Horse (Royal Canadians)

The Governor General's Body Guard

The Princess Louise Dragoon Guards (the Regiment dropped the designation '5th' in 1920)

1st Hussars

2nd Dragoons

3rd The Prince of Wales' Canadian Dragoons

The 4th Hussars of Canada

6th Duke of Connaught's Royal Canadian Hussars

The 7th Hussars

8th Princess Louise's New Brunswick Hussars

The Mississauga Horse (known briefly in the 1920s as the Ontario Mounted Rifles)

The 11th Hussars

12th Manitoba Dragoons

13th Scottish Light Dragoons

The King's (Nova Scotia) Mounted Rifles

15th Alberta Light Horse

The 16th Canadian Light Horse

17th Duke of York's Royal Canadian Hussars (Argenteuil Rangers)

19th Alberta Dragoons

The Border Horse

The Alberta Mounted Rifles

The Saskatchewan Mounted Rifles

9th (Grey's) Horse

The 10th Brant Dragoons

The Eastern Townships Mounted Rifles (formerly the 26th Stanstead Dragoons)

14th Canadian Light Horse

The New Brunswick Dragoons

18th Canadian Light Horse

The British Columbia Mounted Rifles

The 5th British Columbia Light Horse

The Manitoba Horse

The Fort Garry Horse

The Prince Edward Island Light Horse

Fort Garry Horse troopers carrying out the traditional military exercise of standing in line for something or other, St. Charles camp, 1921. The cavalry 'camp' uniform issued to Militia units in this period was essentially the same as in pre-war days, cavalry breeches, scratchy woolen shirts and 'cows breakfast' straw hats. (Fort Garry Horse Museum)

was the background to Defence Scheme No. 1, drafted in 1921 by Colonel James Sutherland Brown, and the result was a large number of under-manned and poorly equipped units. Of course, conscription was not retained after the war and there was very little in the way of military resources to outfit fifteen divisions, although Canada did get sufficient war surplus equipment from Britain to equip four infantry divisions and a cavalry brigade.

The Otter Committee came under intense political pressures from many sides. There was, however, no lobby on behalf of the wartime tank battalions, with the result that no tanks were included in the post-war structure. The machine-gunners, though, were heard. A Canadian Machine Gun Corps was formed on 1 June 1919 with a single Permanent Force battalion, called The Royal Canadian Permanent Machine Gun Brigade, and twelve Militia machine-gun battalions spread across the country, along with a mechanized component. The 1st Motor Machine Gun Brigade was raised in Montreal, and a 2nd Motor Machine Gun Brigade was created in Winnipeg. (Although called 'brigades', these were actually battalion-sized units commanded by a lieutenant-colonel.) As two of the original autocars from Brutinel's Automobile Machine Gun Brigade had been shipped over from Europe at the request of the Canadian government, each unit was issued with a single armoured car.

The Permanent Force Machine Gun Brigade was disbanded a scant three years after being formed, and its equipment and personnel were distributed, following the British example, among the three regular infantry regiments. Captain F.F. Worthington, for example, found himself posted to the PPCLI in Winnipeg. The reserve component lasted until 1936 when the twelve battalions were amalgamated with reserve regiments, including some cavalry units.

CAVALRY TRAINING IN A PERIOD OF ADVERSITY

The immediate post-war period was one of retrenchment for the two regular cavalry units. They returned to their pre-war locations and resumed their traditional task of training the reserves. This was done primarily through the operation of schools of instruction, of which there were two types. Royal Schools, essentially the regulars' home stations, contained the necessary facilities and infrastructure to conduct rank qualification courses for officers and NCOs, while Provisional Schools, on the other hand, were established on a temporary basis close to the reserve units being trained. In addition to these formal schools, the regular units supplied officers, NCOs and men to the Militia summer camps to give instruction in equitation and tactical drills.

The regular units in this period had a surplus of over-qualified officers and other ranks, with the inevitable result that promotion was excruciatingly slow. Moreover, they often found themselves doing distasteful tasks. The disruptions of war and re-adjustment to peace had led to a great increase in labour unrest in Canada, and the government looked to the military as its guarantors of public order. Many times in the 1920s the regular cavalry were deployed on Aid to the Civil Power duties, as mounted troops were believed to be the most effective way of containing riotous strikers.

Doctrinally, little had changed since the war. In Britain, cavalry units were now given motorized transports to carry unit stores. As a result it was possible to remove a great deal of weight from the horses' backs and thus improve mobility. A few Canadian reserve units were also thinking along these lines, but officially there was no action taken. The British army was also experimenting with armoured units and formations but Canada only watched with interest, since armour was experimental and expensive, two factors that bred caution in Canadian gen-

erals. Once, eastern Canada had been widely seen as unsuitable country for cavalry; now, because of its vast spaces, Canada was thought to be unsuitable country for armour. There was some justification for such views, for armoured vehicles were slow, mechanically unreliable and of limited range. For many functions, especially mobile operations over long distances, horsed cavalry was a far more reliable alternative. Still, hesitation bred inertia and although many could see that mechanization was the wave of the future there was little urgency in military circles to follow that course. Instead of modernization, the two regular regiments put their energies into developing musical rides. These forms of entertainment were a popular success, and remain so today even though the concept has been largely left to the Royal Canadian Mounted Police.

The Militia units were as poorly off as their regular brethren. Most units were rebuilt in 1920 around a small cadre of war veterans but the government was somewhat cautious about the reserves, fearing that their Great War veterans might side with the social agitators and help to overthrow the state! The military as a whole was not a popular institution in these years, as many blamed the war on the mere existence of armies. Some mothers would forbid their children to become boy scouts or girl guides simply because those organizations wore uniforms.

The pre-war concept of mounted brigades was revived, along with the old pre-war training programme. In a typical year cavalry regiments would conduct training at the local armoury – usually ten evenings in the autumn and ten in the spring – with the occasional weekend scheme. Then, in early summer, the unit would attend a one-week-long camp where the entire gamut of training from individual musketry and riding to troop and squadron-level drills and formations would be

'A' Squadron of the Strathconas on parade in Winnipeg, 1922. Ceremonial duties on public occasions were an essential part of the army's peacetime activities. (LdSH Museum)

taught and practised. The 17th Duke of York's Royal Canadian Hussars, reported on their annual training cycle in these terms:

> Each squadron trained one night per week from September to June, dividing the time and space available between foot and arms drill, troop, squadron and regimental drill, weapon training and miniature range practice and lectures on horsemastership, map reading and tactics. A section competition in collective rifle fire was conducted in the spring on the miniature range. During the autumn and spring mounted training was carried out, each man receiving about six hours in the saddle each season.

The Royal Canadian Dragoons' musical ride, 1923. The tradition of the musical ride was later copied by the Royal Canadian Mounted Police. (RCD Archives)

The perennial tug-of-war between *arme blanche* and mounted rifles tilted dramatically in favour of the latter in 1921. Only six regiments were classified as traditional, sword-armed cavalry in the post-war army: the two regular regiments, and those reserve units located in capital cities where ceremonial escorts formed a part of their duties: the Body Guard in Toronto, the PLDG in Ottawa, the Fort Garrys in Winnipeg and the 19th Alberta Dragoons in Edmonton. All the other regiments were categorized as mounted rifles and thus were not issued with swords. This, however, did not stop them from continuously pestering Ottawa for an allotment of swords, both for training and for ceremonial purposes.

The mid-1920s saw a flurry of formal alliances between units of the Canadian and British mounted arms, intended to foster a sense of Imperial solidarity and to provide, for the officers primarily, an intro-

duction into the other country's services. Members of allied regiments, for example, automatically became honorary members of the other unit's messes. As with all human organizations, some of these alliances withered and died, some merely survived, and still others positively thrived. Overall, however, the system of allied regiments proved successful, and continues to this day.

The Canadian Cavalry Association, from its beginning, supported the practical aspects of cavalry training through the offer of competition trophies and financial incentives to units for collective training. The first of the several trophies donated for annual competition was the Merritt Challenge Cup. This trophy had been donated in 1913 by Lieutenant-Colonel William

'Balaclava Melee', one of the traditional events at cavalry sports meets, where the objective is to remove the tassels from the top of opponents helmets with the sword. In this photo members of the 12th Manitoba Dragoons demonstrate their swordsmanship during a summer camp in 1925. (FGH Museum)

Officer of the Mississauga Horse in camp at Niagara in 1924. (GGHG Archives)

a nebulous force called morale. Good units have a lot of it, and poor units always lack it to some degree, but it is an impossible thing to measure, even though its presence or absence is always apparent. Morale is the force created when a unit's leaders and followers have a mutual trust in each others' competence and personal trustworthiness. The bonding that takes place between the members of a well-run unit is often compared to the social bonding found in a close-knit family. Regimental loyalty, for that is what it is called, is a powerful force for those who have experienced it, and it is this bonding that is the key to understanding why and how the Canadian military – regular and Militia – survived the inter-war period.

As already mentioned, the two post-war Regular cavalry units were filled with over-qualified officers, non-commissioned officers and men. Pay was poor, and promotion was slow. Then, with the onset of the Great Depression, wages were cut. It was taken as common knowledge that there would never be another war; the League of Nations was going to see to that. So why then did the soldiers go through the annual rituals of unit-level training over and over again with little hope of professional advancement? The sustaining ingredient was regimental loyalty.

Hamilton Merritt of the Governor General's Body Guard, a veteran of the North-West Rebellion and the South African War as well as the great-grandson of the leader of the Niagara Light Dragoons in the War of 1812. Originally awarded to the best team of riders in the Militia cavalry, the Merritt Cup was still in use until recently as the award for best reconnaissance squadron or troop in the Corps.

Although not much appeared to have changed from the pre-war era, there was to be one significant advance in this period. In 1923 the Canadian Cavalry Association joined with its sister organizations in launching a new military publication, *Canadian Defence Quarterly (CDQ)*, which became the intellectual link between the officers of a tiny military force scattered across a vast country. Still, even with the advent of *CDQ*, in overall terms the 1920s were a sterile period for the Canadian military. The 'wait-and-see' attitude at the top ensured that no new equipment and precious few new ideas were introduced. At the same time the left-over First World War equipment aged and deteriorated. Then came the Great Depression. A financially-strapped government looked for programmes to cut and quickly focused on the military. Ironically, by the early 1930s the generals had finally concluded that it was time to mechanize the Army, but, by then, there was no money either to purchase or develop the necessary vehicles.

The glue that holds a military unit together has always been

One could understand why a young man might join the regulars. There was a small but steady income, and a pension at the end and, although the work was hard, it was a living. However, this just did not apply in the Militia. The work was similar, if only part-time, but financial rewards were almost totally absent. While militiamen were theoretically paid fifty cents for attending an evening parade, almost all units 'confiscated' this pay to buy dress uniforms and finance other basic expenses that the government would not provide for. Why then, would anyone join the Militia?

The obvious reason was that every Militia unit had all of the attributes of a highly organized community service club. There were uniforms and bands, there were regular social activities such as sports leagues and dances that members could attend at little or no cost, and, during this time of prohibition, there were bars that served beer and alcohol. Service in the Militia provided a welcome change from the work-day grind with weekend exercises and the annual summer camp. Cavalry regiments, especially those in cities, had that extra attraction – men had the opportunity to ride horses. It was fun that was otherwise unaffordable.

But the Militia also took on another aspect during the

(Left) A troop of the Prince Edward Island Light Horse march through Montague, PEI, 1925. (Prince Edward Island Regiment Archives)

(Below) The mounted escort of the Governor General's Body Guard, Toronto, 1926. (Governor General's Horse Guards Archives)

(Bottom) A section of the 17th Duke of York's Royal Canadian Hussars practises a traditional cavalry charge, Montreal, autumn 1927. (RCH Museum)

Depression years, when in most communities the local unit became a sort of social support organization, helping members to find work, and sometimes making loans to those in financial distress. Meals were provided during training camps, and in some city units street car fare was provided to enable members to get to weekly parades at the armouries, and often there were free sandwiches and coffee before they went home. In many ways the Militia unit was a stand-in for the welfare state that did not yet exist.

THE DEVELOPMENT OF ARMOURED WARFARE CONCEPTS

Canada, as always, looked to Britain for its military doctrine, for Canada was a key member of what amounted to an Imperial military alliance, the British Empire. Although the complete integration of all of the Empire's military forces was never achieved, the degree of interoperability in doctrine and weapons systems is one that alliances such as NATO can only envy today.

But at the Empire's centre, Great Britain, there were serious problems with regard to the development of armour. Britain had been the first nation to develop the tank, albeit only narrowly beating the French. They were also the first to raise armoured units and formations (the Tank Corps had twenty battalions and twelve armoured car companies at the end of the Great War), and the first to develop a doctrine for employing armour. This lead continued into the 1920s. After the war, Britain retained four battalions of tanks (one for each infantry division) in its peacetime military establishment, and carried out experiments with totally mechanized formations of all-arms.

Then the British faltered, and their lead was lost due to the so-called 'ten-year rule', a piece of political sleight-of-hand, renewed annually, which postulated that Britain would not be involved in a war with a major power for at least ten years. That lead-time supposedly would be sufficient for Britain to prepare for such a war and, in the meantime, the defence budget could be severely cut. Under those circumstances, experimental concepts such as mechanization went to the back of the queue. By the time the ten-year rule was abolished in 1932, the next war was a scant seven years away and it was nearly too late for Britain to re-arm.

The other dimension of the problem was a serious doctrinal conflict over how tanks could best be used. During the Great War some had prophesied the creation of tank armies that could win wars entirely on their own. Battlefield experience had, however, demonstrated that tanks could not operate inde-

pendently and were most effective when incorporated into all-arms teams. The visionaries of the 'all-tank school', chief among them Colonel J.F.C. Fuller, held to their dreams, pointing to the great leap in technology that had come about since the war and pressing the notion of armies largely comprised of tanks. Their theories gained a significant following, both in Britain and especially in Germany. (It is perhaps interesting to note the symmetry with the advocates of air power who were making similar claims for their arm.) But the advocates of an all-tank army overlooked the very negative effect their evangelizing would have on the rest of the army. The other arms – artillery and infantry in particular – were being told that they were redundant, which they knew intuitively to be nonsense, and they took deep offence. The tank visionaries soon became

Exhibition of 'tent-pegging' – lifting tent pegs with the tip of the sword while at a gallop – by members of the Princess Louise Dragoon Guards, Ottawa, 1929. (RCAC Association Archives)

military outcasts, howling in the wilderness, and the legitimate case for armour development in Britain was severely handicapped.

The post-war survival of the British Tank Corps in light of this doctrinal conflict was perhaps remarkable in itself. It may be remembered that the Americans, like the Canadians, had abolished their tank corps following the war. The decisive factor in the perpetuation of British armour was undoubtedly the armoured car, and the armoured car companies survived primarily because they were needed for counter-insurgency operations in Ireland, India and Iraq.

In 1923 the Tank Corps achieved the title of 'Royal'. Far from being an empty honour, this was official recognition of its status and assurance of its permanent place in the British Army. Along with the Royal designation it acquired another distinction, the black beret.

The origins of the black beret, the hallmark of the armoured corps, lie in the Great War, although no British or Canadian serviceman wore one in that conflict. In 1918, the officers of the Royal Tank Corps became dissatisfied with the various types of headgear issued to their men as they showed oil stains, were uncomfortable in cramped spaces and impaired the use of gunsights. They began to search for an alternative and, admiring the distinctive berets worn by the *chasseurs alpins,* the mountain troops of the French army, decided to find a British equivalent. At this time, berets were very uncommon in the English-speaking world but the Tank Corps officers noted that they were worn by the girls of some public schools. They therefore requested samples from the headmistresses of these schools and chose the most appropriate model. In 1924, the black beret became the distinctive headdress of the Royal Tank Corps and proved so practical and popular that the armoured forces of many nations later adopted it.

The Royal Tank Corps' first new post-war vehicle was the Vickers Light Tank, later known as the Vickers Medium Mark I. It was the first British tank with a revolving turret, mounting a three-pounder gun, and sprung tracks. Its successor, the Vickers Mark II, was even better – it was bulletproof.

In the late 1920s the Royal Tank Corps was also experimenting with 'tankettes'. These were one- or two-man tracked vehicles, originally intended for the infantry as a means of moving their machine guns forward rapidly over broken ground. The most successful design was that produced by Sir John Carden and constructed in the garage of a Mr. Loyd. Their vehicle, known as the

Carden-Loyd, was procured by the War Office as a reconnaissance vehicle for what was called the Experimental Mechanical Force (a brigade-sized organization), which was, however, closed down in 1928 after only two years in existence. While the British had intended to make use of the lessons learned from these extensive trials by creating a permanent armoured brigade, the Depression intervened: there was no money available. It would be another five years before Britain formed its first armoured brigade.

Reconnaissance was still the purview of the cavalry. In 1928 the first two regiments of British cavalry, the 11th Hussars and 12th Royal Lancers, were converted to armoured car regiments. Reconnaissance and shock action, both at one time cavalry roles, were now divided between the cavalry and the Tank Corps, and they would not come back together until April 1939 when the Royal Armoured Corps was created.

By the mid-1930s, its small fleet of tanks increasingly obsolescent, the Royal Tank Corps began a headlong rush into a doctrinal dead end, creating too many specialized tanks for over-specialized roles. In 1934 the Vickers firm was asked to develop a tank impervious to all known anti-tank weapons for the close support of infantry. The result was the A11 or Infantry Tank Mark I, later christened the Matilda. An improved version, the A12, was developed in 1936. It had a four-man crew, a radio and a 2-pounder (40mm) gun, and it was heavily protected with 70 mm of frontal armour. This mark of the Matilda was a tank that the Canadian Armoured Corps would come to know well.

Machine Gun Platoon of the Royal Canadian Regiment in their newly-acquired Carden-Loyd carriers, London, Ontario, April 1933. (NAC C30956)

The diminutive Carden-Loyd carrier entered service in Canada in 1933. It was used for training until the early years of the Second World War, when it was superseded by more modern wartime armoured vehicles. (Drawing by Chris Johnson)

6'

Carden-Loyd Mk VIA Machine Gun Carrier
Country of Origin: Great Britain
Crew: 2 (Commander, Driver)
Length: 8 feet 1 inch
Width: 5 feet 7 inches
Height: 4 feet
Weight: 3,000 pounds

Engine: Ford 4 cylinder, gasoline
Maximum Speed: 28 mph
Range: 100 miles
Armour – Maximum: 9 mm
       Minimum: 6 mm
Armament: .303 inch Vickers MG

Members of the 1st Motor Machine Gun Brigade from Montreal examine one of the new Carden-Loyd carriers at a demonstration at the Connaught Ranges in Ottawa, June 1933. (RCH Museum)

With a top speed of only 25 kph, it was, however, far too slow for the sweeping armoured breakthrough operations that the tank enthusiasts anticipated, so the lighter and faster 'cruiser' tank was developed. Unfortunately, the first cruiser tanks, designated the A9 and A10, proved to be extremely unreliable.

A light tank, the 5.5-ton Vickers Mark VI, was also built to meet the needs of the reconnaissance units. It had a crew of three, was armed with two machine-guns (a .50 and a .303), and was capable of reaching 56 kph on roads. The army recognized that this vehicle was inadequate in many ways, but because the Mark VI was the only British tank ready for mass production when full-scale British re-armament was finally authorized in 1936, 608 were ordered. As with the Matilda, Canada's armoured soldiers came to know this vehicle very well.

Having three types of tanks with markedly different characteristics led to the creation of three types of armoured units, and three variations of armoured doctrine. The Canadians, understandably, followed the British lead. It would take the experience of battle in the 1939-45 war to show that these overly specialized roles for armour were very wasteful of resources.

The Germans, equally inspired by the teachings of Fuller and Liddell Hart, also developed armoured forces in the interwar period, despite the fact that Germany was forbidden to have tanks by the Treaty of Versailles. The first German armoured vehicle of the period was developed in secret in 1925,

and a secret agreement with Russia three years later permitted the German Army to conduct tank trials near Kazan. German doctrine at this point was no different than that of the British: the tank was intended for close support of infantry in an attack on enemy trenches. However, an aggressive young infantry officer, Major Heinz Guderian, had other ideas. Guderian had spent a large part of the First World War commanding a wireless station, experience which convinced him that radio was the key to controlling armoured forces.

In 1933 the German Army ordered its first light tank, similar in size and function to the Carden-Loyd 'tankette'. The *Panzer I* (*Panzerkampfwagen*, or armoured battle vehicle), as it was later called, although really a 'tank trainer', was used in action in the *Blitzkrieg* invasions of Poland and France. It was followed in 1935 by the *Panzer II*, a much-improved three-man light tank armed with a 20mm cannon, and the medium *Panzer IV* with a short-barreled 75mm gun. Another medium tank, the *Panzer III*, armed with a 37mm cannon, was introduced in 1936. Both the *Panzer III* and *Panzer IV* had five-man crews. Mobility was the outstanding attribute of these latter tanks; the *Panzer IV* (often referred to as the Mark IV) could travel 150 km at speeds of over 45 kph.

The *Wehrmacht* created three armoured divisions in 1935. Colonel Guderian, in command of *2 Panzerdivision*, was thus well-placed to influence the doctrine for the employment of ar-

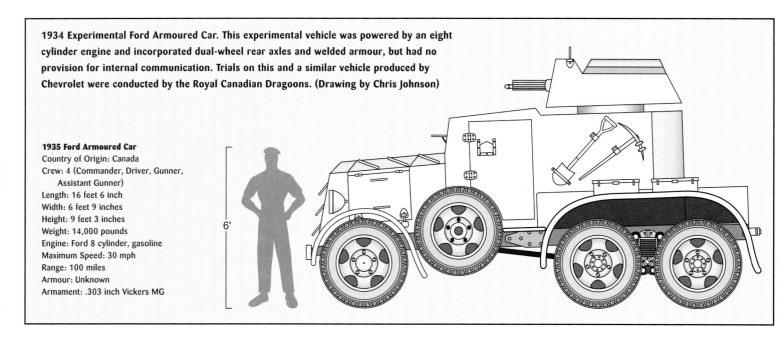

1934 Experimental Ford Armoured Car. This experimental vehicle was powered by an eight cylinder engine and incorporated dual-wheel rear axles and welded armour, but had no provision for internal communication. Trials on this and a similar vehicle produced by Chevrolet were conducted by the Royal Canadian Dragoons. (Drawing by Chris Johnson)

1935 Ford Armoured Car
Country of Origin: Canada
Crew: 4 (Commander, Driver, Gunner, Assistant Gunner)
Length: 16 feet 6 inch
Width: 6 feet 9 inches
Height: 9 feet 3 inches
Weight: 14,000 pounds
Engine: Ford 8 cylinder, gasoline
Maximum Speed: 30 mph
Range: 100 miles
Armour: Unknown
Armament: .303 inch Vickers MG

6'

mour in the German Army. While he advocated that tanks be kept concentrated rather than being parceled out in small numbers to support infantry formations, in contrast to the British he was always a strong advocate of a balanced all-arms approach. But in his approach to structuring this all-arms team, he insisted that the infantry had to be motorized so their mobility at least came close to that of the tanks. Guderian is usually given credit for having initiated the concept of the *Blitzkrieg:* fast, long-ranging, radio-controlled armoured forces supported by motorized infantry, with the final ingredient being close air support from dedicated fighter-bombers.

EARLY MECHANIZATION TRIALS IN CANADA

Just as the Depression struck, Canada, too, took the first halting steps in experimenting with mechanization. The artillery led the way, introducing trucks in the 3rd Medium Battery and the two RCHA batteries in 1929 and 1930. Then in 1931, the government found the money to purchase six Carden-Loyds from Britain, with another six acquired the following year. After a

course for instructors was conducted at Petawawa – attended by Captain Worthington of the PPCLI, and Captain Charles Foulkes of the Royal Canadian Regiment (RCR), among others – the twelve vehicles were split evenly between the three Permanent Force infantry regiments. The four that found their way to the RCR in London, Ontario were soon used 'operationally'; the RCR took them to the city of Stratford on aid to the civil power duties in September 1933. Their arrival there caused a sensation, a *Toronto Daily Star* reporter describing them as "baby armoured military tanks". The small carriers, however, sat unused beside the armoury of the Perth Regiment until November, when they were returned to London.

Cavalry trials began when the RCD were issued two armoured cars in 1934, one built by Ford, the other by General Motors Chevrolet. Both were experimental vehicles, designed and built at the expense of the automotive companies, which undoubtedly accounted for the government's willingness to take them on. Both carried a crew of four, the armament being a Vickers machine-gun, and their range was 160 kilometres, at a maximum road speed of 50 kph. They proved to be a great success and plans were made for two more to be built in 1935, for issue to the Strathconas. The manufacturers were not willing, however, to continue to subsidize Canadian re-armament, and wanted to be paid the full price for their products. When the Liberals won the 1935 election, they quickly torpedoed the entire programme, and mechanization came to a grinding halt, with the Ford being shipped to the Strathconas so that both

Experimental armoured car manufactured by General Motors during trials by the Royal Canadian Dragoons in Petawawa in the summer of 1935. (RCD Museum)

Mounted band of the Governor General's Body Guard, Toronto, 1934. This was the only mounted band organized by Canadian cavalry. (Governor General's Horse Guards)

Permanent Force cavalry regiments could each have one armoured car.

The Militia cavalry units, meanwhile, were not blind to the possibilities of mechanization. In 1934, the 1st Hussars conducted a day-long exercise which involved a mounted squadron providing an escort force to a motor convoy of engineers (riding in civilian automobiles) over a distance of 45 kilometres. Then, in 1936, three cavalry units were converted into 'motorized cavalry regiments' – the 8th (New Brunswick) Hussars, the 7th/11th Hussars and the 19th Alberta Dragoons. That summer the 8th Hussars trained without horses for the first time in their history. Cavalry Regiment (Mechanized) was the designation applied to these units in 1937, but the new title did not bring with it any equipment for the role. Their new mounts, 31 privately-owned vehicles, inspired a camp administrative instruction that stipulated "spurs will not be worn during periods of training when cars are being used."

The three motorized cavalry regiments had a theoretical establishment of three squadrons, each of three troops. Each troop, one officer and twelve other ranks, was to consist of a headquarters of two trucks, and three sections each with one truck and two motorcycles. The operational concept closely resembled that of mounted rifles. In a 1937 paper, Major Gerard Bradbrooke of the Strathconas (a future armoured brigade commander), wrote:

These vehicles are [intended to be] Morris, short wheelbase, large tire, four-wheeled trucks. They carry a section of one NCO and seven men and have a moderate cross-country performance. There is a certain amount of armour plating to protect the engine and driver, and the height, with crew seated, is about six feet. The crew carry a light machine-gun, rifles, grenades, etc., but they do not fight from the vehicle. For action they dismount, a number of exits being provided in order that they may do so rapidly. When the crew is in 'dismounted action', the trucks are kept under cover as near as possible, in much the same way as 'led horses'. With each troop, one of the three trucks carries an anti-tank rifle.

An early attempt at mechanization of the British cavalry was carried out by the 3rd King's Own Hussars. The Morris Cavalry Portée vehicles shown in this photo are the type described by Major Bradbrooke in a 1937 report. (RCAC Association Archives)

The first combined training of cavalry, armoured cars, machine guns and motorized reconnaissance was conducted by the Royal Canadian Dragoons at a 'Royal School' in St. Jean, Quebec, in August and September 1936. (RCH Museum)

FORMATION OF THE FIRST CANADIAN ARMOURED UNITS

Throughout the inter-war period a succession of contingency plans termed 'defence schemes' examined Canadian force requirements for a variety of possible wartime scenarios. Defence Scheme No.1, a plan for war with the United States, was abandoned as being irrelevant in the early 1920s. Scheme No.2 may have been a bit more pertinent, since it anticipated a variety of commitments in the event of a war in the Pacific. Defence Scheme No.3, drafted in 1932, examined the raising of a Canadian expeditionary force of seven divisions for overseas service in another major conflict similar to the Great War, and Scheme No.4, the last in the series, was concerned with the raising of a smaller expeditionary force – something on the scale of the Canadian contingents in the South African War. None of these plans was intended to be an operational blueprint; they were never reviewed, and certainly were never approved, by the government. Instead, they served as a focus for planning and discussion on such issues as force structure and manpower requirements.

Of these plans, Defence Scheme No. 3 was by far the most significant, for it became the basis for the 1936 reorganization of the Canadian Militia. This major shake-up had its roots in a 1931 proposal by the Chief of the General Staff, Major-General A.G.L. McNaughton, for the reduction of the existing fifteen divisions to a more balanced force of seven divisions – six of infantry and one of cavalry. Surplus units were to be disbanded, amalgamated or re-roled.

When McNaughton's plan was implemented in December 1936, the 35 horsed cavalry regiments were reduced in number to sixteen. At the same time, four armoured car regiments were created as part of the Cavalry Corps. The two motor machine gun units raised in 1919 in Montreal and Winnipeg became, respectively, the 6th Duke of Connaught's Royal Canadian Hussars (Armoured Car) and the 2nd Armoured Car Regiment, while the King's Canadian Hussars in Kentville, Nova Scotia, and the British Columbia Hussars also became armoured car regiments.

Perhaps the most notable of the changes aimed at preparing the Canadian Militia for war in an age of mechanization was the designation of six units as tank battalions, to be carried on the infantry order of battle. Four of the six were existing infantry battalions – the Argyll Light Infantry in Belleville, Ontario, the Ontario Regiment in Oshawa, the Three Rivers Regiment, and the Calgary Regiment. One was a machine-gun unit, the New Brunswick Regiment in Moncton, and the junior of these new units, the Essex Regiment (Tank) in Windsor, Ontario, was created from scratch – the only completely new fighting unit raised in 1936. In this era, knowledgeable vehicle mechanics and skilled drivers were just not all that common. The army, therefore, sensibly chose to develop closer links with the nation's automobile industry by selecting Windsor (home to Ford and Chrysler) and Oshawa (home of General Motors) as the location for two of the new tank battalions.

The support that the industry gave to the army during the war years, and to the Armoured Corps in particular, reflected the astuteness of that decision, but that was in the future. In the real world of 1936, having the word 'tank' in brackets, as a part of their name, was about all that the new units received. There were no vehicles of any kind issued to them, only some obsolete

Vickers machine guns. The 2nd Armoured Car Regiment, in Winnipeg, at least had a vehicle of sorts, but it was an engineless mock-up manufactured by the Dominion Bridge Company and the soldiers had to push it onto the floor of Minto Armoury to practice mounting and dismounting drills.

The black beret was introduced to Canada at this time. The new tank battalions wanted the beret because of its association with armour but Ottawa refused, no doubt fearing that giving the units black berets might lead them to expect tanks to go with them! They were told to continue to wear 'traditional headdress', but members of the Essex Regiment, not having a traditional headdress, purchased black berets at their own expense and wore them at the regiment's inaugural parade on 20 April 1937.

When the process of re-organization was completed, the structure and look of Canada's army was very different. The eight existing mounted brigade headquarters were disbanded in 1936 and replaced with five cavalry brigades: the 1st Cavalry Brigade in Toronto (GGHG, 2nd/10th Dragoons), the 2nd in Pincher Creek, Alberta (15th Alberta Light Horse, 19th Alberta Dragoons), the 3rd in Montreal (6th Duke of Connaught's Royal Canadian Hussars, 17th Duke of York's Royal Canadian Hussars), the 4th in Winnipeg (12th Manitoba Dragoons, Manitoba Mounted Rifles, Fort Garry Horse, with

The first occasion when the black beret was worn by a Canadian unit was the inaugural parade of the newly-formed Essex Regiment (Tank) in 1937. (*The Windsor Star*)

2nd Armoured Car Regiment attached), and the 7th – there were no brigades bearing the designations 5th or 6th – in Regina (14th Canadian Light Horse, 16th/22nd Saskatchewan Horse). Each brigade was commanded by a colonel, its headquarters consisting of eight all ranks as well as two horses, one bicycle and a four-seater staff car.

The Canadian Cavalry Association certainly did not ignore the need for mechanization. In 1937, the Association passed resolutions calling on National Defence Headquarters to reimburse owners of private vehicles used and damaged in training, to supply all cavalry units, both horsed and motorized, with wireless (radio) sets, and to provide training films and manuals on the use of armoured fighting vehicles. Of course those old perennial resolutions, more horse shelters and swords for all mounted units, were still being passed as well.

FORMATION OF THE CANADIAN TANK (LATER AFV) SCHOOL

To train and guide the newly formed tank battalions, the Canadian Tank School was created on 1 November 1936 in London, Ontario, under the command of Captain, Brevet Major, F.F. Worthington of the PPCLI. During 1937, Major Worthington, known by everyone as Worthy, attended a twelve-month course at the Royal Tank Corps School in Bovington, England, along with Lieutenant J.H. Larocque of the RCD. The remainder of the staff attended a course on engine maintenance at RCAF Station Trenton, and, by the beginning of 1938, the School was able to make a start on the training of the six new tank battalions. Typical of these training sessions was that conducted in February and March 1938. Worthy's second-in-command, and eventual successor as Commandant, Captain Gordon Carrington Smith, and an NCO, Quartermaster Sergeant Instructor M.M. Philpott, travelled to Windsor, Ontario, to conduct training in the local armoury for the Essex Regiment. For a six-week period on Mondays, Thursdays and Sundays, they lectured the unit on tank tactics and machine-gunnery. In March examinations were held for those who had attended the training.

On 1 May 1938 the Tank School lacking a suitable training area in the London district, was moved to Camp Borden Ontario, which had an abundance of open ground for vehicle training. As well as a change of scene, the School underwent a change of name, becoming the Canadian Armoured Fighting Vehicles School (CAFVS). It was with this title that it undertook its first formal course of instruction but it still did not have much in the way of

The Order of Battle of the Canadian Cavalry in 1937

Cavalry Regiments (Horsed) or Mounted Rifles: Peace Establishment: 25 officers and 397 other ranks, organized with a regimental headquarters, a headquarters squadron, and three cavalry squadrons each consisting of a squadron headquarters and three troops. Each troop consisted of a troop headquarters, three sabre sections (7 men to a section), and a light machine gun section (1 Lewis gun). The unit's mounts included 345 horses, 6 wheeled cars, 7 trucks and 8 motorcycles.

The Royal Canadian Dragoons

Lord Strathcona's Horse (Royal Canadians)

The Governor General's Horse Guards (An amalgamation of The Governor General's Body Guard and The Mississauga Horse)

IV Princess Louise Dragoon Guards (An amalgamation of the Princess Louise Dragoons Guards and The 4th Hussars of Canada)

2nd /10th Dragoons (An amalgamation of the 2nd Dragoons and The 10th Brant Dragoons)

1st Hussars

12th Manitoba Dragoons

15th Alberta Light Horse (An amalgamation of the 15th Canadian Light Horse and the South Alberta Horse)

16th/22nd Saskatchewan Horse (An amalgamation of The 16th Canadian Light Horse and The Saskatchewan Mounted Rifles)

17th Duke of York's Royal Canadian Hussars (Argenteuil Rangers)

The Manitoba Mounted Rifles

14th Canadian Light Horse

The British Columbia Dragoons

The Fort Garry Horse (An amalgamation of The Fort Garry Horse and The Manitoba Horse)

The Prince Edward Island Light Horse

Cavalry Regiments (Mechanized): Peace Establishment: 25 officers and 381 other ranks, organized with a regimental headquarters, a headquarters squadron, and three fighting squadrons each consisting of a squadron headquarters and three troops. Each troop to consist of a troop headquarters (1 wheeled car and 1 light tank), two light tank sections (2 light tanks to a section), and a carrier section (1 armoured carrier). The unit's total number of vehicles was 53 light tanks, 17 armoured carriers, 19 wheeled cars, 10 trucks and 13 motorcycles.

8th Princess Louise's (New Brunswick) Hussars

7th/11th Hussars (An amalgamation of the 7th Hussars and the 11th Hussars)

19th Alberta Dragoons (An amalgamation of the 19th Alberta Dragoons and the Alberta Mounted Rifles)

Cavalry Regiments (Armoured Car): Peace Establishment: 26 officers and 286 other ranks, organized with a regimental headquarters (which also fulfilled the responsibilities of a headquarters squadron), and three fighting squadrons. Each squadron contained a headquarters (two armoured cars, two wheeled cars, one truck and two motorcycles) and three troops. Each troop consisted of 3 armoured cars. The unit's total number of vehicles was 35 armoured cars, 9 wheeled cars, 6 trucks and 10 motorcycles.

6th Duke of Connaught's Royal Canadian Hussars (Armoured Car) (An amalgamation of the 6th Duke of Connaught's Royal Canadian Hussars and the 1st Armoured Car Regiment, formerly the 1st Motor Machine Gun Brigade)

2nd Armoured Car Regiment (An amalgamation of the 1st Machine Gun Squadron and the 2nd Armoured Car Regiment, formerly the 2nd Motor Machine Gun Brigade)

The King's Canadian Hussars (Armoured Car) (An amalgamation of The King's Canadian Hussars and the 6th Machine Gun Battalion)

The British Columbia Hussars (Armoured Car) (An amalgamation of The British Columbia Hussars and the 11th Machine Gun Battalion)

The Order of Battle of Canadian Armour in 1937

Note: Officially there was no such list in 1937, the Mechanized Regiments and the Armoured Car units were on the Cavalry order of battle while the Tank units were on that of the Infantry.

Tank Battalions: Peace Establishment: 33 officers and 453 other ranks, organized with a battalion headquarters (which also fulfilled the responsibilities of a headquarters company), and four tank companies, each consisting of a company headquarters and three sections. Each section to consist of 5 tanks. The unit's total number of vehicles was 66 tanks, 11 wheeled cars, 9 trucks and 12 motorcycles.

The Argyll Light Infantry (Tank) (This unit had a restricted establishment of a headquarters company and two, instead of the normal four, tank companies.)

The Ontario Regiment (Tank)

The Three Rivers Regiment (Tank)

The Calgary Regiment (Tank)

The New Brunswick Regiment (Tank) (This unit had a restricted establishment of a headquarters company and one tank company.)

The Essex Regiment (Tank)

Governor General's Horse Guards

2nd / 10th Dragoons

7th / 11th Hussars

16th / 22nd Saskatchewan Horse

BADGES OF THE 'NEW' CAVALRY REGIMENTS AFTER THE 1936 AMALGAMATIONS

6th Duke of Connaught's Royal
Canadian Hussars

2nd Armoured Car Regiment

The King's Canadian Hussars

The British Columbia Hussars

BADGES OF THE FOUR ARMOURED CAR REGIMENTS CREATED IN 1936

The Argyll Light Infantry (Tank)

The Ontario Regiment (Tank)

The Three Rivers Regiment (Tank)

The Calgary Regiment (Tank)

The New Brunswick Regiment
(Tank)

The Essex Regiment (Tank)

BADGES OF THE SIX TANK REGIMENTS CREATED IN 1936

(Right) The original staff of the Canadian Tank School, November 1936. Rear Row: Sgt R.S. Edwards, PPCLI; Sgt G.H. Pratt, RCR; Sgt G.A. Farmer, RCA; Sgt A. Viel, R22eR. Centre Row: Sgt J.C. Cave, PPCLI; Sgt R.J. Hider, RCD; Sgt A. Pengelley, RCR; Sgt W.V. Leblanc, R22eR; Sgt E.D. Reid, RCA. Front Row: WOII R. Harris, RCD; WOII F. Richmond, LSH; Lt T.G. Gibson, RCR; Capt G. Carrington Smith, RCA; Lt J.G. Andrews, PPCLI; WOII M.M. Philpot, LSH. Absent: Maj F.F. Worthington, Lt J.H. Laroque, RCD; Lt J.A.G. Roberge, R22eR; Lt F.E. White, LSH.

(Below) The first course conducted by the Canadian Armoured Fighting Vehicles School, July 1938. By this stage the black beret was widely used in the School and in tank units.

CANADIAN ARMOURED FIGHTING VEHICLES SCHOOL—CAMP SCHOOL COURSE NO. 1 CAMP BORDEN, ONT. JULY 11–23RD 1938

equipment. The vehicle fleet at Borden consisted of twelve Carden-Loyd tankettes, reclaimed from the Permanent Force infantry regiments, a model-T Ford engine for instruction in motor mechanics, a locally built truck called 'Old Faithful' and a discarded artillery gun tractor known as a Dragon. It did, however, have an interesting, and useful, gunnery training aid called a RYPA, which was an acronym standing for Roll, Yaw, Pitch and Alteration of course. The somewhat erratic movement of this device in all four planes was meant to simulate a tank travelling cross-country over rough ground. The student, sitting in the gunner's seat in a cut-away tank turret, was meant to learn to maintain a lock on a target through the gunner's sight in spite of the often fairly violent movement of the RYPA. The sight was slaved to a sub-calibre .22 rifle and the trainee gunners shot at miniature targets on an indoor sand-table range.

CAFVS Course No. 1 was conducted from 11 to 23 July 1938. The syllabus emphasized trades training, driving and maintenance (more commonly called D&M) and (machine) gunnery, but also included an introduction to communications and tactics. An initial period of garrison training was followed by outdoor practical training, and no more than two consecutive days were spent in a classroom. The trades training completed, a day

of crew training followed, which in turn was followed by a day-long tactical exercise. Tactical training at this time was very rudimentary, since no one really had much idea about how to move tactically with a group of armoured vehicles. This was not a particularly significant problem, however, because the doctrine of the day cast the tank in the role of an infantry support weapon, meant to accompany marching infantry in the assault on enemy trenches, just as they had in France and Flanders.

The School's first tanks, two Vickers Mark VIBs, arrived in September 1938, and CAFVS Course Number 4, conducted from 12 to 23 September 1938, incorporated instruction on the newly arrived light tanks.

While the courses of 1938 may appear somewhat simplistic to the modern eye, at the time they represented innovative military training. Worthy insisted on crew training with no more than six students to an instructor. He loathed lectures and insisted that classroom sessions be immediately confirmed with practical training either in the field or the vehicle bay. Above all he believed in personal example. The militiamen from the Ontario or Calgary Regiments, as well as all the other units, saw a leader with dirty hands and a get-involved attitude. They would remember him and his example in the coming war.

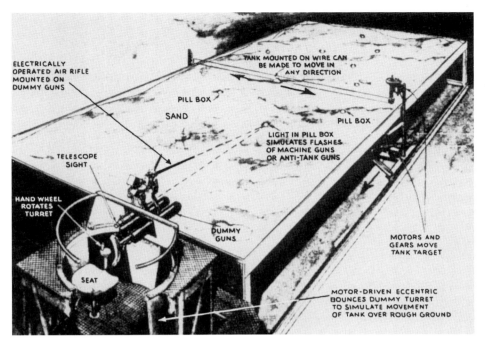

Drawing of a RYPA Range.

THE MILITARY–INTELLECTUAL TRANSITION

The 1930s were not quite the wasted period that the previous decade had been. The army had recognized the need for mechanization; the problem was paying for it. Money gradually became available as the ominous signs of impending war began to appear in Europe, and the formation, in 1932, of the Conference of Defence Associations (CDA), helped to keep military interests and issues fresh in the government's mind. The CDA was a natural outgrowth of the work of military lobby groups like the Canadian Cavalry Association.

The School was an obvious locus for practical thinking about armour doctrine and employment. Because each course was just two weeks long, Worthington and his staff concentrated on first principles, so that the officers and NCOs attending the training could pass them on to others back at their

units. During the summer of 1938 the first armoured exercises were conducted at Borden using the Carden-Loyds, the two Vickers Mark VI B light tanks and the Dragon. In the spring of 1939 an additional fourteen Vickers Mark VI Bs arrived from Britain but, like their two predecessors, without any spare parts.

The main Canadian source of intellectual debate on armoured issues was to be found in the pages of *Canadian Defence Quarterly*. As he watched the British experiments with armoured formations and their organizations, Major E. L. M. Burns, RCE, became concerned that the full capabilities of armour were being dissipated within unworkable organizational structures. Burns was a regular contributor to *CDQ*, and his writing showed that he had a far deeper understanding of armour than most of his contemporaries. In 1933, for example, he reviewed J. F. C. Fuller's book *Operations Between Mechanized Forces*.

In the April 1938 edition of *CDQ*, Burns published an article, 'A Division That Can Attack', calling for a standard division composed of one armoured brigade and two infantry brigades. This went against the newly-introduced British structure of pure infantry divisions with brigades of armour attached to them as necessary. A rebuttal appeared in July with a piece by Captain Guy Simonds of the RCHA, titled 'An Army That Can Attack – A Division That Can Defend'. Simonds thought it wasteful to include an armoured brigade in every division and wanted armour to be concentrated for the counter-attack and breakthrough roles. Burns responded in October with 'Where Do the Tanks Belong', stressing the need for all arms to work

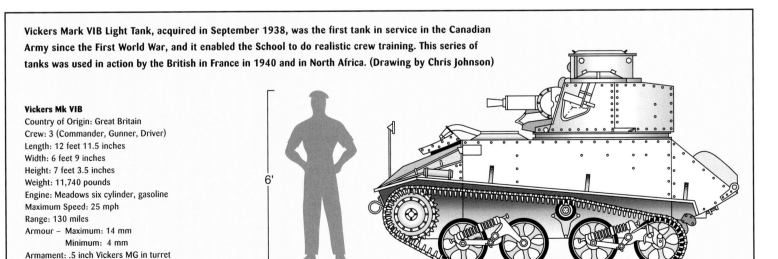

Vickers Mark VIB Light Tank, acquired in September 1938, was the first tank in service in the Canadian Army since the First World War, and it enabled the School to do realistic crew training. This series of tanks was used in action by the British in France in 1940 and in North Africa. (Drawing by Chris Johnson)

Vickers Mk VIB
Country of Origin: Great Britain
Crew: 3 (Commander, Gunner, Driver)
Length: 12 feet 11.5 inches
Width: 6 feet 9 inches
Height: 7 feet 3.5 inches
Weight: 11,740 pounds
Engine: Meadows six cylinder, gasoline
Maximum Speed: 25 mph
Range: 130 miles
Armour – Maximum: 14 mm
      Minimum: 4 mm
Armament: .5 inch Vickers MG in turret
    .303 inch Vickers MG co-axial to .5 inch MG

6'

together on a regular basis – something difficult to do if they belonged to different formations.

Simonds replied with 'What Price Assault without Support' in the January 1939 edition, arguing that the resources allocated to a division on a permanent basis would not be sufficient to make and sustain a breakthrough. Additional resources would have to come from higher headquarters. The debate ended at this point and, with the outbreak of war eight months later, *CDQ* itself died. (It would be resurrected in the post-Second World War era.)

This exchange of opinions on the correct structure and role for armoured formations was subsequently widely praised as the intellectual highlight of the inter-war army. It is interesting to note that it was carried on by a sapper and a gunner, and that both would command armoured divisions in the coming war.

The fact that a gunner and a sapper were the leading intellectual lights in the Canadian army of 1938 was not an anomaly. The key military figure of the inter-war period was General Andrew McNaughton. An engineer by profession, by applying engineering principles to the task, he had turned the business of counter-battery operations into a true science during the Great War. Rapidly rising through the commissioned ranks, over the heads of officers of greater seniority and field experience, McNaughton served as Chief of the General Staff from 1929 to 1935, when he left on secondment to become president of the National Research Council. Throughout his career McNaughton favoured officers, who, like himself, had strong academic credentials.

Thus, in the late 1930s the higher reaches of the army came to be populated with officers who had done well at staff college

Sleeve badge worn by the staff of the Canadian Armoured Fighting Vehicles School, introduced in 1938. This patch was similar to one worn by members of 1st Canadian Tank Battalion in 1918.

or who had good academic backgrounds. Successful leadership in the field, tactical competence and operational experience were less important in competing for promotion, and consequently gunners and sappers tended to predominate in the higher ranks, at the expense of the infantry and cavalrymen. This practice also tended to discriminate against the regulars in favour of reservists. The small numbers of regulars meant that they could seldom be freed from their instructional duties to fill staff positions where they might gain experience outside of regimental soldiering. When senior appointments for an overseas expeditionary force were being considered in 1936, only one of the six infantry brigades was to be commanded by a regular. In the same force, fourteen out of nineteen senior staff positions were allocated to gunners and sappers. It was an army that favoured the Burnses and Simondses over the Worthingtons.

Defence Scheme No.3, described earlier, was revised in 1937. It now included an expeditionary force consisting of a corps headquarters, two infantry divisions and a cavalry division. Known as the 'Mobile Force', the corps was subdivided into Force A and Force B, each portion containing an infantry division and a slice of the other troops. Both A and B were to be recruited simultaneously, but Force B would not be concentrated until A had been dispatched overseas, and provision was made in the plan for the raising of four more divisions, although in the spring of 1939 the plan for a cavalry division was dropped. In light of the worsening situation in Europe discreet preparations for mobilization were made in August 1939. On the 25th some reserve units were called out to guard vital points. Then, on 1 September 1939, the order to mobilize the 1st and 2nd Divisions was issued from Ottawa, and included in the orders of battle were divisional cavalry regiments, respectively the 1st Hussars and the Fort Garry Horse. For the second time in a generation Canadian cavalrymen prepared for war. Twenty-five years earlier they had discovered that the role of horsed cavalry in modern war had become severely curtailed: this time they were to find that it had disappeared altogether.

THE STATE OF THE MOUNTED UNITS ON THE EVE OF WAR

In the twenty-year period between the two world wars, the Canadian cavalry made only slow progress toward the goal of professional competence. This lack of progress is usually ascribed to a sense of inherent conservatism, and ingrained conservatism played a part to be sure, for it is part of the mental baggage of any military force. When your life depends on getting it right

Officers of the 6th Duke of York's Royal Canadian Hussars discuss tactics during a mechanized reconnaissance exercise in October 1937. (RCH Museum)

Changing a tire during an 8th New Brunswick Hussars motorized exercise, summer 1938. The large number of supervisors has always been a part of military life. (8CH Archives)

In the Canadian context, the Canadian Cavalry Association was certainly not a reactionary body. It consistently promoted the use of the latest technology as an aid to cavalry operations and the cult of the horse, which played a significant role in the debate on the future of Britain's cavalry arm, was mostly absent in Canada. The promoters of armour liked to disparage those who were of a more cautious turn of mind by accusing them of being hippophiles and reactionaries, but, broadly speaking, armour was viewed as the coming trend. The staff of the Canadian Tank School, for example, were all enthusiastic volunteers. Many fervently believed in the armour concept, while others could see personal advantage in getting aboard the armour bandwagon at an early stage.

What then was the state of Canada's mounted forces in 1939? The horsed cavalry regiments were, by and large, in good shape. They had survived the cuts of 1936 primarily because

the first time – with no second chance – one tends to stick with tried and proven methods and procedures. The radical promoters of armour in Britain, the Fullers and Liddell Harts, liked to blame the slowness of the mechanization process on a hide-bound army establishment in general and on the cavalry in particular. These views were echoed, in a minor key, in Canada. Recent studies have, however, shown that these arguments were exaggerated. The British staff, like the Canadian, had no fundamental problem with mechanization, and in each army supported the process. The major limitation was severe financial constraint, and the secondary problem was doctrinal confusion. What types of vehicles were needed, and in what numbers? The criticisms and carping of the tank enthusiasts was anything but helpful in this process, since they tended to alienate the people and bodies who should have been their natural allies. The events of 1940, the *Blitzkrieg*, would permit the tank enthusiasts to say 'I told you so,' with the result that the story of mechanization has been distorted, in their favour, ever since.

One of four canvas 'mock tanks' built by the Calgary Regiment (Tank) for field training. The canvas superstructure was mounted over Model A Ford cars. Perhaps the Calgarys were already practising amphibious landings, even though the Model A was hardly an amphibian. (KOCR Museum)

they were the stronger and better-led units. The mechanized and armoured car regiments were, however, not so well off. Their major problems were a lack of equipment – they had no choice but to use privately owned motor vehicles - and a lack of a coherent doctrine. Were they supposed to be a species of mounted infantry or a reconnaissance organization? They had little guidance in their dilemma; some of the Empire's most eminent professional soldiers were still debating these ideas.

The Royal Canadian Dragoons on an exercise near Camp Borden, 1938. A year later the horse would disappear from the order of battle. (RCD Museum)

Finally, there were the six tank battalions. They, at least, had a fairly clear doctrine, albeit one that was twenty years out of date, but they had no tanks. A private motor vehicle could stand in for a scout car, but not for a tank, even though the Calgary Regiment made a valiant effort to do just that. The soldiers of the Essex Regiment, for example, were reduced to practicing vehicle drills by holding two pieces of rope, representing the sides of the tank, between four men.

On the eve of what was to be the first truly mechanized war, Canada's mounted units were poorly prepared. The horsed cavalry, for the most part, were trained for a form of warfare whose time had long passed, and the officers, Permanent Force and Militia, all understood this. The mechanized cavalry and armoured car regiments were really little better off. While four of the six fledgling tank battalions had begun to master some of the basis tenets of armoured warfare, progress was uneven, essentially because they had no vehicles. The Argyll and New Brunswick Regiments (Tank), however, were judged to have accomplished very little.

If none of Canada's mobile troops were ready to go off to war in the late summer of 1939, the same could be said about all of the other arms. But what the cavalry, armoured car and tank units were able to provide, and in considerable numbers, was a cadre of exceptionally dedicated men who, because of their background, were able to adapt readily to serving in the armoured units that were about to be raised.

CHAPTER 4

Creation and Building
of the Corps

The outbreak of the Second World War came as no great surprise to anyone who had been following world events. War clouds had been building over Europe ever since Adolf Hitler and his National Socialist party came to power in Germany in 1933. Within two years Germany began a massive re-armament programme that included the creation of the most modern mechanized and tank formations in the world. Hitler began to expand his Third Reich when Austria was forcibly occupied in 1938, then he browbeat Britain and France into accepting German annexation of the Czech Sudetenland, and only months later the rest of Czechoslovakia was seized. Attention next focused on Poland. By this stage, however, Britain and France had the measure of Hitler. Both gave politically questionable and strategically impossible guarantees that they would go to Poland's aid in the event of a German attack.

The German–Polish situation deteriorated steadily over the summer of 1939. The way was opened for Hitler by the signing of a non-aggression pact with Russia on 21 August and, eleven days later, German mechanized divisions raced across the Polish frontier supported by massive aerial fleets. Few images better capture the essence of this *Blitzkrieg* campaign than that of gallant Polish cavalrymen, armed only with lances, charging hopelessly into advancing German tank formations. Britain and France, acting on the commitments they had made to the Polish government, declared war on Germany on 3 September.

The Canadian government followed these developments very closely. While Prime Minister Mackenzie King may have had a personal preference for neutrality, he understood clearly that Canada could not remain uncommitted when Britain was involved in a major war. On 25 August 'precautionary measures' were taken to call out selected units for the guarding of vital points. Then, on 1 September, orders were telegraphed to district headquarters across the country to place 'on active service' all of the units designated in Defence Scheme No. 3 as part

Recruiting poster. During the Second World War over a million Canadians would serve in the nation's armed forces. Nearly 30,000 served in the Canadian Armoured Corps.

Vickers Mark VI B tanks on field training, Camp Borden, winter 1940. (NAC PA129099)

AN UNCERTAIN BEGINNING

Of 1 and 2 Canadian Divisions. Parliament formally declared war against Germany on 10 September.

Of the units destined to become part of the Canadian Armoured Corps on its formation, only four were affected by the mobilization order. The 1st Hussars in London were called to active service as the divisional cavalry regiment of 1 Division, and the Fort Garry Horse was mobilized in Winnipeg for 2 Division. Two of the six tank regiments created three years earlier were also placed on active service: the Three Rivers Regiment (TRR) for attachment to 1 Division, and the Ontario Regiment from Oshawa for the 2nd. At first there was work enough in recruiting the hundreds of men needed to bring the units up to strength and conduct basic training, but all four units were soon faced with the reality that there was simply no equipment for the mechanized roles they were intended to perform.

The Armoured Fighting Vehicles School at Camp Borden, with its complement of 39 all ranks, was also placed on active service on 1 September 1939, redesignated as the Canadian Armoured Fighting Vehicles Training Centre (CAFVC) – although it was still colloquially referred to as 'the School'. Mobilization had very little immediate effect on the Centre as there were no troops to train as yet. A small increase in strength was authorized, however, and one of the first recruits was Private Jack Wallace, the 18-year-old son of one of Worthy's original school staff. Six weeks later a handful of students arrived from Royal Military College – Second Lieutenants Edward (Ned) Amy, Richard Caldwell, Oliver Hopkins and Stuart Nicol. They had been graduated early because of the outbreak of war and

were quickly put to work learning the basic skills of armoured soldiering so that they could be employed as instructors.

Even though he got no encouragement or assistance from National Defence Headquarters, Worthy, now a lieutenant-colonel, immediately got to work expanding the Centre's training capability. In this he received considerable assistance from an informal group of prominent men in Toronto who called themselves the Armoured Force Association. Among these were Colonel Lockhart Gordon, former commanding officer of the Mississauga Horse, and Colonel Sam McLaughlin of General Motors fame, who was Honorary Colonel of the Ontario Regiment. Arrangements were made for the Centre to receive cut-down engines and spare parts from General Motors, Chrysler and Ford, and instructors went to the automobile plants for specialized courses given by the companies' top mechanics. In addition, the Association bought equipment in the United States for use in training wireless operators, and funded the purchase of three additional RYPAs. Not least, they completely outfitted the Centre's kitchen with modern labour-saving appliances such as electric dishwashers and vegetable peelers, which undoubtedly spared hundreds of young troopers many hours of kitchen fatigues.

If there was one man with the determination and energy to shape the future of armour in Canada, it was Worthy. He was a truly gifted, charismatic leader. Brigadier-General Ned Amy recalled his early days at the Centre.

It was a tremendous experience because of his training techniques. For example, he wanted us to learn all about mechanical things, so we were sent to the D and M [Driving

Captain J.H. Laroque at the gunner's seat in the School's first 'RYPA' gunnery trainer, autumn 1939. (Royal Canadian Armoured Corps Collection, CFB Borden Museum)

Wireless (radio) training class, winter 1940. The mystery of the dots and dashes of Morse Code no doubt is the cause of the puzzled look of the students. (RCAC Collection, CFB Borden Museum)

that the way to avoid being swamped with new tasks was to take the initiative whenever you met him: "Colonel, I've just had an idea." He'd always listen, and say, "That's interesting. Work on it." If you didn't have an idea, he'd give you one.

Worthy also knew his own foibles, and habitually gave newcomers to the Centre a mimeographed thumbnail self-description.

1. I am usually in a hurry and I like to have jobs done quickly.

2. I have a great thirst for information and I expect to be kept informed on all matters. I want my information quickly and when it is 'hot'. Cold information is of little value in war. Note this point carefully.

3. I know that all 'doers' make mistakes. If you pull a boner tell me about it. I may 'brown you off' but will help you out of the hole. Beware if I find out your boner through other channels.

4. I like to talk things over with my staff and when I put a proposition before you or ask you to comment on anything I have written, I want your honest opinion, and not what you think I would like to hear. In other words, do not become a 'yes man' with me.

5. I am inclined to blow off steam, especially to my staff. This is a safety valve. However, do not disregard the storm signals when they fly.

6. The following are my pet aversions, which annoy me greatly: (a) Slackness in military discipline; (b) Failure to comply with orders and instructions; (c) Stupidity; (d) Officers who fail to look after their men; (e) Neglect in the care for or abuse of vehicles; (f) Deception; (g) Disloyalty.

7. I believe there is no absolute limit to perfection, therefore I am never fully satisfied, especially with myself.

and Maintenance] Wing. The corporal instructor had an engine on the floor, and said to us "There are the tools; take it apart." When we had it in pieces, he told us to put it together again, and as we did he explained what the different parts were for. In no time at all we learned a hell of a lot about an engine, and there was no formal instruction.

Worthy's enthusiasm was amazing, and there was always a lesson in everything he did. We soon found out that every time he saw you, you had another job. "I want you to design something for the miniature range; get back to me in a couple of days." "Figure out how to do this, and let me know." One of the captains who knew Worthy pretty well told us

By late September the effects of many years of grossly inadequate military budgets were sadly apparent. Serious deficiencies in such basic items as boots, socks, blankets and beds led to the suspension of recruiting for all but the units of 1 Division, and arrangements were made to send the division to Britain in early December equipped only with uniforms and rifles. While the slowdown in the build-up of the Active Service Force provided an opportunity for the government to arrange contracts for essential stores, for many months there was a serious shortage of every sort of operational equipment. In this dire situation Ottawa had no interest whatsoever in tanks or other mechanized equipment; there were just far too many other pressing problems.

There were, of course, staff officers, such as Colonel H.D.G. Crerar and Lieutenant-Colonel E.L.M. Burns, who were advocates of mechanization of the Army, but too many of the senior officers at National Defence Headquarters at this time gave evidence of being the military dinosaurs the Army is often accused of harbouring. In November 1939, Brigadier E.J. Schmidlin, soon to take over as quartermaster-general, was quoted by the *Globe and Mail:* "No one knows how useful tanks will be.... The Polish campaign was no true indication of the power of mechanized armies." Schmidlin was reciting the position argued by the Minister of National Defence, Norman Rogers.

Worthy, however, remained undeterred by this formal discouragement and, to the consternation of Ottawa, he began to press for the creation of an armoured corps and for practical steps to rectify the lack of modern armoured vehicles. As a result of discussions with his contacts in the automotive industry, he was convinced that tanks could be built in Canada, so he encouraged his technical staff to begin work on the design of a tank with substantially greater firepower than was available on existing light tanks.

He also worked at creating an independent identity for the embryonic armoured organization he was determined to bring into existence. In the autumn of 1939 he asked Ottawa to approve a distinctive cap badge for the CAFVC. It was to be identical to the badge of the Royal Tank Regiment – a First World War tank in the centre, surrounded by a wreath of olive leaves with the Imperial crown at the top, but with the designation 'Canada' being substituted for the RTR motto 'Fear Naught' on a ribbon underneath the tank. NDHQ had turned down a simi-

Driver training in Mark VI Bs, Camp Borden, winter 1940. Grossly inadequate as fighting vehicles, the Mark VI Bs were a good training vehicle. (RCAC Collection, CFB Borden Museum)

lar request a year earlier, but this time the badge was approved, and it was first issued in June 1940. Worthy clearly intended that the badge would be worn by everyone serving in armoured units, just as all members of the artillery wear the same badge, but he never did succeed in supplanting regimental insignia. However, in later years it was worn by officers and men serving in the headquarters of 1 Army Tank Brigade and 4 Armoured Division (4CAD), and throughout the war by all recruits and members of the Corps in reinforcement units. This badge thus served as the *de facto* insignia of the Canadian Armoured Corps until well into 1946.

By November the strength of the Centre had grown to 137 officers and men, and a tactics wing was formed to round out the more technical training provided in the gunnery, driving and maintenance and wireless wings. The first efforts to provide training for the already mobilized units took place early that month, when officers of the 1st Hussars were brought to Camp Borden for instruction as mechanized cavalry. This course was, unfortunately, cut short on orders from Ottawa. The Ontario Regiment suffered a similar experience in early December when NDHQ abruptly cancelled a tank tactics course for officers in its third week. By the end of the year the future of armour looked bleak. A number of Worthy's originals were by this time becoming discouraged, and several began to make arrangements to go back to their parent regiments where the prospects of serving usefully, and perhaps even getting overseas, seemed more likely.

Badge of the Canadian Armoured Fighting Vehicles Training Centre, issued in June 1940. By common usage, it became the de facto badge of the Canadian Armoured Corps during the Second World War, even though it was never formally authorized as such.

A variant of the standard CAFV Training Centre/Canadian Armoured Corps badge. Note the inverted 'V' on the tank. There is no record of this badge ever having been officially approved, nor are there any known photographs showing it being worn.

Officers on course at the School during a 'tactical exercise without troops', summer 1940. A lack of equipment led to heavy emphasis on theoretical tactics. (RCAC Collection, CFB Borden Museum)

Worse was to follow. In January 1940 Worthy was called to Ottawa to be told that the Tank Centre would soon be abolished because the army did not expect to use tanks in this war. He was told that his job was now to train infantry carrier drivers, although he was allowed to run one last course in armoured car driving and maintenance for RCD and Strathcona NCOs. But Worthy simply would not accept defeat. He deliberately failed to carry out instructions to disband the tactics, wireless and gunnery wings of the Centre, and included these subjects in the courses run over the next several months for some four hundred infantry drivers. Moreover, he continued to conduct unauthorized gunnery, wireless and tactics courses for the Ontario Regiment. Several highly innovative training aids were brought into use at a time when gunnery was no longer supposed to be taught, including a 'spotlight gun' for use on the RYPA range which activated photo-electric cells mounted on miniature tank targets to indicate hits.

The winter and spring of 1940 was a period of confusion and frustration for the tank battalions and mechanized cavalry regiments, and indeed for the two Permanent Force cavalry regiments which were 'on active service' but not yet mobilized. Ottawa had not yet made firm decisions about the wartime composition of the Army, and tanks and armoured cars were not on the list of priorities. In England, Lieutenant-General McNaughton, now senior officer overseas and commander of 1 Division, appealed continually for a more balanced force, including a battalion of tanks, and the Minister

of National Defence, Norman Rogers, repeatedly rejected his pleas.

The 1st Hussars were redesignated as the 1st Canadian Cavalry Regiment (Mechanized) on 1 March 1940, but that was to be a composite unit that included one squadron from each of the Permanent Force cavalry regiments – much to the dismay of the RCD and Strathconas. A letter written by Major Harvey McLeod, and quoted in the RCD history, *Dragoon*, commented:

> The general atmosphere of the regiment was fairly strained…. The RCDs and the Strathconas did not like each other very much, but did combine to despise the militia First Hussars. I remember overhearing a militia trooper talking about his "length of service" – something like six months – and a Permanent Force corporal hooting "My God, I've got more Divine Service than that!" We retained our old regimental identities, wore our own badges, kept our own customs, and never did develop any regimental spirit that I could see.

This experiment ended in January 1941 and all three units resumed their own identities. Then, in the late spring of 1940, a directive from Ottawa ordered the TRR and Ontarios converted to infantry, but before that could take place events in Europe caused a change of policy.

The 'phoney war' came to an abrupt end on 9 April 1940 when Hitler invaded Denmark and Norway. A month later German divisions swept into Belgium and Holland and swung around the north end of the Maginot Line to launch their *Blitzkrieg* thrust through the Ardennes. There could hardly have been more dramatic proof of the value of a mechanized army or of the effectiveness of even relatively primitive tanks when properly deployed. The Germans rapidly overran the Allied armies, even though the French had more and better tanks. The British Expeditionary Force was pushed back to the English Channel and on 4 June the Royal Navy concluded the evacuation of what remained of the BEF from the beaches of Dunkirk. Britain, its army nearly bereft of guns and equipment, now faced the daunting prospect of a German invasion.

The Canadian government's immediate reaction to the crisis was to speed the departure of 2 Division and authorize the formation of a third, but even before the Germans reached the Channel coast the staff at NDHQ was looking into the creation of an armoured brigade, while the Minister arranged to meet privately with Worthy in Toronto on 10 June, presumably to discuss the latter's views on the organization and training of armour. This meeting never took place, as Rogers was killed in a plane crash on his way to Toronto, but his successor, Colonel J.L. Ralston, promptly took up the cause. Worthy was asked to resubmit a paper written several months earlier on the

Mounted parade of the Governor General's Horse Guards after being mobilized as the 2nd Canadian Motorcycle Regiment. The motorcycles were an inexpensive replacement for armoured cars, but no one had any idea how to employ them tactically. (GGHG Archives)

"Organization, Training, and Employment of a Canadian Armoured Corps."

In light of the German triumph in France, the public was also beginning to bring considerable pressure. Articles in both the *Globe and Mail* and the Toronto *Telegram* criticized the lack of armour in the army and a full-page advertisement appeared in the Toronto *Evening Telegram* on 27 May blasting the government for not having tanks. In Parliament, the opposition took up the attack. And, following the precedent set twenty-five years earlier by Raymond Brutinel in raising his motor machine-gun battery, Douglas Steubing, a young reporter with the Kitchener *Daily Record* (who later served as a captain in 4 CAD), organized a 'Buy-a-Tank' campaign, and quickly collected more than $37,000. In the meantime, the first of those units destined to be charter members of the Canadian Armoured Corps began to concentrate in Camp Borden. The 1st Hussars, in the guise of the 1st Canadian Cavalry Regiment, moved from London in early May, and later in the month were joined by the Ontario Regiment.

Worthy submitted his historic memorandum on a Canadian armoured corps to the Chief of the General Staff on 19 June. His pointed and pithy six-page paper noted that "the vital importance of armoured troops" was self-evident, and need not be argued, but he pointed out that no "properly trained or equipped" armoured units yet existed and went on to review the unsatisfactory state of training in the four regiments thus far mobilized. He emphasized, however, that the AFV Training Centre was capable of rapid expansion and recommended that it should be charged immediately with the training of all officers and men intended to serve in armoured units. This was essential to ensure "uniformity of purpose and doctrine," as well as common standards for all training.

He added that all armoured units, heavy or light, have common characteristics. If the officers and men are properly trained in the basic armoured trades and elementary tactics, units can be converted with relative ease to other types of armoured equipment or roles, and argued that personnel should thus be completely interchangeable between units. To make this feasible he recommended the creation of a Royal Canadian Armoured Corps, within which all units would be designated numerically, rather than retaining distinctive names. Next, he suggested that all units assigned to the Corps adopt "the dress now authorized for the Canadian Tank units," by which he clearly meant the black beret and probably also the badge now being worn by the staff of the Training Centre.

His memorandum went on to make recommendations regarding the rapid acquisition of light armoured vehicles for training until heavier vehicles (perhaps a made-in-Canada 'wheeled tank') could be made available. Finally, he noted that the "ultimate aim should be the production of sufficient armoured units to form … an armoured division" and outlined a plan for the progressive training of those units. The CGS consulted General McNaughton by telegram and McNaughton concurred, hoping "to develop eventually one Armoured Division plus one brigade of Infantry Tanks." A number of lengthy conferences took place over the next weeks and, in the end, most of Worthy's ideas were accepted.

While waiting for official word about the creation of the Canadian Armoured Corps, other developments affected the eventual structure of the Corps. On 14 July 1940 five motorcycle regiments were formed from former cavalry units as an inexpensive alternative to the creation of armoured car regiments. These units were designated numerically, as Worthy wanted. The 1st Canadian Motorcycle Regiment would be a composite unit raised from the RCD and Strathconas, the 2nd from the Horse Guards in Toronto, the 3rd from the 17th Hussars in Montreal, the 4th from the 8th New Brunswick Hussars, and the 5th was to be raised by the British Columbia Dragoons. Three of these regiments were intended to serve as light reconnaissance units with the brigades of the newly-formed 3 Division, while the Horse Guards were detailed for security duties in southern Ontario and the BCD likewise for the west coast.

Modest improvements in training capability continued at Borden during the summer of 1940. The most significant event was undoubtedly the arrival of two modern British tanks, a Matilda and a Valentine. Along with them came a small contingent of instructors from the 7th Royal Tank Regiment, all with battle experience in France during the *Blitzkrieg*. The Valentine

was the very latest (but still inadequate) British attempt to produce a satisfactory Infantry tank, the first having been built only in May. The British had, in fact, just concluded an agreement to build Valentines in the CPR's Angus shops in Montreal, and the Canadian Cabinet approved an order of 488 for its own 1 Army Tank Brigade.

Anticipating the decision to create a Canadian Armoured Corps, other units which were to become part of the Corps were deployed to Camp Borden. The TRR arrived on 1 August, after nearly a year of guarding prisoners-of-war, and the Horse Guards, as the 2nd Motorcycle Regiment, arrived in mid-month. The Fort Garrys, also relieved of tedious prisoner-of-war duty, deployed to Borden at the end of August.

FORMATION OF THE CANADIAN ARMOURED CORPS

For Canadian armour, the most significant event since the beginning of the war was the formal creation of the Canadian Armoured Corps on 13 August 1940 by General Order 250. The Corps was to consist of "a headquarters and such other formations and units which may later be authorized." Worthy's long-standing dream was beginning to be realized. Even at this very early stage of the Corps' existence the influence of the cavalry was being felt and companies in the tank battalions were officially redesignated as 'squadrons', with the rank of 'trooper' adopted in all units.

Separate general orders, all effective 13 August 1940, gave substance to the official organization order. Four units were allocated to the Armoured Corps: The Fort Garry Horse, the 1st Canadian Cavalry Regiment (Mechanized), The Ontario Regiment and The Three Rivers Regiment. At the same time, seven Reserve units were affiliated: the 2nd Fort Garry Horse, The Argyll Light Infantry (Tank), the 2nd Ontario Regiment, the 2nd Three Rivers Regiment, The Calgary Regiment, The New Brunswick Regiment and The Essex Regiment.

1 Canadian Armoured Brigade under the command of newly-promoted Colonel Worthington was also created on 13 August, to consist of the Fort Garrys, the Ontarios and TRR, with 1st Cavalry Regiment (Mechanized) 'attached' until a second brigade could be formed.

The Corps' first Valentine tank in a fire-power demonstration, Camp Borden. A total of 1,420 Valentines were built in Canada, but only 32 were kept for training, with the rest shipped to Russia. (Photo by Corporal Jack Wallace, RCAC Collection, CFB Borden Museum)

Brigadier F.F. Worthington, the Father of the Corps. Known as 'Fighting Frank', he was most commonly just called 'Worthy'. (Canadian Forces Photo Unit)

In addition to commanding 1 Armoured Brigade and the Centre, Worthy was appointed 'Officer Administering, The Canadian Armoured Corps', with "duties as laid down by the Adjutant-General." In effect, he was given broad authority to function as the *de facto* commander of the Corps, with responsibilities for organizational matters and training standards affecting the Corps as a whole. His right to advise the staff branches in Ottawa on armoured issues, including equipment, was clearly acknowledged. To the regiments, and to individual

members of the Corps, Worthy was recognized ever after as the 'Father of the Corps'.

A temporary solution to the lack of armoured vehicles for training was found as a result of staff talks that took place with American officials in Washington in July. Among the materiel assistance the United States offered were 1918-vintage Renault FT light tanks which the US Army had ceased to use in the 1930s. Despite their primitive design, Worthy thought these American-made Renaults could be useful for training until more modern tanks were available, and in late August he went to the Rock Island Arsenal in Illinois to examine them. On 10 September he advised Ottawa that 250 tanks had been earmarked at "a cost of $20 per ton plus 100 per cent making a total of $240 per tank," and arrangements were made to have them shipped to Camp Borden.

Only 236 Renaults were shipped to Borden, and the majority were soon put in running condition. These vintage vehicles did yeoman, if often stubborn, service as training vehicles for nearly two years, both at the Centre and in the armoured regiments based in Borden. As Jack Wallace notes in *Dragons of Steel*:

There was no question about the value of those relics…. Drivers learned something of the problems of handling armoured vehicles; they and the mechanics received more than ample time to carry out maintenance and repair; officers and non-commissioned officers, despite the lack of internal communication, by using flag or hand signals between tanks, were able to practise minor tactics and formation training. For those of us in Camp Borden at that time, it was an exciting experience.

Some time later, the 8th Hussars' regimental sergeant-major, WO 1 George Lawrence, also commented on them.

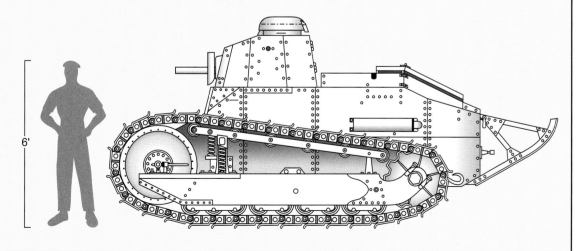

M1917 Light Tank, an American-built version of the Renault FT 17. The Corps acquired 236 of these obsolete, First World War-vintage vehicles from the US Army in October 1940. The Renault FT was the first tank with gun in a rotating turret. (Drawing by Chris Johnson)

M1917
Country of Origin: United States
Crew: 2 (Commander/Gunner, Driver)
Length: 16 feet 5 inches
Width: 5 feet 7 inches
Height: 7 feet 6 inches
Weight: 13,400 pounds
Engine: Buda HU 4 cylinder, gasoline
Maximum Speed: 5.5 mph
Range: 30 miles
Armour – Maximum: 15 mm
        Minimum: 6 mm
Armament: 37 mm Gun M1916 or a .30
   calibre MG mounted in the turret

6'

At least they were good for laughs. They were low-slung things with a sort of pillbox cab for the men. They had no suspension and when you'd go over a log, say, and come down, you'd hit with a whack that was enough to knock your teeth loose. There really wasn't room for two men but we'd cram two in. You needed the extra man; the things kept catching fire and you'd have to have a bucket of water or sand handy to put it out. They could go 8 or 10 miles an hour, but they seldom got very far. They'd break down and you'd fix them up and they'd break down again.

Another significant development in August 1940 was the formation of an inter-departmental Tank Committee in Ottawa. The government had now recognized that the British simply did not have the capacity to supply tanks for the armoured formations being sent overseas, and that the necessary vehicles would have to be produced at home. The task of the Tank Committee was to serve as a centralized government authority to coordinate specifications and design parameters, as well as to control and oversee the production. Colonel E.L.M. Burns was appointed as the first chairman and Worthy was named as one of the original members.

Understandably, the skills needed by armoured soldiers were in very short supply, so training in the basic tank trades was the main preoccupation. The full resources of the Centre were put to work, with first priority given to training sufficient NCO instructors for each unit in order that they could begin to run their own armoured trades courses. Because of the limited number of instructors, classrooms, vehicles and training aids, the Centre ran on a two-shift system for many months in order to qualify as many men as possible in the shortest possible time. Within the units, the focus was on training everyone as drivers, wheeled and tracked, and the regiments were each provided with about ten Renault tanks and a number of trucks for this purpose.

The pattern of training laid down was intended to produce multi-skilled crewmen who could do at least two jobs within a tank squadron. Following basic and advanced general training lasting thirteen weeks, all new crewmen were given four weeks of wheeled driver training followed by two

Arrival of the Renault tanks in Camp Borden, October 1940. (CFB Borden Museum)

Renault tanks, Camp Borden. Although breakdowns were common and their fighting value was negligible, the Renaults were valuable training tools until more modern tanks were available. (CFB Borden Museum)

weeks of tracked vehicle driving. The men were then broken off by primary trade. Gunners got a four week course, mainly theory because there were no tank guns yet available and only machine-guns could be fired; driver/operators received an eight week course, split between tank driving and wireless operator skills, while the driver/mechanics course lasted four weeks. After this, the men were brought together for two weeks of crew training, where they learned to work together, followed by a further two weeks of elementary field training in tactical drills and formations at troop level; but while this training pattern succeeded in producing a crewman with a reasonable level of skill in his own trade and a rudimentary knowledge of at least one other, a great deal of practical, on-the-job experience still had to be gained before anyone was really proficient. At this stage, the Centre made no attempt to teach tactics to crew commanders beyond elementary troop drills.

The Corps urgently needed a cadre of more highly qualified instructors, so a group of officers and NCOs were sent to England in October 1940 for a six month attachment to British regiments. Most also attended advanced instructor courses at Royal Armoured Corps centres at Bovington and Lulworth before returning to Borden in April 1941.

The Armoured Corps Centre, at Worthy's instigation, went to great lengths to further the Corps identity. One of the means used was the publication of a monthly news magazine, entitled *The Tank (Canada)*, which was dubbed 'the official organ of the Canadian Armoured Corps'. The first issue was published in November 1940, and it continued to appear until June 1945.

By early winter, 1 Armoured Brigade began to look like a genuine field formation. The essential support elements were added in December 1940 with the arrival of 1 Armoured Brigade Company, RCASC, the 1st Field Squadron, RCE, and 1 Armoured Brigade Workshop. By this stage Worthy was having to devote most of his time to command of the brigade, and Lieutenant-Colonel Gordon Smith was appointed commandant of the Armoured Corps Centre.

The Canadian Armoured Corps in this early period unques-

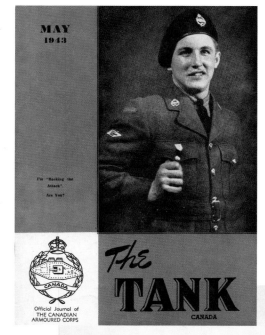

The Tank Canada was published monthly by the School from November 1940 until June 1945. (CFB Borden Museum)

tioningly accepted British doctrine, since no one in the Canadian Army had any operational experience with tanks, and therefore no reason to doubt the concepts developed by the British. Their doctrine split tank units into two quite separate categories. Army tank battalions, whose function was to provide close support for the infantry, were intended to be equipped with heavily armoured, and thus relatively slow, 'Infantry' tanks. Armoured regiments, on the other hand, whose function was to provide fast-moving, cavalry-style striking power, were to be given less heavily armoured, and thus faster, 'cruiser' tanks.

What the Canadians did not know was that this doctrine, which had its origins in the very different modes of thinking in the Royal Tank Regiment on the one hand and the cavalry regiments on the other, was already being questioned by many senior British officers. Even more telling, the British were having great difficulty in producing the two types of tanks called for. This made little real difference when the Canadians had no modern tanks at all, but it complicated training for several years, especially with regard to the need for intimate all-arms cooperation by all units, not just those in the army tank brigades.

EXPANSION OF THE CORPS

The confusion between tank battalions and armoured regiments was soon reinforced. On 17 December 1940, Ottawa was told by the British War Office that they would like Canada to provide an armoured division as soon as possible, which they (the British) would equip for training with American M3 tanks. The British at that time were faced with a requirement for nine armoured divisions and they hoped that a Canadian armoured division could be sent to England in the early autumn of 1941, so as to be trained and available for employment early in 1942.

They also indicated that an army tank brigade would be welcome, and offered to equip it with the Mark III Valentines now being produced in Canada, and, if necessary, additional Infantry tanks from their own production. The Cabinet approved the creation of these formations on 28 January 1941, both to be sent overseas as soon as feasible.

The Tank Committee visited the United States to inspect a prototype of the new American M3 Lee tank. It was agreed that the basic design, with the main gun mounted in a sponson on the hull, was seriously flawed and would never be satisfactory in operations. The Committee then decided that there was no choice but to produce a Canadian-designed tank for the new armoured formations, rather than proceeding with the order for Valentines. This tank, soon designated as the 'Ram', was to incorporate the running gear of the M3, but with a Canadian-designed turret and cast steel upper hull, and mounting a Canadian-made 6-pounder (57mm) gun as the main armament along with a .30 Browning machine-gun. A contract was let with the Montreal Locomotive Works, and a mock-up was ready by the end of February 1941.

1 Canadian Army Tank Brigade was officially formed on 4 February 1941. Worthy was transferred from command of 1 Armoured Brigade to the new formation, and two of the units then in 1 Brigade – the Ontarios and TRR – went with him. The third battalion was to be the Calgary Regiment, personally selected by now-Brigadier Worthington, and it moved to Camp Borden in March, while the brigade headquarters squadron was to be provided by the New Brunswick Regiment. So as to differentiate the units of this brigade from their 'armoured' counterparts in other brigades, they were designated as 'army tank battalions'. The ram from Worthy's personal coat of

Lieutenant-Colonel Gordon Carrington Smith, who succeeded Worthington as commandant of the School in December 1940.

The 'Ram' sleeve patch worn by 1st Canadian Army Tank Brigade, 1941-42. Veterans relate how the animal's rather prominent gonads were often decorated in red lipstick by female friends, a perennial problem for troops preparing for inspections and parades.

(Below) Troops lining up for lunch at the School mess hall, 1941. (CFB Borden Museum)

arms was adopted as the brigade symbol and for over a year it was worn as a sleeve patch and used as a tactical sign, painted on the brigade vehicles. From the outset it was known that the brigade would be sent to England in the early summer and its units were given a degree of priority in the use of the available vehicles and training facilities.

As a result of this rapid expansion, the whole structure of the Canadian Armoured Corps changed dramatically. The official date for the changes was 11 February 1941, but it took several months to bring the new structure into existence and implement the decisions.

1 CANADIAN ARMOURED DIVISION

The most far-reaching aspect of the growth of the Armoured Corps was the raising of 1 Armoured Division (1 CAD). The establishment called for two armoured brigades, 1 (which had been formed in August 1940) commanded by Brigadier T.J. Rutherford, the former CO of the Grey and Simcoe Foresters, and the 2nd, officially organized in early March 1941 although its units did not arrive at Borden until May and June, commanded by Brigadier A.C. Spencer. Major General E.W. Sansom was transferred from command of 3 Division to be the first GOC. At the same time, reconnaissance battalions were formed for each of the three infantry divisions. In England, the IV Princess Louise Dragoon Guards (4 PLDG) was mobilized to serve with 1 Division and the 14th Hussars to serve with 2 Division. In the case of both, two of their three squadrons were recruited from within infantry battalions already in the United Kingdom, while the headquarters and the third squadron were raised by the parent unit in Canada. The 17th Duke of York's Royal Canadian Hussars mobilized in Montreal to serve with 3 Division.

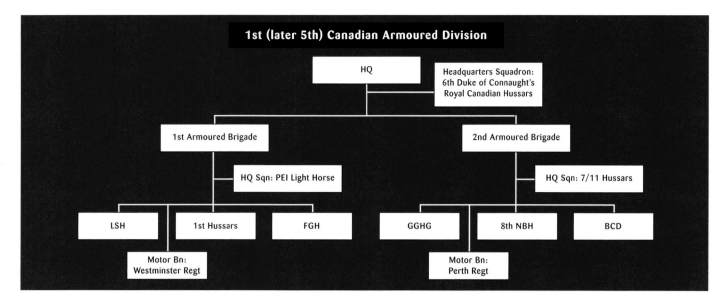

1st (later 5th) Canadian Armoured Division

HQ

Headquarters Squadron: 6th Duke of Connaught's Royal Canadian Hussars

1st Armoured Brigade

HQ Sqn: PEI Light Horse

LSH | 1st Hussars | FGH

Motor Bn: Westminster Regt

2nd Armoured Brigade

HQ Sqn: 7/11 Hussars

GGHG | 8th NBH | BCD

Motor Bn: Perth Regt

Regiments of the Canadian Armoured Corps, February 1941

1st Armoured Car Regiment (Royal Canadian Dragoons)

2nd Armoured Regiment (Lord Strathcona's Horse)

3rd Armoured Regiment (Governor General's Horse Guards)

4th Reconnaissance Battalion (4th Princess Louise Dragoon Guards)

5th Armoured Regiment (8th Princess Louise's (New Brunswick) Hussars)

6th Armoured Regiment (1st Hussars)

7th Reconnaissance Battalion (17th Duke of York's Royal Canadian Hussars)

8th Reconnaissance Battalion (14th Canadian Hussars)

9th Armoured Regiment (The British Columbia Dragoons)

10th Armoured Regiment (The Fort Garry Horse)

11th Army Tank Battalion (The Ontario Regiment (Tank))

12th Army Tank Battalion (The Three Rivers Regiment (Tank))

14th Army Tank Battalion (The Calgary Regiment (Tank))

5th Canadian (Armoured) Division Headquarters Squadron (6th Duke of Connaught's Royal Canadian Hussars)

2nd Canadian Armoured Brigade Headquarters Squadron (7th/11th Hussars)

1st Canadian Armoured Brigade Headquarters Squadron (The Prince Edward Island Light Horse)

Another of the changes that took effect on 11 February 1941 was the formal numbering of the units of the Corps, as Worthy had recommended eight months earlier in an effort to foster a distinctive Armoured Corps identity among units that came from very different backgrounds. The old cavalry units with historic names found this new policy most distasteful, even though unit names continued to be used in brackets behind the new designations. The official name of the RCD, for example, became 1st Canadian Armoured Car Regiment (Royal Canadian Dragoons), while the Strathconas became the 2nd Canadian Armoured Regiment (Lord Strathcona's Horse).

The numbering system adopted was itself somewhat confused, reflecting in some cases seniority in the Cavalry Corps, and in others seniority of entry into the Armoured Corps. Units brought in after 11 February were assigned numbers sequentially, based on date of affiliation. While the numerical designators were used on all official documents until after the war was over, regimental names continued to be commonly used in practice, especially by the former cavalry regiments. With the sole exception of the 8th Reconnaissance Regiment (14th Canadian Hussars), all units continued to wear their own regimental cap badges. The policy on wearing regimental shoulder titles varied from one formation to another, as will be explained later.

The CAFVC continued to evolve to meet the increased training load created by the rapid expansion of the Corps. On 15 February, the Centre was reorganized by creating two separate but similarly organized centres. A8 Canadian Armoured Corps (Advanced) Training Centre, commanded by Lieutenant-Colonel A. McGoun on loan from the Royal Tank Regiment, would handle men for the Army Tank Brigade and the reconnaissance units, while A9, under Lieutenant-Colonel J.A. McCamus, was to deal with personnel destined for 1 Armoured Division. The

H-Huts in the School lines, Camp Borden. Intended only as temporary wartime accommodations, they remained in use for another three decades. (CFB Borden Museum)

term 'advanced' in the titles simply meant that these centres taught special-to-Corps courses, as opposed to basic training. Corps headquarters continued to exercise overall control, as well as co-ordinating the equipment trials and experimental work of the Technical Wing.

In early April 1941, a large advance party from 1 Army Tank Brigade sailed for England. Many of the officers and NCOs from this group were attached to British units for practical training while awaiting the arrival of the remainder of the brigade, which docked in Scotland on 30 June. With the permanent departure of Brigadier Worthington, Colonel E.L.M. Burns was posted to Camp Borden and named Officer Administering, The Canadian Armoured Corps.

The prototype version of the Ram tank, a Mark I with a 2-pounder (40mm) gun, was rolled out of the Montreal Locomotive Works' Canadian Tank Arsenal shop on 30 June. One of the early models was immediately shipped to England for trials, but mass production began immediately.

By the summer of 1941 Ottawa decided to bring some measure of coherence to the organizational structure of the Army, and among the decisions made was that all divisions, regardless of type, should be numbered consecutively. 1 Armoured Division was thus officially re-designated as 5 Canadian Armoured Division (5 CAD).

The units of 5 CAD carried on a programme of intensive trades training in Camp Borden until late September, when it was announced that the division was to proceed overseas. While the individual training of drivers and radio operators had reached a good level, gunnery training was inadequate as there were still no tank guns to be fired in Borden. Tactics training, even at troop level, did not go beyond the practice of elementary drills and movement formations. There was thus a great deal yet to be done before the units would be operationally

The first Mark I Ram to come off the production line at the Montreal Locomotive Works is inspected by the Minister of Munitions and Supply, the Hon. C.D. Howe, and the Minister of National Defence, the Hon. J.L. Ralston, 30 June 1941. Although it never saw service as a fighting vehicle, the Ram gave good service in training and as a chassis for specialized equipment. (CFB Borden Museum)

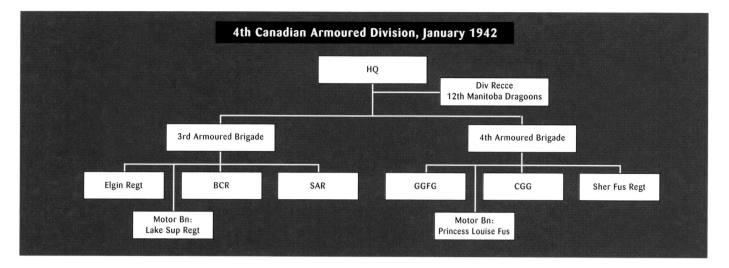

4th Canadian Armoured Division, January 1942

- HQ
  - Div Recce
    12th Manitoba Dragoons
- 3rd Armoured Brigade
  - Elgin Regt
  - BCR
    - Motor Bn:
      Lake Sup Regt
  - SAR
- 4th Armoured Brigade
  - GGFG
  - CGG
    - Motor Bn:
      Princess Louise Fus
  - Sher Fus Regt

competent, and the prospect of having real tanks with which to train in England made news of the move overseas most welcome. The division sailed to Britain in October and early November. An account its training in England continues in the next chapter.

In mid-November, just as the units were settling in at their new bases in England, General McNaughton sent a cable to Ottawa stating that the War Office would welcome a second armoured division and another army tank brigade. This was, of course, in line with government thinking that any additional troops deployed should be armoured formations, so the Minister immediately made the decision to convert 4 Division, located in Debert, Nova Scotia, into an armoured formation. The creation of this second armoured division and a second army tank brigade was approved by Cabinet on 6 January 1942. By that time the war had taken a new course. The United States, in response to a Japanese attack on Pearl Harbor on 7 December 1941, and an ill-judged declaration of war on them by Hitler, had entered the war and the full might of the English-speaking world was now arrayed against the Axis powers in a truly global conflict.

4 CANADIAN ARMOURED DIVISION

Both 4 Canadian Armoured Division and 2 Canadian Army Tank Brigade were officially formed on 26 January 1942. As with 5 CAD, 4 CAD was to have two armoured brigades, the 3rd, commanded by Brigadier A.M. Thomas who had previously commanded 12 Infantry Brigade, and the

4th by E.L.M. Burns, who vacated his appointment as Officer Administering, The Canadian Armoured Corps. Worthy, promoted again, was appointed GOC, but he was still in England and did not formally take command until 8 March.

The immediate problem was that not a single man in 4 CAD knew anything at all about tanks, and there were no tanks or training aids anywhere but in Borden. Moving the entire division there was not a feasible option, as the training facilities for so many men just did not exist. The best that could be done was to train cadres of instructors for each regiment at Borden as quickly as possible, so that they could then return and conduct basic trades training in Debert. The training of instructors thus became the first priority for the CAFVC. This was done in two overlapping six-week sessions, the first beginning on 2 February, the second a month later. Each of the units in the two brigades was given a quota of instructor vacancies. When these newly-qualified instructors returned to Debert, each unit was

The first Ram (a Mark I with a 2-pounder gun) was delivered to the School in Camp Borden in February 1942. (CFB Borden Museum)

expected to run courses for 180 men in each trade and, if all went well, the trades training would be completed by 15 June. By then it was hoped that enough Ram tanks would be available to equip each unit with a half-dozen or more. In the meantime, the Centre also conducted two 10-week courses for officers, to introduce the three Corps trades as well as elementary troop-level tactics.

In February 1942 the first production-line Ram tanks began to arrive at Borden. There had been serious problems during the process of assembling the tanks, and a great many of the original batches were found to be defective in some way. The first fifty, known as Ram Mark I, were equipped with 2-pounder guns borrowed from stocks intended for the British Valentines because production of 6-pounders was well behind

the dock, waiting to be shipped overseas. He was also told that there would be no vessels to carry them across the Atlantic for at least six weeks. Rather than go immediately to Debert, Worthy decided to visit Ottawa in order to persuade the Master General of the Ordnance, Victor Sifton (a son of that Sir Clifford who had been instrumental in creating Brutinel's machine gun battery in the First World War), to let him have at least some of those tanks. He argued that tanks coming off the production line could replace those that had come to him by the time ships were available. Sifton agreed, and arrangements were made to send some sixty Rams to Debert.

When they arrived at Debert in early May, none of the people sent for training to Borden had yet returned and only two men there knew how to drive a tank — Worthy and his GSO 1,

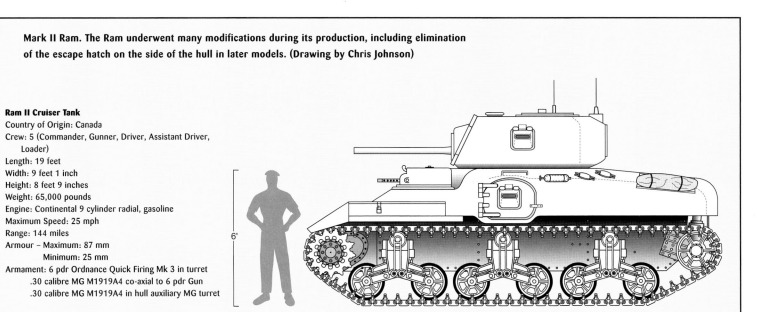

Mark II Ram. The Ram underwent many modifications during its production, including elimination of the escape hatch on the side of the hull in later models. (Drawing by Chris Johnson)

Ram II Cruiser Tank
Country of Origin: Canada
Crew: 5 (Commander, Gunner, Driver, Assistant Driver, Loader)
Length: 19 feet
Width: 9 feet 1 inch
Height: 8 feet 9 inches
Weight: 65,000 pounds
Engine: Continental 9 cylinder radial, gasoline
Maximum Speed: 25 mph
Range: 144 miles
Armour – Maximum: 87 mm
　　　　　Minimum: 25 mm
Armament: 6 pdr Ordnance Quick Firing Mk 3 in turret
　　　　　.30 calibre MG M1919A4 co-axial to 6 pdr Gun
　　　　　.30 calibre MG M1919A4 in hull auxiliary MG turret

6'

schedule. In fact, most of the early Mark II models were accepted without any guns being mounted, as they were urgently needed for training both in Canada and Britain.

Even as the first Rams were brought into service, however, serious doubts were being expressed about their suitability for operational purposes. The Americans had just begun to bring their latest tank, the M4 Sherman, into mass production, and the British had decided to buy it in large numbers. In many respects the Sherman was based on the Ram design, but it was considerably superior in armour and armament. However, production of the Ram II continued for the next year and a half, during which time nearly 1,900 were made, with 1,600 of them being sent to Canadian formations overseas.

Major-General Worthington arrived at Debert in early March to assume command of 4 CAD. On passing through Halifax he discovered that 165 of the new Rams were sitting on

Lieutenant-Colonel George Gaisford. It was thus the 'high-priced help' who had to drive all 65 Rams off the flat cars, much to the amusement of the throng of men who gathered to watch. These were all Mark II versions, missing their 6-pounder guns. They were superb for driver training, but, obviously, less than useful for gunnery instruction. Lieutenant-Colonel Harry Quarton, who at the time was technical quartermaster-sergeant in division headquarters, recalled that one day:

Worthy spotted a train destined for Halifax with complete [i.e., with 6-pounders] tanks on board. He immediately called me to get some crews together and we headed for the railway station. Worthy talked the station master into putting a flat car on the siding, and we proceeded to unload the four tanks on board. Of course, they were all greased for overseas shipment, so a number of us worked all night to

4th Armoured Division's first tank, a Ram Mark II, Debert, Nova Scotia, May 1942. The tank was named 'Robin' for General Worthington's daughter. (Courtesy Lieutenant-Colonel Harry Quarton)

was limited by the boggy ground of the Debert training area. Because none of the regiments had more than fifteen tanks, the vehicles had to be shared amongst the squadrons and few of the crews got to operate actual tanks for more than one or two days a week. The rest of the time 'dismounted drill' was the order of the day. Trooper John Galipeau of the South Alberta Regiment is quoted in Donald Graves' history of the regiment.

> Lengths of 2 x 2 lumber had been fastened together to form a letter H configuration. ... Each crew was presented with one of the H-shaped structures and told to arrange ourselves in the positions we would occupy in a tank. ... We were now imaginary tanks and under the directions and orders of the troop officer, we walked hither and yon over the area forming tank battle formations such as arrowhead, square and line abreast.

degrease and stow the first tank. Worthy named it *Robin* after his daughter. ... It was the first fully equipped tank that we had.

Under Worthy's watchful eye, 4 CAD trained intensively over the spring and summer of 1942, working in two shifts until early June to speed the process of teaching the intricacies of driving and maintenance, and learning to control and apply the fire of the 6-pounder guns. The British Columbia Regiment history, *The Dukes*, notes that "Worthy was to be seen in every corner of the huge camp, inspecting, encouraging, instructing, occasionally giving a brief talk to the officers and men of the division." The Governor General's Foot Guards history tells a similar story:

> The men worshipped Worthy. When he talked to them in his blunt, clipped way, their eyes glistened and they hung on every word. When he cracked a grim joke, they chuckled appreciatively. He completely caught the imagination of the troops. They liked his kind of toughness and because they knew he spared none in his drive for perfection they willingly underwent any hardship.

In June the regiments took turns on the tank gunnery range at Spencer's Point on the Minas Basin, firing the 6-pounders and machine-guns at log targets floating in the water. Crew training began in July and soon progressed to basic field manoeuvres with complete troops of three vehicles, although this

Largely because of the enthusiasm engendered by Worthy himself, 4 CAD accomplished a near-miracle in converting to its new role in less than five months. The bulk of the division sailed for England in August and September 1942, already having achieved a higher level of basic armoured training than 5 CAD had accomplished in over a year. Their story of preparing for war in Britain continues in the next chapter.

Major-General F.F. Worthington, Commander of 4th Armoured Division.

2 CANADIAN ARMY TANK BRIGADE

As noted earlier, 2 Army Tank Brigade was also formally created on 26 January 1942, but it was not until late May that the units arrived in Camp Borden to begin their training. Brigadier G.R. Bradbrooke, a pre-war Strathcona who had recently commanded the Calgary Regiment in England, was appointed to command. At this time the term 'battalion' was abolished in favour of 'regiment'.

The training of the brigade followed the now well-established pattern, but it had the distinct advantage of having most of its crewmen taught by seasoned Centre instructors in facilities that had become increasingly sophisticated. The quality of the trades training was thus at a notably higher level than had been achieved by other brigades. Then too, each of the regiments began their training with six new Ram II tanks, which, by early autumn, had increased to a full squadron per unit.

In mid-September Brigadier Bradbrooke departed to take command of 5 Armoured Brigade in England. He was succeeded by Brigadier N.A. Gianelli, a former commanding officer of the Strathconas, who continued to press an intense pace of training throughout the winter and spring of 1943. By the time that the brigade sailed for England in mid-June 1943, its regiments were among the best trained in the Corps.

The reconnaissance component of the Corps also grew during the course of 1942. Both the 30th Reconnaissance Regiment (The Essex Regiment) and the 31st Reconnaissance Regiment (Alberta Regiment) were raised in May 1942. The Essex Regiment was intended to serve as divisional recce for the 7th Infantry Division, but instead spent most its war service at A27 Reconnaissance Training Centre in Dundurn. The Albertans were raised as the divisional recce for 6 Division on the west coast. Members were recruited primarily from the 15th Alberta Light Horse with others coming from the 19th Alberta Dragoons, and the regiment wore the former's badge. Some months later, in January 1943, the Royal Montreal Regiment was converted into a recce unit and re-designated as the 32nd Reconnaissance Regiment (Royal Montreal Regiment) for service as army troops with First Canadian Army.

A Ram tank crossing a shallow river, Debert, Nova Scotia, June 1942. (CFB Borden Museum)

'Dagger' sleeve patch worn by units of 2nd Army Tank Brigade, 1942-1943.

GROWTH OF THE CORPS CENTRE

Throughout 1942, because of the rapid enlargement of the Corps' training needs, the structure of the Centre in Borden was adapted continually to cope with both the greatly enlarged course loads and the technical changes brought about by new equipment. This process began in mid-March when the Canadian Armoured Corps Training Group was created to take over the functions of the Canadian Armoured Corps Headquarters.

The Experimental Wing, which had been organized on a small scale a year earlier, suddenly found itself conducting tests, trials and experimental work on equipment of every description that the Corps might use. Among the user trials carried out were tests of the first Universal carriers, the Valentine and Ram tanks and prototype armoured cars, as well as extensive testing of new types of tank tracks, synthetic rubber 'bogey' wheels, tank suits, thermos bottles, chemical (gas) protection equipment, food containers and a wide variety of other equipments. Additionally, the wing did experimental work to determine why vital components, such as track sprockets and transmissions, broke down earlier than expected.

Recognizing that the Centre was no longer the only place where members of the Corps were taught the fundamental trades, an Instructors' School was set up in May to train instructors for all formations. Its purpose was to

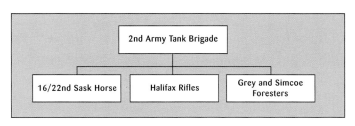

Organization diagram of 2 Army Tank Brigade as at May 1942.

2nd Army Tank Brigade

16/22nd Sask Horse — Halifax Rifles — Grey and Simcoe Foresters

Squadron of Mark II Rams, Meaford AFV Range, spring 1943. Late production models with the counterbalanced 6-pounder gun and the hull doors eliminated, are interspersed with mid-production Ram IIs. (CFB Borden Museum)

standardize the subject matter covered in trades courses throughout the Corps, as well as ensuring professional methods of instruction. Captain Gord Pratt was the first chief instructor, with a staff of ten NCOs. Because of ever-growing demands, two additional training centres – A27 and A28 – were established within the Corps Training Group in early May, although they were not officially created until 1 September 1942. A27 was designated as the Reconnaissance Training Centre.

By this time, the Centre had outgrown the maximum capacity of Camp Borden, in quarters for the men, in classrooms and in space for manoeuvre in the training area. An advance party was sent to Saskatchewan to make arrangements for the estab-

lishment of a branch of the Corps Centre at Camp Dundurn, south-west of Saskatoon, to accommodate both A27 and A28 Training Centres. The acquisition of a large tract of farmland near Meaford, Ontario, some 110 kilometres west of Borden, changed the picture, however, and it was decided to keep all tank training centred in Camp Borden, although A27 moved to Dundurn as planned and, in October, began training reinforcements for the reconnaissance units in Britain and Canada. It remained in Dundurn until the autumn of 1944, when, the need for replacement recce crewmen being far less than anticipated, the centre was disbanded in November.

In July, Colonel Roland Wood, a British officer on loan to the Canadian Army who had served as an instructor in reconnaissance operations, was appointed commander of the Corps Training Group, and Officer Administering, The Canadian Armoured Corps. By this time the Training Group controlled the Tactical School, the Instructors' School, the Experimental Wing, the Armoured Fighting Vehicle (AFV) Range Detail and two demonstration troops, as well as the Training Centres.

By mid-October 1942, nearly 7,200 hectares (18,000 acres) of new training area at the Meaford AFV Range was available for use. The Halifax Rifles had the honour of christening the ground when they conducted a tactical exercise with a full squadron of Ram tanks. The tank gunnery range opened on 1 November, with the first shots being fired downrange from a Mark II Ram by Brigadier Spencer. The Grey and Simcoe Foresters spent much of that same month conducting tactics training there. From that time on, the Meaford range was in constant use, and the Tactics Wing was established there for the remainder of the war years. For some unknown reason, however, the range was not officially opened until a year later, in October 1943, by which time over 10,000 men had already

Embarkation. Painting by George Tinning, depicting the departure of the 2nd Army Tank Brigade from Halifax, June 1943. (Canadian War Museum 13878)

passed through it. Brigadier-General Pat Grieve, then a troop leader in the Halifax Rifles, remembered that unit's training:

> While eventually we did get a full regimental complement of tanks, the Halifax Rifles initially had only one squadron of Rams. This meant that the squadrons had to take turns using them. One week a squadron would be on the tanks, the next week that squadron would do fatigues for the whole regiment, and the third week small arms and other training.
>
> After the Meaford Range opened we spent a lot of time there doing tactics and gunnery. We would live in the empty farm houses, with the tanks parked right beside us. The tactics training was all done within the troop, and troop leaders were pretty much free to decide what to do and where to go. No one even talked of squadron-level training. Much of the time we practised formations – one up, two up, line, and so on. We also did 'fire and movement' drills where, for example, two tanks in fire positions would support the third tank as it moved to the next 'bound' a few hundred metres forward, and then that tank would support the other two as they moved. We also practised fire and movement while firing the 6-pounder guns during battle runs on the gunnery range, and this was as close to working under live fire as you could get.

Worthy and the two centre commandants crewed a vehicle called a 'swamp buggy' which mounted a 2-pounder gun. Unfortunately, they had a misfire on the "official first round", and none of them knew the misfire drill. Finally this was sorted out and the "first" round was fired. During the speeches, it was said how the soil at Meaford was excellent for manoeuvre due to the rock close to the surface, so there would be little chance of getting stuck. When the swamp buggy moved down range to fire again, it got stuck!

Tank Manoeuvres, Camp Borden. **Painting by A.J. Casson. (Canadian War Museum 14083)**

A further reorganization of the Centre took place in mid-April 1943, when it was re-named the A33 Canadian Armoured Corps Training Establishment while the three Training Centres, A8, A9 and A28, were restructured as Armoured Training Regiments. Each of the regiments was organized into gunnery, wireless, and driving and maintenance squadrons for basic trades training, and each was designed to handle an intake of 18 officers and 360 men per month. A 'Trained Soldier Regiment' held men until they were shipped overseas to one of the Corps Reinforcement Units in England. Colonel S.A. Lee (who had won a Military Cross with the Fort Garry Horse during the First World War) was appointed as the first commandant of A33 and Officer Administering, The Canadian Armoured Corps. At this time the Centre (A33) had a staff of nearly 2,300 all ranks, and a student population of over 3,000.

Overseas armoured units had begun to complain about the relatively low standard of training of replacements, so a conference on training took place in June 1943. Among the key decisions taken were that all trades courses needed to be substantially extended in order to conform to standards

The Canadian-designed and built Ram tank was depicted on 13 and 14 cent postage stamps issued in July 1942.

established by the Royal Armoured Corps. The driver/mechanic (tank) course was extended from twelve to sixteen weeks, the gunner/operator course was also extended to sixteen weeks, while the operator course was set at fourteen weeks. The number trained in each trade was also adjusted, so that 25 percent were trained as driver/mechanics (tank), 25 percent as gunner/operators, 39 percent as wheeled vehicle drivers, and the remainder as motorcyclists, technical storemen, clerks and cooks.

By the summer of 1943, the Corps Training Establishment was operating at the peak of its wartime efficiency. The number of students graduated and posted overseas varied somewhat from month to month, but production was sufficient to build a solid reserve of men of all trades in the reinforcement units in England. Drafts of trained personnel despatched overseas included 40 officers and 500 men in April, 23 officers and 70 men in May, 75 officers and 287 men in June, 6 officers and 355 men in July, 32 officers and 600 men in August, 27 officers and 521 men in September and 22 officers and 400 men in November. These numbers diminished somewhat in 1944, but even then the average strength of the monthly overseas draft was 20 officers and 200 men.

(Left) Otter light reconnaissance cars at A27 Canadian Armoured Corps Advanced Training Centre, Camp Dundurn, Saskatchewan, 1944. (CFB Borden Museum)

(Left) The Canadian Armoured Corps Band, 1944. (CFB Borden Museum)

(Below) Grizzly tanks, the Canadian version of the Mark I Sherman, on the firing point in Meaford, autumn 1944. (CFB Borden Museum)

(Right) Bombing up with 6-pounder ammunition, Meaford AFV Range. (Canadian Forces Photo Unit)

(Below) The summer vehicle park at 'Last Chance Saloon', Camp Borden training area, summer 1944. Note the M-10 anti-tank gun and the 'Kangaroo' personnel carriers in the foreground. (CFB Borden Museum)

By the summer of 1943, the Corps had matured sufficiently that ceremonial matters could be given some emphasis and, in the early autumn, the Canadian Armoured Corps Band was established with thirty bandsmen under bandmaster WO 1 C.H. Fowke. The band was a magnificent complement to parades at the Centre, and its members also put together a revue entitled 'The Black Berets', which toured the training camps in Ontario over the next year.

In August 1943 Colonel J.A. McCamus, who had served continuously at Borden since 1941, was appointed to succeed Colonel Lee as commandant of A33. Major-General Worthington returned to Camp Borden as camp commandant in May 1944 after relinquishing command of 4 CAD. With Worthy's return, the appointment of Officer Administering, The Canadian Armoured Corps appears to have become dormant, for there was no question in anyone's mind where the real authority rested in the Corps. That same month Colonel C.E. Bailey, who had commanded the British Columbia Regiment in England, took over from Colonel McCamus as commandant, and continued in the position until after the end of the war.

* * *

From extremely modest beginnings in 1939 – little more, in fact, than a dream of a modern mechanized army in the minds of a small group of determined and dedicated men – the Canadian Armoured Corps grew enormously in size and operational capability in the first three years of its existence. By the end of 1942, at the height of its strength, when 26,000 Canadian soldiers wore the black beret, the active service components of the Corps consisted of four reconnaissance regiments, two armoured car regiments, eighteen armoured regiments in two armoured divisions, and two independent tank brigades. In addition there were four training centres in Canada and three reinforcement units in Britain. With the bulk of the Corps overseas, the centre of gravity of Canadian armour quite naturally shifted to Britain, and it was there that the units and formations honed their understanding of armoured operations and their war-fighting skills before going into action.

CHAPTER 5

Training the Corps in Britain: Sharpening the Swords

Political and military leaders knew that Canadian troops would go into battle as a distinctive Canadian Army, following the precedent set during the First World War by the Canadian Corps. However, there was never any doubt that they would fight alongside British formations, and under senior British commanders. Many other factors – among them the threat of a German invasion of the British Isles until the end of 1941, and, not least, the lack of armour in Canada – made it essential that the armoured formations be concentrated in Britain for their training and indoctrination for battle.

As explained in the previous chapter, a significant part of the Armoured Corps was deployed overseas in 1941, beginning with 1 Army Tank Brigade in July and continuing with the two armoured brigades of 5 CAD in October and November. However, the first units of the Corps in Britain were the two divisional reconnaissance regiments officially created on 11 February 1941, IV Princess Louise Dragoon Guards and the 14th Canadian Hussars. In the autumn of 1942 the armoured brigades of 4 CAD would join these earlier arrivals, and the last of the Armoured Corps formations to move overseas, 2 Army Tank Brigade, would do so in June 1943.

By the end of 1941 there were four distinct types of ar-

moured units in England. Two of these were reconnaissance units: the light reconnaissance regiments attached to the infantry divisions, and the armoured car regiments which, initially, served with the armoured divisions. There were also two varieties of tank units: the army tank battalions and the *pur laine* regiments of the armoured division. Each type of unit was structured and equipped for specific tasks on the battlefield, and each was subject to a different set of doctrinal principles which affected their training. After a reorganization of the Corps in January 1943, a third category of reconnaissance unit was added: the heavy armoured reconnaissance regiments equipped with a combination of tanks and carriers.

THE DIVISIONAL RECONNAISSANCE REGIMENTS

The reader will recall that when 1 and 2 Canadian Divisions were mobilized in September 1939, two regiments – the 1st Hussars and the Fort Garry Horse – were mobilized as divisional cavalry to serve as reconnaissance units. Both divisions were, however, hastily shipped to Britain without their intended recce capability, and this became a serious operational deficiency when, after Dunkirk, the Canadians were tasked with the defence of part of the south-eastern coast of England. In June 1940, in each brigade of the two divisions an *ad hoc* recon-

For most Canadian tank units in Britain, the Ram tank was the workhorse that enabled the crews to become highly proficient before going into battle. (Canadian Army Photo)

Cyclists and carriers of 4th Princess Louise Dragoon Guards, Worthing, England. (NAC PA160030)

Carriers and Beaverette scout cars of the 17th Duke of York's Royal Canadian Hussars. (RCH Museum)

naissance company was formed, with each infantry battalion contributing one platoon. These companies were initially equipped with Norton motorcycles mounting Lewis guns on side-cars, but these were replaced in early 1941 by Universal carriers and Beaverette scout cars. In January 1941 Canadian Corps Headquarters authorized the formation of a reconnaissance battalion in both divisions.

On 11 February 1941, 4 PLDG was mobilized in Ottawa as the 4th Reconnaissance Battalion, the 14th Canadian Hussars from Swift Current were raised as the 8th Reconnaissance Bat-

talion, and the *ad hoc* recce units in the two divisions immediately adopted the new regimental titles. Lieutenant-Colonel Harry Foster, a pre-war Strathcona who would later lead 4 CAD, was given command of 4 PLDG in the 1st Division, and Lieutenant-Colonel C. Churchill Mann, from the RCD, was sent to the 14th Hussars in the 2nd Division. 'Church' Mann, who had married into the wealthy McLaughlin family, quickly concluded that he would have difficulty in making a cohesive regiment out of men who had come from nearly twenty different units, so he personally designed a distinctive 8th Recce Bat-

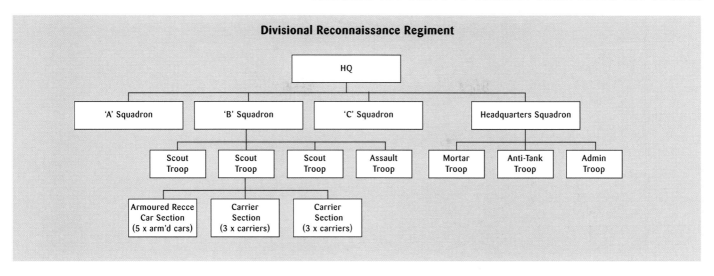

Motorcycle troops of the 8th Reconnaissance Regiment (14th Canadian Hussars), England, 1941.

talion badge, a silver maple leaf with gilt 'VIII Recce' scroll, and paid for it out of his own pocket. This was the only unique badge created for any of the armoured corps units during the war, and Mann's unit was also distinctive within the Corps for preferring to be known by its numerical designation rather than as the 14th Hussars.

A reconnaissance component was provided for 3 Division when, in February 1941, the 17th Hussars were converted from a motorcycle regiment to become the 7th Reconnaissance Battalion. They sailed for England in September 1941 with the other units of the division, to be equipped, once there, with a succession of different armoured recce cars – first Otters, then Foxes and Dingos, and later a combination of Humber armoured cars and scout cars.

The main task of the divisional reconnaissance units was to collect information for the division commander about enemy locations, movement and strength, as well as ground conditions that could affect operations, such as the state of roads, tracks and bridges and, especially, potential obstacles such as rivers, marshes and woods. Intelligence of this nature is especially vital at the stage in operations before contact with the enemy has been established. Reconnaissance units are thus in greatest need during the offensive phases of war – the advance to contact, the attack, and the pursuit of a retreating enemy. Once contact with the enemy is established by main combat forces, reconnaissance units usually revert to their secondary role of providing protection for the division, performing tasks such as screens, flank guards and rear guards.

While initially no one was quite certain how best to employ a combination of scout cars and carriers to do the job, traditional cavalry concepts provided a sound basis for what was required of reconnaissance troops: a large measure of dash and daring, great initiative and imagination on the part of crew commanders who often had to function independently, well-

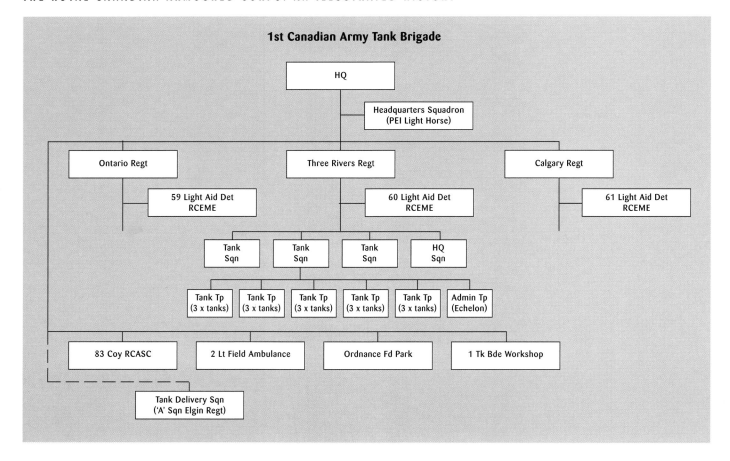

1st Canadian Army Tank Brigade

honed observation skills, thorough training in recognition of enemy vehicles and equipment, a very high standard of map reading and absolute integrity in reporting precisely what was observed, (and in many cases what was *not* observed). To be of any value to the division commander and his intelligence staff, information had to be collated and passed back through squadron and regimental command posts virtually immediately. Reliable radio communications was thus one of the hallmarks of a competent recce unit, and this in itself gave these units enormous flexibility to perform a host of other, less glamorous but equally vital, tasks such as convoy and traffic control.

The lack of Anglo-Canadian doctrine on the tactical employment of the recce units was in large measure resolved by Colonel Mann, who wrote his own training manual on reconnaissance operations. This pamphlet soon became the standard doctrine, and it heavily influenced the tactical procedures developed independently by the two armoured car regiments. While the divisional recce units prided themselves on having more fire power than an infantry company, in reality they were neither armed nor equipped to fight in order to gain information. The weapons mounted on the vehicles – 37mm guns on the armoured recce cars and Bren light machine guns on the carriers – were essentially for self-protection. They were heavy enough to force an enemy position to reveal its location, or per-

haps to get a patrol out of trouble, but not enough to engage in a serious fire-fight with the enemy. The tactics developed were thus based largely on fire and movement and what is known as 'sneak and peek', where the lead vehicle in a patrol advances from one observation position to another while being protected by other vehicles in fire positions immediately behind.

1 ARMY TANK BRIGADE

As already noted, the first Armoured Corps formation to be deployed to Britain was 1 Army Tank Brigade. Advance parties of officers and senior NCOs had been despatched in April 1941, so that a core of instructors from each unit could spend about two months on attachment with units of the Royal Tank Regiment for familiarization with real tanks before the arrival of the brigade. The main body docked in Scotland on 1 July 1941 and within days all units were established, somewhat uncomfortably, in a tented camp near Lavington, on the north-western edge of Salisbury Plain.

By mid-July each unit of 1 Army Tank Brigade was the proud possessor of a half-dozen brand new tanks, a similar number of Universal carriers and about eighteen trucks of various sizes. The Ontario Regiment was supplied with Churchill tanks, the very first that had come off the British production line, while the Three Rivers Regiment and the Calgarys were

Matilda tanks of the Three Rivers Regiment demonstrating anti-tank ditch crossing for General Sir Alan Brooke and Lieutenant-General A.G. L. McNaughton on Salisbury Plain, September 1941. (Canadian Army Photo)

issued Matildas. By early August all units had nearly a full squadron of tanks, enough to undertake a rigorous if improvised programme of basic vehicle training on the manoeuvre area of Salisbury Plain. The Ontarios had constant problems with the mechanically unreliable early-model Churchill tanks, which their regimental history describes as "having bugs in their guts". The Matildas, on the other hand, gave very little trouble, and were well liked by their crews.

The meagre quantity and dismal quality of British Army wartime rations was the source of enormous discontent among units arriving in wartime Britain. Even the most skilful of the cooks had difficulty producing palatable meals out of things that most Canadians found to be essentially distasteful – mutton, Lord Woolton sausage (which many were convinced contained sawdust), powdered eggs, and margarine with an unpleasant taste. For many weeks it seems that the Ontario Regiment survived on wild rabbits snared in the tent lines. Morale was, however, greatly boosted when the first tanks appeared.

By late September 1941, Worthy judged that his regiments had mastered their new tanks, and it was time to move into more complex training. Accordingly, in early October the regiments were sent, one at a time, to the tank gunnery range at

Linney Head in south Wales, where for the first time crewmen had the opportunity to fire their 2-pounders. Working under the tutelage of British gunnery instructors, every member of a tank crew fired at a number of stationary targets, while the gunners fired a more extensive series of shoots at both stationary and moving targets. Within each squadron, the final practice was a troop battle run, with the troop leader controlling the fire of his three tanks as they moved down-range in tactical formation. The Ontario Regiment's last day of shooting was observed by a group of distinguished visitors, and as all too often happens on such occasions, things went awry. The regimental history relates:

Lieut. Ned Amy's troop moved up to the start line on a troop battle run. The crews were to fire at stationary targets while the tanks moved forward together. The wireless in Lieut. Amy's tank broke down just as he passed the line. The troop ground forward, firing strenuously, oblivious to the apoplectic efforts of the range officer to stop the tanks. Range crews had dived to cover, a scant jump ahead of the observers. Amy's troop was only brought to a stop by brisk 'Very light' fire athwart his line of advance.

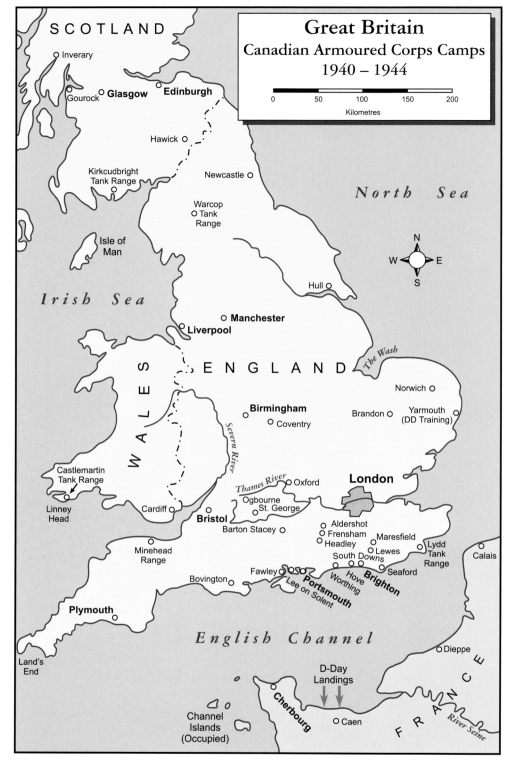

Great Britain
Canadian Armoured Corps Camps
1940 – 1944

0   50   100   150   200
Kilometres

vre areas, needed at a particular time in their training development, but it was always a puzzle to the men. The Ontarios' history remarks:

Much time has been wasted in trying to find a reason for the Gargantuan game of draughts played by Higher Authority in moving Unit A to Little Snorting in the Wold and taking Unit B from its billets in Little Snorting and dumping it in the camp just vacated by Unit A. No very conclusive deduction has been reached. It is, perhaps, merely done for practice.

While based in the Headley area, units began to move beyond individual crew trades training and into what was termed 'collective training', beginning at the troop level and progressing through squadron, regimental and then brigade field exercises. During this period a beginning was made at all-arms training with infantry units of 3 Division, a move that was brought to a premature halt in late November when Churchill tanks were issued to both the Three Rivers and the Calgary Regiments. The conversion made it necessary for the Ontario Regiment to act temporarily as a training regiment, which a brigade report noted had "disastrous results as far as their tanks were concerned".

In late December 1941 the brigade became part of I Canadian Corps, and was given an operational role in the defence of Sussex. This brought another move, this time to Brighton, Worthing and Seaford, on the Channel coast. The brigade remained in this area for much of the next year, taking full advantage of the proximity to large, open tactical training areas on the nearby South Downs.

On departing from Linney Head in mid-October, the brigade moved to a new base in the area of Headley and Tilford, south of Aldershot. The practice of moving armoured formations and units from one camp to another was something that happened with great frequency. In some instances this was done to give units access to training facilities, such as manoeu-

On 28 January 1942, Brigadier R.A. Wyman, a pre-war gunner then serving as commander of the Support Group of 5 Armoured Division, succeeded General Worthington.

By this time, the regiments of 1 Army Tank Brigade had their full complement of Churchill tanks and other vehicles and equipment: 50 tanks, 13 carriers, 9 scout cars, 6 motorcycles and 37 trucks to each unit. Emphasis was now given to field tactics, and to understand the context of this training it may be useful to review briefly the tactical doctrine for the employment of 'army tanks'.

Heavy 'infantry' tanks such as the Churchill were intended to provide intimate support to infantry operations in all phases of war. Army Tank brigades were 'independent' formations, controlled at Army level and parcelled out to infantry divisions as the operational situation demanded. Their sole function was co-operation with infantry, and one might reasonably assume that the tactics developed for their employment on the battlefield would reflect this, and that

General McNaughton and Brigadier Worthington inspect an Ontario Regiment Churchill tank. (Canadian Army Photo)

procedures and drills would have been worked out in considerable detail at least down to tank troop/infantry company levels. Strangely, this had not been done, except in very general terms, even though the concept had been part of British thinking since before the war began. There was thus not very much guidance for brigade or regimental commanders on which to pattern their training, and even less for squadron commanders and tank troop leaders. Lieutenant-Colonel Jim Cameron, then a young lieutenant with the Ontario Regiment, described his experience on a troop leaders' tactics course:

> Along with a group of newly arrived reinforcement officers, I was sent down to Headley Common to attend a course for tank troop leaders. We crewed our own tanks, alternating as drivers, gunners, crew commanders and troop leader, and that was good experience. The two instructors – one was an elderly major who had been a sergeant in the Strathconas before the war – were never very sober. The tactics training consisted of doing cavalry drill with the tanks. Can you imagine, forming fours or doing cavalry-style charges with tanks on the common!

The official doctrine for "The Employment of Army Tanks in Co-operation with Infantry" was contained in Army Training Instruction No. 2 of August 1941. This instruction dealt with all phases of war – the advance to contact, the attack, the defence and the withdrawal. Our examination of its contents will, however, focus only on the attack, as this was to be the predominant phase of war in the invasion of *Festung Europa* [Fortress Europe].

Calgary Regiment troops on a map reading exercise, England, 1941. (NAC PA193939)

The doctrine for the attack called for an advance against an enemy position in three 'echelons'. In the first echelon, tanks were to lead, in order to neutralize both enemy automatic weapons and anti-tank guns so that infantry could later advance without undue casualties. A second echelon, also composed of tanks, would then come forward to break passages through wire obstacles and neutralize enemy small arms fire from the defended locality, and infantry would follow on, mopping up by-passed enemy and consolidating the position overrun by the tanks. A third, reserve, echelon was to consist of tanks retained to exploit success or for counter-attack if necessary. Some exceptional circumstances were outlined when the infantry might be required to take the lead, especially if the enemy's gun area was reached or there was an anti-tank obstacle.

This instruction is notable for the total absence of any

The Calgary Regiment on parade before going to Dieppe, July 1942. (NAC PA116274)

discussion of armour and infantry functioning as an integrated team on the battlefield, and thus very little emphasis was placed on joint operations in the training conducted by 1 Army Tank Brigade. It never got beyond basic familiarization with what the other arm could do on the battlefield and, while tanks and infantry may have aimed at capturing the same objective, the doctrine anticipated that they would fight quite separate battles to do so.

This 1941 doctrine capitalized on the relative invulnerability of the heavily armoured 'army tanks', such as the Churchill, to artillery, mortar and machine-gun fire, and even to most contemporary anti-tank weapons. It is perhaps noteworthy, however, that their main armament at this time was strictly an anti-tank weapon, since it fired only a solid-shot round. High-explosive rounds had not yet been developed for either the 2-pounder or 6-pounder gun, so that in an infantry assault on an enemy position the tanks would, in effect, be limited to using their machine-guns to give fire support.

Beginning in April 1942, the brigade began to participate in a series of major field exercises. The first of these was Exercise *Beaver III*, a three-day scheme where 2 Division and 1 Army Tank Brigade defended against an invading force simulated by 1 Canadian Division. As with most large-scale manoeuvres, *Beaver III* was intended mainly to train the staff officers at division and brigade headquarters and give unit commanders practice in battle procedure and command techniques. Rarely are exercises of this nature of much value to soldiers on the ground. The Ontarios history noted that "For the tank crews, Beaver III provided some change of scene but no excitement. The tanks

were moved from one harbour to another … the whole thing was a bit of a bore." A report on the exercise prepared by the brigade headquarters noted that "the [technical] shortcomings of the Churchill tanks became very obvious and very serious," as at one time or another during the exercise 119 of the brigade's 139 tanks were "off the road" with either major or minor breakdowns. The Ordnance Corps (later RCEME) mechanics thus got a lot of practice in vehicle recovery and field repair.

It was during *Beaver III* that tank crews were introduced to the British ration pack known as 'Iron Rations'. The Three Rivers' war diarist commented:

The Regiment was issued its first "Iron Rations" yesterday. Issued on a 5-man basis, they consist of 5 tins of 'hard tack' (these biscuits may be the reason the rations are called 'iron'), 5 tins of 'bully' beef, 1 1/2 tins of beans, 3 tins of sardines, 1 1/4 tins of jam, 3 tins of tea per person, sugar and milk powder. The men seem to find them very satisfactory, which reflects rather sadly on the standard fare.

Exercise *Beaver IV*, conducted in mid-May, pitted 2 Division and the tank brigade against 3 Division. The scenario was much the same as in *Beaver III*, but with increased air activity, so that the tanks spent much of the exercise hidden in woods. "The tank crews waited and waited. It rained. Then a series of quick moves brought the tanks to the Downs… The final move teed up the tanks at the edge of a wheat field, prepared to advance." Brigade headquarters noted that this was one of the few occasions on which the brigade actually launched an attack, as most exercises ended just as the tanks were positioned for their assault. On this occasion "the brigade did attack, but the resulting damage to the English countryside had repercussions which lasted for many weeks after the exercise."

In June 1942, immediately following *Beaver IV*, the Calgary Regiment was sent to the Isle of Wight to train in secret for the raid on Dieppe, training in assault landing techniques and preparations for the operation that will be reported in the next chapter.

Since the creation of the brigade, in February 1941, the tank units, as readers may recall, had been formally designated as 'battalions', when all other equivalent units of the Armoured Corps were 'regiments'. This distinction, a reminder of the pre-war period when tank units were part of the Infantry Corps, was formally changed on 15 May 1942: the tank battalions were henceforth to be 'army tank regiments'.

Exercise *Tiger*, conducted over an eleven-day period in late May 1942 was a scheme organized by General Montgomery's Southeastern Command to test the stamina of Canadian troops. It involved six divisions, pitting I Canadian Corps against XII British Corps in an advance to contact and encounter battle. From 1 Army Tank Brigade only the Ontario and Three Rivers regiments participated, as the Calgarys were busy training for the Dieppe operation. It was a strenuous exercise, involving constant movement as the tanks followed up the attacking infantry. The second phase involved the conduct of a withdrawal, in which the tanks covered the retreating infantry on a broad front and successfully prevented a superior enemy force from overrunning them. While there were still significant problems with the mechanically unreliable Churchill tanks, at least some of the troops for once came away from an exercise with a sense that they had learned something useful about armoured operations.

The British showed renewed interest in tank-infantry cooperation following their brief-lived 1942 reorganization of the infantry division to include an army tank brigade. A Royal Armoured Corps Wing was opened at the GHQ Battle School to teach a modified form of battle drill for tank/infantry work. Colonel Jack English described the revised British concept in his book, *The Canadian Army and the Normandy Campaign:*

Three Rivers Regiment Churchills cross a stream during Exercise Spartan, March 1943. (NAC PA133968)

The attack was foreseen as beginning with artillery concentrations and air strikes, to be followed immediately by teams of infantry and assault engineers breaching minefields and anti-tank ditches. A first echelon of tanks, massed for maximum effect, would then assault to achieve a breakthrough by sheer speed and weight of numbers. Next would come a tank and infantry second echelon, the "Shepherding Wave", working at "infantry speed" to reduce pockets of resistance. A third echelon, also mixed, was later to exploit success. ... The "real scope for infantry-tank cooperation" was considered to lie in "second echelon work", for which a battle drill had been worked out. According to this drill, infantry were to move forward making best use of ground, preceding tanks that in the case of a platoon-troop were to be treated much like a bigger "Bren Group" for purposes of manoeuvre. On contact with an enemy, the tanks were to move forward to a position as nearly as possible right-angled to the infantry "fire line" to provide fire support for flanking or pincer movements by the latter.

These new concepts had little immediate effect on tactical training within 1 Army Tank Brigade and there is no evidence that any attention was paid to this thinking until much later in the year when a few officers of the Canadian Armoured Corps were sent on courses at the GHQ Battle School.

In the latter part of August 1942 units each spent just over a week firing on the Minehead Tank Gunnery Range in Somerset, the first occasion in nearly a year for the crews to fire their main armament. Tactical battle runs, planned and coordinated by each troop leader, demonstrated that great strides had been made in crew proficiency, but the brigade headquarters staff noted that "there were many points which had yet to be learned before the troops could be considered really battle worthy." This was also the first time that gunners in the Ontario and Three Rivers Regiments fired the 6-pounder, and both regiments reported problems with the fire control systems and with accuracy.

The autumn of 1942 was given over to troop and squadron training in all units. One of the major concerns was the rebuilding of the Calgary Regiment which had lost the better part of two squadrons at Dieppe. In this period a new version of the Churchill tank – one with many of the faults rectified and with a 6-pounder gun – began to appear, bringing the brigade to a much higher standard of battleworthiness.

Distinguishing patches for formations and units received a great deal of attention at First Canadian Army during the course of 1942, essentially because of the complete lack of standardization. The matter of shoulder patches for the tank brigades – there were now two – was decided in late October 1942. Independent army tank or armoured brigades were authorized to wear a patch based on a black diamond shape with a three-quarter-inch-high horizontal coloured bar: 1 Brigade a red bar, 2 a blue bar, and 3 (which did not yet exist) a French grey bar, and abbreviated regimental titles were to be embroidered in gold on the bar. The Ram patch was taken out of wear in late 1942 when the new patch was issued, and shortly afterwards 'Canadian Armoured Corps' printed cloth shoulder titles were also issued for wear on battle dress tunics.

By the end of November 1942 the commander and operations staff of I Canadian Corps had become concerned about the rather dismal state of 'tank-cum-infantry' capability within

Canadian Armoured Corps shoulder title, worn by 1 Army Tank Brigade in Britain, and later by men serving in the Corps reinforcement units.

the Corps. This was attributed, in part, to the heavy emphasis placed on low-level battle drill in the training done by infantry units, but it is also true that the tankers had been preoccupied with their own technical and tactical training. Corps Headquarters therefore directed that a two-month programme of training be carried out to achieve "a satisfactory standard of cooperation between army tank sub-units and infantry sub-units."

Within 1 Army Tank Brigade, the task fell to the Three Rivers Regiment. 'A' Squadron was to train with the units of 1 Division, 'B' Squadron was to work with 3 Division, and 'C' Squadron with 2 Division. Corps laid down a three-day programme. On the first day the participating troops were to receive briefings on the principles of tank-infantry cooperation, there was to be a cloth-model exercise demonstrating how tanks and infantry were to work together in the attack and defence, and practice at the tank troop/infantry platoon level in giving "practical and suitable orders." On the second day the infantry battalions and tank squadrons would rendezvous on the South Downs for a series of troop/platoon exercises, each of which was critiqued in detail by the senior officers of the battalion and squadron. On the third day the exercises continued at squadron/company level.

Nine such three-day sessions were conducted in December and January, but this meant that there were only two days of actual field training with each infantry battalion, certainly not enough to develop even a rudimentary degree of tactical proficiency. The well-intentioned aim of the Corps directive was, of course, not met, and this was indicative of the general lack of interest or concern about all-arms cooperation in the Canadian Army at this time. Only 3 Division had enough interest to comment, and they recommended that increased stress be put on communications, such as the netting and use of the infantry's No. 38 sets, and on training at troop/platoon level. It is also interesting to note that these sessions involved only the Three Rivers Regiment. Brigadier General Ned Amy, a troop leader in the Ontarios at the time, has stated, "In the Ontario Regiment we never actually exercised on the ground with the infantry where we practised deployment drills and married up and had a combined exercise."

Sleeve patches of the Army Tank Brigades

1 Army Tank Brigade (later 1 Armoured Brigade). Abbreviated unit names were shown on the coloured band.

2 Army Tank Brigade (later 2 Armoured Brigade). Unit titles were not used on the patch in this brigade.

3 Army Tank Brigade.

Tank-infantry cooperation training exercise conducted by the Three Rivers Regiment in early December 1942. This was one of the rare occasions when this took place. (NAC PA154304)

Troops of 1 Army Tank Brigade lined up for an inspection by HM King George VI, 11 February 1943. (NAC PA37480)

King George VI inspected the brigade, drawn up in the South Downs, on 11 February 1943. The King reviewed a dismounted parade, after which the Ontario Regiment did an impressive mounted march-past in highly polished Churchill tanks. It seems that the headquarters squadron of the Three Rivers Regiment was well known for its lack of parade skills, so arrangements were made for the somewhat scruffy squadron to stand in line along the top of a dike. The *Chronicles of the Three Rivers Regiment (Tank)* recorded this aspect of the Royal inspection:

... We had been marched into place hours early, and the Royals arrived hours late. So there came a time when our level of body liquid brought tears to our eyes. It was dance or wet our pants. R.S.M. Jack Davy, after a very brief consultation with higher and higher ups, finally relented. "About turn!", he barked. "Unbutton! Fire at will!" We performed to

a man with remarkable precision and grace. ... And – suddenly – there to behold it was His Majesty, with his cortege making a hiccup of a halt in a vain attempt to stop at a diplomatic distance.

"About turn!" ... The scramble can best be described as 'buttons and bends'. Finally a semblance of order and decorum. The dike helped. The Royal cortege lurched forward. Given our endless wait it seemed to sweep by our end of the parade with unseemly haste. But not so fast that we failed to see a wide grin on the kingly countenance.

Following Exercise *Spartan* (described later in this chapter), the units of the brigade traded their Churchills for new Ram tanks, but they barely had time to 'shoot-in' the guns at Minehead before the brigade was moved to Scotland for training on Sherman tanks prior to sailing for the Mediterranean. The story of 1 Army Tank Brigade in Sicily is continued in Chapter 7 below.

The Fox Armoured Car was a Canadian-built copy of the British Humber Mark III. Generally considered too high and too lightly armed, the Fox was used for training the armoured car regiments in Britain before being replaced by the Staghound. The Fox saw service in Italy and North-West Europe with the reconnaissance regiments. (Drawing by Chris Johnson)

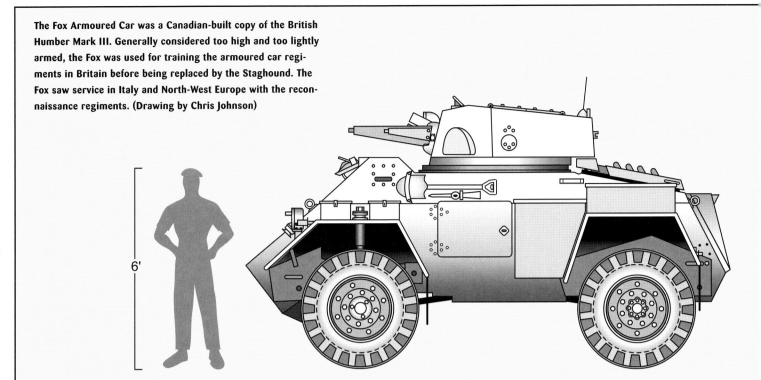

Fox Armoured Car
Country of Origin: Canada
Crew: 4 (Commander, Gunner, Driver, Wireless Operator)
Length: 15 feet
Width: 7 feet 7 inches

Height: 8 feet
Weight: 17,159 pounds
Engine: GMC 6 cylinder, gasoline
Maximum Speed: 44 mph
Range: 210 miles

Armour – Maximum: 15 mm
Armament: .50 calibre MG in turret mount
        .30 calibre MG coaxial to .50 calibre MG

The Humber I Scout Car, produced to supplement the more popular Daimler Scout Car, was found alongside the Lynx II in the Intercommunication Troop of Canadian armoured regiments in North-West Europe. It was used primarily for liaison work. (Drawing by Chris Johnson)

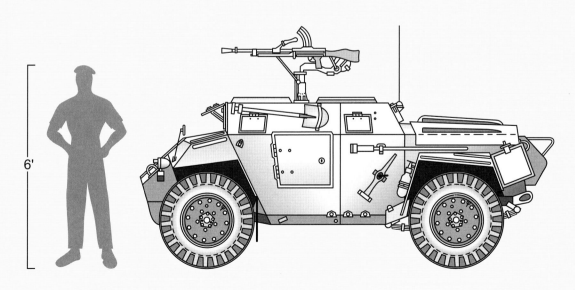

Humber Scout Car
Country of Origin: Great Britain
Crew: 2 (Commander, Driver)
Length: 12 feet 7 inches
Width: 6 feet 2 inches
Height: 6 feet 9 inches

Weight: 7,800 pounds
Engine: Humber 6 cylinder, gasoline
Maximum Speed: 62 mph
Range: 200 miles
Armour – Maximum: 14 mm
Armament: .303 inch Bren MG

The M3 Lee Medium Tank, an interim type before the appearance of the M4 Sherman series, was the first American tank to mount a dual-purpose 75mm gun. Canadian M3s often incorporated mud chutes under the top track, extra stowage boxes on the rear deck and an externally mounted auxiliary fuel tank. (Drawing by Chris Johnson)

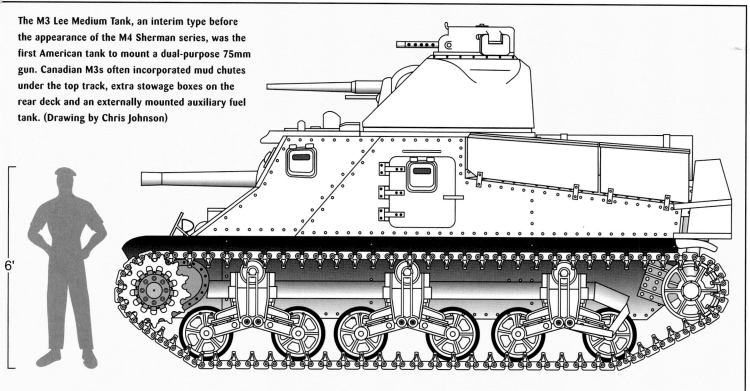

M3, Lee Medium Tank
Country of Origin: United States
Crew: 6 (Commander, 2 x Gunners, Driver, 2 x Loaders)
Length: 18 feet 6 inches
Width: 8 feet 11 inches
Height: 10 feet 3 inches

Weight: 61,500 pounds
Engine: Continental 9 cylinder radial, gasoline
Maximum Speed: 24 mph
Range: 120 miles
Armour – Maximum: 37 mm
         Minimum: 12 mm

Armament: 75 mm Gun M2 in sponson mount
    37 mm Gun M6 in turret
    .30 calibre MG M1919A4 in turret cupola
    .30 calibre MG M1919A4 co-axial to 37 mm in turret

The Otter Light Reconnaissance Car was loosely based on the British Humber III Light Reconnaissance Car. Some 1,761 Otters were built in Canada and, although superseded by better designs, they served in reconnaissance regiments in Italy and North-West Europe. (Drawing by Chris Johnson)

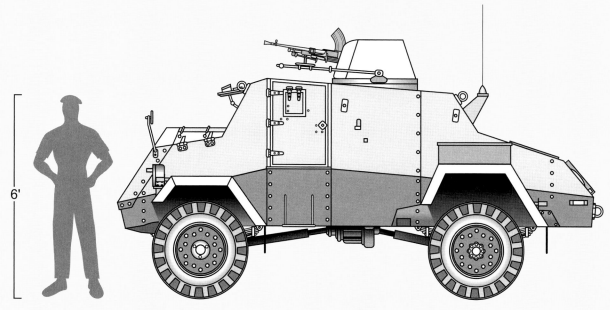

Otter Light Reconnaissance Car
Country of Origin: Canada
Crew: 3 (Commander, Gunner, Driver)
Length: 14 feet 9 inches
Width: 7 feet

Height: 8 feet
Weight: 11,000 pounds
Engine: GMC 6 cylinder, gasoline
Maximum Speed: 45 mph
Range: 261 miles

Armour – Maximum: 12 mm
          Minimum: 8 mm
Armament: .303 inch Bren MG in turret mount
    Boys Anti Tank Rifle in hull when not fitted with wireless

Fort Garry Horse troops with a newly-issued Lee tank, April 1942. Armed with a 75mm gun in a hull sponson and a 37mm gun in the turret, the Lee was a British variant of the American Grant tank. (Canadian Army photo)

Soldiers of the 30th Recce Regiment (Essex Regiment (Tank)), Britain, 1943. Dispatched overseas in July 1943, this unit from Windsor, Ontario, one of Canada's automotive centres, was tasked with the assembly of military vehicles that had been shipped to Britain in parts. Although the task was deeply resented it was nevertheless well done. In April 1944 the unit was broken up to supply reinforcements to other reconnaissance units. (Courtesy of the *Windsor Star*)

5th ARMOURED DIVISION

To follow the development of 5 CAD, we must return to its arrival in Britain in the autumn of 1941. 1 Armoured Brigade was concentrated in Aldershot, along with the division headquarters, while the 2nd occupied more remote quarters on the bleak and windswept Marlborough Downs on the north side of Salisbury Plain. The RCD, the divisional armoured car regiment, was based in Blackdown, just outside Aldershot.

It had been intended that the division would be equipped with Ram tanks almost immediately after arrival in England, but production had fallen far behind schedule. Overseas Headquarters thus had to turn to the British Army with a request for at least a few tanks for the division so that training could be started on a limited scale. The British, having their own serious problems with tank supply, managed to put together a motley collection of M3 Lee tanks, M3 Stuart light tanks, M2 light tanks (the forerunner of the Stuart) and a few Daimler Dingo scout cars. These were parcelled out to the regiments of 2 Brigade in early December, when the Horse Guards got five Lees and one Stuart, and the 8th Hussars eight Lees, while the BCD received three Lees and two scout cars. In January a further batch of American tanks were issued to the units of 1 Armoured Brigade. The RCD found themselves in possession of two Humber armoured cars and four Dingo scout cars. The shortage of vehicles, which was to last until well into the summer of 1942, severely limited the pace of the essential conversion training of crewmen, and substantially delayed the beginning of the collective tactical training phase in all units.

Before reviewing the tactics training conducted by 5 CAD during the course of 1942, it may be of value to return briefly the doctrinal background – the officially sanctioned rationale and concepts for the battlefield employment of a British armoured division – since, more than anything, it was that which determined the scope of training. It is perhaps worth noting that this doctrine evolved during a period when what was called the 'all-tank' school was predominant within the Royal Armoured Corps

In British thinking during the early years of the war, armoured divisions were designed for fast-paced, offensive manoeuvre warfare, exploiting the inherent characteristics of armoured forces – firepower, mobility, armour protection and shock. While the division was, of course, meant to be capable of cooperating with infantry divisions when required, its structure was intended primarily for independent operations in two phases of war, the advance to contact, and the attack, and especially for the engagement of enemy armoured formations. The cruiser tank was the central element of a concept that stressed the principles of flexibility, mass, and rapid concentration of force at the decisive point on the battlefield.

In this grand view, infantry were seen as playing relatively minor roles. The principal task of the motorized battalion in the armoured brigades was the restoration of mobility if the armour was engaged by anti-tank defences which it could not deal with alone; that of the support group battalion was the occupation of a defensive position to form a firm base or 'pivot' around which the armour could manoeuvre; and both battalions were expected to 'mop up' the battlefield in the wake of the armoured units. Because they were rarely intended to manoeuvre together, little need was foreseen for the development of detailed tank-infantry cooperation procedures. The organization of the division reflected this orientation.

The British recognized that there were limitations inherent in this organizational structure. The armoured division was considered to be "unsuitable for attack on highly organized defences." It could not hold ground, and was thus unsuitable for defensive operations, and, because tank crews could not see to manoeuvre or fire their weapons in the dark, it was deemed incapable of fighting at night. It became accepted principle that armoured units would move well back from the front during hours of darkness for replenishment, maintenance and rest.

The tactics developed to put the doctrine into practice envisaged the division operating on a broad front, often as wide as fifteen kilometres in 'open' country. In an advance to contact, the armoured car regiment would patrol well to the front to find the enemy, and then probe for gaps and weak spots while the leading brigade closed up. After being briefed on the details of the enemy deployment, tank units would manoeuvre into position to engage the enemy with fire. The armoured car regiment would then withdraw, through the tank units, while the tanks would continue to manoeuvre from one fire position to another so as to be able to destroy the enemy with "overwhelming firepower". The second brigade would usually be kept in reserve to reinforce the attack if necessary, to defeat a counter-attack that might develop, or to exploit success and continue the advance.

Within the armoured regiments, the tank squadron was the primary manoeuvre element. The squadron consisted of a headquarters (with four tanks), and four or five tank troops, each with three tanks.

HM Queen Elizabeth, accompanied by Brigadier C.R.S. Stein, inspects the Governor General's Horse Guards, 24 April 1942. (NAC PA193937)

(Readers might note that squadrons in regiments of the armoured divisions had *four* tank troops, while those in the independent army tank brigades had *five* troops.) This combat part of the squadron was sometimes called the F (for 'fighting') Echelon. In addition there was an administrative group called A Echelon, equipped with trucks, which carried the supplies of ammunition and gasoline needed for immediate battlefield replenishment, along with a small group of mechanics who were able to do minor repairs to the tanks. A Echelon was commanded by the second-in-command but normally run by the squadron sergeant-major. A second administrative group – B Echelon headed by the squadron quartermaster-sergeant – held other supplies not urgently needed by troops in battle, such as the men's personal kit bags and stocks of clothing.

Tactics manuals of the period tend to emphasize bold and rapid movement of a squadron from one fire position to another, and there is more discussion of the appropriate 'formation' to adopt while manoeuvring – whether it might be better to have one troop or two in the lead – than of how the principle of 'fire and movement' might be applied. Within tank troops,

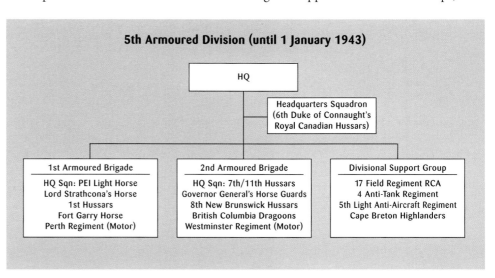

5th Armoured Division (until 1 January 1943)

HQ

Headquarters Squadron (6th Duke of Connaught's Royal Canadian Hussars)

1st Armoured Brigade	2nd Armoured Brigade	Divisional Support Group
HQ Sqn: PEI Light Horse	HQ Sqn: 7th/11th Hussars	17 Field Regiment RCA
Lord Strathcona's Horse	Governor General's Horse Guards	4 Anti-Tank Regiment
1st Hussars	8th New Brunswick Hussars	5th Light Anti-Aircraft Regiment
Fort Garry Horse	British Columbia Dragoons	Cape Breton Highlanders
Perth Regiment (Motor)	Westminster Regiment (Motor)	

Stuart M3 light tanks were issued in limited numbers to units of the 5th Armoured Division in May 1942. This tank, indicated by the tactical sign number painted on the fender – 62 – belongs to the 8th New Brunswick Hussars. (Canadian Army Photo)

The Division commander, Major-General Sansom, inspects the British Columbia Dragoons' Lee tanks, Headley Down, March 1942. The sponson-mounted main armament of the Lee severely limited its use in action, but the chassis was used for both the Ram and the Sherman tanks.

individual crew commanders were expected to make the best use of ground for cover and concealment while moving rapidly between fire positions, and to adopt 'turret down' positions, where the entire tank remained behind cover from enemy observation, to search for likely enemy locations before moving into a 'hull down' position, where only the turret was exposed, to bring fire to bear on the enemy.

A severe shortage of tanks continued to hamper individual and crew training in 5 CAD until well into the late spring of 1942, when Ram tanks began to arrive from Canada. Even then, however, the units had to contend with a mix of Lees, Stuarts and Rams, and conversion training for the crewmen on the Ram tanks further delayed the completion of individual training. In May 1942, for example, the division's total holding of tanks consisted of 96 tanks – 33 Rams (Mark I), 47 Lees, 8 Stuarts, and 8 M2s – out of an establishment of 320. It was not until the beginning of June 1942 that regiments began tactical training at tank troop level, and this was possible only by giving all of a unit's tanks to a single squadron at a time.

The introduction of the No.19 wireless set in the early summer of 1942 was one of the technological advances of this period which contributed significantly to the effectiveness of armoured and reconnaissance units by providing a usually reliable means of communications. Developed in Britain by the Pye Radio Company and extensively field tested for the Canadian Army in the autumn of 1941 by a team working under Lieutenant George Bell of the Three Rivers Regiment (a future Colonel-Commandant of the Corps), the 19 set incorporated three components: an 'A' set operating in the High Frequency band which had a range of up to fifteen kilometres, a very short-range 'B' set which could, under ideal conditions, broadcast about one kilometre, and an intercommunications mode that for the first time allowed all members of the tank crew to talk to each other.

The 'A' set, which allowed for normal voice communications

Sleeve patch worn until about 1943 by troops temporarily posted to one of the Canadian Armoured Corps Reinforcement Units (CACRUs).

Sleeve patch of Canadian Military headquarters which was also worn from late 1943 by men serving in the Armoured Corps Reinforcement Units.

The regiments of 1 and 2 Armoured Brigades got their first opportunity to fire the main armament on tanks in July 1942 when each unit in turn was sent for a week to the Castlemartin Tank Gunnery Range at Linney Head in Wales. There the units took over 28 Ram Is and six Lees, and proceeded to fire a series of set practices with the 2-pounders and Browning machine-guns. All members of a crew fired a basic 'familiarization practice' of ten rounds of 2-pounder armour-piercing ammunition and two belts of machine gun ammunition, while tank gunners fired a more extensive programme. In each unit six tank crews were selected to fire the 75mm guns of the Lee tanks, using both armour-piercing and high-explosive rounds. In the final three days on the range, each tank troop was put through a five-kilometre 'battle run', engaging both moving targets and stationary 'pop-up' targets that would appear briefly at different distances. All units made a very respectable showing, proving that theoretical gunnery instruction on the RYPA and miniature ranges had been most effective.

for the passage of information and orders within a regiment, largely eliminated the need for radio operators to be proficient in Morse code, although it could transmit Morse if necessary. Tuning in to the allocated frequency (which changed daily) was, however, a bit of an art, as each radio had to be individually 'netted' to a transmission from the control station at squadron or regimental headquarters. Moreover, the set had several inherent limitations: it operated on a different frequency band than radios carried by the infantry, it was always noisy, it was less effective at night when it would pick up all manner of interference from the ionosphere, and a 'net' could be totally jammed if a crew commander or operator forgot to release the pressel switch after making a transmission.

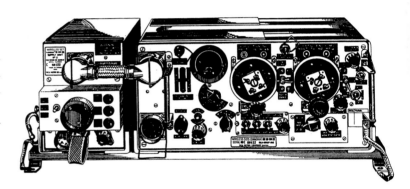

(Above) The introduction of the No. 19 Wireless Set radio in the summer of 1942 brought a significant improvement in tank-to-tank communications, and in the battlefield employment of tanks.

(Left) The first Canadian-built Ram Mk I to arrive in Britain in 1942 is proudly displayed in this public relations photo. Most of the Rams later shipped to Britain were Ram IIs, armed with a 6-pounder gun in place of the 2-pounder shown in this photo. (Canadian Army Photo)

The training situation improved considerably when 5 CAD was moved from the area of Aldershot to camps in East Sussex, near the south coast of England, in mid-August 1942. There the units had ready access to relatively large, open manoeuvre areas on the nearby South Downs, and over the autumn months each unit's holding of new Ram II tanks grew progressively. To make up for the earlier inability to carry out effective tactical training, General Sansom extended the time allotted to troop and squadron-level field training to the end of December.

THE ARMOURED CORPS REINFORCEMENT UNITS

Three reinforcement units were created in England on 1 April 1942 as training and holding units for reinforcements for the units of the Corps in Europe. No.1 Canadian Armoured Corps Reinforcement Unit (1 CACRU) was to provide trained reinforcements for the armoured car and reconnaissance regiments, 2 CACRU served the army tank units, while 3 CACRU held the officers and men destined for the armoured divisions. After April 1943 a Headquarters Group, under Brigadier Tom Rutherford, coordinated the efforts of all three units. For the remainder of the war, all Armoured Corps reinforcements, officers and men, coming from the schools in Canada were first posted to one of the CACRUs until they were needed as replacements in the units. In that they were responsible to ensure adequately trained soldiers for the operational regiments, each CACRU held close to a regiment's worth of equipment so that training could take place.

Major-General E.W. Sansom, DSO, Commander of the 5th Armoured Division March 1941 to January 1943. (Canadian Forces Photo Unit)

4th ARMOURED DIVISION

4 CAD began its move to Britain in late August 1942, and was initially stationed in and near Aldershot. Because of the intensive training carried out in Debert, the division arrived in a more advanced state of training than 5 CAD had done, and the division headquarters decreed that tactical training to troop level was to be completed by mid-February 1943. Ram tanks were still in short supply, however, so units were issued a training scale of Universal carriers until Rams became available, but Worthy, impatient to get on with 'proper' training, used his influence to ensure that some of the Rams coming into England were diverted to his division. Before much had been accomplished, however, the division was swept up in a massive reorganization of the Corps.

RESTRUCTURING THE CORPS

The British experience in North Africa in 1941 and early 1942 had revealed that tank and infantry formations all too often tended to fight quite independent actions in the same battle. Tank-infantry cooperation was virtually ignored, in some instances with disastrous results, such as at Halfaya in April 1941 after the *Afrika Korps* began to deploy 88mm anti-tank guns in mutually supporting screens. Then too, the two-brigade armoured division proved "unwieldy" and clearly did not have enough organic infantry. The British examined these problems very thoroughly and, in the summer of 1942, restructured their

The Camouflage Net. Painting by Bruno Bobak of training in 3 Canadian Armoured Corps Reinforcement Unit, Surrey, England. (Canadian War Museum 11907)

divisions by replacing one of the armoured brigades with a motorized infantry brigade. General McNaughton recommended that the Canadians should conform to this reorganization, and in this he took account of a projected manpower shortage that had been identified as likely to affect the flow of armoured reinforcements in 1943.

This restructuring meant that two armoured brigades – six armoured regiments – were about to become surplus. In an effort to forestall the disbandment of any of the existing units, McNaughton initially recommended that a third army tank brigade should be authorized, along with the two reorganized armoured divisions. New roles were also identified for three units: two were to become Corps troops – armoured car regiments for I and II Corps – and one was needed as an armoured delivery regiment for First Canadian Army. At the same time, the numbering of the brigades of the Armoured Corps was to be simplified, with the numbers 1 to 3 allocated to independent brigades, such as the army tank brigades. The reorganization took effect on 11 January 1943, based on McNaughton's plan. It entailed a wholesale reshuffling of affiliations for many of the units of the Corps, other than those in 1 Army Tank Brigade and the recce units with the infantry divisions.

In 4 CAD, the 12th Manitoba Dragoons were designated as the Corps armoured car unit for II Canadian Corps, while the South Alberta Regiment from 3 Armoured Brigade became the

Brigadier Tom Rutherford, who coordinated the training of Canadian Armoured Corps reinforcements in England from 1943 until the end of the war. (Photo courtesy of Colonel The Hon. Robert Rutherford)

divisional armoured recce regiment, to be re-equipped with a combination of tanks and Universal carriers. 3 Armoured Brigade now disappeared: the Elgin Regiment became the tank delivery regiment, while the British Columbia Regiment was shifted to 4 Armoured Brigade, which retained the Foot Guards and the Grenadier Guards, but the Sherbrooke Fusiliers were moved to the newly created 3 Army Tank Brigade.

5 CAD suffered a similar upheaval. The RCD became I Canadian Corps armoured car regiment, while the Governor General's Horse Guards were shifted from 2 Brigade to become the divisional recce regiment, the counterpart to the South Albertas in 4 CAD. 1 Armoured Brigade was disbanded and the 2nd was renumbered as the 5th, retaining the 8th Hussars and British Columbia Dragoons and adding the Strathconas from 1 Armoured Brigade. The 1st Hussars and the Fort Garry Horse joined the Sherbrooke Fusiliers in 3 Army Tank Brigade.

II Canadian Corps headquarters was created on 15 January and General Sansom was promoted and appointed commander of the new corps. His successor at 5 CAD was Major-General C.R.S. Stein, who had commanded 2 Armoured Brigade for some seven months in 1942.

Also disbanded at this time were the squadrons provided by the 6th Duke of Connaught's Royal Canadian Hussars and the 7th/11th Hussars for the headquarters of 5 CAD and 2 Armoured Brigade. The headquarters squadron of 1 Armoured Brigade, supplied by the Prince Edward Island Light Horse, was assigned as the defence company for II Corps headquarters.

Amidst the turbulence of this process, yet another reconnaissance regiment was

Removing Engine. Painting by W.A. Ogilvie of repairs to a Ram tank in a workshop in England. Units of the Armoured Corps were totally dependent on the RCOC/RCEME mechanics to keep their tanks running throughout the whole of the war, and they became as much a part of the Corps as men who wore regimental badges. (Canadian War Museum 13528)

Members of the 4th Princess Louise Dragoon Guards taking part in a 1 Division exercise near Hastings in January 1943. (NAC PA177142)

Ram tanks of the Canadian Grenadier Guards training in England, 1943.

being created to serve as organic reconnaissance for First Canadian Army. On 25 January the Royal Montreal Regiment was converted from a machine-gun battalion and brought into the Canadian Armoured Corps as the 32nd Reconnaissance Regiment.

There is no doubt that this reorganization adversely affected the orderly progression of training in all units, especially in the new armoured reconnaissance regiments, the Horse Guards and the South Albertas. The theory behind their creation was indisputable: armoured divisions needed tank-heavy recce units for close reconnaissance tasks that could involve fighting

(Left) The divisional sleeve patch of 5 Armoured Division. Unit titles were embroidered on the patch. Division patches measured 7 x 5 cm.

(Right) The divisional patch of 4 Armoured Division. Units within this division wore their own regimental shoulder titles.

The Canadian Armoured Corps in Britain, January 1943

First Canadian Army
Army Recce Regt:
Royal Montreal Regiment

Armoured Delivery Regt:
The Elgin Regiment

I Canadian Corps

Corps Recce Regt:
Royal Canadian Dragoons

II Canadian Corps

Corps Recce Regt:
12th Manitoba Dragoons
Corps Defence Coy:
PEI Light Horse

5th Armoured Division

Div Recce Regt:
Governor General's Horse Guards

5th Armoured Brigade
Lord Strathcona's Horse
8th New Brunswick Hussars
British Columbia Dragoons
The Westminster Regiment (Motor)

11th Infantry Brigade
Perth Regiment
Cape Breton Highlanders
Irish Regiment of Canada

4th Armoured Division

Div Recce Regt:
South Alberta Regiment

4th Armoured Brigade
Governor General's Foot Guards
Canadian Grenadier Guards
British Columbia Regiment
The Lake Superior Regiment (Motor)

10th Infantry Brigade
Lincoln and Welland Regiment
Algonquin Regiment
Argyll and Sutherland
Highlanders

1st Division
Div Recce Regt:
4th Princess Louise Dragoon
Guards

2nd Division
Div Recce Regt:
8th Recce Regt (14th Hussars)

3rd Division
Div Recce Regt:
17th Duke of York's Royal Canadian
Hussars

1st Army Tank Brigade
Ontario Regiment
Three Rivers Regiment
Calgary Regiment

3rd Army Tank Brigade
1st Hussars
Fort Garry Horse
Sherbrooke Fusilier Regiment

to gain information. However, how they were to do the job with their bizarre mixture of tanks and Universal carriers had not been thought through, and several months were spent in each of the units developing workable procedures and tactics.

Perhaps among the most disenchanted were two of the units assigned to the *ad hoc* 3 Army Tank Brigade, a temporary formation which was never formally authorized by the Minister. Both the 1st Hussars and the Fort Garrys, old, well-established cavalry regiments and the first units mobilized at the outset of the war, deeply resented their designation as 'army tank regiments'. The status of this brigade remained very much in doubt for the next six months, but the units carried on with training while temporarily attached to 4 CAD.

Canadian Tanks Manoeuvring. Painting by W.A. Ogilvie depicting Ram IIs on exercise. (Canadian War Museum 13268)

EXERCISE *SPARTAN*

The reorganization had just been completed when 5 CAD and 1 Army Tank Brigade deployed into the field with much of the remainder of First Canadian Army for Exercise *Spartan*, the largest Canadian manoeuvres ever conducted in Britain. 4 CAD did not participate because it had only just begun a period of individual trades and crew training, but many of its officers served as umpires, and 3 Army Tank Brigade was also excluded because, as an *ad hoc* formation, it had no formal operational role.

Spartan took place between 27 February and 12 March, 1943, and was intended to practice First Canadian Army in the role of breaking out of a bridgehead that had already been established by other forces. This would be, of course, its actual task in the forthcoming invasion of France. The Army's invasion force consisted of an unusual and very unbalanced grouping of I Canadian Corps, with an all-infantry force of 2nd and 3rd Divisions, the newly formed II Canadian Corps, with an all-armoured force consisting of 5 CAD and the British Guards Armoured Divi-

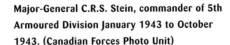

Major-General C.R.S. Stein, commander of 5th Armoured Division January 1943 to October 1943. (Canadian Forces Photo Unit)

sion, along with XII British Corps and 1 Canadian Army Tank Brigade. A total of nineteen air squadrons were tasked in support. The defending 'enemy', simulating the German Sixth Army, consisted of two British corps.

General McNaughton described *Spartan* as "a strict test of the physical condition and endurance of the troops, their proficiency in movement and tactics and of the ability of commanders and staffs to administer, handle and fight their formations and units." This aim was grossly overambitious, but typical of the inexperienced Canadian commanders and staffs of the day. There is a rule of thumb that no more than three levels of command can be tested or trained effectively during any field exercise but *Spartan* planners intended to involve at least seven.

For the armoured regiments, the exercise was a severe test of their endurance: they moved nearly continually from one harbour to another, almost always on roads. The troops got little sleep and little opportunity to eat because of a seemingly endless succession of orders to "move

Churchill tanks of the Three Rivers Regiment during Exercise *Spartan,* March 1943. (NAC PA146661)

A Ram II belonging to the Governor General's Foot Guards on exercise with infantry near Hindhead, England, April 1943. Many of the early Ram tanks shipped to Britain came without guns. (NAC PA146662)

now, out!" Orders from higher headquarters were routinely countermanded and traffic was often snarled because of poor staff planning. Other than toward the end of the exercise there was no tactical deployment, and thus few operational lessons were learned at unit level. The units were in fact little more than training aids for the senior headquarters staffs. If anything useful was gained by the men in the tank crews, it was to learn how to live in their tanks for long periods.

There is no doubt, however, that *Spartan* proved to be a good training vehicle for commanders and staff at brigade, division and corps levels, if only because it brought out many weaknesses in operational and logistics procedures that needed to be fixed. First Army headquarters, for example, on many occasions issued orders which they expected to be implemented by troops on the ground within six to eight hours, demonstrating a total lack of understanding by the staff of the time needed for routine battle procedures at each subordinate level of command. Several gross errors were committed by the untrained staff at II Corps headquarters, including the regrouping of the armoured divisions so that both infantry brigades came under 5 CAD and both armoured brigades were placed under the Guards Division. Nevertheless, they had an excellent introduction to the detailed staff planning that must be done at that level if troops are to be successfully committed to battle and then provided with the necessary administrative and logistics support.

DIVISIONAL COLLECTIVE TRAINING

Immediately following the conclusion of *Spartan,* both 4 and 5 CADs began a long period of intensive collective training, starting with squadron field training and rapidly progressing to exercises at brigade and divisional levels.

4 Armoured Brigade had deployed to camps in the vicinity of Hove, near the south coast, in mid-January 1943, and within a month all of the regiments had their full complement of Ram II tanks and Universal carriers. By the time *Spartan* ended, in mid-March, all units had reached a level of tactical proficiency that allowed 4 CAD to conduct two major exercises on the South Downs in May. *Hotspur* focused

primarily on squadron-level operations, beginning with squadrons advancing to seize a 'pivot of manoeuvre' in the face of light resistance, and then practising deployment of the tanks on the objective and the subsequent hand-over to an infantry company. Exercise *Quattuor* took the tactical scenario to brigade level with emphasis on breaking into and overrunning a strongly-held enemy position by both armour and infantry, as well as on the use of massed flamethrowers as a close assault weapon in support of the tanks. In June and early July the division exercised the South Albertas in the roles of the armoured recce regiment as divisional advanced guard and rearguard.

The units of 5 CAD had already reached a more advanced stage of training, so 5 Armoured Brigade concentrated on regimental-level tactics during the spring of 1943 and the division conducted only one short major exercise, *Flankem,* in this period, when the aim was to practice armoured regiments in tactical movement.

While training was, of course, the main preoccupation in both armoured divisions, there was time for other diversions. Regimental, brigade and divisional sports meets were always popular activities and many of the men took every opportunity to take leave. London, only an hour away by train, always had a magnificent selection of plays, vaudeville and musical entertainment, and Glasgow and Edinburgh, while further afield, were also popular destinations. The one thing that Canadian troops remembered with greatest affection of their time in England, however, was the British pub. Regardless of where they were based, there was always a favourite pub, "the pivot of their social migrations and adventuring" as the 8th Hussars regimental history recalls.

> In Headley, there were two, the Wheat Sheaf and the Holly Bush. ... The Holly Bush was run by a lady named Sally, a fat lady of ruddy countenance, straight unpretentious hair-do, and a habit of speaking the King's English out of the corner of her mouth. ... In Crowborough, the Crow and Gate was their home away from home. They liked Mr. and Mrs. John Dean, the people who ran it, and they liked Mrs. Dean's mother whom everybody called Mum, a lady who saw not a few Hussars through financial difficulties. Nightly they descended and were warmly welcomed and passed a satisfying time or, after a quick one or two, went on to other things.

At the beginning of July 1943, the whole of 5 CAD moved to a sparsely populated area near Thetford in Norfolk, where a battle training area large enough to accommodate full-scale divisional exercises had been set aside. The units were housed in Nissen-hut camps along the perimeter of the training area, and for two months they participated in one field exercise after another. The Strathcona history describes the experience:

A Strathcona Ram is bombed up during firing practice, April 1943. (NAC PA162757)

The tanks were made ready for the strenuous work ahead, and, on the morning of July 6th, the schemes got under way. From that day until August 10th there was virtually no let up from the exercise which started on a regimental level and worked up to full divisional battles. The country was by far the best we had encountered for tank training…. The first exercises … were regimental and consisted of river crossings, minefield breaching and infantry-tank cooperation. The second group … lasted two days each and were more complicated in that they were based on more difficult tactical situations and involved the use of Regimental Groups for the first time. Then followed Exercises *Rabbit, Sherman* and *Hardtack* which lasted one, two and three days respectively, and these involved the whole of 5 Armoured Brigade. Finally came the divisional schemes, *Grizzly* and *Snaffle,* lasting four days each; these brought all the lessons covered in the preliminary training together with problems of road space and traffic control.

When the manoeuvres in Norfolk came to an end, in mid-September 1943, 5 CAD again moved south, this time to camps at Barton Stacey, near Winchester, to take part in Exercise *Harlequin*, the first detailed test of the intricate plan to move a large force, in comparative secrecy, through a series of staging areas to ports on the English Channel where embarkation for the invasion force would eventually take place. 4 Armoured Brigade

South Alberta Regiment crews get a briefing from their troop leader during a tactical exercise, April 1943. (NAC PA146663)

A British Columbia Regiment tank crew cleaning guns, July 1943. (NAC PA167116)

was also part of this enormous pre-invasion movement scheme. The troops involved in *Harlequin* did not know it, but the exercise was also part of a major deception scheme intended to convince the Germans that a cross-channel invasion, aimed at the Pas de Calais, was about to take place.

In early September it was the turn of 4 CAD to move to the battle training area in Norfolk. The pattern of the training was very similar to that of 5 CAD, with only the names of the major exercises changed. The first two weeks were given over to squadron operations, as noted in the regimental history of the Governor General's Foot Guards:

Daily the squadrons swept across the moors in deployed formations while gunners laid on imaginary anti-tank guns. ... In harbours the gunners cleaned their guns and drivers did maintenance while the co-drivers bent their backs to their unhappy task of digging slit trenches in the hard chalky ground. Here the tanks first became homes from which the crews lived as well as fought, and the refreshing brew of tea characterized each halt.

Following a short period of 'inter-arms' demonstrations, where tank crews and infantrymen briefly lived together in each others' camps, the field training continued at a hectic pace — first weeks of regimental-level schemes, then brigade exercises, and finally the divisional exercises *Grizzly II* and *Bridoon*. Brigadier-General Pat Grieve, then a lieutenant with the Canadian Grenadier Guards, recalled that "there wasn't much tactical realism in these exercises; it was all this naval formation-type of manoeuvre. I can't remember any exercise where we worked in support of the infantry. On the final exercise we simply drove to the objective, everyone moving at once."

In *Bridoon* 4 CAD was pitted against the 9th British Armoured Division in a relatively 'free-play' manoeuvre to practise the meeting engagement. Led by the South Alberta Regiment, 4 Armoured Brigade was tasked to conduct a rapid advance over a distance of some 25 kilometres to seize an imaginary chromium mine before the 'enemy' got there. It appears that Worthy may have indulged in a wee effort to deceive his British opponents about how this would be carried out, allowing a copy of a fake division operation order to fall into British hands. When the exercise began on 2 November, Canadian tanks literally raced through to the objective, and within 24 hours nearly half of the British tanks had been 'destroyed'. The

British complained of the Canadians' "unorthodox and un-sporting" methods, but even when the umpires insisted on a re-play the outcome was much the same and the exercise was called off three days ahead of schedule.

Bridoon was undoubtedly a turning point for 4 CAD and Worthy proclaimed that he had "complete confidence in his division." But for reasons that have never been satisfactorily explained, *Bridoon* proved also to be the last major field exercise ever conducted by the division. One might question, as DND historian Stephen Harris has done in his history of the Foot Guards, "that something as complex as an armoured division could be perfectly refined and honed after just one such test."

In the meanwhile, it was a busy and exciting time for those serving in 5 CAD. While still based in Barton Stacey, yet another divisional exercise was conducted over the Lambourne Downs near Oxford. Exercise *Ditto* focused on the use of the armoured recce regiment to obtain information on opposing troops by fighting, on liaison between engineers and the assaulting troops, and on the conduct of a deliberate attack. The exercise ended on 12 October and the units moved back to familiar billets in Hove, on the south coast, only to learn that the division was to be deployed to Italy almost at once, along with I Corps Headquarters, under a plan code-named Operation *Timberwolf*. As a security cover the troops were told they were going to Northern Ireland, but the issue of tropical uniforms made many suspicious of this story.

Major General C.R.S. Stein was relieved of command of the division on 18 October, "owing to ill health". Brigadier R.O.G. Morton, the divisional Commander, Royal Artillery, was appointed to temporary command until the division arrived in Italy. The story of 5 CAD in Italy is continued in Chapter 8.

After its exercises in Norfolk, 4 CAD moved back to Sussex in November. A training instruction for the period January to March 1944 directed that tank-infantry cooperation was to be stressed by both the armoured and infantry brigades, but this never happened in the intended way; the only tank-infantry training carried out was done by the South Albertas with 10 Infantry Brigade. By early February, the process of crew conversion received heavy emphasis when operational 75mm-gunned Sherman tanks began to arrive in the regiments.

It was a major blow to the division when, on 29 February 1944, Major-General 'Fighting Frank' Worthington was re-

Major-General George Kitching, DSO, commander of 4th Armoured Division March to August 1944.

lieved of command of the division. Worthy was deeply disappointed that he was not going to be allowed to lead the division he had founded and trained when it finally went into battle. But he had expected that this might happen, as all too often he had been highly vocal in expressing views unpopular with the higher command. The official reason was that, at 55, Worthy was too old, but the truth was that Lieutenant-General Guy Simonds, his immediate superior, disliked Worthy, and did not want him. So Worthy was sent back to Camp Borden as the camp commandant. Subsequent events, in Normandy, suggest that it might have been better for everybody (except the Germans!) had he remained in command.

Simonds' good friend Major-General George Kitching succeeded Worthy. General Kitching had been Simonds' GSO 1 (chief operations staff officer) in 1st Division Headquarters during the early stages of the Italian campaign, and then, for a brief but costly period, had commanded 11 Infantry Brigade. He brought with him from Italy two new brigade commanders. Brigadier Leslie Booth, who had commanded the Three Rivers Regiment in Italy, took over 4 Armoured Brigade from J.D.B. Smith, and Brigadier J.C. Jefferson, former commanding officer of the Loyal Edmonton Regiment in Italy, was appointed to command 10 Infantry Brigade. There was at this time also an attempt to provide some operational leavening in the regiments of 4 CAD by cross-posting a few senior officers with battle experience. Major Hershel 'Snuffy' Smith of the Ontario Regiment, of Casa Berardi fame, and Major Ned Amy of the Calgary Regiment were sent to the Canadian Grenadier Guards, while Captains Bill Mooers and Pim Watkins went to the Foot Guards. At the same time several Three Rivers officers were posted to 2 Armoured Brigade.

On taking command, General Kitching pleaded with Simonds to be permitted to conduct a series of field exercises with 4 Division, both to hone the division's skills and to allow him to get to know the abilities of his subordinates, but he was refused. He later wrote in his memoirs, *Mud and Green Fields*:

We were not allowed to hold any divisional exercises with everyone participating and I think that was what was needed. While the individual regiments had reached a good standard of training, the essential cooperation between armour, infantry and artillery had not been practiced to the

Starting on Manoeuvres. **Painting by E.J. Hughes depicting Fox armoured cars and Dingo scout cars of the Royal Canadian Dragoons preparing to depart on an exercise. (Canadian War Museum)**

regiments of the armoured brigade also added a 17-pounder 'Firefly' Sherman to each tank troop, as well as a troop of Crusader anti-aircraft tanks.

And at this time the newest of the recce regiments, the Royal Montreal Regiment, was disbanded. The manpower shortage was beginning to hit home and First Canadian Army could no longer justify maintaining its own organic reconnaissance capability. The officers and men of the RMR were dispersed, primarily to other recce units, although many were also sent to reinforce units in 4 Armoured Brigade despite their lack of training on tanks.

THE ARMOURED CORPS STAFF AT FIRST CANADIAN ARMY

When the first Canadian Armoured Corps formations arrived in Britain in 1941, the Canadians for good reasons looked to the Royal Armoured Corps for policy on doctrine and training and for technical guidance and assistance. The RAC, in turn, tended to regard the Canadian formations and units as being part of their extended family, even though there was always tacit acknowledgement of their distinct national identity, and they were most generous in providing training and technical facilities. There was, however, always a problem in that there was no central Canadian Armoured Corps authority in Britain to deal with such things as standardization of training or the dissemination of distinctly Canadian armour information or lessons. In some respects, the Director, Royal Armoured Corps filled these functions, but in most instances things 'armoured' were simply dealt with by Overseas Military Headquarters in London, the staff of First Canadian Army Headquarters, and by the divisional and brigade staffs. Important policy issues were usually referred back to Canada, and in some instances the Officer Administering the Corps, in Camp Borden, was consulted. One of the results of the lack of a central Canadian Armoured Corps authority in Britain was, for example, a considerable difference in training standards in the units of the two armoured divisions and in the independent armoured brigades.

This general problem was, to a degree, rectified in August 1943 when the staff position of 'Brigadier, Royal Armoured Corps' (BRAC) was established at First Canadian Army Headquarters. The BRAC organization began with a staff of two majors, but eventually grew to include a lieutenant-colonel, a

extent it should have been. Nor had the Brigade and Divisional headquarters enough experience of command and control, on exercises of some duration, that would have taxed their resources and taught them lessons.

In early May 1944 the division was ordered to waterproof all of its vehicles in preparation for the invasion of Normandy, a procedure that prevented them being driven until the waterproofing could be removed. Thus, in the three months prior to the division going into battle, no training could be done other than map exercises, small arms range firing and route marches. This was hardly the best way to bring a formation to peak efficiency on the eve of its first battle.

A final bit of restructuring took place in March 1944, when General Montgomery decreed that all armoured reconnaissance regiments in 21 Army Group were to be organized as standard armoured regiments, even while retaining the recce designation. Accordingly, the South Alberta Regiment replaced only recently issued Stuarts with Shermans in all three squadrons, retaining 'Honeys' only in the RHQ recce troop. Almost at the same time the South Albertas were permanently placed under command of 10 Infantry Brigade, thus creating the only such brigade group in the Canadian Army during the war. The

major and a captain, along with a separate technical staff of a lieutenant-colonel and a major. The BRAC was, strictly speaking, only an adviser to the Army Commander, but he had broad authority for liaison with subordinate formations and armoured units, he could raise questions with the Army staff, and he was allowed to communicate on training matters directly with the Officer Administering the Corps. He was also the principal point of contact with the major-general, RAC at 21 Army Group Headquarters, and thus received information on British armour developments and lessons learned which were passed down to Canadian armoured formations.

The first BRAC was a British officer who only held the post for a week. He was succeeded on 27 February 1944 by Brigadier Robert Wyman, newly returned to England from commanding 1 Armoured Brigade in Italy. When Wyman moved to command of 2 Armoured Brigade in April 1944, he was replaced by Brigadier Norman Gianelli, and finally, in December 1944, Brigadier John Bingham was appointed, holding the post until July 1945.

THE ARMOURED CAR REGIMENTS

With the reorganization of the Armoured Corps in January 1943, Canada's two armoured car regiments – the RCD and the 12th Manitoba Dragoons – were given a new role as reconnaissance troops for I and II Canadian Corps respectively. As Corps troops, their task was now the conduct of 'medium' reconnaissance. This was officially described as the collection of information on enemy strengths and deployment, and on vital topographic features, out to a depth of some eighty kilometres forward of the leading combat elements, in order to enable the corps commander to make timely plans.

The new role had little immediate effect within either regiment, on organization or on tactical training. Both, with a strength of 858 all ranks, had identical organizations: four fighting (reconnaissance) squadrons and a headquarters squadron. Each of the recce squadrons was made up of five armoured car troops and an assault troop. The armoured car troops, with fourteen men, had two armoured cars and two scout cars, while the 35-man assault troop was mounted in ten quarter-

ton trucks. During the time when the units were conducting crew trades training, they had been equipped with a variety of vehicles, Daimler, Humber and Fox armoured cars and Daimler Dingo and Ford Lynx scout cars, but shortly after being tasked as Corps troops, the Dingos were replaced with American-built Staghound armoured cars.

The tactical employment of an armoured car regiment was one of those things that the British had never quite sorted out. When the RCD had begun to conduct troop-level training in the late spring of 1942 it was well-understood that standard reconnaissance principles would apply, but as there were no tactics manuals in existence there was some uncertainty as to how their heavier capability ought to be used. To rectify this deficiency, and explain to senior commanders and staffs how the regiment should be employed, Major Jim Roberts, the second-in-command, put together a tactical handbook in the autumn of 1942. *A Canadian Armoured Car Regiment* was published in August 1943, and when Roberts became commanding officer of the 12th Dragoons a month later, it was taken into use there, becoming a quasi-official doctrine and tactics manual.

The basis for armoured car recce tactics was the concept that each troop was in fact an 'officer patrol', which could effectively cover one route in an advance or withdrawal. The fast-moving scout car section would usually lead, moving accordion-fashion from one observation position to another, while the armoured car section, led by its troop leader, would move one tactical bound behind the scout cars, ready to deploy and engage the enemy with their 37mm and machine-guns if the scout cars came under fire, or lay a smoke screen with the 2-inch bomb thrower to assist the scout cars in breaking contact. (There was some thought at this early stage of training that an armoured car troop could, to a degree, fight to gain information, and, by bringing in the squadron's assault troop, clear a lightly-held

A 12th Manitoba Dragoons Staghound armoured car on exercise, December 1943. (NAC PA144146)

A Fort Garry Horse troop during a live-firing battle run, July 1943. (NAC PA146665)

enemy position or seize and hold ground of tactical importance for a limited period of time.) With twenty such 'officer patrols', an armoured car regiment was, in theory, able to cover a front of about forty kilometres.

Equipped with wheeled vehicles, the armoured car regiments were not limited, as the tank units were, to doing field training and exercises in the few designated manoeuvre areas. Both units were thus able to train extensively along the intricate road network of England, occasionally ranging as far away as Scotland. When the RCD, without their vehicles, deployed to Italy with I Canadian Corps in October 1943, the regiment was both tactically proficient and highly skilled in the gathering and passage of information. The 12th Dragoons carried on with their programme of training until May 1944, by which time they, too, had built a reputation within their corps for exceptional competence.

2 ARMOURED BRIGADE

The final step in the restructuring of the Canadian Armoured Corps was not taken until the end of July 1943. 2 Army Tank Brigade, which had been training in Camp Borden for more than a year, arrived in England in late June, when General McNaughton's hope of being able to retain three independent tank brigades – in theory one for each of the infantry divisions – had been rejected by Ottawa. It thus became necessary to disband one of the tank brigades then in Britain. Logically this might have been the fate of the *ad hoc* 3 Army Tank Brigade, as it was the most recently created formation. But McNaughton had been very careful to include in that brigade the only two Militia cavalry regiments that had been mobilized at the very outbreak of the war, the 1st Hussars and the Fort Garry Horse, and both were by now among the best trained units in the Corps.

To give at least the appearance of impartiality to the disbandment process, First Canadian Army decided that a comprehensive competitive test of operational capability would be held, and at the conclusion of these tests it was decided that 3 Brigade – the 1st Hussars, the Fort Garry Horse and the Sherbrooke Fusiliers Regiment – would be retained. The unfortunate units of 2 Brigade – the Grey and Simcoe Foresters, the 16/22nd Saskatchewan Horse and the Halifax Rifles – however well trained they were, would be disbanded. The announcement came on 29 July 1943, and to this day it is a controversial issue. Reporting the event, the Halifax Rifles history comments that, "Today the Regiment is disbanded, but the spirit of the regiment will live on in the deeds that will be performed by its former members in the units they are reinforcing. The honours they will win for other units will accrue to their old Regiment, The Halifax Rifles, after the war."

3 Army Tank Brigade was redesignated as 2 Armoured Brigade on 1 August 1943 and almost immediately earmarked for participation in the assault landings in France in support of 3 Canadian Division. An intensive eight-month programme of training had already been mapped out for the Normandy invasion force and from the outset armoured regiments were paired with an infantry brigade, both for training and for the planned operation: the 1st Hussars with 7 Infantry Brigade, the Fort Garrys with 8 Brigade and the Sherbrookes with the 9th.

The first phase of training for the invasion force consisted of intensive familiarization with the mechanics of amphibious assault operations, conducted at special bases at Inverary and Castle Toward in Scotland between August and October. Training was organized so that each regiment progressed from learning basic drills and procedures through to full-scale brigade assault landings. Each, in turn, spent three weeks at one of the

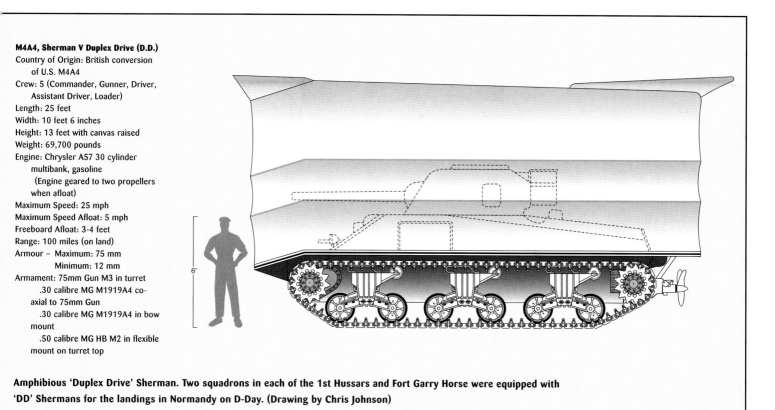

M4A4, Sherman V Duplex Drive (D.D.)
Country of Origin: British conversion
   of U.S. M4A4
Crew: 5 (Commander, Gunner, Driver,
   Assistant Driver, Loader)
Length: 25 feet
Width: 10 feet 6 inches
Height: 13 feet with canvas raised
Weight: 69,700 pounds
Engine: Chrysler A57 30 cylinder
   multibank, gasoline
    (Engine geared to two propellers
   when afloat)
Maximum Speed: 25 mph
Maximum Speed Afloat: 5 mph
Freeboard Afloat: 3-4 feet
Range: 100 miles (on land)
Armour – Maximum: 75 mm
      Minimum: 12 mm
Armament: 75mm Gun M3 in turret
   .30 calibre MG M1919A4 co-
   axial to 75mm Gun
   .30 calibre MG M1919A4 in bow
   mount
   .50 calibre MG HB M2 in flexible
   mount on turret top

6'

Amphibious 'Duplex Drive' Sherman. Two squadrons in each of the 1st Hussars and Fort Garry Horse were equipped with 'DD' Shermans for the landings in Normandy on D-Day. (Drawing by Chris Johnson)

Combined Operations centres with their affiliated infantry brigade, and the tank crews initially focused on loading and unloading with Tank Landing Craft (LCTs) and Tank Landing Ships (LSTs), and then repeatedly practised landing on a variety of beaches, both in daylight and in darkness. Realism was added in the later exercises by live fire from artillery aboard LCTs, and smoke screens laid by aircraft.

Back at their home bases in southern England, the officers and men of the regiments got to know their infantry counterparts during the course of a series of battalion and brigade-level amphibious exercises at a variety of locations along the Channel coast. The tank crews also got their first introduction to the Sherman tank over the autumn months. Each regiment spent ten days at the advanced tank gunnery range at Kirkcudbright in southern Scotland, where RAC instructors ran conversion courses and supervised the firing of the 75mm guns. The Sherbrooke Fusilier Regiment assisted in the training of artillery drivers who were to crew gunless tanks to be used by forward observation officers of the division's field artillery regiments.

In mid-November, 2 Armoured Brigade units were relocated to camps on the coast north-west of the Isle of Wight so they could more readily participate in a further series of amphibious training exercises. The 1st Hussars were housed at Sway, the Fort Garrys at Milford-on-Sea, and the Sherbrookes at New Milton. While most of the exercises understandably concentrated on putting troops ashore in the right place and at the right time, Exercise *Roundabout,* conducted in early December,

focused for the first time on the breakout from a bridgehead. A number of important lessons came out of this experience, the most important of which was that tank-infantry cooperation skills, so essential in the breakout battle, were notably lacking even in the otherwise well-trained units of both the armoured and infantry brigades.

In the year after the ill-fated Dieppe raid a herculean effort had been made to overcome the many weaknesses that had been revealed in amphibious assault-landing capability, and this was especially true in the case of specialized armoured vehicles needed to support the infantry in an assault on a heavily-defended beach. Among the desirable specialist equipment that had been identified was the need for a 'swimming' tank, one that could go ashore with, or even before, the infantry to provide the pinpoint-accurate heavy firepower needed to overcome beach defences. The Duplex-Drive tank was thus conceived by British engineers with the 79th Armoured Division. Its very existence was one of the best-kept secrets of the war.

The DD-tank, as it was known, was a standard M4A3 Sherman fitted with a retractable canvas-screen flotation device attached to the hull to provide buoyancy, and two propellers in the rear which could be engaged on entering the water by a spade grip lever in the driver's compartment. In the water the tank was steered by swinging the propellers, either from the driver's compartment or from the back deck by means of a long pole. When afloat in a relatively calm sea, the DD-tank could reach a speed of 4.5 knots.

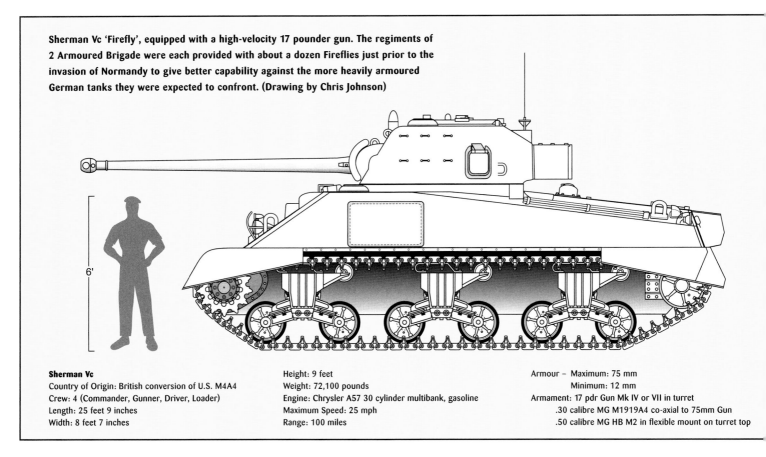

Sherman Vc 'Firefly', equipped with a high-velocity 17 pounder gun. The regiments of 2 Armoured Brigade were each provided with about a dozen Fireflies just prior to the invasion of Normandy to give better capability against the more heavily armoured German tanks they were expected to confront. (Drawing by Chris Johnson)

6'

Sherman Vc
Country of Origin: British conversion of U.S. M4A4
Crew: 4 (Commander, Gunner, Driver, Loader)
Length: 25 feet 9 inches
Width: 8 feet 7 inches

Height: 9 feet
Weight: 72,100 pounds
Engine: Chrysler A57 30 cylinder multibank, gasoline
Maximum Speed: 25 mph
Range: 100 miles

Armour – Maximum: 75 mm
Minimum: 12 mm
Armament: 17 pdr Gun Mk IV or VII in turret
.30 calibre MG M1919A4 co-axial to 75mm Gun
.50 calibre MG HB M2 in flexible mount on turret top

As 7 and 8 Brigades had been selected to form the assault wave of the Canadian landing, their affiliated armoured regiments, the 1st Hussars and the Fort Garry Horse, were to accompany them onto the beaches. Two squadrons of each regiment were thus designated to be equipped with DD-tanks, and the training of crews in the use of the equipment began in greatest secrecy in late December 1943.

Trooper (later Sergeant) Jim Paisley was the driver of one of the 1st Hussars' DD-tanks:

We started our training at Great Yarmouth, where there was a lake, using DD-Valentine tanks, and my first reaction when I saw them was to think 'they'll never float!'. One of the first things the crews had to do was underwater escape training using the same apparatus submarine crews trained on, a big tank that could be filled with water in a few seconds. There was a Valentine hull at the bottom that the crews had to take their place in, the instructors would then flood it, and we had to come to the top. After that we learned to inflate and deflate the screens, and practiced swimming the tanks out on the lake. Later, at Gosport, we did a lot of loading onto landing craft, launching the tanks off the ramps, swimming the tanks out on the Solent, and landing on beaches – all kinds of manoeuvres.

Before going to Great Yarmouth every man was told how important it was to maintain absolute secrecy about what they were doing, and it is to their credit that the secret was never revealed, even within the two regiments, until D-Day. The DD-training continued until the end of April 1944 at Stokes Bay, Lyme Bay and a highly secret installation near Fawley codenamed *Shangri-la*.

It was only after we drew our battle tanks at the factory in Birmingham that we started training with the DD-Shermans, but the techniques were almost the same except the landing craft ramps had to be extended so we could get further out in the water when we launched.

To launch the tanks we would first inflate the pillars and put the struts in place. When the ramp was down, we would creep down into the water in low gear. As soon as the tank had full flotation the driver would engage the props and third gear, and we'd be under way.

3 Division and 2 Armoured Brigade formally came under command of I British Corps for training and subsequent operations on 30 January 1944. Among the early effects of this new chain of command was a directive to resolve the tank-infantry cooperation problems that had been noted over the past months. Accordingly, in February each of the armoured regiments began a nine-day period of intensive training with their

affiliated infantry brigade, devoting three days with each infantry unit. The first day with each battalion was devoted to an impressive firepower demonstration and general familiarization when the infantry soldiers were encouraged to crawl inside the vehicles, go for rides and even drive the tanks. On the second day there was a discussion with infantry officers of a tactical situation about a deliberate attack on a heavily defended area, where each officer was called on to explain the type of support he might need and what he could do for the other arm. Following this discussion the scenario was played out on the ground with a full tank squadron and company of infantry, and great emphasis was placed on how targets could be indicated to the tanks by means of bursts of machine-gun tracer rounds.

On the final day, a squadron of tanks went through the same exercise with each infantry company in turn, using live ammunition. This three-day training session with each of the battalions was undoubtedly of value but it was of far too short a duration to instil any depth of understanding of how the two arms needed to cooperate intimately on the battlefield, or to work out useful tactical drills. For the Hussars and Garrys it proved to be the last such training session before going into action, although the Sherbrooke Fusiliers were able to conduct several additional exercises with units of 9 Infantry Brigade.

While each of the regiments of 2 Armoured Brigade were issued a handful of Sherman tanks beginning in January, it was not until early April that the re-equipment was complete, including some of the new Fireflies, one of which was issued to each tank troop (except in the DD-squadrons) to help cope with the heavy armour of the German Mark V Panther and Mark VI Tiger tanks. Firefly gunners and crew commanders had only one opportunity to fire these new guns on the Warcop range. The tanks had to be 'run-in' for a hundred or more kilometres, after which they were waterproofed and then put into well-camouflaged storage at Fort Gomer, near Lee-on-Solent, until orders came for loading onto LCTs for the invasion.

Brigadier Robert Wyman arrived to take command of 2 Armoured Brigade on 15 April 1944, replacing N.A. Gianelli who had departed on 23 March. Wyman had commanded 1 Amoured Brigade in the early stages of the Italian campaign, and was one of several seasoned veterans brought back to England to take command of formations for the invasion of Normandy

There was general anticipation that the day of the invasion was drawing near when on 25 April the brigade was mustered near Fort Gomer for an inspection by a "distinguished visitor," who turned out to be His Majesty The King. This was the first occasion when all members of the brigade wore the black and blue diamond sleeve patch on their uniforms.

Fabius III, the last invasion exercise, began on 29 April. While it was intended to practice the entire operation from marshalling and embarkation through to landing and breakout, weather conditions caused it to be cancelled before the landings took place. Finally, on 25 May, the brigade was put in quarantine near Gosport, and a day later the officers were briefed on Operation *Overlord.* This story continues in Chapter 12.

* * *

In the years since the Second World War historians and veterans alike have asked whether formations and units of the Canadian Armoured Corps were as well prepared to go into battle as they might have been, given the relatively lengthy period of training in Britain. There is no simple answer, in part because the standard of training achieved varied from one formation to another, even from one regiment to another, within the same formation. Generalization may thus be unfair to some. Then, too, training can never replicate actual combat, so there will always be a painful period of learning and adjustment by green troops when put into battle. However, the question can not be evaded, because there were instances in early battles, both in Italy and Normandy, when armoured units did not perform especially well.

The Defence Medal, awarded after the war for six months of service in Britain.

Technical and crew trades training carried out in Britain clearly was of high quality. The tank, armoured car and scout car crews knew their vehicles and equipment extremely well and were proficient in using and maintaining them. This was an aspect of training that everyone could relate to, even commanders who themselves were not technically inclined. Results of training were obvious – tanks ran or they didn't, targets were hit or they weren't, radios operated or they didn't. It was old cavalry stuff. Everyone understood that if the 'mount' didn't work, the gun it carried was of no use. If the gun couldn't hit the enemy target first, the vehicle mounting it would probably be knocked out by the enemy.

Tactical training was a different story. Training in manoeuvring the 'mount' on the battlefield was hampered by a combination of misguided, if not totally erroneous, doctrine, and by a general lack of understanding of armoured operations by the senior officers who organized and directed training, both at unit and formation levels.

From the perspective of sixty years later it is easy to forget that no one in the Canadian Armoured Corps in 1941 had any experience of employing tanks on the field of battle and the British experience in North Africa was not of much help in preparing Canadian regiments to operate on the very different battlefields of Italy or Normandy. It is probably fair to say that most units, especially the armoured regiments, were not adequately prepared for their first battle. They did, however, have the essential skills that enabled them to learn from their early mistakes and adapt relatively rapidly to the ground over which they were to fight and the tactics employed by the enemy.

If there was one major failing in the training carried out in Britain, it was that the all-arms nature of modern battlefield was almost entirely neglected. British doctrine, which governed the tactical teaching of the day, had tried to absorb the lessons of the *Blitzkrieg,* but failed to understand the all-arms nature of German operations, and the wrong conclusions had been drawn. Everyone – armour, infantry and artillery – seemed content to train to fight their own separate battles, and the blame for this shortsightedness must be widely shared. Tank-infantry cooperation, given little emphasis by the doctrine of the day, got lip service during training: a few days of familiarization, but no extensive practice except in a very few units. There were thus no well-tried drills or standard operating procedures in place for armoured, infantry and artillery working together. The separate arms did not understand the others' needs or expectations, or, more importantly, what could be accomplished by working as a close-knit team. That had to be learned the hard way, on the battlefields of Italy and France, and there was a high price that had to be paid for that neglect.

This cartoon was presented to Major-General Worthington on 1 February 1942 by the men of 1 CATB Ordnance Field Park, RCOC, to mark his departure from the brigade. It no doubt reflected the attitude of many troops to formal inspections by the 'brass'.

CHAPTER 6

The Raid on Dieppe

For Canadians, the raid on the French port of Dieppe on 19 August 1942 is one of the worst military disasters of the Second World War, and the events surrounding that day still spark controversy. This operation might have been an occasion of great national pride since it was the first commitment of Canadian troops in a land battle against German forces on the Continent, and the first combat action for Canadian tanks. But Dieppe was a badly botched operation from the moment of its conception. The troops who loyally tried to carry out the flawed plan – willing, determined and brave beyond imagination – never had the least chance of success.

The Dieppe Raid. **Painting by Charles Comfort. (Canadian War Museum 12276)**

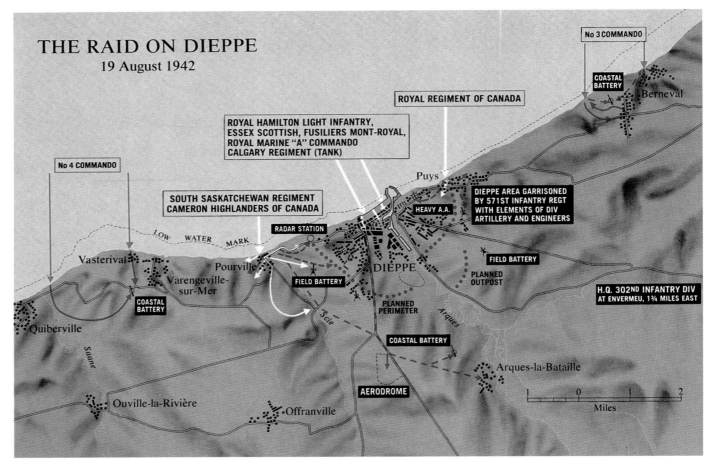

THE RAID ON DIEPPE
19 August 1942

No 3 COMMANDO

COASTAL BATTERY

Berneval

ROYAL REGIMENT OF CANADA

ROYAL HAMILTON LIGHT INFANTRY,
ESSEX SCOTTISH, FUSILIERS MONT-ROYAL,
ROYAL MARINE "A" COMMANDO
CALGARY REGIMENT (TANK)

No 4 COMMANDO

Puys

DIEPPE AREA GARRISONED
BY 571ST INFANTRY REGT
WITH ELEMENTS OF DIV
ARTILLERY AND ENGINEERS

SOUTH SASKATCHEWAN REGIMENT
CAMERON HIGHLANDERS OF CANADA

HEAVY A.A.

RADAR STATION

LOW WATER MARK

FIELD BATTERY

Vasterival

Pourville

DIEPPE

PLANNED
OUTPOST

FIELD BATTERY

H.Q. 302ND INFANTRY DIV
AT ENVERMEU, 1¾ MILES EAST

Varengeville-
sur-Mer

FIELD BATTERY

COASTAL
BATTERY

PLANNED
PERIMETER

Scie

Arques

Quiberville

Saane

COASTAL BATTERY

Arques-la-Bataille

AERODROME

Ouville-la-Rivière

Offranville

1   0   1   2
Miles

Map of the Dieppe Raid area. (DND)

Dieppe had its origins in the politics of grand strategy. The war had not been going well for the Allies. In the Far East, the Japanese had taken Hong Kong, Malaya, the Dutch East Indies and much of Burma, while in North Africa the Germans seemed poised to take Alexandria and the Suez Canal. In the Soviet Union the Germans were continuing their relentless onslaught into the Caucasus and there was serious concern that the Russians might soon collapse and make a separate peace. Stalin was clamouring for the Americans and British to open a 'Second Front' in Western Europe to relieve the pressure on his own armies, but, while the Western Allies had already agreed that the defeat of Nazi Germany was their first priority in a war that was now global, there was considerable disagreement about how that was to be done. The Americans favoured a return to the Continent in 1942 but the British took a more realistic view, recognizing that the resources needed for an invasion of France – the trained manpower and the equipment (especially specialized amphibious shipping) – were not yet available. Perhaps a major raid, something on an entirely new scale, would satisfy both the Russians and the Americans.

PLANNING FOR OPERATION *RUTTER*

Combined Operations headquarters, under the King's cousin, Lord Louis Mountbatten, had in fact already formulated a plan, codenamed *Rutter*, for a division-size raid on Dieppe. Ostensibly intended to test techniques and procedures for landing a large force on a hostile shore, the raid was also to determine whether it was possible to seize an intact port before the enemy could destroy its facilities. Churchill gave his approval and, as senior Canadian officers had been pressing the British to allow Canadian participation in cross-Channel raids since the autumn of 1941, General Montgomery offered the leading role to First Canadian Army. General McNaughton accepted, subject to satisfactory conclusion of detailed planning, and 2 Division's 4 and 6 Brigades were chosen for the task; and, as an armoured regiment was required to test the feasibility of landing tanks as part of an amphibious force, 1 Army Tank Brigade detailed the Calgary Regiment to take part.

In the grand scheme of things, the town of Dieppe had no strategic significance. It was chosen as the target mainly because it was close. Amphibious ships and landing craft, still relatively primitive, could travel the hundred-kilometre distance in darkness, and the area was well within range of fighter aircraft based in southern England. Moreover, intelligence reports indicated, quite erroneously as it turned out, that Dieppe was only lightly defended.

The outline plan for *Rutter*, presented to First Canadian Army at the end of April 1942 provided only the essential parameters, leaving details to be worked out by the assigned sea, land and air commanders, but the main features of the plan were well in place. While the raiding force was crossing the Channel during the hours of darkness, German defences in the town and the surrounding area were to be hit by heavy bomber strikes. Then, at "morning first nautical twilight," an infantry battalion was to be landed on both the left and right flanks of Dieppe, at Puys and Pourville, with the key task of destroying weapons emplacements located on the high headlands overlooking both ends of the two-kilometre-long beach in front of the town. At the same time, heavy coastal gun batteries further off on the flanks were to be captured and destroyed by paratroopers.

An hour later, just after first light, the main force of two infantry battalions and two squadrons of tanks was to be landed at Dieppe, covered by fire from destroyers, bombers and fighter aircraft. Once the town had been captured, engineers would systematically destroy port facilities and defences. While that was happening, the Calgary Regiment's tanks were to move through the town, rendezvous with a second infantry battalion landed at Pourville, three kilometres to the west, and proceed to attack an airfield some four kilometres inland. Later in the day, the entire raiding force was to concentrate in Dieppe to be withdrawn at high tide.

It was in many respects an audacious plan, but it incorporated all of the risks and disadvantages inherent in a frontal attack. Everything would depend on the suppression of enemy firepower while the landing craft approached the beaches, and in the vital period when the assaulting troops disembarked and got off the beach.

This outline plan was reviewed at 2 Division headquarters by the senior operations staff officer (GSO I), Lieutenant-Colonel Churchill Mann. While he pronounced the plan "to have a reasonable prospect of success," much of his analysis focused on the "almost … fantastic conception" of landing Calgary Regiment tanks on the main beach. His major concern was that the damage likely to be done by heavy bombers would prevent the tanks from moving through the town to carry out their task at the airfield but, after weighing the pros and cons, he concluded that putting the tanks in on the Dieppe beachfront "offers the best opportunity to exploit the characteristics of A.F.V. [armoured fighting vehicles] in this operation," and he commented especially on their value as a rearguard during the withdrawal phase.

Almost at once the assigned units were deployed for specialized training on the Isle of Wight. Throughout the latter part of May and early June the tank squadrons worked at preparing themselves for an entirely untried form of operation, and there was a great deal of improvisation and trial and error in the training. For the first several weeks the training focused on technical matters related to waterproofing the Churchill tanks so that they could wade to a depth of two metres, and on mastering techniques peculiar to amphibious landings. The crews were shown how to install box-shaped extensions on the engine air-intakes, how to extend the exhaust pipe above the expected water line, and how to seal the turret ring and all openings in the hull with rubber balloon fabric and thick grease.

Each crew was also given practice in loading and unloading from LCTs and experiments were carried out in using

Churchill tank of the Calgary Regiment disembarking from a landing craft during training for the Dieppe raid. (NAC PA133965)

The Calgary Regiment in Exercise *Yukon II*. (NAC PA158010)

'chespaling' (thin slats of metre-wide chestnut wood wired together much like a snow fence) to improve the traction of the tanks on a pebble beach. Demonstrations showed how the Churchill tanks could scale a sea wall that was higher than the usual 1½-metre 'step' capability. Finally, a limited amount of training was done with companies of the Royal Hamilton Light Infantry and the Essex Scottish, the battalions which the Calgarys were to support in the assault landing. Several exercises were conducted, each of which included securing a beachhead, attacking inland for several kilometres to capture an objective such as an airfield, and then covering the withdrawal of the infantry to the beach, and re-embarking the tanks. In light of later events, it is worth noting that the assault landing phase of these exercises always portrayed a weak enemy who was quickly overcome.

By early June the level of training had reached the stage where a full-scale exercise was laid on to test the capability of the entire combined operations team. *Yukon I* was conducted on the Dorset coast on 11 and 12 June as a rehearsal for the assault landing phase. It went badly awry. Some units were landed many kilometres from their intended destinations and many of the landing craft, including those carrying the tanks, were a full hour late in reaching the beach. A second rehearsal, *Yukon II*, was carried out ten days later and, while the results were somewhat better, many problems remained. Nevertheless, the decision was made to proceed with the actual operation.

Under the guise of yet another exercise, now code-named *Klondike*, the troops were assembled on 2 July and loaded aboard landing craft and ships. Once on board, the men were told that this was the real thing and were given detailed briefings as to their destination and tasks. The weather declined to cooperate, however, and on each of the next several days the operation was postponed for 24 hours. Finally, on 8 July, with the sea still too rough for the Channel crossing, Operation *Rutter* was cancelled and the units re-deployed back to their home camps.

OPERATION *JUBILEE*

Within a week of *Rutter*'s cancellation, the raid was revived by Combined Operations headquarters under the code-name *Jubilee*. Some historians have claimed that this was done without proper authorization, as a means of salvaging the reputations and positions of Mountbatten and his senior planners. Whether or not this is true, the Canadian military authorities immediately accepted the renewal of the task and were given full military authority over all ground aspects of the operation. The units involved were, of course, not informed until much later that the raid was being remounted, but were instructed to continue developing amphibious landing procedures. By this stage an important change in the plan had been made: there was to be no preliminary heavy bombing: fire support for the operation would be limited to what light bombers, fighter-bombers and fighters, together with the four destroyers, could provide.

A variety of schemes were used to cover the re-assembly of the troops involved. On 10 August the Calgarys were ordered to Gosport, near Portsmouth, on the pretext of taking part in a combined operations demonstration, while other units were apparently committed to a month-long series of movement exercises. Actual loading of the landing ships and landing craft began on 17 August, final orders for the operation were issued the following morning, and convoys bound for Dieppe started out from five different ports in southern England after dark on the 18th.

According to plan, at close to 0450 hrs on 19 August the Royal Regiment of Canada was landed at Puys, on the left flank, and the South Saskatchewan Regiment on the right at Pourville. The Royals never got off the narrow beach at Puys. The South Saskatchewans fared better during the landing phase but were soon halted by machine-guns as they tried to take the German radar station on the headland between Pourville and Dieppe. The Cameron Highlanders of Canada, following them ashore, penetrated a kilometre or so inland towards the German airfield that was their objective, but with no tanks joining them eventually began to fall back.

The assault on the main beach in front of Dieppe began at around 0520 hrs with the landing of the Essex Scottish on the

'Burns', the 'B' Squadron commander's tank, was one of the first ashore. The tank was hit by anti-tank fire, and the right track was blown off. As the tank was pointing downward into the trench in front of the sea wall, it could not use its weapons. Part of the Promenade can be seen beyond the concrete sea wall. (Hugh Henry and the KOCR Museum)

left and the Royal Hamilton Light Infantry on the right. However, the LCTs carrying the tanks had navigation problems and the first of them did not beach until nearly fifteen minutes after the infantry was ashore. During that critical time both battalions were without fire support of any kind and they suffered many casualties from heavy machine-gun, mortar and gun fire. Some of this came from weapons sited in caves high up on the headlands – emplacements which had not been detected by British intelligence – all of which had an unrestricted field of fire over the entire beach, turning it into a gigantic killing zone, with light and heavy weapons firing in from three sides. The official history of the Canadian Army noted that "it may be said that during that minute or two the Dieppe battle, on the main beaches, was lost."

Six LCTs carrying eighteen of the Calgary Regiment tanks began their approach to the shore just before 0530 hrs. As they neared the beach they were met by a hail of fire and considerable damage was done. The first to touch down carried 'C' Squadron's three headquarters' tanks. Within minutes of each other, five more landing craft arrived at various points on the beach with 'C' Squadron's 13 Troop, 'B' Squadron headquarters, and three of 'B' Squadron's five tank troops. Only one of the

tanks brought to shore in the first flight was lost during the disembarkation; 'Bull', commanded by Captain Spike Purdy, drove off an LCT ramp prematurely and sank in about four metres of water. While three members of the crew managed to escape, Purdy and Trooper Bill Stewart were drowned.

As the remaining seventeen tanks got ashore, the beach was a scene of carnage and confusion. The tankers' briefing for this phase of the operation no longer had much relevance and, from reports of survivors, there was considerable uncertainty about what should be done beyond getting off the fire-swept beach as soon as possible. The two squadron headquarters that were ashore were having their own problems and neither of the squadron commanders at that moment were in a position to fill the leadership vacuum that had developed. 'B' Squadron headquarters lost the squadron commander's tank very soon after landing when its right track was blown off and it nosed into a ditch near the sea wall. 'C' Squadron headquarters attempted to move two of its three tanks toward the Casino, where they thought the sea wall could be crossed, but both were almost immediately immobilized when anti-tank fire broke their tracks.

The squadron commander, Major Allen Glenn, initially po-

Two of the Calgary's tanks that were disabled on the beach. On the left is 'Calgary', with 'Bob' in rear on the waterline. (Hugh Henry and the KOCR Museum)

sitioned himself just below the sea wall on the central part of the beach, intending to act as a command post and coordinate support, but he was never able to contact any of the infantry commanders to determine what the tanks might best do to help them, so troop leaders were told simply to do what they could by knocking out enemy weapons.

'Calgary' was one of the 'C' Squadron headquarters tanks that had a track knocked off on the beach by a German shell. Trooper Dennis Scott, the loader-operator, described his experience which was typical of many of the crews that day:

We were sitting with no cover and so had a good view of the beach. Lieutenant Douglas found enough targets to keep the gunner busy until we had used up all our ammunition. … Meanwhile we were attracting a lot of gunfire. We took some direct hits on the turret, hard enough that the paint was melting and running down on the inside. The heat inside, along with the smell of the smoke and cordite, was almost

unbearable…. We stayed in the tank until we were ordered to surrender.

Many Churchills were hit by enemy anti-tank fire but it is worth noting that there was not one single casualty to any of the crews while they remained inside their tanks.

The crew commanders quickly discovered that attempting anything but a very gentle turn on the rounded chert pebbles of the beach was a very hazardous manoeuvre that could easily result in a broken track, since the stones tended to be carried up into the drive sprocket if a track dug in at all. Chert proved to be a harder material than the steel of the track pins and five of the tanks were immobilized through losing a track in this fashion.

Eight of the tanks that landed in this first wave did make it over the sea wall and on to the grassy promenade fronting the town, but none of them could get into the built-up area as every entry into the streets was barred by interlocking metre-and-a-half-square blocks of reinforced concrete. Crew commanders

'Betty', one of the tanks to get onto the Promenade, spent much of the morning circling the open area firing at German snipers and other weapon installations in the town and on the headlands. The tank was hit several times, but got bogged in a large hole. (Hugh Henry and the KOCR Museum)

knew about these barriers before the raid and engineer demolition parties (on foot) had been brought along to blow them up, but the sappers were all mown down before reaching the barriers. Some of the tanks tried to shatter the concrete blocks with armour-piercing rounds but that proved fruitless. Acting on Major Glenn's general instructions, most of them roved up and down the length of the promenade for the next several hours, firing at targets of opportunity until their ammunition ran out. Their actions here were effective, in that a number of dug-in machine-gun emplacements sited to fire onto the beach were eliminated, and at least some of the weapon positions on both headlands were destroyed by their fire.

As the first Churchills were moving up onto the promenade, the second wave of four LCTs began to arrive on the beach shortly after 0600 hrs. These carried the regimental headquarters (RHQ) tanks, two more 'B' Squadron troops and 'C' Squadron's 15 Troop. The nine tanks of 'B' and 'C' Squadron disembarked without difficulty, and all but one soon made their way across the beach and onto the promenade. Lieutenant Ed Bennett, whose face had been badly burned when shellfire hit his LCT just before landing, later wrote:

I told Bobby [Cornellsen], my driver, to head for the casino because I had seen other tanks in the centre of the beach stranded in the shingle. We may have had a better chance on the beach because we did not land as high up as the first flight of tanks and the shingle was not as loose. I decided that we would stick to the waterline and go along until we could go over the sea wall, but it was quite something going along the beach because of all the bodies, … and there were places where we had to straddle or go around them.

The landing craft carrying the RHQ tanks, as well as 4 Brigade headquarters, was not so fortunate. The adjutant's tank, 'Ringer', was the first off the ramp, but it immediately got trapped in the chert and blocked the exit of the other two. The

'Blossom', which broke a track in the chert near the Casino (in the background). This tank continued to bring fire to bear on the west headland and on other enemy positions for much of the morning. Note the 'chespalling' in front of the left track; it did not help. (Hugh Henry and the KOCR Museum)

commanding officer, Lieutenant-Colonel John Andrews, went ashore to assess the situation for himself, but returned to the LCT just as it was withdrawing. From there he spoke by radio to Major Glenn and ordered him to assume command of all tanks that were ashore. There was no further effort to land the remainder of 'C' Squadron or to bring in 'A' Squadron, all of whom remained at sea.

About an hour later this same LCT returned to the western end of *White* beach to land the tanks of the CO and the second-in-command, Major John Beggs. Just as the ramp was being lowered an enemy shell hit the front of the craft and broke the ramp chains. Colonel Andrews, probably thinking that the LCT was on the beach, told his driver to advance, and the tank plunged into the water. His crew was rescued but Andrews was last seen in the water and it is believed that he was killed by machine-gun fire although his body was never found. 'Johnny' Andrews was one of Worthington's originals, a founding member of the Canadian Armoured Corps and a highly respected

soldier. His loss was one of many great tragedies on that fateful day, but especially so to the Calgary Regiment and the Armoured Corps.

At 0900 hours, General Roberts, the divisional commander, recognizing the extent of the disaster, ordered the withdrawal to begin by 1100. The tanks still active on the promenade were brought back to the beach, where they did their best to protect the withdrawal of what remained of the RHLI and the Essex Scottish. For the tank crews there was never much hope that they would be taken off the beach since they were needed in action until the very last, and they expended all of their remaining ammunition to give cover to the loading of the landing craft. Lieutenant Jack Dunlap recalled:

Evacuation boats came out of the smoke screen and approached the beach and as they appeared they came under very intense fire from the Germans.... As the boats neared the beach there was a rush of men for the boats. Some were swamped by too many men, sunk by gunfire or forced to turn back with partial loads. Casualties on the beach and in the water were unbelievable.

When no more boats were seen to be coming in, the gunfire dropped off …. The whole beach and shoreline was a shambles of broken bodies, beached boats, derelict tanks. Those of us in the tanks around the Casino had observed troops surrendering west of our position, a movement that gradually swept down the beach toward us. There had been so much killing and destruction that further resistance seemed useless, so as German troops appeared in our sector we raised our hands in the traditional manner and gave up.

Only three men of the Calgary Regiment who had landed got back to England. Twelve members were killed in action and another four were wounded, but 157 officers and men went into German captivity for the remainder of the war, and all of them wore shackles in the German prisoner-of-war camps for the better part of the next year.

The Canadian Army's first experience of battle in Europe in the Second World War was a resounding disaster. All told, 807 Canadians lost their lives on the beach at Dieppe, and 586 were wounded with 1,874 taken prisoner. Only some 30 percent of those who landed were taken off the beaches. It was a very high price to pay for no real purpose and far too high a price to justify the reputations of Lord Mountbatten and his incompetent staff at Combined Operations headquarters. Nor can the senior Canadian officers who accepted the plan avoid a share of the responsibility for what happened that day. Whatever the apologists may say, there were very few lessons learned at Dieppe that could not have been derived more easily in exercises and trials. Perhaps the most important outcome was that the Americans were convinced that an invasion in strength of Hitler's *Festung Europa* was still a long way off.

Aftermath of the battle: the beach at Dieppe, looking to the west headland. The tank in the foreground is 'Calgary'. (RCAC Association Archives)

Mark III Churchill with a 6-pounder gun. Eighteen of the 30 tanks landed at Dieppe by the Calgary Regiment were Mark IIIs; the remainder were mostly Mark Is armed with a 2-pounder gun. (Drawing by Chris Johnson)

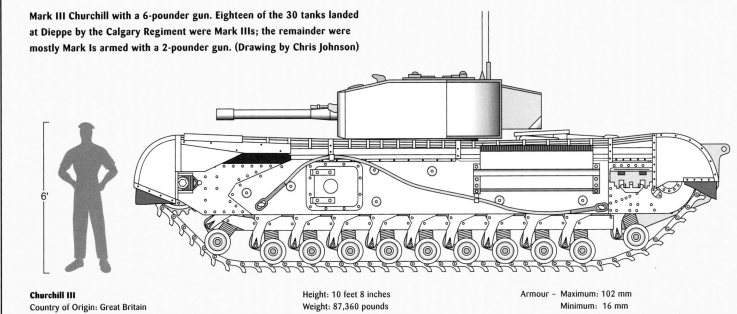

6'

Churchill III
Country of Origin: Great Britain
Crew: 5 (Commander, Gunner, Driver, Assistant Driver, Loader)
Length: 24 feet 5 inches
Width: 9 feet

Height: 10 feet 8 inches
Weight: 87,360 pounds
Engine: Bedford Twin-six cylinder, gasoline
Maximum Speed: 15.5 mph
Range: 90 miles

Armour – Maximum: 102 mm
Minimum: 16 mm
Armament: 6 pdr Ordnance Quick Firing Mk 3 in turret
7.92 mm Besa MG co-axial to 6 pdr
7.92 mm Besa MG hull mount

CHAPTER 7

Armoured Operations in Sicily

While Allied political and military leaders all agreed that the defeat of Nazi Germany, their principal strategic objective, could only be attained through an invasion of France in great strength, the Dieppe disaster brought home most forcefully that this was not going to be possible anytime soon. By the autumn of 1942 it was clear that the enormous logistics build-up necessary for a successful assault on Hitler's *Festung Europa* could not be complete until well into 1944, and questions began to arise as to what could be done in the meanwhile to weaken the German hold on the Continent. The Russians, beating back the Germans at Stalingrad, pleaded with Churchill to establish a 'second front' in the west to relieve the pressure on them.

Until this time the main Allied land operation had been in North Africa, where the British had been fighting an indecisive, see-saw war against the Italians and the German *Afrika Korps* since late 1940. However, Montgomery's victory over the Axis forces at El Alamein, in October 1942, turned the tide and his Eighth Army began to pursue the enemy through Libya and then into Tunisia. Its advance was abetted by an Anglo-American force landed in Morocco and Algeria in November 1942. By early May 1943 the Axis forces in North Africa had been decisively defeated and the Allies controlled the whole south shore of the Mediterranean.

That greatly changed the strategic equation, allowing Churchill to pursue his notion of striking at what he called "the soft underbelly" of Europe; and President Roosevelt reluctantly agreed, at the Casablanca Conference in January 1943, that an invasion of Sicily should be the next step. The Americans believed, at least at that time, that Sicily would be a limited commitment, after which all efforts were to be directed at preparing for a landing in northern France, but what might occur after Sicily was captured was left officially undecided.

Canadian involvement in the Sicilian campaign can be traced back to political clamour in Canada during 1942, when newspaper editorials were asking why large numbers of Canadian soldiers in Britain appeared to be 'sitting on their duffs' while British and American armies were busy fighting. The prime minister's ear was always keenly attuned to potentially damaging public controversy, and in October 1942 he let the British know that his government no longer held to the view that First Canadian Army could not be broken up if there were useful tasks to be done.

The relative inactivity of the army had indeed become a problem. By the spring of 1943, 1 Division had been in England for well over three years, 2 Division had been there for more than two and a half years, and 1 Army Tank Brigade and 3 Division were nearing the second anniversary of their arrival. The threat of a German invasion had passed and there was no longer a vital need for Canadians to garrison the south coast of Britain. Training, therefore, had been the sole preoccupation of all of these formations. Many of the troops were becoming restless, and even intensified training, such as carried out in the divisional battle schools, could only alleviate the boredom. Many senior officers were concerned that the troops were in danger of losing their edge.

However, lack of operational experience was a far more serious problem and 2 Division's brief introduction to battle at Dieppe had not provided much useful experience. While a number of officers and senior NCOs had been attached to British units in North Africa, including about two dozen members of armoured units, the operational leavening within the Canadian formations was very thinly spread. The argument that a commitment in the Mediterranean would improve the overall fighting quality of the army thus had many adherents.

General Andrew McNaughton, still the senior Canadian officer overseas and now Commander of First Canadian Army, held firmly to the principle that his army must be kept intact for the main task, the eventual invasion of France. He resisted any suggestion that part of his force might be hived off for operations in a secondary theatre, even though the prime minister and defence minister Ralston were pressing for that to happen. However, in late April 1943, the British, bowing to pressure from Ottawa, finally asked for a Canadian contingent – an infantry division and an armoured brigade – to participate "in certain operations based on Tunisia," *i.e.,* for the invasion of Sicily. The Cabinet quickly concurred, since it was their idea, and McNaughton, yielding to his political masters, tasked 1 Division and 1 Army Tank Brigade for Operation *Husky.* Like the Americans, he thought this was to be a limited commitment and expected that these formations would be back in England in time for the invasion of France, sometime in the next year.

Within days, the units of the Tank Brigade were moved from Sussex to camps in southern Scotland for training and preparation for the move to the Mediterranean. The Ontario Regiment was located in an isolated camp of damp and drafty Nissen huts near the town of Hawick. The Calgary Regiment occupied slightly more luxurious accommodation on the grounds of the hunting lodge of the Duke of Argyll at Langholm, and the Three Rivers Regiment was based on the coast at Hoddam Castle, in Annan, on the Solway Firth.

Only one of the brigade's regiments was required to provide support for the amphibious landing of 1 Division, and the TRR was selected by Brigadier Wyman for this task. At this time, Lieutenant-Colonel E.L. Booth, who was serving in the 1st

(Department of National Defence)

Hussars, was promoted and given command of the TRR. Booth was one of those officers who had been attached for some months to a British tank unit in North Africa, and other than key members of the brigade headquarters staff, he was one of the few officers who was told where the Tank Brigade would be going into battle.

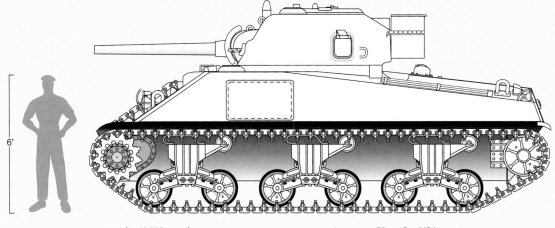

M4A4 (Sherman V). The Sherman V, the workhorse of the Canadian Armoured Corps during the Second World War, was the most widely used Sherman variant in operations in Italy and North-West Europe. (Drawing by Chris Johnson)

6'

M4A4, Sherman V Medium Tank
Country of Origin: United States
Crew: 5 (Commander, Gunner, Driver, Assistant Driver, Loader)
Length: 19 feet 10 inches
Width: 8 feet 7 inches
Height: 9 feet

Weight: 69,700 pounds
Engine: Chrysler A57 30 cylinder multibank, gasoline
Maximum Speed: 25 mph
Range: 100 miles
Armour – Maximum: 75 mm
　　　　　 Minimum: 12 mm

Armament: 75mm Gun M3 in turret
　.30 calibre MG M1919A4 co-axial to 75mm gun
　.30 calibre MG M1919A4 in bow mount
　.50 calibre MG HB M2 in flexible mount on turret top

Almost immediately after their arrival in Scotland the regiments were issued with new M4A4 Shermans, armed with 75mm guns and powered by 30-cylinder Chrysler multi-bank gasoline engines. These were the first Shermans issued to Canadians, and much of the six weeks spent in Scotland was devoted to conversion training, but as the tank crews had already trained on a variety of other tanks they adapted rapidly. The conversion training included extensive firing of the 75mm gun, using both armour-piercing ammunition and the newly introduced high-explosive rounds, on the nearby tank range at Kirkcudbright. TRR crews also spent many hours practising loading and unloading from LSTs.

The final weeks in Scotland were given over (in all three regiments, since they might all have to land over open beaches) to waterproofing the tanks so that they would be able to wade to a water depth of just under three metres. This was a messy and time-consuming task that involved the caulking of every joint and opening into the hull and turret. The final job was to apply a coat of sand-coloured paint, and red, white and blue 'bulls eye' aircraft-recognition markings. By the third week of June all three regiments were aboard LSTs, waiting to be carried to their still-secret destination. Clearly it was to be somewhere warm, as lightweight tropical clothing had been issued. The most persistent rumour among the troops was that they were going to Burma.

ARMOURED OPERATIONS IN SICILY

At 0300 hours on 10 July 1943, 1 and 2 Infantry Brigades of 1 Division landed on *Bark West* beach, near Pachino, on the south-east tip of Sicily. There was little opposition from the Italian defenders and the infantry quickly moved inland. As part of the divisional reserve, the TRR was brought close in to

1 Army Tank Brigade Shermans testing waterproofing in a river bed, Scotland, June 1943. (NAC PA193875)

Landing in Sicily. **Painting by Will Ogilvie. (Canadian War Museum 13420)**

the shore in LSTs, beginning at 0900 hours. It was a calm, sunny morning, quite in contrast with the rough seas of the previous night, and most of the tanks dropped off the LST ramps into about two metres of water and were able to drive ashore. A few were swamped and had to be recovered later by the Light Aid Detachment. 'A' Squadron was declared 'operational' at 1030 hours, and by 1530 the whole regiment was complete in its designated de-waterproofing area, a few hundred metres from the beach.

While the regiment was sorting itself out after the landing, a patrol of the recce troop, under Corporal Bob Gladnick (an American who had served with the anti-Franco forces during the Spanish Civil War), was sent inland in their Universal carriers to check on what was happening. He later wrote:

About three or four kilometres inland we ran into an Italian armoured regiment with about 50 Ansaldo tanks armed with 57mm cannons, any one of which could have blown our Bren gun carriers to kingdom come. With no chance of escaping, I told my driver to head for the centre of the column at full speed. There, I shouted in Spanish, "Donde este el commandante?", which was fortunately close enough to Italian. Soon, a brigadier with a chest full of ribbons marched up to meet us. I told him that I expected him to surrender at once and save himself and his men from being massacred by the huge force following me. He agreed on one condition: that he surrender to an officer of equal rank. At that time my uniform consisted of a pair of shorts and a helmet. So I promoted myself to Generale Maggiore (Major-General). The Italian officer saluted me, proud of the honour of surrendering to a 'higher author-ity'. I ordered him to take his tanks and trucks off the road, and soon the rest of the Recce Troop came roaring through....

Gladnick's skilful handling of this situa-tion won him immediate promotion to the rank of sergeant.

At 1720 hours, Colonel Booth detailed 'C' Squadron to advance with the Carleton and York Regiment in an attack on a height of ground at Burgio, some three kilometres west of the town of Pachino, while the remainder of the regiment moved into a harbour about a kilometre inland. Similar to recce troop's earlier en-counter, 'C' Squadron's first operational mission had an almost comic touch. The squadron duly mounted its attack, 'two troops up', only to find that Burgio con-sisted of a single farm and one miserably poor and frightened Sicilian family.

While the TRR was getting established ashore, the other elements of the brigade remained aboard LSTs well out at sea, in the 'Slow Convoy'. This convoy had been intended to berth temporarily in Malta, but because of the rapid inland advance of the assaulting troops on D-Day, the ships carrying the Ontarios and the Calgarys were diverted on D+1 to make for the Si-cilian port of Syracuse, some fifty kilome-tres north of the landing beaches at Pachino. They disembarked in the con-

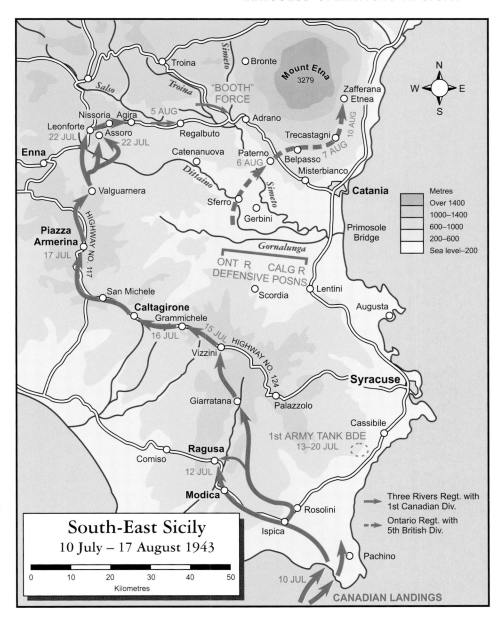

gested port on the afternoon of 13 July (D+3), and the follow-ing day moved to harbours near the village of Cassibile, twelve kilometres to the south, where they waited for tasking for the next week.

Meanwhile, the Canadian infantry marched inland for three days along narrow, unpaved Sicilian roads against only spo-radic and light opposition, and there was no need for the tanks, even though a squadron was placed in support of both 1 and 2 Brigades. The real foes were the intense heat, with daytime tem-peratures reaching 45° Celsius, and clouds of fine white dust, raised even by the boots of the marching infantry. The tank crews, bringing up the rear, covered their mouths and noses with improvised cloth masks, but the dust still filled their lungs, coated their skin and stiffened their clothing.

On 13 July General Montgomery called for a day of rest for

the Canadians. The initial bridgehead boundary had been reached at Modica, beyond which the ground became increas-ingly hilly and rough. The day proved to be anything but restful as Montgomery paid one of his dramatic, morale-boosting vis-its to each of the Canadian units in turn, including the TRR, and the troops spent most of their time cleaning and polishing for the Army commander.

The TRR got its baptism of fire on 15 July. Early that morn-ing, 1 Brigade, supported by 'A' Squadron, was advancing to-wards Grammichele, a town perched along the top of a ridge rising a hundred or more metres above the surrounding coun-tryside. The recce troop was in the lead and infantrymen rode on the back decks of the tanks that followed close behind. As the column reached the outskirts of the town, the lead carriers and tanks were met with a sudden burst of fire from tanks and anti-tank guns belonging to the Hermann Goering Division. The squadron immediately lost a Sherman and three of its carriers, but in the ensuing fight destroyed three Mark IIIs and a number of anti-tank guns of various calibres. The Hastings and Prince Edward Regiment stormed the town with three companies, and the Germans quickly pulled back, the TRR and the 48th Highlanders pursuing them vigorously. In this brief engagement the first armour casualties of the Italian campaign were suffered: one trooper was killed and eight men were wounded.

The gradual advance continued over the next days, with the TRR providing support to the leading battalion of whichever brigade was committed. This continual switching of brigades and battalions made effective tank-infantry cooperation somewhat difficult, at least initially. As there were no practised standard procedures, commanders did not know or necessarily trust each other and neither tanker nor infantryman knew what was wanted or could be ex-

Princess Patricia troops pass a Three Rivers Regiment tank near Valguarnera, Sicily, 19 July 1943. (NAC PA166755)

pected from the other arm. Their attempts were not helped by communications problems, which worsened as the countryside became increasingly rugged, difficulties due in part to the very weakly-powered, short-range, and often unreliable infantry man-pack radios as well as the unreliable No. 38 sets mounted in some tanks to net into the infantry frequency.

German opposition stiffened considerably in this period. The Canadian advance had begun to threaten the east-west highways needed by the Germans to maintain the line of communications and supply with their formations in western Sicily, as they began to withdraw those troops toward the port of Messina , in the north-east corner of the island.

As the fighting intensified and the division penetrated deeper into the mountainous hinterland, the less suitable the country was for armoured operations. Much of the time there was no room of any kind to manoeuvre, since the roads were often cut into the sides of hills, with solid rock on one side and a steep drop on the other. In these circumstances the lead tank was extremely vulnerable both to anti-tank fire and to mines, and mutual fire support from the following tanks was difficult, if not impossible. A single major obstacle, a crater or a blown

bridge, could and often did bring the entire column to a halt. The experience was but a foretaste of what all units of the brigade were to encounter for much of the next eighteen months.

By noon on 16 July, 2 Brigade, led by 'C' Squadron of the TRR, reached the area some five kilometres south of the large town of Piazza Armerina. Here the main road bent sharply as it descended into a narrow gully, and as the leading tanks entered the defile they ran into a German ambush. One tank was destroyed. The Loyal Edmonton Regiment mounted company-size attacks to dislodge the enemy and in a series of hard-fought actions the infantry eventually managed to capture the high ground overlooking the town, but the German defenders tenaciously held their ground in the built-up area until long after dark.

Piazza Armerina was captured the next morning, after the enemy had pulled back during the night, and the advance toward Enna and Valguarnera continued early in the afternoon of 17 July. 'B' Squadron of the TRR moved off in the lead, carrying troops of 3 Brigade's West Nova Scotia Regiment on their back decks. Six kilometres north of Piazza Armerina, a blown bridge brought the advance to a halt. While the engineers worked to create a by-pass, 'B' Squadron's tanks deployed along the crest of a hill and succeeded in driving off enemy outposts that had halted the infantry's dismounted advance. But soon after the road-bound advance resumed it was discovered that an area known as the Grottacalda Pass was held by the Germans in considerable strength. General Simonds decided at this point that a set-piece attack by two brigades would be needed to clear the way to Enna and Valguarnera.

The battle for Valguarnera lasted for the whole of the next day, but it was essentially a dismounted infantry fight, and the tanks were able to play only a small role. 'B' Squadron worked with the West Novas, carrying companies forward to their start line and then providing fire support as they moved cross-country to their objective. The enemy put up very determined resistance from prepared defensive positions all along high ground south and west of the town, but Valguarnera finally fell after dark on 18 July.

At this time XXX Corps headquarters decided that the Canadian division should press on to the north, to take the towns of Leonforte and Assoro, and then swing eastward along the north side of the Catania Plain to outflank the strong German defences still holding firm against the British along the east coast. The town of Enna, 1 Division's objective until now, was assigned to the Americans, who were pushing forward on the left. Meanwhile, 'A' Squadron of 4 PLDG, the only part of the reconnaissance regiment to accompany the division in Sicily, pushed a patrol along the road to Enna. Blocked by a deep crater about eight kilometres from the town, a party of NCOs and troopers continued on foot, arriving in Enna just as the first Americans arrived from the west.

The advance to Leonforte and Assoro would take the Canadians into

by-pass the obstacle by moving along the dry river bed to a point downstream, where it appeared his tanks could scale the far bank. Once into the river bed, however, the tanks came under ferocious machine-gun and mortar fire, and to their dismay the crews soon discovered that some of what they thought was mortar fire was in fact the explosion of anti-tank mines. In this first encounter with mines, nine Shermans were put out of action in a matter of minutes with their tracks blown off. Much of the squadron spent a very uncomfortable night inside their tanks because the mortar fire made recovery impossible until the next morning.

Meanwhile, the other two regiments of 1 Army Tank Brigade, the Ontarios and Calgarys, moved on 20 July from their base camp at Cassibile into defensive positions on the River Gornalunga, between Lentini and Scordia, on the southern edge of the Catania plain, where the British advance had been

Tank at Cross Roads. **Painting by Will Ogilvie. (Canadian War Museum 13609)**

even more difficult, mountainous countryside, which severely limited the mobility of the tanks. For the attacks on 20 July, 'A' Squadron was tasked to support 2 Brigade's assault on Leonforte, while 'C' Squadron was to support 1 Brigade's move on Assoro. 'C' Squadron of the TRR and the PLDG recce squadron were to protect the division's left flank.

In its move forward from Valguarnera, 'C' Squadron found the way blocked by a demolished bridge over the River Dittaino. The squadron commander, Major Mills, decided to

stopped by fierce resistance. Here they were placed under command of 13 Brigade of the British 5 Division which was preparing to support an attack by 51 (Highland) Division on their left.

The area occupied by the two regiments gave their men experience of the worst of the torrid Sicilian summer. The ground was a treeless expanse of undulating, boulder-strewn country, covered with dry, yellow grass and populated by dense swarms of flies. There was no escape from the intense sun, and the steel of the tank turrets and hulls became so hot that it was painful to touch. Thick clouds of dust were raised every time a vehicle was moved. This dust could be observed by the Germans on the far side of the plain, and often resulted in shelling, so no vehicle movement was allowed in daylight. This part of the front, however, proved to be very quiet for the next ten days, and only a few rounds of main armament high-explosive were fired by the Ontario Regiment during this time.

The infantry attacks on both Assoro and Leonforte went in on the 21st, and both ran into difficulties. The Hasty P's captured the ancient Norman castle on the heights overlooking Assoro by a daring silent night attack in which the battalion

Universal carrier, as used by 4 PLDG during the push through the Sicilian highlands. (NAC PA131368)

climbed up the steepest part of the mountain, but after daybreak they could not penetrate the German hold on the village itself. They were cut off, under nearly continuous counter-attack, and they ran desperately short of ammunition and water.

The 48th Highlanders were ordered forward for an attack the next morning to relieve them, and in this operation a TRR troop of 'A' Squadron gave exceptional support. Early on the morning of 22 July, the troop leader, Lieutenant Waldron, led his crews up a steep boulder-strewn cutting that seemed completely impassable to tanks, but the drivers gradually inched their way into positions from which their gunners could fire onto enemy machine-gun posts dominating the approaches to the high ridge south-west of Assoro. Using high-explosive rounds, Waldron's tanks neutralized the well-entrenched

enemy covering the road into Assoro, enabling the Highlanders to clear the ridge and make contact with the beleaguered Hasty P's.

At Leonforte, a deep ravine had to be crossed to get to the hill where the town was located, but the bridge crossing the ravine had been blown and the approach to the bridge site was swept by enemy fire. It was not until evening that the Edmonton Regiment was able to fight its way up a steep cliff and into the town, but a German counter-attack soon isolated the men in the village and a wild night battle raged in the streets. The engineers worked all night under continual fire to construct a Bailey bridge over the ravine and by first light it was completed. The brigade commander, Chris Vokes, then decided to send a 'flying column' across the bridge and into the town. This column – a troop of TRR Shermans in the lead, followed closely by a troop of anti-tank guns and a company of the PPCLI – made its mad dash at mid-morning.

Colonel Stacey's early history of the campaign, *From Pachino to Ortona*, described how, "at breakneck speed the column raced down the road, 'galloped' the bridge and tore up the long switchback hill into Leonforte. Machine-gun fire raked it, but such was the speed of the rush that this caused only one casualty. A moment later the enemy posts near the entrance to the town, stunned and overwhelmed by the suddenness and power of the attack, had surrendered." Two more companies of the Patricias were rushed into the town, and bitter fighting continued in the streets for the next several hours, including several tank-versus-tank engagements at point-blank range. Sergeant W.R. Campbell, who at the time was a troop sergeant in 'A' Squadron, subsequently reported on this action:

We flushed out a German tank on a side street, and, followed by Sergeant Gallagher in 2B, we chased it through a maze of narrow back streets until the German tank commander set a trap at a major intersection. In a close range exchange of gunfire, the German Mark IV tank damaged my Sherman, starting a fire in an ammunition bin. Trooper Lund, the driver, smartly reversed and backed the tank around the corner. The German tank was also hit, but managed to escape along the main street and get out of town…. Shortly after, a second German tank attempted to escape town, but, emulating the strategy of the first German tank, I trapped and destroyed it at the same intersection….

The TRR lost one Sherman, but accounted for three Mark IVs. The Germans finally abandoned Leonforte in mid-afternoon but continued to hold dominant positions on the east side of the town. By now, the Americans, who had been clearing the western side of the island, had begun a thrust eastward, along the north coast, and it had become clear that the Germans were no longer content simply to delay the Canadian advance; they were now prepared to stand and fight for every inch of ground in a last-ditch effort to keep open a line of retreat for their forces in western Sicily. The Canadians' north-eastward push thus gained greater strategic significance to both friend and foe, and they were ordered to press on with all possible speed.

Agira, twelve kilometres to the east, was the next major objective, but halfway along the road was the small village of Nissoria, "an abject collection of hovels," according to Farley Mowat, and fierce fighting there was to make the name reverberate in many regimental histories.

Patrols from 4 PLDG, moving towards Nissoria on the morning of 23 July, came under heavy fire, so General Simonds decided that a set-piece attack, with overwhelming artillery support, was needed. His plan called for a slow, inflexible advance behind a rolling barrage, reminiscent of the worst of First World War attrition tactics, which seemed to appeal to senior gunner officers such as Simonds.

At 1500 hrs the next day, the attack on Nissoria was launched by the Royal Canadian Regiment, with 'A' Squadron of the TRR in support. The infantry soon lost the rolling barrage, as almost always happened, but there was initially very little opposition. On the western outskirts of the hamlet a German tank and an anti-tank gun were encountered, but these were rapidly dealt with by TRR tanks. It was a very different story as the infantry and tanks emerged on the eastern side of the village and the infan-

try companies were mowed down by an enemy barrage of mortars and artillery. 'A' Squadron's tanks continued to advance, but they too were soon stopped by fire from several 88mm guns sited on high ground on the left flank.

In but a few minutes the TRR squadron lost ten tanks (six of which were later recovered and put back into service). Two of them were 'brewed up' – the first time the TRR had seen the results of ammunition inside a tank being set on fire by armour-piercing rounds. The infantry and the remaining tanks then withdrew into the village. Simonds' set-piece attack had come to nothing. Two further attempts were made over the next day

Mountain Stronghold. **Painting by Will Ogilvie, depicting the tortuous terrain of central Sicily. (Canadian War Museum 13457)**

by battalions of 1 Brigade to break through the enemy positions on the ridge east of Nissoria, but neither met with any greater success, and 2 Brigade was brought up on the evening of 26 July.

Its attack, mounted by the PPCLI together with the Three Rivers' 'C' Squadron and the 90th Anti-Tank Battery, went in at 2000 hours, along with the heaviest artillery barrage yet fired in

Three Rivers tanks passing through the ruins of Regalbuto, 3 August 1943. (NAC PA170290)

the Sicilian campaign. This time the effect on the enemy was "paralysing", according to the official history, and the ridge that had given so much grief the previous day was rapidly taken. Continuing on in the dark, two Patricia companies moved forward without tank support against a second objective – another ridge line that intersected the highway a thousand metres further on – but they got lost *en route*. Brigadier Vokes then committed the Seaforth Highlanders, who set out shortly after midnight with 'C' Squadron tanks in support, the latter playing a significant role in the battle for this second ridge, codenamed *Tiger*, in knocking out two German tanks threatening the operation. The Seaforths and Edmontons then continued on toward Agira, with TRR tanks supporting their move from *Tiger*. Agira was taken later in the day by the Patricias and 'C' Squadron, and there they learned that Mussolini's Fascist dictatorship had been overthrown on 25 July.

In the period 31 July to 2 August, 'A' Squadron supported

231 (Malta) Brigade in an advance on Regalbuto. Two troops were kept forward at all times to give covering fire as the infantry advanced. Close observation by crew commanders revealed that the Germans were concealing their tank positions by driving tanks into the ground floor of houses on the outer edge of the built-up area, and fire from these was a serious problem for the infantry as they moved toward the town until the tank crews found that an effective way of dealing with them was to fire a high-explosive round set at 'delay' through the wall of a house, which then collapsed the structure on top of the enemy. Throughout the fight for Regalbuto the Germans put up a determined effort to hold the town, but persistent attacks made it untenable and they finally withdrew. The 48th Highlanders entered the town on 2 August only to find it abandoned.

Further to the south, the Ontario Regiment was redeployed with the British 13 Brigade to protect crossings of the Dittaino River at Sferro, and on 3 August provided two squadrons to

A carrier from 4th Princess Louise Dragoon Guards enters Catanzaro in southern Italy, 10 September 1943. (NAC PA136807)

was a momentous day for another reason: that evening the Italian surrender was announced, and the local citizens staged a riotous celebration. Progress was a bit slower when the column continued on the next morning, because of blown bridges and mines. PLDG patrols exchanged fire on several occasions with small demolition parties left behind by the Germans, but more than seventy kilometres were covered and Marina di Badolato was taken on the 9th, the same day as the assault landings at Salerno. On 10 September, *X Force* pushed on to Marina de Catanzaro and then moved eight kilometres inland to occupy the outskirts of Catanzaro, a city of 20,000 inhabitants. This was the last of its exploits, however, as 1 Division, to avoid a now-unnecessary slow march through the mountains, switched its axis of advance to the coast road.

Led by 'A' Squadron of the PLDG, 3 Brigade set out on 11 September on a 160-kilometre drive that brought the Canadians to the instep of the Italian boot, at Castrovillari, four days later. While the remainder of the division caught up, patrols from the PLDG drove another sixty kilometres along the coast and established contact with elements of the British 1 Airborne Division that had landed at the port of Taranto a week earlier.

THE DRIVE TO POTENZA

The operational situation in Italy was changing dramatically. By 14 September the German high command had acknowledged the failure of their counter-attacks on the Salerno bridgehead, and had begun to withdraw the forces remaining in southern Italy in order to create a temporary defensive line

Infantrymen of the West Nova Scotia Regiment get a ride on the back deck of a Calgary Regiment Sherman during the advance from Villapiana, 17 September 1943. (NAC PA177155)

For the advance on Potenza, General Simonds created *Boforce*, named after its commander, Lieutenant-Colonel Bogert of the West Nova Scotia Regiment. It consisted of the West Novas and a squadron of Calgary tanks, along with a battery from 1 RCHA and detachments of engineers, machine-gunners and anti-tank guns. 'A' Squadron, PLDG, was not included in this group because too many of its vehicles had broken down during the long run from Reggio de Calabria. A second, composite squadron arrived in Villapiana from Sicily on 18 September.

Boforce set out from Villapiana, on the Gulf of Taranto, on 17 September, turning inland at Nova Siri, and reaching a point just short of Sant' Archangelo by nightfall, having met no opposition. Next day, with the Calgarys in the lead, the column moved on to Corleto, where it was delayed for many hours by a blown bridge and rubble-choked streets caused by Allied bombing. Fifteen kilometres further on, *Boforce* was brought to a stop at Laurenzana by a bridge that was blown just as the leading troops arrived.

When the march resumed, on the morning of 19 September, movement was considerably slower; German rearguards put up sporadic fights all along the way, but the biggest problem was a road "studded with Teller mines." Despite these difficulties, just after dusk the column reached the heights on the south bank of the River Basento, overlooking Potenza across a broad valley.

The West Novas mounted a night attack with two companies and succeeded in penetrating into the south-western part of the town by daybreak, but enemy paratroopers, many

stretching from Manfredonia and Foggia in the east to Avelino and Naples in the west. During their withdrawal, the German formations were to fight delaying actions, demolish all bridges and disrupt lines of communications. Their purpose was to buy time for the construction of a more substantial defensive line some 120 kilometres further north, hinged on the River Sangro on the Adriatic coast. It would be known as the Winter Line.

On the Allied side, the British and American corps in the Salerno bridgehead were preparing to break out to the east and north. To facilitate this move it became increasingly important to control the city of Potenza, a communications hub in the centre of the peninsula between Salerno and Taranto, and General Alexander, the supreme commander in the Mediterranean theatre, made it the main objective in the next phase of the offensive. The task was given to the Canadian division.

The terrain of southern Italy made it relatively easy for German engineers to delay the Canadian advance. Here the Calgarys and 4 PLDG move around a blown bridge near Anzi, 19 September 1943. (NAC PA144114)

equipped with automatic weapons, held firm in the built-up area throughout the morning. For several hours the Calgarys could not get into the town because of mines and demolitions blocking all approaches but, shortly after noon, the last of the obstacles was cleared and the squadron moved forward along the main road. As the tanks climbed the long hill to the centre of the town, the Germans beat a hasty retreat. The capture of Potenza enabled the Canadians to link up with the British 5 Division, which had taken Auletta, thirty kilometres to the west.

Elsewhere, while *Boforce* was closing on Potenza on 19 September, 4 PLDG, now with two squadrons working in support of 1 Infantry Brigade, sent patrols forward over a wide area between Potenza and the sea. They had a noteworthy clash with the enemy at Miglionico, where they attacked a bivouac area by approaching through a railway tunnel and inflicted a large number of casualties before they withdrew. Over the

'Adjunct', a Sherman of 'A' Squadron of the Calgarys, gives covering fire to the West Novas in their advance into Potenza, 20 September 1943. (NAC PA144103)

next week PLDG patrols significantly extended the area controlled by the Canadians, taking Canosa and Melfi by the end of the month.

At this time a concerted effort was being made to reunite the units of 1 Armoured Brigade, which had been widely dispersed during operations in September. The Three Rivers Regiment, which had remained in general reserve in Sicily, was moved to the mainland in LSTs beginning on 12 September and, after a brief stop in Taranto, landed at the Adriatic port of Manfredonia on 30 September. The Ontario Regiment, which had been concentrated in the western seacoast resort of Praia Mare since having been withdrawn from support of the British 5 Division on 18 September, sent its wheeled vehicles across the peninsula by road convoy on 27 September, while its tanks were moved by sea to Manfredonia, where they were put ashore on 7 October.

As the operational commitments of the armoured brigade increased, there was a requirement to streamline the functioning of the tank delivery organization. No.1 Tank Delivery Squadron was reorganized as 'A' and 'B' Squadrons of the Elgin Regiment. 'A' Squadron, under Major W.D. King, served as the

forward squadron, responsible for the immediate delivery of replacement tanks complete with crews to the regimental 'B' echelons, while 'B' Squadron took on duties as the rear squadron, holding the bulk of the replacement tanks received from Ordnance or RCEME workshops. Each of the regiments attached one of their officers to the Elgins to look after the organization and training of crews destined as unit replacements.

ON TO MOTTA AND CAMPOBASSO

The Allied high command now set its sights on Rome. On the western side of the peninsula, the Fifth US Army was to push northward from Naples, while on the Adriatic side the British Eighth Army was to continue its thrust northward to Pescara and then swing westward across the Appenines. In this grand scheme, the Canadians were given the mission of advancing westward from the Foggia plain, into the mountains, to capture the city of Campobasso and a vital road junction at Vinchiaturo.

The task of leading the Canadian advance was given to yet another *ad hoc* battle group, commanded by Cy Neroutsos and

Tanks carrying infantry in the main square of Potenza, 20 September 1943. (NAC PA144113)

made up of his Calgary tanks, 4 PLDG, and the RCR mounted in trucks along with two artillery batteries in support. The vanguard of this force, led by Lieutenant-Colonel Fred Adams, the CO of the PLDG, consisted of his own regiment with one squadron of the Calgarys and a company of the RCR, and they started out from Lucera early on the morning of 1 October, making rapid progress over the first fifteen kilometres of the flat Foggia plain. As they began to climb into the foothills of the Daunia Mountains they sighted the first major town along Highway 17, Motta Montecorvino (usually referred to simply as Motta), perched at the top of a thimble-shaped hill, where PLDG scout cars came under intensive machine-gun fire. Patrols were sent out for about eight kilometres left and right of the main axis, and all reported that the ridge line was heavily defended. It was clear that the Germans intended to defend Motta, and that an attack by tanks and infantry would be needed to dislodge them.

At 1600 hours the attack went in, led by 'A' and 'B' Squadrons of the Calgarys. The tanks moved "with great dash" up the ridge, all the while being fired upon by 88mm and 37mm anti-tank guns. While a number of tanks were knocked out or damaged, several

Tank transporters hauling Shermans, Manfredonia, Italy, 3 October 1943. (NAC PA142076)

Shermans, making good use of folds in the ground, were able to fight their way into the outskirts of the town. But the operation had already gone badly awry, or, as the official history notes, "… infantry-tank co-operation broke down." The RCR companies, which were intended to move immediately in rear of the tanks, lagged behind, and found themselves pinned down by machine-gun fire.

Only two 'A' Squadron tanks, commanded by Lieutenant Arni Charbonneau, penetrated into the centre of Motta, having destroyed an 88mm gun just as they reached the outskirts of the built-up area. As the two tanks moved along the main street, the second, Andy, was hit on the right side by a 37mm anti-tank gun and was brought to a halt. Charbonneau's own tank,

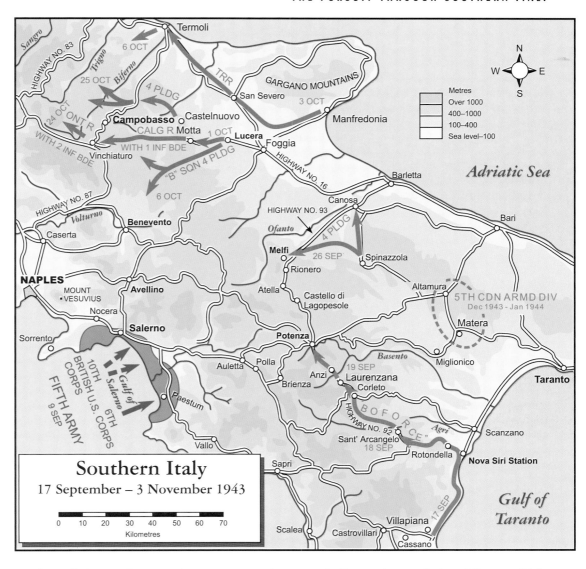

Southern Italy
17 September – 3 November 1943

Amos, continued on. Trooper Peter Reimer, who was the loader-operator, recalled his experiences:

> We passed the crippled 88mm gun [which they had just knocked out] and entered Motta. We hadn't gone more than a hundred yards when one helluva bang lifted the tank and we lurched into a stone building on our left. Must have been some mine to lift the tank, but it didn't blow off the track! … We then turned a fairly sharp corner to the right and dead ahead, in the middle of the road, sat one of those [37mm] anti-tank 'squeeze' guns. This gun's profile is quite squat, and we were so close to it that Ted [Court, the driver] decided to run right over it. Unfortunately for us, the tank "bellied up" on the gun, and there we were, no traction, totally immobile….
>
> …We spotted troops around us wearing khaki coveralls, and thought they were RCRs. I opened the pistol port and shouted out. The answer came back immediately and in no

uncertain terms: bullets and grenades! … We were fairly close to a house with a balcony and Jerry was spraying submachine-gun fire down on us. Jack [Haase, the gunner] cleared the balcony with our turret guns and things smoothed out for a while. Then we heard Jerry climbing onto the tank and the hatch covers started lifting. Lieutenant Charbonneau reacted quickly and held onto the covers for dear life, literally. Duke [Ross, the co-driver] passed up a wrench and 'Charby' secured the hatch by inserting the wrench through the loops on the underside of the covers. We did some frantic traversing and firing until we got them off the tank.

For well over a half hour the German paratroopers rained down a hail of mortar bombs and machine-gun fire on *Amos*, but the crew continued to return fire until they ran out of ammunition for the main armament.

Jerry then began to roll hand grenades under the tank. I guess he knew the Sherman tank had an escape hatch on the floor. These grenades kept coming pretty steadily until Jack and I got smart. We lined up the 75mm gun, I opened the breech and sighted down the barrel and we got the next grenade-thrower in the act. Other than sporadic fire, nothing much then happened until it got dark. By this time we'd heard on the No.19 set that the attack had been called off and we were on our own.

Just before dusk, Neroutsos gave orders for the tanks to withdraw from Motta, while the RCR prepared for a night attack. *Amos* was eventually brewed up by a beehive charge, but Charbonneau and his crew managed to get out and escape to a line held by the RCR east of the town. The infantry finally captured Motta just before dawn. The fighting here, fierce and costly, was the first major battle fought by the Canadians since landing in mainland Italy and the Calgarys lost ten Shermans on 2 October. The daring determination of Charbonneau's crew was recognized by the award of a Military Cross to their commander, which he firmly maintained was really for his crew.

After the battle at Motta, Colonel Neroutsos' battle group was broken up and 1 Brigade took the lead as the Division's axis along Highway 17 became increasingly mountainous and heavily wooded. It was an infantry struggle for the remainder of the distance to Campobasso, with the Calgarys simply providing fire support when and where possible. Campobasso finally fell on 14 October.

Throughout 1 Division's ad-

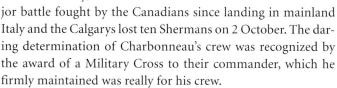

(Above) Calgary Regiment Sherman near Motta, 1 October 1943. (NAC PA167138)

(Right) PLDG crewmen examine a destroyed German staff car during a regimental sweep of the flanks of the Canadian advance toward Campobasso, 26 October 1943. (NAC PA145016)

A PLDG Otter armoured recce car on an isolated Italian trail during the advance on Campobasso. (NAC PA201359)

vance to Campobasso, the PLDG did yeoman service in providing flank protection as the brigades fought their way forward. The reconnaissance squadrons ranged many kilometres on either side of the main thrust, searching out isolated enemy outposts and providing valuable intelligence to division headquarters. This active patrolling, often in the face of mortar and machine-gun fire, greatly expanded the breadth of the sector brought under Canadian control during this period.

TERMOLI

While the Calgary Regiment was recovering from its fight at Motta, brigade headquarters, located south of Barletta on the Adriatic coast, was waiting anxiously for the arrival of its other two regiments that were being shipped to the area in LSTs. The Three Rivers arrived in the port of Manfredonia, fifty kilometres to the north, on the morning of 3 October, but by the time the TRR had finished unloading its tanks, it had been placed under command of 78 Division and committed to reinforce a British amphibious landing that had gone in that same day further up the coast, at Termoli. Termoli was significant in that it was the Adriatic hinge of the interim German defence line along the Bifurno River, and the Germans were known to be rushing *16 Panzerdivison* into the area to counter the expected seaborne landing. The division was reported to have about thirty Mark IV Special tanks, equipped with long-barrelled 75mm guns, so there was an urgent need to reinforce the single British armoured regiment then *en route*.

The TRR began an eighty kilometre march northward within hours of having disembarked. It was an arduous trek, in heavy rain, most of the way along a muddy cross-country track, but by mid-afternoon on 5 October two squadrons had arrived at the Bifurno river, just south of Termoli. It was none too soon, for the Germans had counter-attacked the bridgehead earlier that day and had nearly driven the British back into the sea. The two squadrons rushed across the Bifurno on a Bailey bridge that had been completed only hours before, and their arrival had an immediate effect: the enemy pulled back slightly, while 78 Division made plans for an attack the following morning by two brigades, supported by TRR tanks.

In the first phase of the attack, on the morning of 6 October, 'C' Squadron worked as the third squadron of the County of London Yeomanry, operating on the right flank of that unit. The objective was to capture the small village of San Giacomo, four and a half kilometres due west of the start line. The terrain appeared to be ideal for armoured operations, a most unusual situation in the Italian campaign, the ground being relatively open and rising gently in a series of progressively higher plateaus. The 'C' Squadron crew commanders did, however, operate that day at one disadvantage: they had no maps and could thus not give precise locations of either themselves or whatever

enemy they met. Lieutenant Jack Wallace, recalled that "the leading troops of tanks would simply head west hoping they were going where they were supposed to."

Crossing the start line at 0725 hours, two troops advanced over the first thousand metres without encountering any opposition, but then fire from a ridge line another thousand metres in front brought their movement to a standstill. Enemy infantry were all around them, and one of the tanks was hit five times by fire coming from a small wood to the left rear, but before the crew baled out they destroyed the Mark IV tank that had fired on them. Wallace, who was awarded a Military Cross for his gallantry in this action, related the story:

> For some time the situation appeared to be a stalemate, with no less than five 'C' Squadron tanks out on the proverbial limb and the remaining 12 positioned in comfortable hull-down positions behind. Although the enemy infantry weapons could not cause any great damage, some of the more venturesome kept up a continuous nuisance fire on the exposed tanks. Somewhat more dangerous was the hail of steel fragments raining down on tank commanders' steel helmeted heads coming from ... artillery shell bursts overhead. Around 1500 hours the squadron commander (Major Mills) asked us to make an attempt to get further forward, ... which if successful would put the squadron up onto Croce Plateau. The lead tank (Lt Wallace) did not move more than a hundred yards when it was hit several times in the rear, with the shells killing the driver, the gunner and smashing the leg of the crew commander.

Several enemy tanks were knocked out and the advance continued in the company of British infantry for another 2,000 metres, until brought to a halt by a deep ravine. However, being on high ground, the squadron was able to give effective fire support to the infantry as they continued to the objective.

'B' Squadron had begun the day in a defensive position immediately to the west of Termoli, and for five hours endured heavy artillery and mortar fire which put one of their tanks out of action. The squadron commander, Major J.R. Walker, finally got permission to launch an attack against a factory complex about a thousand metres south-west of the town. Two troops went forward under the battle captain and, while one tank was destroyed soon after starting out, the others continued on, knocking out three Mark IVs. Reaching the factory, they took up hull-down positions and were able to fire on enemy tanks, infantry and transport as they pulled back.

Using the initiative expected of armoured commanders, Captain D.F. Major, the battle captain, asked for and got authority to pursue the retreating Germans. In a bold move that took them to San Giacomo on the Croce Plateau, 'B' Squadron

The Battle of Termoli, 6 October 1943. **Painting by W.S. Scott depicting the Three Rivers Regiment action in Termoli. (Courtesy 12e Régiment blindé du Canada (Milice))**

destroyed another five Mark IV tanks and many other light vehicles. In the words of the official history, "this well executed thrust was the key to success in the battle for Termoli." Shortly afterwards, the German high command issued orders to withdraw from the area.

Meanwhile, 'A' Squadron, commanded by Major C.B. Van Straubenzee, was brought forward to clear the area along the coast immediately to the west of the town of Termoli, in cooperation with the 2nd London Irish Rifles. This too was a very successful action, with the tanks "clearing out mortar and machine-gun nests located in houses, bridge embankments, woods and ditches." By late afternoon, the ground for three kilometres west of the town was in Canadian hands.

On the morning of 7 October, the commander of 38 Brigade presented his brigade pennant to Major Walker as a tribute to the excellent work done by the TRR in the fight for Termoli, and many other commendations followed. It was a significant battle in the history of the Canadian Armoured Corps; being

the first real tank-versus-tank action it fought during the war, and the Canadians, mounted in Shermans that were reputed to be not quite as good as German Mark IVs, especially their Mark IV Special, found that skilful tactical employment of the Sherman made it the equal of any German tanks yet encountered on the battlefield. There was also an important lesson learned: the enormous value of the commander on the spot seizing the initiative when a momentary opportunity was presented.

5th ARMOURED DIVISION DEPLOYS TO ITALY
Operation *Timberwolf*, the plan to deploy a second division to Italy, along with a Corps headquarters and appropriate Corps troops, was set in train in early August 1943 when Prime Minister Mackenzie King raised the matter with Winston Churchill just before the opening of the *Quadrant* Conference in Quebec. When Churchill brought the proposal to his Chiefs of Staff, it was initially rejected on the basis that there was no military justification for such a move and, in any case, shipping simply was

A view of the difficult terrain over which the Canadians advanced in October 1943. (NAC PA141867)

Major-General G.G. Simonds, Commander 5th Armoured Division November 1943 to January 1944. Painting by Charles Comfort. (Canadian War Museum 12384)

Soldiers of the Governor General's Horse Guards, part of the 5th Armoured Division advance party, buy trinkets in the market in Naples. (NAC PA204150)

not available. The Canadian government did not, however, accept this decision as final and, recognizing the political imperative, the CIGS, Sir Alan Brooke, changed his mind, but with conditions attached: the movement of the Canadians was to be based strictly on an interchange of personnel and, in order to save on shipping, they would have to take over equipment left behind in Italy by British formations which were being returned to England.

General McNaughton met with Brooke on 7 October and they agreed that an armoured division would be sent, mainly because to send an infantry division would leave II Canadian Corps in England with one infantry and two armoured divisions, which was thought to be highly unbalanced. McNaughton thus named 5 CAD to go to Italy and become part of I Canadian Corps. The British government made a formal request for this exchange of troops on 12 October, and it was approved by the Canadian Cabinet War Committee that same day. The advance parties were to leave for Italy in the last week of October.

Advance parties from all of the units involved in *Timberwolf* left England in late October, while they completed the return of all vehicles, stores and equipment accumulated over the past two years. The advance parties arrived in Naples in early November, to arrange for the reception of the fighting elements over the next month and it was their distasteful task to take over an inventory of thoroughly decrepit wheeled vehicles that had belonged to the British 7 Armoured Division, which was returning to the United Kingdom in order to prepare for the invasion of France. British ordnance officers openly admitted that many other units had already had first pick, swapping their 'crocks' for the better of 7 Armoured's vehicles.

One of the decisions made by General McNaughton in the early stage of planning *Timberwolf* proved fortuitous: he was given the choice of accepting immediate delivery of the well-used, diesel-powered Shermans that had been through much of the fighting in North Africa, or waiting for new M4A4 Shermans – the same model used in 1 Armoured Brigade. He chose commonality of equipment, even though it meant a delay of several weeks to equip 5 CAD. The wait proved longer than promised but it was worth some degree of frustration to avoid getting worn-out British tanks.

The main bodies of the division arrived in Naples in early December, to be greeted by their new commander. Major-General Guy Simonds, who had commanded the 1st Division throughout the campaign in Sicily and southern Italy, had been named on 1 November to replace Major-General C.R.S. Stein in order to give him experience with an armoured formation prior to taking command of II Canadian Corps; but as no major operation was conducted in his brief three-month tenure, any broadening of his understanding of armour was very limited.

General Simonds had arranged that the division would be concentrated in southern Italy, in the vicinity of Altamura and Matera in the mountains south-west of Bari. There it was to spend December and January in tents and makeshift billets in the surrounding towns while the regiments waited for their tanks. In nearly six weeks without tanks very little useful training could be done.

CHAPTER 9

The Battles of the Moro and Ortona

Throughout the latter part of November, 1 Division struggled against weather, rugged mountainous terrain and innumerable enemy demolitions to extend its hold on the countryside north-west of Campobasso. Finally, it managed to reach the River Sangro, where it encountered the forward positions of the German Winter Line, now usually referred to as the Bernhard Line. Along the Adriatic coast, the British 78 and 8 (Indian) Divisions fought their way across the Sangro, broke through the Bernhard Line, and, by 30 November, were on the ridge north of the river. In these operations the Three Rivers Regiment supported 78 Division, while the Calgary and Ontario Regiments worked with the Indians.

At this point, 1 Canadian Division was called upon to relieve 78 Division in the continuation of the Eighth Army's northward thrust towards Pescara. Its initial task was to force a crossing over the Moro River and then move on to capture the small port of Ortona.

At midnight on 5/6 December, attacks across the Moro were put in at three widely-separated locations: the PPCLI, on the left, were ordered to capture the village of Villa Rogatti; in the centre, three kilometres eastward, the Seaforths were to take San Leonardo; and the Hasty Ps were to establish a bridgehead along the coastal highway. Only the Patricias met with success, supported by tanks of the 44th Royal Tank Regiment, although the Hasty Ps also managed to keep a perilous toe-hold on the far bank of the river despite vicious German resistance. General Vokes gave up his intention of reinforcing the Patricias' success on the left when he was informed by his engineers that it would be impossible to construct a bridge over the Moro at that point, and decided instead to focus on establishing a crossing at San Leonardo.

Recovery of two of the Calgary Regiment's tanks that had rolled over a cliff during the attack on San Leonardo by Major Ned Amy's squadron. (NAC PA131644)

167

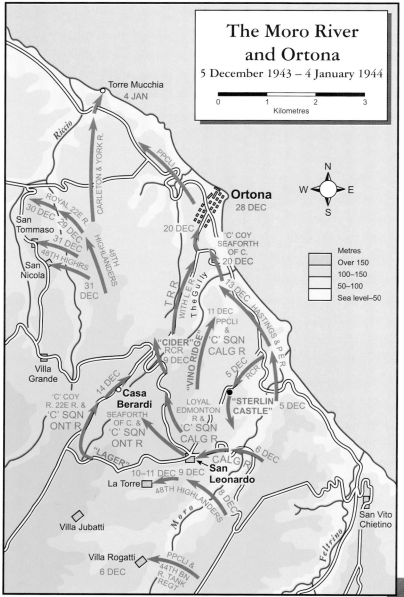

The Moro River and Ortona
5 December 1943 – 4 January 1944

Vokes decided to exploit this new crossing and the job of securing San Leonardo was given to 'A' Squadron of the Calgarys, now commanded by Acting Major Ned Amy, who had recently transferred from the Ontario Regiment. Amy was given 'D' Company of the Seaforths and told only that, "they haven't taken the bridgehead. You do it now."

With the infantry riding on the back decks of twelve Shermans, Amy's squadron moved off at best speed along the exposed, winding road down to the Moro, but two of the tanks failed to make a sharp bend in the road and rolled over a ten-metre cliff. Once in the valley, they came under heavy artillery and mortar fire, forcing the infantry to dismount and continue on foot. Negotiating the steep far bank of the river, they continued along the switchback road and climbed up to the village, only to have the lead tank disabled by a mine. Amy then led his remaining tanks off the road and continued through a muddy olive grove, until, with only four tanks still running, he managed to penetrate into the outskirts of San Leonardo. A much depleted Seaforth company, down to 39 men, arrived and cleared the enemy from the town.

Amy's small force was counter-attacked almost immediately by twelve tanks supported by infantry, and for nearly three hours the Canadians fought off repeated attempts to push them out of the town. He recalled one of the incidents during this battle:

The adjutant of the Calgary Tanks, Captain F.M. Ritchie, climbs down from a straw-camouflaged tank, San Leonardo, 10 December 1943. (NAC PA167659)

A two-pronged attack went in on the afternoon of 8 December. On the left, the 48th Highlanders quickly took the village of La Torre, just over a thousand metres southwest of San Leonardo, but the RCR, attacking out of the small bridgehead taken two days earlier by the Hasty Ps, were far less successful as they tried to take San Leonardo from the east. However, by first light on 9 December, engineers working under continual shellfire and sniping had constructed a diversion around a blown bridge on the main road over the Moro, and had carved out a passable exit for heavy vehicles on the far bank. This exceptional work by the engineers was possible in part because of effective covering fire provided throughout the night by a troop of Calgary tanks which had kept enemy machine-gunners at bay.

The enemy set fire to a haystack in front of my own tank and as I changed position I saw a German tank moving toward us from the north. It was a Mark III and we knocked it out at about 150 yards.... This all took place less than 100 yards in front of Lt. Charbonneau, who asked if he could move the position of his tank. I refused him and within minutes he himself knocked out a German Mark IV tank at about 40 yards.... This incident caused a Seaforth soldier who had been lying in the path of the oncoming German tank to run up to Charbonneau's tank, pat it on the side and say, "You big cast-iron son-of-a-bitch, I could kiss you".

For his determined and gallant leadership in taking and holding this vital bridgehead over the Moro, Major Amy was given an immediate award of the Military Cross.

The Germans now conceded the line of the Moro River but began to rush in reinforcements and redeployed *90 Panzergrenadierdivision* to a new defensive line, just south of the main road between Ortona and Orsogna. This line was hinged on a deep, narrow ravine that would soon bear an infamous name in Canadian military history – The Gully. Here, well protected from both direct and indirect fire, the Germans dug in on the reverse slope of the south bank; and many days and nights of vicious fighting would pass before The Gully was firmly in Canadian hands.

The bridgehead having been consolidated, the operations staff of 1 Division expected the Germans to withdraw northward for several kilometres, probably to the line of the River Arielli, the next obvious location where another stand could be made. Anticipating only light resistance, General Vokes decided to continue the advance almost immediately to the next tactical objective, a key crossroad two and a half kilometres north of San Leonardo which was given the codename *Cider*, control of which would allow the division a clear run at Ortona.

The first attack was put in on 10 December, by the Edmonton Regiment with support from the Calgary Tanks, but it failed to get anywhere near *Cider* before it was halted by German defenders concealed in The Gully. A second attack by the Patricias also came to nothing in the face of withering fire, but Vokes nevertheless continued to mount a series of frontal attacks in battalion strength over the next two days. This was a notable example of reinforcing failure, and frittering away the lives of many men in attacks that were always too weak to have any chance of success. Little by little, and at great cost in casualties, the Canadian infantry clawed their way forward onto what came to be known as Vino Ridge – the near side of The Gully. But the German defenders in The Gully itself could not be budged.

In mid-afternoon on 13 December, a probing attack by what remained of 'C' Company of the Seaforths and 'C' Squadron of the Calgarys, by now down to four operational Shermans,

Major-General Chris Vokes, commander of 1 Division, with Brigadiers Hoffmeister and Wyman, December 1943. (NAC PA131064)

moved along *Lager* Track from San Leonardo, near the division's left flank. This small force managed to cross The Gully on a culvert the Germans had neglected to demolish and, encountering no opposition, reached the Ortona highway and turned north-east, toward Casa Berardi and Ortona. In the process they knocked out two German tanks and captured 78 prisoners. But the force was clearly too small to press an attack on the Casa, and at dusk they were ordered to withdraw. Their relative success prompted Vokes to try the same flanking manoeuvre the next day, this time in force. The Germans had, however, also taken note of this gap in their line and moved quickly to fill it.

The Ontario Regiment's fitters spent a long night recovering bogged tanks from along *Lager* Track, and by morning 'C' Squadron had seven serviceable Shermans. At 0730 hours on 14 December, after an hour-long artillery bombardment, Major H.C. 'Snuffy' Smith set out with his squadron and a company of the Royal 22ᵉ Régiment under Captain Paul Triquet, but the thick mud was again a serious problem for the tanks and they initially lagged behind the Van Doos. One Sherman was knocked out by a Mark III soon after crossing the culvert they had traversed the previous day, but the enemy tank was promptly blasted at a range of less than a hundred metres. Major Smith felt certain that there would be more enemy tanks lying in wait, and he decided to 'wait them out' below the crest line. The brief pause proved worthwhile and the squadron destroyed another three German tanks in that location.

Smith then pressed on along the Ortona highway to catch up with Triquet's company of Van Doos. No sooner had he joined them than more enemy tanks appeared. In a tank-versus-tank fire-fight three Mark IV Specials were destroyed but two of the six remaining Shermans were also disabled.

Smith and Triquet, their force now drastically reduced, persisted in an increasingly difficult advance towards Casa Berardi. By 1400 hours, seven hours after they had set out, they had penetrated to within two hundred metres of the farm, where they were met by a wall of artillery, machine-gun and sniper fire. The Shermans fired smoke shells and HE, and the Van Doos charged. In a hand-to-hand fight against the paratrooper garrison, Triquet's men captured Casa Berardi and the ground beyond, and then prepared for the inevitable counter-attack. They were ordered to hold on, and, despite being desperately short of every form of ammunition, they did exactly that. The remainder of the Van Doos reached them in the small hours of the next morning, but the enemy was still all around. The Canadians remained cut off and under nearly continual fire for the next two days.

Casa Berardi. Painting by Arnold Hodgins, depicting the actions of Major H.C. 'Snuffy' Smith's squadron of the Ontario Regiment during the bitter fighting alongside the Royal 22e Régiment at Casa Berardi on 14 and 15 December 1943. During this action Major Paul Triquet of the 'Van Doos' won a well-deserved Victoria Cross. (Courtesy The Ontario Regiment Officers' Mess)

The Germans mounted a strong counter-attack on the afternoon of 15 December, with some two hundred paratroopers supported by tanks and, for a time, the situation was very tenuous. The artillery saved the day, raining 1,400 rounds on the attacking Germans within a span of fifteen minutes. The paratroopers reeled back, and during the night a mule train brought in desperately needed supplies. Also, seven additional Ontario tanks arrived, each loaded with all the ammunition they could cram inside their turrets and co-drivers hatches. This strengthened garrison continued to hold Casa Berardi until 18 December.

The extraordinary gallantry displayed by all in this action is one of the great feats in Canadian military annals. Captain Paul Triquet was later awarded the Victoria Cross for his valour and exceptional leadership. No doubt equally deserving of the highest decoration, Major Smith was given a Military Cross. Triquet always insisted that his VC was for all of the men who fought so bravely at Casa Berardi, but especially for 'Snuffy' Smith's valiant endeavours that day.

Operation *Morning Glory,* an attack by 1 Brigade, supported by the TRR, was launched on the morning of 18 December, to drive a deep wedge into the defensive line that the Germans still held south-west of Casa Berardi. The most notable feature of this assault was the meticulous preparations made to ensure effective tank-infantry cooperation. Each of the squadron commanders was detailed to move with the CO of the supported battalion, and, to ensure that communications were maintained, an infantry officer was assigned to ride in each squadron commander's tank with a radio set tuned to the battalion frequency. Additionally, troop leaders met with company and platoon commanders to sort out precisely what was to take place during the attack, and how each arm could best support the other.

This preparation proved to be very effective: tanks fired on every building and haystack that could hide enemy machine guns and, on occasions when soft ground forced the tanks to take a different route than the infantry, communications were such that fire support never faltered. There is no doubt that the TRR was one of the first armoured regiments to master the complex techniques needed for effective battlefield cooperation between tanks and infantry, and these were soon adopted by the Ontario and Calgary Regiments. Throughout its subse-

Reinforcements Moving Up in the Ortona Salient. **Painting by Lawren Harris. (Canadian War Museum 12712)**

quent service in Italy, 1 Armoured Brigade, whose purpose had always been to support infantry operations, was known for its competence and reliability in providing direct fire support.

Morning Glory cleared the remaining enemy from The Gully and established control over the dominating ridge to the northwest. However, a second operation, aimed at taking *Cider* crossroads by advancing parallel to the Ortona highway, was a near disaster for the RCR and a squadron of TRR tanks. The artillery support, planned from grossly inaccurate maps, fell on our own troops and had to be lifted prematurely, then the RCR were caught in the open by heavy crossfire and suffered a large number of casualties. The operation continued the next day, however, and this time they quickly took *Cider*. The way was now open to Ortona.

ORTONA

No-one really expected that the Germans would put up much of a fight for Ortona, a relatively insignificant fishing port, and the question has often been asked why the Eighth Army did not simply by-pass it and force the enemy to withdraw by an outflanking manoeuvre. But 1 Canadian Division was given the task of taking the place, and the advance up the highway from *Cider* crossroad began at noon on 20 December. The Loyal Edmontons, supported by twelve tanks of 'C' Squadron of the TRR, were tasked to occupy buildings on the southern outskirts of the town, but Major Frank Johnson's tanks were slowed by mines early in this move. Lieutenant Melvin's Sherman was literally blown to pieces when it ran over a huge demolition charge buried in the roadway and the entire crew was killed. While attempting to by-pass the resulting crater, three other tanks had tracks blown off in a minefield. Fortunately there was little other opposition and this force reached its objective at 1430 hours. Later in the day they were joined by a Seaforth company that had moved toward Ortona along a coastal track.

Ortona was garrisoned by two battalions of paratroopers and they clearly intended to hold the town. They had prepared

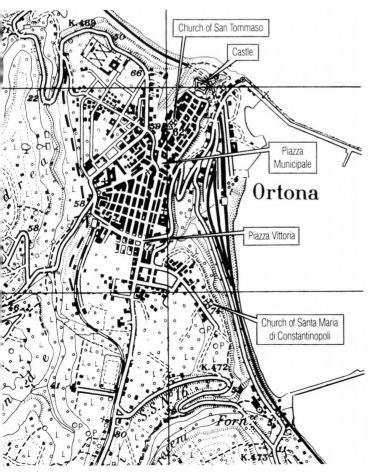

Map of the town of Ortona, part of a 1:25,000 map issued to participating troops. The main road from the south becomes the Corso Vittorio Emanuele, the main street.

Captured German paratroopers pass a Three Rivers Regiment Sherman, Ortona, 23 December 1943. (NAC PA152835)

their defences in the older part of the town with great care. The main street leading into the town from the south, the Corso Vittorio Emanuele, had been left clear, so as to lure the attackers into a killing ground in the main square in the centre of town, the Piazza Municipale. Almost all of the side streets not too narrow for the passage of a tank had been blocked by mounds of rubble from demolished stone buildings, and anti-tank guns were sited behind many of these. All along the Corso, machine-gun posts had been prepared in the upper floors of the sturdy stone buildings.

The Edmontons moved into the southern part of the built-up area on the morning of 21 December, with one company clearing buildings on either side of the Corso. TRR Shermans moved somewhat cautiously, adopting a 'staggered column' formation wherever possible – the lead tank on one side of the street, the next twenty or more metres behind on the other side, so that it could provide covering fire to the tank ahead, with the third tank, on the same side as the first, bringing up the rear and providing more covering fire.

As they advanced the tanks fired HE shells into every building and, as they crossed side streets, crew commanders remembered the gap drill they had learned in basic troop tactics in England, but neither tankers nor infantry had experience of fighting in a built-up area, so much of what they did was simply common sense improvisation. By nightfall, they had reached the Piazza Vittoria, which was where the 'old town' really began. There one of the tanks lost a track to a mine, the only armoured casualty of the day.

Early the next morning, the attack moved into the old town, and the hard fighting began. Here sturdy, thick-walled, stone buildings, usually four stories high, were nestled one right against the other. Machine-gun nests dominated the deserted streets, and every other

A solitary Three Rivers' Sherman advances into the centre of Ortona, 23 December 1943. (NAC PA114029)

Canadian Armour Passing Through Ortona. Charles Comfort's painting vividly depicts the enormous damage to the town during the siege. (Canadian War Museum 12245)

building seemed to contain a small party of paratroopers armed with semi-automatic rifles, submachine-guns and grenades. The infantry could not move in the streets without suffering severe casualties, so they endeavoured to stay inside the buildings while clearing from block to block, 'mouse-holing' their way from one building to the next by blowing holes in the interior walls. This vicious, often hand-to-hand fighting went on for a week.

Ortona's streets were not what anyone would call good tank country but the TRR gave stalwart support throughout the battle. For the most part, tanks served as mobile pillboxes, firing HE rounds to knock down walls and destroy machine-gun posts, while suppressing snipers with machine-gun fire. They provided cover when the infantry had to venture into the streets, brought ammunition forward, took out casualties, and on at least one occasion deliberately crashed into a building to crush an anti-tank gun crew. All the while, they had to contend with anti-tank guns, mines and snipers who took great relish in picking off crew commanders or crews foolhardy enough to dismount. They were also plagued by grenades and 'beehive' charges lobbed from the upper stories of ruined buildings.

The Germans finally withdrew on the night of 27 December, bringing to an end the most ferocious battle the Canadians had yet experienced. In a week the TRR crews had become masters of the art of armoured warfare in built-up areas, but the regiment lost twelve men killed in action and 21 wounded.

Derelict Sherman Tank Beside the Berardi Road. **Painting by Charles Comfort. (Canadian War Museum 12274)**

WINTER IN THE MUD AND RAIN

By late December 1943, as the countryside turned into a sea of mud, Canadian soldiers understood perfectly why the Romans, some two thousand years earlier, had constructed hard-surfaced roads through the length and breadth of the peninsula. Movement off main roads became close to impossible, as the men of 1 Armoured Brigade found during their support of operations aimed at clearing out the Germans remaining immediately west of Ortona. In fact, with the exception of a continuation of the difficult offensive in the mountains around Cassino and an Allied amphibious landing at Anzio on 22 January, operations in the whole of the Italian theatre wound down into static holding actions because of foul weather and soaked ground. 1 Division spent the winter on the line of the Riccio and Arielli rivers and, until the end of March, the regiments of 1 Armoured Brigade took turns occupying defensive positions in support of the division. Occasionally they were employed in futile minor offensive operations serving little real purpose.

Senior officers were well aware that there was a risk of a serious morale problem due to a combination of miserable living conditions and the long period of relative inactivity, compounded by slow delivery of mail from Canada. One of the measures taken to counter the problem was to produce a daily newspaper for the troops. *The Maple Leaf* began publishing in mid-January 1944, and among its most popular features was a cartoon depicting the misadventures of a sad-sack soldier named Herbie, who was always getting into scrapes. Herbie was the product of Bing Coughlin, a PLDG sergeant, who had served through Sicily and southern Italy. The troops identified strongly with the wryly humorous situations Coughlin created for Herbie and *The Maple Leaf* published two booklets of Herbie cartoons to cope with the many requests for copies. Herbie soon became so well known that many daily newspapers in Canada also carried the cartoon.

After what seemed like an endless delay, the regiments of 5 CAD finally began to receive their new tanks. The Stathconas

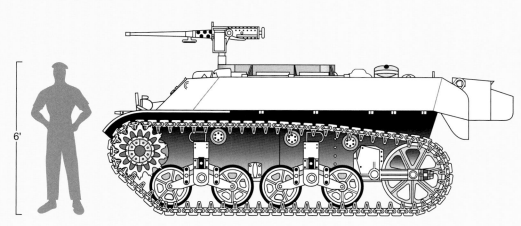

De-turreted Stuart tanks were widely used by the regiments of 5th Armoured Division in Italy. The Stuart was generally called a 'Honey' tank, a name that had originated with the British in North Africa. (Drawing by Chris Johnson)

M3A3 Stuart Recce
Country of Origin: British/Canadian conversion of U.S. M3A3
Crew: 4 (Commander, Gunner, Driver, Assistant Driver)
Length: 16 feet 6 inches
Width: 8 feet 3 inches
Height: 6 feet (approximately)
Weight: 31,752 pounds
Engine: Continental 7 cylinder radial, gasoline
Maximum Speed: 36 mph
Range: 70 miles
Armour – Maximum: 51 mm
　　　　　Minimum: 10 mm
Armament: .30 calibre MG M1919A4 in bow mount
　　　.50 calibre MG HB M2 in flexible mount on top of hull

6'

"What d'ya mean, look out for the tree? I thought you were driving."

"What a helluva time to run out of ammo!"

'Herbie' cartoons by Sergeant Bing Coughlin of the 4 PLDG appeared weekly in the Army newspaper, *The Maple Leaf.*

(Above) 8th Hussars tanks lined up for an indirect shoot on the German-held Tollo crossroads, 4 February 1944. This was the first occasion when indirect fire from Shermans was employed in operations. (NAC PA204152)

(Right) Brigadier G.R. Bradbrooke, commander of 5th Armoured Brigade from September 1942 to February 1944, talking to Major-General Guy Simonds while he was commander of 5th Armoured Division. (NAC PA132782)

(Above) Major-General E.L.M. Burns, commander of 5th Armoured Division January to March 1944. Burns was no stranger to the Armoured Corps, having served as Officer Administering the Corps in 1941 prior to taking command of 4th Armoured Brigade. (NAC PA134178)

got the first batch, and by 12 January had their full complement of 52, along with eleven M5 Stuarts for the recce troop. The 8th Hussars were fully equipped a week later, and the British Columbia Dragoons had two complete squadrons by the end of the month. The Horse Guards, however, had to wait until mid-February before they received their Shermans and Stuarts. Conversion training was a relatively simple matter because each of the units had been issued six Shermans several months before leaving England, and within days of getting the new tanks the regiments were busy firing the 75mm gun on improvised ranges near Matera. The Stuarts, generally known in the division as 'Honeys', had their turrets removed to lower their silhouette and improve cross-country mobility, with a .50 calibre Browning mounted on the turret ring. The Strathconas were the first to be sent north to gain experience, and they spent the last weeks of January with 4 (Indian) Division in the vicinity of Guardiagrele on the River Sangro.

When I Canadian Corps was activated on 1 February, the infantry of 5 CAD took over a section of front west of Ortona, and 5 Armoured Brigade was deployed as divisional reserve, housed in makeshift, boggy camps along the Moro River. For five weeks the rain was unceasing; "fog to drizzle to torrential downpour" is the description given in the Strathcona history. Only the Hussars saw any 'action' in this period. They persuaded Brigadier Bradbrooke to try some indirect shooting and, after proving that this could be done very effectively, the whole regiment lined up for a shoot on to enemy positions at the Tollo crossroad. The demonstration worked to perfection; in less than two minutes 720 high-explosive shells landed on the crossroad and the practicality of indirect tank fire was firmly established.

A number of changes in key personnel took place at this time, many of them related to preparations for the impending invasion of Normandy. Major-General E.L.M. Burns replaced Simonds in command of 5 CAD on 30 January, when the latter was promoted to command II Canadian Corps in England. Later in the month, there were new commanders in both armoured brigades. On 22 February, Brigadier Bradbrooke, the

The Canadian Volunteer Service Medal, awarded with a silver bar in January 1944 to all men who had completed 60 days of overseas service. The medals themselves were not issued until after the war, but the ribbon was worn. The troops often referred to it in a somewhat disparaging manner as the 'Spam' medal, since it 'arrived with the rations'.

highly respected former Strathcona, was relieved of command of 5 Armoured Brigade, ostensibly because of age, and replaced by Desmond Smith. It is likely, however, that Bradbrooke had paid the price for being too independent of mind for General Simonds' liking. In his book, *Mud and Green Fields*, George Kitching reported how Bradbrooke incurred Simonds' wrath during a divisional cloth model exercise when Simonds was critical of Bradbrooke's failure to halt his formation in order for the artillery to catch up, only to be told by Bradbrooke that he had no need to wait for the artillery since he already had more than enough guns on his tanks! Apparently Simonds, the gunner, could not forgive this heresy and Bradbrooke simply had to go.

In 1 Armoured Brigade, Bob Wyman was replaced on 27 February by newly promoted Bill Murphy, a former commanding officer of the BCD, and Wyman returned to England to take command of 2 Armoured Brigade for the invasion of Normandy. At the same time, Lieutenant-Colonel Leslie Booth, commanding officer of the Three Rivers Regiment, was promoted and returned to the UK to take command of 4 Armoured Brigade. Several units lost some of their best officers, such as Majors Amy and Smith and Captains E.R. Watkin and E.F. Mooers, in order to provide battle-experienced leaders in units which were destined for Normandy.

CHAPTER 10

The Battles
of the Liri Valley

By early February 1944 it had become apparent that the Allies' somewhat overblown hope of forcing the Germans to pull back to the north of Rome had failed. The offensive in the Adriatic sector had ground to a muddy halt. On the other side of the peninsula, the Americans had gained a small toehold in the outer defences of the Gustav Line, but had then been stalled at Cassino. The Anglo-American bridgehead at Anzio had been effectively contained by the Germans and a revamping of the strategy for the Italian campaign was clearly needed.

By the end of the month, the high command had decided to give overriding priority to the capture of Rome and concentrate the bulk of the Allied forces west of the Appenines for a major offensive to begin in May. The gradual redeployment of troops for this offensive began in March. I Canadian Corps was relieved in the Ortona sector on the 7th and 5 CAD moved into reserve in the area of Castelnuovo, just north of Motta, to train and prepare for the coming offensive.

For the regiments of 5 Armoured Brigade, March and April were by far the busiest months since their arrival in Italy. Desmond Smith, nicknamed "Sixteen Cylinder" by the troops, very quickly set his stamp on the brigade, and intensive training was the order of the day. Regimental schools were set up to hone the skills of drivers and radio operators, and a tank gunnery range was established where each of the units had exclusive use of its own firing point and target area. As it was deemed that "tank-cum-infantry" tactics within the division needed significant improvement, a great deal of time was slated for squadron/company training and tactical exercises with the units of 11 Infantry Brigade. Unfortunately, too little of this training actually took place.

This was also the time for technical innovation. To give the brigade's nearly two hundred tanks some

measure of extra protection, strips of steel track were welded to the front of the hulls, and sections of steel plate were added over the gas tanks. To aid in communications with the infantry, all tanks got a 'tank telephone' mounted externally on the rear of the hull, a No.38 set radio – which had a frequency compatible with the infantry's No.18 man-pack radios – was installed in the co-drivers compartment of some tanks, and a second No.19 set was placed in all command tanks. And, adopting an idea originating in the BCD to make camouflage easier, short sections of two-inch pipe were welded on the sides of the Sherman turrets and on the hulls of the 'Honey' tanks, into which branches and foliage could be inserted easily to break the shape of the vehicle. The men soon dubbed these bits of pipe "flower pots".

General Burns' tenure as commander of the division proved to be very short, for on 20 March he was promoted and appointed to command of I Canadian Corps when General Crerar was recalled to England to take command of First

Brigadier J.D.B. Smith, DSO, OBE. Painting by Charles Comfort. Brigadier Smith served as commander of 5th Armoured Brigade from February to June 1944, and earlier, between June 1942 and May 1943 he had commanded 4th Armoured Brigade. He subsequently served as Brigadier General Staff in I Corps Headquarters. (Canadian War Museum 12385)

Canadian Army. Major-General B.M. Hoffmeister, a militiaman from Vancouver who had commanded the Seaforth Highlanders and 2 Infantry Brigade in quick succession, became the new division commander, a post he was to hold with great distinction until the end of the war.

One of Hoffmeister's greatest strengths was a clear perception of the limitations of his own knowledge or understanding. When taking command of the division he told Des Smith that he "knew nothing about tank operations," and asked for his help, and members of his staff have stated that he was always ready to listen to the views of the staff and of his brigadiers. All of his soldiers soon learned that he was a man who cared very deeply about their well-being.

In the meanwhile, 1 Armoured Brigade had been placed under the command of XIII British Corps and, at the end of March, was moved across Italy into tented camps at Venafro, on the Volturno River. Here the brigade organized tank-infantry cooperation schools for units of the British 4 and 78 Divisions, and later 8 (Indian) Division with whom it was to go into battle in the assault on the Gustav Line.

With the exception of a brief period during the fight for the Liri Valley, 1 Armoured Brigade was to spend the rest of the war in Italy in support of British or Indian formations, rather than

Major-General Bertram M. Hoffmeister, Commander of 5th Armoured Division from March 1944 to June 1945. General Hoffmeister is widely considered to be the best of the Canadian general officers who served during the Second World War. (Canadian Forces Photo Unit)

Canadian. This strange situation apparently had its origins in a personality conflict between General Vokes and Brigadier Wyman which prompted Vokes to state, after the Ortona battle, "… if at any time there was any armoured brigade in support of my division, I would be pleased if it were NOT the 1st Canadian Armoured Brigade;" after Wyman's departure, however, Vokes admitted that he regretted having made this judgement about a formation that higher British commanders termed "the best armoured brigade in Italy".

During much of this time of tank-infantry training, the Three Rivers Regiment had squadrons attached to British brigades opposite Cassino for possible counter-attacks. TRR crews also temporarily manned tanks of the New Zealand armoured brigade, positioned in the rubble of Cassino where they were only metres away from the nearest German positions, in order to give the New Zealand crewmen a rest. These changeovers were carried out at night, very furtively.

In mid-April, I Canadian Corps began to move under a veil of great secrecy to a concentration area near Caserta, on the Volturno River, to be in position for the upcoming offensive in the Liri Valley. All regimental insignia and vehicle markings were removed in the interests of security, and for several weeks all units were hidden away in tiny olive groves.

Men of the Calgary Regiment instructing troops of the 8th Indian Division in tank-infantry cooperation, Castelfrentano, Italy, 30 March 1944. (NAC PA144108)

Jeep train carrying supplies on what was known as 'Inferno Track' to Three Rivers Regiment tanks on Monte Cairo, overlooking Cassino, 18 April 1944. (NAC PA140132)

THE BATTLE OF THE LIRI VALLEY

From its beginning south of Cassino, the Liri Valley runs north-west for 24 kilometres, to Ceprano, where it joins with the valley of the River Sacco that runs much of the way to Rome. The valley is six to ten kilometres wide throughout this length. The Liri River runs generally along the south-western side of the valley, with a range of low mountains between it and the coastal plain. On the north side of the valley is Highway 6, the main road to Rome and, beyond it, a rugged mountainous massif centred on 1,700 metre-high Monte Cairo which dominates the first sixteen kilometres of the valley. General Alexander proclaimed it to be the "gateway to Rome", but the Germans also understood this and they had taken advantage of every natural barrier in the valley to ensure that it would not be the easy route to Rome that the Allies hoped it might be.

There were many natural barriers for the Germans to exploit in preparing their defence. At the entrance to the valley ran the Gari River, also known as the Rapido in the area of Cassino, and as the Garigliano south of its junction with the Liri. The Gari was roughly twenty metres wide and more than two metres deep, with a swift current, making it a tank obstacle throughout its length, and for nearly a hundred metres on both sides of the river the ground was wet and boggy. Immediately beyond the Gari, the ground rose to a series of hills that overlooked and dominated the river line, and behind these hills, the ground, even though heavily cultivated with olive groves and vineyards, was rough country – small hills, meandering steep-sided ravines, scattered woods, narrow sunken farm trails, innumerable small streams and isolated stone farm buildings. Nine kilometres beyond the Gari lay a deep gully named the Forme d'Aquino, another tank obstacle over much of its length, and five kilometres further on came the River San Martino. Seven kilometres beyond that was the Melfa river.

The Germans had constructed two formidable defensive lines. The Gustav Line, anchored on Cassino, followed the line of the Gari. The second, Adolf Hitler Line, its complex of anti-tank gun positions and machine-gun posts never quite completed but still a major barrier, ran just in front of Aquino and

The ruins of the town of Cassino, with the rubble of the Monte Cassino Abbey above. (NAC PA136204)

Pontecorvo, eleven kilometres behind the Gustav Line. By and large, the ground between was not good tank country, but in comparison with much Italian countryside it was as good as it got.

The Liri offensive, code-named *Diadem,* was to be carried out in three broad stages. XIII British Corps would make an assault crossing of the Gari and break through the vaunted Gustav Line, while, at the same time, II Polish Corps was to capture the town of Cassino and the ruins of the Benedictine monastery atop Monte Cassino. Then the Canadian Corps would be brought in to take over the southern half of the valley and 1 Canadian Division would carry the attack through the Hitler Line. Finally, 5 CAD would exploit to Ceprano, opening the way to the beleaguered Anzio bridgehead and then to Rome.

For the Canadian Armoured Corps, the Liri Valley offensive was to be the most important operation of the Italian campaign. It was to be the only battle in which every Canadian armoured regiment in the theatre participated, and it was the real baptism of fire of 5 CAD.

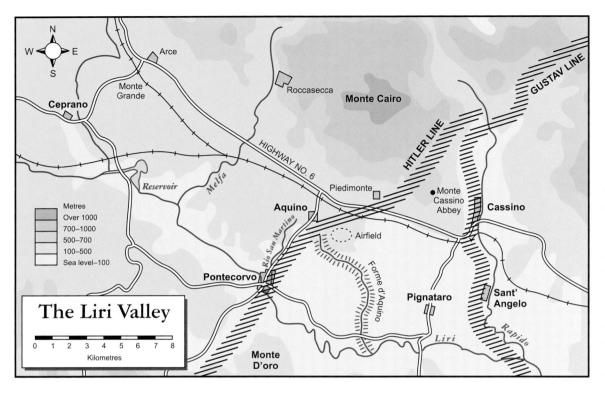

The Liri Valley

Metres
Over 1000
700–1000
500–700
100–500
Sea level–100

0 1 2 3 4 5 6 7 8
Kilometres

use by coating the cross-hairs with luminous paint, and the crews had been trained in night firing.

The heaviest artillery barrage fired since El Alamein opened up on the Gustav Line positions along the Gari at 2300 hrs on 11 May, and 45 minutes later British and Indian infantry began to cross the river in assault boats, supported by the fire of three troops of the TRR. The Ontarios and Calgarys began to move forward from hides behind Monte Trocchio, but as the Gari could not be forded they had to wait for engineers to construct Bailey bridges. Four bridges were to have been built in the usual fashion, two for the use of the Ontarios, designated *Cardiff* and *London,* and a third, *Oxford,* for both regiments; the fourth, *Plymouth,* was to be laid in a new and very different way designed to work under heavy fire.

A devastating weight of machine-gun and mortar fire caused the first two sites to be abandoned before first light, but *Oxford,* south of Sant' Angelo was ready for traffic at 0830. 'B' Squadron of the Ontarios moved across at once but immediately ran into difficulties in the muddy flats on the far bank, where more than a half of the tanks became bogged or lost tracks to anti-tank mines. Shortly afterward 'C' Squadron followed and ran into the same problem. The Ontarios' commanding officer, Lieutenant-Colonel Purves, described the situation as a "considerable shambles".

Plymouth was the brainchild of Captain Tony Kingsmill, commander of the Calgarys' Light Aid Detachment (LAD). It was a 25-metre-long bridge mounted on rollers, its forward end set on top of a de-turreted Sherman which would carry

THE ASSAULT ON THE GUSTAV LINE

In the first stage of the battle, the assault crossing of the Gari river, 1 Armoured Brigade provided the tank support. The Ontario Regiment was with 17 (Indian) Brigade, crossing the Gari opposite the town of Sant' Angelo, and the Calgary Regiment with 19 (Indian) Brigade, assaulting a kilometre further south. The Three Rivers Regiment had a unique task in this phase, something that had not been tried before, the provision of direct fire support to the infantry crossings at night. The sighting telescopes of the three troops involved were adapted for night

Line of heavily camouflaged 1st Armoured Brigade Shermans preparing to advance across the Gari River, 11 May 1944. (NAC PA139891)

1 Armoured Brigade Sherman crossing a Bailey bridge over the Gari River at Sant' Angelo, 12 May 1944. (NAC PA173362)

it to the near bank of the river. At that point a second Sherman, fitted with a bracket supporting the rear end of the bridge, would push it forward on the rollers until it extended far over the first, carrier, tank. The carrier would then drive into the river until the front end of the bridge was in place on the far bank, and the pusher tank would disengage, leaving the bridge ready for use.

Trials conducted along the Volturno River had shown that the idea worked well, but it very nearly did not in the early morning of 12 May. Assembly of the bridge on the carrier tank was slowed considerably by heavy shelling, and by the time it was ready to be driven to the river bank the entire area *was* blanketed in a thick smoke screen, making movement to the launch site slow and difficult. It was after 0900 hrs when Captain Kingsmill began to guide his bridge down to the launching position. His actions that morning earned him a Military Cross, and the citation describes what happened:

… Under direct observation and subject to intense mortar and machine gun fire Captain Kingsmill, with no thought for his own safety, coolly walked backward over a distance of 500 yards in front of the tank-borne bridge. He directed it successfully into place at the first attempt. Wounded by an exploding shell he dauntlessly remained at the river crossing during the final securing of the span. When an enemy counter-attack developed from

the opposite side of the river … he climbed into one of the two supporting tanks, methodically proceeding to machine gun the German fire position. … Not until the counter-attack was beaten off did Captain Kingsmill consider leaving to have his wounds attended.

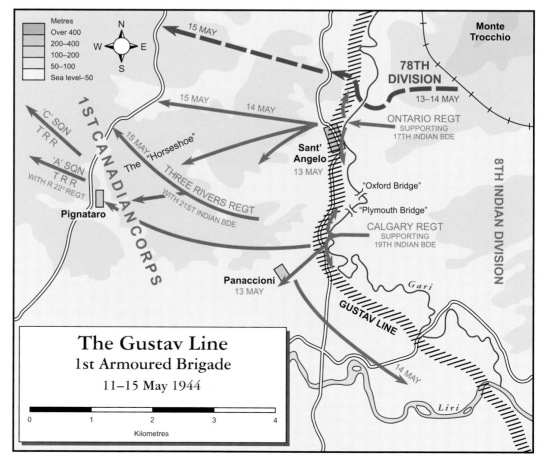

The Gustav Line
1st Armoured Brigade
11–15 May 1944

Sherman on the road near Sant' Angelo, 12 May 1944. (NAC PA139890)

(Above) Bridge on the Gari at Sant' Angelo, where the Ontario Regiment and most of the Calgary Regiment crossed the river. (NAC PA193898)

(Right) Valentine-mounted Scissors bridge, with destroyed Stuart tank in the foreground. (NAC PA204156)

However, only four Shermans got across *Plymouth* before it was badly damaged by enemy artillery, and the rest of the Calgary Regiment's tanks had to be diverted to cross the Gari at *Oxford*. The situation there was only marginally better. By noon sixteen of the Ontarios' 'B' and 'C' Squadron tanks were mired in the mud on the far bank. Gradually, however, fourteen of them were recovered, largely through the efforts of Captain G.L. Patton, RCEME commander of the Ontarios' LAD, and his recovery section commanded by Sergeant F.L. Carson, all of whom worked under continuous fire.

'B' Squadron, working with the Indian Frontier Force Regiment, cleared the immediate area to the first objective line which was about 800 metres from the Gari, but was unable to move northward into Sant' Angelo because of a blown bridge and muddy ground. However, for the rest of the day the two Ontario squadrons across the river continued to destroy pockets of the enemy, and by nightfall 'B' Squadron tanks were in positions where they could bring fire down in support of the Royal Fusiliers who were holding, very tenuously, north of Sant' Angelo.

'C' Squadron of the Calgarys eventually got across the bridge at *Oxford*, but only four of its sixteen Shermans got through the mud to the north-south lateral road just beyond the Gari. By firing on enemy positions on high ground to the west, these four were able to assist the Punjabis in widening the bridgehead. They then moved on to the north-west of the village of Panaccioni. Meanwhile 'A' Squadron had also crossed at *Oxford* and worked its way southward. The tanks, however, failed to make any contact with the infantry, the Argyll and Sutherland Highlanders, and eventually linked up with the remnants of 'C' Squadron at Panaccioni.

By nightfall the slender bridgehead over the Gari, still only a few hundred metres deep in some places, was considerably

Vehicles of a squadron 'A' Echelon moving forward to replenish tanks in the forward area. Behind the Sherman tank, which is probably a replacement for a casualty, is a White half-track and a105mm Priest self-propelled gun. (NAC PA177098)

more secure, with two infantry brigades and five squadrons of tanks across the river, even though the enemy still held key terrain at Sant' Angelo and the whole of the higher ground to the west, termed the Sant' Angelo 'horseshoe'.

The situation was considerably better on the morning of 13 May. Kingsmill's bridge at *Plymouth* crossing had been repaired and reinforcements were moving into the bridgehead. However, there was hard fighting all day as the Germans contested every piece of ground. Sant' Angelo was taken in a deliberate attack during the early afternoon, even though only two of the Ontarios' tanks were able to provide support. Corporal L.J. Toye's crew destroyed a Mark IV positioned in a cellar, shot up several fortified houses, and in general contributed greatly to the clearing of the village. The two tanks then went forward with the Indian infantry to clear a plateau to the north.

By mid-afternoon a scissors bridge had been positioned over a blown culvert, and the whole of 'C' Squadron moved through Sant' Angelo to assist the Royal Fusiliers, on the right of the Indian Division's sector, clear the entire area as far as the Colle Romano. 'B' Squadron, by last light, held the western part of the Colle Vittiglio. In the south end of the bridgehead, the Calgarys

assisted the Punjabis in taking the village of Panaccioni. By nightfall the bridgehead was 1,500 metres deep and the Germans no longer commanded the high ground overlooking the Gari River.

The battle was carried into the depths of the Gustav Line defences on the 15th, even though German resistance intensified and there was considerable confused fighting. The TRR was brought in to support attacks by 21 Indian Brigade, in the south-centre of the Indian division's sector. Here the ground "was hilly and rough, cut by ravines and contained a lot of scrub and other cover. There were no roads except the occasional sunken wagon track and these were worse than useless as they provided the enemy with excellent defensive positions." On at least three occasions the Three Rivers' tanks got beyond their initial objective, only to be called back to assist the infantry in clearing by-passed machine-gun posts.

Despite these setbacks, by mid-evening the lead squadron reached the village of Marchisella, 1,300 metres north of Pignataro, where they set up a defence. The CO, Lieutenant-Colonel Fern Caron, later commented that tank-infantry cooperation in this attack was very poor, in large measure because they had never had the opportunity to tee-up drills with the battalions of this brigade.

The Ontarios supported attacks by Gurkhas early in the morning, and for the first time encountered enemy anti-tank guns, losing three Shermans. The Germans then launched a counter-attack and the infantry and most of the tanks were forced to pull back. Lieutenant Bob Mulcaster, however, did not get word to withdraw and held his ground, calling in artillery on the advancing enemy with great skill. The German attack was broken up, enabling a counter-attack by 'B' and 'C' Squadrons to push the enemy completely off the high ground, and eight anti-tank guns, one Mark IV tank and one self-propelled gun were destroyed. In the southern part of the bridgehead, the Calgarys assisted in the clearing of the town of Pignataro.

1 Canadian Division went into the action on 16 May and during the course of the day Canadian infantry brigades took over ground held by the Indians. As a British armoured brigade had been allocated in support, the Ontarios and Calgarys were relieved during the afternoon of 16 May. For the moment, however, the TRR, however, remained in positions north of Pignataro in support of 3 Brigade because heavy traffic moving into the bridgehead had delayed some of the British armour.

On 17 May units of 3 Brigade, supported by the Three Rivers tanks, exploited in a north-westerly direction over very difficult ground, and by nightfall, after an advance of nearly five kilometres, had secured positions overlooking the Forme d'Aquino ravine. It was a hard fight, and while the TRR took 128 prisoners they lost fifteen tanks during the day. By this time the sense of accomplishment in the whole of 1 Armoured Brigade was justifiably high: the Gustav Line had been broken and all three regiments had played important parts in this vital first stage of the battle for the Liri Valley.

BREAKING THE HITLER LINE

By 18 May the British 78 and 1 Canadian Divisions had all but closed up to the second defensive line in the Liri Valley – the Hitler Line. This position, about 800 metres deep, was not based on any natural obstacle, but rather on a continuous line of barbed wire stretching from the foot of the mountains, two kilometres east of the village of Piedimonte and zig-zagging south-west across the valley, passing in front of Aquino, crossing the Forme d'Aquino about 1,500 metres south of Aquino

and east of Pontecorvo, and crossing the Liri 1,500 metres below that latter town. Anti-tank ditches blocked the most obvious tank approaches, and there were a considerable number of anti-tank gun emplacements, including eighteen *Panzerturm* – tank turrets with long-barrelled 75mm guns, installed on a base of reinforced concrete and brick rubble. Each of these *Panzerturm* positions was protected by smaller anti-tank guns, self-propelled guns and machine-guns.

The first attempt to penetrate the Hitler Line came in the 78 Division sector, where the commander thought there was a fleeting chance to break through at Aquino before the Germans had time to man all their positions. This initiative led to the

Panzerturm on the Hitler Line. Painting by Charles Comfort. The Germans had emplaced about 18 Panther turrets, with long-barrelled 75mm guns, in concrete emplacements topped with brick rubble, covering the main approaches to the Hitler Line. Many Canadian and British tanks succumbed to their fire. (Canadian War Museum 12341)

Ontario and Calgary Regiments being hastily recalled to the battle, from a rest area fifteen kilometres east of the Gari which they had just reached, on the afternoon of 18 May.

The Ontarios were ordered to move off at once to a holding area north-east of Sant' Angelo, but almost immediately on arriving there they got orders to continue to an assembly area south-east of Aquino airport, and to be prepared to support an attack at first light on the 19th. The move forward in darkness was exceptionally difficult, as much of the route allocated consisted of narrow dirt tracks and trails, many of which were not even shown on maps, and the route was often clogged with other traffic. They arrived in the appointed assembly area at 0200 hrs, just in time for orders, and learned that the regiment was to support the 5th Buffs in an attack on the town of Aquino at 0500 hours.

When the tanks moved out at H-Hour a thick morning fog blanketed the area, muffling the sound of a barrage being fired on suspected enemy positions in and near the town. Two troops of 'B' Squadron moved with an infantry company along a road leading directly from the Aquino airfield to Aquino, while 'A' Squadron moved to the northern end of the airfield to reach a position to give covering fire. Almost immediately the advance had to be delayed because of restricted visibility, but shortly after 0700 hours 'B' Squadron reached a cemetery mid-way between the airfield and the town. Here they ran into spirited resistance by German infantry, who fought tenaciously between the graves as the tanks tried to winkle them out.

With the advance stalled, 'A' Squadron was sent north, to the railway track, with the intention of outflanking the enemy, while a 'B' Squadron troop moved through thick vineyards south of the axis, to within three hundred metres of the town. Then the fog suddenly cleared and German anti-tank guns opened fire. One gun at the edge of the town was destroyed, but a well-camouflaged *Panzerturm* came into action at nearly point-blank range, hitting each tank of the troop at least twice and setting them on fire. The British infantry were heavily shelled at this time, and when their CO was killed all contact with them was lost for the remainder of the day. 'C' Squadron, which had moved in behind 'A' Squadron, north of the airfield, soon lost two tanks to an anti-tank gun on high ground beyond the railway.

78 Division headquarters then sent a message urging the

Camouflaged Sherman belonging to the Ontario Regiment, near the Aquino airfield, 19 May 1944. (NAC PA114462)

regiment to hold its ground, and throughout the day, despite constant shelling and mortaring, the tanks continued to engage the enemy. They were protected to some degree by a smoke screen laid by the artillery to the north and west of their positions. Finally, at dusk the regiment was pulled back to a harbour south of the airfield, having lost twelve tanks to anti-tank fire and one to a mine, while every tank had received at least one hit from a mortar or artillery shell. The main lesson learned was that the Germans were indeed holding the Hitler Line in strength; it would take a concerted effort to break through, and it was decided that the division would mount a set-piece attack on 23 May.

Meanwhile, 4 PLDG, who had moved into the area south of Pignataro on 18 May, had been tasked with providing flank protection for the division in the area

Night Attack Before the Hitler Line. Painting by Lawren Harris. The Harris painting gives some sense of the atmosphere in the short time before the critical attack to penetrate beyond the Hitler Line. (Canadian War Museum 12706)

Knocked out Calgary Regiment Sherman IIs, along with a damaged German ammunition carrier, near Pontecorvo, 22 May 1944. (NAC PA143903)

Three Rivers Regiment tank moving up for the assault on the Hitler Line, 23 May 1944. (NAC PA204153)

of the Liri River. The regiment was ordered to probe forward and maintain contact with Free French forces operating on the south side of the river line. By the morning of 20 May, PLDG patrols were in contact with the forward edge of the Hitler Line south-east of Pontecorvo, collecting information about the enemy in that sector.

On 22 May, 'A' and 'B' Squadrons, supported by British tanks, attacked along the road leading into Pontecorvo with the intention of breaching an enemy minefield. Despite coming under very heavy fire, the two armoured regiments succeeded in penetrating the enemy position to a depth of more than four hundred metres before being halted by mines. 'A' Squadron took sixty prisoners that morning, and the 'Plugs' gained the distinction of being the first unit in the Eighth Army to penetrate the Hitler Line.

The Canadians attacked the Hitler Line defences on a 3,000 metre front. Following a barrage of unprecedented proportions, the Patricias and Seaforths of 2 Brigade, and the Carleton and Yorks of 3 Brigade followed a rolling barrage into the enemy lines, supported by Churchill tanks of the North Irish Horse and the 21st Royal Tank Regiment. In the 2 Brigade sector, the North Irish were stopped by a minefield, and were systematically picked off by a *Panzerturm*. The Patricias tried valiantly to go on alone, but their companies were decimated by enemy fire as they emerged from a wood on their line of advance. The Seaforths, on the left of the Patricias, fared only a little better and, by 0900 hours, it was apparent that the assault had failed. The British armour in support had suffered heavily: 41 of their 58 tanks had been knocked out.

In the 3 Brigade area, an attack mounted by the Carleton and Yorks had a much different result. Their objective, astride the Pontecorvo–Aquino

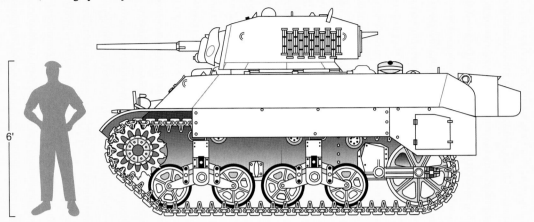

M3A3, Stuart V Light Tank. Entering production in early 1943, the Stuart V was the final production variant of the series. It was widely employed by Canadian armoured regiments in their reconnaissance troops. Affectionately known as the 'Honey', a name that had originated with the British in North Africa, the Stuart was a rugged and reliable tank. (Drawing by Chris Johnson)

M3A3, Stuart V Light Tank
Country of Origin: United States
Crew: 4 (Commander, Gunner, Driver,
    Assistant Driver)
Length: 16 feet 6 inches
Width: 8 feet 3 inches
Height: 8 feet 5 inches
Weight: 32,400 pounds
Engine: Continental 7 cylinder radial, gasoline
Maximum Speed: 31 mph
Range: 135 miles
Armour – Maximum: 51 mm
    Minimum: 10 mm
Armament: 37mm Gun M6 in turret
    .30 calibre MG M1919A4 in bow mount
    .30 calibre MG M1919A4 in flexible
    mount on turret

6'

road, was gained within an hour and a half of setting out, even though most of the supporting British tanks were quickly destroyed by anti-tank fire. Because of this success General Vokes decided to commit his divisional reserve here, rather than in the 2 Brigade sector as originally intended. The Three Rivers Regiment – the only Canadian armour involved in the assault – and the West Novas were thus ordered forward.

When 'A' and 'C' Squadrons of the TRR arrived in their assembly area they may have had some trepidation about their mission, for there were "30 to 40 Churchill tanks burning immediately to their front." At 1640 hours, together with the Royal 22e Régiment and the West Novas, they moved forward through the gap in the Hitler Line taken earlier by the Carleton and Yorks. To everyone's surprise they met only scattered resistance. The tanks had a difficult time crossing the River San Martino, but the infantry continued onward for nearly two kilometres and, by early evening, had consolidated on their objectives. The West Novas were counter-attacked but the timely arrival of a troop of tanks brought an end to the enemy action. During their brief involvement in the battle, the tank squadrons lost a total of six Shermans and thirty officers and men in destroying four Mark IVs, one self-propelled gun and a 75mm anti-tank gun. The regiment's report on operations notes that heavy thunderstorms that evening made roads impassable for wheeled vehicles and the recce troop's Stuart tanks "did a magnificent job, working all night to bring up adequate petrol, supplies and ammunition" – a role that fell increasingly on the Honeys in this difficult terrain.

The way was now paved for the introduction of 5 CAD to exploit to the line of the Melfa River and then to the Liri at Ceprano.

PENETRATION TO THE MELFA

In the exploitation beyond the Hitler Line, General Hoffmeister assigned the task of securing a crossing over the Melfa to 5 Armoured Brigade, and the subsequent drive to take Ceprano to 11 Infantry Brigade. He recognized, however, that the standard armoured/infantry separation within the division was totally unsuitable for the missions, so the grouping within the brigades was altered to provide better operational balance. For its task on the Melfa, 5 Brigade had the Irish Regiment of Canada under command, to supplement its own motorized infantry, the Westminster Regiment. The matching armour component for 11 Brigade in the second phase, the advance to Ceprano, was left undecided at this point.

Within the armoured brigade, Brigadier Des Smith had a number of problems in making his plan. Because of the limited number of troops available for an advance of some fifteen kilometres, the thrust to the Melfa was going to have to be pushed on a very narrow front with essentially unprotected flanks, especially on the north. The Germans still held the town of Aquino and the mountainous high ground north of Highway 6, making it likely that they could observe all movement during the advance and thus bring down accurate artillery and mortar fire. Smith therefore decided to create two *ad hoc* striking forces. *Vokes Force*, commanded by Lieutenant-Colonel Freddie Vokes, commanding officer of the British Columbia Dragoons (and brother of 1 Division's commander), would consist of his own regiment and the Irish Regiment of Canada, while *Griffin Force*, commanded by Lieutenant-Colonel Paddy Griffin of the Strathconas, was composed of the Straths and 'A' Company of the Westminsters.

Each group was given a battery of the 4th Anti-Tank Regiment equipped with M10 tank destroyers and a detachment of

Major-General Hoffmeister briefing officers of 5th Armoured Division prior to the attack beyond the Hitler Line. (NAC PA189922)

engineers in Honeys borrowed from the regimental recce troop. Vokes was to lead off, pushing forward roughly halfway to the Melfa, to a farm complex known as Mancini, where he was to establish a firm base for the subsequent advance of Griffin's men to the line of the Melfa. To secure the vulnerable and open flanks during this phase, and to mop up by-passed enemy positions, the division's armoured recce regiment, the Governor General's Horse Guards, was to deploy a squadron on each flank.

On learning of the successful breaching of the Hitler Line by 3 Brigade, Hoffmeister got permission from Corps Headquarters to begin 5 Brigade's advance on the evening of 23 May. Heavy rain, however, had its inevitable effect; by early evening all routes forward from the Forme d'Aquino had simply become impassable for the tanks, so the attack was delayed until the next morning.

Leading *Vokes Force*, the BCD moved up to their start line, the River San Martino, shortly after 0600 hours on 24 May. It was a cold, misty morning, and visibility was very poor. The engineers were supposed to have built a Bailey bridge over the steeply-banked river, but it had not been completed because of heavy shelling, and the recce troop was sent out to find a place

where tanks could avoid having to climb the steep and muddy far bank. It was thus close to 0800 hours when the BCD squadrons got across the river obstacle and began to shake out into battle formation. Two carrier-borne companies of the Irish Regiment accompanied 'B' and 'C' Squadrons, which fanned out on either side of the axis toward the first objective. The men of the other two Irish companies rode on 'A' Squadron's tanks, bringing up the rear.

This neat formation did not last long. The ground was rough and covered with scrub brush, olive groves and vineyards. The BCD history, *Sinews of Steel,* records that:

> The vineyards gave considerable trouble to the tanks. Innumerable strands of wire attached to posts supported the trees, and these were at a height which would have decapitated the tank commander had he stood with his head and shoulders out of the tank turret. Moreover, as the Shermans charged through these groves, each tank inevitably became entangled in some of the wire which resulted in it trailing behind a length of tangled wire and vines.

The infantry dismounted from the tanks when snipers began to inflict casualties. There seemed to be scattered pockets of Germans at every turn and, as the weight of enemy mortar and artillery fire increased, the tanks and the infantry gradually became separated, each arm fighting its own battle, with the tanks soon well ahead of the infantry. The fight to the first objective was thoroughly confused, caused in part by extremely poor quality maps that were hard to read and in part by the crew commanders' very limited range of vision in the olive groves and vineyards, which meant that identifiable landmarks could rarely be seen. The three squadron commanders had a slight advantage, in that each had a 1:12,500 scale air photo mosaic with a superimposed map grid, but they rarely knew where their tank troops were located during this advance, and that everybody actually reached their intended objective was clearly due to a certain amount of luck.

Sergeant Bill Kurbis, a crew commander in 'A' Squadron's 1st Troop later recalled:

> … the orders came to move off … through a deep ravine covered with olive groves and in between grapes were strung and you couldn't see 20 feet in front of you. Our orders were to shoot at anything that moved and knock down any building we saw. This we proceeded to do, and we had gone forward about half a mile or so when all of a sudden there was a big bang on my left. I looked over and there was Corporal Wendall's tank hit by a bazooka and there were Jerries all around it. So we wheeled our gun over and sprayed them good…. We kept going through the olive groves when … we

came out in a little clearing and my troop leader's tank went into a tank trap. We gave him covering smoke fire and then we got close to him and hooked a cable on to him and pulled him out.

Not long afterwards, Sergeant Kurbis' own tank was hit several times, and the crew had to bail out. There were Germans all around, but in short order, with support from other tanks, he had thirty prisoners.

As the Dragoons continued their cross-country advance toward the second objective, they came under increasingly heavy artillery fire, and as 'B' Squadron, on the left, began to cross a grain field, it was fired on by a group of Mark IVs and Panthers. Lieutenant Nigel Taylor, whose troop found itself in the thick of a vicious battle, wrote:

I got almost to the banks of the Melfa River when I came on the most enormous tank I had ever seen. Fortunately for me its gun was traversed at right angles to our approach. I promptly reported this beast as a "Tiger". It turned out of course to be a PzKw V Panther.

I suppose he saw me at about the same time I saw him, and he started backing down a road. My gunner, Tpr. Cecil D. Shears, was a crack shot and I gave him the distance as a thousand yards. Two quick shots and the Panther was finished! Cecil's last words in this world, poor fellow, were "I got him, sir." Two German anti-tank guns were flanking the Panther and had commenced firing at us like mad. I remember yelling "smoke" to the loader and "reverse" to the driver: seconds later we were hit and Tpr. Shears was instantly killed....

... the two anti-tank guns also got my corporal's tank, killing him and his loader. My Sgt's tank, under command of Sgt. W.J. Range, got both these guns....

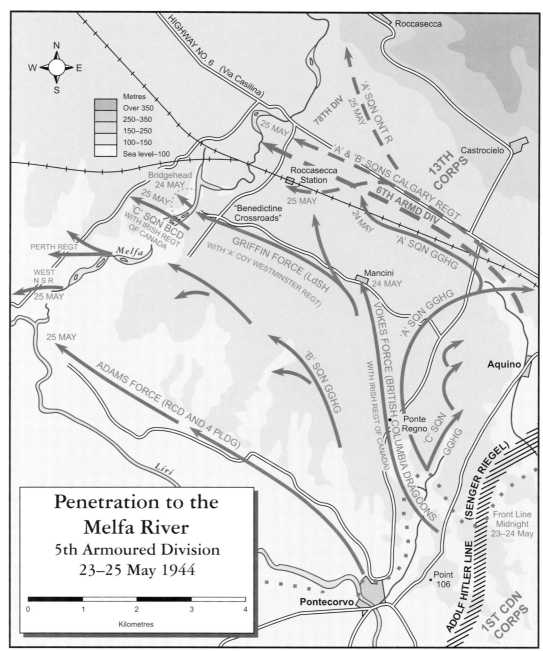

Penetration to the Melfa River
5th Armoured Division
23–25 May 1944

Major-General Bert Hoffmeister in the turret of his Divisional command tank. (NAC PA204155)

BCD Sherman knocked out during the advance to the Melfa River. Note that the turret has been penetrated by six armour-piercing rounds, and the hull by another. (NAC PA204154)

reached the San Martino they found that the crossing site "had been wrecked by the tanks of the Armoured Brigade," and a great deal of time was wasted while they searched in vain for an alternative crossing. In the end they had to repair the original crossing, and it was thus close to 1100 hours before the squadron was able to move out on the left flank of *Vokes Force's* axis. 'C' Squadron crossed the San Martino immediately behind 'B' and swung to the right, towards the town of Aquino, where a large concentration of enemy tanks had been reported. Their movement was severely hampered by shelling, but they got to within a thousand metres of Aquino and then deployed to an area west of the town where they could give protection to the right-rear of the attacking infantry. 'A' Squadron joined 'C' Squadron on this highly vulnerable right flank in late afternoon, initially taking up positions overlooking Route 6 near Aquino Station. Through the afternoon, the Horse Guards fought sharp battles with isolated pockets of the enemy remaining in the area behind the Hitler Line, but gradually the brigade flanks were firmed-up.

Major Allan Burton recalled the experience of his squadron of the Horse Guards:

> … As my last vehicles descended into the small ravine and struggled up the steep slope on the far side to re-form around me, we were alone at last in enemy territory. … I ordered the advance to proceed slowly, keeping in visual contact and together as a unit. We saw the heavy tank-tracks of vehicles recently departed when we came to our first clearing, an inviting open space with a house about two hundred yards away. … I ordered every tank available to open fire on it simultaneously with machine guns and high explosives.

The Panther destroyed by Shears was the first of its kind to be knocked out during the Italian campaign.

At the same time, a similar battle was being fought by 'C' Squadron on the regiment's right and, in the rear, the recce troop's Honey tanks were assisting the infantry to get forward by using their .50 calibre machine-guns on enemy outposts, pointing out targets to the self-propelled guns and rounding up prisoners. By shortly after noon the BCD squadrons reached the area of Mancini farm, code named *Kummel*, but it was some time before the Irish companies caught up and, meanwhile, the Dragoons set up a defensive perimeter to await the passage of the Strathconas.

The Horse Guards, tasked with protecting the flanks, began to move forward into the gap in the Hitler Line soon after 0830 hours, but their advance was very slow because of heavy traffic. When 'B' Squadron

A German Panther, knocked out on 24 May, is examined by Canadian infantrymen. Arguably the best tank design of the war, the Panther had thick, well-sloped armour, together with a high-velocity long-barrelled 75mm gun. (NAC PA169112)

Tank Advance, Italy. **Painting by Lawren Harris of the Governor General's Horse Guards advance on the flanks of the Canadian penetration to the Melfa River on 24 May 1944. Note Monte Cassino Abbey high in the background, indicating the view the Germans had of the Canadian advance from the heights on the mountains. Before becoming a war artist, Harris was a lieutenant in the Horse Guards. (Canadian War Museum 12722)**

Lieut. Cyrus Gaskin ran his tank up to the house and jumped down. A small figure in black tank coveralls and beret, he kicked in the door, threw in a grenade, and nearly fainted in amazement as over seventy Germans crawled out, tears streaming down their faces and thoroughly demoralized.

We found a 75mm anti-tank gun on one side of the house and a huge tracked anti-tank vehicle with an 88mm gun called a Ferdinand on the other, both knocked out by our speculative barrage…. We had the foresight to make a note of the frequencies on their radio equipment and found a code book that appeared to be current.

… Finally, after many small encounters, we reached our allotted positions. We had been lucky. The fact that we steadily advanced and overcame the rearguard positions left by the

Germans seemed to convince them we were supported by a large force coming up behind us. In fact, there was no one. …We found ourselves by late afternoon in an unenviable position for tanks, with individual troops a mile apart guarding vital spots to protect the right flank of the main divisional advance. … Resigned to staying in our exposed positions, we took as much of a defensive position as we could, literally in full view of the Germans on Monte Cassino….

Meanwhile, even before the leading squadrons of *Vokes Force* had secured their objective at Mancini, Griffin had been ordered to begin the move forward from the assembly area. Led by the Strathcona recce troop, his tanks and men made rapid and almost unhindered progress and, at 1340 hours, they

Honey tank of the Strathcona Recce Troop at the 'Benedictine' crossroads, on their way to the seizure of a bridgehead over the Melfa River. (NAC PA204157)

passed through the firm base that had been established by the BCD and the Irish, fanning out as they struck for the Melfa. The BCD were still engaging enemy tanks as *Griffin Force* went forward.

When planning the thrust to the Melfa, Colonel Griffin had seen from air photos that there were two possible crossings sites over the river. The obvious one was a ford already being used by the Germans and Griffin was certain that it would be well defended, so he focused on a second location a thousand metres to the north. While it would be much more difficult to get vehicles across at that point, there was at least some prospect of achieving tactical surprise. This, then, was the objective given to the recce troop.

Lieutenant E.J. Perkins, commanding the Strathcona recce troop, wrote an account of his battle shortly after the action. He described his drive to the Melfa:

I headed up the centre line. The country was close and visibility limited.... The first enemy I saw was about 1000 yards beyond the BCD. A half-tracked vehicle was parked behind a house with its crew about it.... About 2000 yards further on a Panther tank suddenly came across my right front travelling very quickly at a range of about 300 yards. The crew commander was standing in the turret with his chest exposed. I immediately opened up on him with my .50-inch Browning and had the satisfaction of seeing him slump forward in his cupola.... A little further on I saw two more enemy tanks on my left. On the wireless, I heard 'A' Squadron planning to go for them so I kept on going.

The Strathconas had reached what was called *Benedictine* crossroads, a track junction five hundred metres short of the Melfa. Here they encountered two groups of German tanks and self-propelled guns. One group of Mark IVs and SP guns was off to their left, on both sides of the Melfa, protecting the ford that the Germans were using, and the other, the better part of a company of Panthers, was to the centre right. What ensued over the next hour was one of the most hard-fought tank-versus-

Infantrymen, with a Honey tank about to pass them, near the Melfa bridgehead, 24 May 1944. (NAC PA135904)

Melfa River Crossings. **Painting by Lawren Harris. This painting has been criticized by some veterans as not accurately representing the terrain in which the battle took place. (Canadian War Museum 12705)**

tank engagements of the Italian campaign, "a very hot battle", and the first in which a number of Panthers were pitted against Shermans.

The Panthers first fired on the lead troop of 'A Squadron, commanded by Lieutenant Bob Gartke. As 'C' Squadron came up on the left of the centre line they too were engulfed in the fight. The many clumps of small woods severely restricted visibility, so that mutual support between troops was next to impossible and most of the tank duels were fought out at ranges of less than four hundred metres. Captain John Windsor, second-in-command of 'A' Squadron, who was permanently blinded when his tank was hit, later wrote an account of this action in his book *Blind Date:*

> Slowly but relentlessly we pushed on …. crashing through tangled woods and trim orchards, racing across open fields, all the time scanning the country ahead through our glasses, looking for the German Panthers and self propelled guns, which, shooting from concealed positions, were beginning to make us pay a heavy toll in 'brewed up' tanks and dead and wounded crews.

We must be close to the Melfa, maybe it was on the far side of this orchard. I could only see one of our tanks now, the rest were hidden among the trees. … We went forward again, edging through the orchard, and a feeling of exhilaration began to take hold. Others had been hit, but I was indestructible. Then it happened. One moment the world around me was full of vivid colour … then suddenly, in the fraction of an instant, everything turned to inky blackness…. At the same instant, from what seemed a long way off, there came a mighty metallic clang as though some great anvil had been struck by a giant sledgehammer.

At these short ranges the tank that fired first usually came out the victor, but several Strathcona crew commanders quickly discovered that their 75mm AP rounds would not penetrate the frontal armour of the Panther turret, and sometimes glanced off the Panther's sloping front glacis plate. However, they also found that the Sherman's power traverse often gave them a brief advantage over the Panther, which was fitted with a much slower manual traverse system.

By 1630 hours the stiff fighting in and around *Benedictine* crossroads had ended; all enemy vehicles, except one SP gun, having been destroyed. When a count was done somewhat later, the 'bag' included seven Panthers, four Mark IV tanks, nine SP guns, five anti-tank guns, five *nebelwerfers,* four multi-barrel anti-aircraft guns and some 21 wheeled vehicles. But the Strathconas had also lost heavily: sixteen Shermans were destroyed, and among the 55 casualties were many of the senior officers in 'A' and 'C' Squadrons.

While this fierce battle at *Benedictine* was raging, another smaller but more significant fight was taking place five hundred metres further on, on the far bank of the Melfa.

The three Honey tanks of the Strathcona recce troop had raced through the crossroad just before the battle there had begun, and by 1500 hours were on the near bank of the Melfa. Leutenant Edward Perkins and his troop sergeant, Sergeant G.N. Macey, dismounted to find a place where the Honey tanks could cross over:

We posted three men with Bren guns to cover us and began our search. Towards the left the bank was impassable, but about 75 yards to the right there was a sort of ledge leading down into the river bed. This was very steep and difficult but still passable to tanks. All along the river bank were very well prepared enemy positions, which we searched as we went along. The enemy had obviously vacated them in great haste as there was kit and equipment lying about in profusion. …

The track on the far side was even more difficult than that on the near side. I decided, however, that it could be made passable, though a dint of hard work would be necessary… There was an obstructing bank upon which we exploded three prepared charges. It was also necessary to widen the track in one place and to do this we built a sort of retaining wall using several tree trunks and then filled up the gap with dirt. We did some furious work with pick and shovel…. In retrospect, I think this was the most ticklish part of the whole business. … We knew that the enemy must have an idea of what we were about and might be expected to do something quickly.

Within thirty minutes of arriving at the Melfa, Perkins and his men had their three Honeys across the river and in hull-down positions on the far bank. Their immediate priority was

Lieutenant Edward Perkins, DSO. Perkins was the only Armoured Corps subaltern in the Italian campaign to be recommended for a VC, but got a DSO because two VC's could not be awarded for a single action. (LdSH Museum)

to prepare to defend this tiny bridgehead, and the first task in securing it was to capture an enemy-occupied house a hundred metres to the left of the crossing site. By approaching from the back, eight very surprised enemy paratroopers were taken without a fight, but other Germans in the area had noted the location of Perkins' small group. Soon afterward two Panthers and an 88mm SP gun appeared on the left and fired on the house they had just captured. They were fortunately distracted for a time by the appearance of 'A' Squadron tanks on the far bank, but the Canadians were subjected to periodic machine gun fire from an enemy infantry platoon less than two hundred metres away, and to the occasional shell from German tanks moving in the vicinity. Even though the troop had now been reinforced by a fourth Honey, the Straths were in a very awkward situation and Perkins knew that his twenty-man garrison could not hold on if the Germans mounted a serious attack. Nevertheless, hoping to deceive the enemy about his real strength, he was determined to hang on until the Westminster company could get forward, into his bridgehead, and his men kept up a heavy volume of fire with their small arms and the .50 Brownings on the Honeys.

The Westminster company, led by Major John Mahony, began to arrive at about 1700 hours and the position was considerably improved when the infantry captured a second house on the left, along with twenty prisoners. Shortly afterward, Trooper Jacob Funk crawled out along the river bank to engage an 88mm SP gun that was firing both on the bridgehead garrison and on 'A' Squadron on the far bank. At a range of less than a hundred metres, Funk fired at the gun with a PIAT (Projector, Infantry, Anti-Tank, a very short-range weapon), killing it with the fourth round he fired.

Shortly before dusk the Germans mounted an attack with three Panthers and about a hundred infantry. There was still no artillery available, but the Strathconas and Westminsters fired everything they had, including more PIAT rounds, hoping desperately that the enemy would believe they had anti-tank guns. The bluff seemed to work. The enemy tanks "swerved off at about 175 yards and did not press the attack." They returned in a second attack a short while later, but again they broke off before getting to the perimeter of the position, perhaps because visibility had become too limited in the growing darkness.

The bridgehead was reinforced by the arrival of 'C' Company of the Westminsters, while 'B' Company attempted a crossing well off to the right, but it had a very difficult time in the face of stubborn enemy resistance and, unable to progress, were eventually withdrawn.

A lone German SP gun remained on the Canadian side of the river at this stage, and it continued to cause considerable damage, especially to the troops in the small bridgehead. The Strathcona second-in-command, Major G.J.H. Wattsford, decided to do something about this. He relates what happened:

We made our way off to the left rear of our position and I got my tank up close in behind what I found out was an SP gun partly hidden behind an old barn. I could see its rear end sticking out. We were right on top of it, probably not more than a hundred yards away. I said to my gunner, "Make sure your first shot is right on, because we won't get a second chance", and I told him to fire when his aim was dead on. But he didn't fire. Again I said, "Get that shot away or they're going to spot us". Nothing happened. No reply. The SP gun began to back out to aim in our direction. Again, "Get that shot away, we've only got another five seconds". The German gun continued to back out and then slowly traversed onto us. A moment later a shell came through the driver's compartment, into the turret and out the back of the tank. I found myself sitting on the bottom of the tank, with all our ammunition on fire. My gunner, who had been knocked out, came to, said he was getting out and he climbed over me. I thought that's not a bad idea, so I bounced out of the tank too.

Wattsford's gunner did get his shot away at precisely the moment that the German gun fired, and the SP gun also 'brewed up', but Wattsford, one of the longest-serving Strathconas in the regiment, was badly wounded and burned.

The Strathcona regimental history describes the aftermath of this, their first battle of the campaign:

As far as one could see through the trees and hedges [around *Benedictine* crossroads], the eerie light from burning tanks blended grotesquely with the glow of the setting sun; smoke from burning oil and petrol mingled with the dust that hung over the valley to give the effect of a partial eclipse. Now and then the ammunition in the burning tanks caught fire, the sharp staccato crackling of the small arms and the loud re-

ports of the 75mm shells seemed as an echo of the afternoon's tumult, punctuated by the steady whine and explosion of the 'Moaning Minnies' landing in the river bed, by the sickening 'carumph' of heavy shells landing between 'Benedictine' and the [Regimental Aid Post].

To the immediate north of the 5th Armoured Division thrust across the Melfa, units of 1st Armoured Brigade were supporting the advance of the British 38th Brigade. This photo shows the Calgary Regiment in an attack on Castrocielli. (NAC PA177096)

On the far side of the Melfa, Major Mahony's Westminsters and Perkins' recce troop held out through the night, under continual machine-gun fire and shelling by *nebelwerfers* and artillery, and casualties grew steadily during the hours of darkness. Several times the Germans fired smoke rounds in front of the position, and everyone was kept in a state of constant alertness in case the Germans attacked once again. The position was greatly strengthened, however, when the Westminsters succeeded in man-handling three of their 6-pounder anti-tank guns into the bridgehead, and Perkins finally made contact with the forward observation officer of a battery of Jeep-towed 75mm pack howitzers on the other bank. Now there was, at last, some light artillery fire to inhibit enemy activity, but it was a very uncomfortable night waiting for the enemy to do something. They never did.

Major Mahony received the Victoria Cross and Lieutenant Perkins, to whom much of the credit is due for taking and then holding the bridgehead until the infantry arrived, was given a well-deserved Distinguished Service Order, very rarely awarded to a subaltern. Sergeant Macey was awarded the Distinguished Conduct Medal for his bravery and determination, and Trooper Jacob Funk got the Military Medal. Colonel Griffin's exceptional leadership throughout this vital operation was appropriately recognized with the Distinguished Service Order.

5 Armoured Brigade headquarters appeared to have been gripped with paralysis during the night of 24/25 May, and was extremely slow to do what was necessary in order to expand the fragile toehold across the Melfa. Brigadier Smith did make plans for an early morning crossing on 25 May, but this attack was delayed for many hours because there were no artillery units in position to provide fire support – the gunner regiments had been hopelessly caught in traffic jams as they tried to move forward. An inexperienced divisional staff must undoubtedly bear the brunt of the blame for the inadequate movement control which caused such confusion and congestion, but why there was no effort by 5 Brigade to maintain momentum by putting tanks across at first light, even without artillery support, has never been explained. It was not that there was a shortage of armour immediately available: the BCD were within 4,000 metres of the bridgehead, and the 8th Hussars, involved the previous day only in brief skirmishes while clearing out by-passed enemy, were not much further to the rear, in harbours just west of Ponte Regno.

It was almost noon on 25 May when an attack was finally put in at the main crossing point, south-west of the bridgehead, by the Irish Regiment and 'C' Squadron of the BCD. The planning and coordination of this operation were very badly handled. The Dragoons were not informed until 1000 hrs that one of their squadrons was to support the infantry and, by then, there was simply no time for any of the essential 'marrying-up' drills with the Irish. 'C' Squadron thus went into battle without knowing the locations of the troops in the bridgehead, without any clear understanding of their task or of the infantry objectives, and without radio communications with the infantry companies.

German anti-tank fire claimed seven of their Shermans almost as soon as they moved beyond the Melfa, but the infantry advanced rapidly and within an hour were firmly in control of the lateral road 1,000 metres beyond the river. At the same time, a Westminster company broke out of the bridgehead and linked up with the Irish on the line of the road. Then the mission of exploitation beyond the Melfa passed to 11 Infantry Brigade, whose inexperienced headquarters was having serious problems in the planning and coordination of the passage of lines through 5 Brigade.

This first attack was fortunately a relatively straightforward affair. At 1630 hours the Cape Breton Highlanders and the 8th Hussars were to attack through the Irish Regiment and push forward to an objective another 1,000 metres away. Once again, however, there were difficulties in effectively linking up the tanks and infantry before crossing the start line, mainly because insufficient time had been allowed for orders and pre-battle coordination at squadron and company levels. 'C' Squadron led the Hussars over the Melfa on a track that had been bulldozed by the engineers, and the troops spread out on the far side to join the advancing Highlanders. Then, as Douglas How wrote in *The 8th Hussars:*

In a matter of seconds, the raw swirl of action had touched everything. Out of the places where the guns were hidden, the Germans whipped the field with the whining thunderclaps of armour-piercing shells, with yellow spikes of flame stabbing toward the river bank. When a tank was hit it squatted back upon its haunches, suddenly and drunkenly, as though its steel were wounded flesh. In some of them, tongues of flame broke out of the engine hatches and the crews, feeling the heat against their sweating flesh, scrambled out in panic and fled. Oil-black columns of smoke spewed upwards into the sunlight, curled and plumed and tinged with fire and in time the tanks burned like great iron pots of fuel.

Inside the tanks, the gunners searched feverishly for targets through their telescopic sights. The turrets swung back and forth. They fired at anything they suspected. The 75's cracked, reeled back and hurled out spent casings. The loaders plunged home new shells. The breeches clanged shut. The guns flared back across the field; streaks of white-hot tracer above the grass. The machine-guns chattered. The belts fed them and curled away. The guts of the Shermans were a riot of noise and smells, acrid with the gas, the cordite, the hot gun oil, the engine fumes. The men were wet with sweat.

There was no lack of zeal or initiative on the part of either tank crews or infantrymen in this brief hour-long battle, but although the two units were going in the same direction they were not working together. The objective was taken, but it was well after dark before the Hussar squadrons managed to find the positions held by the Highlanders. There was still much to be learned about tank-infantry cooperation in 5 CAD. In this

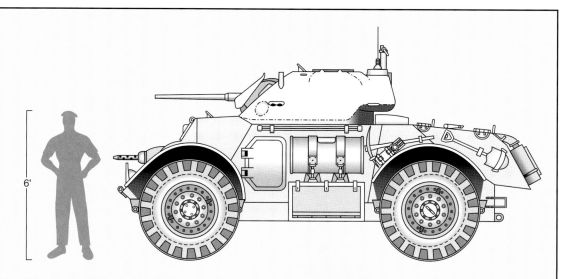

Staghound Armoured Car
Country of Origin: United States
Crew: 5 (Commander, Gunner, Loader, Driver,
    Assistant Driver)
Length: 17 feet 8 inches
Width: 8 feet 10 inches
Height: 7 feet 9 inches
Weight: 26,600 pounds
Engine: 2 x Chevrolet 6 cylinder, gasoline
Maximum Speed: 55 mph
Range: 500 miles
Armour – Maximum: 1 3/4 inches
        Minimum: 1/4 inch
Armament: 37 mm M6 Gun in turret mount
    .30 calibre MG M1919A4 co-axial to 37
    mm Gun
    .30 calibre MG M1919A4 in bow mount

6'

Staghound Armoured Car. Originally designed for desert fighting, the Staghound was somewhat large and heavy for European terrain. Nevertheless, it was a popular armoured car in the Canadian service and it equipped both the Royal Canadian Dragoons and the 12th Manitoba Dragoons in the Italian and North-West European campaigns. (Drawing by Chris Johnson)

brief action, the Hussars lost four Shermans, three of them 'brewed-up', while accounting for one 88mm SP gun and three 75mm anti-tank guns. The gain of a thousand metres, however costly, was nonetheless important, for it meant that the line of the Melfa was at last securely in Canadian hands.

On 5 CAD's right flank, XIII British Corps was finally able to move forward in the area of Highway 6 on 25 May. Soon after the bridgehead over the Melfa had been established, the Germans occupying Aquino had been ordered to withdraw during the night of 24/25 May. During the afternoon of 25 May the Calgary Regiment supported units of the British 38 Brigade in a push to the Melfa along the axis of Highway 6, but they were unable to force a crossing of the river because of heavy enemy opposition. 'A' Squadron of the Ontarios, meanwhile, working with a British recce regiment, found that the enemy had abandoned their positions in the towns of Castrocielo and Roccasecca.

The Germans still held the high slopes of Monte Cairo, on the northern flank of the battlefield. This gave them one very significant advantage: their artillery and mortar observers could see clearly the whole panorama of the Liri Valley below and locate precisely where every Canadian unit was concentrated. All the Canadians had suffered the effects of deadly accurate shell fire during the advance to the Melfa on 24 May, and the troops continued to endure this plague the following day. Early in the afternoon, just as replacement tanks and crews were being taken on from the Elgin Regiment's tank delivery squadron, the Strathconas suffered what was later described as "the greatest tragedy in its history":

Without warning, there suddenly rained down upon the entire area an incredible concentration of heavy shells. Landing only a few feet apart, in and around the tank lines, and exploding at the rate of several per second, they threw the Regiment into a state bordering upon chaos. … Strathconas lay wounded and dying, some of them literally blown to bits, while others, with complete disregard for their own personal safety and with the unselfishness that breeds heroism, rushed about administering first aid and bearing their fallen comrades to the Medical Officer.

The Canadian thrust beyond the Hitler Line was greatly assisted in the south of their sector by another composite battle group called *Adams Force*, commanded by Lieutenant-Colonel F.D. Adams of 4 PLDG. Colonel Adams led his own men, two squadrons of RCD armoured cars, one squadron of the TRR tanks, and the Carleton and York battalion, in thrusting forward to the junction of the Melfa and the Liri rivers, lifting mines, taking prisoners and reporting areas where resistance was encountered.

Late on 24 May, once they were able to get through the rubble and mines that blocked the streets of Pontecorvo, the push began, 'C' and 'D' Squadrons of the RCD leading in the Staghounds that had replaced their Daimlers. The Dragoon historian quotes the regimental report on operations:

No one will ever know exactly what happened during this advance, or in what sequence…. Time and again the lead cars were left 'in the blue' as the supporting cars took pris-

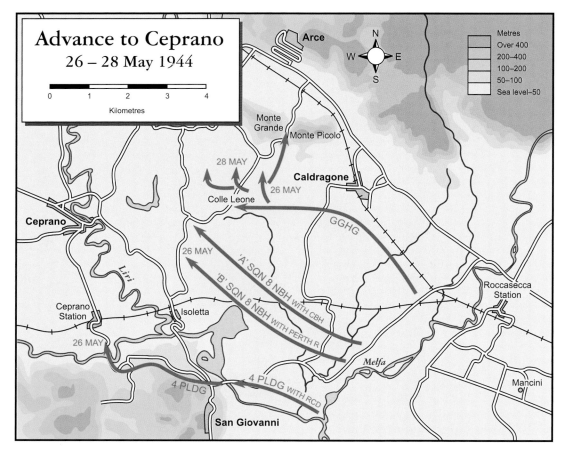

THE ADVANCE TO CEPRANO AND FROSINONE

11 Brigade began its advance toward Ceprano early on the morning of 26 May, led by the Perths on the left and the Highlanders on the right, and each with a squadron of the 8th Hussars in support. While the infantry were hindered by incessant mortar and artillery fire, only scattered pockets of enemy troops were met for much of the day; but at a time when boldness and speed were required to take advantage of a weakened and dispirited enemy, this attack moved very slowly. The problem was the terrain – ground covered by scrub brush and small woods, with innumerable ravines and small streams running across the axis of advance. Almost at the outset the Hussars had difficulty crossing two streams where many tanks bogged down; then a steep railway embankment blocked forward movement until early afternoon. Without tank support to deal with machine-guns, the infantry were reluctant to go forward on their own and the attack ground to a halt when the Hussar squadrons ran out of fuel, a likelihood predicted by their CO when his 'A' Echelon had been denied permission to come forward the night before to replenish the squadrons. Not until early evening were the tanks refuelled. By nightfall, the brigade had advanced only some 4,000 metres, and was still no more than halfway to Ceprano and the key crossings over the Liri River.

oners who came up to the roadside after the leading cars had passed. Other Germans, who were surprised lolling half-way out of their trenches, leaped back in and opened furious fire, while not one hundred yards to the flank another group was trying to work its way through the fire to surrender.

By nightfall *Adams Force* had taken the advance some three kilometres beyond Pontecorvo, having dealt with a spate of mines, a few anti-tank guns and numerous small groups of enemy soldiers, some who were prepared to fight, and many others who had no fight left in them. While the main body of the force harboured for the night, a PLDG patrol continued on foot to the Melfa without encountering any enemy.

Early on the morning of 25 May, they reached the confluence of the Melfa and the Liri, but were confronted by fifteen-metre cliffs on the far bank. A ford was soon found about 1,000 metres upstream, and the Carleton and Yorks, covered by the tanks, crossed over and caught the remnants of a German battalion by surprise. Eventually the Three Rivers' squadron was able to make its way across, but the force on the west bank was kept pinned down for much of the rest of the day by shell-fire and mortars. Later, however, patrols were able to tie in with the Perth Regiment and the West Novas when they moved up on the left of the Irish Regiment.

While 11 Brigade was still approaching Ceprano, *Adams Force* had penetrated to the south end of the Isoletta Reservoir. A bridge across the Liri, below the dam, had been blown but PLDG patrols were sent forward on foot to scout possible crossings over the River Sacco, south of Ceprano Station. The next day the regiment provided a screen on the far bank of the Liri to protect engineers while a bridge was built.

When patrols of the Irish Regiment reached the Liri on the night of 26 May, they found that all bridges had been destroyed and the Germans still held high ground overlooking the river. The next day the Perths and Cape Breton Highlanders crossed the Liri in commandeered row boats. Engineers got to work immediately on a 40-metre Bailey bridge, but while it was being pushed onto the far bank on the morning of the 28th it collapsed into the river, delaying all movement beyond Ceprano for another day.

While 11 Brigade and the 8th Hussars were slowly making their way toward Ceprano, 'B' Squadron of the Horse Guards had been deployed to protect the right flank of the advance. The squadron moved from the Melfa along the line of the railway, toward the village of Coldragone, and then westward to take up positions where crews could observe Monte Grande and Monte Piccolo, two high features on the south side of Highway 6 overlooking the approaches to Ceprano. A considerable enemy force of infantry, tanks and SP guns was seen in the area of both hills.

Because of concern that the Germans might attempt to strike the right flank of the brigade as it neared Ceprano, the Horse Guards were instructed to take up a defensive position near a low hill known as Colle Leone, four kilometres east of the town. 'A' Squadron moved forward during the evening of the 26th to relieve 'B' Squadron, and the following day patrolled actively toward the Liri, north of Ceprano and around the base of both hills, destroying a number of enemy infantry positions. After dark on 27 May, 'C' Squadron was brought in, and the next day was engaged in heavy fighting on Monte Grande.

While a replacement Bailey bridge was hastily built over the Liri south of Ceprano, orders had come from Eighth Army giving XIII Corps priority for its use. The first vehicles over this bridge were tanks of the Ontario Regiment, who were leading the advance of 78 Division to positions west of Ceprano.

5 Armoured Brigade, hard pressed to get on with the move toward Pofi and Frosinone, diverted a battle group consisting of the BCD and two companies of the Westminsters to bridges that had been erected by 1 Division south and west of the Isoletta Reservoir. It took the better part of the night to make the long trek around the reservoir

8th Hussars Sherman approaching Ceprano, 26 May 1944. (8th Hussars Archives)

but, at first light on 29 May, the advance on Pofi began, although as the British had been given priority on the use of Highway 6, the Dragoons were confined to moving along narrow trails and farm roads south of the highway. It was very difficult country for tanks, "practically impassable" according to a report by the brigade commander, as two major rivers, several streams and a series of razor-backed hills ran at right angles to

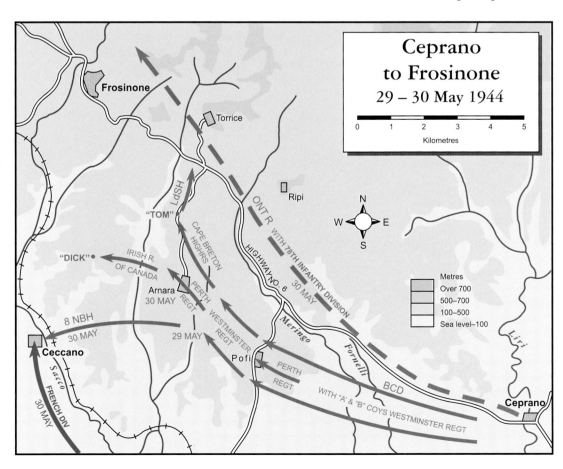

199

Inspection of 5th Armoured Brigade by HM King George VI. This photo shows the King passing in front of the Governor General's Horse Guards. (NAC PA204158)

the line of advance. The group struggled forward for nearly ten kilometres, encountering enemy rearguards only when they neared Pofi. By 1900 hrs they were on their objective, between Pofi and Arnara, but with only about half their Shermans; four had been lost to anti-tank fire and many more were "bogged down or up-ended in the innumerable ditches, tree stumps, and other obstacles."

Units of 5 Brigade continued the hopelessly slow, cross-country push towards Frosinone on 30 May. The 8th Hussars, on the left, "found themselves confined to a narrow track through very thick country and spent most of their time clearing mines off the road." Eventually diverted in the direction of the village of Ceccano, they linked up with the French but could make no headway towards Frosinone because of mines.

The Strathconas, on the right, eventually found their way blocked by a cratered road and, in mid-afternoon, they too were diverted toward Highway 6 to cut off retreating German forces. At a crossroads just south of the village of Torrice, the Straths fought a pitched battle against tanks and anti-tank guns of the *26th Panzerdivision,* destroying three Panthers, one Mark IV, one SP gun and a variety of other vehicles. The actions of one 'B' Squadron crew commander, Corporal J.B. Matthews, merit special mention. His troop leader's tank had been knocked out while coming into the position, and the troop sergeant's tank bogged down further back, but Matthews took up a fire position on an exposed bank, and proceeded to take on the Germans by himself. *A Record of Achievement* relates how, "although under direct fire … Corporal Matthews manoeuvred his tank back and forward, changing positions each time, and all in all, turned a truly remarkable performance, highly deserving of the award he received – the Distinguished Conduct Medal." Matthews knocked out one Panther and an SP gun, and probably accounted for a second Panther and a Mark IV.

The Strathconas held their position at the crossroads while under heavy shelling until reinforced late that night by the Cape Breton Highlanders. By now, General Burns had recognized that the countryside was so unsuitable for armoured operations that he ordered 1 Division to take over the advance. 5 CAD was relieved on 31 May and, for the next two weeks, occupied harbours and camps in the area of Ceprano. The next day 1 Division continued to press forward to Anagani, but was then ordered to halt so that French forces could pass through, and, on 4 June, as the Americans entered Rome, was placed in Army reserve.

5 CAD: INTROSPECTION AND REORGANIZATION

While there was, understandably, a lot of well-deserved satisfaction among the units of 5 CAD about their overall performance in their first significant action, General Hoffmeister was very aware that much had gone wrong during the Liri battles. Div HQ had, in many instances, botched important aspects of plans, and the exercise of control during the fighting had often been inadequate; passage of information, up and down, had been poor at best, and almost non-existent at times; standard battle procedure drills had often not been followed, leaving companies and squadrons with too little time to give orders or brief their men; many units had been far too cautious during the advance; and tank-infantry cooperation procedures were well below the standard needed. The catalogue of problems was long, and his division came in for a lot of criticism from Army and Corps.

Intent on taking steps to improve its operational capability, Hoffmeister issued instructions as soon as the division was re-

lieved that all headquarters and units were to carry out a thorough and critical examination of every aspect of the operation just concluded. Thus, in the first few days of June, each unit brought its officers together to discuss what had happened, and identify problems and their solutions. Based on reports submitted by commanding officers, the division and brigade staffs then worked out detailed plans for training to fix the shortcomings.

A few heads rolled in the aftermath of the battle, mainly among the staff at I Corps headquarters, but the commander of 11 Brigade was also replaced. The shake-up at Corps resulted in Des Smith being sent there as Chief of Staff and his replacement as commander of 5 Brigade was the newly promoted Brigadier Ian Cumberland, who had come to be highly regarded as commanding officer of the Governor General's Horse Guards.

However, the most significant change to come out of the detailed examination of the conduct of the Liri operation was in the structure of 5 CAD. The one armoured brigade, one infantry brigade, organization was based on a doctrine and concept of fast-moving and far-reaching operations that had no applicability in the Italian theatre. When employed in relatively rugged, close country against a determined enemy in prepared defences, as was the case in the Liri Valley, the division had proven to be tactically unbalanced; it simply did not have enough infantry for the type of operation foreseen in Italy. Commanders from Army level and down all agreed that an additional infantry brigade was needed, but finding that brigade was the difficult part of the equation.

A request to provide one from among the Canadian formations still in Britain was rejected outright. The invasion of Normandy had begun on 6 June, and north-west Europe was the decisive theatre of operations for the defeat of Germany, so that if another infantry brigade were needed in Italy, it would have to come from resources already there. For a brief time the Corps staff worked on a concept of 'equalizing' the two divi-

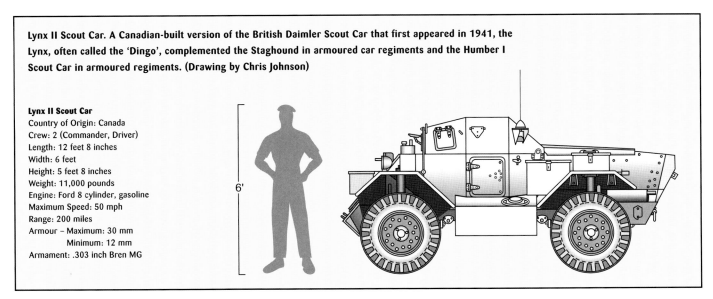

Lynx II Scout Car. A Canadian-built version of the British Daimler Scout Car that first appeared in 1941, the Lynx, often called the 'Dingo', complemented the Staghound in armoured car regiments and the Humber I Scout Car in armoured regiments. (Drawing by Chris Johnson)

Lynx II Scout Car
Country of Origin: Canada
Crew: 2 (Commander, Driver)
Length: 12 feet 8 inches
Width: 6 feet
Height: 5 feet 8 inches
Weight: 11,000 pounds
Engine: Ford 8 cylinder, gasoline
Maximum Speed: 50 mph
Range: 200 miles
Armour – Maximum: 30 mm
Minimum: 12 mm
Armament: .303 inch Bren MG

6'

sions by giving the 5th one of the infantry brigades from the 1st and replacing it with 1 Armoured Brigade. This notion was turned down by Eighth Army, however, for the independent 1 Armoured Brigade had become too valuable a resource for XIII British Corps. The only other solution was to create an infantry brigade out of troops already in I Corps.

The transfer of the Westminster Regiment from 5 Brigade to a new 12 Infantry Brigade was the easy part. A second infantry battalion, eventually to be named the Lanark and Renfrew Scottish, was created out of two anti-aircraft artillery regiments which were no longer needed since the enemy air threat had all but disappeared. The nucleus of a third battalion was to come from one of the recce regiments – either the RCD or 4 PLDG – since it was judged that there was a surplus of reconnaissance capability in the Corps.

General Burns personally made the decision: 4 PLDG was selected for conversion into an infantry unit, purportedly be-cause it already had some experience in the role. There was bit-terness, anger and a sense of enormous betrayal when this deci-sion was announced to the 'Plugs,' as they were affectionately known. The regiment had served as 1 Division's eyes and ears with great distinction ever since its first squadron had landed in Sicily a year earlier, and it had taken part in every one of the division's actions. They termed the day of the announcement 'Black Thursday' and the officers held a wake, with a mocked-up a grave in front of the mess and a marker that read "RIP 4 Cdn Recce Regt (4 PLDG) 13 Jul 44 – STABBED IN THE BACK." The RCD, heaving sighs of relief, ceased to be part of the Corps Troops and replaced the PLDG as 1 Division's recon-naissance regiment.

In mid-July 5 CAD was moved southward, back into camps on the Volturno River, where intensive training was carried out to rectify operational faults identified in the searching self-examination conducted by all units earlier in the month.

CHAPTER 11

The Advance into Northern Italy

After the fall of Rome, on 4 June 1944, battered and much reduced German divisions were rapidly pushed back from one improvised position to the next. The German high command had decided to make a firm stand in a new defensive line, known to the Allies as the Gothic Line, which ran across the Italian peninsula, over the Appenine Mountains north of Florence, to Pesaro on the Adriatic coast. To buy time for the completion of bunkers and gun emplacements in this line, the Germans intended to delay the Allied advance with the Trasimene Line, some 75 kilometres south of Florence.

THE 1 ARMOURED BRIGADE ADVANCE TO FLORENCE

On 18 June the regiments of 1 Canadian Armoured Brigade were concentrated with the British 4 Division near Viterbo, sixty kilometres north of Rome, and three days later the Ontario Regiment supported 78 Division in an attack on the Trasimene Line at Sanfatucchio, near the western shore of Lake Trasimene. In two days of stiff fighting, the Ontarios greatly helped the British infantry to break through the German positions but the enemy held still out on the left and the British 4 Division, supported by the Three Rivers Regiment, was brought in to deal with that. Rain-soaked ground and high stone vineyard terraces made movement very difficult for the tanks, but over the next few days the Germans were slowly pushed back. The most intense fighting took place on 28 June, just in front of the village of Casamaggiore. Here 'C' Squadron of the TRR, in a bold move, seized vital high

ground in the strongest part of the German defences and for seven hours stood off repeated counter-attacks by Panther tanks and infantry while the British fought their way forward to join them.

Captain Ian Grant, who took over when the squadron commander's tank was knocked out early in the engagement, showed great personal courage throughout the day, while leading what remained of the squadron. For more than five hours, dismounted from his own tank, he directed the fire of the three re-

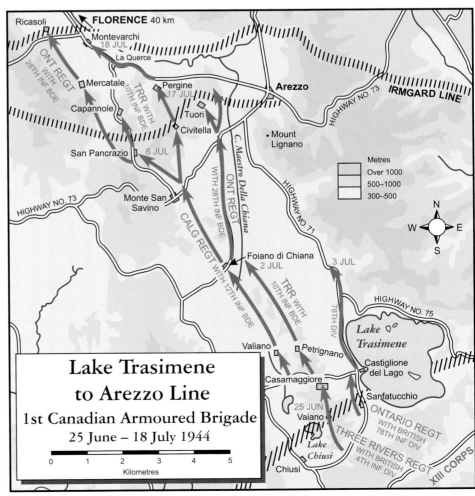

Lake Trasimene to Arezzo Line
1st Canadian Armoured Brigade
25 June – 18 July 1944

1 Armoured Brigade Sherman moving through the village of San Pancrazio, 16 July 1944. (NAC PA115031)

maining Shermans onto enemy paratroopers who continually attempted to infiltrate the position. Later, having identified a well-camouflaged Panther which was threatening 'A' Squadron, he brought his own tank into the open in order to bring accurate fire to bear, and his action forced two Panthers to withdraw.

Under continuous fire, Grant's small group then held their ground until reinforcements arrived late that night. For his superb leadership, Captain Grant was given an immediate Distinguished Service Order, and Lieutenant F.A. Farrow, the only troop leader to survive, was awarded a Military Cross.

The battle for the Trasimene Line was won, but the cost to the TRR was very high: 94 officers and men were casualties, and 26 tanks were lost. The war diary noted that 'the Regiment is suffering more casualties than in the Gustav and Hitler shows! And personnel and tank reinforcements are very short, mainly because the tank rail-head is about 200 miles back at Cassino, and transporters and road space are very limited.'

In the July heat the regiments of 1 Armoured Brigade fought their way forward in support of British infantry brigades, inching along toward the Arno River and Florence. German resistance was stubborn the whole way, fighting fiercely from one position, then withdrawing a few kilometres to the next. All the while the countryside became increasingly hostile for tanks. In this extremely rugged terrain the 1st Canadian Assault Troop, created in early June to give the brigade its own indigenous armoured engineer capability, proved its worth in lifting mines, filling craters, and, on one occasion, blasting a route for tanks along a sheer cliff face. Without their excellent work, it is unlikely that the tankers could have continued effective support of the infantry units.

On 23 July the Brigade again passed under command of 8 (Indian) Division. Support was provided to all three Indian brigades in fighting that every day increased in intensity as they neared the Arno. Finally, on 5 August the south bank of the

A tank-infantry cooperation exercise conducted by the Calgary Regiment for soldiers of the Mahratta Light Infantry, near Florence, 28 August 1944. The 8th Indian Division looked on the 1st Armoured Brigade as being 'their' tanks. (NAC PA141745)

river was taken and the Canadians were sent for a much-needed rest south of Florence. In early August the Ontario Regiment worked briefly with 1 Canadian Division, in a counter-attack role in the southern suburbs of Florence, at a time when there was an attempt to convince the enemy that I Canadian Corps had been committed in this sector.

THE GOTHIC LINE

Just as Allied troops were about to enter Florence, a major change occurred in the strategic plan for the Italian campaign: the main thrust to break through the Gothic Line was now to take place on the Adriatic front, instead of northward from Florence towards Bologna. There were many reasons for this shift, not least being that General Alexander had just lost seven French and American divisions to Operation *Anvil*, the invasion of southern France to be launched on 15 August. Additionally, making the main effort in the centre of Italy would have meant a slow and ponderous advance confined to mountain roads and constricted valleys through the Appenine Mountains. That would concede an enormous advantage to the Germans, as the regiments of 1 Armoured Brigade, who were to remain on this front in support of XIII Corps, were soon to discover. Serious problems in coordinating the operational efforts and styles of the Americans and British could also be avoided by separating the two Allied armies. By the time this new strategy was revealed to senior commanders, 5 CAD had already been moved northward to an area centred on Foligno, some fifty kilometres south-east of Lake Trasimene.

The plan finally adopted envisioned a rapid advance by three corps of Eighth Army along the coastal plain and into the Po Valley, beginning from the line of the Metauro River, II Polish Corps on the Adriatic coast, I Canadian Corps in the centre, and V British Corps on the left. The necessity of a rapid advance was stressed, for by early October the usual heavy winter rain could be expected to turn the ground along the coast into a sea of mud. The redeployment of the Canadian and British corps began almost immediately.

Units of 5 CAD began their road move to the Adriatic coast on the morning of 16 August, with the slower tank convoys of the regiments of 5 Brigade moving in advance of the division's wheeled

The units of 5th Armoured Division moved from Florence to the Adriatic coast along this road through the Appennine mountains in mid-August 1944. (NAC PA204147)

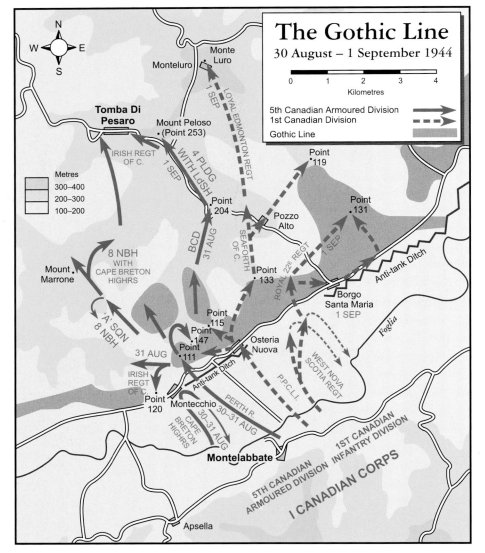

The Gothic Line
30 August – 1 September 1944

0 1 2 3 4
Kilometres

5th Canadian Armoured Division
1st Canadian Division
Gothic Line

… We could look down on the anti-tank ditch and a lot of open ground between where we were and the Gothic Line…. We could, by careful examination, pick out the odd concrete gun emplacement, and we could see the barbed wire, and we saw the minefields; but there was no life around the place at all. I did not expect German officers to be swanking up and down but the whole thing looked terribly quiet. There was not a shell coming our way, and the road that led out of the position that we were occupying at that time, due north, crossed the anti-tank ditch. Undoubtedly we assumed it was prepared for demolition but the road was still in operation and you could see it going up through the line itself, obviously still in use by the Germans. I remember turning to [Brigadier] Ian Johnston and saying that there's something wrong with this whole situation, it just does not sit right with me….

In fact, the Germans had not yet completely occupied this part of the Gothic Line defences. They were, however, on their way, and by next morning battalions of *26 Panzerdivision* were in pre-prepared positions in and around the town of Montecchio, on the far bank of the Foglia. But, based on the evidence available to him at the time, Hoffmeister decided, on the morning of 30 August, that he would try to 'bounce' the defences rather than wait another two days for the deliberate attack that had been laid on.

Orders were issued at 1330 hours: the Cape Breton Highlanders and the Perth Regiment, each with a squadron of the 8th Hussars, would attack across the Foglia at 1730 hours. The Cape Bretons, with 'B' Squadron, were to take Montecchio and Point 120, a high cliff-feature on the left of the town, while the Perths and 'A' Squadron were to capture Point 111, five hundred metres to the right.

Even before H-Hour things began to go awry in the CBH battle group on the left. As they formed up for the attack the Highlanders were subjected to heavy mortar and artillery fire, but the attacking companies nonetheless crossed the river at the appointed time to begin their move on Montecchio and Point 120. The plan called for the 'B' Squadron tanks to follow close behind the infantry after engineer work parties had cleared lanes through a minefield on the far bank. However, the tanks were delayed during their approach to the river by an officious

vehicles. For this often difficult move – much of the distance covered during hours of darkness and sometimes over improvised roads hacked through the mountains – the tankers had been provided with rubber-padded tracks for their Shermans, giving greater speed and better traction. By 20 August the whole of the division was near Jesi, thirty kilometres south of the Metauro.

In the Canadian Corps sector, 1 Division was to lead off, with an advance from the Metauro to the Foglia River, a distance of about seventeen kilometres. On the night of 25/26 August, 1 Division attacked over the Metauro and, four days later, the Canadians were on the south bank of the Foglia. The infantry battalions of 11 Brigade moved up on 29 August to ensure that 5 CAD was positioned for the deliberate attack planned to break into the Gothic Line positions, and many years later General Hoffmeister spoke about a reconnaissance he made that evening by crawling forward on a hill overlooking the Foglia.

5th Armoured Brigade Sherman fording a shallow stream while moving forward toward the Foglia River, 31 August 1944. (NAC PA204149)

military policeman who insisted that the Hussars pull off the road as another regiment, the Horse Guards, had been given priority use of the route.

Nearly an hour later, after having decided to ignore the traffic control post, 'B' Squadron's tanks were able to manoeuvre into positions facing the 100-metre-high rocky promontory, from where they could give fire support to the Highlanders' assault. But the Germans were waiting in their skilfully sited positions. Three times over the course of the bright moonlit night Cape Breton companies got up on to parts of the Point 120 feature, but each time they were thrown back by withering fire from German machine-guns. Point 120 simply could not be taken in a frontal assault, and finally, at 0430 hours, the much reduced Highlander companies and the Hussar tanks withdrew to the Foglia to regroup.

Initially the Perth Regiment attack on Point 111, supported by 'A' Squadron of the 8th Hussars, was also met by very heavy fire, but tanks and infantry slowly advanced together and, by dusk, after two anti-tank guns had been knocked out by artillery, the battle group was part-way up the hill. One company, along with a single Sherman, gradually inched their way to the crest of the hill and silenced German machine-guns blocking the advance of other companies of the battalion. By 2230 hours Point 111 was held, albeit tenuously, and the remainder of 'A' Squadron's tanks were then brought forward to bolster the defence. The Perths continued their advance northward by some 700 metres during the night, expanding their toehold to include Point 147, but they were unable to penetrate further. When morning broke on 31 August, the 'A' Squadron tanks still on Point 111 found themselves in the midst of a host of scattered German positions and several crewmen were wounded by sniper fire before the enemy were eliminated.

During the night, the commander of 11 Brigade, Ian Johnston, had decided to reinforce the Perths' success by bringing in the Irish Regiment, supported by 'C' Squadron of the 8th Hussars, to make a flanking attack from Point 111 onto the rear of Point 120. At about this same time, Brigadier Ian Cumberland, having decided to launch his tank regiments before the infantry had completely taken their objectives, issued orders to the BCD to move forward immediately to a rendezvous just below Point 111. There they were to pick up the Perth Regiment, and then push to the north-east as quickly as possible to seize Point 204, some four kilometres beyond. This key terrain controlled access to the high Tomba de Pesaro feature which anchored the whole Gothic Line system in the area.

Dug-in German anti-tank gun emplacement near Monte Marrone. This gun overlooks the ground crossed by the British Columbia Dragoons and Strathconas during their advance to Points 204 and 253. (Photo courtesy of Major Hunter Dunn)

While the flanking attack on Point 120 was still being 'teed up', 'A' Squadron of the Hussars was sent off from Point 111 to capture Monte Marrone, a high feature near the division's left boundary which, if left in German hands, threatened to block further movement into the depth of the Gothic Line defences. Because there was no uncommitted infantry available to accompany them, the tanks were on their own. They started out at 0830 hours. The nearly bare slopes leading toward Monte Marrone rose sharply north of Point 111, and the tanks moved carefully. The value of fire and movement within a tank squadron was one of the lessons learned from experience in the Liri Valley, and one troop was always in static positions ready to provide covering fire as the others advanced.

After about half an hour one of the leading tanks was hit by fire from an anti-tank gun in a concrete emplacement concealed by a haystack. The indomitable Major 'Frenchy' Blanchet gave instructions to his battle captain to cover him, then turned and raced toward the enemy, his 75mm gun blazing fire. When he reached the German gun, its crew were all dead. Then, off to the left, another Hussar tank went up in flames. Sergeant Bill McIntee and his crew bailed out, but nearby German infantrymen rushed toward the crew and bayoneted every man before other tanks could bring fire to bear.

As the squadron pressed on toward a hill shown on the map as Point 136, half-way to Monte Marrone, the situation worsened. The Shermans got caught in intense fire from interlocking anti-tank positions, and a barrage of heavy mortar bombs rained down. Blanchet called down artillery fire on the anti-tank guns he could see, but it had little effect. Sergeant Billy Bell manoeuvred his tank onto a steep side slope of the Point 136 hill, but just as he cleared the crest "an 88mm shell cleaned the entire suspension off the left hand side. The tank lurched back, turned over and began to roll." Somehow the crew got out; Sergeant Bell was known to say later that it wasn't too difficult, since "every time the turret came up, one of us got out."

The squadron was stopped cold, with only seven Shermans left out of eighteen. 'Frenchy' Blanchet had no thought of pulling back, however, and he positioned his few remaining tanks in a close defence while awaiting the arrival of friends from the rear.

Meanwhile, the BCD had hastily left their harbour before dawn. No orders had been issued to the squadrons by the commanding officer, other than to move to the assembly area, so there was some confusion about what was to come. Colonel David Kinloch, then a major commanding 'B' Squadron, stated in an interview that he had no knowledge of what the BCD had been tasked to do, and that his squadron "went into this with our muzzle covers on." It was close to 0800 hours when the regiment arrived at the appointed rendezvous with the Perth Regiment, just below Point 111, only to find that it was still occupied by a platoon of German paratroopers, and that the Patricias, on the right, had not yet taken the village of Osteria Nuova or Point 115 immediately to the right. The Dragoons thus found themselves involved in a totally unexpected and nasty fight to hold their assembly area. The Perth Regiment was not at the rendezvous, for they were still struggling to consolidate their hold around Point 147.

After waiting for more than an hour, Colonel Vokes, gruff and sometimes unpredictable in his behaviour, decided to push ahead without the infantry and ordered 'C' Squadron, just arrived at the RV, to take the lead toward Point 156, with the other squadrons following on. The orders passed by radio to the squadron rear-link (battle) captains were brief and somewhat vague: when 'C' Squadron reached Point 156, 'A' Squadron was to take the lead to Point 204. It is noteworthy that the BCD regimental history states plainly that Vokes had no direct contact with his squadron commanders at any time in the assembly area or in the ensuing battle as the regiment advanced toward Point 204. While Colonel Vokes might indeed be commended, as he has by some historians, for pressing on with bold initiative, his failure to brief his squadron commanders on the mission so that they, in turn, could give appropriate orders to the troops, might be categorized as an inept way to launch a regiment into battle.

'A' and 'C' Squadrons fought a somewhat confused battle as they struggled toward their objective on Point 204. They were dogged the whole way by fierce mortar and artillery fire and crew commanders had no choice but to keep their hatches closed, so that their view of the battlefield around them was severely limited. Few ever knew precisely where they were; the steep-sided, sparsely wooded hills all seemed to look alike. A number of Shermans 'threw' their tracks as they tried to negotiate sideslopes that were too steeply inclined, and enemy mines also took a constant toll. But the most serious problem was the large number of well-sited German anti-tank guns over the whole depth of their advance, and many BCD tanks fell victim to their deadly fire.

While the other two squadrons moved out, 'B' Squadron under Major David Kinloch was kept waiting in the re-entrant for the Perths. Kinloch later wrote:

The CO and I were out of our tanks, with the headphones hanging out of the turrets. He was listening to the progress made by the other two squadrons, and getting 'antsier' by the minute. I was standing beside him when he decided to leave and he told me explicitly to stay there until the Perths arrived. I waited and waited, and then he called me on the wireless and said that the Perths must have by-passed the assembly area, and that I was to move forward and join up with them.

I moved out, and we had not gone far when we came under fire and one of my HQ tanks was hit. We could not tell where the fire was coming from. There was no sign of our infantry. By this time we were going down a slight slope. Then Vokes came on the air and told me that he had heard that the Perths had just arrived in our assembly area, and that I was to return immediately and bring them forward. So I had to turn the whole squadron around and grind back up the slope still in full view of the enemy gunners. They picked off a couple more of my tanks, and when I got back to the re-entrant, the Perths were not ready to move. … It was a bitter day for me. I had lost good men killed and wounded; not a shot was fired by my squadron, and we accomplished nothing.

Tank Convoy. **Painting by Bruno Bobak. (Canadian War Museum 11992)**

At about 1230 hours the BCD arrived on Point 204, but between the two squadrons they mustered only twelve serviceable tanks and perhaps sixty men. The squadron commanders busily organized a hasty defence.

Back at Montecchio, the Irish Regiment's attack on Point 120 did not get underway until nearly noon because traffic congestion at the single crossing over the Foglia had delayed its move to the start line at Point 111. When the assault went in, however, it was a model of tank-infantry cooperation. Two Hussar tanks shepherded the dismounted infantry during the approach from the north-east and then provided pinpoint direct fire support for the attack, while another company with two Hussar troops circled wide to come in from the left rear of the German position. All the while Point 120 was bombarded by artillery and direct fire from 'B' Squadron, down in the

Burned-out Sherman near Point 204. This is probably one of the BCD regimental headquarters tanks. Note that the turret is some distance from the hull, indicating that the ammunition in the turret exploded. (Photo courtesy of Major Hunter Dunn)

the course of the battle for the Gothic Line. While the Dragoons suffered very heavy casualties in the process, 5 CAD had driven a four-kilometre-deep salient into the German defence line, and in most respects the Gothic Line had been broken. On the right, opposite 1 Division, the Germans had already begun to pull back. But the enemy still held Monte Peloso (Point 253), the commanding heights of the Tomba di Pesaro feature. The battle was not yet quite over.

The Perths and the Strathconas spent a very uncomfortable night on Point 204 as paratroopers repeatedly tried to infiltrate into the position, and the Strathcona tanks, lit up by still-burning BCD Shermans, were sniped at by SP guns that got close in on the left. Much of the fighting was done at 'hand-to-hand' level, and there was a lot of confusion because of the difficulty in distinguishing friend from foe. Major Bill Milroy, then commander of the Strathconas' 'B' Squadron, later recalled:

> When we got to the top of the hill, it was obvious that we were going to have to stay there. There were no infantry with us at the time – the Perths didn't come up until last light – so I deployed my troops with that in mind. The tanks were sited so they could fire across each others' bows, and we dismounted the bow [machine-] guns. When the Germans counter-attacked that night it was a real donnybrook. The forward elements of the Perths drew back to the tank lines, and everyone essentially protected his own tank. There were a tremendous number of bullets flying around, and we kept shooting until it all died down.

Foglia valley. The Hussars cut down an entire enemy company trying to escape to the west, and the Irish captured 130 prisoners.

While this assault on Point 120 was carried out, Colonel Vokes was taking his four regimental headquarters tanks to join 'A' and 'C' Squadrons, but he appears to have lost his way, leading the RHQ troop well forward and to the left of Point 204. There, three of the four, including his command tank, were knocked out by anti-tank fire. However, riding on the back deck of the remaining Sherman, Vokes managed to get to Point 204 just as 'A' and 'C' were beating off a counter-attack by enemy tanks and self-propelled guns. In mid-afternoon, they all came under attack by enemy mortars and artillery and Vokes was severely wounded by a mortar shell, but before being evacuated in a Honey tank he gave firm instructions that there was to be no withdrawal. Later in the day, he died of his wounds.

Relief for the beleaguered Dragoons was already on the way. The Strathconas had been moved up to a laager near Point 111 in late morning, waiting for instructions to advance. That order came at about 1400 hours: the Strathconas were to proceed as quickly as possible to relieve the BCD. The push forward, led by the recce troop, was almost unopposed, although nearly fifty paratroopers were taken prisoner and one Panther tank was knocked out on the way. The relief of the BCD began shortly after 1700 hours, and the arrival of the Perth Regiment just before last light greatly bolstered the position on Point 204.

The significant risk taken by Colonel Vokes earlier in the day – sending his regiment 'into the blue' – had a notable effect on

Trooper Harold Boettcher won a Military Medal for his bravery that night. Even though already wounded by small arms fire after his own tank was knocked out, Boettcher ran to a neighbouring Sherman and manned the anti-aircraft machine gun on the turret of that tank until he had repelled the enemy attack on his troop.

During the night the Strathconas received orders to support the Perths in an attack on Point 253 early the next morning. The Perths, however, were in no fit condition to carry on, so the task was given to that new infantry unit, 4 PLDG, which had been attached from 12 Brigade. While the 'Plugs' were moving forward to Point 204, in order to link up with the Strathconas, the situation on 5 CAD's left flank was stabilizing. The Cape Breton Highlanders had joined 'A' Squadron of the 8th Hussars, which had taken up a defensive position 1,500 metres short of Monte Marrone after losing so heavily in its attack the previous day. This battle group then advanced on to Monte Marrone, by then only lightly held by the enemy, and this key feature in the Gothic Line defences was captured just after first light on the morning of 1 September.

The PLDG attack on Monte Peloso did not begin auspiciously. The assembly area near Point 204 was heavily shelled shortly before the scheduled H-Hour. The resulting casualties among senior officers and

The Gothic Line – Tomba di Pesaro. This painting by G.C. Tinning vividly portrays the barren hills where the tank regiments fought this battle, and the commanding views of the terrain from German anti-tank gun positions. (Canadian War Museum 13903)

NCOs caused considerable disruption within the unit, and the start time had to be postponed until leadership problems were sorted out. When the attack was finally launched, at 1310 hours, it proved, however, to be a text-book example of good tank-infantry cooperation. While 'A' Squadron of the Strathconas provided covering fire from static positions atop Point 204, 'C' Squadron moved immediately in behind the leading PLDG platoons, spraying "every hedge and wheat stook with machine-gun fire." Not long after setting out a large force of German paratroopers was encountered concealed in the surrounding wheat fields, quite obviously readying to counter-attack Point 204. The Strathcona tanks literally mowed them down by the score; 120 dead were counted after the battle, and an equal number of wounded prisoners were taken.

As the 'Plugs' and Strathconas continued their advance toward Point 253 they met determined resistance and heavy machine-gun cross-fire, and PLDG casualties mounted with every metre of ground gained, so that that when the final assault was made only the CO, Lieutenant-Colonel Darling, and forty all ranks remained. The only Sherman that managed to climb the exceedingly steep slope to support this gallant attack was commanded by Lieutenant Brick Brown. The hilltop,

crowned by a church, was thus taken, and the way was now open for the Irish Regiment to capture the town of Tomba di Pesaro later in the evening.

Soon after Point 253 fell, the German high command gave orders to abandon all remaining positions in the Gothic Line, including the other prominent height of ground, Monte Luro, in 1 Division's sector of the front. With both of these dominating high hills, which together had served as anchors to the Gothic Line defences, now firmly in Canadian hands, the reconnaissance regiments of both 1 and 5 Divisions were ordered forward to pursue the Germans as they hastily withdrew to new positions north of the River Conca.

In 5 CAD, the Horse Guards were tasked to spearhead a six-kilometre advance by 12 Brigade to seize a crossing over the Conca just beyond the town of San Giovanni. 'B' and 'C' Squadrons moved off from an assembly area near Monte Marrone at first light on 2 September, planning to link up with the Westminster Regiment on an intermediate objective, code named *Carry Duff*, north-west of Tomba di Pesaro. From the outset it proved to be rough going. Shortly after starting out, 'C' Squadron, in the lead, lost a Honey tank to a mine in crossing a stream, temporarily blocking forward movement, and much of

A Horse Guards Sherman II near the River Conca. (NAC PA168022)

the remainder of their advance was met with heavy enemy mortar fire that inflicted a growing number of vehicle and personnel casualties. As had so often happened over the past months, German rearguards had been left behind to hinder movement by Allied troops on all avenues of approach.

By mid-morning, however, the Horse Guards established contact with the Westminsters north-west of Tomba di Pesaro, and a joint attack on *Skeena*, a hill overlooking San Giovanni, was organized for late afternoon. The terrain to be negotiated during this advance was very rough – a succession of steep, rocky ridges and deep gullies – but there was very little enemy resistance, and the objective was captured by 1630 hours. The Horse Guards and Westminsters then coordinated plans to seize two crossings over the River Conca, their original task. Just before they moved off, however, division headquarters sent instructions that they were to remain back from the river line by at least 1,200 metres because bomber strikes were about to be launched on enemy positions just north of the Conca.

While 'B' Squadron and a Westminster company made a foray through San Giovanni and reached the coastal highway during the night, encroaching seriously into 1 Division's territory in the process, it was not until the following afternoon that the enemy was pursued across the Conca by any unit of 5 CAD.

In the 1 Division sector, after the Monte Luro feature had been occupied by 2 Brigade, the RCD were brought up for rapid exploitation behind the retreating Germans – their first mission as the divisional reconnaissance regiment. I Polish Corps

had now been 'squeezed out' of the advance, and 'A' Squadron was to be part of a mixed Anglo-Canadian force of tanks and self-propelled guns ordered to cut the coastal highway near the town of Cattolica, which, it was hoped, would block the escape of at least some of the withdrawing German units. At the same time, 'B' and 'D' Squadrons were to advance north-west, along the inter-divisional boundary, to find crossings over the Conca just beyond San Giovanni, and then move to the east to join up with 'A' Squadron on the coastal highway. It took many hours to marry-up the units involved in the coastal road mission, and the column did not move off from Monte Luro until 0400 hours on 2 September.

Soon afterward 'D' Squadron, followed by 'B', set off toward San Giovanni. On 'A' Squadron's eastern axis, all the British tanks soon became victims to anti-tank fire or bogging, and the squadron pressed on, supported only by a company of the Van Doos. However, movement was very slow because of road craters and interference by enemy rearguards, and when the coastal road was finally reached in late afternoon dug-in machine-guns blocked any further advance. Meanwhile, 'D' Squadron had an adventurous journey to San Giovanni, capturing several very surprised Germans on the way. The Dragoon regimental history recounts:

On reaching San Giovanni, the lead troop heard the roar of a tank starting up. As Corporal C.J. Paterson's car cautiously edged into the central square, a Panther lurched out from the other side. Paterson let loose with his machine-gun at the crew commander sitting on the tank's turret, causing its driver to swing erratically and drop a track, and then the Dingo [scout car] reversed smartly into cover as the Panther's enormous gun swung to smack the fly causing it so much bother. But with their target gone, the Germans panicked, scuttled their tank and fled.

Later in the day, Corporal Paterson encountered another Panther in the village of Monte Albano, but fortunately the crew had dismounted. Once again he opened fire with his light machine-gun, this time inflicting nearly a dozen casualties on German infantry alongside the tank as he forced his way past them. Once beyond the village, he observed another two Panthers covering the withdrawal of enemy infantry over the River Conca, so he prudently decided that it was time to rejoin the rest of his squadron. The only route back, however, was through the centre of the village, and so, for a second time, he had to run the gauntlet through the enemy position. In the process he managed, however, to add to the number of German casualties. Corporal Paterson's daring exploit won him a Military Medal.

Unquestionably, the breaking of the Gothic Line defences by 5 CAD was an extraordinary feat of arms. The tactical proficiency demonstrated time and again by the units – both armour and infantry – stood in marked contrast to the brave but often inept performance of the division in the Liri battles. The standard operating procedures (SOPs) developed and practised in training prior to the Gothic Line operations had paid enormous dividends: armoured and infantry units understood what the other arm could do for them, and, perhaps even more important, how the two arms needed to work and move together on the battlefield. The 're-grouping' of units and sub-units, i.e., changing the affiliation of tank squadrons from one infantry battalion or company to another, could now be accomplished quickly and without disruption. Attacks could be 'teed up' rapidly at all levels of command, and units were able to react promptly to the constantly changing demands that were an inherent part of a hostile battlefield environment. Perhaps as important as anything else, there was a much greater level of confidence, within and between units, that leaders at all levels knew what they were doing (provided they were not new reinforcements), and that all members of the team, including the troopers and privates, could be trusted to do their part.

It was not only the 'F' Echelons that had developed this thoroughly professional outlook to soldiering. Every regiment has its own stories of how the NCOs and men in the support echelons never failed to bring up the ammunition, fuel, rations and water without which the tank crews could not fight the next

One of Strathcona Major Bill Milroy's 'B' Squadron headquarters tanks, disabled on Point 204. (Photo courtesy of Major Hunter Dunn)

day; how they would always find the tanks despite the dark and the shelling. Stories also abound about the mechanics who worked under fire to repair disabled tanks on the battlefield, or tow tanks to the rear when they needed more extensive repairs. And regimental legends include the devoted padres who always had the right words of comfort for men who were often frightened and lonely, and who, sharing in the unit's grief, always lent that essential measure of dignity in conducting burial services for regimental comrades.

Nor should the contribution of 'G' Squadron of the Elgin Regiment, the division's tank delivery squadron, be ignored in any assessment of 5 CAD's operational achievements. 'G' Squadron's task was to replace all vehicle casualties with serviceable tanks or scout cars fully kitted for battle – fuelled, stowed with ammunition, and complete with all tools and equipment – within 24 hours of a unit demand. It was permitted to hold a forward reserve stock of 12.5 percent of the total number of tanks allocated to the armoured regiments of the

'B' Squadron of the Strathconas lined up in the area of the Gothic Line. (LdSH Museum)

division, or approximately thirty Shermans and ten Honeys, but an additional twenty Shermans and five Honeys were always readily available in the rear.

The source of these holdings was a combination of repaired tanks coming out of the division and corps workshops and new tanks issued through Ordnance channels. Replacement tanks, complete with fully trained crews, were delivered directly, sometimes as far forward as the regimental A1 Echelon when operational conditions made this necessary. The work of the tank delivery squadron was never easy, and this was especially true during the fighting through the Gothic Line and at Coriano – a story yet to come. In the period 31 August to 15 September 1944, 'G' Squadron replaced a total of 197 tanks in the armoured regiments, of which 145 had been repaired in the workshops. Division records indicate that even in the periods of the heaviest tank losses, no regiment was ever at less than 80 percent of its war establishment tank strength at the end of any 24 hours. The Elgins kept 5 CAD operationally effective in its most difficult hours.

THE BATTLE FOR CORIANO

With the Gothic Line defences now broken at the Adriatic end, it appeared that the fighting in the Italian theatre had entered a new, potentially decisive phase. The distance between the Conca and the beginning of the flat, wide valley of the River Po was a mere twenty kilometres, and the Germans had only a single, partially-prepared line of defence in that whole sector – the so-called Rimini Line along the San Fortunato Ridge. If the Eighth Army could penetrate to the Po valley before the onset of the heavy winter rain, then perhaps the enemy might be forced back into the Alps.

There was more than a lot of wishful thinking here, and perhaps also a great deal of bad military intelligence. A considerable amount of rough, defensible terrain still had to be taken before the valley would be reached, and the valley itself was intersected by an endless succession of tributary streams, many with high, diked embankments, that would have to be crossed. Even a cursory examination of the standard topographical maps should have revealed these difficulties. And then there was the matter of the inevitable wet autumn weather that everyone knew would swell the rivers and streams running down from the Appenines, and create a sea of mud.

I Canadian Corps issued orders for the advance beyond the Conca on 1 September. Four 'bounds' were established for the advance to Rimini: the first, a ridge line some two kilometres north of the Conca; second, the Marano River, some ten kilometres further on; third, the San Fortunato Ridge south-west of Rimini; and, finally, the Rimini–Bologna railway immediately north of the Marecchia River. 1 Division was to remain on the right, in the relatively flat coastal plain, while 5 CAD would advance on the left, over the more rugged ground. Getting beyond the first bound was the immediate problem. 5 Brigade was to spearhead the thrust. The Strathconas, with the Westminsters in support, were to lead off, with the 8th Hussars and the Lanark and Renfrew Scottish following to mop up and consolidate. Once the brigade was across the Conca, the Horse Guards were to move up on the left to provide flank protection along the boundary with V British Corps.

The attack by the Strathconas, initially planned as a night assault, began from an assembly area south of San Giovanni just before 0600 hours on 3 September. By 0700 the regimental recce troop had established a bridgehead on the north bank of the river, and 'C' Squadron pressed on, two troops up. Low vines

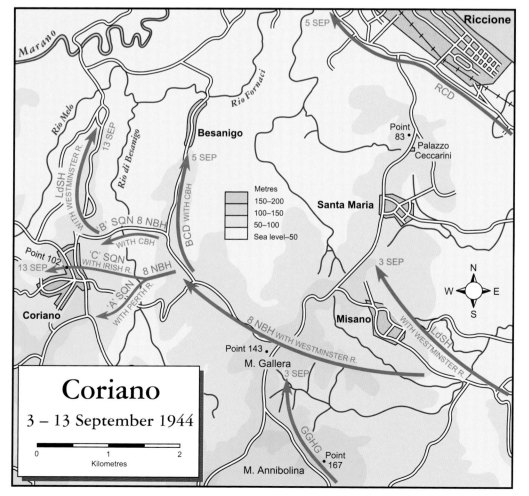

Coriano

3 – 13 September 1944

and fruit trees severely limited visibility during the advance and steep-sided hills restricted radio communications, but fortunately very little enemy opposition was encountered until just short of the village of Misano, where a single anti-tank gun was put out of action by a PIAT. 'C' Squadron by-passed Misano on the right, and by 0930 had established a defensive position on a ridge about a kilometre north of the village, and 'A' Squadron very soon arrived to take up positions to the west of 'C'. The Westminsters moved into the area at around noon and dealt with the few Germans remaining in Misano, but it was becoming apparent that there was still a considerable number of enemy troops on the higher ground to the north and west of the village, especially in the area of Monte Gallera, 1,500 metres to the west.

By early afternoon the Germans had begun to react to this incursion with intense shelling and mortaring. The Strathcona regimental history notes that the tankers "… had a very uncomfortable afternoon: every tank in 'B' and 'C' Squadrons was forced to keep 'waltzing', moving a dozen or more yards back and forth, as extremely accurate shelling was brought to bear." Somehow the regiment escaped any serious casualties, but it was very clear that the Germans were preparing to resist any attempt to advance beyond Misano.

The 8th Hussars had started to move across the Conca soon after the Strathconas were clear of the crossing, with the intention of picking up the Westminsters and pushing forward. When they arrived south of Misano it was already obvious that any further advance was likely to be delayed and the CO, Lieutenant-Colonel G.W. Robinson, and the commander of 'C' Squadron, Major Cliff McEwan, stopped and dismounted to confer with one of the Westminster company commanders. On returning to their tanks, Colonel Robinson recalled:

Knocked-out German self-propelled anti-tank gun. (NAC PA144728)

A German tank suddenly came out on the road. Just like that. I figured the only thing I could do was lie down in a ditch and not move. I did this and the tank came and passed me, still without a shot being fired by our tanks. He got 100 yards down the road before our squadron woke up and knocked him out.

I was just recovering, having overcome my shaking, and was just starting back for my tank when to my amazement a short-barrelled 88 started coming through the hedge in the same place as the previous one. It also had a German tank on the end of it. The only thing I could do was lie down in the ditch and hope I'd get away with it a second time. Just as he came opposite me one of our tanks hit him with an H.E. shell. Things began to fall on me and I was sure the crew commander had thrown a grenade at me….

This second tank got about 50 yards down the road before it, too, was knocked out…. By now our tanks were all wide awake and shooting at anything that moved. Every time I'd try to get out of that ditch someone would let fly at me. Eventually, however, I managed to get out of the ditch and saw a tank across the road, about 75 yards away. I started to run towards it and the thing that impressed me most was that his guns were trained right on me and at the back of the tank was Cliff McEwan with his helmet half on, pounding the turret with his fists and shouting 'shoot the bastard, … kill the s.o.b.'

I thought Cliff could not possibly be referring to me as he had never spoken to me in such disrespectful terms before. However, not taking any chances, I shouted at him, 'You bastard, if you shoot me I'll break your goddamn neck.'

In the official record, the Hussars were credited with knocking out two German tanks that day. It did not note that a squadron commander had mistaken his CO for one of the enemy!

'A' Squadron of the Horse Guards moved across the Conca

shortly after noon with the immediate objective of taking Monte Annibolina (Point 167), 1,500 metres south of Monte Gallera, near the inter-Corps boundary. The squadron encountered German machine-guns soon after crossing the river and several men were wounded while taking them out. As they moved on toward Point 167, "shooting up houses, haystacks and other likely targets," an 88mm anti-tank gun was destroyed and four prisoners were taken.

On several occasions during the move, the leading troops had reported seeing "very wide tank tracks" and the source of these was discovered when two Tiger tanks were suddenly encountered by the troop leader of 1st Troop, Lieutenant Bill Base, as he rounded the corner of a house some five hundred metres short of the Monte Annibolina objective. Fortunately, the Tigers were moving slowly in the opposite direction, with their guns traversed away. Base had an HE round already 'up the spout', which he let loose while shouting orders to his gunner to load an AP round. When the gunner instead stepped on the co-axial machine-gun trigger pedal, Base instantly concluded that his wisest course of action was to tell the driver to reverse and take cover behind the house. For whatever reason, the Tigers, unscathed in the engagement, were obviously not interested in getting into a fire fight, and they continued to move off. By the time Base got his other two tanks into position to take them on, the Tigers had disappeared. Continuing on, perhaps somewhat more cautiously, the squadron arrived on Point 167 at 1500 hours. There they came under continuous heavy mortar fire for many hours, while deployed into a defensive position facing north-westward toward the Coriano feature, awaiting reinforcement.

It was close to 1930 hours when 'C' Squadron of the Horse Guards arrived just short of Point 167 after being held up for several hours trying to cross the Conca behind the 8th Hussars. 'A' Squadron then moved off toward its next objective, Monte Gallera. Before they had gone half way, a 75mm anti-tank gun opened fire, destroying a Honey and a Sherman. Although other tanks quickly knocked out the German gun, the squadron commander, Major Appleton, decided it was time to take shelter for the night. 'A' Squadron then worked its way into a nearby re-entrant on the south slope of Monte Gallera which promised to give some protection from the incessant shelling, and, since they were deep in enemy-held territory, moved into a 'close laager' – a formation, usually adopted in open country at night, in which the tanks are positioned for all-round-defence.

The Canadian Corps was to have no easy march to Rimini, nor to the Marano River line for that matter. While the Germans were making an enormous effort to bolster and thicken the prepared defences along the Rimini Line, orders were given to all formations on 3 September that held the Canadians well to the south of Rimini. *Ad hoc* blocking groups were created out of the remnants of depleted units, and reinforcements were rushed to the front throughout the day on 4 September. Most significant for the regiments of 5 CAD, a fresh enemy division – *29 Panzergrenadierdivision*, albeit badly understrength – was deployed on to Coriano Ridge. While this six-kilometre-long feature was in the British V Corps sector, its garrison overlooked and dominated almost all the ground that would have to be crossed in the Canadians' advance.

At first light on 4 September the 8th Hussars passed through the Strathcona positions near Misano in a thrust to the Marano River, some five kilometres beyond. The Westminster Regiment, in support, followed immediately behind. The Hussars first cleared the area of Monte Gallera, 1,000 metres from the start line, where they destroyed several anti-tank guns that had fired on them. The regimental recce troop and 'B' Squadron then began to move cautiously along the western slope of Besanigo ridge. However, once exposed to observation and fire from German positions on the parallelled Coriano ridge, 2,000 metres to the west, they began to lose one tank after another to anti-tank and mortar fire and the advance came to a grinding halt as crew commanders desperately searched out whatever immediate cover was available. 'A' Squadron, still considerably understrength after the Gothic Line fight, was sent forward to help extricate 'B' Squadron, and all of its tanks' smoke shells were expended to screen the enemy's direct observation while the exposed tanks moved to the eastern slope of the ridge.

Late in the afternoon, the BCD were brought up in support of an attempt by the Lanark and Renfrew Scottish to push farther along the Besanigo ridge. 'B' Squadron, advancing in front of the infantry, ran into the same heavy shelling and fanatical resistance by the German paratroopers that had stopped the Hussars and Westminsters earlier that day. In the vanguard of the squadron, the troop commanded by Lieutenant James Looney experienced very sharp fighting in attacking a strongly-defended German position well forward of the infantry. The light was beginning to fail, and Looney recognized that this objective had to be taken before dark. He also knew that the Germans were well-supplied with hand-held anti-tank weapons, as several of the squadron's tanks had already been knocked out, so he dismounted from his tank and took on a group of paratroopers with grenades and his pistol, killing two and capturing another three. A short distance away, Sergeant Bill Fleck, his troop sergeant, was involved in a similar dismounted action to clear a way for the tanks. In leading the Shermans forward, Fleck, even though seriously wounded while advancing, killed five Germans and took another eight prisoners on the objective. The personal bravery demonstrated in this action earned Sergeant Fleck the Distinguished Conduct Medal, the first DCM given to a member of the Dragoons, and Lieutenant Looney received the Military Cross.

Coriano Ridge Under Bombardment. **Painting by Campbell Tinning depicting the valley between Besanigo Ridge and Coriano, crossed during the attack by 11th Brigade and the 8th Hussars on 13 September 1944. (Canadian War Museum 13867)**

During the night 'A' and 'C' Squadrons of the BCD were brought forward to relieve the Hussars and 11 Brigade took over command of the sector. The Cape Breton Highlanders pressed forward in the darkness another 1,000 metres, and at first light on 5 September the Dragoons moved to support the Highlanders as they advanced doggedly along the top of Besanigo ridge. Every metre of the way the tanks and infantry were in clear view of the German garrison on Coriano ridge to the west, and they were constantly shelled and subjected to anti-tank fire from across the narrow valley between the ridges. Nonetheless, the Dragoons and Highlanders persistently edged forward and, by late morning, reached the northern extremity of the ridge. But they were still under direct observation from Coriano, and under almost continuous fire. The BCD regimental history relates:

In a situation such as this where [the infantry] could not manoeuvre without incurring heavy losses, the tank crews had to fend for themselves. Those who could dug a fairly large slit-trench and drove the tank over it, thus providing

themselves with excellent protection against almost constant shellfire. The tank was then camouflaged to the best of their ability....

These perilous conditions were to last for the whole of the next week, although the risk and discomfort of the exposed position was shared when the BCD were relieved by the Hussars two days later.

While 5 CAD's thrust to the Marano River had ground to a halt, in large part because of the strength of the German positions on Coriano ridge, the V British Corps attack toward Coriano from the south had simply made no headway at all and further attempts by the British to break through on 7 and 8 September also failed. By then another hindrance to the Canadians' momentum appeared on the night of 6 September in the form of heavy rain. The resulting torrents flowing down from the hills made significant obstacles of what until then had been only shallow streams, and deep, slippery mud began to slow all movement, whether by vehicle or on foot.

The Canadian Corps boundary was shifted to the west on 9

September, and Coriano ridge became a 5 CAD problem. That day General Hoffmeister went forward to an observation post on Besanigo ridge to study the ground and come up with a plan. In a night attack beginning in the small hours of 13 September, all three battalions of 11 Brigade would attack westward from Besanigo ridge, each supported by a squadron of the 8th Hussars. The Perth Regiment would assault south of the village of Coriano, the Cape Breton Highlanders would take the area to the north, and the Irish Regiment would go through the centre to clear the village itself. The tank squadrons were to follow as soon as engineers had prepared crossings over the Besanigo, a small stream at the bottom of the valley with very steep banks that tanks could not climb. In support of this attack, the British 1 Armoured Division's Gurkha Brigade was to assault the southern end of Coriano ridge two hours before the Canadian H-Hour; and once Coriano was taken the Westminsters, with a squadron of the Strathconas, would be brought in to exploit to the northern end of the ridge.

5 CAD's attack began promptly at 0100 hours on 13 September, as the massive firepower of the whole of the Eighth Army's artillery rained down on the area. While many of the problems inherently associated with a night operation arose at one time or another, the attack by the Perths on the left flank of the village progressed much as had been planned and by around 0430 hours they were consolidating the positions taken on the ridge. There were many more problems on the right flank, where the forward companies of the CBH went astray in the dark, and only one platoon arrived on the intended objective. By dawn, however, the Highlanders had re-assembled most of their missing troops and secured a toehold on the ridge, although for some time they continued to have difficulties on the slope nearest the village.

What very nearly went wrong was the preparation of crossings over the Besanigo for the 8th Hussars' tanks. This was to be done by three Sherman tanks fitted with bulldozer blades, but two of them broke down, so much of the work of filling-in the bed of the stream had to be done by engineers using picks and shovels, all the while under heavy shell fire. The first crossing site was not ready until 0630 hours, when 'A' Squadron quickly got across to join the Perths in ongoing battles on the south edge of Coriano. 'C' Squadron, which had been intended to support the Irish Regiment in its clearance of the built-up area of the town, soon afterward moved through the 'A' Squadron crossing site and went forward to assist the CBH until 'B' Squadron was able to

move up. When Major Tim Ellis was finally able to get 'B' Squadron across the valley about an hour later, his tanks immediately joined the Highlanders in fighting through their objective.

By this time the Irish Regiment had begun their assault on the rubble-filled streets of Coriano. It was a bitter and costly battle, fought street-to-street and house-to-house, much like at Ortona, and it lasted the whole of the day and well into the night. The German defenders had dug a myriad of tunnels from one narrow street to another and between houses, and time and again they used these tunnels very skilfully to reoccupy buildings that the Irish had already cleared. At one early point the Canadians thought that the Germans had pulled out entirely, and the Hussars 'C' Squadron sent in two troops of tanks to help in consolidation. On reaching the central square, however, the lead troop came face to face with a German tank, reported as being a Panther, cleverly concealed among the buildings. The Panther quickly knocked out two Shermans, one of which 'brewed up', and several of the other Hussar tanks were engaged in vicious close-in fighting with German infantry. When a third Sherman was disabled by a *Faustpatrone* – a much-superior PIAT – 'C' Squadron was directed to pull out of

German Mark IV tank captured by the 8th Hussars in Coriano. The tank was later presented to General Hoffmeister, but there is no record of what became of it. (8CH Archives)

the built-up area. For the rest of the day, the tanks remained on the outskirts of the village to provide whatever fire support they could as the Irish pursued the Germans through cellars, tunnels and attics. Major Cliff McEwan later wrote:

The Jerries had some damnably clever positions dug into the cellars of houses, places we couldn't get at with our tank guns. It was tough to have to sit there and watch them nail one infantryman after another and not be able to do anything about it. We could fire but it didn't do much good. Then you'd see a Canadian making a break from one place to another. There'd be a burst of fire and, like as not, he'd go down.

While these street battles were still raging, the Westminster Regiment, led by 'C' Squadron of the Strathconas, passed through the Cape Bretoners to exploit to the northern end of the ridge. While they encountered heavy mortar fire and a substantial number of German infantry, by mid-afternoon they were firm on their objective overlooking the Marano River.

Just after first light on the morning of 14 September, the Hussars went back into the village with a company of the Irish. The Germans had evacuated the town during the night. The Hussars gained a rather large trophy-of-war that day: the Germans had abandoned an intact Mark IV Special near the central square. It had been prepared for demolition but the fuse to the charges had sputtered out. The Hussars towed the tank back to their 'A' Echelon, and a few days later it was presented to General Hoffmeister.

The 8th Hussars also gained another, quite different, prize. Regimental fitters were working in the valley of the Besanigo repairing tanks abandoned in the attack. The Germans were still shelling the area periodically, and on one such occasion, huddled under a tank, the fitters heard what sounded like a scream. When the shelling stopped they went out to investigate, and soon came across a young filly, about three months old, "half starved and bleeding … wounded in the leg and stomach." Nearby was her mother, killed by a shell several days earlier, and the frantic little foal had worn a path around her body. Somehow the old cavalry instincts were aroused in these 'mechanized veterinarians', and they took the colt back to the Hussars' harbour. The medical officer, even while protesting that he was no horse doctor, bandaged her wounds. "She was given a shot of rum. From the beginning she was a true Maritimer in her appreciation of a shot of rum. From that day on, she was first on the sick parade until her health was restored. Almost at once she was called Princess Louise and no one thought of anything but keeping her." Princess Louise became the regimental mascot. She travelled with 'B' Echelon up the Adriatic coast and, at the end of the Italian campaign, she was smuggled from Italy to north-west Europe, well hidden in a stall built in the back of a truck.

The wounded filly rescued by the 8th Hussars after the Battle of Coriano. She was named Princess Louise, and was the regimental mascot until she died in 1973. (8CH Archives)

For 5 CAD this battle was over. A British division was brought forward during 14 September to relieve 5 CAD's very tired units for the attack across the Marano. On the right, 1 Canadian Division, having had a very hard struggle to get past Riccioni, was now also on the banks of the Marano. Over the next week they faced some of the most intense fighting of the Italian campaign in battles at San Martino and San Fortunato. Meanwhile, 5 CAD pulled back into the area around San Giovanni for rest and refitting.

1 CANADIAN ARMOURED BRIGADE: NORTH FROM FLORENCE

While the units of 5 CAD were being readied for the attack on Coriano, 85 kilometres to the west the regiments of 1 Armoured Brigade, still supporting XIII Corps north of Florence, were being positioned to support a Fifth US Army thrust against the sector of the Gothic Line high in the rugged mountains of the central Appenines. In the first week of September, the enemy had been slowly pushed back from the historic city by nearly twenty kilometres, the Ontarios supporting the British 1 Division and the Calgarys with 8 (Indian) Division. By 10 September, this advance had reached the line of the Sieve River, and the next morning the Ontarios supported an infantry brigade attack across the Sieve and captured the village of Borgo San Lorenzo. The Germans at this point withdrew the bulk of their forces into prepared positions in the Gothic Line, a further twelve kilometres to the north, leaving behind an almost unending succession of roadblocks, craters and demolished bridges. As was now the enemy's usual practise, small but well-armed rearguards remained in place to obstruct the pursuing Allied troops. It was to be a difficult and frustratingly slow pursuit.

XIII Corps launched its attack toward the Gothic Line on the morning of 13 September. The Ontario Regiment moved in support of 66 Brigade, northward from Borgo San Lorenzo along the main road to the Casaglia Pass, one of the anchor points in the Gothic Line. In the early stages of the advance, two troops of 'B' Squadron moved behind the British infantry and, while opposition was light, the tanks provided a considerable weight of direct fire onto enemy positions. The Calgarys, backing up 21 Indian Brigade in an attack along a secondary axis three kilometres to the east, had a more difficult beginning, having to manoeuvre a squadron of tanks over several kilometres of tortuous mule track to get into position where they could bring fire to bear on the Indians' initial objective,

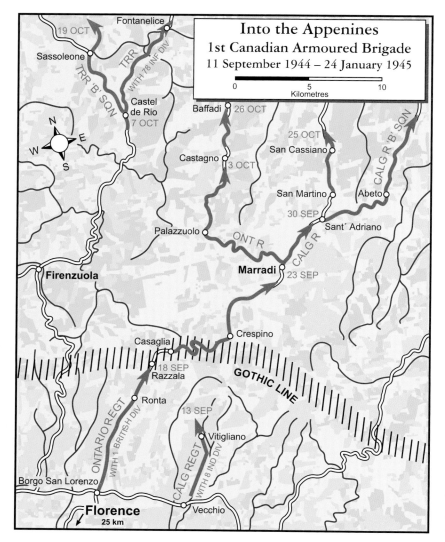

Into the Appenines
1st Canadian Armoured Brigade
11 September 1944 – 24 January 1945

0　　　　5　　　　10
Kilometres

Monte Veruca, that dominated XIII Corps' main axis of advance. When the attack went in, fire support from the tanks was so devastating to the enemy on the exposed mountain top that the infantry were able to take their objective with only very light casualties.

XIII Corps continued to make moderate gains over the next several days, but the mountainous terrain became increasingly impenetrable. Roads and tracks deteriorated, and enemy demolitions frequently prevented the tanks from keeping up with the supported infantry. By 25 September the main employment of the forward tanks was to provide protection for engineers who were clearing demolitions and road blocks, so all but one squadron in both the Ontarios and the Calgarys were withdrawn into reserve. All this time the Three Rivers Regiment was in Corps reserve, employed in traffic control duties on the main supply routes.

In late September, the XIII Corps boundary was shifted to the west to accommodate a thrust by II US Corps on the left, and this entailed a shift for both the Ontarios and Calgarys, as well as bringing in the TRR to support 78 Division on the Corps' new left-hand axis. A combination of extraordinarily heavy rain and a succession of German demolitions on all three routes severely limited the ability of the tanks to provide intimate support to the infantry, however, and increasingly they were used to provide indirect fire. On 27 October Fifth Army suspended its offensive.

The Gothic Line had been broken in the east but the Germans simply could not be budged from the centre. All three regiments of the brigade maintained a squadron in forward locations, often in precarious and exposed positions, until the end of the year, when the Calgarys were taken out of the line. The Ontario and TRR squadrons remained in place until late January.

Cleaning the Gun. Painting by Campbell Tinning of an Ontario Regiment crew scrubbing their tank's 75mm gun with a bore brush. (Canadian War Museum 13861)

Winter quarters for members of the Ontario Regiment: a sand-bag shelter in back of a Sherman, San Clemente, January 1945. (NAC PA151745)

THE BATTLE OF THE RIVERS AND CANALS

In the I Canadian Corps sector, on the Adriatic, the week following the capture of Coriano brought more intense battles. The capture of San Martino and then the San Fortunato ridge by 1 Division enabled the PPCLI to exploit to the Marecchia River and establish a lodgement on the north bank, three kilometres west of Rimini, on the morning of 21 September. The next day, the British crossed the Marecchia further to the west. The stage was now set, or so it seemed, for the long-promised 'debouch' into the flatlands of the Po Valley, where Allied armour could chase the enemy back to the Alps! On 23 September, 5 CAD was brought up to form the spearhead.

5 CAD, operating on the left of New Zealand's 2 Division which had replaced 1 Canadian Division, was given the grossly optimistic mission of advancing to the north of Bologna. The first bound in this eighty kilometre thrust was to be to the Fiumicino River, known in Roman history as the Rubicon. In the six kilometres between the bridgehead and the Fiumicino

ran two other lesser rivers, the Uso and the Salto. The task of leading the division to the Fiumicino was given to 12 Brigade, supported by the Strathconas, and in the first phase of this operation 4 PLDG, with 'C' Squadron of the Strathconas, were to seize a crossing over the River Uso.

The attack went in at 0900 hours on 23 September. Lieutenant-Colonel Jim McAvity, CO of the Strathconas, wrote:

The P.L.D.G. advanced through the village [of Santa Giustina] with two companies leading. One hour later they were stopped ... only a few hundred yards beyond by heavy mortar fire and by machine guns sited in the vines which encompassed every field. Generally these vines were not more than 50 yards apart while the length of the fields did not exceed 400 yards. These, then, were the limits of visibility obtained by our crew commanders. Olive trees and farm buildings added to the difficulty. It was impossible for the squadron commander to exercise control in the usual

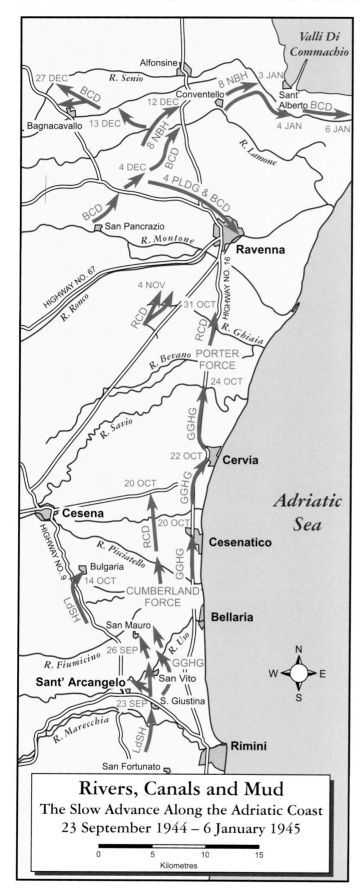

Rivers, Canals and Mud
The Slow Advance Along the Adriatic Coast
23 September 1944 – 6 January 1945

manner with troops supporting one another forward. Each troop (of three Shermans) worked with a company. More than ever before or since, we were dependent upon the infantry to scout ahead for the carefully concealed self-propelled guns.

The 'Plugs' suffered eighty casualties and 'C' Squadron lost seven tanks, five 'brewed up' by anti-tank guns which were never seen. Several flanking operations were attempted over the next two days, all equally unsuccessful, and the Strathconas lost an additional nine Shermans. The Horse Guards were brought in on 24 September to serve as flank protection along the division's right-hand boundary, but they, too, lost several tanks without being able to advance more than about 1,500 metres. Finally, on 25 September, after four days of unexpectedly bitter fighting, three crossings were gained over the Uso. On the most easterly of these, the Horse Guards had sixteen men killed and another four wounded when a series of mines exploded just as they were moving up to give cover to a mine-lifting party. The battle for the Uso River was but a foretaste of the fighting that would plague the Canadians as they advanced over twenty or more river and canal lines in the next two months.

The Fiumicino River was reached on the morning of 28 September by units of 11 Brigade which had advanced without armoured support. There the advance stalled on the south bank; it rained very heavily throughout the day, swelling the Fiumicino to a ten-metre-wide torrent of muddy water, and washing out bridges and culverts on all supply routes to the south. Cross-country movement in the thick, greasy mud of the plain simply proved to be impossible, and all three of the armoured regiments of 5 Brigade were withdrawn from the immediate front to await better conditions.

The severe shortage of infantry reinforcements being sent to Italy was by now having a most serious effect on the fighting capability of the infantry battalions, and all of these units badly needed a period of rest. Even though the offensive had been temporarily halted, there was still a requirement for troops to hold the line, and "where possible, to nibble away with a view to gaining more ground." One solution was to create a series of *ad hoc* forces from units of the other arms to hold portions of the line not considered vital to the overall Corps plan.

Cumberland Force, created on 9 October, was tasked with holding a five-kilometre sector bordering on the Adriatic Sea. While its composition varied over the eighteen days of its existence, it included two of Canada's most illustrious cavalry regiments, the Royal Canadian Dragoons and the Governor General's Horse Guards, serving 'de-horsed', as well as British, New Zealand and Greek troops. When 1 Canadian Division resumed the Corps offensive on 10 October, *Cumberland Force* took on an aggressive 'nibbling' posture, advancing more than eight kilometres in the next ten days, and the Horse Guards liberated the town of Cesenatico.

No sooner was *Cumberland Force* disbanded, than another group, *Porter Force*, was created. It included the RCD, the Horse Guards and squadrons of the Strathconas, as well as that unique British unit, Popski's Private Army, and it continued the by-now familiar, if heartily disliked, task "to hold the line on the Adriatic coast and follow up an enemy withdrawal without developing a particular offensive effort." The RCD, whose excellent reconnaissance capabilities had only rarely been employed in the campaign, especially distinguished themselves while serving in this infantry role. Two of their squadron commanders, Majors Al Brady and C.V. Vickers were awarded the Distinguished Service Order for exceptional gallantry, Sergeant Cliff Saunders, Lance Corporal Thomas Smith and Trooper Jim Papps were awarded the Military Medal, and Sergeant Saunders also received the American Silver Star.

The relentless push against the Germans resumed. It was one river or canal line after another: the Pisciatello, the Savio, the Ronco, the Montone, the Lamone, the Fosso Vecchio, the Naviglio Canal, the Fosso Munio, the Senio. Ground conditions, however, severely restricted the employment of armour. Because of deep, pervasive mud, cross-country movement was often impossible (track-pad extenders, known as 'grousers', which reduced the ground pressure of the tanks, did not become available in Italy until the end of the year) and because of the difficulty in building bridges anchored on the rain-soaked dikes there were often insurmountable problems in getting tanks across water obstacles quickly enough to be of use. Where direct support by tanks was possible, the BCD was usually in the forefront, although at times squadrons of the Strathconas, 8th Hussars and Horse Guards were brought forward. The Strathconas regularly found themselves supplementing the artillery with indirect fire support for the infantry. And, in mid-December, both the Strathconas and Hussars were temporarily employed as infantry.

While they arrived in late October, somewhat too late in the campaign to be of great use, each regiment in 5 Brigade was issued with sixteen 'Firefly' Shermans. While internal distribu-

Strathcona Sherman passing over a Bailey bridge on the River Uso at San Vito, September 1944. (NAC PA173514)

For the tank regiments in the Adriatic sector, mud became the major enemy in the autumn of 1944. This photo shows an 8th Hussars tank bogged in the mud while attempting to cross one of the innumerable streams and rivers that hindered the advance. (NAC PA204159)

tion varied somewhat within the three regiments, in most instances one 17-pounder Firefly was given to each tank troop to replace a standard 75mm equipped tank; and to supplement these welcome additions each of the regiments was supplied with six 105mm howitzer Shermans in early December, giving a greatly increased indirect fire support capability.

On 30 December, after the Germans had withdrawn to the west bank of the Senio River, the Allied offensive in Italy was halted for the winter, although Corps commanders were instructed to 'tidy up' their sectors before going over to the defensive. As part of this clean up in the Canadian Corps area, 5 CAD was ordered to secure the area still held by the Germans south of the Valli di Comacchio, a shallow, twenty-kilometre-wide enclosed lagoon.

'Ground' was the major factor affecting General Hoffmeister's plan for Operation *Syria*. All but one major water obstacle could be avoided by selecting an axis of advance parallel to the Fosso Vecchio, and by deliberately waiting until the muddy ground was frozen, he could ensure that his tanks would be able to move rapidly. The operation was to be done in two phases: first, 11 Brigade, with an 8th Hussars squadron, was to break through the enemy position at the village of Conventello, then 5 Brigade, supported by the Cape Breton Highlanders, would secure a bridgehead over the Bonifica Canal and move on to capture the village of Sant' Alberto. The plan was straightforward and simple; its execution was not.

The assault on Conventello began in the pre-dawn darkness of 2 January 1945, the sky dimly lit with artificial moonlight. The tanks of 'B' Squadron, 8th Hussars, followed closely behind the Perths and the Irish Regiment. As they got closer in to the stone houses of the village at first light, "a German anti-tank gun barked, and then another, and another. One tank began to flame. The shells spat viciously at the others." The quick reaction of one crew commander undoubtedly saved the day, as their history recounts.

[Sergeant Daniel McAskill] halted his Sherman where it was and took on the nest of German guns at close range. He was in a dangerously exposed position but it was his aim to draw upon himself the attentions of the enemy so the rest of the squadron could escape the trap. Single-handed, he and his crew stood their ground and dominated the Germans' positions until his aim had been achieved. The enemy did try to check the other tanks with 50 or 60 rounds of armour-piercing shells but their fire was inaccurate, and it was inaccurate because Dan McAskill was raising havoc among their crews.

Sergeant McAskill knocked out four anti-tank guns and a Panther tank, and information he passed to the squadron com-

(Above) Strathcona troopers un-crating ammunition in preparation for an indirect shoot in support of infantry operations, October 1944. (LdSH Museum)

(Right) BCD Shermans in the mud of the Po Valley, 13 October 1944. (NAC PA17321)

Sherman tanks in the Mud. This painting by Campbell Tinning depicts one of the 17-pounder-equipped Sherman 'Fireflies' that were brought into service in Italy in October 1944. (Canadian War Museum 13846)

mander enabled the squadron to outflank the remaining Germans and destroy them. For his bold action, he was awarded the Military Medal.

With Conventello secured, the Hussars and BCD moved through toward Sant' Alberto shortly before noon. The advance proved to be considerably slower than had been anticipated, in part because of hedgerows and thick vines that were "webbed together by strong, heavy wires which persisted in striking the hatches of the tanks and making it difficult to rotate the guns." Both regiments encountered many small groups of Germans firing at them from ditches, hedgerows and farm buildings, and the liberal employment of 'speculative fire' – the use of machine-gun fire and HE against "anything liable to conceal or protect enemy positions" – was especially noted in both units' after-action reports.

The Hussars, on the left, also had to contend with fire from positions to the west of the Fosso Vecchio. By late afternoon both regiments reached the Strada Molinazza, a major road some 1,500 metres north of Conventello, but here the Hussars

were halted by a deep ditch stoutly defended by self-propelled guns and Panther tanks. Because it was getting dark by then, a further advance in the close country was deemed unwise and the Cape Breton Highlanders were brought forward to protect the tanks.

During the night an armoured bulldozer carved a path through the five-metre-high banks of an abandoned canal, known as the 'Dry Lamone', and that enabled the BCD to position 'A' Squadron on the east side of the canal bed for the continuation of the attack. About an hour after first light on the morning of 3 January the push toward the Bonifica Canal was resumed. The pace was slow and cautious because of "fire from infantry in dug-in positions around farm houses and from well concealed enemy tanks and self-propelled guns." The Dragoons encountered no less than five separate groups of enemy armour and dealt with each by using the lead tank, pushing through succeeding rows of vines, as a decoy to draw fire while the other tanks waited to fire at the flash of the enemy weapon. No fun for the leaders!

The Hussars, on the left flank, made good use of their newly-acquired 105mm Shermans to blast enemy-held positions. 'C' Squadron of the Hussars arrived at the key bridge over the Bonifica Canal, 2,000 metres south-west of Sant' Alberto, just before 1400 hours, and to their surprise it was intact. They could not get at it, however, because of an anti-tank ditch, and, as they watched, a lone German soldier climbed onto the bridge, made a dash across, and dodged underneath on the near side. Everyone knew what he was doing: the bridge was pre-

pared for demolition, and he was lighting the fuse. Sergeant Alf Baughan, who was awarded a Military Medal for his actions later that day, recalled that "he stayed down there for maybe three minutes and then he came up again. He began to run for the far bank. You got a strange, empty feeling even as your machine-gun went at him. Damned if you didn't want to see a guy like that get clean away. But he didn't. We killed him half-way across the bridge."

Almost immediately an explosion shattered the near end of the bridge. The way to Sant' Alberto was blocked, at least on this route. When brigade headquarters was informed of the situation, the BCD were ordered to make a dash the next morning for the only other bridge remaining over the canal, 3,500 metres to the east. That night the Germans made a last, desperate attempt to disrupt the 5 Brigade thrust by means of a four-battalion counter-attack directed toward the base of the operation, south of Conventello. However, they were beaten back by the Westminsters and a British battalion, supported by an enormous weight of artillery fire.

As the remnants of these German battalions were being mopped up, the leading troops of 'B' Squadron of the BCD arrived at the Sant'Alberto bridge. It was obviously prepared for demolition, for wire could be seen "all over the roadway on the

(Left) BCD tank crew preparing a meal in front of their tank, Conventello, January 1945. (NAC PA193869)

(Below) *Sherman Tanks Refuelling in Harbour.* **Painting by Campbell Tinning. (Canadian War Museum 13997)**

top of the bridge". While the troop leaders wanted to go across at once, the squadron commander, Major R.B. Sellars, was concerned that the Germans might blow the bridge while tanks were on it. He dismounted from his tank with wire cutters in hand, ran out onto the bridge, and proceeded to cut the leads to the charges and re-move whatever detonators he could find, under enemy mortar and small arms fire all the while. "When he returned to his tank his clothes had been torn to shreds by mortar bomb splinters, although he escaped with slight scratches." This gallant squadron commander received the Distinguished Service Order for his bravery and initiative in capturing the bridge intact.

Within hours 'B' Squadron and two companies of the Perth Regi-ment had a firm bridgehead on the north bank of the Bonifica, and 'C' Squadron was put across and sent westward along the canal to link up with the Cape Bretoners, who had waded across opposite the bridge the Hussars had failed to capture the previous day. Sant' Alberto was taken with com-parative ease early on 5 January and the Dragoons exploited along the south shore of the Valli di Comacchio as far as the Adri-atic coast. 5 Brigade thus ended its final action of the Italian cam-paign with a notable victory.

END OF THE ITALIAN CAMPAIGN

After the successful operations south of Comacchio, the regi-ments of 5 Brigade returned to rest billets in Cervia, where they expected to spend the winter in the relative luxury of heated buildings, hot showers, clean clothing and regular meals, and with leaves to visit Florence and Rome. But, with the campaign in north-west Europe still not won, there was a great need for reinforcements in that theatre. The opportunity for the Cana-dian Army to be reunited in a single operational theatre, for which the government had been pressing British authorities for many months, was eagerly grasped by Canadian military au-thorities, and plans were approved to move the whole of I Ca-nadian Corps and 1 Armoured Brigade to north-west Europe.

By 11 February, the units of 5 CAD and 1 Armoured Brigade were being moved in great secrecy by rail and road convoy to camps near Livorno (Leghorn), to await transport to southern

(Above) Men of the 1st Ar-moured Brigade waiting in Livorno to board LSTs for the voyage to Marseilles, March 1945. (NAC PA177535)

(Left) The Italy Star, awarded for operational service in Sicily and Italy.

France. There it became obvious to the staff that many of the units had brought with them far more vehicles and equipment than were authorized in official scales of issue – stuff that had been 'acquired' over the previous year to add to the comfort of the troops. With shipping space already severely cramped, units were duly informed that, unless special authority was granted, they could take only the vehicles and equipment listed in the war establishment equipment issue scale. Major-General

George Kitching, who had commanded 4 CAD in France and had since returned to Italy as Brigadier General Staff, later wrote, in *Mud and Green Fields*:

> One of our armoured regiments asked if they could have special permission to take with them four extra tanks which they had fixed up as command tanks. [Lieutenant-General] Charles Foulkes [the Corps commander] paid an unexpected visit to the regiment one morning and asked to see the four tanks. Somewhat embarrassed, the regimental commander led him over to four rather scruffy tanks which were grouped together and isolated from the rest of the unit's Shermans. Charles' suspicions were aroused when on approaching them he heard faint clucking sounds which greatly increased in volume when he hit the side of the first tank with his stick. Charles had a good sense of humour on these occasions but he wouldn't allow the regiment to retain their egg-laying tanks, in each of which were about fifty hens supplementing the daily ration with fresh eggs.

Units went to great length to circumvent the strictures imposed by the staff and a great deal of contraband stores and souvenirs of war were surreptitiously included in the official baggage. The 8th Hussars smuggled Princess Louise aboard and the Calgary Regiment brought their regimental piano.

When they sailed, both formations had earned enviable reputations of great competency on the field of battle, amongst their Canadian brother soldiers, amongst all the Allies with whom they had served, and, perhaps as telling as anything, amongst the Germans against whom they had fought. As had their comrades of nearly thirty years earlier in France and Flanders, they had become the storm troops of the Italian campaign. The excellent leadership within the regiments, and in brigade and division headquarters, from crew commander on up, deserve a great deal of credit, but it was the men who served so loyally, so selflessly – the tank crews, the drivers of the echelon vehicles that carried the supplies, the mechanics, the recovery crews, the storemen, the medical assistants – who really made the reputation of which everyone was so proud.

The first convoy of ships carrying men and equipment of 5 CAD left Livorno on 18 February, and the sea move to Marseilles continued for the next six weeks. At Marseilles, tanks were loaded on flat cars, while wheeled vehicles set out on the journey northward through France in convoy. By early March, the division was re-assembled in staging camps in southern Belgium, and 1 Armoured Brigade followed a week later.

Seven hundred and thirty-six members of the Canadian Armoured Corps remained behind, in Canadian military cemeteries at Agira, Cassino, Cesena, Coriano, Montecchio, Ortona, Ravenna and Villanova. They are the lasting tributes on Italian soil of great and valiant deeds by magnificent men in regiments that will never be bettered.

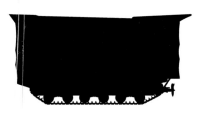

CHAPTER 12

The Battle of Normandy: The Landings and Break-in

The Allied invasion of France, beginning on 6 June 1944, was undoubtedly the most significant operation of the entire war on the Western front. It was an exceptionally risky enterprise that could have gone badly wrong at almost any stage, and failure would have been a catastrophic setback for the Allied cause. But it succeeded and Canadian troops, including three armoured regiments, played a major part in that success.

A large-scale invasion of the continent was the centrepiece of Allied grand strategy from the time the British and Americans met in December 1941 to coordinate the global conduct of the war. The two major allies may have disagreed on how quickly the invasion should be mounted, and on how best to contain the Germans in the interim, but they never wavered on this central principle.

The COSSAC (Chief of Staff, Supreme Allied Commander) outline plan for Operation *Overlord* – the invasion of Normandy in May or June 1944 – was approved at the Quebec Conference in August 1943, and responsibility for detailed operational planning was then passed to the senior naval, air and land force commanders. At this time, 3 Canadian Division, with 2 Canadian Armoured Brigade under command, was selected as the Canadian contribution to the assault force, and the training conducted by the units of 2 Armoured Brigade for this task has already been described in Chapter 5. The materiel requirements were even more complex than the operational problems. Literally thousands of landing craft were needed. Specialist armoured vehicles, such as 'swimming' tanks, mine-clearing 'flail' tanks and engineer demolition tanks (AVREs), had to be designed and tested. Artificial harbours, supplemented by a fuel pipeline under the ocean (PLUTO), were necessary in order that the invasion force could be supplied until a functioning port was captured.

OPERATION *OVERLORD*

Operation *Neptune* was the name given to the actual landing operations. Following an airdrop of three parachute divisions on the flanks, five divisions were to be landed on a 55-kilometre stretch of Normandy coast. Two American divisions were to land on *Utah* and *Omaha* beaches, on the western flank. A British division was to come in on *Gold* beach in the centre, with 3 Canadian Division to its right, on *Juno* beach, and another British division on *Sword* beach on the eastern flank. Once the bridgehead was secure, a further twenty-three divisions were to be brought in, including 2 Canadian Division and 4 Canadian Armoured Division. In addition to the ground troops, huge naval and air components would be involved. The assault was to be supported by nearly 7,000 ships and landing craft and about 600 bomber and 5,000 fighter aircraft.

Juno beach extended over some eight kilometres. On the right, 7 Infantry Brigade, with the 1st Hussars under command, was to land at Courseulles-sur-Mer, with the Royal Winnipeg Rifles and the Regina Rifles leading the assault, each accompanied by a squadron of DD amphibious tanks. 8 Infantry Brigade, with the Fort Garry Horse, would be on the left, at Bernières-sur-Mer and St. Aubin-sur-Mer, where the assault battalions would be the Queen's Own Rifles and the North Shore Regiment, each again supported by a squadron of DD tanks. The third, non-DD, squadron of both the Hussars and Garrys was to come in with their respective brigades' reserve battalions about an hour after H-Hour, and 9 Brigade, supported by the Sherbrooke Fusiliers, would be landed as soon as the coastal villages were secured.

Three phase lines were established as divisional objectives on D-Day. The first, codenamed *Yew*, ran along the southern limits of the coastal villages. The second, *Elm*, followed a line running from the village of Creully in the west, through Pierrepont, to Colomby-sur-Thaon and high ground immediately south of the village of Anguerny. Once *Elm* was attained, 9

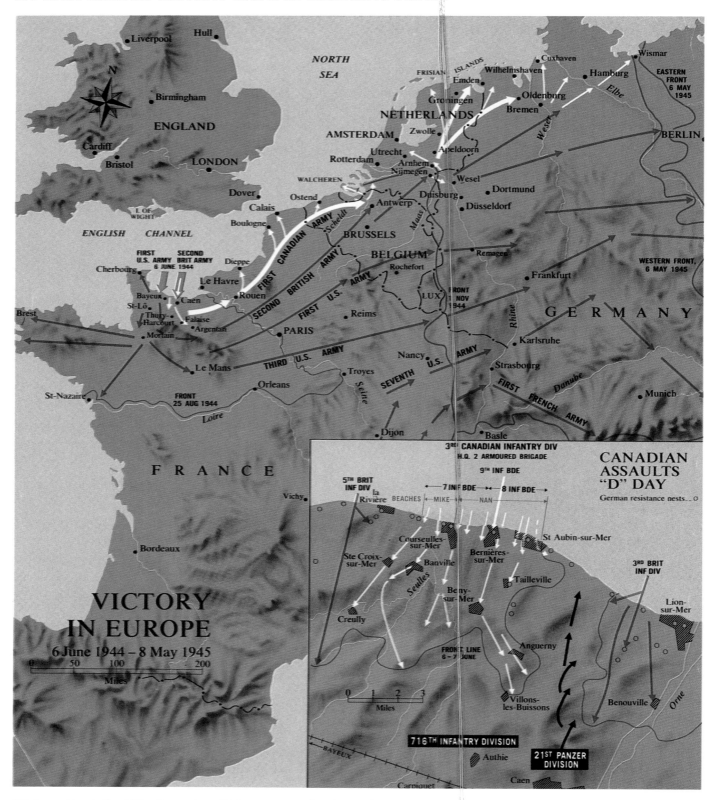

Allied operations in North-West Europe, June 1944 to May 1945. The advance of First Canadian Army is shown in white arrows. (Department of National Defence)

Camouflaged Shermans aboard Tank Landing Craft (LCTs) on D-1, waiting for the order to go to sea. (NAC PA132653)

Brigade and the Sherbrooke Fusiliers were to replace 8 Brigade. The final objective, *Oak* – roughly sixteen kilometres from the coast – was the railway line just south of the Caen–Bayeux highway between the villages of Putot-en-Bessin and Carpiquet. When it was secured, 2 Armoured Brigade was to be prepared to exploit a further ten kilometres to seize high ground around the village of Evrecy.

At the end of May the regiments of 2 Armoured Brigade were quarantined in their camps at the edge of the Solent, and the troops could then be told what they were about to do. The Fort Garry history records that "special maps were used of the actual ground but with code names and a false grid to baffle attempts to discover the actual locality. 'Briefing rooms' were set up with maps, air photos, pictures and plaster models – all with bogus or code names." Squadron commanders were briefed on the entire divisional plan, and all officers attended orders given by the CO of their affiliated infantry battalion.

By noon on 3 June the tanks were all aboard their designated landing craft, tied up in the Solent. There were two days of tense waiting for the order to go, but the tank crews had ringside seats watching the great invasion armada being assembled. Only the brigade staff and unit COs knew that on 4 June D-Day had been postponed because of severe weather conditions in the English Channel.

The signal to proceed was finally passed down on the afternoon of 5 June and one group of vessels after another sailed to form up off Portsmouth harbour. Once out of the sheltered waters the strength of a near gale-force wind made itself felt, and the flat-bottomed LCTs rolled and pitched severely. Captain Bill McAleese, rear link captain in 'C' Squadron of the Fort Garrys:

… as the ships passed through the boom outside Portsmouth, actual maps of the invasion beaches and of inland were produced from their sealed containers, with real place

D-Day. **Painting by Tom Wood, depicting landing craft approaching Courseulles-sur-Mer. (Canadian War Museum CWM 10558)**

names imprinted on top of Code names already so well committed to memory. By this time sea sickness was well past the possibility stage, and green faces, weak knees and prostrate forms increased hourly. ... As the night wore on the wind and waves continued to lash at the small craft with unabated fury.

As dawn broke the landing craft were being tossed about violently by the rough sea, and many of the tank crewmen were extremely seasick. Heavy bombers and fighters were heard overhead, and soon the troops could see bright flashes of light as bombs exploded on the still-distant enemy coast. The fireworks display intensified when the naval bombardment opened a short time later.

D-DAY: THE 1st HUSSARS AND 7 INFANTRY BRIGADE

H-Hour was set for 0740 hours on *Juno* Beach, with the four squadrons of Hussar and Fort Garry DD tanks scheduled to land first. 'A' Squadron of the 1st Hussars was tasked to land with the Royal Winnipeg Rifles on the western side of Courseulles-sur-Mer on *Mike Red* beach, while 'B' Squadron was to support the Regina Rifles landing directly in front of the village on *Nan Green* beach. 'C' Squadron, equipped with standard Shermans and the only Hussar 17-pounder Fireflies to come in on D-Day, was scheduled to land at H+45 minutes.

The tanks were to launch from the LCTs some 7,000 metres out from shore at about 0645 hours but, as the time approached to begin the swim, the seas were simply too rough. The decision was then made to land the tanks directly on to the beach. For the Hussars, however, this decision was reversed by the senior

232

squadron commander, Major Stewart Duncan, who, when less than 5,000 metres from shore, ordered the tanks to swim. The regimental history relates:

> The 'down doors' bell rang and the DD-tanks were ordered to launch. The order took most of the crews by surprise because they were expecting a dry landing in accordance with the most recent orders. ... Much of the bulky extra DD equipment, occupying so much vital space in the tanks, had been discarded. Consequently some time was lost while the nautical instruments, life-saving apparatus etc. were restored. The sea-sick crews climbed into the tanks and started off in first gear, moving from the rolling, pitching LCT's into the choppy, white-capped sea.

Only ten of 'A' Squadron's DD Shermans were able to launch from the LCTs. On one landing craft the chains supporting the ramp were shot away after the first tank got away, and there were problems lowering the ramp on another. 'B' Squadron, however, succeeded in launching all nineteen of its tanks. As the canvas flotation screen provided just over a metre of freeboard, the swim to the beach was rough and perilous.

> ... It was immediately apparent to all crew commanders that the screens were in great danger of collapsing as the struts began to bend from the pounding of the giant waves. Most of the commanders called the turret crews from the tanks to stand with them on the decks to support the screen. In addition, the size of the waves made steering exceptionally hard. ... On approaching land ... the waves increased in size and it was doubtful [if] any DD's would touch down on the beach because all began to ship water in considerable quantities.

Eight tanks were lost during the run-in. In 'B' Squadron, Major Duncan's tank was sunk when hit by a mortar shell, another had to be abandoned when its engine failed, and two sank when their flotation screens collapsed. Three of 'A' Squadron's

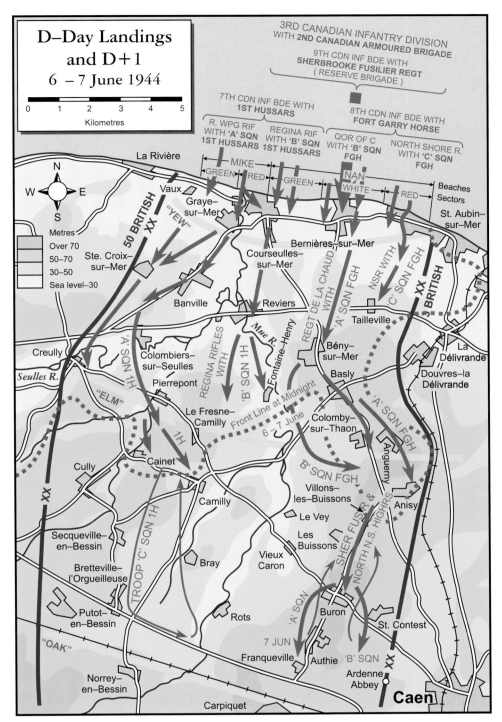

tanks went down when their LCT blew up on a mine, and Lieutenant W.R.C. (Bill) Little's was swamped, as described by the driver, Trooper (later Sergeant) Jim Paisley:

> We got some screen damage above the water line from gunfire, but not serious enough to prevent us from gaining the beach. Lieutenant Little got us all out on the deck just in case, and we were steering from the deck tiller. ... We were just off the beach obstacles when one of our LCTs fitted out as a rocket ship came in behind us and fired its broadside.

A DD-tank, the canvas flotation screen still in place, coming ashore on D-Day. (First Hussars Museum)

screens were deflated so that the 75mm guns and machine-guns could be brought into action. In the first few minutes after landing, however, the tank crews were so busy firing at the many enemy positions that some neglected to watch the incoming tide and, to their horror, found their engines and electrical systems suddenly drowned.

…The launch complete, it turned away from the beach and its bow wave came over us from the rear and we went under.

Years later, in 1970, this tank was recovered from the seabed by men of the RCD Light Aid Detachment and is now proudly displayed as a D-Day monument in the main square in Courseulles.

While seven of 'A' Squadron's DD tanks landed a few minutes after the Royal Winnipeg Rifles got ashore, 'B' Squadron touched down with fifteen Shermans about fifteen minutes before the first Regina Rifles' landing craft came in. Because of the shallow gradient of the beach, in most cases the tracks of the tanks touched bottom while the turrets were still below the water line, protected by the flotation screen. This allowed the tanks to crawl toward the beach between the mined beach obstacles until the turret was above the water, much like in a standard 'hull down' fire position. At that point the flotation

The 1st Hussars DD-tank recovered from the seabed off Courseulles in 1970. It is now a monument in the main square of the town. (Author's collection)

In 'A' Squadron's sector, to the west of Courseulles, the German defences included three blockhouses mounting large-calibre guns, and no less than thirteen concrete machine-gun emplacements. The 50mm guns posed the greatest threat, and they had to be neutralized before the tanks could give effective support to the infantry by taking on the machine-gun posts. Lieutenant 'Red' Goff's troop took on a well-camouflaged concrete fort on the left, but in the attack lost one tank to an AP shell. A 50mm gun was taken out by Captain Jake Powell, the squadron second-in-command, but there were still many enemy machine-guns in action and the Winnipegs suffered a large number of casualties as they struggled up the beach and on to the high sand dunes in rear. Meanwhile, the number of tanks on the beach was significantly boosted when the LCT that earlier had had problems with its ramp came in and unloaded five Shermans. For the next half-hour, the ten tanks cruised up and down the beach assisting in the destruction of the remaining enemy machine-gun nests.

When the Winnipeg reserve companies landed and advanced inland, the tanks were unable to accompany them as the engineers were having great difficulty preparing an exit from the beach. Three flail tanks of the British 22nd Dragoons were initially unsuccessful in beating a path through the five metre-high sand dunes, which were heavily mined and wired. The engineers were then faced with an anti-tank ditch, a crater about six metres deep, and a stretch of flooded secondary road. Nonetheless, a clear path and a causeway were completed by about 0920 hours and 'A' Squadron's tanks began to move toward their first objective, Graye-sur-Mer.

On the other side of the mouth of the Seulles River, fourteen of 'B' Squadron's tanks arrived on the beach in front of Courseulles at about 0755 hours. (One other landed some distance away.) The two assault companies of the Regina Rifles were late, so for nearly twenty minutes the tanks fought their own intense battles against the German emplacements, none of which had been at all damaged in the preliminary bombardment. Just inland from the beach on the north-west corner of the village was a major strongpoint mounting a 75mm gun,

The beach at Courseulles-sur-Mer on D-Day. The large house to the left of the church steeple was a camouflaged German strong point. (NAC PA 135959)

camouflaged to look like a house. Closer to the River Seulles there were two more bunkers, one containing an 88mm, the other a 50mm gun. All three emplacements had thick concrete walls facing the sea, and were designed to fire only along the beach, in enfilade, which, fortunately for several tank crews, limited their fields of fire. The Sherman crewed by Captain Wildgoose, the battle captain, landed immediately in front of the camouflaged strongpoint, and fired at least 25 rounds at it before the tank was swamped by the rising tide. Sergeant Leo Gariépy, beached just in front of one of the other bunkers:

As soon as we touched down, I crawled inside the tank since the bullets were clipping the water all around. I closed one half of the hatch and kept my head out of the open half looking for mines and underwater obstacles. When I felt safe I deflated and engaged a pill-box on my immediate front. I fired five rounds of HE then advanced 50 yards through the water and fired five more of AP at a distance of perhaps 150 yds. from the target. … I began to engage the MG nests dotting the dunes back of the beach, which were playing merry hell along the water line. Finally I got my tank in hull down position by the pill box and looked around for my squadron.

There were also a large number of machine-gun positions atop the sand dunes and on the second floors of stone buildings overlooking the beach.

The reserve squadron of the 1st Hussars landing at Courseulles on D-Day. (NAC PA 128791)

Painting by O.N. Fisher, *D-Day, The Assault*. (Canadian War Museum CWM 12469)

By the time the Regina Rifles' companies arrived, at about 0815 hours, the battle for *Nan Green* had been at least partially won by the Hussars' Shermans. The Reginas were thus able to move quickly into the built-up area of the town. The clearance of Courseulles, however, took somewhat longer than anticipated. There was a considerable amount of street fighting, and it was discovered the hard way that the German positions around the strongpoint were all connected by underground tunnels. Several times the infantry and tanks had to go back to clean out pockets of enemy resistance that resurfaced in areas already cleared once.

Once beyond the area of Courseulles, the tank squadrons reunited with their affiliated infantry battalions as they worked their way inland against relatively light opposition, mainly an occasional machine-gun nest and entrenched infantry. Just be-

yond Reviers, however, 'B' Squadron lost five Shermans to a well-handled 88mm anti-tank gun before it was destroyed.

As it grew dark, the units of 7 Brigade and the 1st Hussars were on the line of the intermediate objective, *Elm*, between Pierrepont and Fontaine-Henri, although one of 'C' Squadron's troops, commanded by Lieutenant Bill McCormick, failing to make contact with the infantry, continued to advance swiftly inland to Bretteville l'Orgueilleuse, where it crossed the Caen–Bayeux railway line and continued eastward toward Carpiquet before turning back to rejoin the regiment. This was the only element of the entire Allied invasion force to reach the D-Day final objective!

After dark, the regiment rallied in a harbour on high ground south-west of Pierrepont.

Damaged Fort Garry DD-tank on the beach near Bernières-sur-Mer, D-Day. Note the concrete bunker behind the Crusader III anti-aircraft gun. (NAC PA132897)

German 75mm gun emplacement on the sea wall at Bernières-sur-Mer, D-Day. Some of the many Canadian casualties it caused have been collected at the base of the sea wall to await evacuation. (NAC PA132384)

LCTs carrying Sherbrooke Fusilier Regiment tanks approach the beach at Bernières at about noon on D-Day. (Canadian Forces Photo Unit CT-305)

D-DAY: THE FORT GARRY HORSE AND 8 INFANTRY BRIGADE

Meanwhile, a kilometre to the east, 8 Brigade, supported by the DD squadrons of the Fort Garry Horse assaulted the coastal villages of Bernières-sur-Mer and St.-Aubin-sur-Mer. The squadrons both had twenty tanks instead of the usual nineteen, the extra tanks being manned by spare crews.

The DD tanks coming in on *Nan White* and *Nan Red* had a very different experience than that of the 1st Hussars. Instead of having to swim, they were brought close in to the beaches by the LCTs in what was termed "a wet wade". Sergeant John Shineton, in 'B' Squadron, recalled being launched about 1,000 metres off the beach at Bernières.

> … When the ramp door went down and the tanks went off the end, we were afloat, but it wasn't very far 'til we touched down on the sand. … We were fortunate that by the time we reached [the belt of booby-trapped stakes and obstacles just off the beach] we were able to direct the tanks with track-steering levers, rather than propellers, and were able to zig-zag through them.

The landings at Bernières, which the official history describes as "… the only Canadian assault … front where tank support was reported as ineffective," has always been engulfed in controversy. According to the official historian, the weight of evidence suggests that the Garrys landed late, with the result that they were not in position to support the assault companies of the Queen's Own Rifles at the critical moment. Captain Bob Grant, who was the battle captain (rear link) in 'B' Squadron, challenged this in an interview in which he insisted, "We were the initial troops on the beach at Bernières," noting that none of the Germans' heavy weapons fired on the tanks until after

the infantry had landed. The view expressed by Sergeant Shineton, however, is probably more accurate:

> In some instances, our amphibious tanks were on the beach 5 minutes ahead of the infantry, and on part of the beach infantry and the Garrys landed at the same time. On another section, the infantry were on the beach before the Garrys … but in the centre … the flails and special armour were just ahead of the Queen's Own and the Fort Garrys.

At about 0812 hours, 'B' Company of the Queen's Own had the misfortune to land directly in front of the main German strongpoint in the centre of the beach. This thick concrete structure had not been touched in the preliminary bombardment, and the company lost nearly half its men in the initial dash across the beach and the subsequent attack on the bunker. The Fort Garry war diary reports that 'B' Squadron provided fire support during this action but the three-metre-high sea wall prevented the tanks from moving in with the infantry and that limited what could be done to assist them. Fortunately, once the blockhouse was captured, the Queen's Own had little difficulty clearing out the few enemy troops remaining in the town.

The tanks were stuck on the beach for over an hour while waiting for the engineers to blow a gap in the sea wall to enable them to move inland. In the meanwhile, beginning about 0830 hours, the brigade reserve – 'A' Squadron of the Garrys and the Régiment de la Chaudière – began to disembark, and the narrow beach in front of Bernières became jammed with tanks and vehicles of every sort. The tanks were tasked to take the lead during the advance inland from Bernières, but they had a very difficult time making it even to the southern outskirts of the town. Captain Eddy Goodman, battle captain of 'A' Squadron later wrote:

> When I finally got ashore I encountered an enormous SNAFU on the beach, [with the single road out of Bernières completely clogged]. Anxious to reach our objective, I decided to cut across some open fields and circumnavigate the infantry vehicles. I came to one ploughed field and saw a sign reading Achtung Minen (Beware of Mines). Somewhere in the back of my mind I remembered an intelligence officer

saying that often instead of mines the Germans put up signs to slow the enemy's advance. I decided that this was one of those times and went bowling across the field, only to blow up my tank, completely destroying the right track. … I grabbed another tank and [led the squadron] to my support position with the Régiment de la Chaudière.

Meanwhile, shortly before noon, the divisional reserve – 9 Brigade and the Sherbrooke Fusiliers – came ashore on the already clogged beaches at Bernières.

After a halting start when 'A' Squadron's lead tanks were held up by a minefield and an 88mm anti-tank gun, the Chaudières battle group finally moved off just before 1400 hours toward its first objective, the village of Bény-sur-Mer, five kilometres inland.

The beach at St. Aubin-sur-Mer. Note the destroyed Fort Garry Sherman near the sea wall and the American Thunderbolt that had made an emergency landing. (US Air Force Photo 72625 AC)

land. Bény was taken about an hour later, and the advance continued toward 8 Brigade's D-Day objective, a hill feature south of the village of Anguerny. While 'A' Squadron continued to support the thrust of the Chaudières and the Queen's Own, 'B' Squadron was sent off to protect the brigade's right flank, from Fontaine-Henri to Thaon.

Both squadrons pressed on without much difficulty, encountering primarily snipers and a few isolated artillery emplacements. The QOR history pays tribute to the Garrys: "The tanks ranged far and wide and did valuable work in locating and destroying pockets of the enemy. It was a tank-infantry fight against scattered nests of enemy resistance and never did

(Facing) The congested beach at Bernières-sur-Mer as the reserves were landed. (Canadian Army Photograph courtesy of The Fort Garry Horse Museum)

the cooperation work more smoothly." By nightfall, 8 Brigade was consolidating positions centred on the Anguerny heights, with the Queen's Own holding Anguerny and Anisy, and the Chaudières near Colomby-sur-Thaon. After dark, the tank squadrons were pulled back to a harbour near Bény-sur-Mer.

At St. Aubin-sur-Mer, the North Shore Regiment's assault was supported by 'C' Squadron of the Fort Garrys. As at Bernières, an offshore reef prevented the LCTs from coming directly onto the beach, so the squadron's DD tanks were launched about 1,000 metres from the shoreline. During this relatively short run-in, the tanks came under intense shelling and small arms fire, and four were knocked out while still in the water. One of the LCTs was badly holed by shellfire and was ini-

Drawing depicting the attack on the blockhouse in St. Aubin. (Author's collection)

tially only able to launch two of the five tanks it carried, but fourteen of the twenty Shermans touched down just minutes after the first wave of the North Shore Regiment.

The German bunkers and concrete emplacements at St. Aubin had escaped damage during the bombing and naval shelling prior to H-Hour, so the fighting for *Nan Red* was among the most intense of anywhere on *Juno* beach. Lieutenant (later Lieutenant-Colonel) W.D. (Bill) Little, in 'C' Squadron (not to be confused with W.R.C. Little of the 1st Hussars' 'A' Squadron, whose tank had been swamped off Courseulles) related his experience of the landing:

After my troop launched mortar shells were bursting all around, and bullets were coming through the canvas [flotation screen]. I felt very exposed, standing on the back deck steering the tank with the tiller, and it seemed a long way in. Just before we got ashore Sergeant Parkes, my troop sergeant, was killed by sniper fire, and his operator, Lance Corporal Stevenson, was also killed when he took over the tank....

My troop landed right under the high sea wall in front of St. Aubin. The rest of the squadron was well off to my right, and I had noticed a breach in the sea wall in that direction. As my troop moved along the beach we were engaged by a [50mm] gun on the sea wall on the western edge of the town, but it went quiet after I fired on them.

In a relatively short time most of 'C' Squadron had linked up on the beach about five hundred metres west of St. Aubin, where the sea wall was only about a metre high. This part of the beach was, by then, fairly quiet and flail tanks had beaten a lane through a minefield that lay just beyond the beach. The tank troops were immediately sent through to link up with North Shore companies which had already penetrated into the town, but they lost an additional three tanks to mines that had not been exploded by the flails.

By late morning, 'B' Company of the North Shores with the support of 'C' Squadron's tanks had cleared through to the south edge of the town. Only one major German position – a huge concrete blockhouse in the centre of the village, protected by road blocks, trenches and minefields – continued to hold out. It was not apparent until much later that this blockhouse was connected by a network of underground tunnels to many of the other German emplacements, and a great deal of effort had to be made later in the day to retake positions that suddenly 'came to life.'

It was not until late in the afternoon that a concerted attack was made on the blockhouse complex. Working under intense fire, engineers cleared a roadblock which allowed two tanks to close in, and Lieutenant Robson and Sergeant Walterson "blew up two 75mm guns in cement emplacements, two light A.A. [anti-aircraft] guns, a sniper's tower and various trench positions." Sergeant Walterson's exceptional performance and personal bravery was recognized by the award of a Military Medal.

In the early evening, after a wall was blown in by one of the engineers' large-calibre 'petard' guns, the blockhouse itself was finally captured, along with nearly sixty prisoners.

While the operation to clear the blockhouse was just beginning, 'C' Company of the North Shores, along with Captain Alex Christian, the 'C' Squadron battle captain, and Lieutenant Little's troop, advanced four kilometres inland to attack the village of Tailleville. This was another German strongpoint, one that intelligence reported as being the headquarters of a German battalion. Before getting heavily engaged in the battle for the village, Little's men seized the high ground just beyond Tailleville, destroying an 88mm and a 75mm gun, along with about fifty German infantrymen, in the process. Christian, who had been slightly wounded at the outset of the fighting in the town, reported:

… The enemy was concentrated in a walled area of the village using the chateau as their HQ. Despite heavy shelling [we] could not dislodge them. … [There was] a large, solid wooden gate which was the entrance of the chateau's courtyard. I ordered my driver to advance and we battered down the gate and entered the area to which the Germans had withdrawn. [There was fierce close-range fighting for about three-quarters of an hour.] The Germans, for the most part, had gone underground into a bunker in the courtyard. My gunner fired a couple of rounds of HE down the entrance and eventually a white flag emerged, followed by a large number of the enemy. … During our foray around Tailleville, we had destroyed a 75mm anti-tank gun and several other artillery weapons… as well as an ammo dump.

Once Tailleville was taken it was too late to move on and tackle the German radar station just two kilometres to the south, so 'C' Squadron spent the night in harbour with the North Shore Regiment.

By last light on D-Day, the Canadian assault force was consolidating in positions along the general line of the intermediate objective *Elm*. There had been many casualties, but in this, their first action, the green troops of 3 Division and 2 Armoured Brigade had acquitted themselves remarkably well in what is undoubtedly the most difficult of military operations, an amphibious assault on a hostile shore. If they did not reach their final objective, it deserves to be reiterated that none of the assaulting forces got further inland on D-Day than did the Canadians.

On the left of 3 Division sector, the Sherbrooke Fusiliers and the North Nova Scotia Highlanders of 9 Brigade relieved 8 Brigade at Anisy, and pushed on to Villons-les-Buissons just before dusk, in position to carry the penetration even deeper on D+1. Everyone dug in to await the expected counter-attack and the appearance of German tanks, which had been notably absent on D-Day. They spent a sleepless night, as German troops repeatedly tried to infiltrate their positions, and some of the prisoners captured were from *21 Panzerdivision*, heightening the concern that German tanks were somewhere nearby.

CONSOLIDATION OF THE BRIDGEHEAD, 7–11 JUNE

Operations on the second day of the invasion began auspiciously on the right. The Winnipegs and Reginas encountered very light resistance as they marched forward to Putot and Norrey-en-Bessin, and by noon both battalions were firmly in possession of their objectives. The 1st Hussars did not move with them because of their heavy losses on D-Day.

It was to be a different story in the 9 Brigade sector, on the left. At 0745 hours the Sherbrooke Fusiliers and North Novas began their advance from the vicinity of Anguerny. Their mission was to take the airport at Carpiquet, one of the division's D-Day objectives that had not been reached. The Fusiliers recce troop led in their Stuart tanks, with a company of the North Novas in Universal carriers, and behind the vanguard the infantry rode on the back decks of the Fusiliers' Shermans. For the first four kilometres there was only scattered enemy resistance but as the head of the column approached the village of Buron it came under fire from the village and from machine-guns and snipers hidden in the long grass. At the same time, mortars and artillery began to pound the Canadians from the open left flank.

While 'C' Company of the North Novas moved directly into Buron, supported by fire from 'C' Squadron, 'A' Squadron, carrying 'A' Company on its tanks, looped around to the right of the village, near Gruchy, while 'B' Squadron and 'B' Company circled to the left. The recce troop was still well out in front approaching Franqueville and reported being able to see the hangars on Carpiquet airfield. However, as the tank squadrons came level with the village of Authie, enemy small arms and mortar fire forced the North Novas to dismount and one company fought its way through to the south edge of Authie while 'A' Squadron continued to move cautiously toward Franqueville.

No one in the Canadian division knew at this time that the leading elements of *12 SS (Hitlerjugend) Panzerdivision* had arrived in the northern outskirts of Caen the previous evening. On the morning of 7 June about thirty Mark IV tanks, along with two *Panzergrenadier* battalions, deployed in the area of St. Contest, Authie and Franqueville with the intention of counter-attacking that afternoon into the broad gap that had developed between 3 Canadian and 3 British Divisions.

Before the Canadians appeared, Colonel Kurt Meyer, commander of *25 SS Panzergrenadiers*, had established a command post in the tower of the old church at the Ardenne Abbey, overlooking the entire area into which 9 Brigade was advancing. Meyer watched as the North Novas and Sherbrookes moved into Buron and then toward Authie, waiting until the Canadians presented a long open flank. He soon saw the North Novas/Sherbrooke Fusiliers battle group dispersed over nearly three kilometres directly to his front and just after 1400 hours he gave the order to attack. A company of Mark IV tanks struck at the lead troop of the Fusiliers' 'A' Squadron near Franqueville, while another two companies and a grenadier battalion attacked from Cussy into the Canadian flank between Authie and Buron. A second battalion pushed out from St. Contest toward the north side of Buron.

'C' Company of the North Novas, at Authie, was quickly overrun and soon nearly wiped out. The other companies, closer to Buron, also came under heavy attack and there was often vicious hand-to-hand fighting in the wheat fields. This dire situation was not helped by the fact that there was no field artillery within range to help stem the onslaught, and communications with the powerful naval guns offshore had broken down. 'C' Squadron of the Sherbrookes was sent out on the left flank, forward of Buron, and the tankers did their best to support the isolated infantry positions, but crew commanders rapidly discovered they had their own desperate fight to contend with.

For the next two hours a fierce tank-versus-tank battle raged in the area between Authie and Buron. Lieutenant Norman Davies, in 'B' Squadron, was moving into position on the left of Authie when the German Mark IVs appeared. His experience was not unlike that of many other Sherbrooke crew commanders that day:

Sherbrooke Fusiliers Sherman Firefly moving into action near Buron. Note the not very effective attempt to camouflage the length of the 17-pounder gun barrel. (NAC PA131391)

Ruins of the Abbaye Ardenne. From an observation post in the tower of the Abbey Colonel Kurt Meyer was able to watch the Canadian troops assembling for the attacks on Buron and Authie. (Canadian Forces Photo Unit PMR82-082)

I spotted seven or eight enemy tanks at 1,000 yards on my left. I halted, stopped two of them with the 17 [pounder gun], advanced, halted and fired again scoring another hit, then all hell seemed to break loose. There were tanks coming up at full speed to my rear (our own), tanks to my left firing at us, anti-tank blazing away from our left and rear, and tracer and 75mm gun flashes all over the place. … Tanks were hit and burning all around us by then, and it was impossible to keep track of who was who. One was hit directly in front of me, one right beside me. 88 tracer was cutting down trees all over the place, so I decided to withdraw with what was left of 2nd and 3rd Troops. 1st Troop had meanwhile stood to and covered our flank but had left themselves open by doing so and Lt Steeves' tank went up in flames a couple of hundred yards away.… At Les Buissons, we counted noses and found we had 5 tanks left out of the 20 which had gone in.

The Germans recaptured both Authie and Buron before they were stopped in late afternoon by heavy bombardment from naval guns and artillery that had finally moved within range. Buron was briefly retaken in a counter-attack by the Sherbrookes, but was abandoned when the whole of 9 Brigade was concentrated in a 'brigade fortress' near Les Buissons to prevent any further German advance into the still-vulnerable bridgehead. This first major action after the D-Day landings had been a costly setback to the Canadians. The North Novas had 242 casualties and 128 men were taken prisoner, and the Sherbrookes had 26 men killed and 34 wounded. Twenty-one tanks were knocked out, and another seven damaged but the enemy also lost a significant number of his tanks; perhaps as many as 31 Mark IVs.

The operational consequence of the tactical defeat at Buron was that the momentum of the drive to expand the Canadian sector of the bridgehead was lost. It would be a full month before Buron and Authie were again in Canadian hands. There were also other serious repercussions. From one of the knocked-out tanks the Germans recovered a signal instruction detailing the Canadian allocation of radio frequencies and codes for the month of June, which their radio intercept units quickly put to good use. And near Franqueville, in a damaged Sherbrooke recce troop scout car, they found a map with German defensive positions accurately marked, revealing how much the Allies knew of their dispositions.

One of the most disconcerting aspects of the aftermath of the fierce fighting at Buron and Authie was the first instances of atrocities against Canadians captured by SS troops. On 7 and 8 June no less than 34 Canadian prisoners of war were brutally murdered by their SS guards, either on the battlefield or at the Ardenne Abbey. At least four of these were members of the Sherbrooke Fusiliers, discovered long after the war to be buried in a secluded garden at the Abbey. After the war Kurt Meyer would be convicted by a Canadian court-martial of war crimes for permitting the killing of these men.

In these first days of battle, the enormous value of the 17-pounder-equipped Sherman Firefly in tank-versus-tank encounters was proven beyond any doubt, especially when the Germans introduced Mark V Panthers. The 17-pounder's 2,900 feet-per-second muzzle velocity gave its AP round nearly double the penetrating power of the standard 75mm Sherman gun, and a hit on an enemy tank virtually ensured its destruction. The bigger gun was not without its problems, however, as Captain Harvey Theobald, gunnery officer of the Fort Garrys, reported:

In England we had only fired about six rounds per tank before landing on D-Day. In action in Normandy, when the tanks were firing almost continuously, we found that the gun would jam. It wouldn't eject the empty cartridge. The problem was in the buffer system that controlled the recoil. I remember that one of my first tasks was going around and telling the crew commanders to release oil from the buffer as soon as they started to heat up, and that cleared the problem.

The greater lethality of the 17-pounder was not lost on the enemy. The Fireflies were easy to pick out because of the much longer gun barrel, and the Germans quickly learned to focus their anti-tank fire on them. As in all three regiments the Fireflies were commanded by troop leaders, this enemy tactic resulted in a disproportionate number of casualties among junior officers and consequent leadership problems at critical times in action. Brigade headquarters decreed that troop sergeants were to take over the Fireflies and, as sergeants the world over are known for their ingenuity, all sorts of schemes were quickly devised to camouflage the length of the 17-pounder barrel.

D+2, 8 June, was a busy if somewhat confused day for the units of 2 Armoured Brigade. The Germans shelled the Canadian positions continuously, and mounted several violent but apparently uncoordinated counter-attacks, especially against 7 Brigade positions in the area of Bretteville and Norrey-en-Bessin. The 1st Hussars, who

Transporter and Burnt-Out Sherman. Painting by William Ogilvie. (Canadian War Museum CWM13629)

had lost nearly half their tanks in the first two days of the battle, worked throughout the day to assist 7 Brigade units in holding firm. Their regimental history reported:

> As requests for tanks came in to RHQ, tanks were parcelled out by troops and even individually. The tanks rushed to that part of the brigade perimeter where the Germans were attacking … and remained there until the scare was over. Then the weary crews returned to RHQ usually to be rushed off to another spot.

Later that afternoon what remained of the Sherbrooke Fusiliers were also deployed to support 7 Brigade in repulsing repeated enemy attacks.

On the morning of 9 June a composite Sherbrooke squadron under Major Vincent Walsh was sent out on a raid to the southeast of Bretteville l'Orgueilleuse. Soon after setting out, a company of twelve Panthers was spotted advancing rapidly across the open fields toward Norrey-en-Bessin, then held by a single company of the Regina Rifles. The Sherbrooke gunners quickly brought this foray to a halt, knocking out seven Panthers in quick order. Later in the day, 'C' Squadron of the Hussars had similar good shooting against another attack by German tanks just west of Bretteville:

Trooper A. Chapman, crack gunner in Lieut. G.K. Henry's tank, established a bridgehead record. When six tanks penetrated his position he held his fire until all were visible; then with Tpr. 'Sass' Seaman slapping the rounds into the 17-pdr…. He fired five times. Five rounds – five Panthers. Before he got to the sixth one, another "C" Sqn. tank, commanded by Sgt. Boyle, had accounted for it.

At the end of the third day of fighting all three regiments of 2 Armoured Brigade had lost more than half of their tanks and were rapidly approaching a state of ineffectiveness. 'C' Squadron of the Elgin Regiment, the brigade's tank delivery squadron, had not yet been landed, but the brigade staff arranged for a British delivery regiment to supply 74 Shermans on the morning of 10 June. The Hussars got 26, the Garrys 21, and the Sherbrookes 27.

3 Division's hold on the Canadian sector of the bridgehead appeared to be firming up. 7 Brigade held the Bretteville-Putot-Norrey area, astride the Caen–Bayeux road, against several counter-attacks, and 9 Brigade was well established in its 'fortress' position centred on Les Buissons. But the Germans still held a narrow strip along the wooded valley of the River Mue between the villages of Cairon and Rots, leaving a potentially dangerous gap between these forward brigades. Before any fur-

ther advance could be made, this enemy pocket had to be cleared, and the task was given to the British 46 (Royal Marine) Commando, supported by 'A' Squadron of the Fort Garrys.

This battle group set out at mid-morning on 11 June, and only small parties of Germans were encountered until it reached the outskirts of Rots in late afternoon. Two troops and two of the squadron headquarters tanks moved into the village in support of the Marines. Sergeant Harry Strawn reported:

The opposition really started to get tough now, and the Commandos took quite a beating.... As we were getting into the centre of the town with Lieut. McPherson in the lead, his driver reported fresh Panther tracks.... They just got across the church square when from a road no further than 30 yards away a 75mm barked from a Panther and hit Lieut. McPherson's tank in the front. The crew immediately bailed out, [but the Germans] from a concealed position started throwing grenades.

By this time all the tanks were in the small square with the wounded under cover to one side.... A Panther snuck around to the rear by another road leading into the square and shot up [Lieut. Mitchell's] scout car.... Confusion was really great, and they sure had us bottled in. Capt. Goodman was backing up and so was Sgt. Crabb.... The Panther knocked out both of them.... The Panther that shot them up became very nervy and started to come up the road into the square. I shot through a building with my 17 pdr. and scored him off. I also shot a machine gun nest up that was trying to shoot our wounded.

The youthful SS troopers fought with the brave tenacity their opponents had come to expect. Rots was not cleared until after 2200 hours. The Royal Marines took 61 casualties and the Fort Garrys had six tanks destroyed. When troops from the Régiment de la Chaudière came in the next morning they reported that bodies littered the streets and counted 122 dead Germans amongst the rubble. In trying to make his way out of the village near dusk, Sergeant Strawn knocked out a second Panther, but his own tank was soon destroyed near the village of Villeneuve. Strawn's gallantry was recognized with the immediate award of a Military Medal.

1st HUSSARS AT LE MESNIL-PATRY

By 10 June the division commander was becoming extremely concerned about the relative stalemate developing on his front, so 2 Armoured Brigade was warned to get ready to mount a brigade attack on 12 June. This operation, aimed at taking high ground near the village of Cheux, some six kilometres directly south of Bretteville l'Orgueilleuse, was similar to the brigade's D-Day contingency plan for exploitation beyond the division's final objectives. Brigadier Wyman met with unit COs at his headquarters near Bray late in the evening of 10 June to discuss preliminary plans. While no detailed orders were issued, Lieutenant-Colonel Ray Colwell was told that the 1st Hussars would lead the attack with two companies of the Queen's Own Rifles.

Things began to go wrong from the very outset. Early the next morning, 11 June, brigade headquarters got orders from 3 Division that the attack would have to be made that very afternoon, so as to coincide with a British attack on the right flank. This information was passed to the Hussars at 0800 hours, and H-Hour was to be at 1300, giving less than five hours to get ready. The Queen's Own, digging in near the village of Neuf Mer, was not warned of this change in timing for another three hours.

Brigadier Wyman gave his orders at 1100 hours. In the first phase 'B' and 'C' Squadrons of the Hussars, with 'A' and 'D' Companies of the QOR, were to advance from a start line just east of Norrey-en-Bessin and secure the village of Le Mesnil-Patry. 'A' Squadron, with the Queen's Own 'A'

Destroyed Fort Garry Sherman in the main square of Rots. (NAC PA115533)

Company, would then by-pass Le Mesnil on the left and continue on to the high ground south of Cheux, followed by the Garrys and the other two Queen's Own companies. There was little time remaining when brigade orders were finished, and Colonel Colwell gave his orders to squadron commanders with less than an hour until H-Hour. There was no time for the squadron commanders to give their troop leaders anything but a bare outline of what was intended, and there was no time to brief the tank crews before moving off. Nor

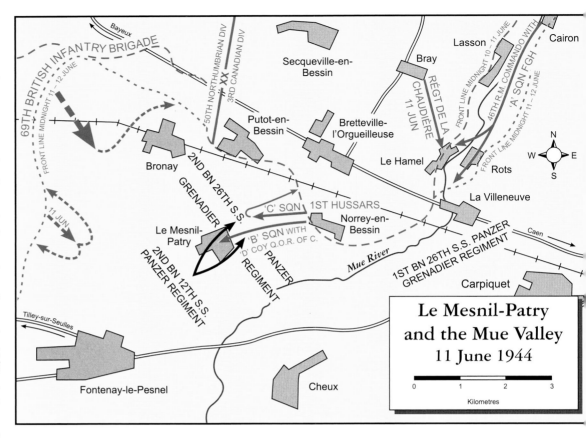

Le Mesnil-Patry and the Mue Valley 11 June 1944

was there time for any reconnaissance, or for any liaison between the infantry and the tankers, and, equally serious, no time to prepare a proper artillery fire support plan.

The chaos got worse. As 'B' Squadron, with the infantrymen of 'D' Company riding on the back decks, approached what was to be the start line, east of Norrey, they found that a minefield laid by 7 Brigade blocked their way. The tanks had to be rerouted, single-file, through the narrow streets of Norrey, which meant that H-Hour had to be delayed. Then, the new start line on the east side of the village was at right angles to the direction of attack.

All the while, the radio monitoring service of *12 SS*, armed with the 2 Armoured Brigade codes and radio frequencies captured near Authie on 7 June, had been listening in on the Hussars' wireless net, gaining a clear picture of what was happening and a German operator, using proper Canadian voice procedure, is reported to have been able to imitate Colonel Colwell's voice perfectly.

Norrey came under heavy shelling just after 'B' Squadron passed through, but the fire caught 'C' Squadron and the RHQ tanks. The German garrison in and around Le Mesnil – three *Panzergrenadier* companies north of the village, several anti-tank guns on the edge of the town, two companies of Pioneers (engineers) to the south, and two companies of Mark IV tanks to the south-west – were lying in wait when 'B' Squadron's tanks

advanced into the wheat field west of Norrey just after 1435 hours. Le Mesnil was not quite 2,000 metres away.

The squadron shook out into a 'box' formation, two troops in the lead, two in the rear, with squadron headquarters in the centre. The two rear troops still carried Queen's Own soldiers on their rear decks, so could not traverse their turrets or use their guns, but the forward tanks immediately began to lay speculative fire on hedges, haystacks and buildings as they moved. Meanwhile, 'C' Squadron moved to positions just east of Norrey, but being directly behind 'B' Squadron they were not well placed to provide support.

The Germans held their fire until the tanks were about half way to Le Mesnil. Sergeant Leo Gariépy recalled how "Small arms resistance was tremendous, enemy infantry in great numbers were lying in the fields on the centre of the advance." At this point the squadron commander, Captain Harrison, gave orders to his tanks to hurry on toward the village. Sergeant Gariépy again:

By that time we had by-passed a strong contingent and were being fired upon from rear as well as from the front. Pandemonium broke loose, our own infantry jumping off the tanks to avoid getting shot, and the German infantry desperately trying to get away from under the tracks of the Shermans.... Knowing that A and C Squadrons were coming up behind me, I gave my driver the order to speed up and, ignoring the German infantry, pushed on for Le Mesnil-Patry. Our own infantry were all mixed up in battle with the Germans in the cornfield behind, so B Squadron headed on, blazing away with machine-guns at various pockets around.

Part of the squadron, probably the two troops on the right, headed directly into the village, while the remainder moved toward an orchard on the south-eastern corner. As the first group neared the village they came under intense fire from anti-tank guns concealed behind a slight rise and most of the tanks in this right-hand group were destroyed in this fire-fight. The half-squadron in the orchard fared little better. Almost at once they were met with a counter-attack by three Mark IV tanks and six Shermans were quickly knocked out in the orchard, and another two were hit as the German tanks continued on. Soon afterwards, however, all three Mark IVs were themselves destroyed by AP rounds from 'C' Squadron tanks near Norrey.

'C' Squadron was then ordered forward. What they saw in front of them – a field of burning Shermans – was not a sight to inspire confidence. However, their advance initially went well and a large number of German infantrymen were cut down, but the second company of enemy Mark IVs then hit at the squadron's right flank and, again, many Shermans were hit and 'brewed up'. Fearing that the Hussars would be outflanked, and with the better part of two squadrons apparently lost, Colonel Colwell ordered a pull-back to Norrey. Only four tanks from 'B' Squadron and nine from 'C' made it back. Three Fireflies and 34 standard Shermans were lost.

Over the next several days a number of men made their way back through enemy lines but 61 members of the 1st Hussars were officially listed as killed in action, six were missing and presumed killed, and sixteen were taken prisoner. Among the dead, at least seven were murdered by SS troops after being taken prisoner. In a sad quirk of fate, two of the officers killed had joined the unit only the day before and no one really knew them. The Queen's Own Rifles also suffered heavily, with 96 casualties, half of whom were missing. For the Hussars, 11 June has always been known as the "black day of the regiment".

LOOKING AT WHAT WENT WRONG

Following the stand-off at Buron and the disaster at Le Mesnil, Brigadier Wyman was asked to report to the commander of 3 Division on the operational lessons that could be derived from the first weeks of action. The regiments of 2 Armoured Brigade were thus asked to respond to a questionnaire dealing with the whole range of problems they had encountered, and make practical suggestions to improve unit fighting capability. The flaws in existing tank-infantry cooperation procedures featured heavily in their responses, reflecting the inadequate level of

1st Hussars tanks moving forward. The lead tank is a Sherman Firefly with the storage bin moved from the rear hull to the front glacis. (NAC PA133749)

training in Britain. Fundamental things such as developing effective communications between the infantry and the tanks featured large – methods of indicating targets, use of radios and liaison officers, and the need for a workable telephone on the back of the tanks. Tank commanders complained that infantry officers wanted to 'site' tanks without knowing their capabilities. However, squadron commanders admitted that their crews had learned a great deal about effective use of ground to conceal their movement from enemy anti-tank guns and how important the practical application of 'fire and movement' really was.

The decision to adopt a four-tank troop – three 75mm Shermans and a Firefly – was one of the most important decisions to come out of this analysis. The additional tank permitted far more effective fire and movement within a troop, and the loss of a single tank would not seriously affect the troop's fighting capability. The new organization was implemented gradually over the next month as the supply of reinforcement tanks improved. The momentum of the early days of the invasion had, however, been lost in the British/Canadian sector of the bridgehead, and for much of the next month the Canadians simply adopted a threatening, but still defensive, posture, as

Captain Alex Christian and his crew ('C' Squadron of the Fort Garry Horse) prepare a meal in a tank harbour, Normandy, June 1944. (NAC PA132870)

commanders on both sides gave their attention to what was happening in the American sector.

Montgomery's plan of inducing the Germans to concentrate the bulk of their armour against the British Second Army in the area of Caen had been successful. By the end of June the Americans, on the right of the Allied bridgehead, had captured the Cherbourg peninsula and were preparing to swing inland. The relatively small area of the bridgehead was, however, becoming uncomfortably congested as more men and logistics stocks were landed every day. This was especially so in the British/ Canadian sector, where there was little space left for manoeuvre. The planned reinforcement of the invasion force consequently had to be slowed, even though it was already well behind schedule, and expansion of the bridgehead became essential for the further development of operations. The city of Caen, which was meant to serve as the hinge of the Allied thrust northward out of Normandy, now had to be taken.

CARPIQUET

The western approach into Caen was blocked by the village of Carpiquet and its adjoining airfield, stoutly defended by *Panzergrenadier* troops. As a preliminary to the assault on Caen from the north and west, 3 Canadian Division was ordered to capture the village and the airfield, and that task fell to 8 Brigade, reinforced by the Royal Winnipeg Rifles and supported by the Fort Garry Horse.

In the first phase of the operation, the North Shores and the Régiment de la Chaudière, each supported by a squadron of Garry tanks, were to take the village and a series of hangars on the north side of the aerodrome, while the Winnipegs attacked hangars 1,000 metres further to the south, on the other side of the airfield. The third squadron was to be a mobile reserve while providing covering fire, and when the initial objectives were secured, the QOR were to move through the village to capture the airfield control buildings at the east end of the field.

Early on the morning of 4 July, Operation *Windsor* began with an exceptionally heavy artillery and naval bombardment on enemy positions in and around Carpiquet. The Germans, however, had been warned by their radio monitoring service, and they were ready. As the infantry crossed the start line behind a rolling barrage, the Germans opened up with their own counterbarrage. All three assaulting battalions suffered heavy casualties as they advanced across flat, open, wheat fields.

On the left, the North Shores and Chaudières pressed forward relentlessly, by-passing a number of concrete bunkers which were then reduced by fire from the tanks. By 0630 hours both battalions were in

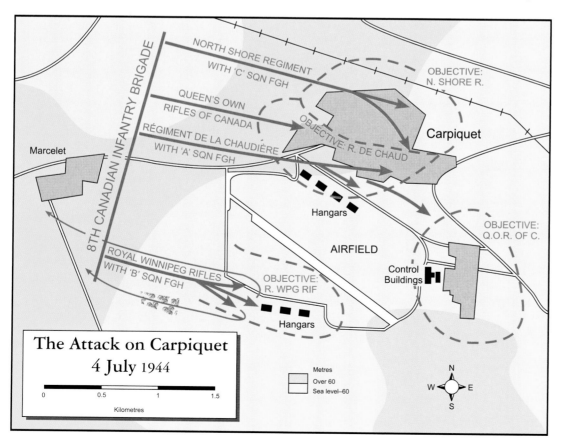

The Attack on Carpiquet
4 July 1944

Battle for Carpiquet Airfield. **Painting by O.N. Fisher. (Canadian War Museum CWM12421)**

the outskirts of the village, and here the fighting began in earnest. In his book, *1944: The Canadians in Normandy,* Professor Reg Roy described this action:

> … The S.S. troops had prepared strong defensive positions. Well-camouflaged machine-gun posts, reinforced by earthen walls several feet thick and well-protected roofs, proved difficult to capture…. The fighting in Carpiquet quickly developed into a bitter, stubborn battle as the Chaudières and North Shores fought their way forward house by house and building by building. The town was soon a smoking ruin as tanks blasted down ancient brick and stone walls and slowly overcame one defensive post after another.

On the other side of the airfield the Winnipegs had a much more difficult time getting forward because of thick mortar fire and machine-guns sited in concrete bunkers. Eventually a troop of 'C' Squadron Shermans was released from brigade reserve to assist the Winnipegs, and about 0900 hours the infantry and tanks got to the first of the three southern hangars. A vicious fight ensued, but the determined young SS soldiers could not be budged from their well-protected positions by tank fire or by flame-throwers. Two of the Shermans were brewed up by anti-tank guns firing from positions on the right flank and the Winnipegs CO ordered his men to withdraw.

A second attack was put in later in the afternoon, this time with four of 'B' Squadron's tank troops. While the infantry advanced directly toward the hangars, the tanks made a wide

A DD-Sherman of 'B' Squadron of the Fort Garrys near a ruined hangar on Carpiquet airfield. (NAC PA131418)

sweep around to the right in an attempt to outflank the defences. While making this move, 'B' Squadron came under fire from the area of Verson, on the right of their axis. Then, as the regimental history describes

> Whilst trying to contact [the Winnipeg Rifles], they were attacked by a superior force of Pz Kpfw IVs and Vs [Panthers]. In the ensuing battle, conducted at ranges from 200 to 800 yards, by good gunnery they were able to knock out half their own number of enemy tanks, and put the enemy to flight....

Once again, however, the Winnipeg battle group had to be withdrawn.

By nightfall on 4 July, 8 Brigade and the Garrys had established a firm hold on the village and the hangars on the north side of the airfield, but the Germans simply could not be dislodged from the control buildings at the west end of the runway or the southern hangars. The situation remained very tenuous as the Canadian-held salient was exposed to enemy fire from three directions. The enemy mounted a series of strong counter-attacks supported by Panther tanks on the 5th and 6th, but all were beaten off after very hard fighting. At that point, the enemy appeared to concede the loss of Carpiquet village, but continued to bombard it heavily for much of the next two days.

BURON AND AUTHIE AGAIN

The next episode in 3 Division's attack on Caen began on the morning of 8 July in what was called Operation *Charnwood*. In the first phase, 9 Brigade, supported by the Sherbrooke Fusiliers, was to take the villages of Gruchy, Buron, Authie and Franqueville, where they had suffered so heavily a month earlier. When this was completed, 7 Brigade, with the 1st Hussars, was to pass through to take Cussy and Ardenne Abbey, preparatory to an advance into Caen itself.

The *12 SS* troops holding this area expected the attack and they had prepared elaborate mutually-supporting defensive works in the thick stone Norman buildings and between the villages. But on the other side of the coin, the Canadian units tasked for the operation, despite their many casualties since D-Day, were now battle-hardened veterans who had learned how to work effectively with their brothers-in-arms. In the early evening of 7 July the squadron commanders of the Sherbrooke Fusiliers brought all their crew commanders to a vantage point near Rosel, two kilometres west of Buron, for a detailed look at the ground they would have to cross. While this was happening, back in squadron harbours the tank crews stowed the standard mix of ammunition, AP and HE, in the bins and ready racks and did last minute maintenance. Just as dusk fell the sky was filled with an armada of Halifax and Lancaster bombers targeted on the city of Caen.

The 9 Brigade attack went in at 0730 hours on 8 July. On the left, the Highland Light Infantry was supported by 'A' Squadron of the Sherbrookes in an assault on Buron, while to the right the Stormont, Dundas and Glengarry Highlanders moved with 'B' Squadron against Gruchy. Major S.V. Radley-Walters, in later years Colonel Commandant of the Corps, but then commander of 'A' Squadron, recalled the battle.

> Both units suffered – the Glens at Gruchy, and at Buron the H.L.I. and Sherbrookes took heavy casualties. ... I got up as far as Buron and there were two tremendous anti-tank ditches. When I got to the other side I had only two tanks left. ... I swung along the north-east side [of Buron].... A German company was dug in within 25 or 30 yards of the H.L.I. We managed to clear that out and come up through the orchards east of Buron and got through to our objective on the east side and this is where I held, with myself and three tanks, for about four hours. We were counter-attacked many, many times, but held on until we got support from our own 'C' Squadron when they attacked toward Authie with the North Nova Scotia Highlanders

Meanwhile, in mid-morning the SDG battle group thrusting toward Gruchy was all but brought to a halt in the open wheat fields by well-placed machine-gun nests and a raging storm of German artillery and mortar fire that caused very heavy casualties. This impending disaster gave a troop of the 17th Hussars' 'B' Squadron an opportunity to make a notable contribution to the outcome of the action. The regimental history records:

At Gruchy the S.D.G. had been stopped by very heavy machine gun fire just outside the town. Lt. Don Ayer, who, with his 15 or 16 carriers, was waiting for the S.D.G. to push on saw this. So, without hesitation, he charged right through them, in real old cavalry style, right into the middle of an enemy company position. With grenades and Bren guns firing at point blank range, they drove the enemy from his dug-outs, killing dozens, wounding others and capturing 25 or 30 prisoners.

This gallant charge momentarily shattered the equilibrium of the *SS* men and allowed the SDGs to continue their advance into the village. The battle continued to rage around the village for several more hours, however, as the Sherbrooke's 'B' Squadron encountered a succession of German tanks and anti-tank guns.

By mid-afternoon the situation around Buron and Gruchy had stabilized sufficiently that 9 Brigade's reserve battalion, the North Novas, was brought forward to launch an attack toward Authie and Franqueville. 'C' Squadron of the Sherbrookes, along with the remnants of 'A' and 'B' Squadrons provided support. German opposition during this phase was considerably lighter, however, and Canadian troops in Carpiquet reported that the enemy was withdrawing in small groups toward Caen.

Shortly after 1815 hours, once Authie was firmly in the hands of the North Novas, 7 Brigade, supported by the 1st Hussars, pushed westward to assault the next line of German positions. The Canadian Scottish, with 'C' Squadron, moved on the village of Cussy, while the Regina Rifles and 'A' Squadron attacked Ardenne Abbey. If the Germans in Authie appeared to have lost heart, this was certainly not the case at Cussy or at the Abbey, where Kurt Meyer, who still had his command post

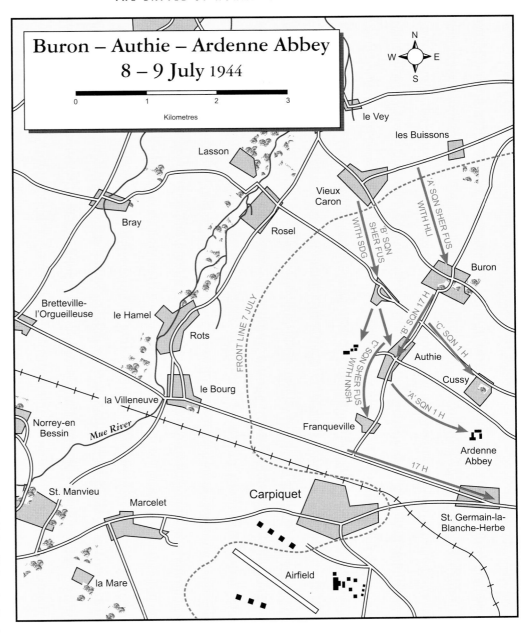

Sherbrooke Fusiliers tank going into action near Gruchy, 8 July 1944. (NAC PA 132658)

Sherbrooke tank in the village of Buron. Note the white Allied star on the hull. These were soon painted over as they made excellent aiming points for German anti-tank gunners. (NAC PA136846)

The commander of a 17th Hussars scout car pauses to talk to a photographer in Caen. (NAC PA140142)

located at the Abbey, personally directed the battle. The Hussar history recounts:

> On approaching the Abbey 'A' Squadron was subjected to heavy shelling, mortaring and small arms fire from well dug-in troops…. As the tanks opened up, the crumbling stone walls around the Abbey revealed Panthers. One of them was destroyed but the rest managed to escape. Two Panthers on the left flank at Cussy held up the advance considerably until Major D'Arcy Marks was able to manoeuvre his tanks to destroy them.

The Canadian attack stalled, if only temporarily, and the official history noted, "At nightfall the ruined Abbey buildings, surrounded by luridly burning German and Canadian tanks, remained in the enemy's hands." But Meyer had given up hope of holding the area north and west of Caen with what little remained of *12 SS* and, during the night, his troops withdrew into the rubbled city.

The northern part of Caen was liberated the next day, 9 July, in a combined thrust by Canadian and British troops. The honour of being the first Canadians into the city went to a patrol of the 17th Hussars, which had to work its way gingerly through a maze of rubble-blocked streets to reach the only intact bridge over the River Orne, held in strength by the Germans. That morning the Sherbrookes led the SDG into the ruins of the built-up area, where they spent the day mopping up "small pockets of enemy diehards." In the meantime, the Fort Garrys assisted in the capture of the rest of Carpiquet aerodrome and then advanced to take Bretteville-sur-Odon.

Despite this notable advance, the liberation of Caen was

thirty-three days late, and it was far from complete. The Germans still held a large part of the city lying to the south and east of the Orne River, and prying them out of the built-up area threatened to be a daunting task.

The units of 2 Canadian Division began to arrive in Normandy on 7 July and, on the afternoon of 11 July, II Canadian Corps became operational, taking over an eight-kilometre sector of the front. At the same time, 2 Armoured Brigade came under command of the Corps.

General Montgomery's next major move was intended to seize the open ground immediately to the south of Caen, in part to open the way for an advance in the direction of Falaise, but also to prevent the Germans from shifting their armoured formations to block the continuing expansion of the American sector of the bridgehead. Operation *Goodwood* was to be mainly a British show, with three armoured divisions thrusting forward on the east side of Caen. The Canadian involvement, code-named *Atlantic*, set 3 Division to attack on the right flank of the British advance, in order to capture the town of Colombelles and an extensive steelworks complex on the east side of the Orne River, and then secure the southern suburb of Vaucelles. 2 Division, in its first operation, was to capture crossings over the Orne on the south-western side of the city and, if possible, seize high ground between Fleury-sur-Orne and St. André.

Operation *Atlantic* went in on the morning of 18 July. The Hussars had two squadrons supporting 8 Brigade, as its infantry advanced on Colombelles and Giberville. It was a hard fight throughout the day, as the ground to be taken consisted of many built-up areas, and the tanks worked closely with the assaulting battalions where they could but the infantry took very heavy casualties. By midnight, however, units of 9 Brigade had succeeded in taking the eastern part of Vaucelles and, next morning, 7 Brigade crossed the Orne to 'firm up' the Canadian hold on most of the city.

On the British front it was a very different story. The British armoured divisions confronted a heavy weight of German anti-tank guns and Tiger tanks on ground that favoured the defenders, and nearly 270 Shermans were destroyed before the front was stabilized south-west of Caen. The vast number of burned-out tanks littering the battlefield south of Cormelles were not much of an inspiration to the Canadian tank crews that would pass through this area in the next weeks.

On the right of the Canadian Corps sector, 2 Division came into action on the evening of 18 July, securing a toehold across the Orne River on the western side of Vaucelles. Next morning, units of 5 Brigade moved through Vaucelles and by late afternoon had taken Fleury-sur-Orne and a dominating hill feature – Point 67 – which overlooked the twin villages of St. André-sur-Orne and St. Martin de Fontenay. When the Black Watch captured the village of Ifs that evening, II Canadian Corps was firmly established on the open ground immediately south of Caen.

Roughly two kilometres to the south lay a kidney-shaped feature shown on maps as Verrières ridge. It was not a particularly imposing feature; fields planted with wheat and sugar beet sloped gently upward to the crest, which was, at most, thirty metres higher that the ground now held by Canadian troops. But the ridge was of enormous tactical importance, as it overlooked all of the open, lower ground the Canadians would have to cross; the Germans had turned it into an interlocking chain of mini-for-

Tanks Moving Through Caen. **Painting by William Ogilvie. (Canadian War Museum CWM13619)**

tresses, the first line in a formidable defensive belt in the rolling countryside south of Caen.

This ridge was the objective for units of 6 Brigade on the afternoon of 20 July. On the right, the Cameron Highlanders attacked St. André; the South Saskatchewan Regiment (SSR) moved against the centre of the ridge; and Les Fusiliers Mont-Royal (FMR) attacked Beauvoir and Troteval farms as intermediate objectives on the way to the village of Verrières, on the left end of the ridge. Two squadrons of tanks were allocated in

Sherbrooke Fusiliers Sherman in Caen, 10 July 1944. (NAC PA162667)

Tank Passing Under a Destroyed Railway Bridge. **Painting by O.N. Fisher depicting 1st Hussars tanks moving through the suburbs of Caen, 19 July 1944. (Canadian War Museum CWM 12635)**

support, 'A' Squadron of the Sherbrookes with the Camerons, and 'A' of the 1st Hussars with the FMR, but their primary task was to be ready to defeat German counter-attacks and neither squadron moved in intimate support as the infantry set out.

Initially, the attack progressed relatively well. The Camerons captured the northern part of St. André and the FMR took both Beaurevoir and Troteval farms. However, the SSR in the centre encountered determined resistance. When they eventually got two depleted companies onto the ridge, the Germans counter-attacked with tanks and, after taking exceptionally heavy casualties, the battalion pulled back in disarray. The FMR were also pushed out of the Beaurevoir and Troteval farm complexes, but these were retaken later in the evening with support from the Hussars' Shermans, while from positions near St. André the Sherbrookes knocked out two of the Panthers that had done so much damage to the SSR companies.

The next three days were marked by repeated counter-attacks by the Germans, mainly by Panther and Tiger tanks of *1 SS Panzerdivision*. These often vicious tank-versus-tank battles are described by Major Radley-Walters, who was in the thick of them:

Early the next morning [21 July] we headed into position with the Camerons, and on arriving we saw two groups of tanks.... One group had eight tanks, the other six, about 300

yards apart. ... After an hours exchange of fire we took up different positions and moved around St. André and the fight really got going. Finally, after two hours the enemy was engaged on three sides, with the battle going in our favour.

Around 1430 hours we'd accounted for eight Panthers. However, we had some tanks a little further into St. André and their position wasn't very good. Two had been knocked out, three of them had their turrets jammed, and another had its crew commander killed. The enemy infantry started moving in with the equivalent to our bazookas and got to within 25 yards of us. So I laid down smoke again and moved some tanks up to assist them....

As I didn't get any reinforcement tanks during the night, the next morning I was down to six tanks. Again an enemy force appeared at about 0545 hours. Enemy tanks again appeared at about 1000 hours, about fourteen this time, on the high ground just south of St. André. We engaged them for about an hour, and five or more were burning. At about 1600 hours they appeared again.... Around 1800 hours, when we were trying to get a 17-pounder into position, they caught us by surprise. At least two of their tanks got to within a hundred yards of us through the heavy cover of broken buildings and trees. There was a quick exchange of fire and we destroyed two of them, but they knocked out one of ours.

One of the many formidable German Panther tanks knocked out in the fighting in the outskirts of Caen. (NAC PA130149)

The rubbled ruins of St. André-sur-Orne, around which the Sherbrooke Fusiliers fought vicious tank-versus-tank battles on 20 and 21 July 1944. Note the destroyed Panther. (NAC PA 145562)

OPERATION *SPRING*

Atlantic was called off on 21 July, with the Canadian front stabilized along the general line of the road running between St. André and Troteval Farm and the Germans resolutely holding on to the Verrières ridge. Almost immediately planning began for yet another deliberate attack, scheduled for 25 July and code-named *Spring*, this time involving both Canadian divisions. 3 Division was brought in on 2 Division's left and the British 7 and Guards Armoured Divisions were to be in reserve for exploitation.

The first phase of *Spring* called for the capture of a line from Tilly-la-Campagne to Verrières and then to May-sur-Orne, an advance of about 1,800 metres on a front of roughly six kilometres. 3 Division's 9 Brigade, with the Fort Garry Horse, were tasked with taking Tilly. To the right of the Caen–Falaise highway, which would figure prominently in operations over the next weeks, 4 and 5 Brigade attacks on Verrières ridge were to be supported by the 1st Hussars. The British 22 Armoured Brigade was deployed in depth as a counter-penetration force, also available, if needed, to exploit success by thrusting forward to another ridge some 2,000 metres beyond.

TILLY-LA-CAMPAGNE

At 0330 hours on 25 July, three companies of the North Nova Scotia Highlanders moved off from the village of Bourgébus toward the village of Tilly-la-Campagne. It consisted of a few dozen old stone houses, many of which were already in rubble from earlier bombardments. The ground that the North Novas had to cross in their 1,500-metre advance was absolutely flat, the fields covered in ripe wheat that stood perhaps a metre high.

The German defenders in Tilly – a *Panzergrenadierbattalion*, along with a pioneer (engineer) company and a company of Mark IV tanks – were exceptionally well-prepared. Defensive positions had been dug in the wheat fields in front of the village, and the stone houses had been turned into veritable fortresses, with concrete-reinforced machine-gun positions scattered throughout the rubble, and carefully sited anti-tank guns. Some of the Mark IVs were well dug-in, others had fire positions between the buildings, while still others were in orchards beyond the village.

As the North Nova companies advanced they were silhouetted against the night sky by 'artificial moonlight' which was supposed to aid their movement. The Germans allowed them to come within a few hundred metres of the village and then opened fire. Within minutes, two of the three attacking companies were nearly annihilated, and when the fourth company was brought in to attack from the west, it, too, was pinned down and took very heavy casualties. There were no reports from the companies about their dire situation, but when the battalion

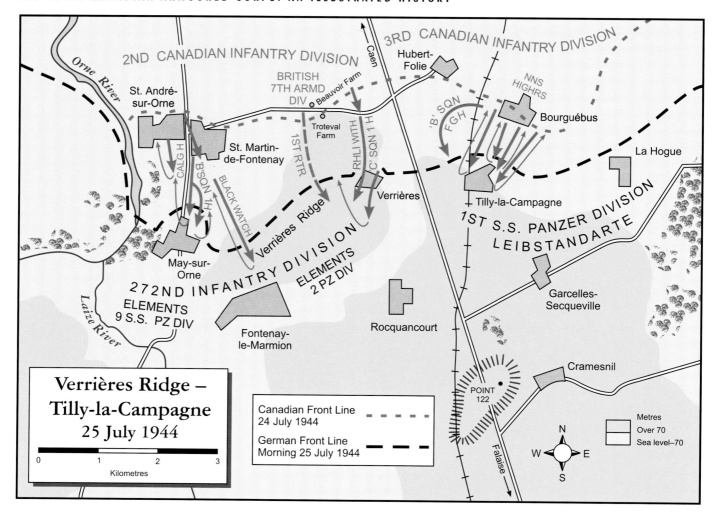

Verrières Ridge –
Tilly-la-Campagne
25 July 1944

0 1 2 3
Kilometres

Canadian Front Line
24 July 1944
German Front Line
Morning 25 July 1944

commander finally recognized, shortly after 0600 hours, that the operation had gone badly awry, he asked for support from a squadron of the Garrys.

'B' Squadron, under Major Alex Christian, set out almost immediately even though three of the troop leaders had been seriously wounded by a mortar bomb during the orders group. By the time they started out it was broad daylight. The tanks drove through the wheat fields at top speed in an arc meant to bring them into positions on the north-east side of Tilly where they hoped to be able to give fire support, but almost at once they came under fire. The North Nova's history records the effect from the perspective of one of their men:

Shortly after a tank appeared … Miller shouted at him that an 88 was trained on the spot, and his only hope was to move fast and get back. The had tank barely started when a shell took the turret off. … The tank caught fire and burned. … A second tank came and Miller shouted warnings at it as he lay among the wheat. Before it could turn it, too, was hit. … A third tank arrived and Miller saw it hit before it reached them. It burned at once.

Major General Michael Reynolds, in his history of *1 SS Panzerkorps* in Normandy, *Steel Inferno*, records the experience of a German tank driver who was part of the force at Tilly:

Three of the eleven Fort Garry tanks knocked out in the attack on Tilly-la-Campagne on 26 July 1944. The lack of any form of cover in the open fields made the Shermans extremely vulnerable to German anti-tank guns. (Canadian Forces Photo Unit PMR 82-386)

Our Panzer was well camouflaged, huddled up against the wall of a house. … the three [Canadian] tanks had not seen us yet. … We moved along the road to the east, out of Tilly … turned south again, back toward Tilly. … When we were about 20 m[etres] from the tanks we opened fire. The first one burst into flames and the other two took some hits. The crews bailed out.

Within a half hour, 'B' Squadron lost eleven of its sixteen tanks, and those remaining pulled back into whatever cover they could find in the open fields. Tilly-la-Campagne was never taken in an assault, even though many attempts were made over the next two weeks. It fell into Allied hands only when the defenders withdrew.

THE ATTACK ON VERRIÈRES RIDGE

Some two kilometres to the right of Tilly, in the centre of the Canadian Corps sector, the Royal Hamilton Light Infantry (RHLI) spearheaded the 4 Brigade thrust toward the village of Verrières. This attack had a shaky beginning. The start line at Troteval Farm had not yet been secured by Les Fusiliers Mont-Royal as had been planned, and at least three enemy tanks were still on the position. H-Hour thus had to be delayed for nearly forty minutes while the Panthers were taken out by tank-hunting teams. Typical of the time, the planned artillery barrage could not be altered, so when the RHLI moved out in the dark toward Verrières, it had no fire support. Nonetheless, just as dawn broke the leading companies, seriously weakened by heavy casualties during their approach, broke into the village and soon consolidated their hold.

At about this time 'C' Squadron of the 1st Hussars moved forward to support them in Verrières. As the Hussars advanced, Captain Brandy Conron, the second-in-command, spotted eight Panthers positioned on the ridge just beyond the village and quickly gave orders over the radio – a detailed plan of which troops were to engage which enemy tanks. His own tank opened fire on a Panther in the centre, and within seconds all of the German vehicles were set ablaze.

Continuing on toward the crest of the ridge, the squadron came under intense fire from other German tanks and from a 'Ferdinand', a huge tank destroyer mounting an 88mm gun that the Germans had just introduced in Normandy. Lieutenant Valdi Bjarnason, a troop leader at the time, described his recollection of this engagement:

There was no cover, and the Germans had the advantage of the higher ground and they could manoeuvre behind the crest. It was one hell of a fight, and the fire from the tank guns on both sides was absolutely ferocious. I remember firing at the Ferdinand [the tank destroyer] and seeing the ar-mour-piercing rounds just bounce off, but I did get two of the Panthers, and I saw them both burn. One of the most awful moments was when one of our own airplanes came in and knocked out one of our Shermans.

When the Royal Regiment of Canada arrived to carry the attack on toward the village of Roquancourt they saw the effects of this battle. Their regimental history records:

On the ridge at Verrières, the advancing Royals saw one Sherman burst into flame as they approached. The hatch flew open, emitting clouds of black smoke…. One man came out backwards, catching his knees on the edge of the hatch, and hung there for a moment, blazing like a torch, before he fell to the ground…. Soon there were burning tanks and vehicles throughout the entire area of advance.

Soon afterward the squadron pulled back, but only five tanks remained, and three of them had been hit.

The Germans counter-attacked as the Royals attempted to advance beyond Verrières and the Canadian attack ground to a halt. By this time there were reports of at least thirty German tanks in positions on the ridge.

Further to the right, the attack by 5 Brigade from the area of St. André was a far more complex operation, and it fared even worse. In a preliminary move, the plan called for the Queen's Own Cameron Highlanders (6 Brigade) to complete the capture of St. André and take the adjoining village of St. Martin to secure the 5 Brigade start line. Then the Calgary Highlanders were to attack southward to seize the village of May-sur-Orne, a distance of some 1,500 metres. When May was secure, at 0530 hours, while it was still dark, the Black Watch of Canada were to launch an attack south-westward, across open ground, to take the western heights of Verrières ridge and the village of Fontenay just beyond the crest. The operation was to be supported by 'B' Squadron of the Hussars.

The plan began to fall apart right from the outset as the Camerons had a very difficult time fighting through the village of St. André. Even before the start line south of St. Martin was secured, the Calgary Highlanders moved through the Camerons en route to May-sur-Orne, but they immediately encountered extremely heavy mortar, artillery and machine-gun fire and never did take their objective. Two troops of Shermans, moving on the right of the Calgarys, did penetrate to the village, where they lost four tanks, but without infantry support they were soon compelled to pull back.

As the Black Watch came forward to begin their assault on Verrières ridge the situation was as confused as it gets in battle, caused in part by small parties of Germans continually infiltrating through mine tunnels into areas that had already been cleared. When the Black Watch CO was killed, command of the battalion devolved on one of the company commanders, who decided to carry on with the original plan, even if somewhat delayed, and shortly after 0900 hours, in broad daylight, the Black Watch started out across the grain-covered slope, four companies in box formation. They were slaughtered, nearly annihilated, by a hail of fire from well-camouflaged positions on the ridge and in May-sur-Orne, on the right flank. Lieutenant Teddy Williamson, one of the "B" Squadron troop leaders, reported that "my troop was belting away with machine-guns at anything that looked like a Gerry position but I'm afraid it was mostly blind shooting as Gerry had turned in his usual efficient job of camouflaging."

With this second failure to penetrate the German positions along Verrières Ridge, General Simonds called off the operation.

It is perhaps too easy in hindsight to find fault, but it would appear evident that there was a serious lack of understanding in 2 Division infantry battalions about elementary tank-infantry cooperation. That should come as no surprise; the training in Britain had not allowed for it, and a high price was paid for this failing. At the same time, one might detect an element of hesitation on the part of the tankers of 2 Armoured Brigade to take risks; by now all of the crew commanders knew from bitter experience that their Shermans were vulnerable to the deadly fire of the Germans' 88mm anti-tank guns and that their tanks were no match for the Tigers that they were just beginning to encounter.

The units of 4 CAD had begun to land on the beaches at Courseulles and Bernières. The Governor General's Foot Guards came in first, on 24 July, followed by the South Alberta Regiment on the 25th, the Canadian Grenadier Guards on the 26th, and the British Columbia Regiment on the 28th. As they were complete, these regiments, with their infantry counterparts in 10 Brigade, were moved into reserve positions southeast of Caen. The stage was being set for another, this time serious attempt to break out of the bridgehead.

CHAPTER 13

The Battle of Normandy: The Breakout

By the end of July 1944, II Canadian Corps had gained little more than a toe-hold in the rolling countryside south of Caen, and all attempts to penetrate the formidable belt of German defences anchored along Verrières ridge had ended in costly failure. The enemy had every tactical advantage: he held the dominating ground which gave an enormous advantage to his deadly-accurate anti-tank weapons, his defensive positions were well-prepared and in great depth, and the Canadians were limited (by the very necessary presence of British forces on both flanks) to conducting a frontal attack in a very narrow corridor. The ridge had already proven to be a hard nut to crack but it was now urgent that the Canadians do so, in order to keep the Germans from moving formations to counter the American advance on the far right of the Allied bridgehead. A new, innovative approach was needed, and Operation *Totalize* would mark the beginning of the Canadian Armoured Corps' most significant battles in the northwest Europe campaign.

OPERATION *TOTALIZE*

The plan for *Totalize* combined massive firepower with surprise and unprecedented battlefield mobility in a two-phased operation. The first phase – a night attack to limit the effectiveness of the enemy's direct-fire weapons – was intended to break through the crust and penetrate the heavily-defended German forward zone. The second phase would be a daylight thrust to exploit the penetration. Both phases were to be preceded by intensive strikes on enemy gun positions and strong points by Allied heavy bombers, but, on the ground, armour was to play the major role. The breakthrough phase was to be carried out by 2 Armoured Brigade and 4 Infantry Brigade of 2 Division,

and by the British 33 Armoured Brigade and elements of 51 (Highland) Division, with the Canadians assigned the sector west of the Caen–Falaise highway and the British to the east of it.

By mid-afternoon on 7 August, the tanks of the Sherbrooke Fusiliers and the Fort Garry Horse had begun to move to assembly areas near Fleury-sur-Orne and Ifs, where they 'married up' with the infantry battalions of 4 Brigade. The infantry were, for the first time, mounted in improvised armoured personnel carriers called Kangaroos, hastily manufactured in RCEME workshops over the previous week using the hulls of Priest self-

The South Alberta Regiment crew of Major David Currie's command tank, 'Clanky', near Cormelles, 28 July 1944. (Canadian Forces Photo Unit ZK 869-1)

Forming-Up Place of the Fort Garry Horse in preparation for Operation *Totalize*, 7 August 1944. (NAC PA113658)

propelled guns, and crewed by men seconded from 2 Armoured Brigade and divisional artillery units.

The main force was formed into three similarly structured columns. Each had a 'gapping force' of two troops of Shermans from the Sherbrookes, with two troops of flail tanks to beat through minefields if they were encountered and a troop of armoured engineers whose job was to mark the route for the main body. Each column formed up four vehicles abreast, about a metre apart, making each column only about fifteen metres wide. Less than three metres to the rear was the next row of four vehicles, and this pattern continued for nearly a kilometre back to the end of the column.

Immediately behind the gapping force in each column came the assault force – two troops of Sherbrooke Shermans in the lead, an infantry battalion in Kangaroos and other assorted tracked armoured vehicles, two troops of M-10 self-propelled anti-tank guns, and a section of engineers. Two squadrons of the Garrys followed immediately in rear as a 'fortress force'. A fourth, smaller column composed of 'C' Squadron of the Garrys and the 8th Recce Regiment would protect the left flank by moving along the Caen–Falaise road.

The three columns in the main force were to move together, in the dark, on a narrow, 150-metre-wide thrust from a start line just short of Verrières ridge across the open ground west of the village of Roquancourt. Then, having passed beyond the main belt of German defences, the columns would split off to seize objectives on features between the villages of Gaumesnil and Caillouet. The enemy positions bypassed during this thrust were to be mopped-up later by units of 5 and 6 Brigades, supported by the 1st Hussars.

Infantry of 4th Brigade mounted in the newly manufactured 'Kangaroo' armoured personnel carriers, 7 August 1944. These were surplus 'Priest' self-propelled artillery from which the guns had been removed so infantry could be carried. This ad hoc armoured personnel carrier proved so useful in the battle that they were made a permanent part of II Canadian Corps, and later formed into a separate Armoured Corps unit known as 1st Canadian Armoured Carrier Regiment. Note the plated-over gun aperture of the vehicle on the right; two plates of steel were used with sand poured in between to give as much protection as possible. (NAC PA129172)

PHASE ONE

Shortly after 2100 hours, when it had become dark enough to prevent enemy observation, the gapping and assault forces moved forward to a forming-up place just short of the start line. Here they waited for the heavy bombers to do their job of pounding German positions on the flanks of the attack route. Then, at 2330 hours, the massive armoured columns began to move forward. Fifteen minutes later, just as the lead vehicles approached the crest of the ridge, the sky above the battlefield lit up, searchlights providing 'artificial moonlight' as a rolling barrage was brought down just in front of the columns and Bofors guns started to fire bursts of tracer rounds along the right and left boundaries to mark the front of attack.

It was not long, however, before the three columns of the main force began to encounter severe problems with keeping direction. Captain (later Colonel) M.H. 'Bomber' Bateman, battle captain of 'B' Squadron of the Sherbrookes, who was leading the centre column, recalled:

At first everything seemed to go just as we planned. But the ground was extremely dry, and a combination of the bursting shells of the artillery barrage and the tracks of the large number of tanks, flails and APCs threw up a dense cloud of dust that soon obscured everything for all but the lead tanks. These problems were made even worse shortly after midnight when a thick smoke screen was laid across the whole front. Then not even the vehicles at the head of the columns could see much. The artificial direction aids didn't really help a great deal either. The tracer shells fired by the Bofors guns went off course after about 3,000 metres and the radio direction signal was hard to hear after we got over the first hill.

It helped somewhat when an order was passed down to turn on the shrouded marker lights mounted on the rear of the tank turrets, but there was still a great deal of confusion.

The Protective Troop of Headquarters 4th Armoured Brigade are briefed on the upcoming operation, 7 August 1944. While the brigade headquarters personnel may have known what was about to happen, Brigadier Booth did not give orders to his regimental commanders until late that night. (NAC PA131364)

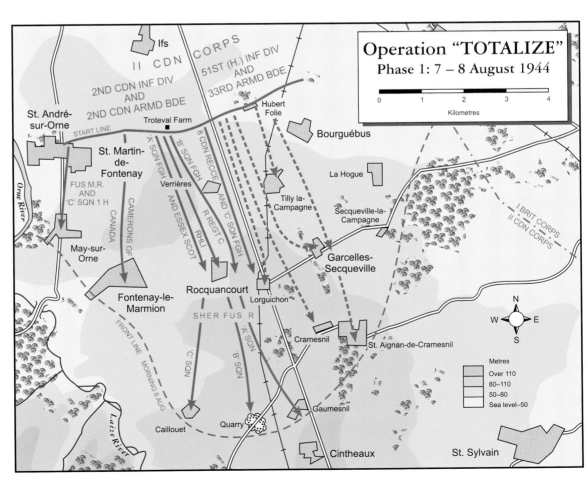

261

Tanks Moving Up for the Breakthough. Painting by George Pepper, depicting the night advance during the first phase of Operation *Totalize.* (Canadian War Museum CWM13795)

In this near-zero visibility there were countless instances of vehicles colliding, and every obstacle on the ground – bomb and shell craters, sunken roads, ponds, and ditches – added to the difficulty because they could not be avoided. A number of vehicles strayed away from their column and some tagged on to another. In these trying circumstances two of the three columns got considerably off course: the left column went around to the east side of Roquancourt; the centre column found itself in the middle of the village, where its infantry got separated from the Fusilier tanks when they got involved in a sharp fight with the German defenders. The right-hand column was the only one that kept more or less to its planned route, west of the village.

During the whole of this phase of the operation there was remarkably little opposition by the Germans, who were equally hampered by the poor visibility and had little idea what was happening. Veterans remember a lot of unaimed small-arms

2nd Armoured Brigade Sherman (probably belonging to the Sherbrooke Fusilier Regiment) which nosed into a bomb crater during the night march. (NAC PA324124)

fire and shelling, and several tank crew commanders recall seeing the glowing tracers of AP rounds, most of which went high. Some tanks and vehicles were hit and set alight, but somehow all three columns continued to inch their way forward, and before dawn broke elements of all but the right column were in the vicinity of their objectives, where they reorganized to await the inevitable counter-attacks.

TOTALIZE, PHASE TWO

If Phase I had gone relatively well, the same could not be said for the early stages of the second phase, involving 4 CAD. At least some of the difficulties experienced by the units of 4 Armoured Brigade, which was to spearhead the exploitation, can be attributed to last-minute

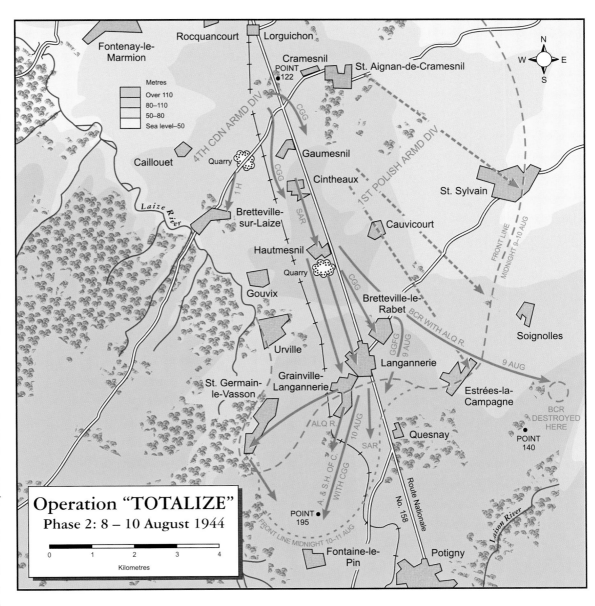

Operation "TOTALIZE"

Phase 2: 8 – 10 August 1944

changes of plan on 6 August by General Simonds, including the substitution of 1 Polish Armoured Division for 3 Canadian Infantry Division on the east side of the Falaise highway. Among other things, this meant altering boundaries to accommodate two armoured divisions on an already congested, narrow battlefield, and thus alteration in operational and administrative plans at every level. Probably even more critical, it appears to have totally disrupted the normal sequence of time-sensitive battle procedure within 4 Brigade.

It was not only at brigade level where there was 'finger trouble' in passing on vital information. In the Canadian Grenadier Guards, for example, a warning order issued by brigade early on 7 August to be prepared to go into action the next morning was never passed down to squadron commanders. All they were told was that the unit would be moving to a new location later in the day.

At 4 Brigade headquarters, Brigadier Booth did not issue detailed orders for Phase II to unit commanding officers until the

early evening of 7 August (in marked contrast to 2 Armoured Brigade, where final orders for Phase I had been given in good time), thus severely limiting the time available for orders and briefings at lower levels. *Halpenny Force*, consisting of the Grenadier Guards and the Lake Superior Regiment (the division's motor battalion), with supporting artillery, flails and engineers, was to lead the thrust through positions already taken in Phase I. It was to begin its forward move from the concentration area south of Caen at 0030 hours on 8 August, just an hour after Phase I had been launched, and seize the area of Bretteville-le-Rabet, then capture two key features – Point 195, some four kilometres further on, and Point 206, beyond Potigny.

Colonel Halpenny, CO of the Grenadiers, did not begin to give his orders for the operation until 2200 hours. This event was described by George Stanley in his history of the Lake Superior Regiment:

The dramatic effects of the bombing that preceded Phase II of Operation *Totalize*, as seen from well behind the front line. (NAC PA154826)

As Lieutenant Colonel Halpenny began to read his orders, his voice was drowned by the roar of heavy bombers passing overhead. At this point a rather cautious officer extinguished the lights. In the noisy darkness the Orders Group lost whatever sense of cohesion it might ever have had, and when the lights were finally turned on again, the place was in a state of the utmost confusion. ... As he returned to his own lines each officer possessed but the vaguest notion as to what was going to happen on the morrow and what his own role was going to be.

Major Ned Amy, now commanding No.1 Squadron of the Grenadiers, was tasked to lead the advanced guard of *Halpenny Force*:

When our Orders Group concluded, very little time remained [to give my own orders], and since I had no idea where my squadron was then harboured, the nightmare began. When I finally found the squadron, my attempt to brief the troop leaders was a shambles. We had but one small flashlight, and the din of gunfire was deafening. This ... made it impossible for them to study the map or hear what I said. Since we had to move [forward] under a rigidly con-

trolled movement plan ... my orders to the troop leaders were limited to an order of march and mount up and follow me. None of the supporting troops had found us, and God alone knew where they were. ... As a result, the troops were launched into their first battle inadequately briefed and under chaotic circumstances.

Amy led his squadron forward in the dark of night along a track already clogged by vehicles of 2 Armoured Brigade's administrative echelons. He was convinced that his commanding officer had told him to be prepared to launch his attack at first light (approximately 0500 hours). Unfortunately, Halpenny had made no mention in his orders of the bomber strike – set to begin at 1300 hours – that was to precede Phase II, or that Amy's squadron could not possibly begin their operation until the bombing was completed nearly an hour after that.

In the meantime, Major S.V. Radley-Walters, commanding 'A' Squadron of the Sherbrookes, was consolidating his position just north-west of the village of Gaumesnil:

I've lost only two or three tanks in this whole night push, and the infantry [the Royal Regiment] lost nine men. At that time there just wasn't anybody in front; you could have gone through in a Volkswagen. The CO, Mel Gordon is saying to the brigade and division commanders 'let's keep going,' but the plan was that we were supposed to halt there.

Only minutes after his discussion with Gordon, Brigadier Wyman was wounded by a sniper and command of 2 Armoured Brigade passed to Colonel John Bingham, who held the unusual position of deputy commander of the brigade.

At about the same time as the Sherbrooke squadrons reached their objectives, *Generalmajor* Kurt Meyer, now commander of *12 SS Panzerdivision*, rushed forward to take personal control of the crumbling defence. From a vantage point near Cintheaux, a mere 1,000 metres from the forward-most Canadian positions, he saw that the attack had halted, and set about redeploying his remaining troops. Meyer knew the ground well, having served in the area two years before as a reconnaissance battalion commander. Among his decisions were to position his 88mm *Flak* battalion astride the Caen–Falaise road at Bretteville-le-Rabet, bring forward a battle group reinforced by thirty-nine Mark IV and eight Tiger tanks for a counter-attack on the west side of the highway, and send another reinforced battle group to occupy positions on the heights near Potigny – Point 195 and Point 206 – which were 4 CAD's objectives.

The bomber strikes by US Army Air Force Liberators and Flying Fortresses came in on schedule just before 1300 hours. Meyer spotted the marker aircraft and gave orders that the counter-attack against the British, on the left of the highway, was to begin at once. By thus closing in, many of the German tanks were inside the 'bomb line' – the safety zone for the Canadians and Poles – when the first bombs were dropped. (As an aside, the Tiger commanded by tank ace Captain Michael Wittmann was destroyed near Gaumesnil during this counter-attack. Radley-Walters thinks it may have been knocked out by one of the Sherbrooke Shermans, but other evidence points to a kill by a Typhoon fighter armed with 3-inch rockets or by Fireflies of the Northamptonshire Yeomanry.)

Some 1,500 tons of bombs were dropped in the raid but there is considerable doubt that they had much effect on the German defenders, and a number of bombers released their loads well short of the intended targets, causing a great deal of

damage and confusion in the rear of both the Canadians and the Poles. The headquarters of 3 Division and 2 Armoured Brigade were both hit by stray bombs and 3 Division's commander, Major-General Rod Keller, was one of several hundred casualties. For units of 4 CAD committed to Phase II, the most disruptive effect of the bombing was the destruction of the communications vehicles of the supporting Army Group Royal Artillery, which severely limited the artillery support available at this critical time.

As soon as the bombing finished, orders came down to the Grenadier Guards to begin their attack. Because of the extremely narrow divisional frontage – little more than about 900

Camouflaged Tanks in a Wheatfield. Painting by William Ogilvie depicting tanks of the Canadian Grenadier Guards prior to their attack on 8 August 1944. (Canadian War Museum CWM13261)

metres at the start line – the actual spearhead of the 4 Division assault was a single tank squadron – Ned Amy's squadron of the Grenadier Guards:

> Without any knowledge of where the enemy might be, my focus was instinctively drawn to the open ground left of our centre line [the highway] where I expected to see elements of the Polish Armoured Division, but they were not visible. While we had good observation across this area, there was adequate cover to conceal both tanks and anti-tank guns, and with this flank wide open I was reluctant to push forward without further information on not only the enemy but where our own troops were located as well.

We were being subjected to some sporadic shelling, but

4th Armoured Brigade tank advancing during Phase II of Operation *Totalize*. The tactical sign (the number 40) identifies this as a headquarters tank. (NAC PA131373)

Column of 4th Armoured Brigade Shermans moving forward toward Cintheaux, 8 August 1944. (NAC PA140822)

nothing serious, and I recall firing at the most likely looking enemy observation post which was the church tower in St. Sylvain which had a commanding view of the entire area.

......

[Lieutenant] Craig Smith's troop was hull down in the forward position with two of his tanks disabled on mines. He had reported two German tanks on fire half way down the hill. [The] constant proddings for me "to get cracking", which were heard on all tank radios, prompted him to charge over the brow of the hill with support from his remaining tank. His tank was hit and brewed....

Lieutenant Smith remembered the hit from the point of view of a surviving 'hittee'.

I started down the hill supported by one tank at the crest. The next thing, I was fired on from the orchard. He missed, but it must have been close as it was like a clap of thunder.

We started to 'jink' and opened up all our guns at the orchard. ... The only cover was to put the burning German tank between us and the other tank. He hit us through the left glacis plate and the right sponson, instantly killing Moe Taylor, the wireless operator, and Bob Puttock, the gunner.

Amy's caution was, in hindsight, fully justified: the entire open area his squadron would have had to cross was thoroughly covered by concealed anti-tank guns and tanks. Had his squadron pressed on, the result would probably have been as disastrous as it had been for the British armoured divisions that had lost hundreds of tanks south-east of Caen a few weeks earlier during the ill-fated Operation *Goodwood*.

The failure of *Halpenny Force* to advance understandably caused great consternation at the superior headquarters. Major-General George Kitching wrote about this situation in his memoirs, *Mud and Green Fields*:

When his brigade was held up at the beginning of our Phase II, I looked for [Brigadier Booth] to hear what was wrong. I had the greatest difficulty locating him and he would not answer calls on the radio. When I finally found him he was nearly two miles away from the battle and fast asleep in his tank. I personally had to climb up on the tank to wake him and tell him to go and see what was happening. I was so angry that I ordered him out of the tank and gave him a tongue-lashing for five minutes.

In a later interview with historian Donald Graves, Kitching stated that Booth was drunk, passed out on the turret floor when he found him. Judging from this highly inappropriate conduct at such a critical time in his brigade's first action, it seems clear that Brigadier Booth was simply not up to the pressures of field command. It is also likely that many of the problems encountered by 4 Armoured Brigade in *Totalize* were the result of his ineffective leadership. Kitching, for his part, never did give a satisfactory explanation as to why he did not immediately relieve Booth.

Shortly before 1600 hours 'Snuffy' Smith's No.3 Squadron of the Grenadier Guards was sent forward with orders to press on toward Cintheaux at all costs, but soon after passing through Amy's No.1 Squadron near Gaumesnil, Smith's tanks met the same murderous weight of anti-tank crossfire on the east (left) side of the highway and were pinned down. He instructed the troop leader of 4th Troop, Lieutenant Ivan Phelan, to "make an end run on the right," between the highway and the railway embankment.

By this time the Royal Regiment of Canada (2 Division) had cleared the village of Gaumesnil. From this vantage Lieutenant Phelan pinpointed the location of an anti-tank gun in an orchard on the north edge of Cintheaux – one of the guns which had stopped the advance on the left of the road. After hitting the gun position with a high-explosive round, Phelan led his troop in a dash across the open field and found the entire gun crew dead. His subsequent action is described in the Grenadier Guards history:

Then … Phelan swung his troop right, accounting for a 2cm gun in the orchard and two more of the same calibre in the farm buildings at the western corner. On turning the corner he came into full view of a prepared defensive position – a fortified hedge running southwestwards for 500 yards from Cintheaux along the secondary tree-lined road, from which half-a-dozen guns opened fire on the three tanks as they charged over a slight rise with all guns blazing. Phelan knocked out one [88mm] gun; Sgt. Hurwitz, crossing from the left rear, knocked out another … and a third, next to the railway, was moving back when it too was blown

up by Sgt. Boucher. The other German guns, liberally sprayed with co-ax[ial machine-gun fire] though unseen, were now silent.

Phelan dismounted his crews to attack on foot and, although several of the men were wounded by the violent explosion of a nearby enemy self-propelled gun, they rushed the German position. In one of the most notable actions by a tank troop in Normandy, 31 prisoners were captured, along with three more 88mm guns and yet another 2cm gun concealed further along the hedge. Sergeant Samuel 'Moe' Hurwitz, destined to become the most decorated man in the Armoured Corps, was awarded the Military Medal for his bravery and leadership this day. Lieutenant Phelan received the Military Cross.

Despite this brief but significant moment of success, despite a continuous flow of messages from brigade to push on boldly and having lost only nine of his tanks, Colonel Halpenny decided to withdraw the bulk of his force into a laager north of Gaumesnil for replenishment and regrouping. Soon afterward, two troops of the South Alberta Regiment supported the Argylls in an advance into Cintheaux, which was captured with little effort. The Argyll companies then continued on for another kilometre to seize the village of Hautmesnil before last light. But by then 4 CAD had run out of steam.

THE BRITISH COLUMBIA REGIMENT'S NIGHT ATTACK

With the second phase of *Totalize* having ground to a premature standstill just south of Cintheaux, the Corps commander, Lieutenant-General Guy Simonds, badgered General Kitching to press on with all possible speed. A hasty plan was cobbled together by the division's operations staff to break through the German's second defensive line by mounting a small-scale version of the attack that had been so successful the previous night. This time, however, there were to be no aids to night navigation, and, as most of 4 CAD's artillery had still not got forward through the traffic jam, there was to be very little indirect fire support.

Worthington Force, consisting of the British Columbia Regiment with three companies of the Algonquin Regiment under command, was tasked to carry the advance to a key feature known as Hill 195, one of the brigade's original objectives. At the same time, *Halpenny Force* – the Grenadiers and Lake Superiors – was to move forward in darkness to launch a first light attack on Bretteville-le-Rabet.

Worthington's plan called for his battle group to advance in column along the left (east) side of the Caen–Falaise highway, so as to avoid a still-intact German strong point in a large quarry immediately south of Hautmesnil. The column was to bypass Bretteville-le-Rabet (which was about to be attacked by

British Columbia Regiment Sherman just prior to going into battle. 4th Armoured Brigade had not yet begun to weld on spare track for extra protection. (Canadian Forces Photo Unit)

the Grenadier Guards) by means of a wide sweep to the left of the village, and then swing 90 degrees to the right, cross the main highway between Langannerie and Quesnay, and make a mad dash over the final three kilometres of open ground onto the objective. 'C' Squadron was to lead, followed by Regimental Headquarters, 'B' Squadron, the Algonquin companies mounted in half-tracks and Bren-gun carriers, with 'A' Squadron bringing up the rear. H-Hour was set for 0330, and the battle group was expected to be on Hill 195 by dawn.

When the BCR/Algonquin column started out the sky was pitch black, and in the intense darkness the few landmarks that existed in the open rolling wheatfields – even the roads and tracks – could not be identified. Behind the lead tanks thick dust thrown up by the tracks of the vehicles in front made map reading impossible, so drivers simply followed the vehicle ahead, as had happened in 2 Armoured Brigade the previous night. There was some confusion not long after the march began when Grenadier Guards tanks, headed for their attack on Bretteville, got mixed up with the column.

As 'C' Squadron approached Bretteville, they came under anti-tank and machine-gun fire from woods on the north-west side of the village. In the brief fire-fight that ensued, a number of houses and haystacks were set alight, causing some concern among crew commanders that their vehicles would be skylined and thus be good targets for enemy gunners. Colonel Worthington gave radio orders to move around the village in a wider arc. It is very likely that this is the time that the crew commander at the head of the column became disoriented, for in-

stead of turning right (south-west) between Bretteville and the village of Estrée-la-Campagne as was intended, the column continued in a south-easterly direction, crossing a secondary highway between Estrée and the village of Soignolles. About 1,000 metres further on, another secondary highway (D 131) was crossed and, given the absence of visible landmarks, it is probable that this road was mistaken for the Caen–Falaise highway. (The relative angles between these two sets of roads is very similar.) Daylight was beginning to break, and directly ahead was a hill that was assumed to be Hill 195. In fact it was a very different feature – Hill 140 – nearly six kilometres to the north-west of Hill 195, and well within the sector assigned to 1 Polish Armoured Division.

Unfortunately for the British Columbia Regiment, Hill 140 was a key part of the new German defensive line forward of the Laison River. The general area was already held by the better part of a *Panzergrenadier* battalion, and another battalion was already heading in that direction from Soignolles. On hearing that there were Canadian tanks on this vital ground, Kurt Meyer ordered an immediate attack, and included in that force five Tigers and fifteen Panthers that were positioned only three kilometres away, in Quesnay Wood.

Almost at the same time as 'C' Squadron arrived on what

Knocked-out BCR 'A' Squadron Sherman near Hill 140. This photo was taken some time after the battle. It would appear that the tank's ammunition exploded after it was hit, blowing off the turret and separating the glacis plate from the hull on the left side. The second photo shows another destroyed BCR tank on Point 111, just below Hill 140. This Sherman was hit by armour-piercing rounds twice on the turret, twice on the hull and once on the gun barrel. It undoubtedly 'brewed up', exploding the ammunition and displacing the turret. (BCR Museum)

was thought to be Hill 195, 'A' Squadron, at the tail end of the now somewhat dispersed column, was attacked by tanks, anti-tank guns and mortars, and all its tanks were disabled or destroyed. 'B' Squadron also had two tanks 'brewed up' in this brief but intense battle, but claimed to have knocked out two Tigers in the process.

Just before 0700 hours on 9 August, the BCR rear link reported to brigade headquarters that *Worthington Force* was on Hill 195, and this was duly passed on to division and corps. By this time Colonel Worthington had been informed of the fate of 'A' Squadron, and deployed his force of twenty-seven tanks and two infantry companies in an all-round defence of a 200 x 400 metre field, surrounded on three sides by woodland, which we now know was centred on Point 111 about 1,500 metres north-west of Hill 140. About a half-hour later the first organized German attack was launched. The artillery forward observation officer with the BCR force called for artillery support but as the map references he gave were related to the real Hill 195 no shells landed anywhere nearby.

During the first of many attacks, a German liaison officer was captured by the Algonquins. Major General Michael Reynolds, in his book *Steel Inferno*, quotes a report the officer later wrote: "I had barely reached the Canadian hedgehog position … when our 88mm guns started to fire on the Canadian tanks and infantry. Tigers [the remains of the Witman force] and Panthers advanced in order to encircle the positions on the hill. One Canadian tank after another was knocked out and ended up in smoke and flames…."

The Algonquin Regiment's history, *Warpath*, quotes the account of Major L.C. Monk, who commanded 'A' Company:

The enemy fire increased in intensity as the morning wore on. It came from all directions, but chiefly from the east and south flanks. By 1030 hours, half of our tanks were in flames; the remainder found it difficult to locate and reply to enemy fire. No targets were offered to the infantry, so we just kept our heads down and took a bad beating from enemy shells and mortar fire which would explode in the hedges and trees above, sending shrapnel showers into the slits.

Brigade headquarters logged the last radio transmission from the BCR at 0856 hours. By that time it had become apparent that *Worthington Force* was not on Hill 195, but where was it? At 1030 hours the Foot Guards were ordered to proceed at once to find and assist the BCR but, showing no sense of urgency, did not start out until 1400 hours. In the meanwhile, Corps headquarters tasked the 7th Recce Regiment and all

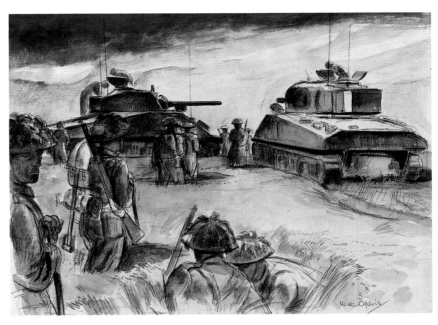

Preparatory to Attack. **Painting by William Ogilvie. (Canadian War Museum CWM13507)**

available Air Observation Post Auster aircraft to carry out a search, but neither came up with any useful information. A Staghound troop from the 12th Manitoba Dragoons was also sent out to the area of Point 195 to find the missing units, but, getting onto the feature from the west, was able to confirm that no Canadians were anywhere in the vicinity.

Meanwhile, the Grenadier Guards and Lake Superiors took Bretteville-le-Rabet in a very hard-fought action, and by early afternoon units of 10 Infantry Brigade, with support from the South Albertas, advanced into the adjoining villages of Langannerie and Granville.

On the left, the Poles were having an equally difficult time getting forward in the face of stiff opposition from *SS* units on their front. By noon they had reached Estrée-la-Campagne, and one depleted squadron of Polish tanks briefly got within about three hundred metres of Point 111. At first they fired on the BCR position, not knowing that friends were in front of them, but after yellow smoke grenades were set off the Poles turned their fire on a group of Germans about to launch yet another attack. Unfortunately the Polish tanks were soon driven off by German anti-tank fire.

Back at Point 111 the battle raged on as the Germans mounted one attack after another and casualties continued to mount. By early afternoon there were only a handful of serviceable tanks remaining, but the gallant men of the BCR and Algonquins continued to hold out. Major Monk again:

By 1730 hours … most of [our tanks] were burning furiously, many with their dead crews still in them. The exploding ammunition in the burning tanks added to the noise and danger. Our mortar detachments were out of action. The field was a mass of shell holes. The trees and scrub were cut to pieces from shrapnel. The smell of burning flesh, the odour of exploding enemy H.E. mingled to make most of us nauseated. … We had run out of morphine and bandages. Many of the wounded men were delirious, shouting and screaming…. Things looked pretty grim.

At about 1700 hours Colonel Worthington was killed by a mortar shell, but the few survivors continued to fight on until last light. Darkness offered cover for at least some of the men to escape by crawling through waist-high wheat toward Canadian lines, but when the Germans finally moved in they captured 34 members of the BCR and 45 Algonquins, many of them wounded. It was a sad day for both Canadian units. The BCR took 112 casualties, 40 of them killed in action, and 47 of its 55 tanks. The Algonquins lost a total of 128, 45 killed in action.

THE FOOT GUARDS AT QUESNAY WOOD

Even though the Foot Guards had been given orders in mid-morning to move immediately to the area of Hill 195 in order to relieve the BCR, the commanding officer, Lieutenant-Colonel M.J. Scott, was not about to be rushed. He was very much aware of the heavy casualties inflicted the previous day on the Grenadier Guards by German anti-tank guns deployed to cover the same exposed ground that his unit faced, and he had absolutely no information on the strength or probable deployment of the enemy on his front. In addition, he knew that there was no smoke to cover the movement of his tanks, limited artillery support, and the infantry he had been promised simply did not arrive until early afternoon.

It is now known, of course, that Kurt Meyer had fully recognized the tactical importance of a large forested area known as Quesnay Wood, where he had deployed a large number of anti-tank guns as well as some 26 tanks, including eight Tigers. This anti-tank phalanx in Quesnay Wood was to prove the undoing of General Simonds' hopes for *Totalize*.

The Foot Guards moved off from Gaumesnil at about 1400 hours on 9 August, bound for Hill 195. As No.1 Squadron passed through the gap between Bretteville-le-Rabet and Langannerie, they were engaged by a tremendous weight of anti-tank fire from Quesnay Wood and four Shermans were destroyed. No.2 Squadron came forward to provide covering fire and No.1 Squadron attempted to move to the right, but even more tanks were knocked out on the table-flat ground that offered no cover for movement and no protected fire positions. Some consideration was given to mounting a dismounted attack with the accompanying Algonquin company, but it was obvious that the enemy in front were too strong to be dislodged

Governor General's Foot Guards Sherman destroyed during the attempted advance to Hill 195 on 9 August 1944. Quesnay Wood, the location of a German anti-tank 'phalanx', is seen in the background. (Canadian Forces Photo Unit PMR82-387)

by a single company. When the Germans began to infiltrate into the Guards' hasty defensive positions, Colonel Scott moved the unit back into Granville-Langannerie. In this brief action the Foot Guards lost twenty-two tanks.

HILL 195

With the villages of Langannerie and Granville secure, attention was focused on one of 4 CAD's key objectives, Hill 195, which, of course, had been the intended objective of the BCR the previous evening. The task of taking it was given to the Argyll and Sutherland Highlanders from 10 Brigade and it was captured before first light on 10 August in a daring, silent, single-file infiltration in the dark. During the night the Lincoln and Welland Regiment advanced to a position overlooking the village of St. Germain-le-Vasson, while the Algonquins occupied St. Hilaire Farm, behind Point 195. Later in the day the South Albertas deployed squadrons to support both battalions.

During the Phase II advance, the 12th Manitoba Dragoons had been tasked to provide flank protection for 4 CAD until such time as the opportunity might arise to exploit southward toward Falaise and Argentan. One squadron served as liaison and reported the progress of the Polish division on the left, while the other squadrons operated on the right flank in the area of the Laize River. Starting out from the area of Urville on 10 August, patrols from 'A' Squadron advanced into the area north-west of Hill 195, where they ferreted out pockets of enemy infantry, while two troops from 'D' Squadron crossed the Laize into enemy-held territory near Mesnil-Touffay, pinpointing German troop locations and directing artillery fire onto mortar and rocket batteries which were bringing down fire on the Canadian positions near Grainville and Hill 195.

(Above) Grenadier Guards tank during the attack on Hill 195, 10 August 1944. Many crews dismantled the .50 calibre machine gun on the commander's cupola as it could interfere with bailing out if the tank was 'brewed'. (NAC PA132963)

2nd Armoured Brigade Sherman during the offensive south of Caen. The lead tank is a 'Sherman, Control', with additional radio sets. The third tank in the line is a 'Ram, Observation Post'. Note the sand bags and tank track welded on the front of the hull. At this time only the regiments of 2nd Brigade were adding this protection. (NAC PA114062)

271

Tanks moving to position for the offensive. NAC PA132904.

Early on the morning of 10 August, the Grenadier Guards were ordered to move forward to bolster the Hill 195 position, and the regiment moved to an assembly area near St. Hilaire shortly after midnight. Just before 0800 hours, No.2 Squadron in the lead, the Guards set out for Hill 195, still shrouded in a heavy morning mist. The hot sun, however, soon burned off the fog, and, over nearly 2,000 metres of open ground that offered no cover or concealment, the squadrons ran a gauntlet of tank and anti-tank fire – from Quesnay Wood on the left, and from concealed German positions on the right and right rear. The commanding officer's tank, *Grenadier*, was one of the first to be knocked out, and another six tanks were destroyed before the remainder got to the Argyll's thinly-held position at mid-morning. The squadrons then fanned out to consolidate the all-round defence of the virtually bald feature.

Lieutenant-Colonel Halpenny gathered his orders group (the squadron commanders and the artillery FOO) just before noon to give a briefing for a subsequent advance aimed at Point 206, 2,500 metres to the south. He had just begun to give his plan when the first of many enemy counter-attacks came in. A regimental Report on Operations (quoted in Roy's *The Canadians in Normandy*) describes what occurred:

The first evidence of [a counter-attack] was the knocking out of one of … 2 Sqn's. Tanks. Lieut. Hill then moved off to the left flank to investigate what he thought were carriers but later proved to be Robot tanks. His tank had not gone 100 yards when it burst into flame. From this point everything happened at once. Two more tanks on the left flank were set ablaze…. The Squadron Leaders' tanks, which had been grouped around the C.O.'s, dispersed but not before Major Williamson's had suffered a fiery fate. Lieut. Stanbury's

troop, which had been guarding the rear and left, now moved to assist. Again a matter of 100 yards had been traversed when his own and Sgt. Forsyth's tanks were destroyed by 88mm fire.

The situation was obviously grave. Some tanks had now withdrawn from the objective and consequently became useless for effective counter fire. The C.O. was frantically endeavouring to re-establish contact with Bde. H.Q. which had been lost one hr. before. Major H.A. Smith, seeing the imminence of the danger, gave orders over the Regimental net and brilliantly succeeded in regrouping the available force and establishing a tight ring around the objective … and we set about the task of dealing with the enemy infantry which, by this time, were advancing upon us under a heavy concentration of machine-gun fire.

For more than an hour the battle raged. Our tanks developed a veritable hail of machine gun and H.E. fire. Elements of the Argyll and Sutherland Highlanders … also on the objective, ably assisted us. Defensive fire was called down by our F.O.O.s, both medium and field. In return the enemy kept up a bitter blanket of mortar, H.E. and machine-gun fire and, although the attacking infantry was halted, they gave no sign of retiring.

At the end of this hour-long fight, the Grenadiers had only fifteen tanks left. Two squadrons of the Foot Guards were brought up in mid-afternoon to reinforce the position. Throughout the day the Germans rained down mortar and artillery shells, and enemy infantry continually pestered the position, sometimes getting to within a hundred metres of the tanks before being detected. The thin garrison on Hill 195 nonetheless continued to hold out, but in the course of these continual small battles both Guards units ran short on ammunition and fuel. Resupply was extremely difficult and dangerous, but the action of Sergeant Charles Fielding of the Foot Guards was typical of the many dedicated men serving in unit 'A' Echelons. Sergeant Fielding's Military Medal citation tells a story of a well-deserved decoration for bravery:

Attempts to reach [the Foot Guards squadrons] by echelon vehicles carrying urgently needed petrol, ammunition and water were fruitless due to intense accurate enemy mortar, artillery and automatic fire. Sergeant Fielding volunteered to run the supplies forward and by skilful use of ground led his three vehicles through to the squadrons in the face of intense enemy fire. Three times he successfully completed this hazardous trip….

Hoping to restore the momentum of the attack, General Simonds brought in 3 Division on 10 August to continue the

THE BATTLE OF NORMANDY: THE BREAKOUT

thrust southward toward Potigny and Epancy. The first task was to clear the troublesome German stronghold in Quesnay Wood, and that evening the Queen's Own Rifles and the North Shore Regiment of 8 Brigade mounted an attack on the wood. Both of these seasoned battalions were met by an overwhelming hail of fire and, after suffering severe casualties, were withdrawn. Operation *Totalize* was over.

Back on Hill 195, the two Guards regiments had a difficult night because of continual shelling. The Germans mounted yet another attack around 0430 hours on the morning of 11 August, but it too was defeated by the Foot Guards and a Lincoln and Welland company. Early that afternoon 4 CAD's units were ordered to pull back to prepare for a "new effort", although getting off Hill 195 was also costly. The German anti-tank guns were still watching over the open ground north of the hill, and another six Grenadier tanks were knocked out during the withdrawal.

THE CONTROVERSY SURROUNDING *TOTALIZE*

While veterans and historians usually agree that the first phase was brilliantly planned and adequately executed, the second phase has been shrouded in controversy, partly because it did not achieve the same measure of clear and measurable success. In some respects, at least, this is unfair to the troops involved, for the gains made on the ground in Phase II were as large as those in Phase I, even though the objectives assigned were never reached. There were, however, serious problems, both in the planning and execution of the operation, that should not be overlooked.

In hindsight it is easy to point to obvious flaws in the planning. The most serious of these was the inordinate delay between the phases, caused by the need to wait over eight hours for the bomber strikes on 8 August (which in the end were of questionable value). This delay allowed resourceful and flexible German commanders time to recover from the initial breakthrough and redeploy forces – especially anti-tank guns – to counter the renewed attack. There were, of course, a host of other planning errors, most at Corps level, which had a cumulative, compounding effect. Chief among them was the last-minute change of plan which brought 1 Polish Armoured Division in on the left of 4 CAD, thus forcing two armoured divisions to advance side-by-side on a frontage barely adequate for a single formation. This precluded any possibility of manoeuvre by either division, and, incidentally, did not in any way actually increase the firepower that could be deployed at the front. Rather, it added to coordination and communications problems, not least because of language differences, across a divisional boundary. The change in plan adversely affected the normal 'battle procedure' in both 4 CAD and 4 Armoured Brigade: orders were late (and in some cases very incomplete) and consequently the troops who were expected to do the fighting were not adequately briefed and there was no time for the armour to 'marry up' with supporting infantry. Administrative plans were also of poor quality. The enormous traffic congestion as 4 Armoured Brigade units tried to make their way forward through the echelons of 2 Division and 2 Armoured Brigade was in large measure the result of exceptionally poor traffic control planning at Corps headquarters, planning which was no doubt compounded by having to fit another division's worth of vehicles into a small, already clogged, rear area.

The planning and coordination problems created at higher levels were not easily resolved or worked around because the staff officers at both division and brigade headquarters, by General Kitching's own admission, had never been trained to work in an operational environment.

Leadership in the field was also an obvious weakness in 4 Brigade. Perhaps reflecting his limited experience in Italy where there was seldom space to employ more than one tank squadron at a time, Brigadier Booth, tended to deploy his units in piecemeal fashion rather than using massed armour as might have been expected in an armoured division. One may also find it difficult to accept the obvious weakness of character demonstrated by Booth when, in a state of drunkenness, he absented himself from the field of battle during his brigade's baptism of fire.

Much has been said (not the least by Guy Simonds) about the "excessive caution" shown by armoured commanders in this battle. There is probably more than a grain of truth in this criticism, but evidence would indicate that it should be applied selectively. In a number of instances caution was fully justified: flat, open countryside dominated by a thick screen of anti-tank guns was nothing less than a 'killing ground'. It might also be recalled that the doctrine of the day assigned the role of taking out anti-tank guns to the infantry. There were, of course, obvious occasions when certain regimental and squadron commanders showed no sense of urgency in reacting to orders and little tactical skill when confronting serious battlefield problems, but this did not apply to all units. It needs to be remembered that the system of training in England rarely gave unit commanding officers any opportunity to exercise their command in a field setting; they did not understand the application of tactics at regimental level, and, like most others in 4 Division, they were learning on the job. In fact, the inadequacy of the tactics training in England showed at all levels, especially the lack of tank-infantry cooperation training. The officers and men in the units of 4 CAD were not the seasoned veterans found at this time in 2 Armoured Brigade, with whom they are often compared. Even with exceptionally good technical and trades training, it is accepted wisdom that no training can substitute for actual battlefield experience. It is also fair to point out that many of the operational problems experienced by 4 CAD in its first action in Normandy had parallels in the experience of 5 CAD in Italy a few months earlier, in the Liri valley battles.

OPERATION *TRACTABLE*, 14–16 AUGUST

Even before *Totalize* ground to a halt in front of Quesnay Wood, General Simonds recognized that the momentum of the attack toward Falaise had been lost, and the staff at Corps headquarters devised a plan for yet another deliberate attack, dubbed *Tractable*. It was to be another massive armoured thrust, designed to break through a new defensive belt the Germans had reconstituted along the general line of the Laison River. It was to be a daylight attack, again preceded by heavy bomber strikes, but this time cover for the attackers would be provided by extensive use of smoke. And to bypass the apparently impenetrable enemy position at Quesnay Wood, the centre line was shifted several kilometres to the west.

On the far left of the II Corps assault sector, the 12th Manitoba Dragoons were tasked to provide flank protection and 4 CAD was assigned a two-kilometre-wide front for its advance, west of an inter-divisional boundary that ran from Soignolles to Rouvres on the River Laison. After seizing crossings over the Laison, 10 Brigade (with the South Albertas) was to take the area of Epancy and Perrières, while 4 Armoured Brigade was to capture the high ground at Versainville (Point 159) overlooking Falaise. 3 Division, with 2 Armoured Brigade under command, was to be on the right, with a final objective on high ground (Point 184) near the village of Potigny. In both divisions the armoured brigades were to lead the thrust, followed by an infantry brigade mounted in Kangaroo armoured personnel carriers and another truck-borne infantry brigade bringing up the rear. The attack was set for mid-day on 14 August.

Following the issue of verbal orders at Corps headquarters on the morning of 13 August, General Simonds gathered the commanding officers of all the armoured regiments in the Corps and stressed "the necessity for pushing armour to the very limits of its endurance," giving firm instructions that tanks were not to be pulled back from the front at night, as was standard practise, but rather must be prepared to move and fight in the dark. Those present have memories of an angry tirade, harsh and accusing. Colonel 'Swatty' Wotherspoon, CO of the South Albertas, recalled that Simonds had "told us we were all rotten, etc., etc.," suggested that the COs were "all yellow," and ordered that they would henceforth command their units in battle from the turret of a tank. It was not the sort of occasion that instilled confidence in the senior leadership on the eve of another major battle.

Meanwhile, in a subsidiary attack intended to draw German attention away from preparations for *Tractable*, 2 Division, with the Sherbrooke Fusiliers under command, was advancing on the right of the Corps sector from Bretteville-sur-Laize toward Clair Tizon on the right bank of the River Laize. This attack began on 11 August but bogged down at Clair Tizon two days later. One of the unfortunate consequences of this was the compromise of the plan for *Tractable*, which took place when an 8th Recce scout car was knocked out as it drove through the enemy line near Clair Tizon on the evening of 13 August. On the officer's body the Germans found a copy of a 2 Division report outlining the Corps plan, and some sources have claimed that this information enabled the enemy to reposition an anti-tank battery along the Laison opposite the intended crossing locations.

On the night of 13 August the armoured brigades moved into their assembly areas near Renémesnil. It was already hot and clear when the regiments began their final preparations for battle on the morning of 14 August. At 1130 hours they began to move forward into forming-up places just short of the start line, which was centred on the village of Soignolles. There the two lead regiments in each brigade deployed two squadrons forward, with the third immediately in rear. Nearly 280 Shermans were poised to advance to the River Laison on a front of just over four kilometres. H-Hour was scheduled for 1200 noon, and at H minus 20 minutes the artillery fired red marker shells to guide RAF bombers on to their targets along the Laison valley. The bombers came in at H minus 10, but some of them dropped their bombs well short, disrupting communications and causing a considerable amount of damage in the support echelons. The artillery began to lay the smoke screen a few minutes later, and just before noon, when smoke obscured the whole front, the order came, "Move now."

The tanks began a "mad charge" to the River Laison over rolling, open wheatfields. They were supposed to maintain a speed of twenty kilometres per hour until reaching the river bank some fifteen minutes later, but this pace slowed very considerably when forward visibility was severely reduced in the dense clouds of dust that mixed with the smoke. "Dust like I've never seen before," said Lieutenant-Colonel Scott, the Foot Guards CO. To keep direction, drivers were reduced to aiming "into the sun," the only thing that could be made out even vaguely, and largely because of this both brigades veered to the left of their intended routes. The neat ranks of armoured vehicles rapidly disintegrated and one historian has noted that, "soon, the advance was by clump, not column." In the confusion, a number of units became intermingled.

Despite the generally adverse effect of the smoke and dust, the smoke screen was not everywhere effective in blocking the enemy's view, most notably in front of the 2 Armoured Brigade regiments. So, expecting the attack, the German defenders – especially those deployed on the upward slope well forward of the river line – took a heavy toll on the advancing units. Before reaching the Laison, the Foot Guards lost six tanks, including the CO's, to anti-tank fire and mines, the Grenadiers had seven knocked out by anti-tank guns, and the 1st Hussars took six tank casualties, including one knocked out by a Tiger. The 'dehorsed' tank crews found themselves fighting stiff battles against dispersed German infantry outposts.

Perhaps the most significant loss in this stage of the battle was the destruction of 4 Brigade headquarters tanks, which had veered well to the right and ran into a German anti-tank screen. In this fight Brigadier Booth was severely wounded and he died a short time later while being evacuated. Major Gerry Chubb, the brigade major – the only officer of the headquarters to survive – had no way of reporting what had happened as all of the headquarters radios had been destroyed. It was nearly three hours before Major Chubb was able to get word back to 4 CAD and, during that critical time, 4 Brigade was leaderless.

The confusion of the "dash in the dust" – the troops had many names for *Tractable* – was exacerbated when the tanks reached the near bank of the Laison, around 1430 hours. While the units had hoped to capture intact bridges over the river, they had been told that the river was, in any case, fordable in most places. As might have been expected, units found that the bridges had been blown, however, and many a crew commander discovered, as he bogged his tank, that the river was a major tank obstacle: the heavily wooded banks were too steep to climb, and the bottom consisted of soft mud. A great deal of time was wasted and many more casualties inflicted by shelling from enemy positions on the far side as commanders searched up and down the river bank for fording sites.

The first to get across were elements of the 17th Hussars, under command of 2 Armoured Brigade, who had been intended to follow behind the leading tank regiments. In the generalized confusion of searching for crossing sites, the recce troops showed their usual *élan* and got the better part of a squadron established at two widely separated sites on the far bank, where they dug in and held in the face of furious enemy fire.

It was close to 1600 hours when the first tanks got over. Seven squadrons – two from the Foot Guards, one from the Grenadiers, two from the BCR, and two from the 1st Hussars – crossed at a single improvised fascine bridge placed by engineers at Rouvres. This was a painfully slow process, made slower when a Foot Guards tank slipped off the

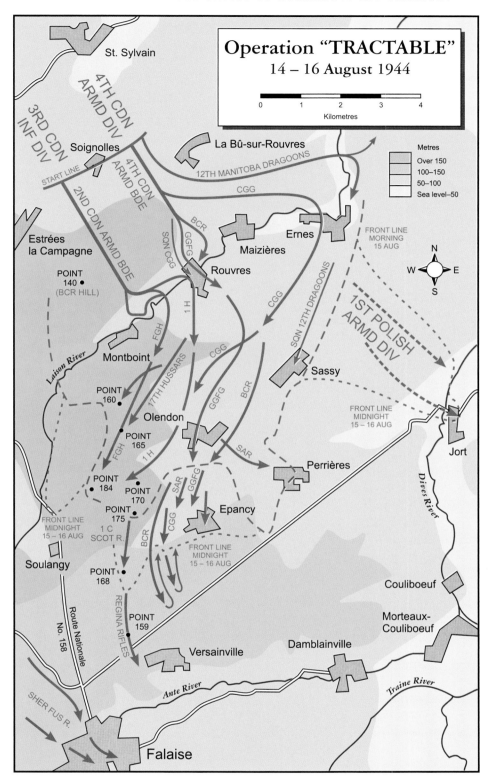

fascines and had to be towed out to clear the way. The makeshift bridge was not the only problem in Rouvres; shelling had damaged many of the buildings and created a maze of rubble. When the BCR were passing through, for example, burning rubble fell from a building onto Captain Jim Tedlie's Sherman. "Corporal

Shermans of 2nd Armoured Brigade moving to their assembly area for Operation *Tractable*, 14 August 1944. In the foreground is a Flail tank belonging to 79 Armoured Division, attached to the brigade for the attack. (NAC PA113659)

Jack Bass, commanding the tank behind, dismounted … and pulled the burning debris off the rear of the threatened tank. For this brave act he won a Military Medal," records the BCR history, *The Dukes.* Two Grenadier squadrons made the crossing four kilometres downstream at Ernes, and the Fort Garrys found an intact minor bridge mid-way between Rouvres and Montboint. Only No.1 Squadron of the Foot Guards and 'B' Squadron of the BCR succeeded in fording the river.

The first to cross at Rouvres was a troop commanded by Sergeant Frederick Kenyon of the 1st Hussars' 'A' Squadron, and his troop immediately became involved in a firefight with five German field guns. The Hussars destroyed all five guns but Kenyon's tank was put out of action. Dismounted, he carried on the battle with hand grenades and his pistol, driving out enemies who could have disrupted the crossing operation. His gallantry was recognized by the award of the Distinguished Conduct Medal.

Meanwhile, three squadrons of the 12th Manitoba Dragoons advanced on the left flank of II Canadian Corps. 'C' Squadron deployed along the left boundary to protect the flank in the sector from St. Sylvain to just short of the Laison River, while 'A' Squadron moved directly to Ernes to picquet the area between Ernes and the village of Vendeuve. 'A' Squadron patrols encountered large numbers of German infantry, most of whom were quite happy to surrender, and at one point several of the troops had more than sixty prisoners. Near Ernes, patrols assisted a few tanks that had gone astray in the dash to the river. 'B' Squadron, which was to pass through when the high ground at

(Above) 4th Armoured Brigade tanks at the beginning of the attack, 14 August 1944. (NAC PA114064)

(Right) Governor General's Foot Guards Sherman bogged in the crossing of the River Laison at Rouvres. (NAC PA131270)

Mont d'Eraines (west of Epancy) was secured, advanced as far as Sassy but was held up as the 4 CAD thrust began to bog down.

Once the Germans were driven off the heights overlooking the Laison, it took nearly an hour for units to gather in their strays and stragglers and reorganize to continue the advance.

In 2 Armoured Brigade, the Fort Garrys moved off at about 1730 hours, but progress was slow mainly because of murderous enemy anti-tank fire. The 2 Brigade account of operations

Sherman recovery vehicle, manned by a crew of Royal Canadian Electrical and Mechanical Engineers, passes through a French village during the breakthough operations. The RCEME technicians who recovered broken-down but repairable tanks from the battlefield were instrumental in keeping the armoured regiments at fighting strength. (NAC PA116535)

noted that "in several places five or six 88mm guns were encountered sited in bits of hedge or woods not more than 200 yards long." The Fort Garry history recounts:

Beyond the river, the country was open and rolling, with numerous small woods and scrub. Both of our flanks were exposed, as there was no one on our right and the only squadron of the 1st Hussars to cross the River was echeloned far behind our left flank. The whole area was stiff with 88mm, 75mm and 50mm anti-tank guns, who pelted us with A.P.; the pockets of infantry we ignored. The enemy guns were impossible to see until they fired…. Unfortunately our losses in tanks were severe and the dreadful sight of tanks going up in flames was common…. Despite this vindictive defence, the crews showed wonderful fighting spirit and pushed steadily on.

While the first of the Fort Garrys' Shermans arrived in the area of their objective shortly before last light, it was not until about 2230 hours that they had firm possession of the height of land south-west of Potigny designated as Point 184. Meanwhile, the Hussars, their number severely reduced, consolidated their hold on the south bank of the Laison with what few tanks were left in 'A' and 'C' Squadrons, while 'B' Squadron pushed forward on the left flank of the Garrys to their objective, a hill feature known as Point 170, about 1,500 metres south-west of the town of Olendon.

In the 4 Armoured Brigade sector to the west, the situation on the south bank of the Laison was perhaps even more con-fused, in large part because of the loss of the brigade headquarters and the subsequent lack of skilled coordination and direction of what the units were to do. At about 1900 hours, while Major Gerry Chubb went to the rear to gather the few staff officers of the brigade headquarters who had been 'left out of battle' and commandeer replacement command tanks to recreate a headquarters, Lieutenant-Colonel Scott of the Foot Guards got word from General Kitching that he was to assume temporary command of the brigade. However, Scott was wounded (which Kitching did not know), he had no means of communicating with the other units, and he was really not up to the job.

All three regiments of 4 Brigade reformed on the heights just beyond Rouvres, and each set out early in the evening toward their intermediate objectives near Olendon. They made slow progress, however. Enemy anti-tank guns had been carefully sited in depth, and they took a dreadful toll. "Everywhere there were knocked out tanks," reports the Foot Guards history. The area around Olendon appeared to be held by the enemy in considerable strength and, shortly before 2000 hours, Colonel Scott decided, in the face of heavy opposition, that it was too late to attempt to push on toward the final objective near Falaise. The Foot Guards, with only nine serviceable tanks remaining, were directed to laager on high ground west of Sassy, while the Grenadier Guards, also having taken a large number of tank casualties, spent an uncomfortable night under continual shelling in a laager close to Olendon. The BCR, which had not yet completely recovered from its near-destruction a week earlier, also harboured north of Olendon. This was not quite the grand, unrelenting, armoured thrust that Simonds had demanded only days earlier, but, given the circumstances, it was probably as much as could have been achieved. There was a measure of relief when the Lake Superior Regiment got forward, and the relief was even more pronounced when 10 Infantry Brigade and the South Albertas captured Olendon and, later that night, moved forward toward Perrières.

The advance toward Falaise was resumed on the morning of 15 August, but it proved to be a day "marked by confusion and lack of coordination," according to the official history. At least some of the difficulties came about because both 3 Division, with 2 Armoured Brigade, and 4 CAD were converging on the same objective – the high ridge just north of Falaise centred on Point 159. Passage of information between the divisions was

This photo depicts a variety of the 'funny' armoured vehicles that supported the attack. In the foreground is an M-10 self-propelled anti-tank gun. Immediately in rear is a 'Crocodile' flame-thrower based on a Churchill tank. In the left rear are Churchill 'AVREs' (Armoured Vehicle Royal Engineers) used by the Engineers to demolish strong-points. Others among the vehicles are Stuart light tanks and Universal carriers. (NAC PA116525)

almost non-existent, and units operating literally next to each other across the formation boundary rarely knew each others' locations or intent. Problems were compounded, at least in the early part of the day, because much of the supporting artillery was not within range to give effective fire support. On top of this, during the night the Germans had been able to bolster their anti-tank defences in front of Falaise.

In the 4 CAD sector, units of 10 Brigade had an early start, with Perrières being captured without difficulty. However, an attack on the village of Epancy, immediately south of Olendon, was a different story; the German defenders fought hard for every building and it was not until early evening, with the assistance of South Alberta tanks, that their resistance was finally overcome.

Colonel Scott, still in temporary command of 4 Brigade despite his badly wounded foot, ordered the brigade to launch an attack aimed at taking the Point 159 feature (codenamed *Idaho*) overlooking Falaise. His mission-oriented radio orders, issued shortly after 0800 hours, were simple, if lacking some desirable detail: "Big Sunray [Major General Kitching] directs move forward to objective now. This is imperative. Take what force you can. Ammunition and petrol now on way to you."

All three regiments desperately needed resupply, as their 'A' Echelons had not been able to get forward during the night, so it was not until 0930 hours that the advance began. The Grenadiers and the BCR led the way, bypassing Epancy on the west. From the outset they were met with mortar, artillery and anti-tank fire and movement was slow and cautious; in mid-afternoon both units were held up by concentrated anti-tank fire while still some 3,000 metres north-east of Point 159. The Grenadier Guards war diary noted that "observation showed

the high ground to be open and flat without cover and it was felt both by the B.C.R. and ourselves that an advance across this ground without infantry and proper artillery support would prove disastrous."

As the tanks pulled back to avoid the deadly fire of the enemy 88s, *Tractable* came to an end in 4 Armoured Brigade. Later that afternoon Colonel Scott went back to the division tactical headquarters north of Olendon to ask to be relieved. General Kitching, unaware until then of Scott's wounds, immediately appointed Lieutenant-Colonel Halpenny of the Grenadiers to take over as acting brigade commander.

In the 3 Division sector, on the right, dawn on 15 August was marked by enemy counter-attacks on the position held by the 1st Hussars on Point 170, which were repulsed after stiff fighting. During the morning both the Hussars and the Fort Garrys reorganized into two understrength squadrons because of the number of tanks lost the previous day.

The first task undertaken on 15 August by 2 Armoured Brigade, temporarily commanded by Lieutenant-Colonel Colwell of the Hussars because the new commander, Brigadier John Bingham was ill, was an early afternoon attack toward Point 168, a high hill some 2,000 metres south of the foremost position taken the day before. This attack, made by the Canadian Scottish and the Hussars, was an exceptionally hard-fought battle in which the Scots lost more men than on D-Day. The ground over which they had to advance consisted of relatively small wheatfields enclosed by high, thick hedges which gave superb cover to enemy tank, machine gun and anti-tank gun positions. Almost immediately after starting to move, the Hussars had several tanks knocked out, and subsequently they could not or would not continue in support of the infantry. The

Canadian Scottish war diary is very critical of this lack of support: "even under great prodding [the 1st Hussars] said they were unable to move beyond the first hedgerow to our front…." By the time the battalion reached their objective, at about 1530 hours, they had suffered 34 killed and 93 wounded.

A short time later 2 Brigade was ordered to mount an attack on Point 159, with the Hussars and Fort Garrys, supported by the Regina Rifles, directed to charge onto the objective through the newly-taken Canadian Scottish position. Planning for this attack was, however, marred by poor all-arms coordination and complicated by unconfirmed information that some elements of 4 Brigade were already in the area of the objective (as noted earlier, this had indeed been reported erroneously by a Foot Guards officer), which severely limited the extent of artillery support. H-Hour was set for 2015 hours. In the event, *en route* to the forming-up place both units informed brigade headquarters of passing through the Foot Guards, who had been reported as being already on Hill 159. And, as they came up to the start line a heavy weight of anti-tank fire hit from the front and the flanks, knocking out four Shermans. It was already getting dark, and with the prospect of any success now very slim, the attack was called-off. Thus ended *Tractable* for 2 Brigade.

FALAISE

The capture of Falaise, the ancient Norman town – birthplace of William the Conqueror – which had been the key objective of II Canadian Corps since early August, was now left to the units of 2 Division that had been advancing with only light opposition from Clair Tizon and Ussy to the north-east. Led by two squadrons of the Sherbrooke Fusiliers, the South Saskatchewans and the Cameron Highlanders of 6 Brigade mounted an attack in mid-afternoon on 16 August. The town had been heavily bombed over the previous week, leaving huge craters and rubble that severely hindered the advance of the Sherbrooke's tanks, but by the morning of 17 August Falaise was in Canadian hands except for a few enemy strongholds that were cleared out the next day.

Even before Falaise was taken the strategic situation in Normandy had altered dramatically. The Americans, even though they had halted temporarily some sixteen kilometres south-east of Falaise, had all but encircled what remained of the German Fifth and Seventh Armies in Normandy. The capture of Falaise, on the north of what was becoming a 'pocket' containing the Germans, tightened the noose, but the Germans had already begun to withdraw elements of their army along roads and trails running eastward in a so-called 'gap' between Falaise and Argentan. If a major part of the German forces could be trapped in the pocket, Allied victory in the West would be a great deal closer. The gap had to be closed, and quickly.

CLOSING THE FALAISE GAP, 17–21 AUGUST

Acting on orders passed down from Montgomery to complete the encirclement of the Germans, on 16 August General Simonds ordered his two armoured divisions to make a broad swing to the south-east so as to link up with American troops advancing from the south. 4 Canadian Armoured Division was tasked to capture a key crossing over the River Ante at Damblainville and then move south-east to secure the area of Trun, on the east bank of the River Dives. 1 Polish Armoured Division was to move in an even wider arc, on the left of 4 CAD, to capture positions in the area of Chambois.

The Argyll and Sutherland Highlanders and 'C' Squadron of the South Albertas deployed to the outskirts of Damblainville during the night, moving into the village at first light. Encountering only snipers, the initial objective – the bridge over the Ante River – was captured intact by mid-morning. Around noon 'A' and 'C' Squadrons of the SAR, with the Algonquins, moved through the town toward the next objective, a high wooded hill some 1,800 metres to the south. Before having got half-way, however, they came under heavy fire from German positions on the hill and it was apparent that a deliberate attack would have to be made to move beyond the small bridgehead.

At this same time word filtered back that an Algonquin company had captured an intact bridge four kilometres to the east at Morteaux-Couliboeuf. Kitching decided immediately to shift

The Break Through Near Perrières, Normandy. Painting by William Ogilvie. (Canadian War Museum CWM13254)

A Sherbrooke Fusiliers Sherman leads men of the Fusiliers Mont Royal into the streets of Falaise, so long the Canadian objective, 17 August 1944. (NAC PA115568)

the division's main thrust – crossing the River Dives at Couliboeuf and driving toward Trun along secondary roads – and he gave the mission to 4 Brigade, which had not yet been committed. The brigade reacted admirably to this sudden change of plan. By 1600 hours the Grenadier Guards were across the bridge at Morteaux-Couliboeuf, followed closely by the Foot Guards. The BCR and the Lake Superior Regiment crossed a short while later. Meanwhile, the Polish division had crossed the Dives at Jort and was advancing some 3,000 metres to the left of the Canadian centre line.

The Grenadiers encountered no opposition until nearing Louvières, but, as the regimental history notes, the following message was frequently heard over the regimental net: "I am being fired on from the left. I think it is the Poles. They are damned bad shots." At Louvières Lieutenant Pat Grieve's troop destroyed two enemy signals vehicles concealed behind haystacks, but 'friendly fire' continued to cause problems. As the regiment turned southward, towards Trun, the lead squadron was attacked by American fighter-bombers, and one crew commander was killed. Despite the delay caused by this unfortunate incident, the Grenadiers were only about two kilometres north-west of Trun by early evening, when, as it had no supporting infantry with it, the regiment was deployed in an all-round defence astride the main road. The Foot Guards and the BCR meanwhile laagered a few kilometres apart near Les Moutiers-en-Auge.

During the night the South Alberta squadrons arrived in the area of Trun with the infantry battalions they were supporting. As radio contact had been lost with both brigade headquarters, it appears that Canadian units did not know each others' locations. In such a fluid situation, with the units of 4 and 10 Brigades well into the area through which the Germans were now moving, all units maintained a high state of alert throughout

the night and patrols reported "swarms of Germans on the move" in the darkness.

The Grenadier history noted: "To the south-east towards Chambois, to the south beyond Trun, and all down the valley towards Falaise the lights of a hundred fires – blazing vehicles, ammunition dumps and buildings – made it evident that the Regiment was out in front, the spearhead in the gut of the gap."

On the morning of 18 August the attempt to link-up with the Americans continued but the situation was, at best, very confused until units sorted themselves out on the ground and brigade headquarters got forward to coordinate operations. Meanwhile, the German exodus from the pocket grew ever larger. In a post-war memoir, Major David Currie of the South Alberta Regiment recalled watching the on-coming horde through his binoculars that morning.

The columns were about three or four miles from our location and seemed to consist of every type of vehicle, gun, tank and horse-drawn equipment that the German Army possessed. The column stretched as far as we could see. It was an awe-inspiring sight, and from the distance, it appeared to be a crushing force. … We … spent most of the day watching the columns inching along in a never-ending stream.

It was a bright sunny day, and the cloudless sky was constantly filled with Allied fighter-bombers that had a field day bombing and strafing the long, slow-moving columns of German vehicles and soldiers on foot. Allied pilots were not always very good at distinguishing friend from foe, and on many occasions Canadian and Polish units became unwitting targets. Yellow aircraft recognition panels or smoke grenades seemed to do nothing, and one South Alberta troop leader is reported to have remarked that setting off yellow smoke "was like poking a hornet's nest, they got agitated and came back twice as bad." On one occasion when the South Albertas' regimental headquarters was being shot up, the padre, Captain Albert Silcox, ran out into the path of an attack to hold up the Union Jack flag he used for burials; his brave deed, which brought the strafing to a halt, won him an MBE.

It was early afternoon on 18 August before a coordinated attempt was made to capture Trun. The village was finally taken by the Lincoln and Wellands supported by 'A' Squadron of the South Albertas, although, almost at the same time, No.2 Squadron of the Grenadiers with a company of the Lake Superiors

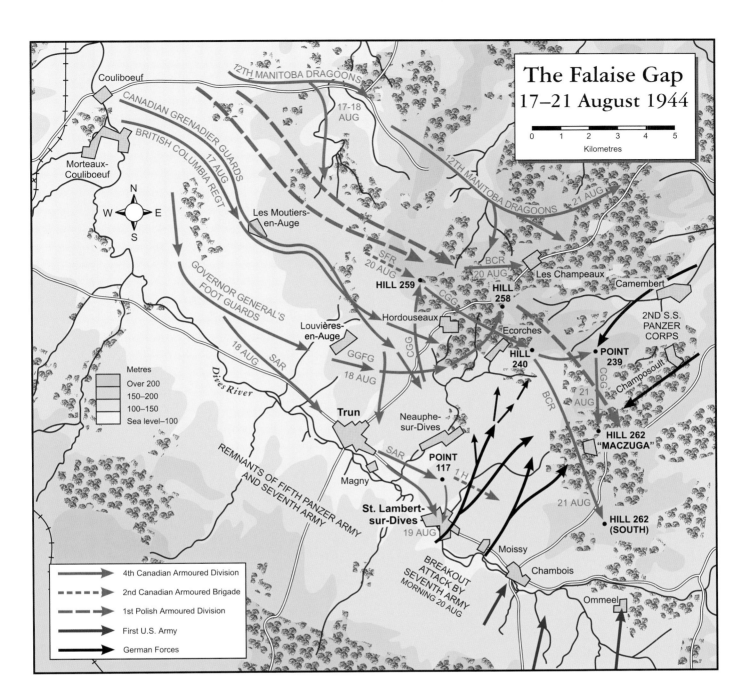

The Falaise Gap
17–21 August 1944

made an approach from the north-east. As hordes of German soldiers had begun to swarm into the area, the main preoccupation of all units was shooting every available weapon at the oncoming enemy to preserve the very tenuous hold on the northern pincer endeavouring to close the so-called 'gap'. At the same time literally thousands of German soldiers were surrendering, overwhelming the capability of most units to guard their prisoners or transport them out of the area.

However, the gap was still open in the five kilometres between Trun and Chambois. Simonds therefore gave new orders on the morning of 18 August: 4 CAD was to continue its advance from Trun to Moissy along the line of the River Dives, with 10 Brigade to complete the 'plug', while the Poles were to

move from Les Champeaux to Chambois to link up with the Americans and occupy the river-line from Chambois to Moissy. But, at the same time, 4 Armoured Brigade was tasked to continue the push to the north-east, in order to cut the highway leading from Chambois to Vimoutiers and 3 Division was brought in to take over the defence of the River Dives line north-west of Trun from 10 Brigade.

In the turbid situation quickly developing in the gap – where both offensive and defensive actions were essential at the same time, and this by units of three different divisions that were already intermingled and functioning without any clear boundaries – some improvisation and unconventional tactics may well have been required. What resulted, however, was a great deal of confusion within the Canadian Corps over the next two days, and the progressive sapping of the fighting capability of all of the divisions. General Kitching remarked in a post-war interview that had the Germans been able to mount a major attack, his division could not have held because it was so dispersed.

ST. LAMBERT-SUR-DIVES

The first step in plugging the still-open section of the gap south of Trun fell to the South Albertas. Major David Currie's 'C' Squadron, reinforced by 'B' Company of the Argylls (only 55 men), set out from Trun shortly after 1800 hours on 18 August. Their mission was to capture and hold the village of St. Lambert-sur-Dives, three kilometres to the south-east. St. Lambert was a typical if undistinguished Norman farming village, for the most part a single line of stone houses and outbuildings along both sides of the main road for nearly 1,000 metres. There was a cluster of houses around a large church at the south end, where a country road crossed the River Dives, and it was this crossing that had taken on enormous strategic importance: the stone bridge was one of only two that remained intact on the Dives, and the retreating Germans were pouring hundreds of vehicles across it. Strangely, no orders were given to take and hold the bridge.

It was dusk when the first troop of tanks arrived at the north end of the village, and almost immediately the lead Sherman was knocked out. At the same moment two RAF Spitfires strafed the column, wounding several of the men. After making a brief recce, Currie considered putting in a dismounted night attack but his CO, Lieutenant-Colonel 'Swatty' Wotherspoon, told him to wait until morning. Wotherspoon then deployed 'B' Squadron to Currie's laager on Hill 117, 800 metres north of the village, along with the regimental recce troop, four M-10 self-propelled anti-tank guns that had been attached to the unit, and his four RHQ tanks.

At about 0630 hours on 19 August Major Currie launched his attack into St. Lambert. A single tank supported the Argyll company as they moved cautiously along the main street, but very shortly the tank was hit by two armour-piercing rounds from a Mark IV and a Tiger at the southern end of the village. When a second Sherman came forward and tried to get past, it too was knocked out. The crew commander, Corporal 'Swede' Thuesen, remembered this incident:

> For years we had practised how to get out of a tank and, if we hadn't … we would never have gotten out. I guess I was knocked down a little on the stand inside the tank. My gunner got out before me … over top of me so I must have been pushed down. I felt something lukewarm running down my chest and stomach. I managed to get out and get the earphones off…. The Germans were shooting at us with small arms fire and we could hear it hitting the tank. We stood be-

hind the tank and none of us got hit but the drivers got burned. The tank brewed.

The Argyll company took over the lead, encountering only light resistance as one building after another was cleared by leap-frogging sections. On reaching the southern end of the village the forward platoon came face-to-face with a German Panther but the intrepid platoon commander destroyed it by climbing onto the tank and lobbing a grenade into an open hatch. By mid-morning the whole of St. Lambert was in Canadian hands, if only briefly.

The River Dives – perhaps three metres wide with steep, two metre-high banks in this area – was certainly an obstacle to vehicles, but men on foot could wade across at virtually any point, and many small parties of enemy troops had already begun to infiltrate through the village and the woods and ravines to the north and south. While some of the Germans were quite happy to surrender, many others were still willing to fight and sniping was a constant problem, so that several crew commanders in their turrets and dismounted tank crewmen were wounded.

By mid-afternoon on 19 August the situation in St. Lambert deteriorated seriously as the on-rush of retreating Germans reached staggering proportions. As the South Alberta history states:

> Hundreds, perhaps thousands of Germans were in and around the village and at one point 'late in the afternoon,' David Currie recorded, 'the tanks were running around in circles firing at one another to keep the enemy from climbing on top of them.' Just to make matters more lively, St. Lambert now began to come under German artillery fire.

Fortunately, 4 CAD artillery had finally come within range, and on several occasions Major Currie called down fire on his own positions to keep from being overrun.

Colonel Wotherspoon found that defending his sector of the gap with a tank force was not going to be easy; for there were simply too many Germans trying to make their way through the position. To better cover the river line he deployed 'A' Squadron in a linear defence on a ridge overlooking the highway and river north-west of St. Lambert. From there the tanks were able to bring fire onto large numbers of enemy vehicles well beyond the Dives and, to some extent, cover an enemy withdrawal route along the Foulbec creek. Later in the day, in a very questionable and risky tactical move, he sent 'B' Squadron out on its own to block a route in a heavily-wooded area northeast of the village, where fields of fire and visibility were rarely more than a hundred metres. What was desperately needed was more infantry for close-in defence and to guard the ever-growing number of prisoners (close to 2,000 were captured on 19

South Alberta Regiment Shermans in St. Lambert-sur-Dives, 19 August 1944. The tank on the right had just been knocked out trying to enter the village, and the other was trying to pass when it too was hit by anti-tank fire. (NAC PA116522)

August alone). In late afternoon 10 Brigade finally sent up a composite company from the Lincoln and Welland Regiment and, later, 'C' Company of the Argylls. Wotherspoon was also told that 9 Brigade would move in to relieve him the next day.

Several kilometres to the north-west, the Poles, at little more than brigade strength, had occupied an important feature at Hill 262 (which they nicknamed *Maczuga* or *Mace*), thus blocking a vital defile on the Chambois–Vimoutiers highway through which most of the withdrawing Germans were going to have to pass. They also got part of their divisional reconnaissance regiment through to Chambois, where they linked up with the Americans late on the afternoon of the 19th, but they made no attempt to move along the River Dives from Chambois to Moissy (one kilometre south of St. Lambert), which they had been ordered to occupy. The Falaise Gap was therefore never actually closed and many thousands of Germans escaped from the pocket in the undefended area between St. Lambert and Chambois on 19 and 20 August.

The South Albertas and their supporting infantry had a most uncomfortable time during the night of 19/20 August as the movement of German combat troops through the gap swelled enormously in the hours of darkness. Close to 2,000 German paratroopers from *2 Fallsschirmjägerkorps*, for example, made their way through 'A' Squadron's area without being detected. The full extent of the enemy withdrawal was, however, felt most intimately by the three tank crews and platoon of infantry deployed in the south end of the village near the church.

Hundreds of German vehicles, including tanks and self-propelled guns, crossed the nearby bridge and passed within metres of the Canadians on their way to the hills and Vimoutiers. The SAR 'B' Squadron crews in their isolated position on Hill 124 were also keenly aware of the huge number of Germans passing all around them, some right beside the tanks, but against such numbers there was little they could do and, sensibly, they held their fire.

If the South Albertas had experienced a traumatic day on the 19th, it was far worse on the 20th. Beginning at about 0800 hours the Germans attacked in mass, as Major Glen MacDougall's 1945 history of the South Albertas describes:

> Waves of infantry began to move against our positions … without fire support and seemingly without hope, only trying to break through to the Seine like some badly wounded animal. Our tanks had a field day, particularly the Crusaders with the Oerlikons. This is a wicked weapon firing some 450 rounds per minute of 20 mm. HE, with a graze fuse, so that if it touches a twig it will explode and blow a man's arm off.

There were even a few tanks with the stampeding horde of enemy infantry. One of these, a Tiger, shot up the building used by the Argyll platoon near the bridge and knocked out two Shermans that tried to engage it. Currie was forced to abandon the southern part of the village soon afterward, concentrating his remaining tanks and infantry in a tight defensive position at

Undoubtedly one of the best-known photos of the war: Major David Currie (third from the left with pistol in his hand) oversees the surrender of a group of Germans in St. Lambert-sur-Dives on 19 August 1944. It has been said that this is the closest we are likely to get to a photo of a man winning the Victoria Cross. (NAC PA111565)

the north end and bringing down heavy fire on any enemy that came in range. At one point Wotherspoon's regimental headquarters position was nearly overrun, and saved only by a counter-attack mounted by 'A' Squadron.

By the afternoon of 20 August the situation was even worse in St. Lambert. Currie was "barely hanging on. He had positioned his five remaining Shermans and his infantry, amounting to about 120 men ... to defend the houses around his headquarters. ... By early afternoon he had lost all four of his troop leaders and only five infantry officers were still on their feet...," states the regimental history.

Throughout the long afternoon Dave's men fired down the length of the village at the Germans, the Links and Argylls trying to hit the German soft-skinned vehicles and infantry, the SAR tanks trying to hit the German tanks and SPGs. Allied artillery fire continued to fall in the area, including a few short rounds that landed on Currie's positions. The streets and lanes at the southern end of St. Lambert became congested with burning vehicles intermixed with dead men and horses. The Germans returned the fire but made no attempt to attack – their goal was to get through the bottleneck....

Some help arrived in mid-afternoon – eight 17-pounder anti-tank guns belonging to the 103rd Battery, RCA, did remarkable work in bolstering Currie's tenuous position. Still the Germans continued to pour through St. Lambert and at a ford downstream at Moissy. During the night 'B' Squadron was literally overrun in their isolated position north of the village and had to pull out.

By the morning of 21 August the fighting on the River Dives had all but come to an end. The British were closing in on the rear of the Germans still in the pocket and there was little fight left in the enemy that remained. In St. Lambert, much of the day was spent rounding up prisoners; no one kept an accurate count, but one report estimates that close to 7,000 prisoners were taken by the South Albertas and their attached companies in the three days of the engagement.

The carnage during this battle was simply appalling, reminiscent of the slaughter of First World War battlefields. Literally thousands of German soldiers were cut down by the tanks' machine guns and main armament, and by the tremendous weight of shellfire fire brought down by the Canadian artillery. One report estimates that 2,000 enemy were killed and another 3,000 wounded on this narrow part of the 'front'. At 1700 hours on 21 August the South Albertas were relieved by units of 9

Troops of the Argyll and Sutherland Highlanders advancing into St. Lambert under the cover of a South Alberta Sherman, 19 August 1944. Note the destroyed Tiger tank on the right side of the road and the gun barrel protruding from the hedge. The turret has been blown off by an internal explosion. (NAC PA131348)

Brigade. In four days of more or less continuous action, they had fought one hell of a battle, losing thirteen of their men killed and 36 wounded.

Throughout the many hours of intense fighting in the village and the surrounding fields there were uncounted instances of bravery and exceptional devotion to duty, but one man stood out above all others. Their leader had consistently demonstrated outstanding courage and exemplary leadership, encouraging his men to carry on the face of overwhelming opposition by his calm and confident demeanour throughout the action and by his obvious sound judgement in directing the battle. For his leadership and valour in the fighting at St. Lambert, Major David Currie was awarded the Victoria Cross. This was the only VC given to a Canadian in all of the intense fighting in Normandy, and the only one ever awarded to a member of the Canadian Armoured Corps. The citation reads in part:

Major Currie's conduct and self-sacrifice were a magnificent example to all ranks of the force under his command. On one occasion he personally directed the fire of his command tank onto a Tiger tank which had been harassing his position and succeeded in knocking it out. During another attack, while the guns of his command tank were taking on other targets at longer ranges, he used a rifle from the turret to deal with individual snipers who had infiltrated to within fifty

Major David V. Currie, VC of the South Alberta Regiment. Major Currie was the only member of the Canadian Armoured Corps to be awarded the Victoria Cross during the Second World War. (NAC PA160836)

yards of his headquarters. On the one occasion when reinforcements were able to get through to his force, he led the forty men forward to their positions and explained the importance of their task as part of the defence. When, during the next attack, these new reinforcements withdrew under the intense fire brought down by the enemy, he personally collected them and led them forward into position again, where, inspired by his leadership they held for the remainder of the battle....

During this operation the casualties to Major Currie's force were very heavy. However, he never considered the possibility of failure or allowed it to enter the minds of his men. In the words of one of his non-commissioned officers, "We knew at one stage that it was going to be a fight to the finish, but he was so cool about it, it was impossible for us to get excited."...

The courage and complete disregard for personal safety shown by Major Currie will forever be an inspiration to his regiment: his conspicuous bravery and extreme devotion to duty in the presence of the enemy will remain an example to the Canadian Army for all time.

To the end of his life, the quiet and unassuming Currie always maintained that his Victoria Cross really belonged to the men who served with him at St. Lambert.

4TH ARMOURED BRIGADE

While the South Alberta Regiment was struggling to hold on to the northern part of the Falaise Gap at St. Lambert, the units of 4 Armoured Brigade were involved in a very different part of the battle to contain the remnants of the German armies in Normandy, and one that perhaps reflected the generally confused conditions that prevailed within much of II Canadian Corps during this fluid and unpredictable battle.

Readers will recall that the regiments of 4 Brigade were at the forefront of the Canadian charge into the area east of the River Dives on 17 August, and that the Grenadier Guards was the first unit to arrive in the area of Trun. Sealing the Falaise Pocket – closing the gap between the Canadian Corps, advancing from the north, and the Americans, coming from the south, so as to encircle and trap the bulk of the German combat forces in France – was the strategic aim. While part of 10 Brigade, with the South Albertas, was deployed forward along the River Dives, in the period 17 to 19 August the regiments of 4 Brigade and the remainder of 10 Brigade were directed to hold the higher ground behind Trun, in the area of Hordousseaux and Ecorches, so as to give depth to the defence. While they all occasionally had 'good shooting' at small parties of Germans that got through to their positions, none of the five major units (three armoured regiments and two infantry battalions) was heavily engaged while there.

Somewhere in the confusion of events and changing orders, the strategic objective seems to have been misplaced, however. The vital gap along the River Dives was never actually closed. While the Poles had been instructed on 19 August to secure the line of the river between Chambois and Moissy (one kilometre south-east of the South Albertas), they never complied, nor could they realistically have done so since they had already become heavily committed in the high ground around Mount Ormel (Hill 262), some five kilometres to the east. Why the relatively uncommitted units of 4 Brigade, or at least some of them, were not sent into this area has never been properly explained, but the consequence of leaving some three kilometres of the gap wide open was that a large part of the German forces in the pocket were enabled to escape unchallenged.

On 19 August, Brigadier Robert Moncel arrived from Corps headquarters to take over command of 4 Armoured Brigade. That evening he gave new orders to the brigade: they were to advance toward Vimoutiers the next day, with two aims: to continue blocking the escape of the Germans, and, at the same time, to

Some of the thousands of German prisoners captured by Canadians during the fighting to close the Falaise pocket. (NAC PA116509)

block an expected attack from outside the pocket by *2 SS Panzerkorps*. This was in line with an earlier directive to II Corps from First Canadian Army "to carry out active reconnaissance … in the direction of Vimoutiers," and it was also a response to intelligence reports (accurate, as it turned out) that the Germans were about to attack from the north to open an escape route.

The Governor General's Foot Guards deployed from positions at Hill 258 to Les Champeaux early on the morning of 20 August to secure a firm base for a brigade attack toward Vimoutiers, and the British Columbia Regiment moved into the same area. However, before the operation got underway it was cancelled and units were told to return to their original locations, in part because of the massive movement of Germans which began that morning through St. Lambert and the undefended area around Moissy.

In what was almost a belated effort to halt the mass cross-country movement of Germans fleeing from the area of St. Lambert, 4 Brigade was now ordered to occupy blocking positions to the east of Hordousseaux. In the early evening of 20 August, the Grenadier Guards, the British Columbia Regiment and the Algonquins moved to the area of Hill 240, east of Ecorches, while the Foot Guards and the Lake Superiors deployed to Point 239, 2,000 metres east of the Grenadiers. The area around Hill 240 overlooked a secondary road leading through a valley which was "littered with corpses and abandoned vehicles," probably as a result of air attacks. The Grenadier war diary describes the experience of

Brigadier Robert Moncel, commander of 4th Armoured Brigade 19 August 1944 to 9 July 1945. (NAC PA113686)

No.2 Squadron: "Every hedge and bush seemed to be filled with Heinies. Browning was sprayed around and the damage must have been very great. About 70 prisoners were taken after the shooting was over. The night was black and raining and the squadron had a sleepless night, their position with eight tanks and so many prisoners not being an enviable one." At Point 239, the Foot Guards also spent a tense night "in a high state of alert, with flares constantly dropping on the flanks.... enemy patrols were active, and two attempts were made to knock out tanks with bazookas."

The Foot Guards had a more lively time on the morning of the 21st, as Baylay's history reports:

At 0815 hours, just as the first crews were dismounting to cook breakfast under the tanks, the hill suddenly became alive with machine gun and anti-tank fire. An escaping German column of tanks was attempting to pass the regiment's position. The only route open to the enemy was the narrow road at the bottom of the hill ... and for once the crews and their friends from the Lake Superior Regiment and the anti-tank gunners were able to enjoy the most frequently encountered German method of doing battle – that of sitting back on a good defensive position and picking off the attackers as they advanced.

At the end of this brief battle the Foot Guards counted the enemy casualties: three S.P. guns, one Mark IV tank and a dozen wheeled vehicles destroyed, about fifty dead Germans, and many more wounded. Nearly 200 prisoners were captured.

RELIEF OF THE POLISH DIVISION

By 20 August, 1 Polish Armoured Division was cut off on *Maczuga*, or Mount Ormel (Hill 262 North). Under heavy attack from both east and west, it was in very serious trouble. Resupply vehicles had not been able to get through for two days, so they were desperately short of ammunition, fuel, food and water, and their many casualties urgently needed medical attention. On the evening of the 20th, General Simonds personally ordered Kitching to send 4 Armoured Brigade to rescue the Poles.

Starting out early on 21 August, the Grenadier Guards in the lead, the brigade (less the Foot Guards) moved off from Hill 240 *en route* to Mount Ormel. The Grenadiers, accompanied by the Lake Superiors, initially moved eastward to Point 239, held

Major-General Harry Foster, commander of 4th Armoured Division, 22 August to 30 November 1944. (NAC PA131220)

by the Foot Guards, from which they intended to attack directly southward, but on the way the lead squadron ran into two concealed SP guns and lost three Shermans before silencing them. From Point 239 Ned Amy's No.1 Squadron led, fighting through strong opposition to reach the Poles. The Grenadiers' history relates the story of this attack:

Throwing smoke to supplement the poor visibility caused by the rain and low clouds, the attacking force sped down into the valley from the far side of which anti-tank fire knocked out another tank, and small arms fire caused the L.S.R. to dismount. With all guns blazing we beat down the enemy infantry; Capt. Ghewey scored direct hits that disposed of a Mark IV tank and a Panther; the L.S.R. supported by half our tanks cleared the enemy from the now burning buildings and gardens, accounting for two more Panthers and capturing the main defensive position. After a short pause the advance continued up the hill into the woods where another Mark IV was set on fire.... Turning off to avoid it, our leading tanks, crashing their way through the bordering trees were suddenly confronted with two advancing Stuarts. Recognition was immediate; these were the last remaining Polish tanks making a final dash for help, and here we were.

Without delay the top of the hill, Point 262, was occupied. Here the scene was the grimmest. Scores of corpses were scattered all about. The road was blocked with derelict vehicles. Several hundred wounded and some seven hundred loosely guarded prisoners were lying in an open field. The Poles, isolated for three days cried with relief.

Just after the Grenadiers broke through to the crest of Mount Ormel, the British Columbia Regiment arrived. They were instructed to carry on southward, with the objective of capturing Hill 262 South, another three kilometres away. The approach was relatively uneventful. Douglas Harker's short history of the BCR relates that:

All available tanks laid a preliminary barrage on objective number one [a cluster of houses at the base of the hill] and then 'B' and 'C' Sqns. switched to the flanks while 'A' [under Captain Jim Tedlie] worked its way down the ravine and into the village. But there was no opposition. The area had been held only by infantry and as a result of our barrage they had all been either wounded, killed or driven into hiding. As soon as Hill 262 had been secured, we withdrew about a thousand yards to a more suitable defensive position.

While 4 Armoured Brigade was fighting its last significant action in the battle of Normandy, Major-General Kitching was called to Corps headquarters. Simonds told him that he was not satisfied with his performance and Kitching was unceremoniously sacked. This was no doubt most unfair; the problems that had occurred in 4 CAD since its introduction on the battlefield were, in large measure, the fault of Simonds routinely making last-minute changes to plans to which battle-inexperienced units could not react quickly. Kitching also had an incompetent armoured brigade commander, who, when killed, was temporarily replaced by officers who were not up to that job. He was deeply hurt, but took his leave with good grace and dignity and was sent back to Italy, where he served with distinction as Brigadier, General Staff in I Canadian Corps until the end of the war. Kitching's replacement was Major-General Harry Foster, a pre-war Strathcona, who came to the division fresh from commanding 7 Infantry Brigade.

4 CAD never had the same opportunity, as did 5 CAD in Italy, of being able to reflect on its operational performance in its first battles and carry out a deliberate training programme to correct apparent faults. There is no doubt, however, that during the actions in the Falaise Gap commanders at all levels showed far better practical application of all-arms cooperation tactics than had been seen, for example, in *Totalize*. The price

paid to learn the lessons that ought to have been brought out in training in England was, needless to say, very high.

Canadian soldiers who participated in the fighting in the Falaise Gap have a common recollection of the Armageddon-like horror of this battlefield. A staff officer in 4 CAD headquarters wrote the following report, which describes it well.

Our route was along a continuation of the German escape route … and which has been aptly termed "Dead Horse Alley". … The sights and smells along the verges of the road are even more frightful than those of last night. Bulldozers have made a pretty good job of clearing wreckage, dead horses and dead Germans to the sides. Both sides for miles are lined with smashed or burnt-out Tiger and Panther tanks, trucks, guns, half-track vehicles, busses, wagons of all sorts and dead horses, now badly swollen and some in the most grotesque positions. In among it all German bodies add to the scene of utter annihilation. The stench is terrific and a constant stream of cigarettes is the only thing that saves one's fifth sense…. It seems as though death and destruction reached out to the Germans no matter how hard they tried to avoid it along here.

The battle of Normandy was now over. A new phase of the war was about to begin – the pursuit of an enemy that had been defeated but would not yet give up.

CHAPTER 14

Normandy to the Scheldt: The Grand Pursuit

As the last battles of the Falaise Gap wound down, the war in North-West Europe took on a whole new character. General Montgomery issued instructions on 19 August for the rapid and close pursuit of the Germans through France and into the Low Countries. The important thing was to keep the enemy off-balance so that he would not have time to reconstitute and re-establish a new defensive line. First Canadian Army was tasked to clear the sector nearest the Channel coast while the British Second Army was to drive for Brussels and beyond. Meanwhile, two US armies were to head in the direction of Paris and then strike eastward.

The initial stage in this new phase of the war was the seizure of crossings over the River Seine, the first major obstacle on which the Germans might position a new defensive line. For this phase of the advance, II Canadian Corps was assigned an axis running from Vimoutiers, through Orbec and Bernay, to Elbeuf on the Seine. Once across the Seine, the Canadians were to dash along the French coast and into Belgium, capturing vital Channel ports along the way. Throughout these fast-paced pursuit operations, the three Canadian reconnaissance regiments – the 12th Manitoba Dragoons, 17th Hussars and 8th Reconnaissance Regiment – came into their own: well out in front of their supported divisions, they played a key part in events.

PURSUIT TO THE SEINE

The sixty-kilometre advance to the Seine began on 21 August, when 2 Division, led by the 8th Recce Regiment, pushed out on a broad front towards Livarot and Vimoutiers. Sergeant Charles Baget of 'A' Squadron described how,

"… the RAF had played havoc with German convoys and the number of destroyed vehicles lying in the ditches was incredible. In Vimoutiers the craters were a mess, and knocked out Tigers, SPs and soft-skinned vehicles cluttered what was left of the streets in the town," in the early stages of this advance.

Advancing well ahead of the infantry, once past Vimoutiers patrols scoured the ground on either side of the main routes assigned to the leading brigades. Other than the odd skirmish with small parties of stragglers, there was no significant contact with enemy troops until reaching Orbec. There, guided by members of the *Maquis* (the French Resistance), the leading troop had several short, sharp battles in the centre of town. Sergeant Baget:

We edged past [a] burning tank and … decided to make a mad dash up to the town square. When we reached the centre of town, lead started to fly and the other cars came up from the flanks…. The carriers were occupying themselves with a troublesome machine gun. They finally silenced it and took the crew prisoners. My gunner, in the meantime, had accounted for a motorcycle combination which came tearing around the corner. His Besa [machine-gun] burst caught them full on and made a gory mess of the three Germans riding on it.

An 8th Recce Regiment Lynx II scout car passes a destroyed King Tiger tank near Vimoutiers during the early stage of the pursuit to the River Seine, 22 August 1944. (NAC PA114370)

17th Hussars Fox armoured car and carrier moving through a French village during the pursuit, 23 August 1944. (Royal Canadian Hussars Museum)

Orbec was the first of many French villages liberated over the next few days. The general advance to the Seine began on the morning of 22 August. 2 Division, which had reached Orbec the previous day, was on the left flank of II Canadian Corps, heading for Bourgtheroulde, south-west of Rouen. In the centre was 3 Division moving on an axis of Orbec-Brionne-Elbeuf, and on the right was 4 CAD aimed at Broglie, Bernay and Pont de l'Arche. For this phase of the operation, the 12th Dragoons served as the division's reconnaissance element.

For the first two days, the recce units, for the most part, encountered only sporadic resistance, although sometimes German rearguards would allow patrols to pass through and then fire on heavier, follow-on troops. As the Canadian columns got closer to the river the number of rearguards increased, for the enemy was determined to protect crossing sites on the Seine until his combat forces were safely across. The 12th Dragoons stumbled into one such determined enemy position near Montreuil-l'Argille, and were stopped by the fire of three 88mm guns and two Panther tanks. The British Columbia Regiment, at the head of 4 Armoured Brigade, came up to clear the route and, in their attempt to push through, lost seven Shermans.

On the morning of 25 August the Dragoons had patrols on the south bank of the Seine at Poses and Pont de l'Arche, and the 17th Hussars, in front of 3 Division, were in Elbeuf. However, 2 Division, on the left, was encountering serious difficulty on the south side of the Fôret de la Londe, where the Germans had deployed elements of three divisions to protect the large body of troops still waiting south of Rouen for their turn to cross the river.

The Sherbrooke Fusiliers, attached to 2 Division, were intended to lead the infantry of 6 Brigade into the Fôret de la Londe on the night of 25 August, but as the lead squadron approached La Cambe they met fierce fire that brought the advance to a halt. The next day the division launched a major attack into the woods by 5 and 6 Brigades accompanied by Sherbrooke tanks. Unfortunately the tanks were only of limited value; because of steep slopes and densely packed large trees, they could not deploy off the few roads and tracks that existed and they were extremely vulnerable to well-concealed anti-tank guns. It took 2 Division four days of desperate fighting and nearly eight hundred casualties before the woods were finally taken, and that occurred only when the enemy chose to withdraw.

By the morning of 27 August, 3 and 4 Divisions had infantry across the Seine at Elbeuf and at Criqueboeuf. There was little opposition at Elbeuf, so this became the main crossing point for both divisions. Tank-carrying rafts were in operation by nightfall, and the first tanks across the river were the combined 'A/B' Squadron of the Fort Garrys, but shortly after first light on the 28th, two Bailey bridges began carrying vehicle traffic. The regiments of 4 Armoured Brigade were among the first to use the heavy bridge and the 12th Dragoons crossed over at mid-morning.

ON TO THE RIVER SOMME

After a stiff series of battles to capture Rouen and clear out a strong rearguard on the heights overlooking the Seine, the pursuit once again got underway early on 30 August. The Dragoons pushed out to the north-east, ahead of 4 CAD, with Forges-les-Eaux as their objective, the Hussars headed in the direction of Neufchatel in front of 3 Division, and the 8th Recce Regiment led 2 Division northward, *en route* to Dieppe. Each of the regiments advanced on two and sometimes three parallel routes and progress was very uneven, depending on how resolute German rearguards were. The *Battle History* of the 8th Recce Regiment describes one incident that is probably typical of the experience of all three:

> Events continued at high speed all morning and it was not long before the leading troops were out of wireless contact…. At Totes the leading troop came to an unexpected but definite halt. Lieut. Paton, in command of 9 Troop, had all he could handle when he contacted a retreating enemy convoy. Some fast shooting took place and one car drove through the enemy while the crew threw grenades right and left. As the following troops came up they joined in the fray, as did the anti-tank troop…. … was a weird scene. The inhabitants of the town, undeterred by the fact that the battle was raging, were plying the troops with champagne, vin rouge, vin blanc, etc. The battle was viewed by Major [Denny] Bult-Francis [the squadron commander] from the top story of the Cygne Hotel … where M. and Mme. Richard, kind-hearted proprietors, kept a steady flow of champagne into the glasses.

Another audacious exploit from this day is recorded in *The Regimental History of the 18th Armoured Car Regiment*. It describes the actions of Sergeant Ross Bell at Bierville, on the left flank of the 12th Dragoons, just after his troop leader had been killed:

> [On entering] the town of Bierville he encountered about sixty infantry and three anti-tank guns. With his vehicle guns ablaze he attacked them and succeeded in knocking the anti-tank guns off the road and liquidating their crews. The infantry were rather different. Some of them were killed by gunfire while the remainder fell victim to the vehicle itself. The crew members later ventured the opinion that a man is likely to be seriously injured when he is struck by a fourteen ton vehicle travelling at high speed. … The armoured car, having been extracted by a great mixture of skill and luck, moved on to find its way blocked by a Tiger tank. It is assumed that the crew of the tank had not paid particular attention to armoured fighting vehicle recognition courses, for the tank obligingly moved to one side of the road and the

Railway ties are unloaded from the back deck of a 12th Manitoba Dragoons Staghound armoured car to stabilize the exit from the pontoon bridge at Elbeuf, 28 August 1944. (NAC PA137296)

1st Hussars Shermans crossing the Seine at Elbeuf on 28 August 1944. (NAC PA113660)

An 8th Recce Regiment patrol, led by a Humber Mark IIIA light reconnaissance car, en route to Dieppe, 30 August 1944. (Canadian Army Photograph)

armoured car passed by. … The next group of the enemy consisted of a horse-drawn convoy with a few anti-tank guns. Sergeant Bell had his gunners open fire and claims to have killed between 70 to 80 horses not to mention 200 to 300 men. By this time all ammunition had been expended and shelter had to be sought.

Sergeant Bell was awarded the Military Medal for his courageous actions.

The rapid advance of all three recce regiments continued the next day, and another typical incident will serve to illustrate the hectic pace. This from *An Historical Account of the 7th Canadian Reconnaissance Regiment*, which describes the action of 1 Troop of 'A' Squadron at Bures on stumbling into some three hundred Germans as they rounded a bend:

The Regiment had learned its lessons long ago, and the one most closely adhered to by the troops was 'Hit the enemy first and hit him with everything you've got; one gets less casualties by inflicting casualties'. So it was with this in mind that the troop leader's car opened up immediately, shooting at everything…. Again all was confusion and surprise on the part of the enemy. … Germans were falling all over the area and lying in grotesque positions. The fire-power of the 37mm and Besa was doing unbelievable damage. After a couple of minutes the surprise was gone and the enemy began to reorganize. Soon, fire was being exchanged hotly. … Sgt. Raich joined the fray and one of the first jobs he did was to knock out the enemy's only anti-tank gun, which was very neatly pointed at Lieut. Pullam's car. …For the next three hours this battle raged…. Finally, the much-needed reinforcements began arriving … none too soon for the cars' ammunition was all but expended.

On 1 September 1944, the 8th Recce led a triumphal return of 2 Division to Dieppe, when Lieutenant L.A. McKenzie, commanding 1st Troop in 'A' Squadron, had the honour of leading the advance into the town:

As we came to the top of the big hill outside Dieppe we got our first view of the city, and dipping down into the valley we came upon an anti-tank ditch which was dug across the road. The civilians were already building a bridge with planks…. We rolled on and were the first troops to enter the city. Thousands of wildly cheering people climbed aboard the vehicles, covering the crews with flowers and plying them with liquor. Two Frenchmen began taking the pretty girls up onto the turrets of the Humbers where they were soundly kissed by all members of the crews.

That same day, the 17th Hussars liberated Le Tréport and the neighbouring town of Eu, and then proceeded inland to Abbeville, on the River Somme, but remained on the south side of the river. Further inland, the 12th Dragoons had also made speedy progress, reaching Warlus, about seven kilometres south of the Somme, before being stopped by an anti-tank screen. British units had also closed up to, and crossed, the Somme to the east of 4 CAD, dashing all German hopes of forming a defensive line on the river.

The 17th Hussars history gives an excellent insight into the daily life of reconnaissance troops at this time:

The most difficult picture to paint is that of the extreme fatigue suffered by the men during this all-out run. The troops were mounted in their vehicles and on the roll at first light each morning, and it was at that time that the high-pitched nervous strain started. Never did the crews of the lead vehi-

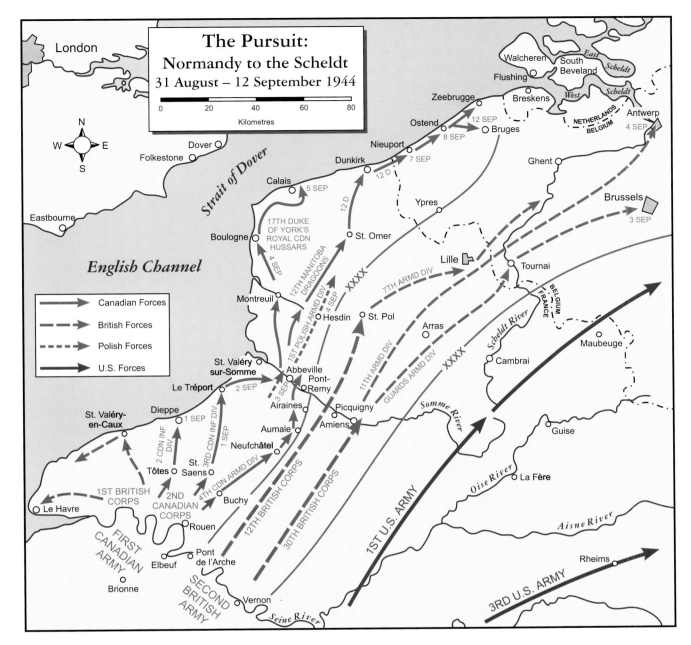

The Pursuit:
Normandy to the Scheldt
31 August – 12 September 1944

cle stop wondering just what was in store for them around the next corner. 'What's that peculiar looking thing under the big elm? An anti-tank gun? Give it a burst of Besa, Joe, and see what happens.' 'Yes, there does seem to be some furtive movement in the next village. Better get the rest of the vehicles in covering positions and we'll go and take a look.' Sometime it was a welcome relief to get involved in a sharp engagement, when only an hour ago you spent a year of your life in three minutes peering at a haystack suspiciously to find out later that the thing was just that – a haystack.

Lunch … usually took place when a troop liberated a town without much of a fight. The natives would go absolutely wild with glee and immediately rush about getting something for the men to eat. Had they had the time, the troopers would have eaten like kings…. However, what it in-

variably boiled down to was scooping a fried egg off a plate, pushing it down with a piece of black bread, washing the mouth out with a few large gulps of wine or cognac, … saying 'Merci beaucoup' to Madame la Grande France, and, with a roar of motors, 'Bashing on.'

This hectic existence of scrapping with the enemy, wondering what to do with large numbers of prisoners, evacuating casualties, sometimes burying friends, scooping up fried eggs, peering at suspicious haystacks, and 'Bashing on' kept up until last light when nightfall closed in on the troops, isolated them and left them wondering just where they were and what was around them. Naturally a good percentage of a troop was forced to keep watch while the remainder slept, at first with one eye open, and finally like babies.

BOULOGNE AND CALAIS

Bridges over the Somme were completed on 3 September, and early the next day 3 Division made a dash up the coast toward the port of Boulogne, which the division was tasked to liberate. Once again probing well forward of the main body for enemy that might hinder or delay its movement, 17th Hussar patrols scoured the terrain covering the main routes. They ran into much more opposition in this move than had been the case a few days earlier, and there were a number of pitched battles. The regiment is especially proud of an action involving 'C' Squadron at Incheville, near Montreuil. Here the assault troop fought bitterly for a bridgehead over the River Canche, and, working under fire, members of a scout troop rebuilt a damaged bridge.

Staghound Armoured Cars in a Smoke Screen, painting by Bruno Bobak. The painting depicts a 12th Manitoba Dragoons vehicle. (Canadian War Museum CWM11986)

The squadron commander, Major Allen, lined up the entire squadron – Humbers, M-10s, carriers, scout cars – and sent them crashing over the bridge in line-ahead and up the hill to take the town, blazing away with every machine-gun, anti-tank weapon, mortar and 37mm as they went. When the smoke cleared away, the enemy was either dead, captured or well on his way home.

While 3 Division was still making its way to Boulogne, the port of Antwerp fell to the British on the afternoon of 4 September. In the flood of good fortune which the Allied cause had encountered over the previous two weeks, this prize was not fully appreciated. The greatest port in north-west Europe had been taken, and with its docks intact. The problem of keeping the advancing Allied armies supplied over a route that led all the way back to the beaches of Normandy was seemingly eliminated at one blow. With his eyes on the Ruhr, Field Marshal Montgomery began to work out a plan for a war-winning offensive into the German heartland. In the meantime, however, the valuable prize of Antwerp was of little use, for the Germans still held both shores of the fifty-kilometre-long Scheldt Estuary which controlled the seaward approaches into Antwerp.

Boulogne and Calais, although not major ports, were thus still vitally important to the Allied cause, but both had been heavily garrisoned by the enemy, and the German commanders had specific orders from Hitler that they were not to capitulate. It would take a deliberate attack, involving heavy artillery and massive fleets of bombers, to take them, and the specialist equipment was not going to be available until after the British attack on Le Havre, so 3 Division was going to have to wait.

Meanwhile, the 12th Manitoba Dragoons continued to work their way northward along the Channel coast. In turn, they liberated Nieuport on 7 September and Ostend the next day. Zeebrugge, clearly, was going to be held at all costs by the Germans, but the Dragoons went on to liberate the magnificent mediaeval city of Bruges on 12 September.

The assault on the outer defences of Boulogne began, finally, on 17 September, and both the Fort Garrys and what was soon to become the 1st Armoured Personnel Carrier Regiment played important roles at several stages of the fighting. After very tough battles, and despite Hitler's orders, Boulogne capitulated on 22 September.

Calais, thirty kilometres to the north, was the next major objective of 3 Division. Here the 17th Hussars had done a superb job of 'encircling' the port and Cap Gris Nez (from which heavy guns had intermittently bombarded Dover since 1940) since 5 September. Beginning on 25 September, the assault got underway. This, too, was a difficult and tricky battle, and support was provided where possible by both the 1st Hussars and the Fort Garrys, but it was not until 1 October that resistance ceased, and by then the Germans had done so much damage to the port facilities that they could not be used for more than a month.

(Right) Carriers belonging to the 17th Hussars liberate yet another French village as the pursuit continued toward the Somme. (RCH Museum)

(Below) French civilians watch as 4th Armoured Brigade Shermans pass along the main street of a village during the pursuit. (NAC PA135957)

(Right) The 12th Manitoba Dragoons, well in advance of the remainder of First Canadian Army, liberated much of the Belgian coast. Here a Staghound is shown moving into Blankenberge, Belgium. (NAC PA140862)

Before an Attack, painting by Captain Alex Colville. (Canadian War Museum CWM12119)

4 CAD: THE BRESKENS POCKET

Although the Allies controlled Antwerp and its docks by the end of the first week of September, they did not control the shores of the West Scheldt estuary that commanded the approaches to the city. The German 15th Army held the south shore, where it had been squeezed into a pocket with its back to the Scheldt and the North Sea. For practical purposes the Leopold Canal on the south, the Braackman Inlet on the east and the Scheldt itself to the north-east, defined the pocket. The enemy's only escape route was through the port of Breskens and across the mouth of the estuary to the South Beveland peninsula that formed the north shore of the West Scheldt.

Approaching the pocket from its western side, the first task facing 4 CAD was the crossing of the Ghent Canal at Moerbrugge. This was accomplished after hard fighting and the Division pushed on toward the towns of Maldegem and Eecloo. It was while they were at Eecloo on 17 September that they saw, passing overhead, the gigantic airborne armada that was the beginning of Operation *Market Garden*, Montgomery's attempt to win a bridgehead over the Rhine. Had it succeeded the consequent fighting in the Scheldt might never have taken place, but once it was known that the airborne assault had involved 'a bridge too far', the struggle for the Breskens pocket was resumed in earnest.

First Canadian Army's two armoured divisions were both put to work. Major-General Maczek's 1st Polish Armoured Division was to clear the area east of the Ghent–Terneuzen Canal, which ran from south to north emptying into the West Scheldt.

8th Recce Regiment 6-pounder anti-tank gun prepared for action, Bergues, Belgium. (NAC PA141720)

4 CAD was to clear the land to the west of the canal as far north as the Leopold Canal and, while it maintained pressure on the Germans from the south, 3 Canadian Division would make preparations for an attack into the pocket.

In front of 4 CAD was its armoured reconnaissance regiment, the South Albertas. As their regimental history notes, the challenges of recce in Holland centred on the crossing of water obstacles:

Lieutenant Ed Reardon's Crusader [an anti-aircraft tank with two 20mm Oerlikon guns] was just approaching a small bridge when his driver skidded to a halt and I [Lieutenant Reardon] hollered "What's going on?" I looked over the side of the tank and there was a sign in English saying "Fresh eggs." So we sent the co-driver over and we covered him very closely and everything seemed fine and he came back with a big basket of eggs and was just handing it in when "powww!" the bridge went up from end to end. If we hadn't stopped for eggs, we would have been in the middle of that bridge.

It was at this time the crewmen of the Canadian Armoured Corps became the happy recipients of new-style rubber ankle boots and the new tank suit – an ingenious piece of kit that could double as a sleeping bag. Called a 'Zoot Suit' by the troops (Zoot suits were a civilian clothing fad), it was covered in zippers and pockets and had a parka-style hood, and it would survive on into the 1960s in Militia regiments. Of equal importance to morale was the institution of a daily rum ration to keep out the raw autumn weather.

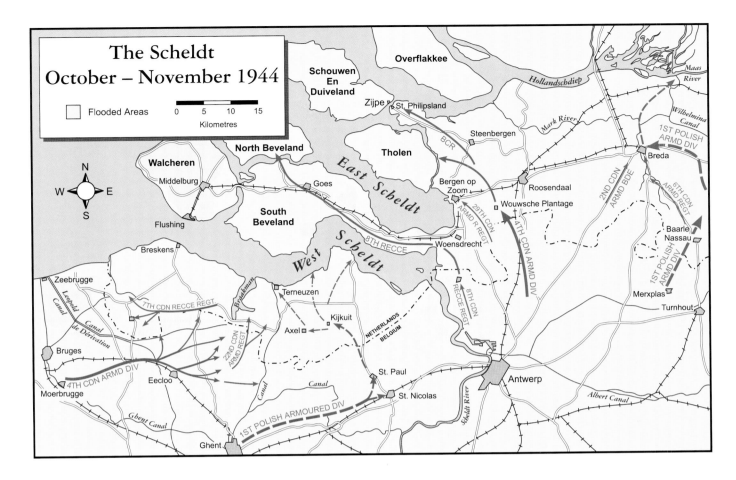

The Scheldt October – November 1944

Flooded Areas

0　5　10　15
Kilometres

Overflakkee

Schouwen En Duiveland

Zijpe · St. Philipsland

North Beveland

Walcheren

Middelburg

Flushing

South Beveland

Goes

Breskens

Zeebrugge

Terneuzen

Kijkuit

Axel

7TH CDN RECCE REGT.

2ND CDN ARMD REGT

Bruges

Eecloo

Moerbrugge

Ghent Canal

St. Paul

St. Nicolas

1ST POLISH ARMOURED DIV

4TH CDN ARMD DIV

Ghent

Tholen

East Scheldt

Steenbergen

BCR

Bergen op Zoom

Roosendaal

Wouwsche Plantage

29TH CDN ARMD R REGT

Woensdrecht

8TH RECCE

West Scheldt

4TH CDN ARMD DIV

8TH CDN RECCE REGT

NETHERLANDS
BELGIUM

Antwerp

Schelde River

Albert Canal

Hollandschdiep

Mark River

Maas River

Wilhelmina Canal

1ST POLISH ARMD DIV

Breda

2ND CDN ARMD BDE

6TH CDN ARMD REGT

Baarle Nassau

1ST POLISH ARMD DIV

Merxplas

Turnhout

3 CANADIAN DIVISION: THE BRESKENS POCKET

On 9 October, 3 Division was introduced to the Breskens battle, their task being to clear the pocket from its eastern to its western boundary, the point where the Leopold Canal emptied into the North Sea near Zeebrugge. It would take them nearly a month of hard fighting to complete the mission, and unfortunately in the course of the fighting a large portion of the trapped German forces would manage to escape, through Breskens, to the north shore of the Scheldt.

During this operation, the 17th Hussars, covered the division's left flank. The regiment's introduction to the pocket came when they were tasked to occupy positions held by the Highland Light Infantry.

Shortly after the troops had got into position, 'first light' broke and, as the degree of visibility increased, the men, peering out of the trenches which lined the dykes they had taken over, looked with interest on their new battle-ground. The polders seemed to stretch for miles in front of them broken only by the few separating dykes and the smashed structure of what had been a farmhouse. Water lay everywhere and, half submerged in it, cattle – some dead and bloated; others alive and miserable. Everything looked dead and, if not so, – doomed. This was the 'Scheldt.'

2 CANADIAN DIVISION: OPERATIONS ALONG THE TURNHOUT–ANTWERP CANAL

While 3 Division was slogging through the soggy polders of the Breskens pocket, 2 Division, with the Fort Garry Horse in support, was involved in operations north-east of Antwerp, at Turnhout. Their activities carried them south-west along the line of the Turnhout–Antwerp canal, clearing the north bank, before, just north of Antwerp, they turned north to close-up to the landward end of the South Beveland peninsula at Woensdrecht. The 8th Recce Regiment had just been re-equipped with Daimler armoured cars in place of the Humbers that had carried them through France and Belgium, and the regiment noted that its soldiers "were loud in its praise mainly because of its lower silhouette and the superiority of the two-pounder over the 37mm.... The armament of the recce regiment now far

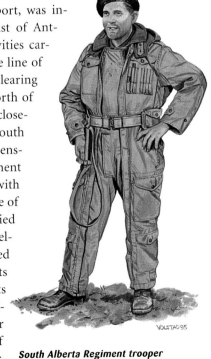

South Alberta Regiment trooper in Winter Crewsuit. **Painting by Ron Volstad. (Directorate of History and Heritage)**

exceeded the laid down establishment and carriers and half-tracks bristled with .50 Brownings which had been obtained through unofficial channels. It's wonderful what a P.38 or a Luger will obtain at a 'Yankee' airfield."

8th Recce's advance north of Antwerp was swift but not without incident:

> We were all astonished by the fruit grown in this part of Holland. The pears were literally the size of boxing gloves weighing between a pound and a pound and a half. Apples were also plentiful as many of the troops can verify. As we passed through the liberated villages the cheering populace threw them to the vehicle crews. Many an unsuspecting crew commander, intent on his map reading, caught a broadside of ripe apples. Considering the velocity of the thrown fruit and the forward movement of the vehicles, it was practically impossible to catch them and we had cause to wonder whether such gifts were delivered with malice before thought.

South Alberta Regiment tank and a 12th Dragoons Staghound destroyed during the attack into the wooded area known as Wouwsche Plantage, south of Bergen-op-Zoom, Holland. Note the Panther track welded to the hull of the Sherman. (South Alberta Regiment Archives)

4 CAD: OPERATIONS NORTH OF ANTWERP

As an aid to 2 Division's advance from Antwerp to Woensdrecht, 4 CAD was tasked to protect its right (eastern) flank, and divided into two battle groups, one group to clear each side of Highway 10 which runs due north to join the cities of Antwerp and Roosendaal. The armoured regiments east of the

highway were the British Columbia Regiment and the South Albertas, while west of it were the Governor General's Foot Guards and the Canadian Grenadier Guards. With their accompanying infantry, the tanks fought their way north, crossing one waterway after another and battling a determined enemy for every hamlet and farmhouse. It was in one such battle for a Dutch village, on 24 October, that the Grenadier Guards lost one of the most highly decorated and respected crewmen of the Corps, Sergeant Samuel 'Moe' Hurwitz, DCM, MM. After taking the objective with only his own tank, the remainder of the troop having been stopped, the sergeant was severely wounded and his tank destroyed. He died soon after in enemy hands.

Sergeant Hurwitz, the only member of the Corps to win both the DCM and MM during the Second World War, had earned his Military Medal in Normandy on 8 August and his Distinguished Conduct Medal in Holland on 20 September. On both occasions he had dismounted from his tank and eliminated enemy strongholds with his vehicle's machine-gun.

4 CAD's advance was slow and difficult as enemy resistance was stubborn and they made extensive use of mines and booby traps, as the South Alberta Regiment's history explains:

Scout Car Making a Crossing on Improvised Ferry. **Painting by William Ogilvie, depicting the crossing of 'A' Squadron of the 8th Recce Regiment to liberate the island of North Beveland on 1 November 1944. (Canadian War Museum CWM13553)**

Column of Fort Garry Horse Shermans along the Beveland Canal in Holland, 30 October 1944. (NAC PA138429)

The defences [of the Wouwsche Woods, south of Bergen-op-Zoom] were elaborate and well-concealed. Tank movement was limited, particularly in fire effect. The enemy possessed, (and, since he planned an eventual retirement, was prone to use) large stores of shells and mortar bombs dumped here for just such a stand. The presence of many anti-personnel mines, wire, and other obstacles concealed in the underbrush made infantry infiltration difficult, particularly at night. To make matters worse the area had been the home of a German mine and demolitions training school and the instructors, specialists in their trade, had supervised the layout of the mine defences.

It took four days of heavy fighting but on 27 October South Alberta tanks, led by Lieutenant Danny McLeod, entered the city of Bergen-op-Zoom.

2 DIVISION: THE BEVELAND PENINSULA

Once the base of the South Beveland peninsula had been secured through the division's capture of Woensdrecht, aided by 'A' and 'B' Squadrons of the Fort Garry Horse, the division turned west. The Garrys noted with amusement, however, that:

Shortly after the town of Woensdrecht had been captured, the provost came dashing up in a jeep and tacked up a sign on one of the first telephone poles leading into the town, warning fellows that the town was out of bounds unless on duty and that the looting penalty was death. During the next five days the majority of the buildings were almost completely demolished by heavy German shellfire.

The advance along the South Beveland peninsula started with an armoured thrust by 'A' Squadron of 8th Recce, supported by a Fort Garry tank troop and an infantry company. It was quickly stopped. All of the armoured vehicles were destroyed, but amazingly the only human casualty was a slightly wounded recce crewman. A second attack succeeded and soon the scout cars were leading the way across South Beveland, encountering water, mud and mines in flushing out enemy resistance. The supporting tanks of the Fort Garrys were hampered by the terrible going and could only be used to help shoot the infantry onto their objectives.

With South Beveland secured, 'A' Squadron crossed the narrow strait to undertake the liberation of the island of North Beveland. They used everything that could float in making the crossing and caught the German garrison of some two hundred men completely by surprise. Lieutenant Earle MacLeod gained a Military Cross by capturing the main town on North Beveland, along with the garrison commander, with just his own troop.

At the western end of the South Beveland peninsula was a 1.2-kilometre-long causeway leading to the island of Walcheren. The crossing of the Walcheren causeway was an epic battle, but

(Above) South Alberta Regiment tanks, led by Captain Danny McLeod, entered Bergen-op-Zoom, Holland, 27 October 1944. (NAC PA140896)

(Below) A Governor General's Foot Guards tank crew get their orders, near Bergen-op-Zoom, 6 November 1944. (NAC PA145519)

it was an infantry epic that opened with 'B' Squadron FGH, supporting the Calgary Highlanders. The tanks were themselves unable to cross because the Germans, near the halfway point, had cratered the 40 metre-wide causeway, and, at the far end, an anti-tank gun was sited to fire straight down it. After last light the frustrated western regiments withdrew and the job was turned over to the British, who found an alternate route through shallow water and established a bridgehead on the far shore. Walcheren would eventually fall to a combined land-based and sea-borne attack. Veterans of 2 Armoured Brigade's 1st Hussars with experience in amphibious operations were detached to 79 (British) Armoured Division to help train the troops who would be involved.

4 CAD: NORTH OF ANTWERP

While 2 Division captured Woensdrecht and then moved onto the Beveland peninsula, 4 CAD had continued moving north, closing first on Bergen-op-Zoom and then Steenbergen. In early

November the British Columbia Regiment and their infantry partners of the Lake Superior Regiment finally reached the sea at St. Philipsland. To their front, across a narrow channel lay the island of Schouwen en Duiveland and its harbour of Zijpe, and in the harbour the Canadians spotted four German naval vessels. Lieutenant R.H. Goepel's troop engaged all four, sinking three and damaging one. A bell from one of the sunken ships was recovered and hangs today in the Officers' Mess of the BCR.

After 2 Division and the Garrys had left Turnhout in their move south-west toward Antwerp, the remainder of 2 Armoured Brigade came under command of the British 49 (West Riding) Division, to pursue operations in a northerly direction leading to Breda. Armoured infantry battle groups were formed, the 1st Hussars and the Sherbrooke Fusiliers working with a battalion of the Lincolnshire Regiment. (During the Second World War, for whatever reason, it was frequently the case that the armour of one nation preferred working with the infantry of another. This seems to have been so with 2 Armoured Brigade and 49 Division, the two formations becoming fast friends.)

1 Polish Armoured Division moved on 2 Brigade's right (eastern) flank and liberated the ancient city of Breda. After the capture of Breda, the soldiers of the three allied armies pushed on the remaining 25 kilometres to the banks of the Maas River. Here they would stay throughout the coming winter.

WINTERING ON THE MAAS

At the beginning of November, 2 Armoured Brigade, minus the Fort Garrys but accompanied by the Lincolnshire battalion, followed the Canadian Armoured Corps Band through the streets of Breda, past thousands of cheering civilians. The next day the Garrys, leaving South Beveland, rejoined the brigade, but *en route* they stopped at Ghent to form a guard of honour as Field Marshal Montgomery presented decorations that had been earned in the Normandy campaign to members of 3 Division and some of their comrades from 2 Armoured Brigade.

The next three months, 8 November 1944 to 8 February 1945, would see First Canadian Army wintering on the River Maas, the monotony broken only by patrol work and the periodic rotation of units and formations into and out of the line. The Canadians occupied the western portion of the Allied line, from the North Sea to a point north of Venlo. Just east of the mid-point of the Canadian front there was a bulge to the north, the Nijmegen salient. This feature was a residue of Operation *Market Garden*, and included two bridges across the Maas, a rail bridge and a road bridge. They were the only crossing points in Allied hands and the Canadians were told that they must hold them at all costs. Despite repeated enemy efforts to destroy them, that is what they did.

Looking at the disposition of the Canadian armoured troops along the Maas from left (west) to right (east), the 12th Manitoba Dragoons were on the extreme left flank, under command of I (British) Corps which, in turn, came under First Canadian Army, and they were tasked with patrolling the lower Maas. A working telephone line was discovered in St. Philipsland (the community on the coast that had been the scene of the BCR's 'naval battle') which was linked with territory still in German control on the north bank of the river. The Dutch underground passed messages over this line which were then conveyed by the Dragoons to higher headquarters. When word arrived that the partisans on the other end of the telephone line were in trouble, a Dragoon rescue party crossed the channel to attempt their rescue. They were, unfortunately, too late.

Canadian Troopers Guarding the Nijmegen Bridge. Painting by Captain Alex Colville depicting men of the 17th Hussars protecting the vital bridge at Nijmegen, Holland, which the Germans repeatedly tried to destroy in early November 1944. (Canadian War Museum CWM12131)

(Below) Canadian Grenadier Guards tank in the mud near Nijmegen, late November 1944. Mud and flooded ground had become the major hindrance to the employment of armour during the winter of 1944-1945. (NAC PA164019)

Further inland, 4 CAD was located in the 's Hertogenbosch area and also under command of I (British) Corps. In late December it was relieved by 1 Polish Armoured Division, the Canadians moving back to Boxtel. In early January the Poles would become involved in fighting at Kapelsche Veer and, at mid-month, the divisions would once again trade places, 4 CAD taking over the struggle at Kapelsche Veer (discussed in the following chapter). Farther to the east, in the Nijmegen salient, 2 Armoured Brigade was tasked with a counter-attack role in support of their, by now, old friends in 49 Division.

The Governor General's Foot Guards history gives the flavour of the times:

> The Regiment was destined to pass most of the cold, wet, Dutch winter in this location [near 's Hertogenbosch], which it left eventually with a feeling of leaving home. It was an area of poor farming country and the troops were billeted in barren little barns and farmhouses along the highway. They were received by the civilians with great hospitality however, and when the tanks departed, they left a community of real friends as well as some broken hearts....
>
> The civilians were very poor and had been just recently liberated. Here one saw for the first time the subtler effects of the 'New Order', listless children covered with nutritional sores and sturdy farmers reduced to the servility of begging for garbage. It soon became the custom for long queues of civilians to attend the meal parades, waiting in bright anticipation for what might remain, and as one walked to the garbage pits one saw eager little hands scooping leftovers from the dirty plates. The NAAFI issue of chocolate bars and cigarettes habitually found themselves in those grateful hands.

Apart from the warm hospitality of the locals, the Foot Guards also got to enjoy their first indoor baths and showers since they had left England, three-and-a-half months previously.

At the beginning of December there were changes in the command structure. On 1 December Major-General Harry Foster exchanged places with the commander of 1 Division, Major-General Chris Vokes – a move that took the former off to Italy. A week later, newly promoted, Brigadier George Robinson arrived from Italy, where he had been commanding the 8th Hussars with great distinction. In taking over 2 Armoured Brigade, Robinson was, in a sense, coming home, for he had been the second-in-command of the 1st Hussars when he had left for Italy. An officer of exceptional talent, according to those who knew him personally, the circumstances of the war were such that he would seldom be in a position to demonstrate his abilities.

On assuming command, one of the important issues Robinson tackled was tank-infantry co-operation. Although one of the tasks of independent armoured brigades was support to infantry divisions, very little training time had been expended on this aspect of armoured warfare. Most of what the tank crews knew about it had been learned the hard way – on the job. Throughout the Corps, speaking in broad terms, those units that had been converted from infantry tended to do better at the combined tank/infantry tasks, primarily because they were already familiar with the infantryman's problems and perspective, but many infantrymen complained long and hard about the support, or lack of it, provided by armour. Sometimes the criticism was justified; sometimes it was not. The tankers, for their part, rarely criticised the performance of the infantry. They knew better.

The other issue Brigadier Robinson tackled was gunnery. Not only direct fire, the bread and butter of tankers, but also indirect fire. Indirect shoots across the Maas became a staple.

Plans were already underway for the next campaign, the clearing of the west bank of the Rhine in anticipation of an assault crossing and the drive into Germany. The date for the opening of the new offensive was 1 January 1945. The Germans, however, had their own plans and struck first, in the Ardennes. The Canadians, with a few exceptions, did not get involved in the Ardennes fighting, but the battle did upset Montgomery's timetable. Five more weeks would pass before they were finally able to start on their own offensive.

CHAPTER 15

The Battles
for the Rhineland

At the 1943 Casablanca conference the Western Allies adopted unconditional surrender as the only grounds upon which they would end the war with Germany. It was a popular decision. In 1918 the First World War had ended with an armistice, followed eight months later by a negotiated peace treaty, and the Nazis had used this sequence of events to claim that the German armies had never been defeated in the field – that in fact their fighting men had been 'stabbed in the back' by traitors at home. By demanding unconditional surrender, the Allies were going to avoid the error of 1918, but they had not completely thought through all of the implications of their policy, and Hitler would fully exploit that oversight.

After the successful landings in Normandy, and as the Soviets came close to East Prussia, the German propaganda machine hammered home the message that peace would bring no relief, but only unknown terror for the German people. The Allies, bent on revenge, would have absolute power, absolute control, over the former Reich. No one, certainly no national government, would be present to speak on behalf of the German people. Better, the Nazis said, to die fighting than to surrender and place your family and your home under the rule of the Communists and their fellow-travellers.

The policy of unconditional surrender meant that in the early months of 1945 yet another series of battles would be fought on the Western Front. Germany had lost the war, but the war was not yet over and some 8,942 Canadian soldiers would die winning the last campaign – the Battles of the Rhineland.

Field Marshal Bernard Montgomery had hoped to end the war in 1944. Using airborne forces to secure three key river crossings and with an army corps as an assault force, he planned to cut a path 110 kilometres deep through Holland, then cross the Rhine and drive towards Berlin. His plan was overly ambitious. The Rhine crossing – 'the bridge too far' at Arnhem – could not be held, and his advance was stopped in its tracks. The Allied armies were thus condemned to spend the winter of 1944-45 on the banks of the Maas River in eastern Holland just a few kilometres from the German border.

II CANADIAN CORPS: FROM THE MAAS TO THE RHINE

II Canadian Corps, fresh from its victory in the Scheldt, replaced British units along the Maas in early November. In static conditions reminiscent of the trench lines of the Great War, there was little for armour to do other than the maintenance of

Grave of a Canadian Trooper. **Painting by Captain Alex Colville. (Canadian War Museum CWM 12164)**

303

observation posts and patrol lines along the Maas. The 12th Manitoba Dragoons, for example, held responsibility for covering 40 kilometres of front. Trooper D.A. Nicholson later recalled that the crewmen on radio watch would share the limited number of frequencies with the enemy, the Germans using the airwaves during certain hours and the Canadians at other times.

A massive armoured operation to clear the western bank of the Rhine was to have started on New Year's Day 1945, but Hitler's December offensive in the Ardennes caught the Allies off guard and upset their timetable. The major attack was now delayed until early February and meanwhile subsidiary operations were undertaken elsewhere to position the Allied armies for the campaign. One such activity was Operation *Blackcock*, mounted to clear out the Heinsberg salient, a thirty-kilometre wide triangle of resistance located north of Aachen. The task was accomplished between 14 and 26 January by XII (British) Corps, who had under their command two Canadian units, 1st Canadian Rocket Battery, RCA, and 1st Canadian Armoured Carrier Regiment (1 CACR), the 'Kangaroos'.

The Rocket Battery consisted of twelve launchers each containing 32 barrels that fired 3-inch rockets each containing 12.5 pounds of high explosive – the equivalent of a 6-inch naval shell. A salvo of 384 rockets landing in a concentrated area was lethal and highly demoralising to any survivors. A plan to use the rockets, combined with other indirect fire weapons, including artillery, mortars, anti-aircraft guns and tanks, was developed. Christened a 'Pepperpot', it would become a Canadian trademark in the battles for the Rhineland.

First developed using the hulls of SP guns during the Normandy campaign, by October 1944 the Kangaroo was a Ram tank with its turret removed. A poor tank, the turretless Ram became a useful armoured personnel carrier. Each vehicle had a crew of two as well as two .30 calibre machine guns, one mounted on the bow and the other on the turret ring. Each of the four troops in a squadron held sixteen Kangaroos, with squadron headquarters employing a further five. A troop could lift an infantry company and a squadron could carry an entire battalion.

For *Blackcock*, 1 CACR supplied two troops from 'B' Squadron, but problems arose because they were 'under command' of the infantry, as opposed to the more usual relationship of 'in

A 'Kangaroo' of 1st Armoured Personnel Carrier Regiment during Operation *Blackcock* near Cleve, Germany, 16 February 1945. (NAC PA137744)

support'. One British infantry brigadier took the 'under command' designation to heart and appropriated a Kangaroo as his personal vehicle, thus condemning some of his men to walking into battle when they should have been lifted in a tracked, splinter-proof carrier. In spite of the difficulties with the command relationship the unit gave splendid support to the infantry and earned high praise for their courage and efficiency.

KAPELSCHE VEER

When the Allied armies closed up to the Maas in November 1944, the island of Kapelsche Veer (nine kilometres long by two kilometres wide), was left unoccupied by both sides, it being of no military value. But in December the Germans moved in a company-sized outpost whose function was to provide a battlefield inoculation for green troops. The Allies, upon discovering the enemy's presence, determined to claim the island for themselves and thus began a series of three attacks, each of which ended in failure. The Polish Armoured Division and the Royal Marines having been shut out, the task was now passed to 4 CAD, and so began the Canadian involvement in one of the most disagreeable and essentially pointless actions of the Second World War. The defenders were German paratroopers, the attackers would be 10 Infantry Brigade (the Lincoln and Welland Regiment, Algonquin Regiment and Argyll and Sutherland Highlanders of Canada) supported by the armour of the South Alberta Regiment (SAR) and the fire support of the British Columbia Regiment (BCR).

Engineers of the 9th Field Squadron, RCE, built a bridge to the island at its eastern extremity which allowed 'C' Company

During the winter of 1944-1945 much of the Dutch countryside was flooded because of damage to the dikes and canals, limiting movement in many areas to roads and the tops of dikes. (NAC PA131221)

of the Lincoln and Wellands to cross. At the same time the Lincoln's 'A' Company landed near the western end of the island by means of amphibious troop carriers called Buffaloes, while a troop of the SAR provided fire support. Both company attacks had to be along the road that topped the dyke running up to the Germans' main defensive position, which was a small harbour located on the island's north side. The initial attack having failed, the following day another attack was mounted, this time using a battalion on each side of the objective, supported by the SAR's tanks. The tanks on the eastern side crossed over 9 Field Squadron's bridge, those on the western side were ferried across on rafts constructed by the ubiquitous, hardworking sappers, but even with the wonderful fire support of the 15th Field Artillery Regiment, RCA, the attacking force was only able to make slow progress along the dyke. As so often happens in difficult circumstances, one man came forward to take command when his leaders had fallen.

Trooper Albert Broadbent was the gunner in his troop leader's Sherman. When his officer was wounded, Broadbent took over command of both the vehicle and the troop, and his effective fire-control permitted the survivors of an aborted infantry attack to withdraw. A new troop officer came forward to take command and a new attack was ordered. A short time later the new officer was wounded and so Broadbent resumed command until the troop was relieved. Broadbent, a Cree Indian from Leedale, Alberta, was awarded the Distinguished Conduct Medal.

The battle on Kapelsche Veer continued for days, the few German paratroopers holding out against an ever-increasing

Shermans of the 1st Hussars during the attack toward Zetten, 20 January 1945. (NAC PA159623)

weight of Allied fire. Because there was little else to report on, the press, on both sides, picked up the story. Pressure mounted on the Canadians to end this increasingly embarrassing little affair, and after five days of fighting and the deaths of 54 Canadian soldiers, the island finally fell into Canadian hands. 'Kapelsche Veer' was awarded to the SAR as a battle honour and

Awaiting Orders. Drawing by Captain Alex Colville depicting scout cars of the 17th Hussars, Holland, January 1945. (Canadian War Museum CWM12116)

rightly so, for few armoured soldiers have ever fought under such severe climatic conditions in an area that offered no room for manoeuvre. It was a soldier's battle throughout, the result depending on courage and tenacity as much as material superiority.

OPERATION *VERITABLE*, 8–21 FEBRUARY 1945

This operation would see First Canadian Army clear the four-mile wide strip of land between the Maas and the Rhine, moving from north-west to south-east. The objective was a two-lane country road that lay at a right angle to the line of advance, the road which ran from Calcar (in the north) to Goch (in the south). Between First Canadian Army and the Calcar–Goch road lay the densely wooded Reichswald, and this eight by fifteen-kilometre area, with trees planted two metres apart in the sandy soil, would prove a formidable challenge.

The Canadians would not be alone in this campaign. Under command of First Canadian Army was XXX (British) Corps consisting of three divisions, and advancing up from the south, in an operation codenamed *Grenade*, would be the First and Ninth US Armies; a force of some 375,000 men. *Veritable*, begun on 8 February, would draw the German reserves toward it thus weakening the forces opposing the Americans. Then, on 10 February, *Grenade* would be launched to form the southern jaw of a pincer that would trap and annihilate the German forces west of the Rhine, opening the way for an assault crossing of the great river.

Veritable started at dawn on 6 February with the roar of 1,334 guns and, of course, the projectiles of the Canadian Rocket Battery. The fire plan had been supplemented the previ-

ous night with the bomb loads of 400 aircraft flying over the target area, raids that reduced the cities of Cleve and Goch and several other Rhineland towns to piles of smoking rubble. To start *Veritable*, XXX Corps advanced with its three divisions forward. Under the British corps commander, Sir Brian Horrocks, and advancing on the left flank, would be 2 Canadian Infantry Division. Still farther left was 3 Division, whose task it was to clear an area of flooded ground equal in size to that being cleared by the other four divisions.

There was little need for reconnaissance in these operations. The two Canadian divisional recce regiments, the 8th Recce and the 17th Hussars, were used for following up the infantry and holding their gains against possible counter-attacks.

Although the recce regiments were held back, there was Canadian armour present in the front lines in the form of 1 CACR, whose Kangaroos were used to carry battalions of British infantry onto their objectives. With their machine-guns blazing, the carriers operated along the north-west side of the Reichswald, where they took the assault elements forward and brought the wounded back, but they were still labouring with the 'under command' relationship, and some of the infantry commanders held the Kangaroos forward, using them as an integral part of their defensive arrangements for the first night. What they did not, or could not, appreciate was that the vehicles required maintenance and vehicle maintenance, involving, as it does, lots of light and not a little noise, could not be properly conducted in the front line. As their regimental history, K.R. Ramsden's *The Canadian Kangaroos in World War II*, notes:

Considerably strong anti-tank defences continued to be encountered. 'Under Command,' the Kangaroos were ordered forward into the anti-tank defences facing small arms fire, mortars, bazookas, and the German tanks. It was this concentrated opposition that caused the loss of seven carriers. They had once again been 'Under Command' and ordered to advance against an objective without tank support.

When General Montgomery was informed of the loss of seven Kangaroos and of the developments that led to the situation, he ordered the change from 'Under Command' to 'In Support.' Lieutenant-Colonel [Gordon] Churchill [the commanding officer] was informed by 79 Division Headquarters that in future 'In Support' would most often be the condition under which the Kangaroos would operate.

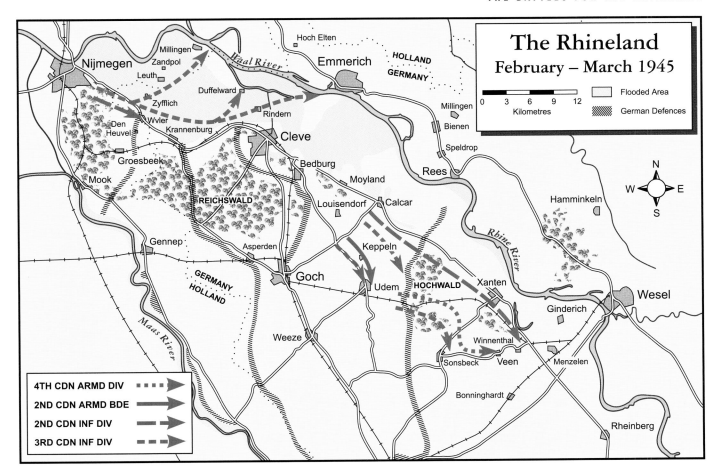

The Rhineland
February – March 1945

0   3   6   9   12
Kilometres

Flooded Area

German Defences

4TH CDN ARMD DIV
2ND CDN ARMD BDE
2ND CDN INF DIV
3RD CDN INF DIV

The ancient city of Cleve fell after three days of heavy fighting. However, the overall Allied plan was in trouble and Operation *Grenade,* due to start on 10 February, had to be postponed. The delay was due to flooding; the Germans had opened the Roer dams and temporarily placed an impenetrable barrier between themselves and the Americans, so that they could now concentrate all of their efforts against First Canadian Army.

In addition to water, the Germans had another valuable ally in the weather. The Allies had originally intended to clear the west bank of the Rhine in January, when their superiority in armour could be brought to bear, their massive armoured formations sweeping forward over the frozen ground. But the delay brought on by the Germans' Ardennes offensive had pushed the start date of *Veritable* into February and an early spring was in the offing. Under the incessant spring rains the frozen ground was quickly becoming a muddy morass and the unbroken cloud and rain served also to neutralize one of the Allies most valuable assets, air superiority. The Rhineland battles would be fought, at the tactical level, on nearly equal terms, one reason for the high casualty rates on both sides.

MOYLAND WOOD

With Cleve in hand, XXX Corps pushed on toward Goch and Calcar but now they had additional help. On 15 February II Canadian Corps was introduced into the battle on the left flank of XXX Corps. Reclaiming its 2 and 3 Divisions, which had been under command of the British formation until now, First Canadian Army also took over that Corps' 43 Division and a brigade of 15 (Scottish) Division that had been stalled for three days in front of Moyland Wood.

For Lieutenant-General Guy Simonds' II Canadian Corps, the first order of business was clearing the wood. 7 Brigade of 3 Canadian Division relieved the Scots, and in preparation for the next attack 1 CACR was brought in to carry their countrymen into battle. 'A' Squadron was tasked to lift the Royal Winnipeg Rifles, whose attack was supported by British tanks of the Guards Armoured Brigade. By now, 16 February, the command relationship problems that had earlier plagued the carrier unit had been worked out and the Kangaroos were 'in support' of the Winnipeggers.

The attack bypassed the wood to the south and captured the village of Louisendorf. Simultaneously, the Regina Rifles attacked the southern face of the wood, but this attack did not

Tanks in Harbour. **Painting by Captain Alex Colville. (Canadian War Museum CWM 12217)**

fare as well as that on Louisendorf for the Germans had been pouring in fresh reinforcements. The Reginas' sister battalions of 7 Brigade, the Winnipegs and the Canadian Scottish, now joined them in a renewed assault. The battle proved a slow and costly one for the infantry and so, on 21 February, the Sherbrooke Fusiliers of 2 Armoured Brigade were brought up to assist.

For this new attack, the Winnipegs would be the assault force, with each company accompanied by two Shermans of the Sherbrookes. Additionally, there were three flame-throwing 'Wasps' attached to whichever was the lead company, the position rotating among the companies. With the aid of these support weapons and the tanks the wood was finally cleared, section by bloody section. The infantry suffered nearly 500 casualties in five days of fighting. The cost to the Sherbrookes was one Sherman destroyed by fire, the driver, Trooper Robert James Elliott, being killed, as well as three crewmen wounded. The death of a single soldier was a relatively inconsequential event in these bloody affairs and so Trooper Elliott has gone unnamed in other accounts of the action. He was but one of the 2,005 fatal casualties suffered by the Canadian Armoured Corps in the course of the war.

THE GOCH–CALCAR ROAD, 19–21 FEBRUARY 1945

The clearing of Moyland Wood had been a preliminary to the securing of the Goch–Calcar road, Operation *Veritable*'s final objective. Once the road was secure it would become the start line for a new operation named *Blockbuster*. Lieutenant-General Simonds' II Canadian Corps would be conducting *Blockbuster*, and the general was anxious to get started. Moyland Wood had been proving to be a sticky obstacle to the start of the new operation; the Goch–Calcar road would prove to be equally as tough an impediment.

2 Canadian Armoured Brigade had been wintering in Holland. Now, in mid-February, they were brought south from the Nijmegen area to a harbour in the recently cleared Reichswald. On 18 February the Fort Garrys were placed 'in support' of 4 Infantry Brigade. 'A' Squadron was then tasked to support the operations of the Essex Scottish while 'B' Squadron did the same for the Royal Hamilton Light Infantry (RHLI). The lead two companies in each battalion would be carried into action by the Kangaroos and would be backed up by the foot-borne companies and self-propelled (SP) artillery.

The commanding officer of the RHLI, Lieutenant-Colonel Denis Whitaker, wrote of his experience in a Sherman in his book *Rhineland*:

I think that was the most frightening part of the battle for me. I never did like riding in a tank – no infantryman does. I was jammed with all my equipment into the narrow co-driver's seat of the squadron commander's tank (Major Harvey Theobald), peering out at the limited field of vision the slits provided. It was quite eerie to watch the enemy shells silently hitting the ground and exploding just a few yards away. You could hear nothing except the noise of the motor of the tank and the explosion of our own gun firing.

The squadron's lead troop of four tanks went ahead of us. Suddenly, two of the tanks burst into flame. Then the same German 88 firing from the left flank knocked out the remaining two. When the squadron leader saw the forward tanks being brewed up he yelled to the driver, 'Driver reverse! Driver reverse!' Two shots narrowly missed us. The driver quickly reversed behind the milk factory, out of view of the 88.

Fort Garry Horse tanks supporting 2nd Division's attack on the Goch-Calcar road pass in front of a destroyed German anti-tank gun, near Calcar, February 1945. NAC PA166592.

The RHLI, with the help of 'B' Squadron, took their objective and then clung to it in the face of fierce counter-attacks for four days. The other side of the Canadian advance, that carried out by 'A' Squadron of the Garrys and the Essex Scottish did not fare as well. The officer commanding 'A' Squadron, Major Bruce Macdonald, later recalled:

I brought the three tanks of Squadron Headquarters well forward, centred between 2nd and 3rd Troops, and we kept up a pretty steady fire into the buildings ahead; while the infantry were debussing, my tank was hit, and we bailed out. While I was on the ground, I talked momentarily with the Officer Commanding 'B' Company, who was pushing his men forward into the nearby houses. My tank was still running, and hadn't brewed, so we climbed back in and found that it would still move but that my [radio] junction box was smashed, with the result that I had no intercommunication or 'A' set control, and was out of touch with the remainder of the Squadron for about five minutes, until we got things inside the tank reorganized. About half an hour after we reached the area, the enemy counter-attack materialized. We were being mortared, and came under tank fire: fortunately most of it H.E. and not A.P. The Boches were closing in, I had no communication except with 1st Troop (who informed me that they and the two supporting companies were held up behind us) and I was almost completely out of ammunition. Finally another direct hit, which may have been either A.P. or H.E. made up my mind for me, and with more alacrity than dignity, we bailed out, for the second time.

There was then little we could do but watch and wait, and look soulfully at a flying O[bservation] P[ost] which hovered over our positions. The sound of our own artillery passing overhead was some solace, and we kept our ears cocked, hoping momentarily to hear the rumble of relieving tanks, plus 'C' and 'D' Companies. They didn't come, but the Boche did, throwing hand grenades into our slits [trenches] from 50 feet away and after most were wounded one stood up with his hands in the air and the rest of us followed suit.

Marched away as a prisoner-of-war, the following day Major Macdonald managed to slip into a trench and elude his escort. He made his way on foot back to the Canadian lines, to virtually the exact spot where he had been captured. The information he was able to give on the defences and ground he had observed during his time as a prisoner proved to be of great value to the Corps Commander and resulted in the award of the Distinguished Service Order.

OPERATION *BLOCKBUSTER*, 26–27 FEBRUARY 1945

Morning, 26 February 1945
The *Blockbuster* plan called for 2 and 3 Canadian Infantry Divisions to advance to, and then occupy, a U-shaped ridge, ten kilometres in depth, which followed the general line Calcar-Üdem-Goch. Once this feature was secured 4 Armoured Division would push through to the Hochwald forest, a total distance of some thirty kilometres from the start line, which was the dearly-won Goch–Calcar road. The wood was located on dominating terrain which led down to the Rhine and the town of Wesel, where a number of bridges crossed the great river.

The battle started prematurely. 2 Division, on the Corps' left flank where it was supported by 2 Armoured Brigade, had all of its units in location awaiting H-Hour, when German parachutists supported by six tanks attacked the right-hand brigade. 'D' Company of the RHLI, supported by a troop of the Garrys, fought off the assault.

The Canadian advance began at 0430 hours and bore a strong resemblance to Operation *Totalize* of the preceding August. On 2 Division's right, the infantry were all carried into battle, either in the Kangaroos or on the back decks of two squadrons of the Garrys and one of the South Albertas. Searchlight beams were bounced off of low clouds to provide illumi-

4th Armoured Brigade Tanks, Xanten. **Painting by Bruno Bobak. The painting depicts the opening stage of Operation *Blockbuster*. (Canadian War Museum CWM 11902)**

Governor General's Foot Guards tanks in an open laager during the battle for the Rhineland. (NAC PA113682)

nation, while tracer, fired from Bofors anti-aircraft guns, marked the direction of advance. 6 Infantry Brigade's objectives were all taken with relatively light casualties, thanks in part to the excellent navigation provided by Lieutenant Lloyd Queen of the FGH, who gained a Military Cross for his night's work. He was unexpectedly tasked with leading three armoured regiments and three infantry battalions forward in darkness and under fire. He did that by frequently dismounting from his tank and leading the force on foot using a compass bearing.

Over on the left, 5 Brigade, supported by 'A' Squadron of the 1st Hussars, was to clear a wood south-west of Calcar, thereby screening the division's left flank. The ground was boggy and there were other problems as the Hussars' regimental history records:

Despite the artificial illumination supplied by searchlights and Bofors tracers fired along the centre line, great difficulty was experienced in finding the way across country because

other Bofors batteries fired at various angles to the centre line, while the searchlights changed the direction of their beam every five minutes. Undoubtedly this intricate code system of giving the proper axis of attack confused the enemy too.

The battle on the front of 3 Division would see that formation win its first Victoria Cross. On the left flank, the Queen's Own Rifles advanced over a mile across open, soggy ground clearing a series of small hamlets and farms supported by 'C' Squadron of the 1st Hussars. When his officer became a casualty, Sergeant Aubrey Cosens of 'D' Company, took command of the remaining four riflemen in his platoon and led them against the defended hamlet of Mooshof. Spotting a 'C' Squadron tank, commanded by Sergeant Charles Anderson, he ran across 25 metres of open ground, under fire, to obtain its assistance. Cosens directed the tank's fire against the German position in a farm building, then ordered the tank to ram the build-

A typical scene just behind the action during the battles for the Rhineland: vehicles of all sorts – infantry carriers, Jeeps, a Kangaroo, a South Alberta half-track, and even a Sherman near the front – all awaiting the call to move forward. (NAC PA138353)

ing to create an opening. Once inside Cosens killed several of the defenders and captured the rest. The tank's driver, Trooper Bill Adams, recalled the action in Jean Portugal's book *We Were There – The Army*:

> I put her in bull-low and advanced. When I hit, I bounced back about two feet and didn't do too much. Then I tried again and this time I did a pretty good job and went in quite a way. I was worried because I didn't know if we were going through the wall whether we'd drop through into the cellar.
>
> From there I was ordered to go to the front of the building, and according to my notebook, we lobbed two or three shells into that building. I'm still driving and after the HE we see a white flag coming out of the house and we got about 20 Germans plus two medical men who had been prisoners since early on. Then we returned to our old position and waited further orders.

Afternoon, 26 February 1945

Thanks in great part to Sergeant Cosens, who was killed shortly afterwards, the QOR consolidated on their objective. Meanwhile, 'C' Squadron was withdrawn to replenish and refuel. Major 'Jake' Powell, who had thirteen of his original nineteen tanks remaining, was told by his commanding officer that his next task would be to support an attack by the North Shore Regiment on Keppeln, the next village on the road to Üdem. Powell, who had won a Military Cross on the D-Day beaches as a squadron second-in-command, conferred with the North Shore's CO. They decided to mount two North Shore platoons on the tanks and rush the village, while two dismounted companies and the battalion's three 'Wasp' flame-throwers would follow the armour. Keppeln was known to contain ten self-propelled guns and four tanks, and as far as Powell was concerned the attack was going to be nothing less than suicide for the Shermans. 'C' Squadron's charge began at 1320 hours. As they raced uphill over the open ground, tank after tank was lost to

Shermans belonging to the South Alberta regiment carrying troops of the Algonquin Regiment through the persistent mud of the Rhineland battlefields, 26 February 1945. (NAC PA113907)

mines, anti-tank guns and the boggy going, so that just four of the thirteen reached the village. Powell's own tank bogged down in a shell hole on the outskirts of the village; however, he continued to fight his tank and direct the fire of the remainder. Under a hail of artillery and mortar rounds, the Shermans fought off one German counter-attack after another, his tiny force accounting for four enemy tanks and a number of the SPs, until, after two hours of bloody struggle, the enemy had had enough and left the ruins of Keppeln to the Canadians. The door to Üdem was now open.

Major Powell was recommended for a Victoria Cross but he never received it. After the citation was approved at every level up to Army Group, Field Marshal Montgomery crossed out the letters VC and substituted DSO, then initialled the change. Few DSOs have been more bravely won than that earned by the modest, gentlemanly Jake Powell.

On Powell's right flank the *Régiment de la Chaudière* and 'B' Squadron of the 1st Hussars captured the hamlet of Hollen in a tough fight, while over on Powell's left the Sherbrookes were supporting the Queen's Own Cameron Highlanders and the South Saskatchewan Regiment in an equally hard-fought action. Interestingly, Major David Rodgers of the Camerons was also recommended for the Victoria Cross for his heroic actions on this day, only to have Montgomery again downgrade the award to a DSO.

While the battle for Keppeln was raging, 4 CAD's *Tiger*

Group, commanded by Brigadier Robert Moncel, was operating a few hundred metres further east. *Tiger* comprised five battle groups. Left front was the British Columbia Regiment (less a squadron) and the Lincoln and Welland Regiment (less a company), and right front was the Canadian Grenadier Guards (less a squadron) and the Argyll and Sutherland Highlanders (less a company). Behind these two groups were two others which comprised the remaining elements of the lead units. In reserve, in the rear, were the Governor General's Foot Guards and The Lake Superior Regiment (Motor). This last group, christened *Smith Force* after its commander, Lieutenant-Colonel E.M. Smith, CO of the Foot Guards, had a special task. It was tasked to secure three pimples of land (the Pauls-Berg and the Katzen-Berg, the third feature was unnamed) on the Calcar–Üdem ridge that lay just north-east of Üdem itself.

As Stephen Harris' history of the Foot Guards in the Second World War noted:

Initially a number of tanks bogged in the muck, but then seven or eight tanks in the lead troop of Number 2 Squadron were hit, and five men were killed outright or fatally wounded. The Regiment nevertheless pushed on, and at about 18:00 hours Number 3 Squadron and a company of Lake Superiors crossed the 'start-line' for Üdem, all the while under heavy fire. Before long, the Superiors' half-tracks had become hopelessly stuck, but rather than give up the infantry gamely climbed on the backs of the Regiment's Shermans. Twice they had to dismount when the columns ran into anti-tank guns, but fighting in what the Guards' history describes as their 'customary fashion,' the Superiors dealt with these smartly. The battle group finally reached the base of Pauls-Berg at about sundown and, after some hard fighting, made their way to the crest.

Evening, 26 February 1945
That evening, 26 February 1945, 9 Canadian Infantry Brigade reached Üdem. Lieutenant-Colonel F.E. White of the 1st Hussars led a group of tanks into Üdem where they took up a defensive position around the church in the middle of the town covering the five roads that radiated out from the town. At first light the tanks were once again in action, helping the infantry in clearing houses on the town's outskirts. Their task completed they left Üdem to re-join their unit at 0830 that same morning.

BLOCKBUSTER PHASE II, 27 FEBRUARY–3 MARCH 1945

4 CAD and the Hochwald, 27 February 1945

The Üdem–Calcar road would serve as the start line for 4 Division's next attack, to be conducted by *Lion Group*, consisting of the South Albertas and the Algonquin Regiment. Their task would be the securing of a hill, Point 73, which dominated the western end of a gap between two forests, the Hochwald and the Balberger Wald. Once Point 73 was taken, by two companies of Algonquins and the South Alberta's 'B' Squadron, other companies would leapfrog through the gap.

The attack began at 0515, an hour before daylight. With 'A' and 'B' Companies dug in on their objective, 'C' Company secured the German positions to the south of the gap, between it and the Goch–Üdem–Xanten railway line. 'A' Squadron and the carrier platoon of the Algonquins set out to conduct a right hook that would secure the group's right flank, but the column met with disaster when it reached the railway line. The area had not been cleared of enemy (although it had been reported as clear) and the group was ambushed. After picking off the first and last tanks in the column the anti-tank gunners took out the remainder at their leisure. The only surviving vehicle was an Algonquin carrier that got away with some wounded. Eleven tanks and twelve carriers were lost, as well as most of their crews.

The operations of the divisions on either side of *Lion Group* were not progressing nearly as rapidly, and the Albertas and Algonquins soon found themselves the main objects of interest for all the German gunners and mortarmen for a considerable distance around. The worst of the battle was in the Hochwald Gap itself, because the force in the gap was in front of its flanking formations, a situation which permitted the enemy to fire at them from three sides. Because of the twists and turns in the Rhine river (the Germans were still occupying the east bank) some enemy artillery was actually behind the Canadians fighting in the Hochwald Gap, and the German artillery gave the Canadians one of their worst poundings of the

war. For five long days the Canadians tried to pass through the gap to reach the town of Wesel, which held what were now the last two bridges over the Rhine.

Instead of going around the forests, frontal assault after frontal assault was made. The Germans at the time, and quite a few Canadian military historians since then, have asked why the two woods were not simply outflanked. The Hochwald battle resembled, in more than a few ways, the battles of the Great War. First there was the mud, which slowed down men and vehicles alike and generally made life very unpleasant. Then there was the failure of communications. Over and over again radio nets failed, the delicate sets subdued by rain, mud and shock. When the radios died, runners were used to ask headquarters for fire support, reinforcements and ammunition but time after time the runners were killed before their messages could be delivered. Back at brigade, division and corps headquarters, the arrows on the maps that indicated progress and the direction of advance were not moving. Information was not forthcoming and the frustration levels of the senior officers steadily grew. Their brilliant plans were not being executed and they did not know why. In their ignorance, commanders continuously reinforced failure, sending out yet another company or squadron to replace ones which had been decimated tying to capture a locale that was just too strongly held by the enemy.

4 CAD and the Hochwald, 28 February–3 March 1945

After a difficult start to the operation, the commander of 4 CAD, Major-General Chris Vokes, decided to restore momentum to the battle by using 10 Infantry Brigade to secure the gap, plus a portion of the Goch–Üdem–Xanten railway line to the south of the gap, the idea being to tear up the rail lines and replace them with a road. That would ease the logistics problem.

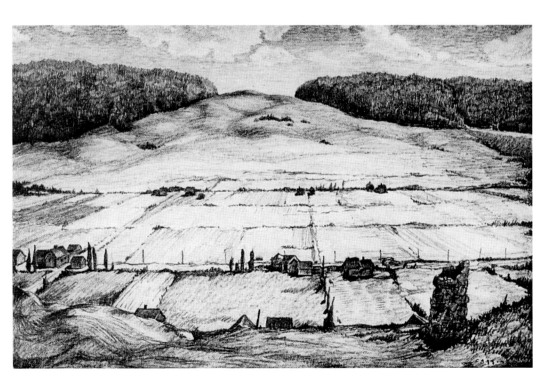

Pencil sketch from the regimental history of the Algonquin Regiment depicting the approach to the Hochwald Gap, the 'pimple' between the Hochwald (on the left) and the Balbergerwald (on the right). (Sketch by Major G.L. Cassidy from *Warpath: The Story of the Algonquin Regiment at War 1939-1945*)

A South Alberta Regiment Sherman Firefly ploughs through knee-deep mud in the vicinity of the Hochwald. The mud created a significant problem in the attack on the Hochwald Gap: the tanks moved so slowly, sometimes bogging completely, that they were especially vulnerable to anti-tank and artillery fire. (NAC PA113675)

tion of fire the 'greatest he had experienced.' By nightfall the fighting had died down and the Lincoln and Welland Regiment was firm in its positions.

2 Division attacked the Hochwald to the north of the gap, while, to the south of it 3 Division's 8 Brigade, supported by the 1st Hussars, made slow progress through the Balberger Wald. When a company of the *Chaudière* was cut off, two troops of 'A' Squadron of the 1st Hussars rode to the rescue along with another company of the French-Canadians. In the words of the Hussars' history, "Using the forest rides as centre lines, the attack went in at 08:30 hours with the tanks leading the infantry and each arm acting as moral support to the other." The frequently unsung heroism of the ordinary soldier was soon illustrated. Again, from the Hussars' history: "Sergeant McLeod's tank was hit twice by an 88mm and the crew bailed out. When it did not catch fire, the driver, Trooper J.E. Jones, got back in the tank and though it was hit three more times he drove it to cover where the crew once again took over, fighting it until relieved." Jones received no official recognition for his courage but he had the respect of his regiment.

Once 10 Brigade had completed its task, a 4 Armoured Brigade battlegroup consisting of the Canadian Grenadier Guards and the Lake Superiors would be passed through to seize a small wood a mile east of the gap.

With grit and determination, the Lincoln and Wellands found themselves close to the western edge of the gap on the morning of the 28th. However, the infantry were alone and armour was urgently needed. The history of the British Columbia Regiment, *The Dukes,* notes:

'A' Squadron, still attached to the Lincoln and Welland's, was now ordered to support a two-company attack to be made by the regiment. So heavy was the going that only three tanks arrived at the start line, the Squadron Leader's and Nos. 2 and 3 Troop Leaders'. This 'high-priced troop' went into action and the enemy shelled the area with the utmost ferocity. Infantry casualties were heavy but the tank force went unscathed. The Squadron Leader called the concentra-

The whole of II Canadian Corps pushed forward on the morning of 2 March. In the gap, Moncel's 4 Armoured Brigade, reinforced with the Algonquin Regiment, made a very determined effort to break through. Three companies of the Lake Superiors, carried in British Kangaroos and supported by a composite squadron from the Canadian Grenadier Guards commanded by Captain Pat Grieve, were to advance 1,000 metres under cover of darkness. Once firm, the Governor General's Foot Guards carrying a company of the Algonquins would advance a further 1,000 metres, to a bridge over a small stream called the Hohe Ley.

Things did not go well. The Kangaroos, held up by the atrocious mud, were late meeting up with the Lake Superiors. The attack, which was meant to be a night operation starting at 0200 hours, instead started just before first light at 0430. Nevertheless, the Lake Superiors took their objectives and the follow-on force was ordered to advance.

The CO of the Algonquins, Lieutenant-Colonel G.L. Cassidy, later recorded in the unit's history, *Warpath:*

> Battalion headquarters group, in four tanks, simultaneously started down the middle of the gap, with the immediate intention of setting up shop in the vicinity of the forward Lake Superior position. The writer was riding with the [GGFG] squadron commander, Captain [C.W.] Conlon. There were three other tanks, one artillery observation tank, and two Armoured Brigade Liaison tanks. We had no sooner emerged from the cover of the trees on the right shoulder when a flurry of 88mm fire began to whistle over. In a matter of seconds the artillery tank and the Liaison tanks were either burning or completely knocked out. The command tank escaped the first few volleys (about seven shots in all came very close), and by skilful manoeuvering and answering fire, succeeded in reaching the lee of a large brick house.

That was as far as the Canadians got on 2 March. An erroneous report that an Algonquin company had reached the Hohe Ley led brigade headquarters to urge on the other Algonquin companies, and the result was the decimation of the battalion, which took 140 casualties. The weary survivors of the Hochwald Gap were relieved on the night of 2/3 March by 5 Brigade, which started its attack at 0300 hours on 4 March only to find the enemy gone. The American advance from the south (Operation *Grenade*) had persuaded the German commander to pull his forces back into a bridgehead over the Rhine at Wesel. That night the main German body crossed the river leaving only rearguards behind. The struggle for the Hochwald had finally ended.

Tanks with Identification Markers. **Painting by Bruno Bobak depicting tanks of the South Alberta Regiment near Sonsbeck, Germany, 9 March 1945. (Canadian War Museum CWM 11996)**

XANTEN, VEEN AND WINNENTHAL, 10 MARCH 1945

The next objective was the ancient town of Xanten, located on the Rhine north of Wesel. In preparation for the battle, the 1st Hussars were concentrated in the Hochwald, which was still infested with mines and subject to fire from the east bank of the Rhine. The Hussars task was part of a 'Pepperpot', that is to provide indirect fire, but even for this relatively undemanding task the unit had little to offer. Its strength in serviceable tanks was now: RHQ, two; 'A' Squadron, one; 'B' Squadron, nine; and 'C' Squadron, five.

5 Brigade, supported by the Sherbrookes' 'B' Squadron, closed on Xanten, clearing the heavily bombed town from north to south. The problem of higher headquarters being left in the dark because of poor communications had been addressed, and a procedure developed to overcome the problem, so that during this set of operations the progress of the action was closely followed by the staff of brigade headquarters and 2 Infantry Division thanks to the efforts of 'A' Squadron of the 8th Recce Regiment. The squadron attached armoured cars to the various headquarters which were in radio contact with other cars monitoring the routes and the fighting. When Lieutenant L.A. MacKenzie, the organizer of this scheme, arrived in Xanten, he came across a large stock of German cigars. Placing a table on the road, he handed out cigars to the soldiers of 6 Infantry Bri-

gade as they filed past him on their way into the town. As the 8th Recce's history notes, 'In the early morning light the progress of the infantry could be followed by the twinkling lights of thousands of cigars.'

In the second phase of *Blockbuster II,* on the right flank the 17th Hussars were told to 'probe towards Sonsbeck.' The unit

The Sherbrooke Fusiliers enter Xanten, 7 March 1945. (NAC PA114966)

found that its Daimler scout cars were virtually useless in the boggy ground south of the Hochwald, and so tried to carry out their task on foot. Two patrols, one by day and one by night, were sent out, both ending with fatal casualties. Sonsbeck was on the inter-divisional boundary between the Canadians and the British and shortly afterwards it fell to 3 British Division, while 3 Canadian Division was pulled back to the area of Üdem. That left 2 Canadian Division on the left and 4 CAD on the right during the final offensive toward Wesel.

4 CAD was driving toward Veen from the north-west, the direction of the Hochwald, and planning for this operation had started as early as 4 March, when 'B' Squadron of 1 CACR married up with the Argyll and Sutherland Highlanders and two squadrons of the South Albertas. The 12th Manitoba Dragoons were to recce the routes through the Balberger Wald to Veen,

but the unexpectedly heavy resistance in the Hochwald Gap prevented any of the force from getting forward. Perhaps it was just as well, since 4 CAD tankers, spotting the Dragoons' Staghounds in the woods, reported them as Panther tanks!

After the Germans withdrew from the Hochwald area, 4 CAD resumed its move toward Veen. Using squadron/company battle groups, they passed by Sonsbeck on 6 March, and following the Sonsbeck–Veen road they then started clearing the countryside towards the objective when the armour found itself stopped by a 70-foot wide crater across the main route. 'B' Company of the Argyll and Sutherland Highlanders pushed on alone, only to be cut-off and captured. The engineers came forward to construct a bridge across the crater, while the commander of 10 Brigade ordered two battle groups to capture Veen.

Advancing along the north side of the road were the Algonquins and the SAR, and on the south side, the Lincoln and Wellands and the British Columbia Regiment, the Lincolns 'A' Company being carried in the Kangaroos of 1 CACR. Veen proved to be a very tough nut to crack. The infantry were pinned to the ground by heavy fire while the armour lost tank after tank to the 88s. Mud and mines conspired to deny the armour the mobility they needed to outflank the defenders and the SAR's history gives a flavour of the action, describing the experiences of Lieutenant W.H. McKechnie of 'A' Squadron:

On his way up, McKechnie ran over a mine which blew in his belly hatch and wrecked his wireless, and his Sherman was then hit twice by an anti-tank gun firing from a woods to the north. He managed to get behind the cover of a building but shortly discovered that 'he could not move his tank a foot either way without being fired on by the anti-tank gun' and, 'being a prudent man, he stayed where he was and engaged what targets he could see from his boxed-in position.' Finally, a third hit forced the crew to bail out but the gunner, Trooper James Forbes, stayed in the tank and fired off all of his ammunition before leaving.

After holding up the Canadians for two days, the enemy suddenly withdrew and 10 Brigade held the ruins of Veen.

While the battle for Veen was being fought, the remainder of

Destroyed Vehicles Near Xanten, Germany. **This painting by Captain Alex Colville shows a 12th Manitoba Dragoons Staghound armoured car blown up on a mine. (Canadian War Museum CWM 12147)**

4 Armoured Brigade pushed on to Winnenthal, just east of Veen. There the Governor General's Foot Guards cleared the approaches for the Canadian Grenadier Guards. The Grenadiers, who had been resting since the breakthrough at the Hochwald on 2 March, came up to fight the last action west of the Rhine, capturing the hamlet in cooperation with the Algonquins. Major George Hale, OC of 3 Squadron, accepted the surrender of the Winnenthal garrison, some 150 paratroopers in all.

Meanwhile, the Allies prepared for an assault crossing of the Rhine, planned for later in March, and the reconnaissance regiments were redeployed along the west bank of the Rhine in their old familiar task of maintaining a line of observation posts. Unlike their experience on the Maas, however, they would have no time to become bored with the task, for within two weeks they would be across the great river and on the final leg of their journey.

The Rhineland battles were an infantryman's fight from start to finish. Even so, the armoured resources of First Canadian Army were heavily stretched. Tanks were frequently parcelled out in penny packets, like the Sherbrookes at Moyland Wood, or re-tasked with little time to rest or plan, like the 1st Hussars at Keppeln. The use and success of squadron/company battlegroups showed, however, that the degree of support between the two arms was never higher, 'each arm acting as moral support to the other.' The absolute requirement for tank/infantry co-operation had been learned; learned the hard way, but learned nonetheless.

CHAPTER 16

Liberation of the Netherlands and the End of the War

Second Lieutenant Emmet Burrows viewed the sight with amazement: an intact bridge spanning the Rhine River. He then crawled back through the bushes to inform his commanding officer of his surprising discovery. Within hours 'A' Company, 27th Armored Battalion, 9th (US) Armored Division had crossed and captured the Ludendorff railway bridge at Remagen.

'A' Company's feat proved to be a bit of an embarrassment for the Allies. Field Marshal Montgomery already had a well-developed plan for a Rhine crossing further north, at Rees, while south of Remagen the Americans under General Bradley were planning to cross at Oppenheim. Both sites had been chosen precisely because they would enable the Allies to by-pass Germany's industrial heartland, the Ruhr valley, but the Remagen bridgehead led directly into the densest conurbation in Europe – definitely not the place for the armoured battle that the Allies sought. The Remagen bridgehead was developed – four American divisions eventually crossed here – but it was never fully exploited and the planned crossings, north and south of Remagen, went ahead as scheduled.

OPERATION *PLUNDER:* THE CROSSING OF THE RHINE, 23 March 1945

Montgomery held to his original plan for an assault crossing at Rees on 23 March. Called Operation *Plunder,* the plan called for four divisions to cross together, two British (15th and 51st) and two American (30th and 79th). The units making up the British forces included an attached Canadian infantry brigade and two regiments of British DD tanks, the 44th Royal Tank Regiment and the Staffordshire Yeomanry. Neither unit had operated amphibious Shermans in action, and to help them with their task D-Day veterans of the 1st Hussars were attached to them.

Instead of leading the assault, as they had in Normandy, the DD tanks' role was to follow the infantry (who were carried in assault boats and Buffaloes) and assist them in securing the

bridgehead while the engineers constructed pontoon bridging and rafts. One of the tanks, commanded by Sergeant Leo Gariépy of the 1st Hussars, had the breech of its main gun removed to make room for a special radio set for communicating with the rocket-equipped Typhoon aircraft supporting the bridgehead. Only the driver remained of Gariépy's original crew, the places of the others being taken by an RAF wing commander and a leading aircraftman. Afterwards, Gariépy reported:

> The Wing Commander then got in touch with his squadron and told them of being across on the enemy shore. Targets were picked here and there, and we had a grandstand show of what the rockets could do. Afterwards, we moved as far as Munster, not firing a single shot, because we could not. But the Wing Commander was enjoying himself like a little boy; he said this was the best observation post he could have had – we could get so close to the targets.

While Sergeant Gariépy, the Yeomanry and the Royal Tanks were in the water, Canadian armour was carrying out a 'Pepperpot' – that is a massive concentration of indirect fire on known and suspected enemy positions, the first organized by Lieutenant-Colonel George Baylay of the Foot Guards. The BCR fired 37,000 rounds over two days while the South Albertas chalked up 38,325. Although the tasking involved only indirect shooting, it was not without cost as German artillery on the east bank returned the fire and several Canadian crewmen were killed and wounded.

Twenty-four hours after the start of *Plunder,* Operation *Varsity* was launched, an airborne assault conducted by two divisions, one British and one American. Dropped just behind the German positions surrounding the bridgehead, they were able to completely disrupt the enemy's defences, leading to a breakout by the Allied forces.

Firing at Enemy Installations. **Painting by Bruno Bobak depicting the use of massive numbers of tanks for indirect fire on German positions on the far side of the River Rhine. (Canadian War Museum CWM11929)**

As a part of Montgomery's deception plan for *Plunder,* First Canadian Army had been instructed to make a feint against the German town of Emmerich, located on the east bank of the Rhine just north of the British crossing sites. Although Emmerich was an obvious target for an assault crossing (it was a major communications hub) it was not selected because of a dominating hill called the Hoch Elten which overlooked the town's northwest side. On 28 March, 2 Canadian Division crossed the Rhine using the British bridges at Rees, 3 and 4 Divisions immediately following it into Germany. The problem of clearing Emmerich and capturing the Hoch Elten feature was given to 3 Division and Brigadier T.G. Gibson's 7 Infantry Brigade led the attack against Emmerich. (Gibson had been one of the originals of Worthy's 1936 Tank School. He had chosen, however, in 1939, to return to his parent regiment, the RCR.)

The Sherbrooke Fusiliers were detached from 2 Armoured Brigade to support 7 Brigade's attacks. The job took two days to complete and, thankfully, casualties were light. On the second day of fighting, 30 March, Brigadier T.J. Rutherford, who commanded the three CACRUs in Britain, arrived in 'A' Squadron's area, and using his not inconsequential powers of persuasion, Uncle Tom, as he was known, talked his way into the gunner's seat of a Sherbrooke tank. Rutherford had commanded 1 Armoured Brigade before taking over the CACRUs. He was a highly respected commander and, by all accounts, made a satisfactory crewman as well.

After having been effectively screened for four days by the Manitoba Dragoons, on 31 March 8 Infantry Brigade, supported by the Sherbrookes' 'A' Squadron, cleared the Hoch Elten feature. This success permitted engineers to begin construction of additional crossing sites at Emmerich, and within a few days there were three new Canadian bridges spanning the Rhine. Morale among the Canadian troops was very high as they prepared for the long anticipated final battle beyond the Rhine. The history of the 17th Duke of York's Royal Canadian Hussars echoes the mood:

> To the 17th [Hussars], the capturing of Emmerich felt as if someone had finally started unclogging the holes of the salt cellar they had been in for the last few months and all that was necessary was for someone to 'tip it' and the fast Recce patrols, shaking the last few bits of mud from their wheels, would begin pouring all over the country. The following day, April 1st, someone, probably the GOC, Maj. Gen. Keefler, tipped that salt cellar and out poured the Regiment.

Montgomery's plan now called for his forces to strike northeast, sweeping across the north German plain and on to Berlin, while First Canadian Army would move north, clearing the east bank of the Rhine and driving on into Holland. The Canadian campaign would serve to protect the left flank of the British forces while further south US armies would perform the same function on Montgomery's right flank, but his plan quickly floundered because (a) the Americans refused to be seen to be playing a subordinate role, and (b) the Supreme Allied Commander, General Eisenhower, told him that the German capital was being left to the Russians. Instead, the British would clear the North Sea coast to Bremen and Hannover.

The quarrels of the senior leadership had no effect on the planned Canadian operations, however, and II Canadian Corps struck north on 1 April, their ultimate goal being the North Sea. Canadian operations would, initially, be conducted on the east bank of the Ijssel River, which bisects Holland flowing north to the Ijsselmeer.

Troops of the Canadian Grenadier Guards unpack 75mm high-explosive shells prior to an indirect shoot, near Emmerich, Germany, 28 March 1945. (NAC PA134433)

Sherbrooke Fusilier Sherman giving cover to men of the Canadian Scottish Regiment entering Emmerich, Germany, 30 March 1945. (NAC PA131818)

I CANADIAN CORPS IN NORTH-WEST EUROPE

After imposing the unwanted 5 CAD on its reluctant allies in Italy in order to create I Canadian Corps, the Canadian government almost immediately reversed itself and started to agitate to have the corps returned to Britain. Leaving Italy proved to be more difficult than getting there, but early in 1945 Canada's allies finally agreed to permit the movement of I Corps to northwest Europe. Under the name of Operation *Goldflake*, the Canadians embarked at Leghorn, crossed the Mediterranean to Marseilles and motored north into Belgium. On 1 April 1945 I Canadian Corps formally came under command of First Canadian Army, replacing I British Corps in the order of battle.

Serving in north-west Europe meant conforming to the local War Establishments. As the regimental history of The Governor General's Horse Guards relates:

5th Armoured Division vehicles awaiting unloading from flat cars in the railway yard at Nijmegen, 27 March 1945. (NAC PA134431)

Reorganization also meant the turning in of a great many vehicles. Of our thirty Stuarts we retained eleven for the recce troop and seven as ammunition carriers, while the remainder were turned over to 5th CAB [5 Canadian Armoured Brigade]. Our old Shermans were discarded and we obtained thirty-three Mark V's, with 75-mm's, from 5th CAB, while the 17-pounders and the 105's were obtained from G Squadron of our Armoured Delivery Regiment [The Elgins]. Our Daimlers [scout cars] went to the infantry. Naturally everyone kept his best, and the wrecks with which we were all presented caused blood, sweat and tears in great profusion. Our tank parks were simply the streets themselves, and maintenance was carried on under the delighted gaze of swarms of local children.

What did the troops think of the move and the consequent hubbub? The Strathcona's history addresses the point:

In England on leave, one was sometimes asked about the reaction of the men in 1st Canadian Corps on being brought to this theatre, and about the attitude of the other divisions already there towards these newcomers. The first question was simply answered: we had had enough of Italy. As regards the attitude of the 'D-Day Boys' and the 'Spaghetti Boys' towards each other, one could find an analogy in inter-colle-

giate football rivalry, or in the harmless bark of the school-boy: "My old man can lick your old man." Of course there was rivalry, good healthy rivalry, as anyone knowing Canadians would expect. But feelings all round were genuinely good.

The first task for I Canadian Corps was to take over the Nijmegen salient. The area between Nijmegen and Arnhem was known as the 'island', although it was not entirely surrounded by water. The north side of the island lay along the Rhine River, Arnhem being situated on the north bank just out of Allied reach. The southern boundary was the Waal River, and the two rivers joined in the east and then nearly rejoined in the west, thus creating the near-island topography. Then, at the beginning of April, I Corps would proceed with the capture of Arnhem. This operation, dubbed *Destroyer,* would be co-ordinated with operations of II Corps which had, in the meantime (and with 1 Canadian Division temporarily under command) commenced clearing eastern Holland, to the east of the Ijssel River.

EAST OF THE IJSSEL

The Canadian advance from Emmerich saw 3 Division moving north with the Rhine on their left and 2 Division on their right. Both divisions had their respective recce regiments in the vanguard heading toward their immediate objective, the Twente Canal, some 25 kilometres north of Emmerich. The canal lay at right angles to the line of advance and was a likely defensive position for the enemy. The 17th Hussars, operating on the extreme left flank, found itself confronting a different type of opposition from that which it had been used to:

The enemy, if he wanted to rescue his divisions in north-western Holland, simply had to stop or slow down the advance of the Canadian Army as it headed up the Ijssel river for Friesland and the North Sea. This task he gave to his most fanatical and Nazi-minded troops – the 'Hitler Jugend,' or 'Hitler Youth.' And it was these youngsters, armed with machine guns and Panzerfausts (Bazookas), that the patrols of the 17th kept meeting up with. Actually, their 'do-or-die' efforts did little or nothing toward stemming the advance of 2 Canadian Corps but their fanatical, absurd daring caused many close shaves for the troopers of the 17th. In the years to come stories will be told of how armoured cars would suddenly be confronted by one of these boy-soldiers, who, standing in the middle of the road a few yards away would open up with a Schmeisser and how the gunner-op, feeling anger, hate and pity all at the same time, would take careful aim and 'let go' with a burst of blazing Besa [machine-gun fire]. Had these lads been properly schooled in war-waging, their 'do-or-die' tactics might have done. As it was they died.

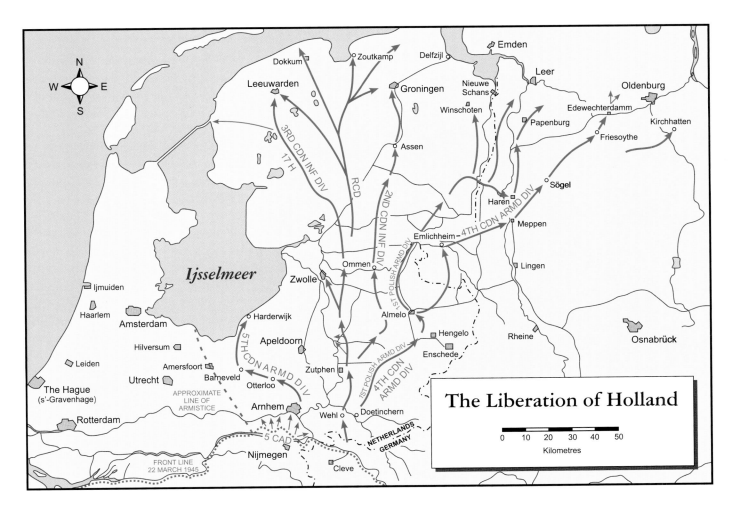

The Liberation of Holland

0 10 20 30 40 50
Kilometres

Farther over to the east, 8th Recce Regiment (14th Canadian Hussars) was in its glory. After skilfully by-passing the town of Doetinchem, which would hold out for a further two days, patrols of 'A' Squadron made a dash for the Twente Canal, hoping to secure a bridge. At speeds of 60 to 65 kilometres per hour the scout cars sped on, firing at any German troops they encountered, but always pushing forward. Finally the bridge was in sight:

Just as we reached the bridge spanning the canal and began shooting up the 'jerries' on the far side, the bridge literally exploded in our faces. As it sank to the bottom of the canal our soaring spirits went with it. In sheer anger we shot up everything we could see on the other side and then moved back and off to the left flank where we took up positions guarding the approaches. An hour or so later 6 huns on push bikes came up the road toward us, we were still boiling with anger at 75 yards 6 M[achine-]G[un]s and 3 Brens made quite a mess of them. We felt better after that and later on we returned to harbour with the rest of the squadron.

The following day the infantry crossed the canal in assault boats and soon the engineers had constructed a bridge. Once

again the Staghounds were turned loose, this time followed up by the tanks of the Fort Garry Horse, who had been attached to 2 Division. Meanwhile, the Garrys' sister regiment, the Sherbrooke Fusiliers, had been attached to 3 Division and, along with the scout cars of the 17th Hussars, were pushing north. The battle groups found themselves passing through Doetinchem, which had just fallen, on their way to the town of Zutphen, a small city on the banks of the Ijssel, just south of the Twente Canal.

To get at Zutphen the assaulting Canadians had to first get across the Berkel River. The Sherbrookes' history records:

In the attack on Zutphen the next day two troops supported Le Régiment de la Chaudière to the first group of buildings, but had to halt because of a blown bridge, whereupon Sergeant [Hubert] Atkinson commanding No.1 Troop in a reconnaissance discovered a spot to the left by which the tanks found a crossing. With his crew, aided by a few infantrymen, he laid enough logs to give a firm footing under intense, highly accurate sniping, and both troops crossed to enter the town and continue to aid against the savage opposition of the enemy paratroopers defending it. Sergeant Atkinson was killed by a sniper and three troopers were wounded.

Barge carrying a Sherbrooke Fusilier Sherman across the River Ijssel, near Deventer, Holland, 12 April 1945. (NAC PA142407)

Atkinson had been selected for commissioning and was about to leave the unit to go on course when he was killed.

With Zutphen taken, the pursuit continued fifteen kilometres north to Deventer, a similar-sized town also located on the east bank of the Ijssel, which fell to 3 Division aided by the Sherbrookes. With these two 'anchors' secure, 1 Division was launched west, across the Ijssel, in an effort to capture the provincial capital, Apeldoorn, which lay roughly another fifteen kilometres away.

THE ADVANCE TO THE SEA: 3 CANADIAN DIVISION

With Deventer in its hands, 3 Division turned its attention once more to the north. The RCD, on temporary loan to II Canadian Corps from I Corps, were inserted between the lead elements of 1 and 3 Divisions to maintain continuity of control across the front. The numerous Dutch canals were the main obstacles to a rapid advance and this meant that the black berets needed help in their work. As the 8th Recce's regimental history notes:

It is fitting at this time to pay tribute to the work of the Royal Canadian Engineers. During these operations, a detachment was always with the leading squadrons and they invariably chose to move with [the] leading troop, accepting all the risks and dangers involved. That they speeded the advance goes without question. On many occasions with only civilian help available and without materials to which they were accustomed they quickly filled road craters, lifted minefields and spanned minor obstacles, enabling the advance to carry on with little or no delay.

To help speed the advance two regiments of French paratroopers were dropped behind the enemy lines but they do not seem to have had much effect on the course of events. After the capture of Deventer the Canadians found little organized resistance and the main problems were mines, blown bridges and the odd die-hard German soldier or soldiers. On Sunday, 15 April 1945, the RCD enjoyed the double pleasure of liberating the Dutch city of Leeuwarden (aided by the 17th Hussars, who entered from the west while the Dragoons came in from the east) and reaching the North Sea near the town of Dokkum. Meanwhile the 17th Hussars swung west to seal off the causeway that linked eastern and western Holland at the north end of the Ijsselmeer. With the causeway blocked, on 18 April, the German forces in western Holland were trapped.

THE ADVANCE TO THE SEA: 2 CANADIAN DIVISION

2 Division, operating to the east of the 3rd and led in its advance by the 8th Recce Regiment, made even better time. Most of the parachute drops, mentioned above, had been made in front of 2 Division, and within two or three days the link-up between ground and airborne forces had been made. The focus of the division's operations was the city of Groningen. This provincial capital was reached on 13 April and cleared by the infantry over a period of three days. The major resistance came from SS troops, including Dutch SS, who knew they would receive little mercy if captured by their countrymen.

Attached to 2 Division from 1 to 18 April was 'A' Squadron, 1st Canadian Armoured Carrier Regiment (the Kangaroos). The maintenance of their Ram carriers was an unending burdensome chore, for the vehicles had been in continual use for years, first as training tanks in Britain, then as personnel carriers on the Continent. As in every armoured unit, RCEME craftsmen performed daily miracles to keep the vehicles moving.

After Groningen, 8th Recce swung east to cover the last fifteen kilometres lying between them and the North Sea. They reached their objective, the tiny port of Delfzijl on 21 April; however, the port was defended by a determined garrison of roughly 3,000 men, flooded surrounding terrain and large-calibre naval guns located on both sides of the Ems estuary. The capture of Delfzijl would not be a walkover. The German forces pushed back into this corner of Holland had only one route out, by sea, and they were determined to hold the port, their last hope for escape to Germany.

RCD Staghounds entering Leeuwarden, 15 April 1945. (RCD Museum)

Kangaroos of 1st Armoured Personnel Carrier Regiment lift infantrymen of the Royal Hamilton Light Infantry into Groningen, Holland, 13 April 1945. (NAC PA130937)

On 20 April, 2 Division was relieved by the 3rd and shifted east to the right flank of 4 CAD, with a battle group based on the South Alberta Regiment tasked to protect the inter-divisional area. The division's objective was the city of Oldenburg but, as described below, the South Albertas decided that they would get there first.

THE ADVANCE TO THE SEA: 4 CAD AND 1 POLISH ARMOURED DIVISION

With 2 and 3 Divisions now clear of Doetinchem, there was room for 4 CAD to move through and join in the general advance to the north. For this campaign the division divided into two battle groups, *Lion* and *Tiger*. *Lion* was comprised of 10 Infantry Brigade, plus the Governor General's Foot Guards and 'B' Squadron of the 'Kangaroos,' while *Tiger* consisted of the remainder of 4 Armoured Brigade, the Canadian Grenadier Guards and the British Columbia Regiment, plus the Lake Superior Regiment less a company.

4 CAD operated to the east of 2 Division's line of advance for the first thirty kilometres, the ground between them being covered by II Corps' armoured car unit, the 12th Manitoba Dra-

goons. At Almelo the Canadians were joined by 1 Polish Armoured Division (Major-General Maczek), which was slotted in between 2 and 4 Canadian Divisions. The Poles, in fact, found themselves following the line of the Dutch/German border on its western side while 4 CAD parallelled them on the eastern side. Generally speaking, opposition was weak, but the low-lying, marshy terrain was anything but suitable for armour. Any fighting that did arise was carried on mainly by infantry forces, but the scout cars of the Manitoba Dragoons were invaluable in these circumstances, being able to clear ground bypassed by the battle groups. As the Dragoons' history notes:

> It is a difficult story to get clearly in one's mind even when one knows what went on. If one can visualise four divisions moving generally north with the one furthest to the east [4th Armoured] well ahead of the others, and then take the exposed flank of that division as a base for the operations of an armoured car regiment, one has a fair picture of the situation. With the whole emphasis of the advance to the north and to the east, the regiment was called upon to work in a westerly direction in an effort to expedite the link-up of these divisions. This had been done and the patrols had almost a free hand in fanning out to the west, south-west, and north-west. To say that these patrols had run amuck or run wild would not be far from the truth....

The Poles reached the North Sea on 15 April, south of Delfzijl. This meant that the substantial number of Germans located to their north were effectively trapped in north-eastern Holland, with their backs to the North Sea. Their only escape now would be by boat.

In connection with 4 Division's advance, mention must be made of the operations of Lieutenant-Colonel 'Swatty' Wotherspoon's South Alberta Regiment in late April 1945. On 13 April this unit was given the task of advancing independ-

British Columbia Regiment crewmen loading 17-pounder high-explosive rounds into a Sherman Firefly during the 4th Armoured Division advance toward Oldenburg, 8 April 1945. (NAC PA113696)

ently between 4 Armoured and 2 Infantry Divisions, but not in close contact with either formation. Wotherspoon was provided with some SAS troops and ordered to move north-west on a 20-kilometre front toward Oldenburg. For nearly three weeks the South Albertas fought a private war, using their own tanks for artillery support, organizing their own engineer troop to deal with the many small rivers and numerous booby traps in the area, negotiating with German civil authorities and, generally, having the best time possible under the conditions.

A high point of this little odyssey was an action near Varrelbusch airfield on the evening of 15 April, when Lieutenant Danny McLeod's troop from 'C' Squadron fought a mixed force of German armour. The troop had no problem taking out a *Hetzer* self-propelled gun and two medium tanks, but then encountered a 68-ton King Tiger, a much more dangerous opponent. Gunner Carson Daley remembered that he hit the German behemoth with three rounds of 17-pounder AP although his "knees were knocking something terrible", but there was no effect. Troop Sergeant Tom Milner remembered scoring eight hits before the King Tiger exposed its flank in attempting to withdraw, which allowed the troop to knock out the monster.

This hard-fought and successful little tank battle resulted in McLeod receiving the Military Cross.

The South Albertas' private war came to an end on 4 May when they entered Oldenburg, which had been secured by 2 Division. They might have got there first had they been able to bridge the broad Kusten Canal, but they were praised by the 10 Brigade historian for "a job unparalleled for initiative".

WEST OF THE IJSSEL

When 1 Division crossed the Ijssel River to attack Apeldoorn, their assault was being co-ordinated with another attack being made by the remainder of I Canadian Corps farther south – a break-out from the Nijmegen salient. The operation was carried out in the staff college standard format of three phases: the clearing of the south-eastern portion of the 'island,' then the clearing of the remainder, an operation that would involve 5 CAD, and finally the crossing of the Neder Rijn (Lower Rhine) to capture Arnhem.

The first phase saw the Ontario Regiment placed under command of the British 49 Division. Begun on 2 April, the operation was completed in one day and, starting on 3 April, 5 CAD began its first operation in north-west Europe. 11 Infantry Brigade, supported by the Governor General's Horse Guards cleared 'the island' against light opposition, also in one day.

The assault crossing of the Neder Rijn took place on 11 April, co-ordinated, as noted above, with the attack by 1 Division on Apeldoorn. British forces, with a troop of the Ontario Regiment attached, made the attack, while 5 CAD and 1 Armoured Brigade's Calgary Regiment supported the operation with indirect fire from the south bank. The next day, 5 CAD was relieved by Brigadier W.C. Murphy's 1 Armoured Brigade, and the division then drove south and crossed the Rhine at Emmerich before proceeding north to Doetinchem. This brief passage along the east bank of the Rhine would be 5 CAD's only incursion onto German soil.

Arnhem was cleared between April 11 and 14, with the Ontario Regiment taking a conspicuous part in the fighting, while the Calgary Regiment noted that they fired almost incessantly for two days and three nights, supplementing the artillery support. Alexander McKee's book, *The Race for the Rhine Bridges*, quotes Lieutenant F.S. (Steve) Wotton of the Ontario's 'C' Squadron:

'C' Squadron took the right hand road through the factory area and did its initial attack over a railway embankment with the British infantry clearing a large factory which I understand was in the cellulose business and was, in peacetime, a competitor to a British firm which employed the Company Commander who I was working closely with. I can recall

Tanks of the Calgary Regiment carry British infantry in the offensive beyond Arnhem. (KOCR Museum)

some interesting comments by the Company Commander prior to the battle that we should ensure a very thorough covering fire for his men as they cleared the factory.

Meanwhile, Apeldoorn had been captured by 1 Division, supported by the tanks of 2 Armoured Brigade's 1st Hussars, who had been attached to the division since 6 April. While the Hussars were fighting alongside the RCR, north of the city, 1 Armoured Brigade's Three Rivers Regiment was supporting the PPCLI to the south. The divisional commander, Major-General Foster, who had commanded 4 CAD in Normandy, had no intention of fighting in Apeldoorn itself, however, preferring to squeeze out the German garrison. By 17 April the Germans had been expelled from Apeldoorn and were being pursued westward by Foster's troops, and with both Arnhem and Apeldoorn in Allied hands the Army commander gave Major-General Bert Hoffmeister's 'Mighty Maroon Machine' just four days in which to reach the Ijsselmeer. After that there would be another task for 5 CAD.

THE ADVANCE TO THE SEA: 5 CAD

Operation *Cleanser* (Dutch Cleanser being a well-known detergent) began on 14 April. 5 Armoured Brigade group, under Brigadier Ian Cumberland, motored north-west, passing Arnhem on their left side, their objective being the town of Otterloo. The brigade moved 'two up' with the British Columbia Dragoons on the right and the 8th New Brunswick Hussars on the left, and following on the centre line was Lord Strathcona's Horse and part of the motorized Westminster Regiment. Led by its regimental reconnaissance troop, each forward armoured regiment had a company of infantry attached, as well as two troops of 'Badgers' (flame-throwers mounted on Ram tanks) and three troops of 'Flails' (mine-clearing Shermans). With these forces the brigade set out to take on the minefields, roadblocks and anti-tank guns that awaited them. Making effective use of their attached infantry and liberal use of the flame-throwers, the forward regiments reached their initial objectives with light casualties. Still, as Douglas How's history of the 8th Hussars tells us, it was not a walkover:

Across a distance of nearly a mile, an 88 cracked at the first tanks to break through the morning haze. Three others joined the chorus.

They were firing on Lieutenant Bill Spencer's leading troop of B Squadron. A good and gallant officer, Spencer at once moved to outflank the position even though it exposed him fully to enemy fire. The Germans struck his tank once; it kept on going. Trooper [D.W.] Boone, his gunner, got one gun in his sights and took it out. The crew fell around it. The crews of another gun fled. The tank wheeled towards the

327

The commander of 5th Armoured Brigade, Brigadier Ian Cumberland (on the left), discusses operations with the commanding officers of the Westminster Regiment and the 8th Hussars, Holland April 1945. (NAC PA131033)

other two. There was a flash of hurtling explosive against the steel of Spencer's tank, a glare and burst of exploding light. He fell mortally wounded. So did his gunner.

The tank began to burn. The three survivors of the crew evacuated but when Lance Corporal James Stanley Stewart saw that the officer and gunner had not made it he seized a fire extinguisher and leaped back into the flaming hulk. He put out the fire that was already eating at Lieutenant Spencer's clothes and then put out the fire itself. After that, he took command of the tank and rejoined the squadron.

On the second day of the advance, the Strathconas, who were now the right forward unit of the brigade, hoped to reach Otterloo before nightfall. They did not succeed. Large enemy forces were reported in and north of Otterloo, and so the 'Straths' harboured for the night with the intention of mounting an attack at first light.

Sergeant H.K. Robertson, Governor General's Horse Guards, briefs his troop during the advance from Arnhem to the Ijsselmeer (Zuider Zee). (NAC PA108015)

The assault on Otterloo, conducted during the morning of 17 April, was successful and casualties were light, as the Strathconas' history, *A Record of Achievement*, tells us.

When the squadron leader (Major J. Smith of 'C' Squadron) got almost to the first road-block, his tank was hit by a bazooka. It set fire to the kit and ammunition on the back of the tank and Major Smith was momentarily stunned. The crew got out quickly, only one wounded – Lance Corporal [R.L.] Pengelly, the driver. The major jumped away from the road and threw himself flat on the open field. Sergeant [P.R.] Switzer, his gunner, got into a round hole which the Germans had dug as a weapon pit; as luck would have it, this hole was directly in the path of the tanks as they cut out to pass the Major's, and every tank that followed passed directly over Switzer's head, wearing down the height of his shelter; the last tank scratched his skull slightly!

5 Armoured Brigade swept on, heading north-west toward the next objectives, the towns of Barneveld and beyond that, Voorthuizen. Meanwhile, the headquarters of 5 CAD moved into Otterloo. However, an entire German battalion, situated in a wood to the north, had been missed by the advancing Canadians, and this battalion had been joined by the survivors of the action at Apeldoorn who had been pushed westward out of that city toward Otterloo. Shortly after divisional headquarters arrived in the town, on the evening of 16 April, the Germans decided to retake it, and a second Battle of Otterloo was fought. In an interview, many years later, with historians Ben Greenhous and Bill McAndrew, Hoffmeister described what happened:

I had selected Otterloo as my headquarters which was, incidentally, also the headquarters of the Irish Regiment [of Canada]. I had deliberately chosen it so that we would have some protection. The Irish Regiment was deployed around us and there was a field regiment there, 17th Field, and our own divisional protective troops, but all of a sudden we were just overwhelmed with Germans everywhere.... This was the occasion, of course, in Otterloo when the 17th Field Regiment got to the point of firing at the Germans over open sights. They were finally overrun, the Germans capturing their guns, and the 17th Field then mounted a counterattack, took their guns back and took on the Germans over open sights again as they were withdrawing.... People were shooting in all directions and I think it was the one and only time in the war when the clerks and batmen and so on around divisional headquarters had the opportunity to fire a shot at anything.... I was moving around the area until such time as the whole thing started closing in and it looked

An 8th Hussars Firefly passes through Putten on the way to the Zuider Zee, 18 April 1945. Note the different varieties of steel track welded on the front of the hull, and also the unique attempt to camouflage the length of the gun barrel. (NAC PA131043)

as though I could have just been nipped off. At that time I got into the armoured command vehicle, locked the doors and prepared to stay there and fight it out. There were batmen and so on underneath the armoured command vehicle shooting at Germans as they were going past, but I had to maintain contact and communications. This was the only way I could, from inside the vehicle, for which it was intended. We kept it up all night and it was a fascinating battle.

5 CAD passed through the towns of Barneveld, Voorthuizen, Putten and Ermelo before reaching the shores of the Ijsselmeer at Harderwijk on 17 April. When the Strathconas arrived they spotted a ship flying a German naval flag and, at the behest of higher headquarters, they engaged it. General Hoffmeister recalled:

It was a German naval supply ship, not a big one, but maybe seven or eight hundred tons. Fortunately it was high tide and the tanks kept the vessel under surveillance. Then, as the tide

went out they sent a patrol out and captured the crew. By that time, unfortunately, the crew had destroyed their code books and various other things, and there wasn't much to be gained from that point of view, but the ship was carrying a full cargo of wine and cheese which the Germans were taking back from Holland… So we quickly mounted an operation when the tide was out far enough and had three-ton trucks go out and unload this vessel before we reported it to anyone else. We made sure we got the wine and cheese for use in the division and then reported that we had captured this ship and turned the prisoners over and said nothing too much about the cargo.

True to his word, the Army Commander gave Hoffmeister fresh orders. His division was now to proceed to the other side of Holland, to the north-east coast, and capture the last remaining port in German hands, Delfzijl. Meanwhile, the division's positions in western Holland were taken over by 1 Division, and with it was the Princess Louise Dragoon Guards, now

Sogel, Germany. Painting by Bruno Bobak illustrating the battle in Sogel on 9 April 1945. From the 'tactical sign' painted on the rear, the tank can be identified as belonging to the Governor General's Foot Guards. (Canadian War Museum CWM11980)

tain a railway line running in the same direction as the Canadian axis of advance.

Corporal Millard Allison, of 3rd Troop 'B' Squadron, would win a Distinguished Conduct Medal in the bridge-head fighting. The BCR history, Douglas Harker's *The Dukes,* relates how:

No sooner had his tank nosed out on to the railway embankment than it was exposed to high velocity fire and heavy shelling. Realizing that he could not take evasive action because of the very soft ground on either side of the embankment, and that he must perforce clear all opposition as he advanced, 'Tex' Allison hit upon the stratagem of shunting a railway goods truck ahead of his tank. The plan was completely successful. The enemy, disturbed by the erratic progress of the truck, turned all guns upon it. He was enabled to liquidate the enemy posts methodically as he advanced. The crazy progress continued for some 2500 yards during which space his guns accounted for over fifty enemy killed. Despite his efforts the infantry gradually closed in with their deadly *panzerfausts.* When he was unable to depress his tank guns sufficiently to deal with them, he held them off with hand grenades and with his pistol, standing in the turret, exposed to unremitting small arms fire. [After rescuing his wounded troop leader] he returned to his own tank where he remained for another forty-eight hours sustaining the infantry against repeated counter-attacks.

restored to their former role of a divisional recce regiment after a period of service as an infantry battalion. At that point, however, a local armistice was invoked in order that food and fuel could be rushed in to relieve the starving Dutch population, and 1 Division and 1 Armoured Brigade spent the last two weeks of the war sitting in static positions.

OVER THE KÜSTEN CANAL

The two armoured divisions of II Canadian Corps, 4 CAD and 1 Polish, reached the thirty-metre-wide, ninety-kilometre-long Küsten Canal, linking the Ems and Weser Rivers, on 14 April. The bridges all having been blown, the Algonquin Regiment crossed the obstacle in boats at 1 a.m. on 17 April, the tanks of the British Columbia Regiment providing the supporting fire. The remainder of 10 Brigade crossed just in time to see off the enemy's counter-attack and, once the engineers had erected a bridge, suitably enough named 'Algonquin Bridge', 'B' Squadron of the BCR was able to deploy into the bridgehead. At that point the enemy managed to destroy the bridge, leaving the rest of the regiment stranded on the 'wrong' side of the obstacle. It took two days to replace the bridge; meanwhile, 'B' Squadron fought on in the isolated bridgehead, which happened to con-

With the construction of a replacement bridge over the canal, the advance resumed, with the Poles heading north-east, toward the port of Leer, while the Canadians travelled east-north-east toward the city of Oldenburg. But then the Poles suddenly stopped. They reported that their advance was being held up but, oddly, they refused all offers of air support to help remove the obstruction. Finally the reason filtered back to Army headquarters. At Niederlangen they had overrun a

(Above) A Grenadier Guards Sherman fires on an enemy position in a farm near Bad Zwischenahn, west of Oldenburg, on 29 April 1945. (NAC PA166805)

(Right) Tanks of the Fort Garry Horse supporting the Royal Regiment of Canada during the final thrust on Oldenburg, Germany, 25 April 1945. Note the use of logs as additional 'armour' to protect against short-range *Panzerfausts*. By this stage in the war it had become almost impossible for the armoured units to salvage steel track to use as extra protection on the hull and turret. (NAC PA166803)

camp for foreign workers containing thousands of Polish women, allegedly including some of the soldiers' wives. The battle stopped while food, clothing and medical aid were rushed forward. On 22 April the Poles finally got back to the war, however, and no one in First Canadian Army complained about the delay.

CLEARING THE DELFZIJL POCKET

The action to reduce the Delfzijl pocket took a week, from 23 April to 2 May 1945. The attack against the port would be a pincer movement with two battalions attacking from the south, supported by the 8th Hussars, while two other battalions approached from the north. The BCD participated in the operations conducted on the northern approaches, but they did so dismounted, acting as infantry for the first and last time in this war.

The civilian population was still in place, so that massive shelling and bombardment from the sea or sky were ruled out, while the sodden nature of the ground meant that attacks were conducted – at night – by infantry, not tanks. Nevertheless the tanks followed the infantry when and where they could. As each day passed the ring around Delfzijl grew tighter; and each night another assault was made. German sorties from the town were met with a wall of steel shot and beaten back every time. Even though everyone, on both sides, knew that the war was all but over, the fighting went on. Douglas How notes an action that took place on 1 May:

Within 800 to 900 yards of the town, the troop [of 'A' Squadron, 8th Hussars, commanded by Lieutenant William Gerrard] was engaged by a battery of three 88 millimetre guns encased in cement positions. The range was extremely close when [Trooper Wallace] Bishop [Gerrard's gunner] opened fire. One of the German guns was destroyed. The others kept firing. They damaged the guns in the troop's other tanks so that Gerrard's was the only one still firing. His was hit once, twice, four times. It began to burn.

The officer piloted the tank into a side road so passage for others would not be blocked. From there, he kept it in action as long as action was possible, meanwhile passing back information on the German position by radio. The tank kept on firing because of Bishop. He had already been hit and thrown from his seat. He was bleeding badly. His gun-loader was also wounded. The heat of the flames was gathering around them. With blood falling from his nose and mouth, Bishop fought his way back into his seat. Somehow he traversed the gun until once more it focused on a German gun, and then he fired. The German gun became a mass of useless, smoking steel.

Only then did Gerrard and Bishop and the rest of their brave crew evacuate their burning wounded Sherman. Their troop withdrew. But, armed with the information Gerrard had channelled back, another troop immediately took over and knocked out the last three German guns.

Then the war was over. On 4 May the message was passed to all units, "Cancel all offensive operations, ceasefire at 08:00 5 May 1945." Most were too numb to celebrate, the predominant emotion being gratitude, thankful that they had survived when so many good and valiant soldiers had not.

On Tuesday, 22 May, 5 CAD gathered in one place, for the only time in its existence, at Eede airport outside Groningen. In General Hoffmeister's words:

I think there was no formation prouder anywhere at any time than 5th Armoured Division was when we concentrated every fighting vehicle in the division on the old airfield, and were inspected by the army commander, and the men were able to see for the first time what a whole armoured division looked like concentrated in one spot. They were able to move around in their own time before and after the inspection, just marvel at what they'd seen, and take pictures with their own cameras and so on. They could take back to Canada an impression of this great division of which they were a part, a division that didn't lose a battle, incidentally.

Another armoured organization that saw its component parts together again for the first time in two-and-a-half years was the 25th Canadian Armoured Delivery Regiment (The Elgins). These often-unsung heroes had performed their duties with great efficiency and had earned the gratitude and respect of the entire Armoured Corps.

Although the war in Europe had ended, there was still a war to be fought in the Pacific. Canada had offered a division for service with the Americans because Prime Minister Mackenzie King, for his own reasons, wanted to avoid further service alongside the British even though elements of the RCN and RCAF were already serving with the British in South-East Asia. Major-General Hoffmeister would command the new 6 Division and volunteers were sought from the ranks of the veterans in Europe, the Prime Minister insisting that only volunteers would fight in the Pacific.

The Canadian armoured regiments were garrisoned around Holland while they awaited repatriation. The Fort Garry Horse, for example, found themselves in Doetinchem, where they made many friends and established a regimental monument in the form of one of their tanks placed in a local park. (As a Regular regiment stationed in Germany, they would return to Doetinchem twenty years later to refurbish this monument.)

The idea of tank memorials became a popular one in 2 Armoured Brigade. The Sherbrookes were asked by the Canadian Army Film Unit to assist in making a picture based on the exploits of a Sherman 75mm named *Bomb*. It was *Bomb's* proud record to have been the only tank in the regiment to make it all the way from the Normandy beaches to VE Day. *Bomb* was recovered from the Ordnance Corps Field Park where all the tanks had been deposited to await turnover to the Dutch Army. Its crew was reunited and taken to the Rhineland, where scenes were shot on the site of the original battles. After the filming the regiment contrived to retain *Bomb,* and arranged, through less than proper methods, to have the tank sent to Canada. Today it sits in front of the Regimental Armoury in Sherbrooke. The 1st Hussars, not to be outdone, also had its senior tank, named *Holy Roller,* returned to Canada. Today it is a focal point of regimental parades and pride.

The atomic bombings of Hiroshima and Nagasaki brought the Pacific war to an unexpectedly quick end, just as the first drafts of Canadian troops had finished their home leave and were departing for Kentucky to receive training on American weapons and to be formed into American-style units.

'THE HOT WASH', JANUARY 1946

For many years it has been customary in the Canadian Army to follow-up an exercise with a discussion on what was learned from the experience. This activity, light-heartedly called the 'hot

A 17th Hussars armoured car watches over a column of disarmed German prisoners as they march home. (NAC PA134287)

wash', is normally conducted immediately after the exercise cease-fire while memories are still fresh. In the aftermath of the Second World War the Royal Canadian Armoured Corps – it had became 'Royal' on 2 August 1945, in recognition of its wartime services – held just such a meeting, the instigator being Brigadier Tom Rutherford, now Senior Advisor, RCAC (UK).

The meeting was held at Rutherford's headquarters on 3 January 1946 and included a virtual *Who's Who* of the wartime Corps. One hundred and fifty questions were put to the assembled officers under two broad headings: the post-war set-up of the RCAC, and matters of organization, equipment, tactical doctrine and training. Naturally enough opinions varied, sometimes widely, but on a number of issues there was unanimity or near unanimity. There were, for example, no dissenting voices to the questions, 'Should there be an Armoured Corps Association?' and 'Do you favour retaining the black beret?' There was also a favourable unanimous vote to the question, 'Should steps be taken to prepare and publish a history of the Royal Canadian Armoured Corps?'

The question of a new RCAC shoulder badge was also raised, but not resolved, at this meeting. Within a year the decision was taken to adopt the Royal Armoured Corps' red on yellow shoulder badge and red over yellow corps 'flash' used for marking corps vehicles. (The red over yellow flash had its origins in the Great War when flags with this design were used to mark the left and right hand sides of a trench crossing made for tanks.) The RAC's mailed fist badge, introduced in 1942, was also adopted with the letters RCAC used instead of RAC.

A rare sight: a Sherman in German markings. This tank was 're-captured' after the end of hostilities, 10 May 1945. (NAC PA115009)

When the meeting got into the realm of the technical, opinions grew farther apart and, not unnaturally, tended to follow the line of experience of the speaker. Veterans of the independent brigades thought that the Corps should, in future, consist of independent brigades, while veterans of the armoured divisions voted in favour of having a divisional structure. The brigade structure was the one eventually adopted. Although the meeting did not resolve many issues relating to the future of the Corps, there was some eminent good sense displayed. For example,

Colonel R.E.A. Morton, late commanding officer of the Fort Garry Horse, when asked his opinion on future organization noted that, 'I am afraid any views for the future organization of the Canadian Army are somewhat of a pipe dream, as I understand it is already decided – though I do NOT know what it is. In any event it is sure to be hamstrung by "insufficient funds"!'

Morton was a better prophet than he knew, for within the year the government's axe would be at work gutting both the Army and the Corps.

THE FINAL ACCOUNTING

Another of Brigadier Rutherford's projects undertaken at this time was the compilation of the Royal Canadian Armoured Corps' Roll of Honour. The Corps' fatal casualties in the Second World War totalled 2,005 – 229 officers and 1,776 other ranks. The only satisfaction to be gained from these grim statistics is the knowledge that the examples of valour and self-sacrifice made by those soldiers would set the standard for their regiments and the Corps in the years to come.

Medals Awarded Following the North-West Europe Campaign

The 1939-1945 Star, awarded for six months on active operations.

The France and Germany Star, awarded for service in North-West Europe between 6 June 1944 and 8 May 1945.

The 1939-45 War Medal, awarded to all full-time service personnel for 28 days service between September 1939 and 2 September 1945. A bronze oak leaf is worn on the ribbon to signify a 'Mention in Despatches'.

The Canadian Armoured Corps Order of Battle: The Second World War

1st Armoured Car Regiment [Royal Canadian Dragoons]

2nd Armoured Regiment [Lord Strathcona's Horse (Royal Canadians)]

3rd Armoured Reconnaissance Regiment [The Governor General's Horse Guards]

4th Reconnaissance Regiment [IV Princess Louise Dragoon Guards]

5th Armoured Regiment [8th Princess Louise's (New Brunswick) Hussars]

6th Armoured Regiment [1st Hussars]

7th Reconnaissance Regiment [17th Duke of York's Royal Canadian Hussars]

8th Reconnaissance Regiment [14th Canadian Hussars]

9th Armoured Regiment [The British Columbia Dragoons]

10th Armoured Regiment [The Fort Garry Horse]

11th Armoured Regiment [The Ontario Regiment]

12th Armoured Regiment [Three Rivers Regiment]

14th Armoured Regiment [The Calgary Regiment] (There was no regiment with the numeral '13.')

15th (Reserve) Armoured Regiment [6th Duke of Connaught's Royal Canadian Hussars]

16th (Reserve) Armoured Regiment [7th/11th Hussars]

17th (Reserve) Armoured Regiment [Prince Edward Island Light Horse]

18th Armoured Car Regiment [12th Manitoba Dragoons]

19th (Reserve) Army Tank Regiment [New Brunswick Regiment (Tank)]

20th Army Tank Regiment [16th/22nd Saskatchewan Horse]

21st Armoured Regiment [The Governor General's Foot Guards]

22nd Armoured Regiment [The Canadian Grenadier Guards]

23rd Army Tank Regiment [Halifax Rifles]

24th Reconnaissance Regiment [*Les Voltigeurs de Québec*]

25th Armoured Delivery Regiment [The Elgin Regiment]

26th Army Tank Regiment [Grey and Simcoe Foresters]

27th Armoured Regiment [The Sherbrooke Fusilier Regiment]

28th Armoured Regiment [The British Columbia Regiment]

29th Armoured Reconnaissance Regiment [The South Alberta Regiment]

30th Reconnaissance Regiment [The Essex Regiment]

31st (Alberta) Reconnaissance Regiment

32nd Reconnaissance Regiment [Royal Montreal Regiment]

1st Armoured Personnel Carrier Regiment

CHAPTER 17

The Early Years of the Cold War, 1945–1955

Between November 1945 and January 1946 the units of the Royal Canadian Armoured Corps serving in Europe came home to Canada, with the exception of a specially-raised 'second' 7th Recce Regiment which served with the Canadian Army Occupation Force in Germany between 1 June 1945 and 24 May 1946.

Although twenty regiments were repatriated, each of their journeys followed much the same pattern. The overseas units were run-down to a few hundred all ranks as volunteers for the Pacific Force departed and others gradually left for home based on an elaborate point system. Vehicles were turned over to the

Dutch and Belgian armies and, after spending many months in *ad hoc* garrisons in Holland, units were moved to Britain, where the men were sent on generous periods of block leave. Finally, they gathered at the docks in England for return to Halifax on the *Lady Rodney*, the *Empress of Scotland* or the *Île de France*. Or, alternatively, they sailed for New York on the *Queen Elizabeth*.

After an ocean voyage of between six and eleven days, they would leave the dockside for the train journey to the regimental home town, shedding soldiers from other communities along the way. Although they had been initially organized on a territorial basis, by war's end regiments were composed of of-

The Ontario Regiment arrives home after more than four years overseas, Oshawa railway station, 29 November 1945. This scene is typical of what happened to all of the armoured regiments coming back to Canada in 1945 and 1946. (Ontario Regiment Museum)

ficers and men from every part of the Dominion. Invariably the returning veterans were met by the home unit, the 'second regiment' which had formed a reserve and sustaining base for the overseas unit. There would be a parade, heartfelt speeches of welcome and thanks, and then the colonel would give the final command – "Dismiss" – and another of Canada's great wartime regiments would dissolve into the welcoming arms of its families.

The performance of armoured and reconnaissance units during the war years ensured the future of the Corps in the post-war Army, even though its structure would not be settled for some time. In the meanwhile, in the midst of the turmoil that marked the dismantling of the wartime force, there was a minor administrative detail to be dealt with. On 2 August 1945 the Canadian Armoured Corps was granted the title 'Royal', and its official acronym became RCArmdC. The reason for this awkward designation was that the abbreviation RCAC already belonged to the Royal Canadian Army Cadets. The Cadets had prior rights, so some delicacy was required. However, in April 1946 Canadian Army Orders published a notice to the effect that henceforth, 'for the purposes of military correspondence,' the RCArmdC would be known as the RCAC, while the cadets would henceforth be known as the RC Army Cadets.

One of the first substantial acts to deal with the Corps' place in the post-war military structure was the appointment of the first Director of Armour in early 1946. This important staff post was given to Colonel Robert Moncel, former commander of 4 Armoured Brigade, who, like many officers who were given the opportunity to serve in the Regular Force, took a reduction in rank to do so. The Director's function was to oversee all aspects of the Corps' day-to-day existence, and especially to advise the hierarchy in Army Headquarters on organization, equipment and training. One of Moncel's initiatives to weld together the post-war Corps was to publish a new bulletin entitled *RCAC Digest*, which contained classified information about what other armies were doing in the fields of organization and training, tactics, and, perhaps most important at this time, the latest in armoured fighting vehicle design and testing.

The school in Camp Borden continued to serve as the focal point of the Corps. Under its wartime designation, A-33 Canadian Armoured Corps Training Centre, it had grown beyond all recognition, with nearly 2,300 officers and men serving in its ranks, but in October 1946 it was placed on a peace-time footing, with a much reduced establishment strength of only 115. Colonel R.E.A. Morton at that time passed command of the newly renamed Royal Canadian Armoured Corps (School) to a fellow Garry, Lieutenant-Colonel Bruce Macdonald. Under Macdonald the School was organized with five training squadrons – Depot Squadron looked after the basic training of new recruits, Driving and Maintenance, Gunnery and Wireless

Squadrons did the trades courses and trained instructors, while Tactics Squadron taught both tank and reconnaissance field operations to NCOs and officers. One of the important innovations at this time was the introduction of Canadian Officer Training Corps (COTC) courses to qualify new officers for both the regular and Militia units, and COTC training was to be the main focus of the School during the summer months for much of the next two decades. Although, in its experienced veterans, the institution held a wealth of talent in 1946, it had little in the way of modern equipment.

As had been the case in 1919, thoughts soon turned to the organization of the post-war Army, and in 1946 the Government announced that the Canadian Army (Active Force), i.e. the regulars, would number 25,000 all ranks. If that figure seems small it should be kept in mind that this represented a five-fold increase over the number in 1939. The Canadian Army (Reserve Force) was to number 180,000.

Apart from numbers, the Army also had a new look. On 1 January 1947 five new 'Commands' were created to replace the venerable Military Districts – Eastern Command, with headquarters in Halifax; Quebec Command, based in Montreal; Central Command in Oakville, Ontario; Prairie Command in Winnipeg; and Western Command with headquarters in Edmonton. Within the Commands were six subordinate Areas: British Columbia Area, Saskatchewan Area, Western Ontario Area, Eastern Ontario Area, Eastern Quebec Area and New Brunswick Area. A Newfoundland Area was added in 1949.

The mobilization plan called for an army of two corps, com-

Militia Armoured Brigades, 1947–1954

19 Armoured Brigade – HQ Toronto
3rd Armoured Regiment [Governor General's Horse Guards]
6th Armoured Regiment [1st Hussars]
10th Armoured Regiment [Fort Garry Horse]
11th Armoured Regiment [Ontario Regiment]

20 Armoured Brigade – HQ Montreal
12th Armoured Regiment [Sherbrooke Regiment]
15th Armoured Regiment [6th Hussars]
21st Armoured Regiment [Régiment de Hull]

21 Armoured Brigade – HQ Moncton
5th Armoured Regiment [8th Princess Louise's (New Brunswick) Hussars]
23rd Armoured Regiment [Halifax Rifles]

22 Armoured Brigade – HQ Vancouver
13th Armoured Regiment [British Columbia Regiment]
14th Armoured Regiment [King's Own Calgary Regiment]
20th Armoured Regiment [briefly Saskatchewan Armd. Regiment, then Saskatchewan Dragoons]

Mounted march-past of the first Canadian Officer Training Corps (COTC) course, in Canadian-made Grizzlies, at the Royal Canadian Armoured Corps School in Camp Borden, 27 July 1947; and another view of the COTC mounted parade showing the Kangaroo armoured personnel carriers used by the School for driver training. (RCAC Archives)

Nineteen forty-six was a milestone year for the Corps for it was then that the Canadian Cavalry Association reconstituted itself as the RCAC Association (Cavalry). Respectful, as always, of tradition, the new Association made plans to carry on the practice of offering trophies for annual competition. The existing awards, the Leonard Challenge Trophy, the Westby Trophy, the Stockwell Challenge Cup, and so on, were given a renewed existence. The Association also tackled the tangled problem of regimental seniority. The RCAC was more than simply the cavalry in armour. It now included many units whose traditions had nothing to do with cavalry: regiments of infantry, machine guns, tanks or artillery. In 1947 the Association decided that regimental seniority would be based on the date that a unit achieved regimental status – not the same thing as a birthday or date of founding, since many regiments had their origins as independent troops or companies and did not become full-fledged regiments until many years had passed. Of course, regimental seniority did not affect the relative standing of Regular versus Reserve units or regiments of guards versus regiments of the line.

With the structure of the post-war army in place, two problems were immediately evident: manpower and equipment. As a peacetime measure the regular units were only permitted to recruit to 75 percent of authorized strength, while the reserves managed to attract only 47,000 in total, a mere 17 percent of their authorized establishment. The Army had disposed of most of its armoured vehicles in Europe, in the expectation of receiving modern replacements, but those replacements were slow to appear.

Fortunately for the future of the RCAC, the wartime units of the Corps had left a valuable legacy – a cadre of highly experienced and capable veterans. The war had been a national effort and had swept up officers and men who would never have contemplated a military career, and many were people of superior intellectual and leadership ability. Their contribution to the Corps over the coming decades would be immense, both those who continued to serve in the regular and reserve units, as well as many who would see no further military service. This latter group, from their positions in government, business, industry and academe, kept a sympathetic eye on the trials and travails of Canada's black hatters and occasionally lent a helping hand.

In keeping with Worthy's wishes and wartime practice, the regiments of the Corps were again numbered, although the numbers were shuffled somewhat in 1946 mainly because a number of units reverted to their pre-war infantry affiliation.

prised of six divisions with 2 and 6 Divisions being armoured formations. The 2nd was to contain Militia units from eastern Canada while the 6th would employ western units. As well there were four independent armoured brigades plus the necessary corps and army troops. The armoured brigades were numbered 19 through 22, these numbers following in sequence from the infantry brigades which were numbered 1 through 18. The regular units formed a notional 23 Brigade.

The effectiveness of the four brigades appears to have been related directly to the physical proximity of the units and headquarters. The regiments of 20 Brigade, being fairly close together, were able to train together at Farnham, Quebec, in July 1947, and at Petawawa in August of the following year. The four-day long exercise at Farnham also included the 7th and 16th Reconnaissance Regiments. The other three brigades began their collective training in 1948, with 19 Brigade following the 20th to Petawawa in an exercise series called *Plunder,* but the 19th was without one of its regiments since the Fort Garrys were located in far-off Winnipeg. The 22nd exercised in Camp Wainwright, although it was a long haul for the BCR, and the 21st trained in Camp Utopia, New Brunswick, even though the Halifax Rifles likewise had a long journey to make. Distance between units, making collective training difficult, was to prove the major weakness in the armoured brigade concept. In 1954 the experiment was ended as a consequence of an Army reorganization.

The officers of the Royal Canadian Armoured Corps School, 1949, on the occasion of the dedication of the Corps war memorial in what was to become known as Worthington Park. All were highly experienced veterans. Back row: Captain W.G. Harrod, MC; Captain J.A. Milbrath; Captain V.W. Jewkes, MC; Captain J.W. Quinn; Captain J.G. Moore; Captain N. Mann, MC; Captain J.C. Chartres; Captain K.C. Kennedy. Front row: Captain W.D. Little, MC; Major F.S. Corbeau, DSO; Major R.J. Graham, DSO; Major G.R. Hale, DSO; Lieutenant-Colonel B.F. Macdonald, DSO; Major J.F. Merner; Major E.V. Schuster; Major A.C. Beckingham; and Major D.G. Green.

In was in October 1952 that the Colonel Commandant donated the Worthington Trophy to the Corps. A silver model of a Centurion tank, the trophy was to be presented annually to the Militia unit acquiring the greatest number of RCAC (Association) trophies. The first winner, in 1954, was the 8th Princess Louise's (New Brunswick) Hussars.

THE REGULAR FORCE COMPONENT

Service in the post-war world provided considerable challenge for the two regular armoured regiments. For the Royal Canadian Dragoons it meant being converted from an armoured car role to that of a tank regiment and it was while they were co-located with the Corps School in Borden that their first shipment of Sherman tanks arrived in early 1947. The other regular unit, the Strathconas, also appeared in Camp Borden in January 1946 before moving back to the West in June to take up a new home at Currie Bar-

Then, too, some units such as the Three Rivers Regiment, the Grey and Simcoe Foresters and the New Brunswick Regiment (Tank) were converted – not always permanently – to anti-tank or anti-aircraft artillery. In the case of the Three Rivers Regiment the process was reversed just over a year later and they returned to the Corps, but this time as the 24th Regiment instead of their previous designation as the 12th. At this same time two units were added to the Corps: *Le Régiment de Hull* and the Queen's York Rangers. There was, as well, a process of rationalization to ensure that each Command had a similar share of armoured and reconnaissance units. By design, although the reasons are unclear, the armoured role was assigned to units in urban areas, while those based in small towns or rural areas were either re-allocated to other arms or given a reconnaissance role.

On 27 April 1948, as soon as he retired from active service, Major-General 'Fighting Frank' Worthington was appointed to be the first Honorary Colonel Commandant of The Royal Canadian Armoured Corps. (The term Honorary was dropped in 1964.) There could, of course, have been no other choice for this prestigious position, and Worthy held it until the end of his life. While the Colonel Commandant's position was intended to be mainly ceremonial in nature – looking after Corps traditions and morale – it came to be one of the truly important factors linking the far-flung regiments across the country, and one with considerable clout in Ottawa when protecting the Corps' broader interests.

racks in Calgary. At this time both regiments were mere skeletons, with just over a hundred soldiers apiece; however, their institutional health would soon be restored. Two months after their arrival in Calgary the Strathconas were driving up the Alaska Highway on Exercise *Muncho*, their task being to inspect and repair airstrips and landing fields along the route. During their absence from Currie Barracks some wartime H-huts were converted into desperately needed married quarters and, at the same time, an important aspect of the regiment's pre-war *raison d'etre* was restored, albeit in a small way, when a riding club was established with a stable and nearly a troop of horses.

It was during this period that Canada, and the Corps, lost its

The Worthington Trophy, donated by the first Colonel Commandant of the Corps, Major-General F.F. Worthington, for annual award to the best Militia regiment.

The Royal Canadian Dragoons taking their new 76mm diesel-powered Shermans into the field shortly after their move to Camp Petawawa in the spring of 1948. (Canadian Army Photo CC3730)

first soldier on United Nations duty. Brigadier H.H. Angle, former commanding officer of the British Columbia Dragoons, was killed in an air crash on 17 July 1950 while serving as Chief Military Observer with the Kashmir Commission.

THE POST-WAR RESERVES

If the regular units resembled skeletons, the immediate post-war period was also one of famine for the reserve units. Over the protests of the Conference of Defence Associations (CDA), in 1946 the Chief of the General Staff (CGS), Lieutenant-General Charles Foulkes, gave the reserve component of the Army a new name: the Canadian Army (Reserve Force). As the CDA pointed out, doing away with the time-honoured title 'Militia' did nothing at all to help recruiting. As had happened after the Great War, the regiments had reorganized around a small core of veterans. In the early years after the war all units had difficulty recruiting members, in part because roles were not clear and equipment was scarce, and part-time soldiering held little appeal for most veterans. The 8th (New Brunswick) Hussars, always one of the strongest regiments, held a summer camp in 1946, the only one in the Corps, but they could muster no more than 120 all ranks. Matters soon improved, however, as organization tables were produced and armoured vehicles began to appear on armoury floors. Soon, units like the Halifax Rifles were showing dramatic improvements in their parade state, going from 74 men in 1947 to 250 all ranks by 1953.

A major reason for this boost in recruiting and retention was acquisition of new Sherman tanks. In 1947 the Army purchased 294 M4A2 (76mm) HVSS Shermans, more commonly (if incorrectly) known as the M4A2E8 Sherman, along with thirty-two M-24 Chaffee light tanks (18 tons, crew of five, with a 75mm main gun). Both were American products. After the RCD and Strathconas were re-equipped, the remaining vehicles were parceled out to the reserve units, usually four to six per unit. Recce regiments were equipped with wartime Staghound armoured cars, as well as Lynx scout cars (armed with a .30 calibre machine-gun) and Universal carriers in an establishment calling for three sabre squadrons, each comprised of two light tank troops and two assault troops manning the Universal carriers. As there was no mechanized infantry in the Canadian army in the late 1940s, this role was carried out with internal RCAC resources.

A new innovation, although it had been long called for by the CDA, was the assignment of a small number of regulars to each reserve unit. Called the 'A&T' staff (Administration and Training), they were an invaluable aid to the Militia, both as examples of proper standards of dress, drill and decorum, and in taking on a great deal of the routine administration that would have otherwise burdened the time-pressed reservists.

Even though the reserves were largely equipped with recycled equipment from the war, still the government fretted about the costs. The 1952 Defence Estimates noted that while it

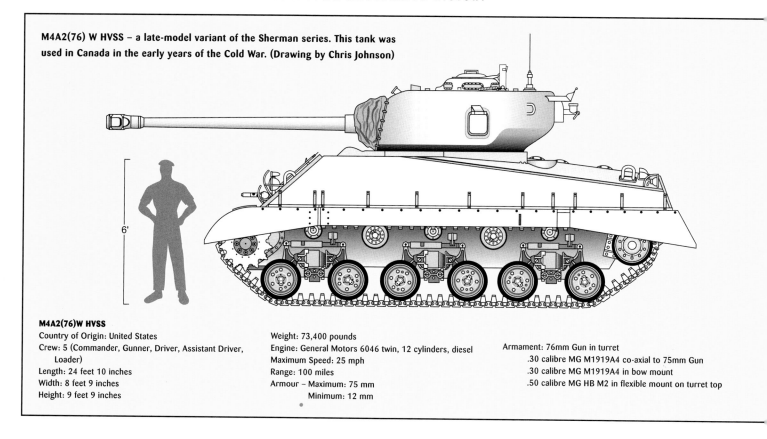

M4A2(76) W HVSS – a late-model variant of the Sherman series. This tank was used in Canada in the early years of the Cold War. (Drawing by Chris Johnson)

6'

M4A2(76)W HVSS

Country of Origin: United States
Crew: 5 (Commander, Gunner, Driver, Assistant Driver, Loader)
Length: 24 feet 10 inches
Width: 8 feet 9 inches
Height: 9 feet 9 inches

Weight: 73,400 pounds
Engine: General Motors 6046 twin, 12 cylinders, diesel
Maximum Speed: 25 mph
Range: 100 miles
Armour – Maximum: 75 mm
       Minimum: 12 mm

Armament: 76mm Gun in turret
    .30 calibre MG M1919A4 co-axial to 75mm Gun
    .30 calibre MG M1919A4 in bow mount
    .50 calibre MG HB M2 in flexible mount on turret top

had cost $82.30 to equip a trooper in 1939, the comparable figure in 1951 was $400.79. Those new Sherman tanks were not cheap either – they had cost the government $62,000 each!

Unit names were to prove to be a constant problem in the early post-war years. The numerical designations allocated in 1946 were as unpopular in the post-war Corps as they had been in 1940, so, in 1949, at the behest of the RCAC Association, the titles of all the units were changed so that the traditional name preceded the number, as in The Halifax Rifles (23rd Armoured Regiment). Adjustments were also made at this time to some unit titles, the Three Rivers Regiment's title was translated into French, and the Essex Regiment, named for its home county, was renamed The Windsor Regiment, for its home city.

Even the Corps itself did not escape the problem. For example, in March 1948 the Corps, to paraphrase one of the more eloquently written regimental histories, gained a slightly pompous, capitalized definite article, to become *The* Royal Canadian Armoured Corps. (It did not last. On 17 February 1964 the title reverted to Royal Canadian Armoured Corps.) This was part of a subtle bureaucratic campaign to add 'The' or 'Le' to the titles of regiments that had names, as opposed to numbers. Over the years only one regiment, Lord Strathcona's Horse (Royal Canadians), was able to resist this trend.

DOCTRINE: THE WAY AHEAD

The Corps' leadership, determined that there would not be a relapse to the pre-war state where progress had floundered because of an absence of doctrine, converted the School at Camp Borden into a 'brains trust' of sorts, and armour doctrine and technological innovations emanated from the RCAC School despite the limitations imposed by existing equipment. Experienced officers and NCOs were hand-picked for this duty, for the survival of the Corps lay in its ability to be agile and that demanded good people who could mentor the next generation.

A similar plan unfolded at the Army Staff College in Kingston, Ontario, since it was essential that the army retain the experience and lessons learned from the hard-fought war years. Experimental field formations were created by the Directorate of Military Training in consultation with the Corps School, so that the Army's future leaders understood the interplay between units and formations on the battlefield. Some of these paper formations influenced future Corps development: for example, the Staff College trained with a 'Divisional Regiment RCAC', a theoretical predecessor to the 1960s Light Armoured Regiment. This notional unit had M-24 Chaffee tanks, armoured personnel carriers based on a light tank chassis, and scout cars as well as portable anti-tank weapons. Although Canada would not field such an organization for another twenty years, the intellectual power was there to generate it in the late 1940s.

Order of Battle of the Royal Canadian Armoured Corps, 1947

1st Armoured Regiment [Royal Canadian Dragoons]

2nd Armoured Regiment [Lord Strathcona's Horse (Royal Canadians)]

3rd Armoured Regiment [The Governor General's Horse Guards]

4th Armoured Car Regiment [IV Princess Louise Dragoon Guards]

5th Armoured Regiment [8th (New Brunswick) Hussars]

6th Armoured Regiment [1st Hussars]

7th Reconnaissance Regiment [17th Duke of York's Royal Canadian Hussars]

8th Armoured Car Regiment [14th Canadian Hussars]

9th Reconnaissance Regiment [The British Columbia Dragoons]

10th Armoured Regiment [The Fort Garry Horse]

11th Armoured Regiment [Ontario Regiment]

12th Armoured Regiment [Sherbrooke Regiment]

13th Armoured Regiment [The British Columbia Regiment]

14th Armoured Regiment [King's Own Calgary Regiment]

15th Armoured Regiment [6th Duke of Connaught's Royal Canadian Hussars]

16th Reconnaissance Regiment [7th/11th Hussars]

17th (Prince Edward Island) Reconnaissance Regiment

18th Armoured Car Regiment [12th Dragoons]

19th Armoured Car Regiment [Edmonton Fusiliers]

20th (Saskatchewan) Armoured Regiment

21st Armoured Regiment [*Le Régiment de Hull*]

22nd Reconnaissance Regiment [Essex Regiment]

23rd Armoured Regiment [Halifax Rifles]

24th Armoured Regiment [Three Rivers Regiment]

25th Armoured Regiment [Queen's York Rangers]

The badge of the Royal Canadian Armoured Corps, approved in July 1949. It is identical in design to that of the Royal Armoured Corps except that the abbreviation 'RCAC' is shown on the gauntlet. Other designs were considered as early as 1945, but it was decided to conform to the badges adopted by the armoured corps of all other Commonwealth countries.

ONSET OF THE COLD WAR

Readers have already seen accounts of the two World Wars and the parts played in them by units of the Corps and its predecessors. These were well-defined conflicts: they have precise start and end dates, a readily identifiable enemy, and clear conclusions based on military achievements. The Cold War, and the Corps' role in it, had very different characteristics than previous wars: the start and end dates are debatable, the nature of the enemy's motives and methods were difficult to determine, and there was no decisive military conclusion. It would thus be easy to dismiss the period as a series of disconnected incidents mainly in obscure parts of the Third World, or merely as a struggle between the Soviet and American superpowers which involved Canada on the margins. But there was much more to it than that.

The Cold War, which was to last for some forty years, was in simple terms the product of the aggressive post-war expansionist drive of the Soviet Union, supposedly in the name of international Communism. At the end of the Second World War, the Russians occupied nearly all of the Central and Eastern European countries, and additionally were allowed large zones of occupation in both Germany and Austria. In one after another of these countries between 1946 and 1948, Communist puppet regimes were installed, subject to Moscow's strict *diktat*. As important as anything, the massive Soviet Red Army in Eastern Europe was never demobilized, as were the armies in all the Western countries, and there were well-founded concerns that Soviet forces, always at high readiness, might one day march westward. In a civil war in Greece, Communist guerillas were only narrowly defeated, and only in Austria did the Russians eventually give up control of their occupation zone. In what was thought of as 'Western Europe', Communist parties, or close sympathizers, had large-scale support in Italy, France and even Britain. Communism was also on the advance in Asia. China fell to Mao Tse Tung's Communists in 1949 and both Viet Nam and Korea were partitioned with Communist governments in their northern sectors. To democratic nations the spread of Communism became *the* great threat. It was a very real threat, a "clear and present danger", backed by the military might of the Soviet Union and China. 'Containment' of Communist expansion thus became a central tenet of the grand strategy of the Western nations in the early post-war years, and direct defence against the Russian military might preoccupied politicians and military men alike.

CONTINENTAL DEFENCE

The first five years of the Cold War produced a great effort between Canada and the United States in continental defence. The wartime Permanent Joint Board on Defence (PJBD), which consisted of Canadian and American military and diplomatic representatives, was already functioning as a clearinghouse for joint operations and facilities, and the Soviet development of the atomic bomb and the introduction of long-range aircraft capable of delivering that weapon over intercontinental dis-

8th Hussars Grizzlies refuelling during summer training at Camp Utopia, 1949. The Grizzly was a Canadian production version of the cast-hull Sherman M4A1. A total of 188 were built. (8th Hussars Archives)

tances redoubled defence planning efforts. A Military Cooperation Committee (MCC) was created in 1946 as the link between the Canadian and American joint planners, and it produced the Canada-US Basic Security Plan, designed to examine every facet of the defence of North America.

Intelligence and analysis conducted by the MCC indicated that there was serious potential in time of war for the Soviets to use portions of its eight airborne divisions to seize the Second World War air staging airfields in the north-west and northeast of Canada. From those sites, Soviet bombers and missiles could then operate against strategic targets in the industrialized southern part of the continent. In response, Canada and the United States created several mobile striking forces, the Canadian one (MSF) consisting of the bulk of the regular Canadian Army. Specifically designed for Arctic operations, the MSF was an airportable formation that could be broken down into sub-units.

One primary target was believed to be the Northwest Staging Route, a series of airfields that paralleled the Alaska–Canadian (ALCAN) Highway, an improved two-lane road that went from Edmonton to Fairbanks. Planning for the defence of the ALCAN Highway was handled by Western Command, which assumed that part of the MSF would be employed along the highway, probably deployed by parachute and glider to disrupt any lodgments that had been identified by tactical support air squadrons. The Strathconas were tasked to move along the highway as far north as possible, make contact with the enemy as he was moving south, then delay him until engineers could blow the bridges and culverts.

By the mid-1950s it had became clear that the intercontinental bomber had made this scenario obsolete. Be that as it may, the reserve units of Western Command and the Strathconas had a task for which they could train, and one that would help them to maintain their recce skills. The use of armoured units in delaying operations was a part of the Staff College syllabus, and the ALCAN defence made a good case study: even Canada's Normandy adversary, *SS General* Kurt Meyer, was brought in to consult with the syndicates, from his prison cell in Dorchester, New Brunswick.

A COMMITMENT IN EUROPE

By 1948 it was abundantly clear to Canadian and other Western political leaders that, because of a Russian veto on every important decision, the United Nations Organization was incapable of serving as the guarantor of world peace and security, as had been so fervently hoped when it was created in 1945. Europe, where so many lives had been recently lost in freeing the continent from Nazi domination, appeared again threatened by imminent warfare. Tension rose markedly in 1947 and 1948, especially after the Soviet-inspired *coup d'état* in Czechoslovakia.

All of the Western European countries felt the effects of Soviet subversive activities, but Germany was the focal point of the struggle. The sole Western outpost in the Communist East – West Berlin – was the catalyst for vitally important decisions by the democracies. Cooperation between the Occupying Powers all but broke down in June 1948 when the Soviets moved tanks to block the *autobahns* and rail lines leading into Berlin, but the city had vital symbolic significance: if the Western nations backed down in the face of the Soviet provocation, they would only encourage further Russian threats. The blockade was broken only by a massive Allied airlift of supplies of every sort, but the danger of Russian military adventure had greatly increased. It was in this environment that the North Atlantic Treaty Organization (NATO) was born in April 1949.

The Governor General's Horse Guards at gun camp in Petawawa in the early 1950s. (GGHG Archives)

Prince Edward Island Regiment troops train on a 76mm Sherman, 1951. (Prince Edward Island Regiment Museum)

The NATO military alliance included Belgium, Canada, Denmark, France, Iceland, Italy, Luxembourg, the Netherlands, Norway and Portugal as well as Britain and the US. Canada, with a growing sense of confidence as a player in international affairs after her major role in the Allied successes of the Second World War, thus chose to take a share in the responsibility for the maintenance of global peace. The only way peace could be kept in Europe was to deter a massive attack by the Soviet Union, and that meant creating a standing military force in peacetime and deploying it to Europe.

Planning for just such a peacetime force was well under way when Communist forces invaded South Korea in 1950. NATO saw this as a feint to draw resources away from Europe, so deployment of the NATO deterrent force was accelerated in 1951.

The main effort of the RCAC during the Cold War years was in Europe, where Canadian armoured units were part of the NATO Integrated Force. Canada had promised to provide a full division to NATO's Central Region in Germany as part of a mixed conventional-nuclear collective deterrent and defence effort. But, mainly because of a later commitment to send a brigade to the United Nations force in Korea, the government decided that only one third of the division – one brigade – would be based in Europe in peacetime instead of the whole formation. Some thought was given to providing an armoured division of one armoured brigade and one motorized brigade, because of the smaller number of personnel in such an organization. However, this was vetoed by Army Headquarters in part because no new Main Battle Tank had been selected to replace the obsolescent Shermans and Chaffees. In any event, the British, under whose umbrella the Canadians would oper-

ate, already had sufficient armour and had requested an infantry division.

The first formation assigned to NATO service was 27 Canadian Infantry Brigade Group, a Special Force formation recruited from reserve units, and its armoured element was intended to be a squadron of the RCD composed of reservists. Five reserve units – the 8th Hussars, Halifax Rifles, Prince Edward Island Regiment, *Le Régiment de Trois Rivières* and *Le Régiment de Hull* – were each tasked to supply a complete troop, including officers, NCOs and men. In June 1951, after a month of basic training in their home areas, the five troops, known as 'Y' Troops, were assembled in Camp Petawawa and labeled as the 1st Armoured Squadron of PANDA Force (PANDA being an acronym for Pacific AND Atlantic Force). However, as the squadron's planned sailing date in November 1951 approached, it became obvious that it could not complete the required training in time. As a result, 27 Brigade's armoured squadron came to be made up of regulars from the RCD, grouped in what became 'C' Squadron, RCD, and the 1st Armoured Squadron was re-named 'D' Squadron RCD, although for some time the officers and men continued wearing the badges of their original units.

A Fort Garry Horse sergeant demonstrates the No. 19 wireless set to some new recruits, ca 1951. (Fort Garry Horse Museum)

At the same time that the 1st Armoured Squadron was being raised, the 2nd Armoured Squadron was being created from 'Y' Troops supplied by the GCHG, the BCR, the Calgarys, the BCD and the Fort Garrys. This squadron would, in February 1952, be absorbed into the Strathconas as 'D' Squadron, with some of the personnel joining the force bound for Korea. The 'Y' Troops and the two armoured squadrons were formally disbanded in July 1953. The designation 'Y' does not seem to have any par-

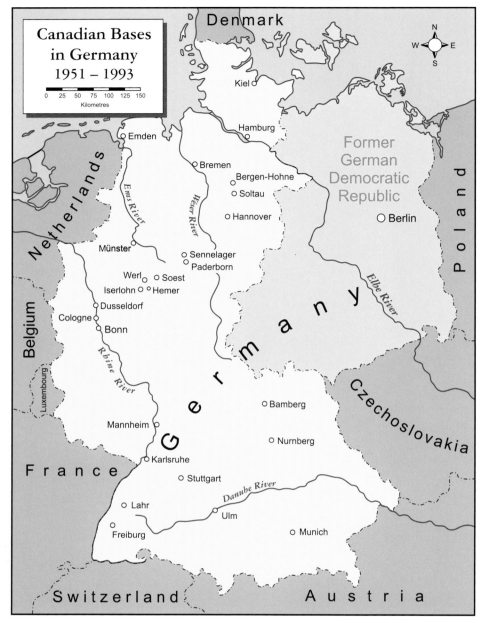

Canadian Bases
in Germany
1951 – 1993

0 25 50 75 100 125 150
Kilometres

Denmark

Netherlands

Belgium

Luxembourg

France

Switzerland

Germany

Austria

Former
German
Democratic
Republic

Poland

Czechoslovakia

Kiel

Hamburg

Emden

Bremen

Bergen-Hohne

Soltau

Hannover

Berlin

Münster

Sennelager

Paderborn

Werl   Soest

Iserlohn   Hemer

Dusseldorf

Cologne

Bonn

Mannheim

Bamberg

Nurnberg

Karlsruhe

Stuttgart

Lahr

Ulm

Munich

Freiburg

Ems River

Weser River

Elbe River

Rhine River

Danube River

phalia. The Canadian camps were given the names of well-known colonial forts, and until 1957 the armoured squadron was 'stabled' at Fort Victoria near the town of Werl.

'C' Squadron, RCD, was equipped with 21 Centurion Mark III tanks, with a 20-pounder (83.4mm) main armament, in January 1952. The decision to re-equip the RCAC with the Centurion was the product of much Anglo-American-Canadian wrangling. The Canadians' first choice for the new tank was the American M-48 Patton – three divisions worth – with the M-47 as a back-up, but production problems prevented delivery of the vehicles in the 1951-52 time frame that was required, so the order was cancelled. The Corps then focused on the British Centurion, which had by this time developed an exceptionally good reputation in Korea, to the point that even the Americans were contemplating an order.

The immediate Canadian requirement was for 280 Centurions, 20 for 27 Brigade, 140 for the two Regular armoured regiments and the School in Canada, and 120 for a war stock. Cabinet initially approved the purchase of a total of 247, but later increased the total to 347. Then the CGS, Lieutenant-General Guy Simonds, got into the act, deciding that 850 Centurions were now required: 609 to equip two infantry divisions, an independent armoured brigade and a reserve armoured division, and an additional 241 as war stocks. The CGS recommended that the first batch of 300 should be acquired immediately and the rest later.

The actual number of Centurion gun tanks purchased, at $126,344 a copy, was 274, far fewer than were wanted, but all that could be afforded. A decade later, in 1964, an additional nine Armoured Recovery Vehicles were acquired, and four Centurion bridge layers were purchased in 1966. Bought as Mark IIIs, the Corps upgraded the Centurions to Mark V standards by replacing the original Besa co-axial machine-gun with a .30 Browning. This was just the first of many modifications in the nearly twenty years the Centurion was in Canadian service.

At this time, Simonds reorganized the now expanded Regular Army. The brigade groups were reorganized into a divisional organization, a division headquarters was formed, and artillery and support units were regrouped accordingly. Each of the four

ticular significance; their counterparts in the infantry were designated as 'E' and 'F' companies.

One interesting memento of the 'Y' Troop experiment is a Quebec provincial flag given to the troop from *Le Régiment de Hull* on 20 October 1951. Presented by Brigadier J-P Sauvé on behalf of the Provincial government, the flag still holds an honoured place in the officers' mess.

The units of 27 Brigade arrived in Europe in late November 1951 and were placed under the command of I (British) Corps, part of British Army of the Rhine. For the first two years they were based in and near Hannover, in northern Germany, but in the autumn of 1953 they moved to widely dispersed camps near the towns of Soest, Werl, Iserlohn and Hemer in West-

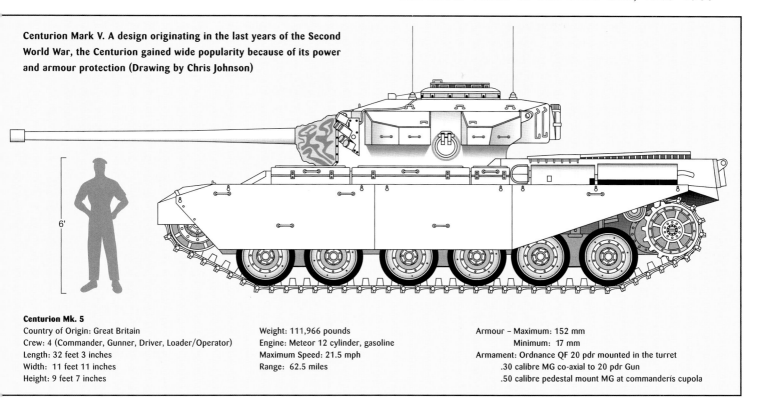

Centurion Mark V. A design originating in the last years of the Second World War, the Centurion gained wide popularity because of its power and armour protection (Drawing by Chris Johnson)

6'

Centurion Mk. 5

Country of Origin: Great Britain
Crew: 4 (Commander, Gunner, Driver, Loader/Operator)
Length: 32 feet 3 inches
Width: 11 feet 11 inches
Height: 9 feet 7 inches

Weight: 111,966 pounds
Engine: Meteor 12 cylinder, gasoline
Maximum Speed: 21.5 mph
Range: 62.5 miles

Armour – Maximum: 152 mm
Minimum: 17 mm
Armament: Ordnance QF 20 pdr mounted in the turret
.30 calibre MG co-axial to 20 pdr Gun
.50 calibre pedestal mount MG at commander's cupola

Centurions of 'C' Squadron of the Royal Canadian Dragoons on exercise in the Munsterlager training area in Germany, April 1952. (NAC PA180054)

RCAC sub-units in Germany, 1951–1957

'C' Squadron, Royal Canadian Dragoons: Nov 51–Oct 53

'D' Squadron, Lord Strathcona's Horse (RC): Oct 53–Oct 55

'A' Squadron, Royal Canadian Dragoons: Oct 55–Aug 57

brigade groups consisted of three motorized infantry battalions, an armoured squadron, and a towed artillery regiment. Though Simonds and others believed otherwise, armour doctrine in the 1950s was wedded to the notion that the infantry in West Germany would fight a covering force battle, well forward of the built-up area of the Ruhr, to prevent the Soviet 'hordes' from crossing the Rhine before NATO could mobilize fully. The role of the Centurion squadron was, therefore, to support the infantry battalions, who would fight from near-static defensive positions, and most of the early NATO exercises in which 27 Brigade participated practiced these concepts. (Readers might be reminded that the Canadian infantry in the 1950s was essentially foot-borne, or at best mounted in 3/4 ton trucks, and that the mechanized combat team or battle group was not possible until APCs were introduced in 1963.)

WAR IN KOREA

On 25 June 1950 the ideological conflict of the Cold War brewing between the Communist 'East' and the democratic 'West' suddenly turned hot. That day six Soviet-equipped divisions of the North Korean Army launched an invasion across the 38th Parallel, the demarcation line between Communist North Korea and pro-Western 'democratic' South Korea. Western political leaders feared that Russian expansionism would be encouraged – that other countries would 'fall like dominoes' to Communist control – if this blatant aggression was not stopped, if necessary by force. The UN Security Council, with the Soviet Union currently boycotting its meetings, passed a resolution on 27 June calling on all members of the UN to "furnish such assistance to the Republic of Korea as may be necessary to repel the armed attack and to restore international peace and security in the area." The ground work was thus laid for the first armed intervention under the *aegis* of the United Nations.

The Americans hurriedly sent a division to Korea from their occupation force in Japan and other countries soon agreed to provide contingents to a United Nations Command. On the ground, however, South Korean and American troops were continually pushed back and, by the first week of August, the North Koreans controlled the whole of the peninsula except a small perimeter around the port of Pusan.

Against this background of near-defeat, the United Nations force began to build up for a major offensive. The first Canadian contribution consisted of three destroyers and an air transport squadron, but on 7 August Prime Minister Louis St. Laurent announced that Canada would raise an infantry brigade with supporting arms and services – the Canadian Army Special Force, later renamed 25 Infantry Brigade – for service in Korea. In addition to three infantry battalions, the brigade was to have an artillery regiment and the usual complement of support services. A short time later a decision was made to add an armoured squadron to give the brigade an anti-tank capability.

The first armoured squadron for service in Korea was formed on 7 August 1950 at the Armoured Corps School in Camp Borden, with Major Jim Quinn as the commanding officer. While a number of positions were filled by volunteers from the Militia, the officers and NCOs came in almost equal numbers from the RCD and the Strathconas, so the squadron was given the official name 'A' Squadron, 1st/2nd Armoured Regiment to reflect its origins in both regular regiments. Lieutenant-General Jim Quinn, in an interview with Colonel John Gardam, recalled:

> Lots of people wanted to go to Korea but the ones selected were senior NCOs in the various teaching wings at the Armoured Corps School and officers who were at the School or who had just left for regimental duty. For equipment we were told we were to get the M-10, an anti-tank gun with a limited-traverse 17-pounder, mounted on a tracked [Sherman] chassis with an open turret. This bit of news, together with our unit designation, quickly made us the brunt of many jokes when we were referred to as "The Half [1/2] Armoured Squadron". It should be understood that from the outset the Director of Armour and others set out to have the M-10 replaced, as it was … totally unacceptable to be used as a tank. The Minister of National Defence, Brooke Claxton – an old gunner – could not see the difference or that it mattered.

The squadron was organized with four troops, each of which was to have four M-10s, a squadron headquarters with three vehicles, and an administrative troop with an armoured recovery vehicle and a variety of trucks to form the 'A' and 'B' Echelons. But before the squadron had completed its initial training in Camp Borden, in Korea the Americans and South Koreans went on the offensive. A large-scale American am-

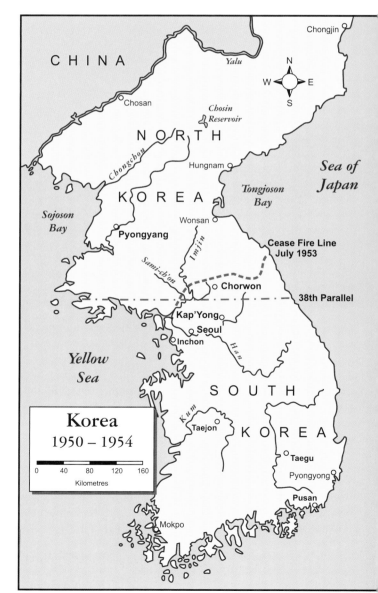

Final parade of 'A' Squadron, 1/2 Armoured Regiment in Camp Borden prior to moving to Fort Lewis, Washinton, November 1950. (Canadian Army Photo CBC 94-043354-9)

phibious landing at Inchon on 15 September outflanked the North Koreans, and by the end of the first week of October UN forces had advanced across the 38th Parallel into North Korea. Before the end of the month South Korean troops reached the Yalu River, the northern boundary between North Korea and China. For a time it seemed that the war was about to come to an end and that the Canadian brigade was not going to be needed. Ottawa nonetheless decided to continue with plans to concentrate the brigade for training at the US Army camp at Fort Lewis in Washington State. 2 PPCLI, assessed as the most battle-ready battalion in the brigade, was immediately shipped off to Korea to provide a nominal Canadian presence, while the remainder of the brigade continued their training.

Along with them, the Armoured Squadron moved to Fort Lewis in early November 1950. Once there, it was equipped with M-10s from US Army stocks, and a programme of intensive training was begun. The M-10s proved to be highly unsatisfactory; the limited traverse of the turret severely constrained tactical employment in support of the infantry, and crews felt

very vulnerable when they heard stories from Korea of enemy troops attacking similar open-top vehicles with grenades and mortars.

Then the war took a sudden strategic swing as the Chinese intervened and the UN Force was thrown back in general retreat. 25 Brigade would be needed after all, and orders arrived for it to embark in Seattle on 19 April 1951. Just prior to boarding, the 1st /2nd Armoured Squadron was given a regimental affiliation – it was now 'C' Squadron of Lord Strathcona's Horse and was given to understand that it would be re-equipped with tanks on arrival in Korea, either American Pattons or British Centurions.

On 4 May, after an uneventful voyage, the squadron disembarked in Pusan harbour. After seeing his men established in the American transit camp, Major Quinn's first mission was to track down the tanks the squadron had been promised. He spoke to the Brigade staff and found that no British Centurions would be available. Quinn and the second-in-command, Captain Ken Kennedy, then went looking at American tanks, first Pattons, which were in short supply and not immediately available, then M4A3 Shermans powered by a 500-horsepower Ford gasoline engine. Major Quinn noted:

> The matter was resolved after discussion with the US Marine Corps, who spoke so highly of their [M4A3] Sherman tanks. We decided to wait no longer but to recommend that they be purchased, the authority to buy thirty tanks having been received from Canada. The conversion was no problem, and our only concern was the radios, which we wanted changed to the Canadian 19 set.

On 16 and 17 May 'C' Squadron drew twenty M4A3 Shermans from a US Ordnance workshop. The next day was

Strathcona M4A3(76) Sherman tanks carrying members of the Royal 22ᵉ Régiment during the push toward the 38th Parallel, Korea, May 1951. These Shermans, acquired from the US Army in Korea, differed from the 76mm Shermans in Canada in that they were gasoline-powered rather than diesel. (NAC PA129108)

spent stowing kit and equipment on the tanks and turning in the M-10s, carefully salvaging the 19 set radios for later installation in the Shermans. Two days later the tanks were sent forward on two trains to join the remainder of the brigade just south of Seoul, while the wheeled vehicles of the echelon set off in a road convoy.

By this stage of the see-saw war the Chinese had pushed south of the 38th Parallel, but then had ran out of steam. The UN Force was about to launch a counter-offensive aimed at regaining the line of the Parallel, and 25 Brigade was brought in as part of 25 (US) Division. Early on the morning of 25 May 1951, the brigade attacked northward along the wide valley of the Pochon River, 2 RCR on the left bank with one troop of Strathcona tanks, and 2 R22eR on the right with two troops. Very little opposition was encountered, and two days later they were just south of the 38th Parallel. On 28 May, Major Quinn led an armoured fighting patrol of two troops, accompanied by Filipino infantry, some 15,000 metres into enemy territory to look for the vanished Chinese, but came back with only four prisoners.

The general advance northward continued on 29 May, but again only lightly-held hilltop positions were encountered until evening, when enemy resistance stiffened considerably as they approached the line of the Hantan River. The brigade's first major action in Korea took place the following morning, when the RCR passed through the Van Doos to mount an attack on Chinese positions in the village of Chail-li and three surrounding hills, one of which – Hill 467 – dominated the entire area.

The attack initially went well. 'B' Company of 2 RCR with one troop captured Hill 162 and thus secured the left flank, while 'A' Company and a second troop took the village of Chail-li about 2,000 metres directly north of the highest feature, Hill 467. 'D' Company's assault onto Hill 467, was, however, beaten off with heavy casualties. When the Chinese counter-attacked the village in early afternoon, there was a danger that the company and tank troop there would be cut off, so the battalion group was ordered to withdraw. The Strathcona tanks became heavily involved in protecting the withdrawal, expending most of their ammunition in the course of stiff fighting. Although several were hit by Chinese short-range anti-tank weapons, none were severely damaged.

The strategic direction of the war began to change dramatically in June 1951. General Douglas MacArthur had been dismissed as Supreme Commander in April, and with his departure also went the risk that the conflict would escalate into general war in Asia through an attack on China, as he had openly advocated. Western political leaders then re-asserted the position that this was a limited war, with the limited aim of reversing the invasion of South Korea, and now that the UN

Infantrymen of 25 Brigade return from a long-range fighting patrol mounted aboard Strathcona Shermans, Chorwon area, Korea, 22 June 1951. (NAC PA145367)

Force had, again, liberated almost all of South Korea, the UN Secretary General proposed a cease fire. The Chinese and North Koreans, now apparently convinced that they could not win, agreed, and negotiations between the two sides began on 10 July.

The Strathconas were involved in a number of long-range fighting patrols in the area of Chorwon during late June, but there were no major operations during the summer. There were, however, a number of significant organizational changes. Major Quinn went back to Canada in July, to attend Staff College, and was replaced by Major Victor Jewkes. Then, on 28 July, 25 Brigade became a permanent part of the newly formed 1 (Commonwealth) Division. In the formation headquarters Canadians held a number of key staff positions, most notably providing the GSO 1 (the senior operations staff officer). Among the Corps officers to fill this position were Lieutenant-Colonels Ned Amy and Mike Dare.

When the Commonwealth Division entered the line, in late July, 25 Brigade was shifted eastward to join the other two brigades of the division in the area of the Imjin and Hantan Rivers. The Canadians were theoretically in reserve until early September, but in fact were employed nearly continually in conducting deep fighting patrols across the Imjin River. Troops of tanks accompanied the infantry companies on most of these forays.

The Chinese broke off the armistice talks in late August, and the UN command stepped up the pace of operations. In the Commonwealth Division sector this resulted in two major operations to push the front back from the Imjin River. Operation *Minden* was launched on 11 September and, after the infantry battalions had gained a firm base across the

Sleeve patch of the 1st Commonwealth Division.

Imjin, 'C' Squadron's tanks were taken over to support a further push on the 12th. That day the Van Doos attacked across a valley to take three hills which dominated the position the battalion was to occupy, and from fire positions atop the hill on the near side of the valley Strathcona tanks provided superb direct fire support, with individual tanks getting target indication from Major Jewkes who sat alongside the battalion commander, Lieutenant-Colonel Jacques Dextraze. With pinpoint accuracy, the tanks fired HE rounds directly into the entrances of the many enemy bunkers that dotted the slope of the objective area, enabling the infantry to take the first of the hills with few casualties.

Operation *Commando,* aimed at taking an even stronger defensive line six kilometres further to the west on a line of hills overlooking an unnamed tributary of the Samichon River, began on 4 October. In two days of very hard fighting in exceptionally rough, hilly countryside, the Canadian battalions, with support from the Strathconas wherever tanks could be manoeuvred in the hills, captured their objectives by late afternoon of 5 October. This position, known as the *Jamestown Line,* was occupied (with only minor changes) for the remainder of the war in Korea.

Armistice negotiations began in earnest in late October, and because there was apparent agreement that the existing front would serve as a demarcation line, it was understood that opposing forces would in future refrain from offensive operations. The *Jamestown* positions were strengthened and, with the exception of aggressive patrolling, the conflict in Korea became essentially static in nature. This brought about a major change in the deployment and method of operation of the armoured squadron. Little by little Shermans were deployed high on the hills in dug-in positions where they could best give fire support to dug-in infantry and still snipe at enemy bunkers across the valley.

Photograph taken during Operation *Minden,* the Commonwealth Division's advance to the 'Wyoming Line', September 1951. (NAC PA178953)

Toward the end of December reinforcements for 'C' Squadron began to trickle in. Trooper (later Chief Warrant Officer) Ron Francis was one of the first of these. Francis has gone to the Strathconas in Calgary with the 'Y' Troop of the Governor General's Horse Guards. In an interview with Colonel John Gardam he described his reception in Korea at the squadron's 'B' Echelon.

[After I had] jumped to the ground with all my kit, the truck immediately drove off into the dark evening, leaving me very much alone to ponder my existence. At this point someone started beating on a final drive sprocket ring with a track pin … the local, improvised fire alarm. From a myriad of small holes in the ground came dozens of troopers in a variety of dress, all running to the tank park. … An hour later, I finally found a van with an orderly officer inside. After taking my name and a few other rather significant details, the young officer led me to one of the holes in the ground, pulled back the poncho covering the entrance and quietly said to those inside, "This man's name is Francis and he will be staying with you until such time as we can figure out what the hell to do with him." Not a very inspiring welcome or introduction.

Trooper Francis went on to recall his introduction to the front lines.

The war was nothing like I had envisioned it to be. The tank was dug in alongside the infantry trenches and bunkers and our role appeared to be that of providing direct sniper fire

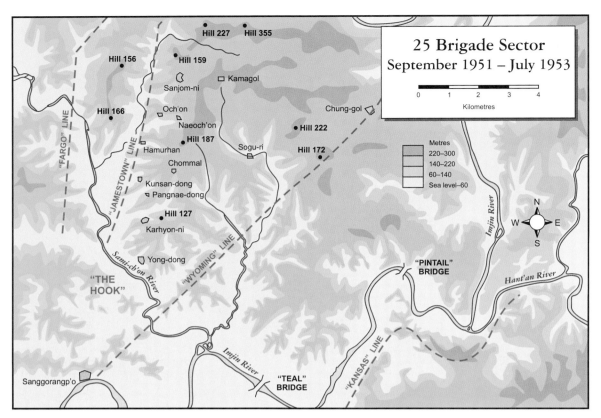

Map labels:

Hill 227 • Hill 355 •
Hill 156 • Hill 159 •
Sanjom-ni • Kamagol
Och'on Chung-gol
"FARGO" LINE
Hill 166 • Naeoch'on
Hill 187 • Hill 222 •
Hamurhan Sogu-ri Hill 172 •
Chommal
Kunsan-dong
Pangnae-dong
Hill 127 •
Karhyon-ni
"JAMESTOWN" LINE
Sami-ch'on River
Yong-dong
"WYOMING" LINE
"THE HOOK"
Imjin River
"PINTAIL" BRIDGE
Hant'an River
"KANSAS" LINE
Imjin River "TEAL" BRIDGE
Sanggorangp'o

25 Brigade Sector
September 1951 – July 1953

0 1 2 3 4
Kilometres

Metres
220–300
140–220
60–140
Sea level–60

N
W E
S

support for the endless infantry night patrols. The nightly turret/radio watches were particularly nerve-wracking, although one would never admit to it. The noise of patrols going out or returning through the wire, the constant thumping of Vickers and .30-calibre [machine guns] firing on fixed lines, the frequent lighting of the sky by some nervous infantryman firing off flares, the shadows created by the searchlights providing artificial moonlight, and every shrub exposed by the flares appearing to move – all had the tendency to make one rather anxious.

'C' Squadron's one-year tour of duty in Korea came to an end in early June 1952. They were replaced by 'B' Squadron of the Strathconas, commanded by Major J.S. Roxborough, which landed at Inchon harbour on 2 June. The squadron took its place in the line a week later.

During its year in Korea, 'B' Squadron experienced much the same conditions as had 'C' Squadron in its last six months: the dug-in tank positions proved to be invaluable in providing close-in fire support to constant infantry patrol activity which was necessary to control the valley approaches to the *Jamestown* positions. The Chinese, on their part, never ceased their harassment of the Canadian positions, shelling our emplacements regularly, and occasionally mounting minor attacks, especially on the flanks. The isolated tank positions became accustomed to being the target of enemy artillery and mortars, and to providing fire whenever called on. To facilitate immediate fire sup-

port, a liaison officer was sent to each battalion headquarters and likely enemy targets or forming-up places were carefully registered. Because so many of the Shermans were in high, isolated spots – sometimes even outside the infantry's defensive localities – additional ammunition was always positioned with the tank so it could fight for some time without replenishment.

To make them more effective in this defensive role, the Shermans were all modified somewhat. The .50-calibre Browning anti-aircraft machine gun was mounted as an anti-personnel weapon in front of the crew commander's hatch so he could fire it from inside the turret. As well, an 18-inch (45-cm) searchlight was mounted on the gun mantlet of some of the tanks to assist the crew in case of night attacks.

Major Roxborough described one instance of effective fire support in an article in *Canadian Army Journal*:

The value of tank defensive fire was aptly demonstrated on 23 October 1952 when the enemy attempted to seize Pt. 355 known as "Little Gibraltar", a feature which commands the surrounding countryside. The signal for the attack was a burst of trace fired by two enemy machine guns from the feature immediately in front of "Little Gibraltar". This trace crossing the sky launched the Chinese attack. However, the tank crews had been alerted during the preliminary shelling and mortaring which preceded the attack, and both these machine guns were knocked out almost before they had completed firing the trace. From then on the tanks engaged this feature, skipping their rounds off the crest on fuze delay which gave the effect of air burst on the reverse slopes. Shortly after the tank fire was thickened by friendly mortar fire and finally the artillery joined the bombardment.

'A' Squadron, under Major Bill Ellis, arrived to take over from 'B' Squadron in June 1953. While Chinese shelling and incursions continued until the last minute, the squadron had a

Incoming. **Painting by Ted Zuber depicting the Chinese attack on 'B' Company of 1 RCR on 23 October 1952. The painting shows a Strathcona Sherman in a typical dug-in position in the Jamestown Line. (Canadian War Museum 198903 28-008)**

relatively quiet tour. The truce was finally signed on 27 July 1953, bringing an end to hostilities. Within 72 hours both sides had to withdraw from a four-kilometre-wide 'demilitarized zone'. For some time, however, considerable caution was exercised, just in case the Chinese failed to live up to their word. Later this gave way to a lesser state of readiness, although for some time defensive positions were manned at a 25 percent level.

'D' Squadron of the RCD, commanded by Major A.L. MacDonald, replaced the Strathcona squadron in May 1954. This squadron was, in large part, made up of men from the 'Y' Troops of *Le Régiment de Hull*, *Le Régiment de Trois Rivières*, the 8th Hussars, Halifax Rifles and Prince Edward Island Regiment. They saw no action, but remained ready to disrupt any North Korean or Chinese thrust into the Canadian brigade area. According to the Dragoon's regimental history, "the closest the squadron got to making real war was during a range firing exercise when their shells began to land uncomfortably close to their own brigade HQ." The brigade commander, Brigadier

Sergeant Bob Slaney and his Royal Canadian Dragoons tank crew during a training exercise behind the demarcation line in Korea, September 1954. (NAC PA131736)

Strathcona tanks along the Imjin River, with the 'Teal' bridge in the background, June 1952. The tanks had crossed the river at 'Loon' bridge – a pontoon bridge on the far side of 'Teal' which was erected at regular intervals in case 'Teal' was destroyed. (Canadian Army Photo)

Major Victor Jewkes, commanding officer of 'C' Squadron, Lord Strathcona's Horse, briefing his replacement, Major J.S. Roxborough, commander of 'B' Squadron. Korea, 4 June 1952. (NAC PA136784)

The Canadian Korea Medal. This medal was awarded to all Canadian troops who served in Korea. In 1998 another medal was awarded to all Canadians who volunteered for service in Korea.

The United Nations Service Medal – Korea. This medal was awarded to troops of all nations' forces under UN command in Korea or Japan. The inscription on medals awarded to Canadians could be in English or French.

Clift, is reputed to have sent a message to Major MacDonald saying, "Dear Laird, Please come up and discuss things quietly before going on the offensive."

In line with a general withdrawal of Canadian troops from Korea, the Dragoons left for home in November of 1954.

THE 1954 KENNEDY COMMISSION

As was noted in discussing the purchase of Centurions, the CGS wanted to equip an army of three divisions even though the Canadian Army was configured for a mobilized force of six divisions. Two things had combined to convince the CGS that a three-division force was what was needed. The first was the experience of recruiting 25 and 27 Brigades in 1951. Although the Reserve Force had responded, the ensuing problems – such as the long time needed to train the 'Y' Troops to an operational standard – indicated that a rapid mobilization based on the reserves was just not going to work. The other factor was the changing nature of the threat. In 1946 a war with the Soviet Union was likely to be a repeat of the Second World War, including enough time to mobilize and train a large army. By 1953, with the deployment of Soviet nuclear weapons, the most likely scenario was now deemed to be a sudden crisis requiring a quick Allied response. In Simonds' mind, that meant that a two-division-strong corps, with a third (armoured) division in reserve, was Canada's most sensible contribution.

The corps that he was proposing would still come from the Reserve Force, but, as in 1936, the existing force structure was too large and would have to be reduced. As in 1936, the groundwork was carefully laid, as the CGS consulted with the CDA to gain their confidence and cooperation. The result was the Kennedy Commission, named for its Chairman, Major-General Howard Kennedy, an engineer, a reservist and a veteran of both World Wars.

When the review was concluded the reserve divisional and brigade headquarters were all disbanded and replaced by 26 Reserve Force Group Headquarters. The artillery lost twenty regiments, primarily coastal defence and anti-aircraft units. The infantry lost twelve battalions, but the RCAC gained four regiments, the latter change due to the transfer of the anti-armour role from the artillery to the armoured corps. In its new format, the Corps' field force, in the event of mobilization, would comprise three armoured car regiments, three reconnaissance regiments and sixteen armoured regiments. An additional seven regiments would, between them, supply a further five regiments and two squadrons as a base for training and reinforcements. Thus the total requirement for armour amounted to 29 regiments and two of the four new regiments were assigned the anti-tank roles they had previously filled with the infantry – the Grey and Simcoe Foresters, and the 15th Alberta Light Horse (soon to join with the South Alberta Regiment to become The South Alberta Light Horse).

Another product of the Commission's work was a return to tradition: the reserve component was renamed the Canadian Army (Militia), while the Active Force was transformed into the Canadian Army (Regular). The Reserve Force Group Headquarters mentioned above became Militia Group Headquarters.

The Kennedy Commission was only one of many reorganizations of the Canadian Army. It had the distinction, however, of being the last reorganization of the century done with the aim of improving the Army's efficiency. All of the subsequent exercises, despite rhetoric to the contrary, had but one real goal – to save the government money.

Following the coronation of HM Queen Elizabeth II, the Corps badge was altered to incorporate St. Edward's Crown.

Order of Battle of The Royal Canadian Armoured Corps, 1955

Royal Canadian Dragoons [1st Armoured Regiment]

Lord Strathcona's Horse (Royal Canadians) [2nd Armoured Regiment]

The Governor General's Horse Guards [3rd Armoured Regiment]

IV Princess Louise Dragoon Guards [4th Armoured Car Regiment]

8th Princess Louise's (New Brunswick) Hussars [5th Armoured Regiment]

1st Hussars [6th Armoured Regiment]

17th Duke of York's Royal Canadian Hussars [7th Reconnaissance Regiment]

14th Canadian Hussars [8th Armoured Regiment]

The British Columbia Dragoons [9th Reconnaissance Regiment]

The Fort Garry Horse [10th Armoured Regiment]

The Ontario Regiment [11th Armoured Regiment]

The Sherbrooke Regiment [12th Armoured Regiment]

The British Columbia Regiment (Duke of Connaught's Own) [13th Armoured Regiment]

The King's Own Calgary Regiment [14th Armoured Regiment]

6th Duke of Connaught's Royal Canadian Hussars [15th Armoured Regiment]

7th /11th Hussars [16th Armoured Regiment]

The Prince Edward Island Regiment [17th Reconnaissance Regiment]

12th Manitoba Dragoons [18th Armoured Car Regiment]

19th Alberta Dragoons [19th Armoured Car Regiment]

The Saskatchewan Dragoons [20th Armoured Regiment]

Le Régiment de Hull [21st Armoured Regiment]

The Windsor Regiment [22nd Armoured Regiment]

The Halifax Rifles [23rd Armoured Regiment]

Le Régiment de Trois Rivières [24th Armoured Regiment]

The Queen's York Rangers (1st American Regiment) [25th Armoured Regiment]

The Algonquin Regiment [26th Armoured Regiment]

The Elgin Regiment [27th Armoured Regiment]

The Grey and Simcoe Foresters [28th Armoured Regiment]

The South Alberta Light Horse [29th Armoured Regiment]

A Ferret scout car belonging to the 17th Duke of York's Royal Canadian Hussars, one of the three units designated as reconnaissance regiments in 1955. (RCH Museum)

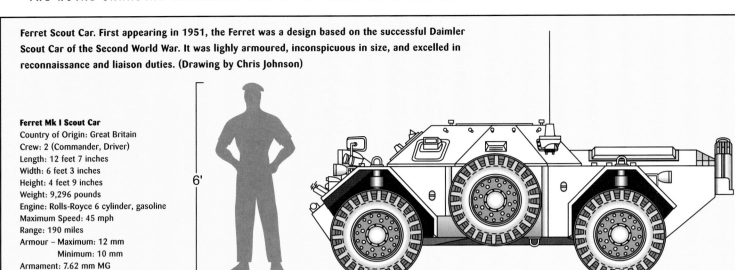

Ferret Scout Car. First appearing in 1951, the Ferret was a design based on the successful Daimler Scout Car of the Second World War. It was lighly armoured, inconspicuous in size, and excelled in reconnaissance and liaison duties. (Drawing by Chris Johnson)

Ferret Mk I Scout Car
Country of Origin: Great Britain
Crew: 2 (Commander, Driver)
Length: 12 feet 7 inches
Width: 6 feet 3 inches
Height: 4 feet 9 inches
Weight: 9,296 pounds
Engine: Rolls-Royce 6 cylinder, gasoline
Maximum Speed: 45 mph
Range: 190 miles
Armour – Maximum: 12 mm
          Minimum: 10 mm
Armament: 7.62 mm MG

6'

UNITS NEW TO THE CORPS IN THE PERIOD 1946-1954

Le Régiment de Hull
April 1946

The Saskatchewan Dragoons
April 1946

The Queen's York Rangers
June 1947

The Algonquin Regiment
October 1954

CHANGES OF UNIT NAME, 1946-1954

The Sherbrooke Regiment

The Prince Edward Island Regiment

The Windsor Regiment

The South Alberta Light Horse

CHAPTER 18

The 'Golden Age', 1956–1970

I n its nearly 150 years of existence the Canadian Army has known three significant peaks of professional success – fleeting occasions when it possessed the skills, manpower and equipment to perform at the level of the world's best military forces and enjoyed a higher than usual level of importance and credibility both within the nation and in the world at large. The first two peaks occurred during the world wars, in 1917-18 and 1944-45, and in both cases the situation was the result of a long, arduous and bloody regimen of on-the-job training.

The third peak was different. The precise time scale is debatable, but it roughly encompassed the period of 1956 to 1968. The background to this era was similar in that it, too, encompassed a war, the Cold War, and was the result of a long and hard, but thankfully not bloody, regimen of training. The equipment was, if not entirely first class, at least of the first rank, with the professional skills of officers and men nurtured in the light of recent combat experience, in both the Second World War and Korea. This mid-century peak is frequently looked upon and spoken of as a 'golden age' in the Army's history.

Most of the senior officers and warrant officers of this post-war period were powerful, colourful personalities as well as being effective leaders. Their standards and ethics derived from two sources, the NCOs of the pre-war era and the officers of the Second World War. Their classic values were passed on to the post-war generation by such men as 'Squint' Armer, Charlie Smith, Pat Forgrave, Dick Cunliffe, Jim Tedlie, Ned Amy, 'Rad'

The United Nations Emergency Force: Ferret scout cars patrolling the sand dunes of the Sinai desert along the demarcation line between Egypt and Israel. (Canadian Forces Photo ME-1197)

Radley-Walters, Bill Little, 'Nick' Nicholson and many others. Nonetheless, Worthy – that long-retired, balding, unpretentious man – was always the boss of the Corps and everyone knew it and was glad of it.

The problem with golden ages is that they are only golden in retrospect, never at the time. The gilt also tends to cover a host of warts and blemishes. As well as the high standards attained, the era is also fondly remembered because of the contrast with the disappointments and disasters that followed, and it is in light of both these factors that the golden age takes on its colouring.

56 RECCE SQN AND THE SINAI SQUADRONS

The month of October 1956 was one of international crisis. In Hungary a popular uprising was suppressed by Soviet armour, while in the Middle East, Israel and Egypt found themselves once again in battle, but this time with the British and French involved as well. Both European nations, the previous owners of the Suez Canal, had joined Israel and reoccupied the Canal Zone in response to its nationalization by the Egyptian leader, Abdul Gamal Nasser. Britain and France were widely condemned for their actions, particularly by the United States, and Lester Pearson, Canadian secretary of state for External Affairs, won a Nobel Peace Prize for his proposal of a United Nations-sponsored intervention force to separate the Egyptians and Israelis, and, not coincidentally, to give the British and French a cover for extracting themselves from an embarrassing situation.

Canada initially offered an infantry unit, the Queen's Own Rifles, as a component of the United Nations Emergency Force (UNEF), but was forced to withdraw this offer when Nasser objected to their British-sounding name. In place of the infantrymen, Canada supplied logistics and communications personnel. The UNEF commander was a Canadian, Major-General E.L.M. Burns, and even though the Queen's Own had been replaced by a Yugoslav recce battalion, Burns wanted a Canadian combat arms unit to assist in patrolling the large tracts of the Sinai which lay between the opposing sides.

So was born 56 Canadian Reconnaissance Squadron, RCAC, an *ad hoc* organization named for the year in which it was conceived. The regular armoured units had only a limited reconnaissance capability (regimental recce troops) because reconnaissance was a role that had been delegated to the Militia in the post-war reorganization. Since it had no parent regiment, the members of the squadron wore the Corps' cap badge with a special 56 Canadian Reconnaissance Squadron shoulder flash. The six officers and 105 other ranks crewed 23 Ferret scout cars which had been withdrawn from Militia reconnaissance regiments. Each of the vehicles carrying a tactical sign with the numeral 56 superimposed on the Corps' *red over yellow* marker. After the crews became acquainted with their new vehicles, during a period of pre-deployment training in Camp Petawawa, the equipment was dispatched by sea, with the personnel following by air; men and equipment reuniting in Egypt in March 1957.

The Canadians patrolled the northernmost 56 kilometres – the distance was purely coincidental – of the boundary/demarcation line between Egypt and Israel, the Yugoslav battalion taking on the longer, southern portion of the line. During the year that 56 Recce spent in the desert, the soldiers had to contend with the harsh climate, baking heat by day and freezing temperatures by night, as well as scorpions and snakes, the military hazards of unmarked mine fields and trigger-happy troops, and the problems of controlling a nomadic Bedouin population who cared nothing for international boundaries.

The tasking also involved casualties: a few soldiers suffered injuries from mine blasts while yet others contracted diseases, particularly malaria. Sadly, the squadron suffered the losses of

An 8th Hussars jeep patrol in the Sinai meets a more traditional form of transport, 1964. (DND Photo ME-64 076-4)

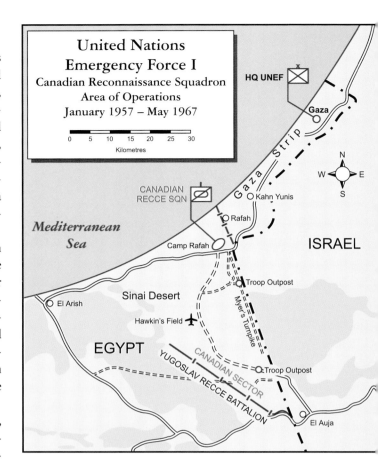

Lieutenant C.C. Van Straubenzee, LdSH, killed when his Ferret rolled in soft sand, and Trooper R.E. McDavid, RCD, killed when his vehicle struck a mine. It is interesting to note that Lieutenant Van Straubenzee was the fourth generation of his family to serve in the Canadian Army. His great-grandfather had been on Middleton's staff in the Northwest Rebellion. His grandfather, Charles, had been killed in action while commanding the RCD at Le Cateau in October 1918 and his father had served in the Three Rivers Regiment during the Second World War.

The 56 Recce experience drove home the need for a regular army reconnaissance component, and in future each regular regiment would have a recce squadron as a part of its establishment. The next unit to serve in the Sinai, the recce squadron of

The RCAC Sinai Squadrons

56 Canadian Reconnaissance Squadron, RCAC: Mar 57–Feb 58

1/8th Canadian Hussars (Princess Louise's), Recce Squadron: Feb 58–Feb 59

The Royal Canadian Dragoons, D (Recce) Squadron: Feb 59–Feb 60

The Fort Garry Horse, Recce Squadron: Feb 60–Feb 61

Lord Strathcona's Horse (RC), Recce Squadron: Feb 61–Feb 62

The Royal Canadian Dragoons, Recce Squadron: Feb 62–Feb 63

Lord Strathcona's Horse (RC), Recce Squadron: Feb 63–Feb 64

8th Canadian Hussars (Princess Louise's), D (Recce) Squadron: Feb 64–Feb 65

8th Canadian Hussars (Princess Louise's), A Squadron: Feb 65–Mar 66

(Right) The United Nations Emergency Force medal, awarded to all who served with the Force for 90 days between November 1956 and May 1967.

1/8th Canadian Hussars, would substitute ¹/₄-ton jeeps for the Ferrets midway through their tour, the jeeps being more suitable for the desert conditions. Reconnaissance squadrons continued to serve one-year tours of duty in the Sinai until 1966 when, as part of a force reduction, the Armoured Corps portion of the mission was ended. The following year, Canadian troops would be unceremoniously chucked out of Egypt as the Middle East once more erupted in war. In addition to the two soldiers mentioned above, Trooper R.H. Allan, RCD, Corporal G.A. Gauthier, LdSH (RC) (attached to 56 Transport Company, RCASC), Trooper R.J. Wiley, LdSH (RC), Corporal P.R. Wallace and Trooper A.A. Bons, 8CH, died during the course of the UNEF mandate.

EXPANSION OF THE REGULAR COMPONENT

By 1956 the regular army included fifteen battalions of infantry, formed into four brigades, but still there were only two regular armoured regiments. That year, however, two battalions of the Canadian Guards, were disbanded and a new regular armoured regiment raised. Rather than create a completely new unit, Army Headquarters determined to build upon the foundations of an existing regiment and selected the 8th Princess Louise's (New Brunswick) Hussars for the purpose, but because regular units recruit nationally, a regional title such as 'New Brunswick Hussars'

The first stage in the post-war expansion of the Regular Army: the new 8th Canadian Hussars (Princess Louise's) badge, issued with the 8th Hussars change of name on becoming a Regular unit.

was deemed unsuitable. After due deliberation, which closely involved the Militia regiment, the name selected was 1/8th Canadian Hussars (Princess Louise's), while the reserve unit would continue under the name 2/8th Canadian Hussars (Princess Louise's). On 29 January 1957, the new regiment was added to the establishment at Camp Gagetown under the command of a wartime Sherbrooke Fusiliers officer, Lieutenant-Colonel S.V. Radley-Walters. The regiment's 'A' Squadron was made up mainly of French-Canadians and stationed at Camp Valcartier. In October 1957 the new unit received its first operational tasking, the relief of 56 Recce Squadron in the Middle East by its Recce Squadron, and within three months the squadron was in the desert.

Three regular armoured regiments were not enough if each brigade was to have one, and on 11 October 1958, George Pearkes, VC, the minister of National Defence, announced the raising of a fourth regular regiment, The 1st Fort Garry Horse (1 FGH). In this case, the regiment was chosen by the RCAC (Association) meeting in its annual session at the School in Camp Borden because of the Garrys' exceptional record of service in both world wars. Apparently the 'Fort Garry' in their title was not viewed as excessively regional and it was not deemed necessary to make any changes to their title. Lieutenant Colonel James C. Gardner, a 1940 graduate of the Royal Military College, who had served with Britain's Royal Tank Regiment during the war, was appointed to command the new regular regiment when it was activated at Camp Petawawa. The reserve unit, in Winnipeg, became The 2nd Fort Garry Horse.

CHANGING TITLES

The title of the regular Hussar regiment posed a problem, sounding as though the unit was an amalgamation of the 1st Hussars and the 8th Hussars. To get around this awkwardness, in February 1960, the names were changed to 8th Canadian Hussars (Princess Louise's) and 8th Canadian Hussars (Princess Louise's) (Militia). A similar change was made to the FGH titles.

Army Headquarters was concerned by the fact that many armoured regiments carried designations that, to the uninitiated, would not immediately identify them as armoured. For example, a foreign liaison officer told to locate *Le Régiment de Hull* or the Elgin Regiment in the field, might be excused for thinking that he was looking for a unit of infantry. The problem did not exist with

Lieutenant Colonel Jim Gardner, RSM Eric Armer and Trooper Goebels crew the first Centurion delivered to the Fort Garry Horse in Petawawa in October 1958. (DND Photo)

The Order of Battle of The Royal Canadian Armoured Corps, 1959

The Royal Canadian Dragoons

Lord Strathcona's Horse (Royal Canadians)

1/8th Canadian Hussars (Princess Louise's)

The 1st Fort Garry Horse

The Governor General's Horse Guards

IV Princess Louise Dragoon Guards

The Halifax Rifles (RCAC)

The Grey and Simcoe Foresters (RCAC)

2/8th Canadian Hussars (Princess Louise's)

The Elgin Regiment (RCAC)

The Ontario Regiment (RCAC)

The Queen's York Rangers (1st American Regiment) (RCAC)

The Sherbrooke Regiment (RCAC)

7th/11th Hussars

Le Régiment de Trois Rivières (RCAC)

1st Hussars

The Prince Edward Island Regiment (RCAC)

The Royal Canadian Hussars (Montreal)

The British Columbia Regiment (Duke of Connaught's Own) (RCAC)

The Algonquin Regiment (RCAC)

12th Manitoba Dragoons

The South Alberta Light Horse

The Saskatchewan Dragoons

19th Alberta Dragoons

14th Canadian Hussars

The King's Own Calgary Regiment (RCAC)

The British Columbia Dragoons

The 2nd Fort Garry Horse

Le Régiment de Hull (RCAC)

The Windsor Regiment (RCAC)

Badge of the Royal Canadian Hussars

names such as The South Alberta Light Horse, since most armies had converted their cavalry regiments to armour while retaining the cavalry names. To resolve any possible confusion, in May 1958 the acronym RCAC in brackets was placed after the name of any unit in the Corps that did not have a cavalry title. A confused clerk once placed the initials in the title of the 1st Hussars in an official document and, like too many administrative errors, this one continued to surface year after year.

An amalgamation of two regiments was completed on 15 September 1958 when the 6th Duke of Connaught's Royal Canadian Hussars and the 17th Duke of York's Royal Canadian Hussars were joined together as The Royal Canadian Hussars

(Montreal). What was interesting, if not unique, about this happy event was that it was instigated by the two units concerned without being imposed by higher authority.

SNAKES AND LADDERS: THE MILITIA'S NATIONAL SURVIVAL ROLE

The 1954 Kennedy Commission had considered making the Militia responsible for aid to the Civil Defence Organizations in the event of war, envisioning the reserve units entering the rubble of major population centres to rescue, succour and evacuate the survivors of a nuclear strike; but the plan was not recommended by the Commission for fear that the Militia would be seen as a safe haven for people seeking to avoid overseas service with the field army.

In a few short years the situation had changed, however. Concerns about nuclear war had grown and in 1957 and 1958 the Army's annual training directives for the Militia emphasized the civil defence role. Then, on 28 May 1959, Order-in-Council PC 656 changed the role of the Militia to one that made civil defence, officially called National Survival Training, its primary task. Summer camps were cancelled, training days were reduced from sixty to forty, and all weapons except rifles and light machineguns were removed from reserve units (although some regiments were able to cling to a few Shermans). In their stead, they received ropes and ladders to use in evacuating casualties from damaged structures. These tools led to the Militiamen nicknaming their activities 'snakes and ladders' after the children's game.

The change to snakes and ladders was a tremendous blow to the armoured regiments for it seemed to confirm that they were no longer field soldiers. It was not all bad news, however, as the 12th Manitoba Dragoons history notes: "… it was a six-week paid course during the winter of 1957 during which the Regiment grew in leaps and bounds with many farmers joining the

(Above) Troops of the newly formed Royal Canadian Hussars in Montreal, shortly after the amalgamation of the 6th and 17th Hussars. As the new regimental badge was not yet available, those in the photo are wearing the Corps badge while posing in front of their Staghounds and jeeps. (RCH Museum)

(Right) A dramatic cloth model exercise for the Militia depicting a simulated nuclear strike on a built-up area, after which the concepts for 're-entry operations' such as radiation monitoring and rescue of survivors were explained to those in the stands. (Canadian Army Photo) In the second photo, the simulated rescue of a victim from a building damaged in a nuclear burst, June 1961. This was the 'snakes and ladders' aspect of National Survival training that damaged the morale of many of the Militia units of the era. (South Alberta Light Horse)

ranks to take advantage of the extra money to supplement their incomes." However, for those who had joined the Militia to soldier, the situation was not so rosy. As the 1st Hussars history notes: "The change from gung-ho armoured manoeuvres back to the slit trench, gas mask and bunker mentality was pretty demoralizing and challenged the ingenuity of commanders to maintain troop interest." To help maintain interest, numbers and morale, armoured units conducted armoured training without pay, and, on occasion, in lieu of the officially sanctioned National Survival Training.

As far as the Militia was concerned, the National Survival Training programme was a failure. Although the government had authorized the change of role, even they generally paid only lip-service to it. Special-to-corps training steadily occupied more and more of the training schedule and, finally, in late 1963 the new CGS, Lieutenant-General Geoffrey Walsh, having seen the damage that snakes and ladders was causing, announced a de-emphasis of National Survival Training and a return to corps training.

The Standard of the Governor General's Horse Guards, the senior armoured regiment in the Militia. Guidons, the 'colours' of other armoured regiments that do not have 'guards' status, are of very similar design except that they are 'swallow-tailed'. (Governor General's Horse Guards Archives)

Her Majesty The Queen presenting the Guidon of the Ontario Regiment, 1967. On the right side of the photo are also seen the Guidons of the 1st Hussars and the Sherbrooke Hussars, awaiting presentation in the same ceremony. (Canadian Army Photo CF-67-405-23)

This episode had weakened Militia morale and undermined its self-image, but, before they had time to recover, another blow would be landed on the shaken citizen-soldiers of Canada in the shape of the Suttie Commission.

HERITAGE AND CEREMONIAL

Amidst the busy pace of training, operations and change in this era, members of the regiments and the School allowed themselves time to remember their heritage, and in many instances this included the presentation of regimental 'colours' – guidons – and, in the case of the 'guards' units, standards.

Guidons are swallow-tailed flags carried by all armoured units except the two regiments designated as 'guards', the Governor General's Horse Guards and IV Princess Louise Dragoon Guards, which carry a rectangular standard. They are made of crimson silk damask and decorated with the regiment's badge, motto and battle honours. Until 1951 only former cavalry units designated as dragoon and 'horse' regiments had been entitled to carry guidons or standards, thus excluding hussar regiments and all of the units that had originated as infantry. That year the British Army ruled that all armoured units, regardless of origin, would be entitled to a guidon or standard, and the Canadian Army adopted this policy. The award of Second World War battle honours further encouraged units to acquire their colours, so in the late 1950s and well into the 1960s there was a steady stream of guidon and standard presentation ceremonies across the country.

At the Corps School in Camp Borden a memorial suite of ten large oak dining tables and 56 matching chairs, each with a carved regimental or corps badge, had been donated in the late 1950s by units or individuals. Then, in 1959, Colonel Jim Tedlie organized the construction of a park, named Worthington Park in honour of the Corps founder and Colonel Commandant, in the area surrounding the Corps memorial. In the tastefully-landscaped grounds were placed an extensive collection of the tanks and armoured cars with which units of the Corps had been equipped in earlier years, along with several German tanks and guns that had been brought home at the end of the war. It was, in Colonel Tedlie's words, "a worthy project", a magnificent display of the Corps wartime heritage.

1964: INTEGRATION

Canada has a long history of experimenting with integrated armed forces going back to 1923 when National Defence Headquarters was first formed with a single minister of National Defence (MND) to look after both the navy and the army.

When Paul Hellyer became MND in 1963, he concluded that the process of integration had to be advanced. His argument was based on the shrinking percentage of the defence budget that was being directed toward operations and maintenance, which included the purchase of new equipment, and, to correct that problem, he decided to reorganize the military and find the funds from internal economies.

Hellyer's first move, in 1964, was to amend the National Defence Act to eliminate the three service heads and their staffs and replace them with a single Chief of Defence Staff (CDS) who would have authority over the three services. The creation of a single professional head of all the uniformed services was a useful innovation and one that was widely adopted in the nations of the Western alliance. Unlike Canada, however, the other nations did not find it necessary to eliminate the three services to make it work. In 1965 the next step followed, the restructuring of the military along functional lines. Six new 'Commands' were established – Mobile, Maritime, Air Defence, Air Transport, Materiel and Training.

The field army now became, for all intents and purposes, Mobile Command. Nevertheless, Mobile Command was not intended to be the army under a different name. It did not, for example, include the ground forces stationed in Europe but it did include tactical air and helicopter squadrons. It was, in Hellyer's vision, to be a rapidly-deployable formation able to go anywhere in the world to fight brushfire wars.

That was a complete departure from the Army's experience of the previous fifteen years. Since Korea, the Canadian Army's major role had been its contribution to NATO's Central Front, a function that required main battle tanks and mechanized infantry, neither of which was particularly easily transported by air. The Mobile Command concept also ran counter to Canada's historic military situation. Never in its history has Canada made war on its own, where a close integration of its land, air and sea forces would be necessary. Canada had always fought as a partner in a coalition in which it was far more important to have Canadian services compatible with those of our senior partners rather than with each other.

There was much unhappiness over the destruction of the traditional services in favour of this radical concept of defence organization. While Hellyer boasted of leading the world in this field some senior officers resigned in protest, and, in order to make the integration concept acceptable to the doubters who remained, the minister had to produce quick results. All along

Officer cadets stack 20-pounder high explosive shells on the firing point during training at the Meaford Tank Gunnery Range in the summer of 1967. (DND/CF-67-1000-70)

Sherman tanks of *Le Régiment de Trois Rivières* during a winter training exercise in the early 1960s. (Canadian Army Photo)

A Halifax Rifles training exercise, early 1960s. (Canadian Army Photo)

he had claimed that integration would free up sufficient funds to re-equip the military with the modern tools and weapons they needed, but now he needed to find that money fairly quickly.

1964: THE SUTTIE COMMISSION

That same year Hellyer decided to reduce the size of the reserves by 60 percent to free up money for the re-equipping of the Regular Force, and to assist in easing the blow he created a Commission under the chairmanship of Brigadier E.R. Suttie, a Militia gunner, to select the units that would be cut. The Commission, having been given their marching orders, first determined that Canada only really needed 30,000 reservists, 40 percent of the existing number. The breakdown of the 30,000 was to be 9,000 to implement the Emergency Defence Plan, which included logistical and special units that were not provided in peacetime, with another 18,000 for the mobilization of three training brigades to replace the three regular brigade groups when they were dispatched overseas. For internal security, that is the guarding of key points, internment camps, and so on, 2,500; for National Survival – augmenting the Regular Army at national survival installations – 1,500.

Over the next two months, the Commission crisscrossed the country receiving testimony and depositions and inquiring into the reservists' problems. Its final report, dated June 1964, made many recommendations designed to improve the Militia's lot such as a reform of the pay system. For the Armoured Corps they recommended: "Armoured units could be provided with obsolete tanks purchased at little cost from other NATO countries to give them the means of familiarizing them with track suspensions, crew space, etc, and would not be that much different from the latest tanks in use."

Badge of the Sherbrooke Hussars

The Commission devised two new mechanisms for handling downsizing – the major/minor unit system and the Supplementary Order of Battle (SOB). The former required that units be assessed every three years as a part of the change-of-command procedure. A major unit was one with an establishment of 300 personnel, commanded by a lieutenant colonel; if, after three years, it paraded on average less than 150 persons, its establishment would be reduced to that of a minor unit. A minor unit had an establishment of 100 personnel and was commanded by a major; if, after three years, it paraded on average over 150 personnel, it would be upgraded to major unit status.

The Supplementary Order of Battle was designed to soften the blow of deactivating units. Instead of being disbanded, a unit would enter a state of suspended animation: it would exist, but only on paper. The Commission's recommendations for the Corps were that four regiments be placed on the SOB – IV Princess Louise Dragoon Guards, the Sherbrooke Regiment, the 7th/11th Hussars and the 12th Manitoba Dragoons. The Algonquin Regiment would revert to infantry. Of the remaining 21 units, nine were to be designated as recce regiments, while one, the Elgin Regiment, was to be a tank delivery regiment although it would continue to be trained on tanks. Finally, the Commission recommended that *Le Régiment de Hull* be switched from Quebec Area to Eastern Ontario Area, so as to be closer to a headquarters and (although it was implied, but not stated) replace IV Princess Louise Dragoon Guards as Eastern Ontario's armoured unit.

It was not enough. In the words of Mr. Hellyer's memoirs, "We followed the Suttie recommendations carefully but not slavishly...." IV Princess Louise Dragoon Guards were cut, but their purported replacement never left Quebec Area. The Halifax Rifles, which the Commission had recommended remain as a major unit equipped with tanks, was cut for unspecified reasons, leaving only one tank-equipped Militia unit in all of the Atlantic provinces. The Sherbrooke Regiment and the 7th/11th Hussars survived, now amalgamated as The Sherbrooke Hussars, and that would prove the only good news as far as the Corps was concerned.

The 12th Manitoba Dragoons were entered on the SOB as expected, but were also joined there by the 19th Alberta Dragoons and the 14th Canadian Hussars. The Saskatchewan Dragoons, recommended by the Commission to remain a major unit with a reconnaissance role, was reduced to minor unit status. When the dust had settled, the Corps had lost six regiments, two regiments had been amalgamated, and one had been reduced to a squadron establishment. Most outlying troops and squadrons were eliminated, depriving many smaller communities of any military presence; a process that furthered the division between the army and the general public. Although some minor improvements were made, the pay reforms and the recommendation to purchase additional tanks were ignored. For a saving to the government of $8,186,549 the Militia had been eviscerated.

WITH NATO IN GERMANY, 1957–1970

The third professional peak in the history of the Canadian Army, mentioned above, was manifested in service with the Canadian brigade in Germany – 4 Canadian Infantry Brigade Group until May 1968, and then 4 Canadian Mechanized Brigade Group. During the years 1957 to 1970 those who had the good fortune to be posted to the Germany-based armoured regiment had the privilege of serving during one of the brief periods in Canadian history when the government was truly committed to meeting its international defence commitments. This included recruiting a large enough army to meet its requirements and giving that army the necessary tools to do its job.

This was peace-time soldiering at its very best. The Canadian brigade in Germany had a true operational role as part of I (British) Corps, which was tasked with the defence of much of the North German plain in the event of a Soviet/Warsaw Pact invasion. And the threat of invasion was, at that time, also believed to be very real: the Russians and East Germans had somewhere around 20 tank and mechanized divisions at a high state of readiness on the other side of the East German border, just over 100 kilometres away. There was thus always a degree of tension, so training for the war that might come tomorrow had a far greater sense of urgency than anything done in Canada.

When the Royal Canadian Dragoons deployed to Germany as a full regiment in September 1957, the regiment occupied an old German army barracks on the outskirts of the city of Iserlohn in Westphalia, which was soon named Fort Beausejour. The camp consisted of five large three-story barrack blocks, a men's mess hall and a canteen, along with two long rows of sheltered tank park hangars. Behind the camp was a small training area, not really big enough, but sufficient for driver training and perhaps troop drills over a couple of tactical bounds. Fort Beausejour was to be the home of Canadian armoured regiments in Germany for almost thirteen years.

The Reconnaissance Squadron of Lord Strathcona's Horse at the same time moved into quarters in a relatively new camp taken over from the British, named Fort Chambly, located six kilometres east of the city of Soest, a delightful mediaeval town which had centuries before been a member of the Hanseatic League. During the time the Canadian brigade served in Northern Army Group, the Recce Squadron was an independent unit working directly for the brigade commander. Fort Chambly was home to the recce squadrons until 1970.

On exercise in the Soltau training area south of Hamburg, Germany, in September 1958. A Royal Canadian Dragoons Centurion working with troops of the *Royal 22e Régiment.*

As in Canada, individual training – tank crew and troop tactics in the 'postage-stamp' training area at Fort Beausejour, annual refresher courses and trades upgrading courses – took up most of the winter months, although it was usual that the regiment was allocated a three-week period in February or March for live firing on the superb British tank gunnery range at Bergen-Hohne, south-east of Hamburg. The entire brigade would deploy for much of the month of May to the Sennelager training area near Paderborn for troop and squadron level exercises. Then, in September, the brigade would hold its training concentration in the Soltau training area, near Bergen-Hohne, where field exercises at regimental and brigade levels were conducted. During these exercises a tank squadron was usually attached to each infantry battalion, while the recce squadron played out its role as the brigade commander's eyes and ears.

The grand finale to the training year was always the British Corps field exercise, where the Canadian brigade would join with the British divisions in a highly realistic three or four-week manoeuvre where there was always a 'live' enemy and hordes of umpires to adjudicate the outcome of 'battles'. So they would not compromise real defensive plans, these exercises often ran in a north-south direction, and it was not unusual for the exercise manoeuvre area to be about 100 kilometres in length. Everything was done as it would be in wartime: tanks moved tactically, across the German countryside, from one fire position to the next. In the process, the tanks caused enormous damage to farmers' fields, even though the Corps exercise was usually scheduled after the harvest, and manoeuvre damage teams

Fort Beausejour. **Painting by Charles Gosbee of the tank park in Fort Beausejour, with the 'A' Squadron barrack block in the background. This painting was done while the Strathconas were serving in Germany, but it is typical of the garrison activities of all the regiments that occupied the camp. (Canadian War Museum CWM16738)**

have been bettered. Canadian tank and recce units in this era were more competent than at any time since the war. For them, it truly was a 'golden age'.

In the period covered by this chapter entire regiments rotated from Canada to replace the units which had completed their three-year tour of duty in Germany. This had many advantages: the units were already well trained when they arrived, and members of the squadrons all knew each other, which made the units what the regimental system was intended to do: they were a family. The one disadvantage of unit rotation was that it took a regiment many months to adjust to serving in a British

would follow behind to pay land-owners for the destruction of crops, fences and even occasionally the walls of buildings that got in the way on narrow village streets.

During the Corps manoeuvres the tank crews experienced life much like the men who served during the Second World War. Lack of sleep was always a problem; if there was a halt in movement, most tank crews worked out an elementary routine to get some rest: if they were told they would not move for at least two hours they would take off their boots before getting into their sleeping bags. Everyone was always very dirty because of the mud and dust and grease, and it was a rare occasion on these exercises for a tank crewman to get to the Mobile Bath Platoon. The troops said you didn't notice the smell after about five days.

The tank crews lived on British Compo ration packs, little improved since the war. They came in 10-man boxes, not quite ideal for a four-man crew, but then much of the contents were barely edible anyway. It was a bad day if your crew was issued the 'Mutton Scotch-Style' pack; people swore the bits of meat still had the wool attached. For a time, crews were able to trade many of the tins of unpalatable 'whatever' to German farmers for potatoes and eggs, but in later years the farmers would have none of it. The wartime practice of stealing chickens and digging up potatoes was not unknown.

Whatever its discomforts, the training of the Canadian armoured units with the brigade in Germany simply could not

operational formation, with real war tasks, and in a country with very different customs and practices.

The Royal Canadian Dragoons and the Strathcona Recce Squadron both set extremely high operational standards for the armoured units that followed them. They trained and exercised to function on a battlefield where tactical nuclear weapons were expected to be used. During exercises, mainly practising defensive operations, a great deal of emphasis was placed on dispersion, on concealing tank squadrons in 'hides' so as to avoid becoming a 'lucrative nuclear target' for Soviet weapons. Squadrons would deploy to defensive positions or for counter-attacks only at the last possible moment.

The 8th Hussars replaced the Dragoons in the autumn of 1959. During the whole of their tour international tension was very high, and the incentive to train effectively was always present. The Berlin crisis, which began in 1958, was still having serious repercussions, and the infamous wall was erected in 1961.

During this period the Hussars modified their Centurion Mark Vs to the Mark XI standard by mounting the 105mm L7 gun in place of the 20-pounders. The Mark XI modifications also included thermal gun sleeves, additional armour on the front of the hull, add-on armoured fuel tanks, and infra-red searchlights and gun sights to improve night-fighting capability. When the Cuban missile crisis broke in October 1962 there was grave concern that the Soviets would mount a surprise attack, so the entire brigade moved to its wartime assembly positions. In preparing for that move, the Hussars discovered that there were insufficient stocks of 105mm ammunition, and a rapid 're-barrelling' was required before the regiment could deploy with a full combat load. The experience proved beneficial in the long run, as no time was lost in getting the tanks up to the standard once the crisis had passed.

In the spring of 1962 a new element was added to the recce squadron – the RCAC Helicopter Troop, equipped with six CH-112 'Nomad' helicopters, piloted by experienced Armoured Corps officers and with senior sergeants as observers. The helicopters added enormous capability to the recce squadron. In most respects the aircraft were used as 'zero ground pressure vehicles': they flew at 'nap-of-

An 8th Hussars Mark VI Centurion passes through a German village in an early morning move during the 1962 autumn exercise. (Canadian Army Photo EF-62-9474-47)

the-earth' level, that is, just above the ground, using folds in the terrain for cover and concealment just as other armoured vehicles in tactical movement. It was extremely dangerous flying, with telephone wires and power lines being the main hazard. The helicopters operated in pairs, and worked in conjunction with one of the ground recce troops. Their great advantage was speed; they could check out an area much more quickly than scout cars, or, when needed, they could remain behind after scout car patrols had been forced to withdraw, and thus maintain constant contact with an advancing 'enemy'. The troop indeed pioneered many aspects of helicopter tactics which were later adopted by the US Army.

The Fort Garry Horse succeeded the 8th Hussars in late 1962, and by the summer of 1963 the regiment was in peak form. One of the many highlights of the Garry's tour in Germany was the opportunity given to the brigade to play 'enemy' during the 1964 Corps exercise, and for much of the year the regiment practised Soviet tank tactics, which included unusual organizations such as tank troop/infantry platoon groups which would advance on many different axes simultaneously. The objective of the Corps exercise was to determine how long a traditional 'beefed-up recce screen' could hold out on the far side of a major water obstacle. When the exercise attack took place, led by widely spread-out tank troops, the Canadians quickly penetrated the defending British divisional positions, and reached their objective – the river obstacle – in less than six hours from starting out. This led to a major shake-up in the

British tactical concept for defending on the line of the Weser River.

It is little recognized that a key component of Canada's success with armour in Germany lay in the introduction of the C-42 family of radios. Although Heinz Guderian had recognized, back in the 1930s, that the mating of armour with radio was the key to *Blitzkrieg*, the technological capabilities of radio had not then reached their full potential. Indeed, up until the early 1960s radios remained delicate and temperamental tools, and commanders preferred to give their orders in person, so that, among other considerations, they could be certain that everyone had heard the plan. Not until the C-42 was it possible to give orders by radio with any degree of assurance that the message would get through. This development, linked with the appearance in 1963 of C-42-equipped APCs, permitted the creation of effective combat teams, and two of the Armoured Corps' major assets, mobility and communications, made regimental headquarters an ideal alternate brigade command post.

Lord Strathcona's Horse rotated to Germany in December 1965, along with 'C' Squadron of the 8th Hussars as the brigade recce squadron. Both added to the laurels achieved by the armoured units which had preceded them in 4 CIBG.

One of the notable Strathcona achievements was to win the 1967 Canadian Army Trophy competition. The Canadian Army Trophy (CAT), a half-metre-long silver model of a Centurion, had been presented to NATO in 1963 for annual award for the highest standard of tank gunnery in the Central Region. The

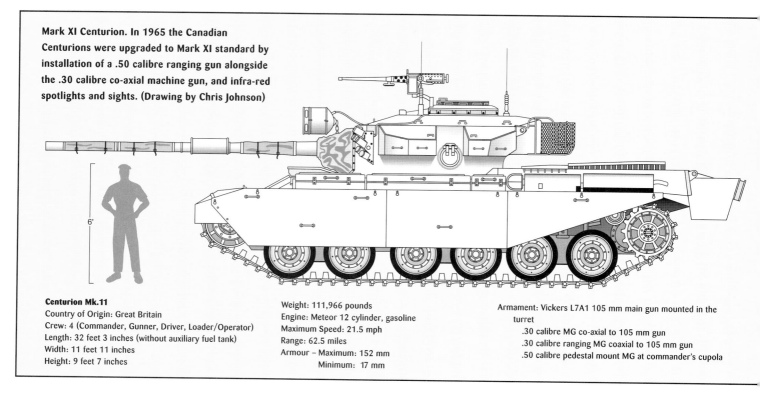

Mark XI Centurion. In 1965 the Canadian Centurions were upgraded to Mark XI standard by installation of a .50 calibre ranging gun alongside the .30 calibre co-axial machine gun, and infra-red spotlights and sights. (Drawing by Chris Johnson)

6'

Centurion Mk.11
Country of Origin: Great Britain
Crew: 4 (Commander, Gunner, Driver, Loader/Operator)
Length: 32 feet 3 inches (without auxiliary fuel tank)
Width: 11 feet 11 inches
Height: 9 feet 7 inches

Weight: 111,966 pounds
Engine: Meteor 12 cylinder, gasoline
Maximum Speed: 21.5 mph
Range: 62.5 miles
Armour – Maximum: 152 mm
Minimum: 17 mm

Armament: Vickers L7A1 105 mm main gun mounted in the turret
.30 calibre MG co-axial to 105 mm gun
.30 calibre ranging MG coaxial to 105 mm gun
.50 calibre pedestal mount MG at commander's cupola

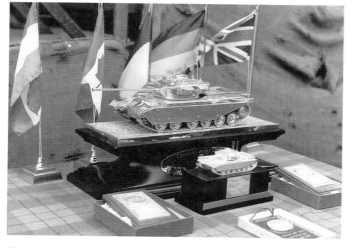

The Canadian Army Trophy, presented in 1963 to NATO's Northern Army Group for annual competition to the unit achieving the highest results in a tank gunnery competition shoot. The competition was later opened to the entire NATO Central Region. It represented the 'Olympics' of tank gunnery. (Fort Garry Horse Museum)

Service in Germany, 1957–1970

Royal Canadian Dragoons; Lord Strathcona's Horse (RC), Recce Squadron: Nov 57–Nov 59

1/8th Canadian Hussars (Princess Louise's): Nov 59–Nov 62

The Fort Garry Horse: Nov 62–Dec 65

Lord Strathcona's Horse (RC); 8th Canadian Hussars (Princess Louise's), C (Recce) Sqn: Dec 65–Jun 70

competition shoot took place on the gunnery range in Bergen-Hohne, and it engendered intense rivalry amongst the tank units of Britain, Germany, Belgium, the Netherlands and Canada. Some countries clearly 'stacked' their teams with gunnery instructors to give a better chance of winning the shoot. It was therefore a major victory when the Strathconas' 'B' Squadron won the CAT. The timing could not have been better – in Canada's Centennial year Canadian tank gunners were lauded as the best in NATO.

Just a few months later, it appeared that NATO, once again, was standing on the brink of battle, as the Soviets led an invasion and reoccupation of Czechoslovakia. But, as before, the tension slowly subsided and the troops returned to barracks.

By 1968 the Armoured Corps had been operating the Centurion for sixteen years and the Ferret for fourteen. They were still viable combat vehicles, but by then were beginning to show the effects of years of hard service. Engines that had been rebuilt too many times routinely broke down after only a few hours use, as did tank transmissions and final drives. The Army began considering a Centurion replacement in 1964, estimating that the fleet would be obsolete by 1971.

At this time the Germans and Americans had begun to develop a new main battle tank called MBT-70, which was intended to have a 152mm Shillelagh gun-missile system. For a brief period Canada participated in the project, but this was cut short because of severe cutbacks to defence spending, and because of some confusion as to the future roles, structure and organization of armoured units. In any event, the project failed. The British Chieftain was then considered, but the more promising discussions were with Krauss-Maffei of Germany who were developing the Leopard tank. Since the Leopard was being purchased by other NATO nations in large numbers, it appeared to be a good choice. In 1967 the negotiations got to the point of dickering over how many tanks Canada would buy – 50, 100 or 150? Then the project was off; the government had no money to spare for tanks.

The Centurion thus soldiered on, but there was an ever-increasing number of unserviceable vehicles. In May 1967, for example, 3 CIBG reported that there were only twelve 'runners' of the 56 Centurions in Gagetown. Even the Militia suffered from the confusion about the future of tanks in the Canadian Army: in 1967 the venerable Sherman was formally declared obsolete, gradually withdrawn from reserve units, then relegated to the roles of gate monuments or hard targets on the tank ranges at Gagetown and Wainwright.

Armoured Corps Helicopter Pilot. Painting by R. Volstad depicting a pilot in an Army flying suit worn in the early 1960s. (Directorate of History and Heritage)

THE MOVE TOWARDS LIGHT ARMOUR

In 1963, the CGS, Lieutenant-General Geoffrey Walsh, did not think that an army based on independent brigade groups was getting the direction and training that it needed to fight in a conventional war in Europe. He wanted a divisional structure, but did not have the money or political mandate to create one. His compromise solution was to create the Army Tactics and Organization Board (ATOB), which was a division headquarters in all but name. Meanwhile, the Board produced doctrine for the Army's field force, doctrine based on a structure of a division that had two mechanized brigades, each with an armoured regiment, and an armoured brigade of two regiments, as well as a divisional reconnaissance regiment. Each armoured regiment was to be equipped with a Main Battle Tank (MBT) and the recce regiment would have an amphibious light tank.

While these concepts were being developed, the new Defence Minister, Paul Hellyer, was looking at what were termed 'brushfire wars' being fought in Algeria, Vietnam and in many parts of the former British Empire. Hellyer saw a role for

Canada here, intervening with light, mobile forces before these wars could spread. Obsessed with 'airportability', he commissioned a study that recommended the creation of a divisional structure that included three light infantry brigades, an 'Armoured Regiment (Airportable)' and a 'Reconnaissance Regiment (Airportable).' The armoured regiment would be equipped with 64 Sheridan light tanks armed with the Shillelagh, while the recce regiment would have Ferrets equipped with .30 machine-guns.

There were thus two radically different views on the future structure, and equipment, of the Army – and especially of the place of armour – one held by the Army hierarchy which focused on heavy, high-intensity combat capability, the other by the Minister who wanted light, air-mobile forces. Neither Walsh's nor Hellyer's plan was ever implemented, primarily because the 1964 federal budget did not allocate sufficient funds for defence. In reality though, Hellyer's views prevailed. 'Mobile Command' was created, and the armour doctrine writers started over, introducing the 'Light Armoured Regiment' concept. The Ferret, useful as it was, was not amphibious, nor did it carry much firepower. A new recce vehicle, it was felt, should have both these capabilities. The M113 ½ Lynx, a derivative of the M113 APC, which

The helicopter-scout car team during a reconnaissance exercise in Germany, 1964. (NATO Photo 3906-12)

A Fort Garry Horse squadron on a tank train in the Iserlohn marshalling yard, 1965. To get the tanks to training areas for exercises or gunnery practice, they had to be shipped from Iserlohn on tank trains. If tanks were moved short distances they were, however, sent on heavy tank transporter trucks manned by Polish veterans of the Second World War. (Photo by Lieutenant-Colonel David Summers)

tions in the Second World War, notably that of the Horse Guards in Italy. He came up with a regimental structure calling for three light armour squadrons and a helicopter recce squadron. In each of the light armour squadrons he envisioned three light armour troops, each with four tracked recce vehicles, two 'direct fire support vehicles' (read 'tanks'), along with an assault troop section for pioneer and infantry support, and two 81mm mortars for indirect fire support. It would have been a formidable force in the low to mid-intensity conflict foreseen by Mobile Command.

Despite the best of intentions, this light armoured regiment concept never quite came about. The 8th Hussars, equipped with a combination of Ferrets, Lynxes and M-113 APCs 'in lieu' of other capabilities, along with a few aged Centurions, tried to get them to work together, but mixing tracked and wheeled vehicles was an insurmountable challenge. Moreover, their Centurions – the only real firepower in the light armour troop – were now unreliable and far from being 'airportable'. The regiment, and the other Regular Force units that were designated as light armour over the next few years, was simply an under-strength light reconnaissance regiment.

THE UN FORCE IN CYPRUS, 1964–1968

From 1964 to 1968 Canada's contribution to the UN Force in Cyprus (UNFICYP) was an infantry battalion supported by a reconnaissance squadron. The Cyprus tasking was anticipated to be of short duration but lasted nearly thirty years, albeit at a much reduced level, before Canada withdrew its contingent. The Cyprus commitment had its origins in intercommunal violence in December 1963. The 18 percent Turkish minority, feeling threatened by constitutional amendments pushed through parliament by the Greek majority, responded with force. Vicious fighting quickly spread and Greek and Turkish military intervention was threatened.

The UN established UNFICYP in March 1964, with Canada offering a contingent to be commanded by an armoured officer, Colonel E.A.C. Amy. HMCS *Bonaventure* departed Halifax carrying *1 R22eR* and the RCD Recce Squadron equipped with 16 Ferrets, the first UN contingent to arrive on the ground. The Canadians were located in an area north-east of Nicosia and in the capital city itself.

The armour task was two-fold. A troop was committed to

Canada had purchased when the Canadian-designed 'Bobcat' APC project was discontinued, was both amphibious and carried a .50 calibre machine gun (original plans had called for a 20mm cannon in a remote-controlled mount) and now Canada bought 175 of them.

The 8th Hussars, part of Mobile Command's new Special Service Force in Petawawa, were made a 'light armoured regiment' in 1967. There was little guidance from Mobile Command about what such a regiment was intended to do, or how it would be equipped, so the commanding officer, Lieutenant Colonel Art St. Aubin, drew on his experience with the US armoured cavalry and a study of Canadian heavy recce opera-

the UN's quick reaction force, while the remainder of the squadron was involved with constant patrolling. As well as keeping an eye on the population, to scotch any outbursts of fighting, they also had to keep the roads open since both sides frequently established roadblocks in attempts to assert control over an area. To cover this wide area of responsibility the Dragoons quickly found it necessary to adjust the organization of the squadron from three 7-car troops, plus two cars in squadron headquarters, to five 4-car

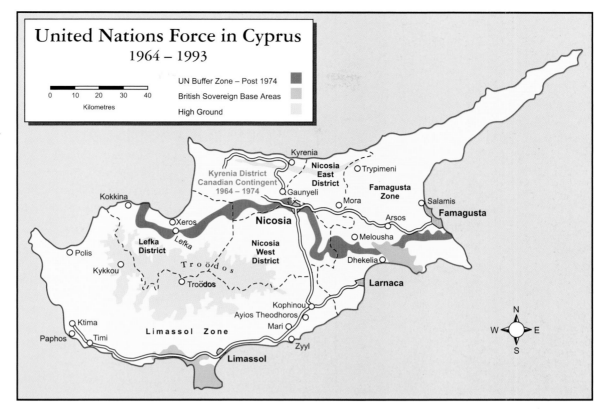

United Nations Force in Cyprus
1964 – 1993

0   10   20   30   40
Kilometres

UN Buffer Zone – Post 1974
British Sovereign Base Areas
High Ground

Kyrenia District
Canadian Contingent
1964 – 1974

Kyrenia

Nicosia
East
District

Trypimeni

Kokkina

Gaunyeli

Famagusta
Zone

Mora

Salamis

Xeros

Nicosia

Arsos

Famagusta

Lefka
District

Lefka

Melousha

Polis

Troödos

Nicosia
West
District

Dhekelia

Kykkou

Troödos

Larnaca

Kophinou

Ktima

Ayios Theodhoros

Mari

Paphos

Timi

Limassol Zone

Zyyl

Limassol

N
W   E
S

troops with three cars in squadron headquarters.

During this first Cyprus tour, Trooper J.H. Campbell was killed when his Ferret scout car crashed over a 12-foot embankment after swerving to avoid an old woman and her flock of sheep on a narrow mountain road. During the four years that Canadian recce squadrons served in this role one additional life was lost, that of Trooper Leonard Nass, of the 8th Hussars, who succumbed to illness in 1966.

During the later tours, the squadrons had two main roles: daily patrolling – to show the UN flag – in areas where the Turk and Greek populations were still intermingled, and the escort of convoys of civilian vehicles between the capital, Nicosia, and the town of Kyrenia, on the island's north coast. The recce squadron also served as the Force reserve, and many times over the four and a half years it was called out to assist in preventing minor confrontations between the Greek-Cypriot National Guard and the Turk-Cypriot 'Fighters' from getting out of hand. On one such occasion Major Art St. Aubin's 8th Hussars squadron deployed to block a National Guard tank company from getting into position to shell a Turk-Cypriot village. On another occasion, one of the most serious prior to the Turk invasion in 1974, the Fort Garry squadron in November 1967 was ordered to the village of Kophinou to intervene when a National Guard company attacked the small Turkish hamlet, and in the process shelled and seized UN outposts that got in the way. The local UN commander would not allow the squadron

RCD Ferrets on patrol in Kyrenia District, August 1967. (Canadian Forces Photo PCN 67-107)

Winning the hearts and minds of at least some Cypriots. Giving candy to the children in the poor villages was a routine part of patrol activity for the scout car crews. (Canadian Forces Photo CYP 67-3-1)

RCAC Squadrons in Cyprus, 1964–1968

The Royal Canadian Dragoons, Recce Squadron: Mar 64–Oct 64

Lord Strathcona's Horse (RC), Recce Squadron: Oct 64–May 65

The Royal Canadian Dragoons, A Squadron: May 65–Sep 65

The Royal Canadian Dragoons, B Squadron: Sep 65–Apr 66

8th Canadian Hussars, B Squadron: Apr 66–Oct 66

The Fort Garry Horse, A Squadron: Oct 66–Apr 67

The Royal Canadian Dragoons, A Squadron: Apr 67–Oct 67

The Fort Garry Horse, C Squadron: Oct 67–Apr 68

The Fort Garry Horse, B Squadron: Apr 68–Sep 68

The United Nations Service Medal. This medal, with a different ribbon for each mission, was awarded by the UN for, in most cases, 90 days service in the theatre. The ribbon shown is for the UN Truce Supervisory Organization. (United Nations Photo)

to position their Ferrets in the path of the Greek attack, which, because they had more firepower than the attackers, could have stopped the affair. This was one of the first occasions when the UN showed itself to be spineless. Other squadrons had less exciting tours, but trouble would usually flare up around the time the United Nations was debating the renewal of the Force mandate, so most had interesting stories to tell about their time on the so-called 'island of love'.

A force reduction in the early autumn of 1968 eliminated the recce squadron role in Cyprus. The Corps had, however, not seen the last of Aphrodite's Island, and several armoured regiments served there in a dismounted role in the 1970s, 80s and 90s.

The fact that both the UNEF and UNFICYP taskings were being filled, simultaneously, by recce squadrons placed a great strain on these soldiers. Men were going back for second and third tours in Egypt, each a year long, interspersed with six-month tours in Cyprus. To ease the strain, regiments converted sabre squadrons to recce so that they could take a turn at fulfilling their units' commitments. The end of these two taskings came as something of a relief.

THE REGULAR/RESERVE RELATIONSHIP

The relationship between regular and reserve components has never been an easy one. In the nineteenth and early twentieth centuries it was the reservists who held the power and who looked down on the few regulars as wastrels and layabouts. The primary function of the regulars was Militia training; their own training and professional improvement being a secondary consideration, and except during wartime this situation did not really change until after the Second World War.

But then it changed dramatically. Following the build-up for Korea and NATO duty in Europe the strength of the regulars grew to the point where, in 1952, for the first time in history, it was larger than the reserve component: 49,000 regulars to 47,000 reservists.

As the regulars grew in numbers and capability, the reserves correspondingly shrank in both categories. In 1951 the CO of the 1st Hussars, Lieutenant-Colonel A.B. Conron, a decorated wartime squadron commander, conducted a ruthless pruning of his regiment, retiring a number of unsuitable officers in the expectation that his unit would be called to active service for the Korean War. He well knew that the battlefield was no place for the physically or mentally unprepared. Twenty years later the concept of mobilizing a Militia unit for active service would have been seen by many as ridiculous. The veterans had been retired and their places largely taken by students. The failure to supply new vehicles and equipment plus the disruptions caused by changing roles such as the snakes and ladders scheme had disrupted the traditional relationship. Meanwhile, absorbed with their role in Germany, where they were at the cutting edge

(Above) The Governor General's Horse Guards taking part in a bridging exercise in Camp Borden, early 1960s. (GGHG Archives)

(Left) Shermans of *Le Régiment de Hull* on a winter exercise. (*R de Hull Museum*)

World War tactics. The Militia's previous motivation – professional competence – had been replaced with an inward-looking, survivalist mentality.

THE ARMOURED TRAINING REGIMENTS

Reductions in headquarters and infrastructure brought on by integration had produced a surplus of senior regulars, officers and other ranks, who, mainly because of age, were not going to receive regimental appointments. These people became the heirs of a new structure designed to support the reserves – in the Armoured Corps the 1st, 2nd and 3rd Armoured Training Regiments. The primary function of these units was the coordination of the collective training of the Militia regiments in one or more regions. For example, a Militia unit would be deployed to a centre such as Wainwright, Borden or Gagetown for a weekend of training and then leave, to be followed the next weekend by a sister unit. In addition to this type of work the Armoured Training Regiments conducted specialized courses, such as crew commander training. Finally, a task that was not to be found in their formal instructions, the Training Regi-

of armour developments in tactics and technology, it was now the regulars who looked down upon the Militia, dismissing them as weekend warriors suitable only as a source of semi-trained manpower to help fill out their ranks in time of emergency.

Both components of the Army, whether they recognized it or not, needed each other. The regulars, primarily focused as they were on NATO's Central Front, were actually living on borrowed time. Circumstances changed and the regulars soon needed political influence and public support only to find that they had largely lost touch with Canadian society and that their strongest link to the broader community, the Militia, had been alienated. The Militia, for their part, traumatized by the cutbacks and reorganizations, had adopted a bunker mentality. Their focus was on the survival of individual units and, in the mid-1960s, they were in danger of becoming an anachronism where Second World War equipment was used to teach Second

ments taught the light armoured concept, the Corps' new mantra.

The Militia at this time were falling farther and farther out of the information/decision-making loop. Even the concept of the Armoured Training Regiment was poorly explained when it was introduced in 1967, and some commanding officers thought that the regulars were being sent in to take over their commands. In one regiment, which shall go unnamed, the commanding officer simply abandoned his position out of a sense of despair, convinced that the turmoil wrought by Hellyer's reforms would result in the imminent disbandment of the Militia, if not the entire army.

The Armoured Training Regiments were a short-lived experiment, lasting approximately five years, but they were successful in helping to re-forge the links between the regulars and Militia and they led to even closer ties with the introduction of the Regular Support Staff (RSS) concept later on.

1968: UNIFICATION

Having reorganized the military along new lines (integration), Paul Hellyer was now ready for the final step – formal unification of the Forces. Among many other things, this process required all military personnel to wear a common green uniform and use a common rank structure. Although the new green uniform was touted for its distinctively Canadian appearance (meaning it did not look British), many were convinced that it was actually modelled on the service dress of the US Air Force, utilized the distinctive colour of the US Army and the officers' rank insignia of the US Navy.

Within the Corps, there were two features of unification that particularly rankled. The honourable rank of 'Trooper' was abolished, to be replaced with the ubiquitous designation of 'Private'. As well, the black beret – the nearly universal symbol of the armoured soldier – was abolished and replaced with a generic Canadian Forces (CF) green one. Unification had many and far more serious faults than these, but the basic problems were not readily apparent at the time and in place of a dispassionate critique of the new system, a great deal of energy was expended in fretting over these matters.

One senior officer who did like the new green uniform was Worthy. Ever the innovator, Worthy was always enthusiastic for change and so earned a great deal of gratitude from the beleaguered Mr. Hellyer. Sadly, though, Worthy did not have long to live, and on 8 December 1967 he died. The Minister whom he had supported responded by approving Worthy's request (which typically was contrary to regulations) to be buried at Worthington Park in Camp Borden, where he would continue to be surrounded by his beloved Corps. Although he obtained his wish it was one tinged with irony. Within three years the Corps School was moved away and soon, except for the dedi-

cated personnel of the Corps Museum and the occasional staff officer posted in to what was now Canadian Forces Base Borden, the Corps' presence in what had been its spiritual home was practically non-existent.

The trials and heartaches of Hellyer's reforms were supposed to be mitigated by new equipment, but in 1970, three years after Hellyer left office, the Corps was still struggling with aged Centurions and Ferrets, the Order of Battle had been cut yet again, and standards throughout the army were sliding as new personnel policies took effect.

The most damaging of these new policies, over the long term, was the removal of promotion examinations for officers. An officer could now obtain the rank of captain merely by serving for five years. There were no objective tests, either practical or theoretical, for fitness for field command and the army staff college, in Kingston, was under near-constant threat of closure because it was supposedly replaced by the new CF Staff College in Toronto. Toronto did not, however, train officers in the intricacies of army staff work at unit and brigade level. Attempting to meet the on-going need, the army staff college changed its name, reduced its course from one year to six months and soldiered on.

The rank structure became bloated. Brigadiers once again became general officers. Trained soldiers automatically became corporals (known derisively as Hellyer corporals) in order to give them a pay raise. Because virtually everyone in the ranks was a corporal it became necessary to create a new rank – actually an appointment – that of master corporal. The use of 'master' in a rank designation (there were also master warrant officers) was reflective of a strong American influence over the new Canadian Forces.

Not all of these problems were of Hellyer's doing, but rather they resulted from the cultural revolution his reforms had unleashed. As a 1980 review of the unification process noted:

The process of unification carried with it two unhealthy side effects. One was that unification for a time was enshrined as an article of faith: it took a number of years before essential environmental differences could once again be recognized and respected. The other effect was characterized by the attitude that any function that could be unified should be, and, if it applied at the national headquarters level it ought to be applied at the field level as well. The end result of this thrust for uniformity was that some policies were introduced more, it seemed, for the sake of unification than for operational effectiveness.

The three combat arms schools were unified in 1968 as the Combat Arms School and subsequently relocated to Gagetown in the summer of 1970. Basic training was centralized with

(Above) A Centurion was placed in Worthington Park to mark the departure of the Combat Arms School from Camp Borden in August 1970, when it was relocated to CFB Gagetown. This move brought an end to 32 years of armour training in Borden. (Courtesy Major General J.P.R. LaRose)

(Left) Throughout his long tenure as Colonel Commandant of the Corps, Major General Frank Worthington – Worthy – was always present at the officer cadet graduation ceremonies on Corps Weekend at the School in Camp Borden. For many years he reviewed the mounted parade in the First World War Autocar which he had commanded in the Motor Machine Gun Brigade in 1918. His driver from that conflict, 'Pop' Saunders, still had that honour. (Armour School Archives)

officer candidates going to Chilliwack, British Columbia, and recruits to Cornwallis, Nova Scotia.

Recruiting ads of this period depicted a lieutenant descending from a 707 airliner carrying a brief case while the viewer was encouraged to join the CF and be a 'junior executive'. Combat arms recruits, no longer trained in their corps schools, started to call themselves 'death techs' as a form of self-parody. Trained alongside future automotive and avionics technicians, they started off their military careers feeling inferior to these individuals, who usually had a higher level of education. Seeing their chosen path as a dead-end holding no realistic prospects of a follow-on civilian career, by the time they started their armoured trades training many were demoralized.

(Above) Recruit training in the Ontario Regiment, summer 1968. (Ontario Regiment Museum)

(Below) A troop of Fort Garry Horse Centurions pause to refuel during an exercise in Wainwright on the day prior to the disbandment of the Regular Force regiment, June 1970.

The Order of Battle of the Royal Canadian Armoured Corps, 1970

The Royal Canadian Dragoons

Lord Strathcona's Horse (Royal Canadians)

8th Canadian Hussars (Princess Louise's)

12e Régiment blindé du Canada

The Governor General's Horse Guards

8th Canadian Hussars (Princess Louise's) (Militia)

The Elgin Regiment (RCAC)

The Ontario Regiment (RCAC)

The Queen's York Rangers (1st American Regiment) (RCAC)

The Sherbrooke Hussars

12 Régiment blindé du Canada (Milice)

1st Hussars

The Prince Edward Island Regiment (RCAC)

The Royal Canadian Hussars (Montreal)

The British Columbia Regiment (Duke of Connaught's Own) (RCAC)

The South Alberta Light Horse

The Saskatchewan Dragoons

The King's Own Calgary Regiment (RCAC)

The British Columbia Dragoons

The Fort Garry Horse

Le Régiment de Hull (RCAC)

The Windsor Regiment (RCAC)

At the new Combat Arms School many armour officer and crewman training courses would start with a number of students asking for reassignment or release on the grounds that "this was not what I expected," before they had done a single day's training.

Although Mobile Command was not intended to be a replacement army headquarters, it soon took on many of those functions. The first commander, Lieutenant-General Jean Victor Allard, had served with the Three Rivers Regiment in the early stages of the Second World War before transferring to the infantry. Then in 1966 he was selected to be Chief of the Defence Staff. Allard had made his acceptance of the position of CDS conditional on Hellyer's agreement to create French-language units throughout the CF. Hellyer agreed, and in 1966-67 *5e Groupe Brigade du Canada* was established in Valcartier. The armoured component of *5e Brigade* was a new regular unit based on the traditions of Allard's former unit, *Le Régiment de Trois Rivières* (RCAC).

As had been the case with the 8th Hussars, the existing regional title was considered inappropriate, however, and so the title was changed to *12ième Régiment blindé du Canada* (*12e RBC*), the translation of the unit's wartime numerical designation. Raised in Valcartier on 6 May 1968, the first commanding officer was Lieutenant-Colonel J.P.R. LaRose who had started his armoured corps career with the Strathconas, serving in Korea, before joining the Garrys as a squadron commander. The regulars, for a brief period, had five regiments on the order of battle.

OPERATIONS *ESSAY* AND *GINGER*: THE 1970 OCTOBER CRISIS
Starting in 1963, an organization called *Le Front de la Libération de Québec*, or *FLQ*, began a campaign of violence with the object of separating Quebec from the rest of Canada. Bombs were planted and weapons stolen. The pattern of violence intensified in 1970 when a bomb exploded in NDHQ, killing a commissionaire. Then, on 5 October 1970, the British trade commissioner, James Cross, was kidnapped and five days later a Quebec provincial cabinet minister, Pierre Laporte, was also taken. Quebec called upon the federal authorities for assistance, which was quickly granted, and the scene was set for the October Crisis.

Two days after the Cross kidnapping, a raid on an *FLQ* training camp provided intelligence to the effect that an ammunition depot at Camp Bouchard, near Montreal, would be attacked. *12e RBC* deployed twelve Ferrets, five M 113s and their assault troop to Camp Bouchard but the attack was not forthcoming.

Operation *Rivet* was then undertaken, the deployment of *12e RBC* sub-units to protect bases containing nuclear air defence weapons and their delivery systems in Bagotville, Val d'Or and La Macaza. The 8th Hussars from Petawawa were committed to Operation *Ginger*, a VIP and Vital Point protection mission in Ottawa. Hussar Ferrets operated out of the Cartier Square Drill Hall while Armoured Corps soldiers provided 24/7 (twenty-four hours a day/seven days a week) personal escorts for Cabinet members and their families.

In Quebec, the military operations were codenamed Operation *Essay*. For a period of ten weeks, soldiers of 'C' Squadron of the 8th Hussars, from Gagetown, joined with *12e RBC* in guarding critical hydro stations. Squadrons of

12e RBC also deployed to Drummondville, Sorel and Trois-Rivières while cordon and sweep operations diligently searched for Cross, Laporte and their kidnappers.

In the end it was too late for Laporte, who was murdered by his kidnappers, but Cross was located and the FLQ exchanged their hostage for a flight to Cuba. The October Crisis had shaken the nation, but the army's ability to deploy quickly helped to maintain public confidence while, at the same time, overawing *FLQ* sympathizers who might have been tempted to emulate the kidnappers.

THE REGIMENTAL SYSTEM IN CRISIS
1970 was a traumatic year for the Corps. The Grey and Simcoe Foresters reverted to infantry, while the Regular Force lost the Fort Garry Horse and saw the wholesale re-badging of regiments. There were two forces behind these events: rampant monetary inflation and the personal views of Prime Minister Pierre Elliott Trudeau.

The financial savings engendered by the processes of integration and unification did not accrue to the Department of National Defence, but were swallowed up by a government dealing with a serious inflation problem. The costs of everything, including military equipment and personnel, were rising faster than government revenues and, in such a situation, defence concerns went to the back of the queue.

The second force was Trudeau. After becoming prime minister in 1968, Trudeau ordered a complete review of, among other government activities, foreign affairs and defence. The review was to re-examine all aspects of these activities from the point of view of first principles. For example, should Canada be a neutral state or part of an alliance? Having decided that Canada's best option was partnership in an alliance, *i.e.* NATO, attention was turned to how Canada could obtain the maximum benefit from membership at the minimum price. The question quickly settled down to a debate about whether Canada should remove its contingent from Germany or not, and in the end a compromise was struck; Canada would maintain troops in Germany, but on a much-reduced scale.

4 CMBG was cut in half – an arbitrary act that made little military sense – and the brigade was moved south to co-locate with the Canadian air bases in Lahr and Baden-Soellingen, just as General Foulkes had argued for twenty years earlier. It may have made more sense to end outright either the army's or the air force's role in NATO and concentrate resources in Canada, but the CDS decided to maintain token elements of both in the interests of keeping peace between the services, a surprising decision since eliminating inter-service rivalry had been one of the major rationales for unification.

Badge of *12e Régiment blindé du Canada*

Back in Canada, Mobile Command, which by default had assumed many of the functions of the former Army Headquarters, was concerned with army reorganization. Falling personnel numbers and the cut-backs in Europe had led to the conclusion that units would have to be disbanded – the only question was, which ones? The delicacy of the situation in Quebec (the October Crisis was only a few months away) led to a quick conclusion that francophone units could not be touched. Therefore, in the Armoured Corps the axe fell on the junior anglophone unit in the Regular Army, the Fort Garry Horse. At one point, consideration was given to disbanding the 8th Hussars as well, but that idea was eventually dropped.

The blow fell on 15 June 1970, when the Fort Garrys instantly became Strathconas, the Strathconas in Germany were 're-badged' to RCD, while the Dragoons in Gagetown either became members of 'C' Squadron of the 8th Hussars or went to extra-regimental duty at the School. Only the Hussars in Petawawa and *12e RBC* in Valcartier were spared from the melancholy business.

The regimental system was twisted to the breaking point, but it, like the Corps, survived. In Ottawa serious consideration was given to abolishing the Army's regimental system. For the Armoured Corps this would have meant generic numbered units not unlike those proposed in 1940 when the Corps was first raised. Happily, as had happened in 1940, the scheme died, but not before someone in NDHQ had prepared drawings of new guidons for these generic regiments.

CHAPTER 19

Regeneration, 1971–1989

The start of this period can be summed up in the words of an oft-quoted phrase from Granatstein and Bothwell's *Pirouette*. "For the Canadian Armed Forces, the Trudeau years were a long, dark night of the spirit. Demoralized, embittered and frustrated, Canada's unified armed forces struggled to understand a government that treated them as an inescapable nuisance." There was, however, a dawn at the end of this long dark night, and by 1989 along with the end of the Cold War a new era would emerge for the RCAC.

THE CAST BRIGADE GROUP

Canada announced in 1969 that it would provide a Canadian Air/Sea Transportable (CAST) brigade group to NATO instead of a division. The CAST brigade was to have pre-positioned equipment in Norway and then fly its troops over to the sites, draw the equipment, and deploy to fight. Except that the Norwegians thought pre-positioned equipment was 'provocative'. Thus, the next evolution of the CAST plan had the brigade group deploying from Canada with its equipment by air and sea.

After negotiations with the Supreme Allied Commander Europe (SACEUR) in 1970, it was determined that the Canadian formation would reinforce either North Norway or Denmark's Jutland Peninsula. 2 Combat Group was tasked by Mobile Command with the CAST role throughout the 1970s. The Group included a light armoured Regiment, the 8th Hussars, which the planners thought would prove useful in either the mountainous environment of north Norway or the open plains of Schleswig-Holstein.

The commitment was not popular with NDHQ and little effective detailed strategic movement planning was conducted. Even so, the brigade commanders did plan and train for the role as seriously as they could, training which included a large air deployment exercise of 2 Combat Group to the Gaspé in 1969, but there was no money for large-scale exercises in the CAST

'B' Squadron of the 8th Hussars deployed with their new tracked Lynx recce vehicles to the Mojave Desert in California on Exercise *Piute Lance* to practise their role in CAST Combat Group operations in an unfamiliar environment, May 1970. (Canadian Forces Photo RE75-794)

role after 1970 and only one partial concentration was conducted near Petawawa. When 2 Combat Group became the Special Service Force (SSF), plans were made to deploy a Cougar squadron to Norway but this idea melted away with time and, in any case, the SSF was primarily interested in Defence of Canada operations and planning to deploy to global hotspots as a UN force.

In addition to the new CAST role, the 8th Hussars, in Petawawa, were also responsible for sovereignty operations in the Canadian north, the purpose of which was to demonstrate *de facto* Canadian control of the area. The Hussars were nothing if not versatile, and in May of 1970 they further demonstrated their capabilities with a deployment by air to California's Mojave Desert. Lieutenant-Colonel P.J. Mitchell, the Hussar CO, had wanted to have his regiment work in a non-traditional area, and the brigade commander, Brigadier-General Radley-Walters, suggested the then-decrepit American facility at Fort Irwin (later home of the famous National Training Centre with its sophisticated computerized training system). The distant location was selected, in part, because the air-portability aspect of the light armoured regiment needed to be tested. Following a deployment by air of some 7,500 kilometres, over the next four weeks Lynx, Ferrets and even a couple of 403 Squadron Hueys, sometimes piloted by ex-RCAC pilots, were scouring the high desert's rocky escarpments and scrub-covered hillocks in search of the Fantasian enemy. The 8th Hussar's RSM, CWO Rutledge, recalled:

During Exercise *Brave Lion* in northern Norway in the summer of 1986, a *12ᵉ RBC* Cougar is recovered from the tidal mud of a Norwegian fiord. (Canadian Forces Photo BLC86-120-64)

> We flew by Hercules from Trenton to Ellsworth AFB in North Dakota and then on to Barstow, California. It was hot! It was dusty! There were scorpions and cacti all over the place. There were almost no landmarks in the desert, which placed a premium on map reading skills. We got really good at using the contours and mountains to navigate by. The guys loved it. It was totally different from the usual training areas around Petawawa, as was the long weekend we had off in Las Vegas. Assault Troop even got to use their full range of explosives against targets which littered the desert training area.

In 1984, responsibility for CAST was shifted from the SSF to *5e Groupe Brigade du Canada (5e GBC)*. *12e RBC* now seized the reins and was tasked to support a mixed wheeled/tracked infantry brigade group in North Norway – the Jutland deployment option having been dropped. As *12e RBC* trained diligently for that role, there was some debate as to whether the role was feasible. Consequently, the first full-scale CAST deployment, Exercise *Brave Lion,* was held in the summer of 1986. Several Norwegian Roll-On/Roll-Off (RO-RO) ships arrived at Quebec to embark *5e GBC* and *12e RBC* prepared its Cougars and Lynx for the long journey across the Atlantic to Sorreisa and Bardufoss, Norway.

Upon arrival, the regiment spent a month operating in a variety of mounted and even dismounted roles. The terrain was forbidding: twisting, winding roads, deep forests, isolated villages and towns, and mountainous fjords. Though not ideal ground for mechanized operations, it was highly defensible. Lynx were used to screen 6 (Norwegian) Division's defensive lines against the Orangeland forces, while the Cougar squadrons, acting as tank surrogates, served as a counter-penetration and rapid reaction force for the vital rear base areas.

PROBLEMS WITH TANKS

In the early 1970s the mood of the Corps was one of frustration. All of the major combat vehicles, save the Lynx, and many of the support vehicles were either obsolete or obsolescent. Worse, there were no replacements in sight, especially for the Centurion. Main Battle Tanks (MTBs) were costly to buy and expensive to operate, and the government was still suffering from the effects of rampant inflation – costs continued to rise while incomes stood still.

Apart from expense, tanks suffered from an image problem; in the Canada of the early 1970s, where the on-going Vietnam War had created a broad public distaste for the military, soldiers and tanks were sometimes objects of derision or protest. The use of armour by communist *régimes* to crush popular uprisings, such as had happened in Czechoslovakia in 1968, created an unfavourable image in the minds of many, and the relatively high Israeli tank losses in the 1973 Yom Kippur War led some experts to declare the MBT obsolete. The tank, of course, was not obsolete; the high casualty rate had resulted from Israeli

This cartoon characterizes some of the arguments about what a direct-fire support vehicle might be. (Cartoon by Lieutenant Colonel Roman Jarymowicz, RCH)

neglect of the all-arms team in favour of tank-heavy formations. Finally, 'light armour,' first developed in the mid-1960s, was increasingly seen, by politicians, as the coming military trend. Lightly armoured, wheeled vehicles that were air transportable would be less intimidating and cheaper for the taxpayer.

The new buzzword was 'direct fire support vehicle' or DFSV, and the 1971 White Paper, *Defence in the 70s*, which would lay the groundwork of defence policy for the next fifteen years, proclaimed that Canada would retire the Centurion in favour of a DFSV.

> The Government has decided that the land force should be reconfigured to give it a high degree of mobility needed for tactical reconnaissance missions in the Central Region reserve role. The Centurion medium tank will be retired, since this vehicle is not compatible with Canada-based forces and does not possess adequate mobility. In its place a light, tracked, direct-fire support vehicle will be acquired as one of the main items of equipment. This vehicle, which is airportable, will be introduced later into combat groups in Canada. The result will be enhanced compatibility of Canadian and European-based forces and a lighter, more mobile land force capable of a wide range of missions.

Like many such *diktats*, this one produced a sense of bewilderment in most soldiers. This sort of vehicle, of course, was of no value on NATO's Central Front where the potential enemy was equipped with state-of-the-art MBTs, but, in the wake of the government's pronouncement, the Canadian-based armoured regiments were now converted to 'light armour' – certainly more appropriate for the CAST Brigade. The only Centurions left were those in Germany with the RCD and those remaining with the School in Gagetown.

Prior to the 1971 White Paper, the Vice-Chief of the Defence Staff, a decorated armoured officer, Lieutenant-General M.R. Dare, had requested that the British Cavalry Vehicle Recce (Tracked) or CVRT family of vehicles be examined with an eye

towards adoption into Mobile Command as DFSVs. The first two vehicles to undergo trials were the tracked Scorpion and the wheeled Fox. Seventy-four Scorpions were initially needed to replace the Centurions in the DFSV role, while the Ferrets also desperately needed replacement. After the White Paper was tabled in 1971, the requirement went up to 134 Scorpions, but many within Mobile Command were opposed to acquiring Scorpion, calling, instead, for an MBT. Dare told them that Scorpion was intended as a tank trainer until he could build up enough political credibility to get an MBT Centurion replacement.

Mobile Command came very close to acquiring Scorpion. A trials team was sent to Bovington in the UK, articles on the vehicle appeared in various journals, and an official vehicle characteristics sheet was distributed within Mobile Command for familiarization purposes. Then, at the last moment, National Defence/External Affairs/British Government machinations relating to other defence-oriented contracts intruded. Apparently, pressure applied by the Supreme Allied Commander Europe (SACEUR) and others in NATO contributed to this delay. At this point two Scorpion and two Fox trial vehicles arrived in Canada and were paraded around to the units.

Lieutenant-General J.A. Dextraze had become the Chief of Defence Staff and *Jadex*, as he was usually called, was not a fan of either Scorpion or Fox. Nevertheless, he allowed a competitive trial to proceed with Fox pitted against the Cadillac Gage V-150, which had a turret mounting a 20-mm gun. The Fox was eliminated in the trials and Cadillac-Gage thought they had the order sewn-up, but the car company would not entertain the notion of production in Canada, which would have driven the price up, and the DND acquisition team subsequently decided

In April 1973 the 8th Hussars celebrated the 125th anniversary of the formation of the New Brunswick Regiment of Yeomanry Cavalry on 4 April 1848. The 8th Hussars are thus the oldest continuously serving regiment in the Royal Canadian Armoured Corps. (8CH Archives)

A Lynx of Lord Strathcona's Horse patrols a street in Nicosia during the deployment of a troop with the Canadian Airborne Regiment in 1974. (Canadian Forces Photo CYPC74-295)

RCAC Regiments in Cyprus, 1972–1991

Lord Strathcona's Horse (Royal Canadians): Apr 1972–Oct 1972

12e Régiment blindé du Canada: Apr 1977–Sep 1977

8th Canadian Hussars (Princess Louise's): Oct 1978–Mar 1979

Lord Strathcona's Horse (Royal Canadians): Oct 1979–Mar 1980

12e Régiment blindé du Canada: Apr 1983–Sep 1983

Lord Strathcona's Horse (Royal Canadians): Feb 1988–Sep 1988

The Royal Canadian Dragoons: Mar 1989–Sep 1989

12e Régiment blindé du Canada: Sep 1990–Feb 1991

to open up the trials worldwide. That led to a requirement for the Armoured Vehicle General Purpose (AVGP). At the same time, Cabinet decided, in 1973, that Scorpion was not for Canada and *Jadex* then pursued the idea of a MBT acquisition that eventually led to the purchase of Leopard C1s.

BACK TO CYPRUS

Although the Corps had ceased posting recce squadrons to the Cyprus UN Contingent in 1968, Canada had continued to send infantry battalions to the island on six-month rotations and the strain on the infantry was growing. In 1972, for the first time, a non-infantry unit was detailed for rotation – Lord Strathcona's Horse (RC). Under Lieutenant-Colonel J.A. Fox, the Strathconas deployed in the spring for a very successful tour, and thereafter all of the combat arms units were tasked in turn.

In 1974 the Strathconas supplied a Lynx troop to accompany the Canadian Airborne Regiment's reinforcements when that regiment was augmented following the Turks' July invasion. When the Airborne/Strathcona contingent was replaced in December by a 1 RCR Battle Group, a troop of the 8th Hussars took over the Strathconas' vehicles.

The events of 1974-75 were an aberration. Most tours on the island saw soldiers combating boredom rather than Greeks or Turks. Both sides had a vested interest in maintaining the *status quo,* and relied on the 'peacekeepers' to ensure that their opponent could not carry out a pre-emptive strike. The theory, of course, was that while the UN maintained the peace, the politicians would reach a settlement, but like many good theories this one foundered in practice. Neither side had an incentive to bargain, and for over a quarter of a century the lines established in the summer of 1974 have remained static.

However, for the Canadian units that served in Cyprus, it was a wonderful training experience. Much responsibility devolved on junior officers and junior NCOs. There was just enough danger from minefields, trigger-happy sentries and wild dogs to keep everyone on their toes, and the *locale* was sufficiently exotic to underline the fact that this was not just another exercise. As time passed, and more and more Regulars were going back for third and fourth tours, reservists were introduced to ease the strain. The idea proved to be a boon to both and the great divide between the two narrowed, but eventually the government grew tired of the expense involved in playing a major role in Cyprus and, in 1993, the commitment was cut back to a couple of officers in UNFICYP headquarters.

BUTTONS AND BOWS

In the early 1970s, dissatisfaction with the green (known as CF) service dress was growing. The only corps or regimental insignia worn were the cap and the collar badges, and once the cap and the tunic were removed no one could differentiate between a tanker, a submariner or an avionics technician. The first crack in the dam of such uniform uniforms was the re-introduction of regimental buttons, followed in 1976 by the officially sanctioned return of the black beret, which had never entirely gone away, whatever regulations may have stipulated! Prior to unification the black beret had been one of two choices of headdress. Officers generally wore the army service dress cap

Badge of the Armour Branch, introduced following unification. While it was authorized in 1970, this badge did not come into use until 1980. Substitution of 'Canada' for 'RCAC' in the plaque on the gauntlet made the badge bilingual.

Officer of The Windsor Regiment (RCAC) in Patrol Dress ('Blues'). Painting by R. Volstad. (Directorate of History and Heritage)

air and special warfare training. Direct Fire Division taught armour and communications, Indirect Fire Division was responsible for artillery and mortar training, while Weapons Division ran infantry and small arms training. Although the system worked, it was difficult for a student to grasp the basic concepts of armour in this divisive environment. He needed to appreciate the role of all of the combat arms, but first had to master the basics of his own arm. The CAS's early commandants in Gagetown, Colonels J.P.R. LaRose and D.A. Nicholson, recognized these problems and within two years the School had been reorganized, with departments based on the individual combat arms.

The first officer in command of the new Armoured Department was Major Jack Dangerfield and under him it was organized into five Wings – Officer/NCO Training, Driving and Maintenance, Communications, Gunnery and Administration. It was at this point that the Armoured Department resurrected the Corps' magazine. It was known under a variety of titles but most commonly as the *Armour Bulletin/Journal de l'Arme blindée*. Within five years the Armoured Department had blossomed into the Armour School under Lieutenant-Colonel Gordon O'Connor.

A MAILED FIST FOR MOBILE COMMAND

Although all of the Canadian-based units were now 'light armour' there were still many unanswered questions as to what exactly they were supposed to be training for. The newest unit, *12e RBC*, was still building and was focused on troop and squadron training in the early 1970s. The Strathconas had determined that maintaining a balance between light armour and

while in service dress; the berets were usually, but not exclusively, worn in the field. In heartfelt relief at the return of the black beret; the Corps decreed it to be the only authorized headdress for all orders of dress. Eventually, regimental shoulder titles were re-introduced and, by the mid-1980s, most of the dissatisfaction over dress issues had subsided.

In the rush to get the Regulars into the new green uniforms, little attention was paid to the reservists. The old patterns of uniforms and badges continued to be worn, in some cases for several years after the Regulars had changed over. The re-kitting took so long that it became yet another, and probably the most conspicuous, symbol of the great divide between the army's components. Both Regulars and reservists paid for their own mess dress and that, therefore, had been 'grandfathered,' *i.e.*, personnel were permitted to continue wearing their old-pattern uniforms until they were worn out. The new unified CF mess dress – a dull midnight blue – took a long time to find its way onto the backs of Regulars and made practically no impression in the messes of Militia regiments.

THE SCHOOL

When the Combat Arms School was created in the autumn of 1968, it was initially organized into divisions and companies based on the nature of their activities. Command Division, for example, was responsible for all the leadership, tactics, tactical

Exercise *New Viking* enabled soldiers from all armoured regiments, Regular and Militia, to gain experience in basic military operations in the Canadian Arctic. Here, troops are seen erecting a navigation marker in the barren landscape. (Canadian Forces Photo ISC 77-399)

tank training was desirable. For example, when Lieutenant-Colonel J.A. Fox arrived to take command he joined a sergeant who was commanding a machine-gun armed jeep and asked him "What's your job? " The sergeant replied: "If I'm a Fox, I'm doing this. If I'm in a Lynx, I'm doing that. If I am in a DFSV, we'd be doing something else which might look like this. "

It was fairly straightforward for the RCD in Germany operating with 4 CMBG in the NATO context, while the 8th Hussars continued with light armoured operations in the defence of Canada and the CAST role in Petawawa. These northern operations, the *Viking* exercise series, saw the deployment of a number of sub-units, usually troops in the case of RCAC units, to various locations in the Canadian Arctic during the summer months. Frequently the patrols built navigation and stocked survival cairns in remote areas and then recorded their location so that the data could be included on survival maps. In some cases, Arctic patrol operations were conducted in conjunction with Inuit of the Canadian Rangers. Innumerable deployments were made throughout the 1970s and 1980s by the Hussars, *12e RBC* and Strathconas.

A patrol of Lynxes passes through a German village during an exercise in 1987. (Canadian Forces Photo ILC 87-111-1)

One of the characteristics of major autumn exercises in Germany was the ability to employ realistic tactics, moving across the countryside as one would in wartime. Here an RCD Centurion 'helps' a farmer with his sugar beet harvest. The absolute disinterest shown by the farmer is typical of this era: he knew he would be paid handsomely for the damage. (Canadian Forces Photo ISC 74-084)

THE NATO BATTLEFIELD: 1970s

4 CMBG's armoured regiment, the RCD, had been slashed in half in the cuts of 1969, which left it with two squadrons of ageing Centurion Mark XIs. Plans were made to keep a third squadron's worth of vehicles near the new base at Lahr in southern Germany and then fly over the personnel in time of crisis, and this 'fly-over' squadron was kept at Gagetown where it supported the School. In some cases, the squadron was deployed during NATO's large annual fall Exercises (*Fallex*) through the 1970s.

Working 'down south' in Germany was quite different from the more comfortable days of 'up north.' Instead of being integrated into I (British) Corps, 4 CMBG now worked with both VII (US) Corps and II (German) Corps, forming part of Central Army Group or CENTAG. Initially, it was to act as a CENTAG reserve which could back up any one of the four corps in the region, but eventually reality set in: 4 CMBG was simply too small to plan for all of these contingencies and, in any event, it lacked the requisite mobility.

The potential NATO battlefield had changed by the 1970s and was no longer based on immediate nuclear weapons use. NATO's conventional forces were expected to fight for as long as possible, to stem the 'Red tide' until reinforcements could arrive from North America, the United Kingdom, and Portugal (and later Spain when she joined NATO in the 1980s) or until NATO authorities decided that limited tactical nuclear warfare

Lieutenant General Jim Fox (second from left), commander of Mobile Command, pays a visit to the Ontario Regiment during their annual range practice in Meaford. (Ontario Regiment Museum)

was to be implemented. This situation reduced frontages and thus increased the importance of conventional forces. Unfortunately, cutting 4 Brigade (and the RCD) in half in 1970 had made it a less militarily useful formation than it had been. That said, the Centurion tanks and mechanized infantry were a welcome addition to a series of smaller but critical contingency plans produced by II (German) Corps. This formation was spread rather thin since it had to cover the vulnerable German-Austrian border. Planners assumed (correctly, as we now know) that Soviet plans involved violating Austrian neutrality to outflank the main defence positions on the Czech–West German border. If II Corps was to extract itself from these positions, the numerous bridges on the Donau River had to be secured from this Soviet left hook, and many exercises had Canadian battle-groups operating in this role, with the Centurions divided up to support the infantry in their blocking positions.

The Arab-Israeli war of 1973 had demonstrated that light anti-tank guided missiles could thwart offensive operations by massed tank and mechanized forces. It also confirmed the fact that helicopters could do more that conduct recce operations and carry troops on a modern battlefield since anti-tank guided missiles could be effectively used from them. Though these were not new theories, the scale of the Middle East battles, aptly underscored by the hundreds of destroyed tanks, was enough to shake up the Western media, politicians, and military authorities.

Once again, light airportable formations were trotted out as a possible replacement for heavy mechanized forces. The role of the tank was again questioned, which, in turn, re-fuelled the debate over a Centurion replacement. What most pundits were missing, however, were the details which the RCAC Association was only too ready to supply in order to counter the anti-tank arguments. The 1973 operations had a number of unique terrain factors which increased the effectiveness of the guided missiles. Similarly, the Israelis did not fully comprehend how to use self-propelled artillery or mechanized infantry combat teams and tended to rely on tactical airpower which was vulnerable to missiles.

Exercise *Lares Team* (1976) ended the notion of a completely airportable and airmobile force. This exercise pitted 4 CMBG with its Centurions and M-113s against the American 101st Airmobile Division. The Americans had standard infantry battalions equipped with portable TOW anti-tank missiles and Huey Cobra attack helicopters (also with TOW) and the ability to move a battalion at a time by transport helicopter, but the purveyors of "light infantryism" were stunned when 4 CMBG's mechanized combat teams simply bypassed the immobile American infantry battalions after the Lynx squadron had picqueted them at the maximum range of the TOW systems. The RCD caught the airportable pack howitzers cold when their transport helicopters failed to arrive on time, while their

Recce Squadron penetrated the division's rear area. Light artillery was deemed ineffective against Centurion armour. The Canadian onslaught was stopped only when it outran the air defence systems and was caught by the Cobras.

In the new NATO conventional environment, quality recce capability once again came to the fore, as Sergeant Bill Hungerford recalled.

We were given a particular area of responsibility. It could be a screen, a [flank] guard or an advance to contact. We'd go in early and establish an OP. Sometimes it got very hairy. You were surrounded, but not detected and you had to be careful about what type of information that you radioed back. The only restriction you had was your imagination or initiative. If you could get into somebody's living room, dress as a German, walk the marktplatz and scope out 'enemy' headquarters, then you did it.

Recce operations achieved some prominence within NATO with the establishment of the Boeselager Cup, a NATO-wide recce competition sponsored by the *Bundeswehr*. This CAT-like competition, which the RCD and then the 8th Hussars continuously participated in from 1977, consisted of a range shoot, AFV recognition and the *parcours* – mounted and dismounted night recce exercises.

THE 1976 OLYMPIC GAMES

RCAC units were involved in Operation *Gamescan 76*, held during the Montreal Olympics from June to August. The mass murder of Israeli athletes during the 1972 Munich Olympics, coupled with memories of the FLQ terrorist campaign, generated extreme concern on the part of the government. The entire world would have its eyes on Canada and it would be an ideal opportunity for extremist groups to make their own demonstration.

Most of the Canada-based Mobile Command units were involved. Task Force 1 (TF 1), based on *5e Groupe de Combat* and led by Brigadier-General René Gutknecht, handled athlete security and the main competition sites in Montreal. TF 1 included *12e RBC*, and HQ Squadron and 'A' Squadron were assigned to Montreal to act as a mobile reserve, while the other two squadrons were deployed to three remote sites: the L'Acadie shooting range, the Joliette archery range and Tadoussac. Notably, TF 1 was bolstered by the addition of seven hundred Militia personnel drawn from *Secteur de l'Est* units. In some cases, soldiers from the Royal Canadian Hussars, *Régiment de Hull* and *12e RBC (Milice)* augmented *12e RBC*, while in others they donned blazers and flannels to act as additional plainclothes security at the competition sites. Combat clothing was not permitted and all Mobile Command soldiers wore

Among the many tasks performed by armoured units during the 1976 Montreal Olympic Games was providing a mobile guard for the Royal Yacht *Britannia* as she moved along the St. Lawrence River during the visit of Her Majesty the Queen. Here a Ferret belonging to *12e RBC* takes its turn at this rather unusual guard duty. (Canadian Forces Photo IMOC 76-637)

summer dress with berets instead of helmets and webbing, to avoid presenting an image of Canada as an armed camp.

Task Force 2 consisted of part of 2 Combat Group. The 8th Hussars deployed 'B' Squadron to CFB Ottawa (Uplands) to act as a Standby Force to support either TF 1 in Montreal, TF 4 in Kingston (a joint task force protecting the yachting site), or to deal with any incident which might happen in the national capital region. 'A' Squadron was split between Dorval and Mirabel airports, where, working alongside 1 RCR, 'A' Squadron's task was to continuously sweep areas around the central air hubs to identify, and place surveillance on possible vantage points from which SAM-7 man-portable missiles could be launched against airliners.

The 8th Hussars and *12e RBC* also provided security for the royal yacht, *Britannia,* which was transporting the Queen through the St Lawrence River system. Ferret scout cars moved from bound to bound as *Britannia* made her way up the river to Montreal.

This show of force and continual presence may well have contributed to the fact that no terrorist incidents occurred during the 1976 games, and reassured the nation that the Royal Canadian Armoured Corps also stood on guard for Olympia.

RENT-A-TANK, AND THE 'PERMANENT PANZERS'

By 1972 the Centurions were showing their age. RSM Doug Seed recalled "I was driving when the damned stickshift came out of it! We'd be going through towns and villages at speed and a stickshift or a tiller bar would break. It was a wonder nobody

was killed!" At one point, the entire fleet in Gagetown was grounded and, supported by a major Armoured Corps, community, staff and media education effort, the CDS finally accepted that there was a need to replace Centurion with a new MBT and not a DFSV. Even so, several studies were undertaken on how to extend the life of the tanks – yet again.

The backup plan, if the CDS could not get the government to buy a new tank, was to retrofit the entire Centurion fleet in the same way the Israelis had when they created their 'Patturions': an Israeli armoured corps general was even brought over to Canada to consult on the project, which involved replacing the engine in a Centurion hull with an M-60 engine and final drive, while a Marconi fire-control system would also be installed alongside a 105mm L7 gun. However, once it became clear that a replacement MBT was not out of the question, a more limited rebuild was authorized. The tanks serving with 4 CMBG in Germany were sent to a Dutch workshop, a spare parts deal with the British was worked out (since they still had large stocks on hand) and Jersey Aviation refurbished the engines. Rubber-padded tracks were mounted and the infra-red sighting system was rebuilt.

The 1974 Defence Structure Review confirmed that Canada was not leaving the NATO Central Region and served as the basis for a MBT replacement programme. The Director of Armour's 'tank team' had been keeping an eye on international armour developments and the Leopard II prototypes were available for examination, while the XM-1 was progressing from the design to development stage. Many felt that the army should wait and then push for Leopard II acquisition. However, the options were 'Patturion,' M-60A3, Leopard I, the Italian Leopard variant, or an upgrade of the French AMX-30.

The West German government was talking about linking future trade with Canada to Canada's continued interest in deploying capable military forces for the defence of the Central Region. This became known as the 'no tanks–no trade doctrine' and a 'walk in the woods' with Helmut Schmidt has been credited with changing Trudeau's mind on the matter of a Canadian MBT. *Jadex* explained what happened next:

They gave me the green light. One thing they didn't know is that the German Minister of Defence and their equivalent of the Chief of the Defence Staff were both good friends of mine. We socialized and this was not generally known to everybody. So I went to see Zimmermann and I said to him, "My Prime Minister has agreed to give us a tank. The only one that is available now is the Leopard Mark I. I know you have got the Leopard Mark II on the drawing boards and that you are not going to have it in production for some time. You have got to sell me a tank."

He said, "We can't. We are re-equipping our armed

RCD Leopards on the firing point in Bergen-Hohne during the 1977 Canadian Army Trophy Competition shoot. To the surprise of the entire NATO armoured community, the Dragoons won the competition in their rented tanks against stiff competition less that four months after beginning to train with them. (Canadian Forces Photo ILC 77-365)

forces." "Well," I said, "OK, we'll have to leave West Germany." Zimmermann protested, "We can't have that." I said, "It's easy for you people, you have so many regiments. In each regiment you have so many squadrons. I only want a regiment's worth. Why the hell can't you work this out?" And he did.

The deal was that a regiment's worth of the older Leopard 1 A-2s would be made available to the RCD in Germany under a rental agreement while arrangements were made with the manufacturer, Krauss-Maffei, for the purchase of the Leopard A-3s, which became the Leopard C-1 in the Canadian lexicon. This would cover the period after which the Centurions were no longer capable of operation and the arrival of the new vehicle. *Jadex's* view was that the Leopard A-2 rent/C-1 buy, as well as the AVGP acquisition, were expedients until a better deal could be made later for an up-to-date MBT. This vision was

supported by some in the Director of Armour's shop but it was not fully understood in all quarters.

The first A-2s arrived in Lahr in January 1977, just in time for the RCD preparations for the Canadian Army Trophy competition that year. The crews did a crash course on the A-2 and, using Centurion fire drills, won the CAT that year.

The 'Permanent Panzers' arrived between July 1978 and July 1979. There were 114 Leopard C-1s, eight Taurus Armoured Recovery Vehicles, and six Beaver Armoured Vehicle Launched Bridges. The bulk of the machines went to Lahr, while a squadron was sent to Gagetown to support the Combat Training Centre and to train the fly-over squadron.

The C-1 was based on the Australian version of the Leopard. It had a Belgian SABCA laser fire-control system and a Low Light Television night-fighting system, all wedded to a 105mm L7 gun. It took some time for the crews to get used to the C-1s, and the CAT miracle was not repeated in 1979. There was a serious fault in the fire control system, the design not taking into account heat expansion of the turret which threw off the linkage between the gun and the sight. It would take some time to correct this fault after the embarrassing CAT shoot in 1979 when all the rounds missed their mark.

Other than this defect (Canadian crews even used a 'field expedient' of keeping the vehicles in the shade to keep the tur-

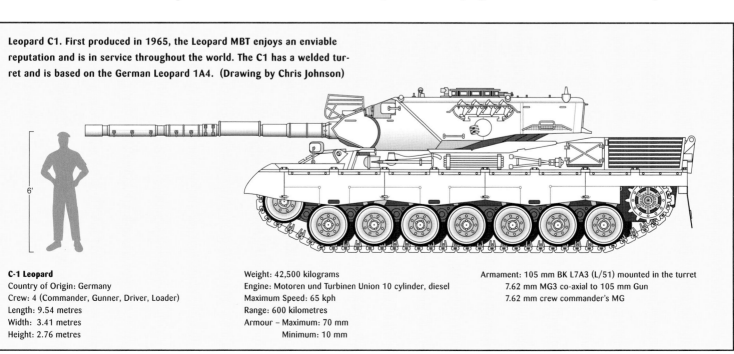

Leopard C1. First produced in 1965, the Leopard MBT enjoys an enviable reputation and is in service throughout the world. The C1 has a welded turret and is based on the German Leopard 1A4. (Drawing by Chris Johnson)

6'

C-1 Leopard
Country of Origin: Germany
Crew: 4 (Commander, Gunner, Driver, Loader)
Length: 9.54 metres
Width: 3.41 metres
Height: 2.76 metres

Weight: 42,500 kilograms
Engine: Motoren und Turbinen Union 10 cylinder, diesel
Maximum Speed: 65 kph
Range: 600 kilometres
Armour – Maximum: 70 mm
     Minimum: 10 mm

Armament: 105 mm BK L7A3 (L/51) mounted in the turret
7.62 mm MG3 co-axial to 105 mm Gun
7.62 mm crew commander's MG

rets cool during CAT), the Leopard C-1 was a superb vehicle. It was easily maintained compared with the Centurion and well liked by its crews. During the 1988 CAT competition, the 8th Hussars team beat 70 percent of the Leopard II and M-1 Abrams-equipped teams.

THE SPECIAL SERVICE FORCE

In 1976, *Jadex* announced that 2 Combat Group in Petawawa would become the new home of the Airborne Regiment, which at that time was in Edmonton. The Combat Group, which also included the 8th Hussars, would henceforth be known as the Special Service Force (SSF) an airportable, rapidly deployable formation. All members would wear a distinctive camouflage smock and sport a winged dagger patch with the motto "OSONS" (We Dare) on their shoulders. It was unclear at the time exactly what role SSF was to fulfil – Defence of Canada operations? North Norway and the flanks? A UN stand-by brigade? If so, what was the role of the armoured regiment? Some thought that *Jadex* had created the SSF to instil some 'machismo' back into the Army, which he thought had been softened by peacekeeping operations.

The relationship between the 8th Hussars and the airborne community was somewhat strained, primarily because of the difficulty of mixing armour with airmobile forces. Later, the members of the Hussars' 1st Troop, Recce Squadron asked to do some adventure training which would incorporate jump training. Next, the troop took the Advanced Recce Course in Gagetown. These men had a 'Let's try this and see if it works' attitude, and wondered why there could not be an armoured recce troop which could work with the Airborne Regiment. Eventually, the merits of the idea were recognized and soon the Recce Squadron's M-113 ambulance, was being extracted by parachute from a C-130 on a landing zone near Edmonton (Low Altitude Parachute Extraction or LAPES). Drop tests from normal parachuting altitudes followed.

The Jump Troop concept stabilized into a seven-car Lynx troop (each with a small black parachute painted on the hull for each drop) which could be LAPES'd or air dropped. Dropping was preferable, seven parachutes being required for a combat-loaded vehicle. The 21 men in the troop parachuted with, but not in, their vehicles. The troop would drop after the Airborne Pathfinders had marked the Drop Zone and then fan out ten to fifteen kilometres like spokes on a wheel, to act as a screen while

The British Columbia Regiment has routinely taken advantage of the opportunity to use the training facilities of the nearby US Army camp at Yakima, Washington, generously provided by Americans. Here a BCR jeep crew practices basic reconnaissance techniques. (Canadian Forces Photo IXC 87-005)

An 8th Hussars Lynx in the field at Petawawa. (Canadian Forces Photo RVC 83-086)

the rest of the Airborne Regiment dropped in. The disbandment of the Canadian Airborne Regiment in 1993 brought an end to any further operations.

THE MILITIA ARMOURED REGIMENTS IN THE 1970s

As we have seen in a previous chapter, The 'snakes and ladders' era wrought significant damage to Militia RCAC units. No sooner had these regiments started recovering their tank skills, using Shermans, than the government cut the funds necessary to carry out such training, eliminated the tanks and converted all armoured Militia units to a recce role by 1972. A plan was drawn up to reduce all Militia units to one hundred men each, which would then provide partially-trained individual augmentees for Regular Force units. No unit training would be authorized.

It was a strange situation in which Mobile Command now had eighteen Militia armoured regiments without tanks. Troopers were trained in a mix of tank and recce tactics at the sub-unit level, but were equipped with jeeps, some of which mounted machine-guns, some of which did not. Was the Mili-

tia to fulfil a light armour function or become a recce force? Was it to attempt to preserve tank skills, or not? What larger role should Militia armour fill in the development of Mobile Command as a fighting force? Were they to augment the forces in West Germany on mobilization? No responsible agency had the ability to answer these questions in the early 1970s.

Nevertheless, as time passed Mobile Command planners came to realize that they had to preserve the Militia for a better day. A start was made by re-introducing troop-level training first, since most units could barely field a full squadron. Then as time went on, squadron-level training was conducted by the Armoured Training Regiments. Collective training with other arms was usually left to the summer concentrations and remained rudimentary throughout the 1970s.

Once the Shermans were gone, however, the Militia units were forced to fall back on learning recce operations using jeeps. The existing Regular/Militia training system was now replaced by the Regular Support Staff, or RSS, whereby several Regular soldiers were posted to Militia armoured regiments, but although this helped, expertise with tank operations declined as that generation of Militia soldiers moved on. Some militiamen with a rather laconic, cynical sense of humour sported T-shirts emblazoned with a black beret-wearing skull and the words "Recce by Death" writ large underneath.

The struggle to retain some semblance of normality led commanding officers to push the envelope of creativity. For example, the British Columbia Regiment worked out an arrangement between the Seaforth Highlanders and a US Marine Corps unit to participate in Exercise *Lumberjack*, a full-blown amphibious operation in which the BCR handled the beach and landing force recce tasks. In another instance, the Queen's York Rangers traveled down to Fort Drum, New York, to participate in a large US National Guard exercise as part of the enemy force, and they wore specially modified cap badges on their black berets which had the regimental title and motto printed in Russian. After the exercise, these were replaced with the normal cap badges and most of the American troops were convinced they were a US Special Forces Ranger regiment brought in to test them!

Another mechanism created to generate closer contact between Regulars and Militia was the Worthington Trophy recce competition. Militia regiments from across the country participated by sending a troop and the winner then sent that troop to train with a Regular regiment's recce squadron, which allowed them to gain some expertise with Lynx vehicles and their armament. In later years, the Worthington Trophy winners completed their training on Lynx and were then flown to West Germany to augment 4 CMBG's recce squadron during *Fallex*.

Providing such incentives went a long way toward keeping the structure intact. *Secteur de l'Est* units, particularly *12e RBC*

A Prince Edward Island Regiment trooper stands radio watch during a 1976 recce exercise. This jeep was not yet equipped with a machine gun. (PEI Regiment Museum)

(Milice), were fortunate to have close links with their Regular counterparts. Similarly, 8 CH (M) in New Brunswick profited by maintaining a special relationship with the 8th Hussars, particularly after the Regulars rotated to West Germany to replace the RCD in 1986.

Summer militia concentrations (MILCONs) brought the Area armoured units together. In the Maritimes, the Prince Edward Island Regiment and 8 CH (M) went to Gagetown, where the latter retained a cadre on call-out with the Armour School to maintain vehicles. The Royal Canadian Hussars, *Le Régiment de Hull* and *12e RBC (M)* all went to Valcartier and then on to Gagetown. The Prairie and Pacific Area units worked with the Strathconas, who maintained two sets of equipment at Wainwright and Sarcee.

In 1981, all Ontario-based Militia regiments were combined into an *ad hoc* unit and deployed to Michigan for a three-day exercise, but a major problem with the emphasis on recce was that there were few opportunities for the Militia to learn critical tank-infantry cooperation or higher-level operational skills. Indeed, armour/infantry links atrophied in the 1970s, both in Militia and Regular units based in Canada, leaving 4 CMBG as the sole repository of such expertise.

THE ARMOURED VEHICLE GENERAL PURPOSE

As noted earlier, *Jadex* had secured slightly more than a hundred Leopards, enough to equip the 4 CMBG regiment in West Germany and a training squadron in Gagetown. There was still the problem of the other three Regular regiments and, in addition, the Militia armoured regiments had progressively lost their ageing Shermans until the last one was retired by 1972. Most of the Militia regiments now operated machine-gun

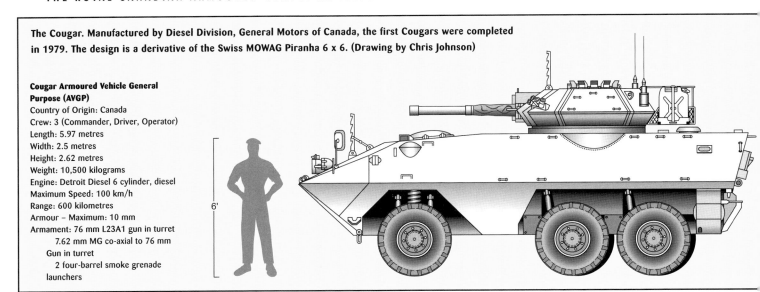

The Cougar. Manufactured by Diesel Division, General Motors of Canada, the first Cougars were completed in 1979. The design is a derivative of the Swiss MOWAG Piranha 6 x 6. (Drawing by Chris Johnson)

Cougar Armoured Vehicle General Purpose (AVGP)
Country of Origin: Canada
Crew: 3 (Commander, Driver, Operator)
Length: 5.97 metres
Width: 2.5 metres
Height: 2.62 metres
Weight: 10,500 kilograms
Engine: Detroit Diesel 6 cylinder, diesel
Maximum Speed: 100 km/h
Range: 600 kilometres
Armour – Maximum: 10 mm
Armament: 76 mm L23A1 gun in turret
    7.62 mm MG co-axial to 76 mm
    Gun in turret
    2 four-barrel smoke grenade
    launchers

6'

Whenever possible Militia units trained with Regular regiments' equipment. Here the Queen's York Rangers are shown training in Petawawa. (Photo by Chris Almey)

equipped jeeps in the recce role. Since the government was unwilling, or unable, to determine what the role of the Militia should be, the CDS and Mobile Command determined that they would attempt to maintain a flexible force structure so that if and when a firm direction was selected, it could be rapidly adopted.

After the demise of the V-150 Commando project in the late 1960s, a new requirement was established for four types of light armoured vehicles by 1974: the WAPC (Wheeled APC); WFSV (Wheeled Fire Support Vehicle); WTMC (Wheeled TOW Missile Carrier) and WMRV (Wheeled Maintenance and Recovery Vehicle). The roles that this family of vehicles would be required to fulfil were to "provide a general purpose combat training capability for [Mobile Command] field units, both Regular and Militia, based in Canada. They will also improve the operational effectiveness of units engaged in internal security and peacekeeping tasks."

These requirements were continuously re-confirmed throughout the AVGP acquisition process. For example, in 1976 and 1977, the primary capabilities of the vehicle family included: (a) direct fire support in combined arms operations and training, (b) reconnaissance and control missions relating to international peacekeeping or to internal security operations, and (c) protection for combat personnel traveling in the vehicle. It was fully understood at the highest levels of NDHQ that:

The ideal programme to ensure a combat ready-armed force is to buy tanks and personnel carriers for Canada-based troops as well as for those based in Europe. The AVGP programme is the next best solution, it is less costly, meets Canada's training needs, and redresses a long-standing equipment deficiency in the Combat Arms.

The selection process for the AVGP was riddled with multinational political intrigue, which was not surprising given that this was a multi-billion dollar deal. Six different trials were conducted. Brazil submitted the EE-11 Urutu, while France fielded three vehicles, the Panhard M4, Berliet 4 X 4 VXB, and Saviem

A *12e RBC* Cougar troop waiting to move with supported infantry during Exercise *Rendezvous 81.* (Canadian Forces Photo IOC 81-114)

Cougar troop of the Governor General's Horse Guards manoeuvring during the 1985 Militia concentration. (Photo by Chris Almey)

the original allocation plan, the Strathconas would get thirty Cougars, nineteen would go to the 8th Hussars, and thirty more to *12e RBC*. The three regional Militia Training Centres (MTCs) at Wainwright, Meaford and Gagetown, would get the balance. This dispersion changed over time as additional vehicles were acquired, but it provides some insight into initial thinking. The immediate impact on the regular regiments and army as a whole was encouraging. Now that Canada-based infantry had the Grizzly and the armoured regiments had the Cougar, equal mobility between the arms was introduced which in turn led to a renewed emphasis on combined arms training.

At the unit level, the Cougar gave crew commanders and gunners a 76mm Alvis turret-mounted gun to train on, and there was provision for a laser sighting system. The acquisition of the RADNIS night-sight and the image intensification driving system allowed units to reconstruct their night-fighting skills with relatively up-to-date equipment. In effect, the Cougar acquisition permitted non-tank units to be 60 percent compatible with tank units, so that if and when a new MBT arrived, conversion time would be reduced. The psychological effect of training on and with a tank-like vehicle should not be underestimated, but there were many limitations. The Cougar was not a tank, only a tank trainer.

The presence of the Cougar in formations like the SSF led to the belief, by some that the vehicle was an armoured car and should be employed as such. In fact, some armoured officers, not content with tank trainers, sought creative means to employ Cougars operationally, even though operational stocks of spare parts had not been acquired; training scales were barely enough to maintain the vehicles in a peacetime situation.

THE IMPACT OF THE COUGAR ON THE MILITIA

Making the Cougar available to the Militia regiments produced an instant and significant boost in morale and retention. 'Recce by Death' was no longer the unofficial motto of those regiments selected to have a Cougar troop. There were several plans for Cougar dispersal. As noted earlier, the original plan was to

Vehicule de l'Avant Blindée. Switzerland's Mowag Company displayed the 6 X 6 Piranha and Cadillac Gage resuscitated the V-150. Saviem dropped out unexpectedly. Trials were then conducted on the Commando V-150, the Piranha, and the Urutu, but it was Mowag's Piranha that met all of the requirements.

The decision was taken to acquire an initial buy of 160 wheeled APCs (nicknamed Grizzly), 120 wheeled fire support vehicles (Cougar) and 16 wheeled recovery vehicles (Husky). In

"It's not very heavily armoured". (Cartoon by Lieutenant Colonel Roman Jarymowicz)

group the vehicles at Wainwright, Meaford, and Gagetown and have Militia regiments rotate through the centres every week. Then, in the summer, the vehicles would be grouped in squadrons to form regiments for the Militia concentrations.

This plan was not implemented and Mobile Command decided that a troop of four vehicles should be parceled out to selected regiments. This appears to have been done for budgetary reasons, lowering the cost of transport for units like the BCD and the BCR who would have to fly to Wainwright every month. By having the vehicles deployed locally, familiarization would be speeded up. The down side was that it did not allow for squadron-level training during the year – only for a few days during the summer concentration.

Another important development with the advent of the Cougar was the inauguration of the Ram's Head trophy. (Donated in 1964 by Worthy for inter-regimental gunnery competition – a ram's head was a part of the Worthington family crest.) All Cougar-equipped units, Regular and Militia, were eligible to compete in this annual competition, which gave a focus to training efforts. In some cases, Militia units even outshot Regular regiments, an outcome that provided an incentive to both organizations to improve.

As the Militia developed Cougar expertise, Mobile Command generated operational taskings for some units. From the mid-1980s, the Militia 8th Hussars, for example, was set to augment *12e RBC* with a Cougar troop. Almost all units retained a list of personnel and their qualifications, so that those not allocated to an operational tasking were available as individual replacements in the event of conflict, or when the West Germany-based units needed augmentees during *Fallex*. Generally, Western

Canada-based Militia units augmented the Strathconas; units in Ontario backed up either the RCD or the 8th Hussars in Petawawa, while *Secteur de l'Est* units had a close relationship with *12e RBC*.

The addition of Cougars to the Militia regiments was accompanied with an increase in funding which, in turn, allowed for more and better training, thus improving recruiting and retention rates. The ability to conduct more exercises meant that the Militia regiments increased not only their visibility, but the visibility of the army as a whole. Where the regular regiments and their vehicles were hidden away on more-or-less remote Canadian Forces Bases, the Militia used local areas for their training. In some cases, route and sector recce exercises (some of them involving Cougars as DFSVs) were deliberately conducted in rural and built-up areas. Dubbed 'hearts and minds' patrols, these exercises in some cases were the only contact the public had with its Armoured Corps.

REGENERATION: THE NATO BATTLEFIELD IN THE 1980s

The Cold War entered a new phase in the late 1970s when the Soviets invaded Afghanistan and, in 1980-81, became embroiled in a serious crisis in Poland. It was clear to NATO authorities that the number of troops necessary to carry out a conventional active defence strategy just did not exist. In many cases the existing forces, which were originally deployed in the 1960s for the nuclear battle strategy, were fewer in number to those needed to cover NATO's vast Central Region.

In addition, they had not kept pace technologically. The Soviets still retained crushing numbers and had modernized from T-55 to T-72 and T-80 tanks, and from BMP-1 to BMP-2 Mechanized Infantry Combat Vehicles. The Soviets also achieved nuclear parity in the mid-1970s, which meant that NATO's threat to escalate to nuclear weapons had become less credible. In addition, chemical warfare appeared more likely, given Soviet use of such weapons in Afghanistan.

The solution was a NATO concept called Follow On Forces Attack (FOFA). A derivative of the American AirLand battle concept, FOFA recognized that the enemy forces were structured in a series of echelons. The key to preventing him from bringing superior numbers to bear was to absorb the ini-

A Sherbrooke Hussars corporal stacks ammunition during annual range practice in Valcartier, March 1984. (Sherbrooke Hussars Archives)

A Royal Canadian Dragoons Leopard during a NATO winter exercise in Southern Germany in February 1979. (Canadian Forces Photo ILC 79-192)

tial onslaught and then prevent the follow-up echelons from moving into the battle area and exploiting gaps into NATO's vulnerable rear areas. Therefore, NATO anti-tank forces equipped with tanks, attack helicopters and precision-guided munitions and positioned close to the Iron Curtain, would reduce enemy armour far forward in a mobile battle while technologically superior NATO air forces would attack the follow-on forces deep inside the Warsaw Pact area.

The problem for 4 CMBG was that the 1978 Leopard C1 acquisition and the constraints placed on future army programmes did not allow Canadian forces to operate within the FOFA concept. The RCD still only had two fully-manned squadrons and the fly-over squadron and the two infantry battalions, mounted in 1960s-era M-113 Armoured Personnel Carriers instead of Mechanized Infantry Combat Vehicles (MICV), also did not have adequate numbers. Thus when the Polish Crisis (1980-81) broke, NDHQ planners scrambled to help NATO but found they had little to offer.

Things started to change, however, when the Mulroney government was elected in 1983. The new administration started out with a robust attitude towards defence policy and money started to flow again. The new attitude also allowed alterations to the force structure in West Germany. Over a thousand new positions were added, which permitted full manning of three tank squadrons and the recce squadron, while retaining a fourth fly-over squadron. 4 CMBG's infantry units got 32 M-113-mounted TOW launchers which had Thermal Imaging

sights, and more thinking was directed towards acquiring an MICV. With 59 Leopards and 32 TOW anti-armour vehicles, 4 CMBG packed a significant punch which could be employed in a wide range of contingencies. Additionally, rotation of complete units was authorized, with Operation *Springbok-Coronet* occurring in 1986 as the 8th Hussars relieved the RCD from the task of guarding the gates to Bavaria.

Once 4 CMBG's deficiencies were identified and in the process of being redressed, the decision was taken to alter the operational role of the formation. Brigadier-General Jack Dangerfield was adamant that "reality had to be injected into an unrealistic planning environment." Given 4 CMBG's anti-armour capabilities and the fact that offensive action with mounted infantry was tactically questionable given the lack of a MICV, the best employment for the brigade was as a blocking force. The most vulnerable part of CENTAG lay on the inter-corps boundary between VII (US) Corps and II (German) Corps, a route known as Highway 14, and the location that 4 CMBG would deploy to in a state of heightened tension.

There were several plans drawn up throughout the 1980s, all of which revolved around the Highway 14 approach. These General Defence Plan positions usually had two infantry battalions dug-in, with anti-tank weapons deployed in layers. The 8th Hussars' Leopards were held back to operate, first, in a counter-penetration role, and then as an exploitation force. The Recce Squadron's Lynx would form part of the screen and flank guard. The Americans and West Germans would handle the covering force battle while 4 CMBG prepared its base of operations.

The 4 CMBG blocking force was flexible enough to be employed anywhere in CENTAG if higher headquarters felt it necessary to do so, but its most likely employment would have

Reconnaissance squadron training, 8th Canadian Hussars, Germany, 1987. (Canadian Forces Photo ILC 87-100-2)

Tank-infantry cooperation training in the Hohenfels training area.

been between the two Corps. This was a militarily necessary and politically salient employment of Canada's armoured forces and went a great way toward redressing the poor state of affairs prevalent in the 1970s. Several exercises subsequently validated the Highway 14 mission.

RAISED EXPECTATIONS: 1986–1989

The Mulroney government eventually tabled its defence policy in the 1987 Defence White Paper called *Challenge and Commitment*, although the new policy was overdue by about three years, which contributed to a series of problems experienced by RCAC forces later in the decade. The most important aspects of *Challenge and Commitment* for the army were the elimination of the CAST commitment and the assignment of *5e GBC* to the NATO Central Region alongside 4 CMBG to form 1 Canadian Division. Conventional defence was a new priority for Canada since the threat of nuclear war was directly linked to the failure of deterrence in Europe:

For the division to be fully effective in a two-brigade posture, a number of other improvements will be necessary. Over time, a large part of the Canada-based brigade's equipment and supplies must be pre-positioned in Europe. Even more important will be the acquisition of new tanks.

There were plans on the books to acquire two more squadrons of Leopard C-1s and deploy them to the planned MTCs so that Militia personnel could learn the Leopard as well as the Cougar. Meanwhile, a Tank Project Office was created to examine the future of Main Battle Tanks in the army. Three avenues were explored: implementing a life extension programme for the Leopard C-1, and the leasing or acquisition of a new tank. Initially it looked like the lease option was viable. General Dynamics was enthusiastic, as was Krauss Maffei. However, the constraints of the Financial Act would not allow the Canadian government to rent capital equipment for longer than a year and the government was unwilling to modify the Act to accom-

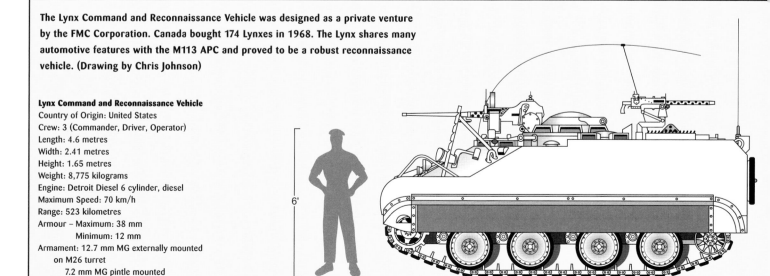

The Lynx Command and Reconnaissance Vehicle was designed as a private venture by the FMC Corporation. Canada bought 174 Lynxes in 1968. The Lynx shares many automotive features with the M113 APC and proved to be a robust reconnaissance vehicle. (Drawing by Chris Johnson)

Lynx Command and Reconnaissance Vehicle
Country of Origin: United States
Crew: 3 (Commander, Driver, Operator)
Length: 4.6 metres
Width: 2.41 metres
Height: 1.65 metres
Weight: 8,775 kilograms
Engine: Detroit Diesel 6 cylinder, diesel
Maximum Speed: 70 km/h
Range: 523 kilometres
Armour – Maximum: 38 mm
          Minimum: 12 mm
Armament: 12.7 mm MG externally mounted
        on M26 turret
        7.2 mm MG pintle mounted

6'

modate MBT leasing. In addition to the legal problems, the Mulroney government wanted offsets, and, of course, tank rentals would not provide any political capital.

The contenders for a new MBT were the M-1A2, Leopard II, Challenger 1, the Leclerc, and the Ariete. Mobile Command wanted between 250 and 280 tanks, which would have been enough to re-equip all four armoured regiments and then some.

The mid-life upgrade option was then examined. The main problem was getting enough performance out of the 105mm gun to defeat future Soviet tanks. The requirement was just not attainable with the L7, though some improvement could be made to the ammunition. This indicated that a 120mm gun was necessary but could the 120mm Rhein Mettall smooth-bore be mounted in a Leopard C-1 turret? The Germans had put one in a cast turret with a ther-

In 1987 the Canadian Leopards were equipped with a combination of mine rollers and mine ploughs to give better capability to cross minefields. This photo shows a tank with mine rollers in front of its tracks. (Canadian Forces Photo ILC 87-100-6)

mal imaging sight, but it was seriously cramped and the amount of ammunition carried was reduced. Moreover, the modifications would be 70 percent of the cost a new vehicle. Throughout this process, according to deputy project director Colonel H.J. Marsh, Deputy Minister Robert Fowler "made life very difficult for us" because he did not believe Canada needed main battle tanks, a view that harkened back to the 1970s debates over MBT acquisition.

The development of the armoured force, and its planned employment, was affected by a future planning study and staff college model generally known as 'Corps 86,' but there was some debate whether it was to be used as a framework for the army's structure or whether it constituted an ideal state. After full mobilization of the Militia, Corps 86 would consist of two mechanized infantry divisions, an armoured division, an independent brigade group, an artillery division, and an armoured cavalry brigade, along with associated Corps troops. In theory, the independent brigade group would already be in Europe (based on 4 CMBG) and the other units would follow during the mobilization period.

One of the structures to emerge from this airy proposition was a fifth armoured regiment and the MND authorized the establishment of the 1st Canadian Division Reconnaissance Regiment in 1988. To create such

an organization, several options were explored. Some thought was given to re-badging all four recce squadrons to Fort Garry Horse but leaving them in place with their parent regiments. Another variant would be to group the three Canada-based squadrons in Kingston, again as Fort Garrys. As for equipment, the planned M-1 or Leopard II buy would free up the Leopard C-1s. This new regiment would not spend time 'sneaking and peeking': it would fight for its information. With Lieutenant-Colonel R.K. Smith nominated to command, the regiment existed as a headquarters cell at 1 Canadian Division HQ from 1990 to 1992, where it participated in exercises and recces.

Throughout the years the Armour School has remained the centre of technical and tactical expertise for the Corps. Here a Cougar is prepared for swimming training in the Gagetown training area. (Armour School Photo)

Another interesting concept which emerged in the Corps 86 process was the planned Chimera tank-destroyer unit. The role of the Germany-based brigade was, simply put, to destroy as much enemy armour as possible should war occur. The tank-TOW team was considered effective, but Canadian armour officers on course at Bovington, in the UK, determined that an anti-tank vehicle with a kinetic energy penetrator would be a useful supplement, and the planners in Ottawa agreed. Preliminary studies projected a Challenger or Leopard II MBT hull with a fixed 120mm gun and the latest fire control system. As with TOW Under Armour, the Chimera would operate alongside the infantry and free up tanks, thus bringing more flexibility to the use of armour in the brigade group. Corps 86 structures saw a divisional anti-tank regiment made up of three squadrons of sixteen Chimeras each, but Chimera was eventually overshadowed by events and inter-arm politics and never built.

TOTAL FORCE

Militia revitalization also took place in the 1980s, in part to support Corps 86. Budgets were increased, which, in turn, increased the ability of the units to conduct interesting and realistic training and improved retention rates. The 1987 White Paper propounded the Total Force Concept in which composite Militia-Regular units of varying ratios would be employed, depending on the nature of the emergency. In wartime, the Militia was to augment the Regular units, contribute to the Defence of Canada and train replacements for overseas operations. Such a concept demanded that the training standards at all levels be equalized and Militia officers also had to understand how to operate at battle group and brigade group levels, not just at the sub-unit level. Several Militia Training Support Centres were established and the existing armoured vehicles pooled at them. The early 1970s training concepts would be reintroduced and a greater effort made to integrate Militia personnel, and even sub-units, into Regular units in West Germany.

The Lynx was showing its age and, in 1984, plans were made to pursue a replacement vehicle that would use a similar chassis to the planned M-113 replacement. Two projects were then advanced: the Armoured Infantry Fighting Vehicle (projected as tracked) and the Canadian Combat Vehicle (CCV-90), which was to be wheeled. These projects were merged in 1986 into the Light Armoured Vehicle Project and 1,700 vehicles of different variants were deemed necessary.

The navy-dominated Programme Control Board set financial priorities and the navy, attempting to get nuclear-powered submarines, did not want any competition. However, the Mulroney Cabinet decided in 1989 that it could not fund continuing modernization of the Canadian Forces, and this, combined with the Cold War warming trend brought on by Soviet *glasnost* (openness), *perestroika* (re-structuring), and the signing of arms reduction treaties by the Warsaw Pact and the NATO member countries, left the MBT and the recce vehicle programmes dangling. In addition, money for the Militia armoured units started to dry up again.

CHAPTER 20

Brave New World, 1990–2000

The Royal Canadian Armoured Corps had, since 1945, existed in a world of two solitudes, the totalitarian Communist systems and the free West, linked by a nuclear balance of terror. All the conflicts which RCAC units had been party to, in Europe, Cyprus, or the Middle East, had been part of a larger state of disagreement and disharmony called the Cold War.

Now, suddenly, things were very different. The Berlin Wall – long the symbol of the Cold War divide in Europe – came down in November 1989, and in 1991 East and West Germany were reunited. Soon the Soviet Union itself had ceased to exist, with most of its constituent parts approaching democracy, but despite celebrations in the West that the Cold War was finally over, an attempted coup in Russia, in August 1991, underlined just how unstable things actually were.

The Cold War had had a dampening effect on local, regional, and ethnic conflicts outside of the NATO area since both sides realized that sparks on the periphery could lead to conflagrations in Europe with nuclear consequences. This *status quo* no longer applied, however, and suddenly smoldering hot spots in Africa, the Middle East and the Balkans began to burst forth in waves of mass savagery. New phrases like 'ethnic cleansing' entered the vocabulary. The immediacy of satellite-transmitted TV news beamed the viciousness right into the living rooms of the West, which, in turn, prompted cries to 'Do something, do anything!'

All this caught the Canadian Forces (and the rest of the world) off guard, and it took some time to regroup. Doctrine, equipment and training which had been focused on a mid-to-high intensity ground war in NATO Europe now had to be modified and supplemented for a new type of conflict – Operations Other Than War. This was more than just classic peacekeeping like the Sinai and Cyprus: new forms of activity involved 'peace support,' humanitarian activities, peace observation, peacemaking, and the oxymoronic, Orwellian term, 'peace enforcement,' which could involve low- or medium-intensity war.

A threat could now consist of a teenage computer hacker with the ability to shut down strategic communications systems, local warlords in a decaying African country using ex-Soviet tanks and artillery to block, or kill, relief workers who were feeding their starving enemies, or the existence of semi-autonomous states-within-states engaging in, or facilitating, drugs and arms smuggling. Fundamentally, it involved anarchy at one level or another.

It took some time for the Canadian Forces to recognize all this, adapt and respond. That said, it was not immediately apparent in the early 1990s that the world had changed so drastically, and there was still a potential for reactionary coups. It was therefore prudent for NATO to continue business as usual,

Night firing with Leopards during Exercise *Rendezvous 89*. (Canadian Forces Photo RVC 89-3260)

'business' being defined as collective training and conventional field exercises.

EXERCISE *ON GUARD 1990*: TOTAL FORCE IN ACTION

The steps taken to revitalize the Militia-Regular Force relationship in the 1980s reached an apex in 1990. Large-scale exercises, dubbed the *Rendezvous (RV)* series, had been held by the Regulars throughout the 1980s at Gagetown and Wainwright, with extensive use of Militia augmentation, particularly during *RV 85*, an exercise that approached division-level size. A Reserve revitalization programme mandated by the 1987 White Paper generated similar ex-

Cougars of the King's Own Calgary Regiment on Exercise *On Guard 90. Canadian Forces Photo.*

ercises for the Militia, called *On Guard. On Guard 90* consisted of a number of almost-concurrent exercises held at Wainwright, Meaford, and Gagetown throughout the summer, with the Militia Areas grouped by region to form brigade groups filled out as much as possible with Regular Force augmentation – the reverse of the *RV* or NATO *Fallex* series.

On Guard 90 was the culmination of nearly a year's training based on the standard progression of individual to troop to squadron, to combat team, battle group and brigade group, very reminiscent of 1950s training. By the time the units deployed to the field, atrophied skills like tank-infantry cooperation were starting to revive. Cougar units were used as tank surrogates in all phases of the battle, including covering force operations, while the recce troops progressed through screens of all types and even rear area security operations. Militia personnel, generally only accustomed to sub-unit activity, could actually see a formation in action, and where his or her unit fitted into the larger scheme of things. With the advent of the new era and its associated budget cuts in the government's quest for a 'peace dividend,' however, *On Guard 91* was conducted at a greatly reduced scale, and as the 1990s progressed the Militia shifted back into its old role of providing individually trained soldiers to augment Regular units.

OPERATION *SALON*: KANESATAKE 1990

In the spring of 1990 at Kanesatake (Oka), Quebec, a dispute arose between municipal authorities and the local Mohawk community over the expansion of a golf course. Soon, barricades went up and members of the Mohawk Warrior Society, a paramilitary group, were advising the native residents of

Kanesatake on how to conduct armed resistance. Then, in the course of an assault by riot police on 11 July 1990, a police corporal was shot and killed. The police retreated and established a perimeter around Kanesatake.

On the other side of the St Lawrence River, at the Kahnawake reserve southwest of Montreal, a mix of locals and Warriors blockaded a bridge leading to the city and set up several barricades. Warrior reinforcements and weapons then flowed covertly into the reserve, based on the claim that the stand-off was a matter of exerting sovereign authority over Mohawk land.

There were an estimated 200 warriors at Kanesatake and 400 at Kahnawake, equipped with AK-47 and M-16 assault rifles, .50 calibre sniper rifles, and RPG-7 and 66mm LAW anti-tank weapons. The Warriors, some of whom had had military training, dug a trench system and erected obstacles covered by fire.

On 6 August, the provincial government informed Ottawa that they could not handle this volatile situation and the army

12e RBC Cougars deployed at Oka, August 1990. (Canadian Forces Photo ISC90-281)

was called in. Its plan, Operation *Salon*, was to display military superiority as a deterrent, surround the two enclaves and squeeze them, while at the same time conducting psychological warfare to discourage further resistance. If the situation seriously deteriorated, the enclaves would be rushed, with armoured vehicles leading the way. The bulk of *5e Brigade* deployed to the region, with the Van Doos on the Oka/Kanasatake side and 2 RCR across the river. *12e RBC* was in the middle of a Cyprus rotation, however, and could only deploy two squadrons, one mounted on Lynx, the other on Cougars. Moreover, additional personnel were needed and the 8th Canadian Hussars (Militia) was asked to provide half of a six-vehicle Cougar troop.

The *12e RBC* squadron and combined *12e RBC*/8th Hussars troop initially operated on the Oka side of the river, but subsequently the troop, led by Warrant Officer Scotty MacDougall, was deployed to the Kahnawake side. Its six Cougars were grouped with 2 RCR's Combat Support Company to form the Quick Reaction Force, on fifteen minutes' notice to move.

A key component of the plan was the prominent movement of, and media exposure to, armoured and mechanized forces. For example, the media were allowed to watch when a troop of Leopards from the RCD squadron in Gagetown, equipped with bulldozer blades and mine plows, was brought in. The Quick Reaction Force was called out several times, in many cases to unnerve and deceive the opposition. In one case, the Cougars escorted an M-113 mounted infantry company through the reserve at night to raid a suspected weapons storage site. Spotlights were strapped to the 76mm guns and were used to illuminate suspected fire positions as the force moved through the darkened streets. The realization came to WO MacDougall as a shock:

> Here I am in a Cougar – a *training* vehicle, not an operational vehicle – driving through downtown Canada bombed up with 40 rounds of HESH and Canister [respectively high explosive and anti-personnel rounds], three boxes of co-ax [machine-gun ammunition] and white phosphorous grenades. We had been trained to fight the Soviets in Europe and here we were, doing what we trained for, back home in the suburbs of Montreal!

After a nasty brawl between 2 RCR and the Mohawks during a weapons sweep, the Cougar crews developed a tactic whereby they would provide flank security to the riot control troops and sharpshooters would be placed on the Cougars' back decks to fire into the crowd if necessary. In the event, when they arrived on the scene of a serious rock throwing incident, the appearance of the vehicles was enough to disperse the rioters.

Plans were also formulated by *5e Brigade* to storm the barricades given certain circumstances, but, fortunately for all involved, the Mohawk resistance eventually collapsed and the situation was defused.

OPERATION *BROADSWORD*, 1990-91:
THE WAR THAT NEVER WAS

While *12e RBC* and the 8th Hussars (Militia) were deploying for Operation *Salon* in August 1990, Iraqi dictator Saddam Hussein invaded Kuwait. Iraq was also pursuing a nuclear weapons programme which, when added to its existing chemical and biological weapons stocks and Hussein's historic willingness to use them, threatened to undermine the stability of the entire oil-rich region, with inevitable consequences for Western Europe, Japan, and North America.

Canadian Forces Europe (CFE) in West Germany put together a contingency plan to provide a battle group that in-

The Royal Canadian Armoured Corps celebrated its 50th anniversary in August 1990. Shown here is Mrs. Clara Worthington, accompanied by the Colonel Commandant, Brigadier General Radley-Walters, unveiling a commemorative plaque in Worthington Park in Camp Borden. (Ontario Regiment Museum)

cluded an 8th Hussar Leopard squadron. At the same time, Mobile Command and NDHQ were examining other scenarios. By mid-August, the deployment of a brigade group was the sixth option generated by these agencies. Dubbed a 'staff check', *Broadsword* eventually took the form of a 'Middle East Brigade Group' that would include a tank regiment (the 8th Hussars), a composite Recce squadron (8th Hussars and Strathconas) and three mechanized infantry battalions.

An 8th Hussars Leopard awaits recovery after becoming 'bogged' during one of the last of the 4 CMBG exercises in Germany. (Canadian Forces Photo)

DISINTEGRATION (AGAIN)

The 1989 'hold' on defence spending imposed by the Mulroney government was only a precursor for deep cuts to Canada's military capability. The major cut was the entire Canadian military presence in Europe, and the last 4 CMB units were disbanded by August 1993. The 8th Hussars repatriated to Canada and melded with their Militia regiment to form Canada's only Total Force armoured regiment, with its headquarters in Moncton, a tank squadron in Gagetown, and two Cougar/recce squadrons in Sussex and Moncton.

Vain attempts were made to acquire new tanks from other sources when the Cabinet chose to sell off the army's Chinook medium-lift helicopter fleet. The Dutch were interested in these newly-refurbished machines and there were attempts to work out a deal whereby Canada would get some of the Dutch Army's Leopard IIs, since the Dutch were downsizing their NATO commitments.

The original CFE plan was based on existing establishments of personnel and equipment, including Leopard C-1s. As things developed, however, Mobile Command and 1 Canadian Division began to adopt a 'we can't go without ____' mind set, and more and more items which had been cancelled after the 1989 budget crunch were included in their wish lists. Naturally, one of them was a new Main Battle Tank.

Some planners favoured going with the Leopard C-1, using the arguments that crew retraining was unnecessary, while Militia personnel could convert from Cougars with no problem and augment the Canada-based regiments if necessary. Others thought that the Americans should be approached. Could Canada get M-60A3s, with the new thermal image sight? There were lots of them in storage, since they had been replaced with the M-1 Abrams. Some less pessimistic planners even thought that the Americans should be approached to provide a regiment of M-1A1s, since the Americans were deploying the more advanced M-1A2, but in the event Canadian ground forces were not sent to fight in the Gulf. The army was represented by a few infantry companies guarding headquarters and a field hospital.

The signing of the Conventional Forces in Europe Arms Control Treaty led to another potential source of MBTs. The terms of the treaty meant that some NATO nations were going to transfer or scrap large numbers of vehicles from the two designated reduction zones in Western Europe. Upgraded Leopard 1 A4s or A5s, and perhaps older versions of the M-1 Abrams or war stocks of M-60A3s, would have to be disposed of. Surely it would be no problem for Canada to acquire 120 or so from some NATO ally? The exact reasons why these acquisitions were not made remain obscure.

Meanwhile, the Leopards were loaded up and brought home, after having all of their running gear inspected by Customs to ensure that potato blight had not adhered to the tracks! A squadron was given to each Regular regiment, since it was felt that having some tanks in all regiments would help keep skills alive across the board. Despite increased maintenance costs, the tanks were parceled out with the understanding that the Armoured Corps was in a 'skills preservation' mode, not unlike the mid-1970s.

The Special Service Medal, first issued in 1992. All members of the Canadian Forces who had served in Europe received this medal with the 'NATO' bar.

Troopers from the British Columbia Regiment preparing to fire a Carl-Gustaf rocket launcher. (BCR Museum)

Members of The Fort Garry Horse having lunch during an exercise. The men are wearing the uncomfortable cast-off air force flying suits used by armoured units as crew suits in the 80s and early 90s. (Fort Garry Horse Museum)

Troopers of the Prince Edward Island Regiment firing the C-7 light machine gun. (PEI Regiment Museum)

An 8th Hussars (Militia) jeep crew practices returning fire on contacting the 'enemy' during a recce exercise in October 1990. (Courtesy Dr. Sean Maloney)

The Governor General's Horse Guards during an exercise in the Meaford training area. (GGHG Archives)

South Alberta Light Horse sergeants give instruction on foreign weapons. (SALH Museum)

SOMALIA, 1993

The precise reasons for Canada's involvement in Somalia in 1993 remain obscure, although TV images beamed *via* satellite portrayed a human disaster with the existing humanitarian aid and observation organizations in Somalia on the receiving end of a variety of forms of military harassment. The UN authorized a military intervention to protect the aid agencies and disarm local military forces within a defined area, but that area embraced only one armed faction. If the faction was disarmed, others outside of the designated Unified Task Force (UNITAF) area would be well placed to win the civil war when the UN forces left, since they would not have been disarmed. This threat brought UN forces into conflict with the local groups within the UNITAF area.

The Canadian unit selected for the initial UNOSOM mission was the Airborne Regiment, which had to reorganize into a mechanized infantry battalion. Consequently, the RCD in Petawawa wound up with five days in which to train sixty airborne soldiers to drive Grizzlies borrowed from 1 RCR. Then the mission changed to a UN Charter Chapter 7 Intervention operation, and an armoured squadron was required. 'A' Squadron, RCD, was selected and given two weeks to prepare.

Only forty per cent of the RCD Cougars were operational due to a lack of spares. Bought as a tank trainer, the Cougar did not have the backup parts that an operational vehicle required, and many parts had to be 'borrowed' from 'B' Squadron. Sights were flown in from the Strathconas and 76mm gun parts came from *12e RBC* – all to make one squadron operational. The Bison eight-wheeled APC was coming into service, something that the echelon appreciated since it received three of them, plus a Grizzly, while two Bison ambulances and two Bison recovery vehicles were brought into the squadron, even though they were untested prototypes. A Bison-mounted mortar platoon from 1 RCR was also added, also using untested prototype vehicles.

The Cougars and Bisons were loaded aboard American C-5B Galaxies (nine per aircraft) for the long haul to Africa in January 1993 – the first time such an operational deployment was made since the Strathconas had flown a Lynx troop into Cyprus in 1974. On arrival at Mogadishu, the Dragoons entered a world that, according to the squadron commander, Major Mike Kampman, was:

> … bizarre. Somalia was a post-apocalyptic nightmare, right out of the movie *Mad Max*. The 'Technicals' drove around in an array of vehicles: we saw 106mm recoilless rifles mounted on the backs of Nissans and twin 30mm anti-aircraft guns lashed to the beds of deuce-and-a-half trucks. There vast numbers of mortars and RPGs present. The supposedly 'backward' Somali factional units had T-54s, T-34/85s, M-47s, M-113s, Italian APCs, and even a few Centurions. Most of

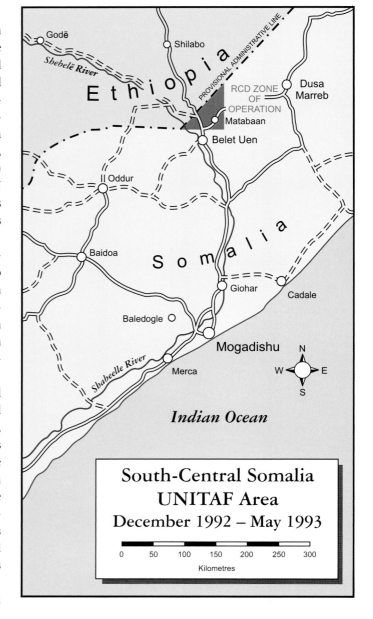

the Somali armoured vehicles I saw were operational, but their war efforts were stalled because of a lack of gas, so the factions would fight over fuel as well as food and ethnicity.

After the Dragoons settled in at the Mogadishu airfield, the Airborne Regiment conducted an airmobile operation to seize Belet Uen, leaving its Grizzlys behind in Mogadishu. The RCD squadron was left to move these vehicles from Mogadishu to Belet Uen, and also to recce and secure the 240-kilometre route. The recce was done with a Maritime Command Sea King helicopter, followed by the Cougars on the ground supported by two US Navy Sea Cobra attack helicopters. When the lead vehicles came under small-arms fire, the attack helicopters 'dissuaded' the opposition from continuing its activities.

An RCD Cougar passes an immobilized Somali JS-3 during a patrol near the Ethiopian border, 1993. (Canadian Forces Photo ISC93-10407)

By mid-January 1993, 'A' Squadron was assigned a zone around Matabaan, a town near the disputed and thus dangerous Ethiopian border. Unlike the Airborne Regiment, in Belet Uen, the squadron and its attached US Special Forces 'A' Team had to deal with a front line area between two of the main warring Somali factions. The humanitarian relief zone covered an area which had part of the battle zone in it: opposing forces were in frequent contact along the line and the Leavenworth and Sandhurst-trained Somali officers conducted their mechanized operations using communications equipment which was superior to that of the Canadians.

There were frequent mine strikes that damaged or destroyed the Cougars but, happily, not their crews. One particularly memorable action involved an attempt to contact a rebel-held town called Balenbale. As the Cougars advanced (they had by this time been reorganized into six-car recce troops) they came

under fire from 120mm mortars, 106mm recoilless rifles, and an M-47 tank. The Cougar crews 'lasered' their target and prepared to fire, but there were many non-combatants – women and children – in the built-up area where the fire was coming from. Fortunately, the translator reached the village elders and the Somali faction troops stopped shooting. Out of this incident came a general cease-fire between the factions in the area, which permitted humanitarian relief to flow.

THE UN PROTECTION FORCE (UNPROFOR), 1992–1995

The most significant operational deployments in the 1990s were to the Balkans. Without Josip Broz Tito's ruthless hand at the helm, Yugoslavia's diverse ethnic matrix could not hold together and 'ethnic cleansing' began, with hundreds of people being killed and thousands driven from their homes. The Conference of Security and Co-operation in Europe, in conjunction with the European Community, formed a monitor mission (which included Canadians) but it proved incapable of stemming the tide of violence. The revitalized Western European Union could not reach consensus on how an intervention force should be structured, and the UN was left to handle a cease-fire between newly-independent Croatia and the Federal Government of Yugoslavia.

The initial mandate of the United Nations Protection Force (UNPROFOR) in 1992 was to disarm and protect the populations of four enclaves in Croatia, a number of which were dominated by Krajinian Serbs, and 4 Canadian Mechanized Brigade in Lahr was instructed to prepare a contingent to deploy to Croatia in the spring of 1992.

An initial recce confirmed that the situation was completely unlike the classic model of peacekeeping – Croatia was not Cy-

This photo of a Royal Canadian Dragoon patrol gives some indication of the continuous problem with dust during the operation in Western Somalia in early 1993. (Canadian Forces Photo ISC93-10168)

prus. There was a tentative peace in existence but it was being used, by all factions, as time to rest, reorganize, and re-equip. The original Operation *Harmony* plan, formulated by CFE and 4 CMBG, envisioned a mechanized infantry battalion mounted in M-113s, several TOW Under Armour vehicles, three troops of Leopard tanks and the 8th Hussar Recce Squadron. This plan went to NDHQ where it was stopped. Ottawa simply did not understand the nature of the environment and disregarded advice from Major-General Clive Addy and Brigadier-General Lewis Mackenzie to 'go heavy', partially out of concern about potential political effects in the UN. The plan was reworked and the tanks taken out. Then the recce squadron was removed, much to the Hussars' chagrin. In the end, a mixed RCR/R22eR force from 4 CMB, dubbed CANBAT 1, deployed from Lahr to Sector West in Croatia in the spring of 1992.

While the situation in Croatia was stabilizing, the tri-ethnic political entity of Bosnia-Herzegovina collapsed into terror. Sarajevo, which was UNPROFOR's base area and headquarters zone, became a hub of violence as Bosnian Serbs, Croats and Muslims vied for control. CANBAT 1 was moved from Croatia to secure the airport and protect UN and non-government organization aid efforts in the middle of what amounted to a three-way Bosnian civil war.

The UN decided to create UNPROFOR II for Bosnia, with a mandate totally different from UNPROFOR I: to escort aid convoys and protect humanitarian efforts within certain regions. In theory, the UN had freedom of movement. In fact, well-armed villages of one persuasion or another would hijack food, while rogue bands would ambush and kill UNHCR drivers. All three belligerents, short of fuel and transport, would simply hijack UN trucks, re-paint them, and use them for their own purposes. The UN wanted a force structure that could deter such acts but, at the same time, they wanted one that was not 'provocative' to the ATGM- and tank-armed belligerents. Some contributing nations therefore sent units equipped with wheeled APCs and no anti-armour capability, while Denmark sent a complete squadron of Leopard A3s!

Canadian military and political officials compromised and decided to send a mechanized infantry battalion with a squadron of Cougar tank trainers to act as armoured cars. The first Bosnia-specific deployment took place in November 1992, CANBAT II being based on 2 RCR and 'A' Squadron, *12e RBC*, the latter organized as a Cougar recce squadron with three seven-car troops. It moved from Canada by ship to the Adriatic and then on to UNPROFOR I's Sector West, but was held up

there when drawn out negotiations between the UN and the belligerents blocked deployment to Banja Luka, deep in the Serb-controlled zone.

While negotiations continued, the volatile situation in Bosnia threatened to spill over into Macedonia, which, in turn, had requested a UN presence to deter ethnic violence. A composite UN force drawn from UNPROFOR was re-named United Nations Preventative Deployment (UNPREDEP) and CANBAT II sent a mechanized infantry company and a *12e RBC* recce troop to patrol the Macedonian border.

After this company group had departed, CANBAT II was ordered into Bosnia. Instead of Banja Luka, it went to Visoko, just north of Sarajevo, which would be the location of subsequent rotations for the next three years. This was a very dangerous area since all three factions converged in it. The Canadians now had the responsibility of escorting convoys through the area, particularly along the vital Sarajevo-Tuzla route to northern Bosnia. 'A' Squadron's Cougars were kept busy making sure UNHCR vehicles got through.

In May 1993, 'D' Squadron, *12e RBC* deployed to Bosnia as part of a R22eR battle group, the new CANBAT II. The area around Visoko was heating up again, particularly the road between Muslim-held Visoko and Croat-held Kiseljak. This road

A *12e RBC* Cougar on patrol in Bosnia, December 1993. (Canadian Forces Photo ISC93-20060-23)

was part of the UNHCR's main supply route, which ran through the Croat-held, but Muslim-surrounded Kiseljak Pocket. It was subject to fire from the Serb side of the line. As Lieutenant J.L.S. Gagnon, a troop leader with 'D' Squadron, recalled:

We had to make sure this road stayed clear. We had to do what we called 'overwatch'. It was kind of like a mounted O[bservation] P[ost]. We had to watch the Bosnian Serbs and, if they were firing at UN convoys on the main road, we were there to respond. We'd put a patrol of two vehicles on this task and then move the other patrol down the road. We were static on the side of the road, maintaining observation and keeping our 76mms aimed at the Serb gun positions. The closest Serb bunker was at 1,350 metres and they would engage with a .50 cal. machine gun…. If it's very aggressive fire, your only choice is to fire the main gun, but only as a last resort. I never had to do this, though I loaded up a lot in some situations. I usually loaded canister in the chamber.

By the next CANBAT II rotation, in November 1993, the Canadian military leadership had determined that there were not enough assets for convoy escort, and that there was an unacceptable degree of wear and tear on the infantry battalion's M-113s. Therefore CANBAT II's organization was converted to an armoured battle group which consisted of two Cougar squadrons (set up as recce squadrons with three seven-car troops), a mechanized infantry com-

pany in M-113s, and a small engineer squadron, with a field surgical team rounding out the organization. The first armoured regiment to be assigned to CANBAT II was *12e RBC*, led by Lieutenant-Colonel David Moore, and Militia regiments in Quebec provided 116 of the 700 soldiers of the two squadrons, while the Van Doos supplied an infantry company.

The Militia also supplied the bulk of the Cougars for the additional squadron deployed to Bosnia, as these were taken from the Militia training centre pools. With most of their Cougars thus suddenly stripped away, the type and quality of training that could be done by Cougar-equipped Militia units was very adversely affected for a considerable length of time.

After moving into Camp Visoko, the situation in the Kiseljak Pocket worsened. Essentially, Croats and Muslims were fighting each other in several locations in central Bosnia, while the Serbs looked on and prepared to exploit the situation. The Serbs would not allow UN forces to be stationed in areas under their control and hampered UN aid convoys moving through, usually in the vital Visoko region. In two cases, Canadian soldiers were disarmed and taken hostage, and in one of them the soldiers were subjected to a mock execution.

The battle group became aware of the existence of two psychiatric hospitals located in the hills overlooking the Kiseljak Pocket, abandoned by their staffs since they lay in the path of the fighting. A force was deployed to protect the hospitals and Sergeant G.P Stevenson was subsequently awarded the Meritorious Service Cross for his actions defending the compounds from Croatian forces who tried to rush them.

As the Kiseljak Pocket disengagement operation was in its final stages, there was increasing concern that the Serbs would use their self-propelled artillery to disrupt the process. These

Cougar belonging to Lord Strathcona's Horse returns to camp following a foray along the line of confrontation between Serbs and Bosnian Muslims. (Canadian Forces Photo ISC94-5007-19A)

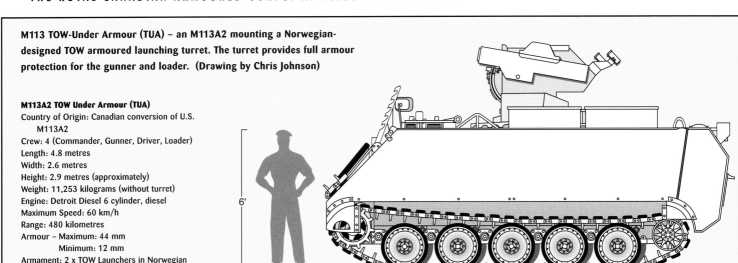

M113 TOW-Under Armour (TUA) – an M113A2 mounting a Norwegian-designed TOW armoured launching turret. The turret provides full armour protection for the gunner and loader. (Drawing by Chris Johnson)

M113A2 TOW Under Armour (TUA)
Country of Origin: Canadian conversion of U.S.
    M113A2
Crew: 4 (Commander, Gunner, Driver, Loader)
Length: 4.8 metres
Width: 2.6 metres
Height: 2.9 metres (approximately)
Weight: 11,253 kilograms (without turret)
Engine: Detroit Diesel 6 cylinder, diesel
Maximum Speed: 60 km/h
Range: 480 kilometres
Armour – Maximum: 44 mm
            Minimum: 12 mm
Armament: 2 x TOW Launchers in Norwegian
            designed turret

6'

guns were also being used to bombard Sarajevo from positions within the Canadian area of operations but outside the Sarajevo Exclusion Zone. Operation *High Jump* was generated by the acting commander, Major J.J.M. Beaudry, and his staff to drive these weapons away from Sarajevo. 'B' Squadron, led by Major J.P.L. Meloche and supported by British special operations forces, seized the Serb-controlled bridge, while engineers disarmed the explosives planted there for demolition purposes. Meanwhile, 'A' Squadron, under Major R.P. Torpe, and the Van Doo company, confronted the hostile artillerymen, and the situation became very tense when the Sarajevo Corps reaction force arrived with its M-84 main battle tanks and faced-off against the Cougars. Nevertheless, negotiations were then completed to remove the Serb guns from the area and the situation returned to normal.

The *12e RBC* battle group was replaced in May 1994 by the Strathconas, led by Lieutenant-Colonel Ray Wlasichuk, who had previously served with the European Community Monitor Mission. The Strathcona group consisted of two Cougar squadrons organized into three seven-car recce troops and RHQ, with a mechanized infantry company from the PPCLI. A new manoeuvre unit, called Combat Support Squadron, was formed by pooling the Strathcona RHQ Recce Troop (eleven M-113s with the 'additional armour' package and machine-guns) with a Mortar Platoon from 1 RCHA mounted in six M-113s and a 'TOW Under Armour' troop of eight vehicles drawn from the Strathcona's 'A' Squadron. Add-on armour packages were also attached to the Cougars to make them more resistant to .50 calibre machine-gun fire.

The operational situation when the Strathconas arrived was very strained, the Serbs being most unhappy with CANBAT II after the Operation *High Jump* encounter. Though the area was now quiet, the Muslim–Serb confrontation line in the area was extremely active. Aid convoy movement which normally transited the Serb areas was seriously impeded and then halted. It was critical that conditions for peace be generated, for UNPROFOR had to move beyond convoy escort in the Muslim and Croat-held areas, and it was vital that the UN forces develop a relationship with the Bosnian Serbs to counterbalance the minimal relationships it had with the other two belligerents. To achieve this aim, Colonel Wlasichuk negotiated the placement of an Observation Post (OP) line into Serb-held territory between Iliyas and Visoko and an agreement by both sides not to target the civilian population. This process took time but eventually led to enough stability that the route to Sarajevo could be re-opened. A Strathcona recce troop then escorted a fifteen-truck aid convoy through. There was a second convoy, then a third, and then a fourth, and power restoration, prisoner exchanges and other confidence building measures followed, all facilitated by the Strathconas.

Another important function was the continual monitoring of the northwestern portion of the Sarajevo Exclusion Zone to ensure that Serb artillery in the area was not used against Sarajevo, and to call in NATO airpower if it was.

The Strathconas then turned to other problems. The Muslim-held town of Breza, opposite Iliyas, was receiving routine shelling from the Bosnian Serbs, usually in retaliation for night attacks conducted by Muslim infantry. The Breza hospital was treating between 150 and 200 casualties per day. Another UN OP was put into Breza and a corresponding OP established on the Serb side. Violations of the cease-fire were brought to the negotiating table for resolution.

Then the situation deteriorated once again. In one incident, WO Tom Martineau was shot in his OP by a Muslim sniper and paralyzed. Being in the middle with blue helmets was not safe by any stretch of the imagination, as David Bercuson has noted in his book *Significant Incident,*

On the night of July 15, Sgt Tom Hoppe and his TOW Troop were again positioned at [OP] Charlie One. This time they had three M-113s parked above the Muslim trenches. A UN flag was flying, illuminated by a spotlight. Cpl Darren Magas had just dismounted one of the vehicles at about [2330 hours].... 'The Serbs opened up machinegun fire just over the top of the tents ... this was about 150, 200 rounds ... it was just non-stop,' he recalled. 'MCpl Phil Ward was outside the tents when the shooting began. He yelled at the men inside to stay down, then dashed around the corner of the position. I could see a muzzle blast from just behind the tree line....'

Ward then mounted one of the APCs and got the engine started. With the bullets cracking around him, he waited for someone to get the other two moving. The machine-gun fire intensified as the Moslems began to shoot back at the Serb positions. Both sides poured fire into Charlie One. Trooper Jason Skilliter ran out of his tent, grabbed his machine gun, and sprawled on the ground facing a Moslem bunker. Then he opened up on the bunker's firing slit. When the shooting from the bunker stopped for a moment, he and Hoppe ran to the other two APCs, got them started, then began to move them out of the line of fire. With Ward's APC as a rear guard, Hoppe and Skilliter then led the troop off the hill and out of danger.

Trooper Skilliter would receive the Medal of Bravery, while Sergeant Hoppe was awarded the Meritorious Service Cross for this action and also a Medal of Bravery for rescuing three Muslim children who were under fire in the Visoko cemetery.

Not having either tanks or mechanized infantry combat vehicles (MICVs) limited the Canadians' ability to conduct some operations. A failed Muslim assault on a Serb defensive position northeast of Visoko resulted in a retaliatory bombardment in which UN OPs were subjected to fire and an observer was killed. With CANBAT II lacking armour, a company of British Warrior MICVs had to be introduced in order to calm things down. In another case, Canada's armoured soldiers watched as the Danish Leopard squadron destroyed five Bosnian Serb tanks in a series of engagements near Tuzla.

The Dragoons, led by Lieutenant-Colonel Bill Brough, re-

Royal Canadian Dragoons Cougars, along with British troops, take part in a live-firing practice, Bosnia, March 1995. (Canadian Forces Photo ISC95-5036-6)

lieved the Strathconas in October 1994. One of the two Cougar squadrons was retrained as a mechanized infantry company and equipped with Grizzlies. The RCD group's area of operations was extremely active, since the Visoko-Iliyas area was an important transportation hub for all three factions. The town of Visko lay in a bowl of hills and there was regular Serb sniping and heavy weapons fire from the hills into the town.

The RCD took over the OP line which the Strathconas had been able to place along the ridge from Visoko, between the Muslim and Bosnian Serb lines near Breza, and then to the Serb town of Iliyas, and put a lot of effort into stabilizing the area through local negotiation. Much time was spent negotiating with both belligerents to move their headquarters assets out of schools and hospitals, and ensuring that the schools and hospitals were equipped to do their normal tasks. Distribution of some humanitarian aid was removed from the overly centralized UN distribution agencies and the RCD ensured that it reached its intended destination.

In November 1994 things started to go wrong. Something irritated the Serb high command and General Ratko Mladic came in person to Iliyas and ordered the local commander to seal the border, leaving an RCD squadron cut off on the Serb side of the line. The men in the OPs were not allowed to leave them, while other support personnel were collected and held in two locations in Iliyas.

A plan was formulated to be implemented if the Serbs either started killing or further humiliating the hostages. Using the Canadian chain of command and NATO authorities in Naples, the operations staff developed an air strike package with 86 targets between Visoko and Iliyas and a special task force was placed on one-hour notice to move. The plan involved seizing the bridge at the border and 'B' Squadron, RCD, under Major R.A. Puddister, making a run from the border to Iliyas, where the hostages were being held. The air strikes would go in simultaneously. The operation was to be conducted at night and was estimated to take less than an hour.

The crisis continued for sixteen days, but fortunately the hostages were not harmed. Then, for some reason, Mladic ordered that Camp Visoko be rocketed. Several 25-pound M-63 rockets impacted in the area, one landing right next to the main barracks building, but fortunately no one was injured. The RCD response was to order the deployed sub-units to establish roadblocks and close all routes emanating from Visoko. That shut down all humanitarian aid to north Bosnia and prevented the Bosnian Muslim army from resupplying its offensive operations further north. Several confrontations were reported, but the Canadians held firm. Finally, the hostages were released.

The situation in Croatia and Bosnia had deteriorated so badly by April 1995 that serious consideration was given to withdrawing both UNPROFOR I and UNPROFOR II under NATO auspices in a plan called Operation *Determined Effort*. A withdrawal of UN forces south, to ports on the Adriatic coast, meant that CANBAT II with its Cougars and TOW Under Armour vehicles, as well as the British Scimitars, would have to hold the exit route near Visoko open. This was a dangerous proposition, given the fact that the belligerents possessed main battle tanks, multiple rocket launching artillery, and anti-tank guided missiles of all types. Fortunately the operation did not have to be executed. Diplomatic breakthroughs and Croatia's military offensive in the fall of 1995 resulted in the replacement of UNPROFOR with a NATO force.

IFOR AND SFOR, 1995-1999

The decreasing credibility of UNPROFOR was brought to a head in the fall of 1995, when Croatian forces initiated a successful offensive into the UN Protected Areas in Croatia, overrunning the UNPROFOR forces there and driving the Serbs out. At the same time, the Bosnian Serbs overran the Srebrenica UN Protected Area and 'ethnically cleansed' the predominantly Muslim population there. Only skillful diplomacy and a real cease-fire, coupled with the deployment of elements of the NATO Allied Rapid Reaction Corps (with airpower) to Sarajevo, prevented a total collapse of the West's position in the region. The Dayton Peace Agreement was signed and it was now time for NATO to take over and the UN to bow out.

The new NATO force was to take over from UNPROFOR II

in Bosnia. Dubbed the Implementation Force (IFOR), it operated with a wider mandate, was equipped with heavy equipment like tanks and attack helicopters, and had unrestricted freedom of movement in Bosnia. Three multi-national divisions were deployed, with the Canadian contingent, 1,000 strong, forming part of Multi-National Division South West. The first Canadian contingent, assembled in Operation *Alliance*, consisted of a brigade headquarters, an RCR infantry company group, an engineer squadron, a field surgical team and, last but not least, an armoured recce squadron from the RCD.

'A' Squadron, whose personnel were drawn from all of the other squadrons in the regiment, deployed in December 1995 and operated as the brigade recce squadron, equipped with three troops of seven Cougars each, plus several Bison variants for the echelon. The squadron conducted sector patrols to monitor treaty compliance in western Bosnia. The belligerents had been stashing unreported weapons around the countryside for future operations, and in many cases patrols uncovered heavy weapons that were supposed to be placed in cantonments supervised by NATO forces. They also observed the cease-fire lines and handled traditional peacekeeping tasks.

'A' Squadron, *12e RBC*, took over in June 1996, when the

Serving with the NATO-led Implementation Force (IFOR). A Royal Canadian Dragoons vehicle on patrol, May 1996. (Canadian Forces Photo COR96-2035-2)

search had begun for war criminals and NATO forces were authorized to track down individuals identified by the UN justice system. Cordon and search duties became the norm, with *12e RBC*'s Cougars providing perimeter security for some of these operations.

Optimists believed that IFOR could bring peace to the region, but more experienced observers knew that, once on the ground, the West was in for the long haul, much like Cyprus. When IFOR's one-year mandate eventually ran out, it was replaced with a Supplementary Force (SFOR) which was smaller, in that each of the three multi-national divisions were replaced with brigade groups. From 1997 to today, the Dragoons, Strathconas, and *12e RBC* have deployed a squadron every six months for Operation *Palladium* tours in Bosnia and, like Cyprus in the 1980s, there appears to be no end in sight.

In December 1998, the Canadian SFOR battle group based on 3 RCR, and including 'A' Squadron, RCD, conducted Operation *Shannon* near Martin Brod in Bosnia. Croatian forces were illegally occupying Bosnian territory near the Una River and the Canadians were tasked to perform an operation similar to Operation *High Jump*.

A Cougar moves through a Bosnian village, January 2000. (Canadian Forces Photo)

Supported by NATO air power (a Croatian tank squadron was nearby), Major M.A. Nixon's squadron, which included TOW Under Armour and an RCR platoon, crossed the bridge and surrounded the main Croatian-held building, and then spread out to deter Croatian forces from reinforcing the area. Croat patrols were turned back in the glare of searchlights mounted on Cougars, while roving mounted patrols established the line of the 'new' border crossing zone.

DOMESTIC OPERATIONS

Canada's armoured soldiers were involved in two major assistance to the civil authority missions during the 1990s. The first of these was the Manitoba Flood. In April 1997, a snowstorm in the northern United States was followed by unseasonably warm weather, which in turn produced widespread flooding in southern Manitoba. Farm evacuations were started on 21 April and a Joint Force HQ was establish to coordinate CF flood operations, labelled Operation *Assistance*. By 12 May, 5,785 troops, the bulk drawn from Land Force units, had been transported to southern Manitoba, and among them were soldiers from all three Regular armoured regiments and all of the western Canada and some Ontario Militia regiments. Traditional military operational techniques were applied. For example, 'dike recces' were conducted to ensure that they held. Armed patrols were sent into evacuated areas to discourage looting, while other soldiers filled and laid sandbags in stricken areas. Citizens who were cut off on higher ground had to be rescued and Bison APCs, which are amphibious, were used to great effect. By mid-May, the water levels had dropped sufficiently for the clean up to begin.

In January 1998 a massive ice storm pelted an area extending from Kingston, Ontario, to Ottawa, to well north of Montreal, and into the Maritimes. Hydro lines crashed down and

Members of *Le Régiment de Hull* study a map of their assigned sector of operations during the deployment to assist victims of the ice storm of January 1998. (Canadian Forces Photo ISC98-42-6)

over three million people were left without power. Downed trees and telephone poles blocked roads, and sheets of ice made walking almost impossible. Then the temperature dropped to below minus thirty degrees, and the situation demanded that the bulk of Canada's land forces be deployed to the region. This deployment once again included all of the Regular armoured units and the reserve armoured units from Ontario and Quebec. Later, more Militia personnel from Newfoundland and Western Canada were brought in to help. The tasks were enormous; roads had to be cleared and temporary patches to the power grid made, while soldiers went door-to-door and farm-to-farm in the rural areas to chop wood for fireplaces and to see if the elderly or sick needed assistance. After several weeks, Operation *Recuperation* wound down as the weather improved and the power system was re-started.

THE LEOPARD C-2 UPGRADE

The scrapping of the MBT replacement programme forced the army to examine its options related to future direct fire support, and the Leopard Life Extension (LLE) programme was approved by Treasury Board in December 1995. It was to consist of four modules: a thermal sight, improved ordnance, applique armour, and an electric turret control system. However, the money was then cut back, and the sole priority became the thermal sight, which was approved in 1996, but when the Minister of National Defence visited an exercise in Suffield, where the Strathconas were preparing to deploy to Bosnia, he asked why they needed better armour. They told him, and in one of his last acts as minister, David Collenette approved the full LLE.

The Conventional Forces in Europe disarmament regime, as we have seen, mandated the scrapping or removal of large numbers of tanks from Europe. Consequently, the Germans were withdrawing many of their Leopard 1A5s from service. Canada acquired 123 of these surplus vehicles in a complex swap arrangement, and the A5 turrets were mated to the Canadian C-1 hulls. Other modifications made at the same time included new radios, better crew configuration, and a muzzle reference system for the gun. This vehicle is known as the Leopard C-2.

THE COYOTE

The demise of the Canadian Combat Vehicle (CCV-90) project in 1989 put the hope of a Lynx replacement into suspended animation. There was, however, recognition that the requirement for such a vehicle would not disappear, and the Multi-Role Combat Vehicle (MRCV) project was initiated in 1990. It involved three vehicle types using the same chassis: an MICV for the infantry, a Cougar replacement, and a Lynx replacement. The MRCV staff, led by Lieutenant-Colonel Ross Carruthers, was able to 'piggy back' on to Norwegian vehicle trials, an undertaking that had the same objectives as the MRCV project. The contending vehicles were all tracked and either mounted, or planned to mount, a 30mm cannon. These machines were the American Bradley, the British Warrior, the German Puma, Austria's ASCOD, and the Swedish CV-90. The CV-90 looked good to the MRCV team.

At that point General Motors Diesel Division intervened. The only producer of armoured vehicles in Canada, it also had contracts to build the LAV-25 wheeled family of vehicles for the US Marine Corps, and it had great influence in Ottawa. In 1992, the MRCV development was cancelled with the exception of the Lynx replacement project, which would continue and be based on the LAV-25. Construction of 229 LAVs was authorized, although this was later reduced to 203 so that more money could be spent on enhancement of the recce capability.

The new recce vehicle was to have the latest sensor and surveillance system, and that system had to be integrated with the hull and turret systems. Dubbed the Coyote, the final version consisted of an improved LAV-25 hull with a 25mm Bushmaster automatic cannon mounted in the turret as well as a coaxial C-6 7.62mm machine gun and a pintle-mounted C-6 for the crew commander. The smoke dischargers were also capable of firing fragmentation devices for local protection. The Coyote also has an advanced threat warning system which tells the crew if the vehicle is being illuminated by a laser designator and from what direction it is coming.

The Coyote's sensor systems include a ten-metre tall retractable mast with a ground surveillance radar, thermal imager and visible spectrum camera, capable of detecting tanks at ranges of

Entering service in 2000, the Leopard C2 is a combination of the existing C1 chassis and the recently acquired German Leopard 1A5 turret. (Drawing by Chris Johnson)

C-2 Leopard
Country of Origin: Germany
Crew: 4 (Commander, Gunner, Driver, Loader)
Length: 9.54 metres
Width: 3.25 metres

Height: 2.61 metres
Weight: 42,500 kilograms
Engine: Motoren und Turbinen Union 10 cylinder, diesel
Maximum Speed: 65 kph
Range: 600 kilometres

Armour – Maximum: 70 mm
Minimum: 10 mm
Armament: 105 mm BK L7A3 (L/51) mounted in turret
7.62 mm MG3 co-axial to 105 mm Gun
7.62 mm crew commander's MG

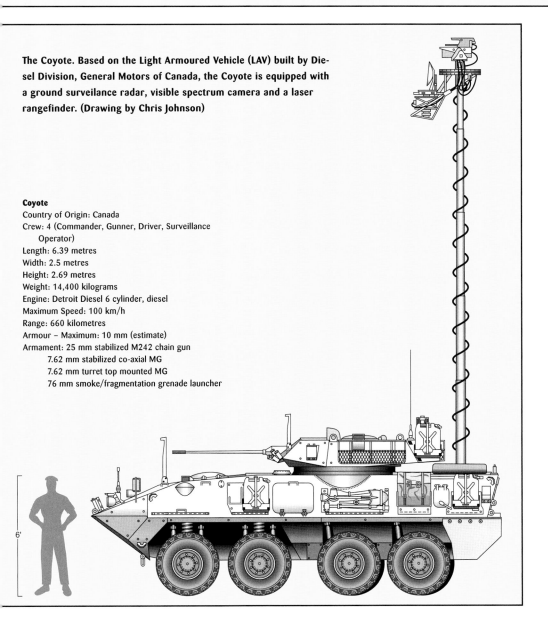

The Coyote. Based on the Light Armoured Vehicle (LAV) built by Diesel Division, General Motors of Canada, the Coyote is equipped with a ground surveilance radar, visible spectrum camera and a laser rangefinder. (Drawing by Chris Johnson)

Coyote
Country of Origin: Canada
Crew: 4 (Commander, Gunner, Driver, Surveillance
    Operator)
Length: 6.39 metres
Width: 2.5 metres
Height: 2.69 metres
Weight: 14,400 kilograms
Engine: Detroit Diesel 6 cylinder, diesel
Maximum Speed: 100 km/h
Range: 660 kilometres
Armour – Maximum: 10 mm (estimate)
Armament: 25 mm stabilized M242 chain gun
        7.62 mm stabilized co-axial MG
        7.62 mm turret top mounted MG
        76 mm smoke/fragmentation grenade launcher

Coyote on patrol in Kosovo, autumn 1999. (Canadian Forces Photo)

KOSOVO, 1999

The first operational deployment for Coyote and upgraded Leopard C-2 occurred in August 1999. The ongoing civil war in the former Yugoslavia surged once again in early 1999, this time in the one-time semi-autonomous province of Kosovo where the population was predominantly Albanian. The Yugoslav government had begun a merciless campaign of persecution and 'ethnic cleansing', and Western leaders decided that they could not permit Kosovo to become another Bosnia. When the Belgrade government ignored a series of diplomatic ultimatums, a NATO air campaign was launched to stop the mass deportations and killing, and bring the Yugoslavs to the bargaining table. The peace restoration effort that resulted led to the deployment of a NATO-led Kosovo Force (KFOR).

Canada's contribution to KFOR, which lasted from August 1999 to June 2000, was made up of a Coyote-equipped recce squadron from Lord Strathcona's Horse, an infantry battle group and a tactical helicopter squadron. The battle group, formed around 1 PPCLI, included a troop of five Leopard C2s from the Strathconas. The recce squadron worked directly for the British brigade headquarters, and was especially useful in keeping track of infiltration from across the Serbian border with the Coyotes' sophisticated surveillance systems. The battle

twelve kilometres. Coyote also has two autonomous dismountable systems in another ground surveillance radar and a combination laser range finder, thermal imager and camera. All the surveillance systems are linked to a sensor operator's position in the rear of the vehicle, which can share data with adjacent vehicles or transmit the data back to higher headquarters.

The introduction of Coyote and the Leopard C-2 resulted in an altered structure for the three Regular Force armoured regiments. By the summer of 1999, each consisted of three squadrons, an RHQ and RHQ Recce Troop. 'A' Squadron – called the cavalry squadron in the RCD and Strathconas – consisted of four four-car Coyote troops operating in the 'direct fire support vehicle' role. (These Coyotes were not equipped with the sophisticated sensor suite). 'B' Squadron was a traditional tank squadron equipped with Leopard C-2s. Recce Squadron had three five-car Coyote troops and an Assault Troop mounted in Bisons. The recce squadron Coyotes, plus those in the RHQ recce troop, were equipped with the sensor package.

Kosovo

Canadian Area of Operations

Senior Corps Appointments

Colonel-Commandant

1948–67	Major-General F.F. Worthington, CB, MC and bar, MM and bar, CD
1968–73	Brigadier G. de S. Wotherspoon, DSO, ED, CD
1973–77	Major-General B.F. Macdonald, DSO, C de G, CD
1977–80	Brigadier-General E.A.C. Amy, DSO, OBE, MC, CD
1980–87	Brigadier-General S.V. Radley-Walters, CMM, DSO, MC, CD
1987–90	Major-General W.A. Howard, CMM, CM, CD
1990–93	Brigadier-General G.G. Bell, OC, MBE, CD
1993–96	Lieutenant-General J.A.R. Gutknecht, CMM, CD
1996–99	Major-General J.P.R. LaRose, CD
1999–	Major-General C. Milner, OMM, MSC, CD

General Officers Commanding 1st/5th Armoured Division

14 Mar 1941–14 Jan 1943	Major-General E.W. Sansom, DSO
15 Jan 1943–18 Oct 1943	Major-General C.R.S. Stein
1 Nov 1943–29 Jan 44	Major-General G.G. Simonds, CBE, DSO
30 Jan 1944–19 Mar 1944	Major-General E.L.M. Burns, OBE, MC
20 Mar 1944–6 Jun 1945	Major-General B.M. Hoffmeister, CBE, DSO, ED

General Officers Commanding 4th Armoured Division

2 Feb 1942–29 Feb 1944	Major-General F.F. Worthington, CB, MC, MM
1 Mar 1944–21 Aug 1944	Major-General G. Kitching, CBE, DSO
22 Aug 1944–30 Nov 1944	Major-General H.W. Foster, CBE, DSO
1 Dec 1944–5 Jun 1945	Major-General C. Vokes, CBE, DSO

Commanders 1st Army Tank Brigade/1st Armoured Brigade

14 Mar 1941–1 Feb 1942	Brigadier F.F. Worthington, MC, MM
2 Feb 1942–26 Feb 1944	Brigadier R.A. Wyman, CBE, DSO, ED
27 Feb 1944–25 Jun 1945	Brigadier W.C. Murphy, DSO, ED

Commanders 2nd Army Tank Brigade

2 Feb 1942–21 Sep 1942	Brigadier G.R. Bradbrooke, MC
22 Sep 1942–11 Jun 1943	Brigadier N.A. Gianelli

Commanders 3rd Army Tank Brigade/2nd Armoured Brigade

26 Jan 1942–11 Jun 1943	Brigadier A.M. Thomas
12 Jun 1943–23 Mar 1944	Brigadier N.A. Gianelli
15 Apr 1944–8 Aug 1944	Brigadier R.A. Wyman, CBE, DSO, ED
9 Aug 1944–8 Dec 1944	Brigadier J.F. Bingham
9 Dec 1944–25 Jun 1945	Brigadier G.W. Robinson

Commanders 1st Armoured Brigade

15 Mar 1941–30 Jan 1943	Brigadier T.J. Rutherford, ED

Commanders 2nd/5th Armoured Brigade

15 Apr 1941–31 Jan 1942	Brigadier A.C. Spencer
1 Feb 1942–14 Sep 1942	Brigadier C.R.S. Stein
15 Sep 1942–22 Feb 1944	Brigadier G.R. Bradbrooke, MC
23 Feb 1944–6 Jun 1944	Brigadier J.D.B. Smith, OBE
7 Jun 1944–11 Nov 1945	Brigadier I.H. Cumberland, DSO, OBE, ED

Commander 3rd Armoured Brigade

2 Feb 1942–10 May 1943	Brigadier A.M. Thomas

Commanders 4th Armoured Brigade

2 Feb 1942–5 May 1943	Brigadier E.L.M. Burns, DSO, OBE, MC
6 May 1943–22 Feb 1944	Brigadier J.D.B. Smith, CBE, DSO
23 Feb 1944–14 Aug 1944	Brigadier E.L. Booth, DSO
19 Aug 1944–9 Jul 1945	Brigadier R.W. Moncel, DSO, OBE

Officers Administering the Canadian Armoured Corps

Aug 1940–Feb 1941	Colonel F.F. Worthington, MC, MM
Feb– Apr 1941	Lieutenant-Colonel S.A. Lee, MC (Acting)
Apr 1941–Feb 1942	Colonel E.L.M. Burns, MC
Jul 1942–Apr 1943	Colonel R. Wood, TD
Apr–Aug 1943	Colonel S.A. Lee, MC
Aug 1943–May 1944	Colonel J.A. McCamus, MC
Jun 1944–1946	Brigadier T.J. Rutherford, CBE, ED (Officer Administering the CAC in Britain)

Brigadier, Royal Armoured Corps, First Canadian Army

Feb–Apr 1944	Brigadier R.A. Wyman
Apr–Dec 1944	Brigadier N.A. Gianelli
Dec 44–Jul 45	Brigadier J.F. Bingham

Directors of Armour

1946	Colonel R.W. Moncel, DSO, OBE
1946–47	Colonel E.F. Schmidlin, MBE
1948–49	Colonel R.I. Purves, DSO
1949–50	Colonel F.E. White, DSO
1950–51	Colonel R.I. Purves
1951–55	Colonel A.G. Chubb, DSO, CD
1955–57	Colonel B.F. Macdonald, DSO, CD
1958–59	Colonel M.R. Dare, DSO, CD
1959–60	Colonel M.H. Bateman, CD
1960–61	Colonel A.J. Tedlie, DSO, CD
1961–64	Colonel E.A.C. Amy, DSO, OBE, MC, CD
1964	Lieutenant-Colonel J.A. Milbraith, CD
1964–65	Colonel S.V. Radley-Walters, DSO, MC, CD
1965–66	Colonel C.A. Greenleaf, MC, CD
1966–67	Colonel F.W. Wooton, CD
1967–70	Colonel J.W. Quinn, CD
1970–73	Colonel G.R. Hale, DSO, CD
1973–74	Colonel P.A. Neatby, CD
1974–77	Colonel J.A. Fox, OMM, CD
1977–80	Colonel J.K. Dangerfield, CD
1980–83	Colonel C. Milner, CD
1983–85	Colonel R.S. Billings, CD
1985–88	Colonel D.M. Dean, CD
1988–90	Colonel D.G. Taylor, CD
1990–92	Colonel N.B. Jeffries, CD
1992	Colonel P.J. Leentjes, OMM, CD
1992–93	Colonel H.J. Marsh, OMM, CD
1993–96	Colonel J.O.M. Maisonneuve, CD
1996–2000	Colonel W.J. Fulton, MSC, CD

School Commandants

Colonel F.F. Worthington, MC, MM	Cdn Tank School, CAFV School, CAFVTC, CACTC	Nov 1936–Nov 1940
Lieutenant-Colonel G. Carrington Smith	CACTC, A8 CACTC	Nov 1940–Jun 1941
Lieutenant-Colonel A. McGoun, RTR	A8 CACTC	Jun 41–May 43
Lieutenant-Colonel J.A. McCamus, MC	A9 CACTC	Jun 41–Aug 43
Lieutenant-Colonel J.A. Macdonald, MC	A27 Cdn Recce TC, Dundurn	May 42–Feb 44
Lieutenant-Colonel N.H. Macauley, DSO	A28 CACTC	Jan 42–Oct 42
Colonel R. Wood, TD	CACTG, A33 CACTE	Jul 42–Apr 43
Colonel S.A. Lee, MC	A33 CACTE	Apr–Aug 43
Colonel J.A. McCamus, MC	A33 CACTE	Aug 43–Jun 44
Colonel C.E. Bailey, DSO, MC	A33 CACTE	Jul 44–Jul 45
Brigadier J.F. Bingham, OBE	A33 CACTE	Oct 45–Mar 46
Colonel R.E.A. Morton, DSO	A33 CACTE	Mar–Sep 46
Lieutenant-Colonel B.F. MacDonald, DSO	RCAC School	Oct 46–Oct 49
Lieutenant-Colonel E.A.C. Amy, DSO, MC	RCAC School	Oct 49–May 51
Colonel G.J.H. Wattsford, CD	RCAC School	Sep 51–Jul 54
Colonel M.R. Dare, DSO, CD	RCAC School	Sep 54–Jan 58
Lieutenant-Colonel M.H. Bateman, CD	RCAC School	Jan–Aug 58
Colonel A.J. Tedlie, DSO, CD	RCAC School	Aug 58–Aug 60
Colonel W.A. Milroy, DSO, CD	RCAC School	Aug 60–Jul 62
Colonel S.V. Radley-Walters, DSO, MC, CD	RCAC School	Jul 62–Aug 65
Colonel C.A. Greenleaf, DSO, CD	RCAC School	Aug 65–Nov 66

RCAC School absorbed into the Combat Arms School 1966–1972

Colonel J.P.R. LaRose, CD	Combat Arms School	1969–1971
Colonel D.A. Nicholson, CD	Combat Arms School	1974–1976
Major J.K. Dangerfield, CD	Armour Dept, CAS	Sep 72–Jun 73
Lieutenant-Colonel C.A. Conway, CD	Armour Dept, CAS	Jun 73–Jun 76
Lieutenant-Colonel G.J. O'Connor, CD	Armour School	Jun 76–Jun 78
Colonel H.B.E. Lake, CD	Armour School	Jun 78–Sep 79
Lieutenant-Colonel W.J. Coupland, CD	Armour School	Sep 79–Jul 81
Lieutenant-Colonel R.N. Lawrence, CD	Armour School	Jul 81–Jul 84
Lieutenant-Colonel I.D. Barnes, CD	Armour School	Jul 84–Jul 86
Lieutenant-Colonel K.L. Thornton, CD	Armour School	Jul 86–Jul 89
Lieutenant-Colonel P.J. Leentjes, OMM,CD	Armour School	Jul 89–Jul 91
Lieutenant-Colonel W.J. Fulton, CD	Armour School	Jul 91–Jul 93
Lieutenant-Colonel C.J.R. Davis, CD	Armour School	Jul 93–Feb 95
Lieutenant-Colonel J.W.G. Rousseau, CD	Armour School	Feb 95–Apr 98
Lieutenant-Colonel C. Fletcher, CD	Armour School	Apr 98–Jul 2000
Colonel C. Hazelton, CD	Armour School	Jul 00–

Corps and School Regimental Sergeants Major

WOI F. Richmond	Canadian Tank School, CAFVTC	1938–40
WOI R.J. Hider	CAFVTC, CACTC, A8 CACTC	1940–42
WOI F. Flood	A8 CACTC	1942–44
WOI D. Watson	A9 CACTC	1941–42
WOI W.H. Young	A9 CACTC	1942–43
WOI C.T. Carnie	A27 CACTC	1942–43
WOI E.C. Caswell	A28 CACTC	1942–44
WOI E.E. Burke	A9 CACTC	1943–45
WOI E.S. Coleman	A27 CACTC	1943–45
WOI N. Lystar	A28 CACTC	1944–45
WOI F.G.A. Blackman	A9 CACTC	1945
WOI P.A. Garvin	A28 CACTC	1945
WOI C.W. Smith	RCAC School	1946–48
WOI S. Heindrich, MBE	RCAC School	1948–50
WOI W. McCullough	RCAC School	1950–51
WOI F.R.J. Prevost, MBE	RCAC School	1951–53
WOI R.M. Davies	RCAC School	1953–56
WOI A.E. Piper, CD	RCAC School	1956–61
WOI B.K. MacKay, CD	RCAC School	1961–63
WOI J. Lank, CD	RCAC School	1963–64

WOI E.J. Armer, MBE, CD	RCAC School	1964–65
WOI H. Wright, CD	RCAC School	1965–66
WOI T.F. Begley, CD	RCAC School	1966–67
WOI C. Cowden	RCAC School	1967–68
WOI J. Harnols	RCAC School	1968–70
CWO V. Geldart	RCAC School	1970–72
CWO E.E. Eros, CD	Armour Dept, CAS	1972–74
CWO V. Geldart, CD	Armour Dept, CAS	1974–75
CWO C.W. Yeomans, CD	Armour Dept, CAS	1975–76
CWO W.L. Prouse, CD	Armour Dept, CAS	1976–77
CWO J.E. Grenon, MMM, CD	Armour School	1977–79
CWO W.L. Prouse, CD	Armour School	1979–81
CWO G.R. Bennett, CD	Armour School	1981–82
CWO A.L. MacAdams, MMM, CD	Armour School	1982–84
CWO P.E. Cady, CD	Armour School	1984–87
CWO T. Urbanowsky, CD	Armour School	1987–89
CWO S.R. Ballard, CD	Armour School	1989–91
CWO A. Currie, MMM,CD	Armour School	1991–93
CWO J.D. Vienneau, CD	Armour School	1993–94
CWO J.E.R. Munger, CD	Armour School	1994–96
CWO R.J. Slaney, OMM, CD	Corps RSM	1970–73
CWO E. Dzioba, CD	Corps RSM	1973–76
CWO R.B.E. Clarke, CD	Corps RSM	1976–78
CWO V. Geldart, CD	Corps RSM	1974–75
CWO D.A. Beattie, CD	Corps RSM	1980–82
CWO J.L. Perron, CD	Corps RSM	1982–85
CWO J.E. Baldwin, CD	Corps RSM	1985–88
CWO J.K. Duffney, CD	Corps RSM	1988–91
CWO B.W. Prendergast, CD	Corps RSM	1991–93
CWO D.F. Seed, CD	Corps RSM	1993–94
CWO R.M. Charest, CD	Corps RSM	1994–96
CWO J.G. Brown, CD	Armour School/Corps RSM	1996–00
CWO D.R. Harvey, CD	Armour School/Corps RSM	2000–

Glossary of Terms and Abbreviations

A-1 Echelon *See* 'echelon'.

A-2 Echelon *See* 'echelon'.

AFV Armoured Fighting Vehicle, a general term denoting an armoured vehicle, wheeled or tracked, used in combat.

AP Armour-piercing, a solid-shot projectile capable of penetrating armour or concrete.

APC Armoured Personnel Carrier.

ARV Armoured Recovery Vehicle, an armoured 'tow truck' manned by RCEME mechanics in the administrative echelons of an armoured unit to recover disabled vehicles.

AVRE Armoured Vehicle, Royal Engineers, a specialist armoured vehicle used by engineers usually mounting a large calibre, short range gun to destroy concrete emplacements.

B Echelon *See* echelon.

BCD British Columbia Dragoons

BCR British Columbia Regiment

brewed up Set on fire, as in a tank set on fire when hit by an enemy shell.

Brigade Operational formation consisting of two or more regiments or battalions, commanded by a brigadier or brigadier-general. A cavalry brigade in the First World War consisted of three cavalry regiments, an artillery regiment, a machine-gun squadron and support services units. A motor machine-gun brigade was of regimental size. An armoured brigade in the Second World War consisted of three armoured (tank) regiments and, in independent brigades, a motorized infantry battalion.

Browning .30 calibre A belt-fed, air-cooled medium machine gun used as an auxiliary weapon mounted alongside (co-axial) the main armament in most tanks.

CAB Canadian Armoured Brigade

CAC Canadian Armoured Corps

CACRU Canadian Armoured Corps Reinforcement Unit

CAD Canadian Armoured Division

Calg R Calgary Regiment

CAR Canadian Armoured Regiment

CAS Combat Arms School

CB Companion of the Order of the Bath

CBE Commander of the Order of the British Empire

CD Canadian Forces Decoration

CGG Canadian Grenadier Guards

CIBG Canadian Infantry Brigade Group

CM Member of the Order of Canada

CMM Commander of the Order of Military Merit

CMB Canadian Mechanized Brigade

CMBG Canadian Mechanized Brigade Group

CO Commanding Officer

co-driver Junior member of a tank crew who acted as an assistant driver and manned a .30 calibre machine-gun in the 'bow' of a tank.

Company A sub-unit of an infantry battalion, usually consisting of about 125 men, organized in three rifle platoons.

Corps An operational formation consisting of two or more divisions with additional artillery and support units, usually commanded by a lieutenant-general. Also used in a generic sense to mean the units of a single arm, such as armour, infantry, artillery, etc, as in Canadian Armoured Corps.

Crew commander Individual in command of a tank, armoured car or scout car.

Crusader AA tank A British manufactured anti-aircraft vehicle armed with twin 20mm Oerlikon guns.

CTC Combat Training Centre

DCM Distinguished Conduct Medal.

Division, armoured Prior to 1943, a Canadian armoured division consisted of two armoured brigades and supporting services. After 1943, it consisted of one armoured brigade of three armoured regiments, an infantry brigade of three battalions, a motorized infantry battalion, an armoured recce regiment and supporting arms and service units.

Division, infantry A Canadian infantry division usually consisted of three infantry brigades, each with three infantry battalions and supporting arms and service units. During the Second World War each division also had an armoured recce regiment.

Driver Tank, armoured car or scout car crew member responsible for driving and maintaining the vehicle.

DSO Distinguished Service Order

echelon The service support component of an armoured or reconnaissance unit, responsible for supplying the fighting elements with ammunition, fuel, food, water and other stores as needed, the repair and recovery of vehicles, guns and other equipment, and immediate battlefield medical care. The echelon is usually sub-divided into A and B Echelons; A Echelon being responsible for immediate resupply of battlefield requirements, and sometimes split into A1 and A2 Echelons; B Echelon holding all other supplies and stores not immediately required in battle.

ED Efficiency Decoration

8th Recce 8th Reconnaissance Regiment (14th Canadian Hussars).

8CH 8th Canadian Hussars.

8 NBH 8th New Brunswick Hussars.

FGH Fort Garry Horse.

Firefly Sherman tank armed with a 17-pounder (76.2mm) gun.

1CACR 1st Canadian Armoured Carrier Regiment

1H 1st Hussars

Fitter RCEME mechanic

Flail tank A specialist vehicle designed for mine clearance by means of a rotating drum fixed in front of a tank, to which weighted chains were attached to beat the ground as the tank advanced and thus explode anti-tank mines.

FOO Forward Observation Officer, an artillery officer who accompanied combat arms units in battle to direct artillery fire.

4 CMBG 4th Canadian Mechanized Brigade Group

4 PLDG 4th Princess Louise Dragoon Guards.

Forming-Up Place (FUP) An area close to a Start Line where units 'formed up' into battle formation just prior to beginning an attack.

GGBG Governor General's Body Guard

GGFG Governor General's Foot Guards

GGHG Governor General's Horse Guards

Gunner Member of a tank or armoured car crew responsible for aiming and firing the main armament of the vehicle.

Harbour A defensible location behind the battle area offering concealment, often in woods or villages, used by armoured units for rest and replenishment.

HE High explosive

IFOR Implementation Force (the NATO force in Bosnia)

Indirect fire Fire in which the target is not within view of the firing weapon(s), usually involving plotted direction and range and correction of fire by a forward observer.

Kangaroo Armoured personnel carriers made from the hulls of Priest self-propelled guns or Ram tanks.

KFOR Kosovo Force (NATO force in Kosovo)

KOCR King's Own Calgary Regiment

Laager (Leaguer) Usually a defensible location in the open, immediately in rear of a battlefield, used by armoured squadrons for hasty battlefield replenishment.

LAD Light Aid Detachment. The Royal Canadian Electrical and Mechanical Engineers unit (at one time Ordnance Corps) permanently attached to an armoured or reconnaissance unit which undertook second-line repair of vehicles, guns and technical equipment.

LCT Landing Craft, Tank.

LdSH Lord Strathcona's Horse. Abbreviated LSH prior to the Second World War.

LST Landing Ship, Tank

M-10 A self-propelled gun on a Sherman chassis, armed with a limited-traverse 17-pounder gun in an open turret.

MBE Member of the Order of the British Empire

MC Military Cross

MM Military Medal

MMM Member of the Order of Military Merit

Militia The reserve component of the Canadian Army.

Mark IV tank The standard German tank during the Second World War. It was a 30-ton vehicle armed with a 75mm gun.

NCO Non-Commissioned Officer (up to the rank of sergeant).

OBE Officer of the Order of the British Empire

OC Officer Commanding (usually referring to a squadron or company commander); Officer of the Order of Canada

OMM Officer of the Order of Military Merit

Ont R Ontario Regiment

Orders Group A gathering of sub-component commanders at which a commander gives orders for a forthcoming operation.

Panther tank A German Mark V medium tank. It was a 45-ton vehicle with heavy, sloped armour mounting a long-barrel 75mm gun.

PEILH Prince Edward Island Light Horse

PEIR Prince Edward Island Regiment

PIAT Projector, Infantry, Anti-Tank. A very short range, spring-loaded hollow-charge anti-tank weapon.

Platoon A sub-unit of an infantry company commanded by a lieutenant, consisting of about 35 men.

Ram tank A medium tank designed and manufactured in Canada in the period 1941-42. The Ram I was armed with a 2-pounder (40mm) gun, while the more numerous Ram II had a 6-pounder (57mm) gun. It was used by the Canadian Armoured Corps in training in Canada and Britain, but was replaced by the Sherman for operations in Italy and North-West Europe. Some Rams were used in operations as artillery observation post tanks, while others, without turrets, were used as Kangaroo armoured personnel carriers.

RAC Royal Armoured Corps

RCAC Royal Canadian Armoured Corps

RCACA Royal Canadian Armoured Corps Association

RCACS Royal Canadian Armoured Corps School

RCD Royal Canadian Dragoons

RCEME Royal Canadian Electrical and Mechanical Engineers.

RCH Royal Canadian Hussars

Rear link captain The 'battle captain' in an armoured squadron who maintained radio contact with RHQ and was prepared to take over operational command should the squadron commander be killed or injured.

Recce Reconnaissance.

Recce Troop A regimental headquarters recce troop in armoured regiments. During the Second World War these consisted of eleven Stuart (Honey) light tanks.

Regiment A cavalry unit of approximately 600 officers and men, usually consisting of three mounted squadrons, each of four horsed troops. An armoured unit (of battalion size) consisting of three tank squadrons and a headquarters squadron. In the Second World War an armoured regiment had a complement of some 60 tanks.

R de Hull Régiment de Hull

Renault FT tank A small two-man French tank of First World War design. A number of obsolescent American-manufactured tanks of this design were purchased to train the CAC in 1940.

RHQ Regimental Headquarters.

RMR Royal Montreal Regiment

RSM Regimental Sergeant Major

SALH South Alberta Light Horse

SAR South Alberta Regiment

scout car A small, usually four-wheeled, lightly armoured car used for reconnaissance and command and control. Scout cars usually mounted a machine gun.

17 DYRCH 17th Duke of York's Royal Canadian Hussars.

SFOR Stabilization Force (NATO force in Bosnia)

Sher Fus R Sherbrooke Fusilier Regiment

Sherman tank An American-designed medium tank of about 30 tons which became the standard tank of the Allies during the Second World War. It mounted either a 75mm or 17-pounder gun.

6 DCRCH 6th Duke of Connaught's Royal Canadian Hussars

Squadron A sub-unit of a cavalry, armoured or reconnaissance regiment. A cavalry squadron, with a strength of about 140, usually consisted of four cavalry troops. In the Second World War a tank squadron, with a strength of 110 to 125 men, consisted of four tank troops (five troops in the independent armoured brigades), and a squadron headquarters with three tanks.

SSM Squadron Sergeant Major

Start Line A line selected for the beginning of an attack, usually an easily recognized feature such as a road or tree line. In principle, a start line was meant to be secure, but contact with the enemy could be expected anywhere beyond it.

Stuart tank A light tank of American design, armed with a 37mm gun, used in recce units. It was often called a 'Honey' tank. In Canadian units, many had their turrets removed to lower the silhouette and give faster speed.

TEWT Tactical Exercise Without Troops

Tiger tank A German heavy tank introduced in 1944, armed with an 88mm gun. The Tiger 1 weighed 56 tons, while the 'King Tiger' weighed 68 tons.

Traverse Term used to describe the rotation of a tank turret to align the gun onto a target.

Troop The basic sub-unit of cavalry, armoured and reconnaissance units, commanded by a lieutenant. A cavalry troop consisted of four sections, each of eight men and horses. In the Second World War an armoured (tank) troop consisted of three tanks until mid-1944, when a fourth (a Firefly with 17-pounder gun) was added. Post-war tank troops had four tanks.

Trooper The lowest enlisted rank, equivalent to private, in cavalry and armoured units.

TRR Three Rivers Regiment.

12D 12th Manitoba Dragoons.

12e RBC *12e Régiment blindé du Canada.*

UNEF United Nations Emergency Force

UNFICYP United Nations Force in Cyprus

UNPROFOR United Nations Protection Force

VC Victoria Cross

wireless Second World War term meaning radio.

Sources

At the request of the History Committee of The Royal Canadian Armoured Corps Association (Cavalry), this book does not contain endnotes citing specific sources of information. Where direct quotations are used, however, the individual or source is in most instances given in the text. The authors have in all instances attempted to satisfy themselves as to the accuracy of the information used, and the manuscript was read prior to publication by a number of outside historians and veterans in an effort to eliminate errors of fact and interpretation. This list cites the principal sources of information for this book.

Official Documents

War Diaries, Operational Reports and other files of, *inter alia*, the Canadian Cavalry Brigade and its component units (1915-1919), 1st Canadian Motor Machine Gun Brigade (1916-1918), 4th Canadian Armoured Division (1943-45), 5th Canadian Armoured Division (1942-45), 1st Canadian Armoured Brigade (1942-45), 2nd Canadian Armoured Brigade (1942-45), 4th Canadian Armoured Brigade (1943-45), 5th Canadian Armoured Brigade (1942-45) and their component units; in Records Group 6 and Records Group 24 in the National Archives of Canada.

Canadian Army tactical doctrine and equipment pamphlets and manuals (1936 to 1971), Canadian Army Training Memoranda (1939 to 1945), Canadian Forces training manuals (1972 to 1999), RCAC School training précis, Combat Arms School précis and manuals; in authors' collections, The Fort Garry Horse Museum and Directorate of History and Heritage library.

Information on the technological developments, policy decisions, procurement and operations in the post-Second World War period was acquired from the Raymont Collection at DHH, Records Group 24 at the NAC, the Fort Frontenac Library's archive section and personal primary source collections of Capt John Grodzinski, LCol Wayne Pickering, Dr. Peter Archambault and Dr. Sean Maloney.

Official Histories

Nicholson, G., *The Canadian Expeditionary Force 1914-1919*. Queen's Printer, Ottawa, 1962.
Stacey, C.P., *Six Years of War: The Army in Canada, Britain and the Pacific*. Queen's Printer, Ottawa, 1955.
Nicholson, G., *The Canadians in Italy 1943-1945*. Queen's Printer, Ottawa, 1956.
Stacey, C.P., *The Victory Campaign: The Operations in North-West Europe 1944-1945*. Queen's Printer, Ottawa, 1960.
Wood, H.F., *Strange Battleground: The Operations in Korea and Their Effects on the Defence Policy of Canada*. Queen's Printer, Ottawa, 1966.

Interviews

The authors interviewed or corresponded with 247 veterans and serving members of the Royal Canadian Armoured Corps, all of whom provided very useful information. Among these were: BGen E.A.C. Amy, Trumpet Major A. Banner, Maj J. Barr, Col M.H. Bateman, BGen G.G. Bell, Col J.R. Beveridge, Maj A. Bolster, CWO J.G. Brown, LCol N.A. Buckingham, LCol J. Burns, Col A. Burton, LCol J.A. Cameron, BGen P.H.C. Carew, LCol R. Carruthers, LCol M. Cessford, MWO E. Cheney, LCol A.S. Christian, Capt B.J. Corbiere, LCol J.D. Crashley, LGen J.K. Dangerfield, LGen M.R. Dare, Capt F. Davidson, LCol J. Dorfman, Capt A. Dugas, Maj R.H. Dunn, Col H.R.S. Ellis, MWO W. Elms, Charles Fearne, Col B. Finestone, LGen J.A. Fox, Col D.N.D. Deane Freeman, Col W. Fulton, Col J.A. Gardam, MGen J.C. Gardner, LGen J.C. Gervais, LCol J.W. Graham, LCpl Canon R. Green, CWO D.J. Greene, BGen P.V.B. Grieve, Maj E.R. Griffith, LGen J.A.R. Gutknecht, Maj J.K. Hjalmarson, Maj R.M. Houston, LCol R. Jarymowicz, LCol F.W. Johnson, Maj R. Kennedy, Col D.F.B.

Kinloch, MGen C.G. Kitchen, LCol W.T. Lane, MGen J.P.R. LaRose, MWO D. Levesque, LCol W.D. Little, LCol W.R.C. Little, BGen O.W. Lockyer, LCol A.F. Lungley, Maj I.D. MacKay, BGen M. Maisonneuve, Maj J.E. Malone, WO M. Maloney, Col H. Marsh, Maj D. McLeod, Tpr R. Mercer, BGen R.S. Millar, MGen C. Milner, LGen W.A. Milroy, MGen P.J. Mitchell, Maj R. Moreau, MGen P.A. Neatby, LCol C. Oliviero, Sgt J. Paisley, LCol W. Pickering, Charles Prieur, LCol H. Quarton, BGen S.V. Radley-Walters, Brig C.A. Richardson, LCol R. Roach, Maj B.C. Rutherford, Col The Hon R.C. Rutherford, CWO W.C. Rutledge, LCol C.R. Sharp, LCol H.A. Smith, MGen J.A. St. Aubin, BGen J.A. Summers, MGen A.J. Tedlie, Capt G.P. Thatcher, Maj R. Thomas, Col J.W. Toogood, CWO J. Tuffin, MCpl G. Wallace, BGen G.J.H. Wattsford, Maj J. Whitton, LCol L. Zaporzan. The authors ask the forbearance of those not named.

Corps and Regimental Histories

Royal Canadian Armoured Corps
Wallace, John., *Dragons of Steel: Canadian Armour in Two World Wars*. General Store Publishing, Burnstown, Ont., 1995.
Worthington, L. *Worthy*. Macmillan, Toronto, 1961.

RCD
Fetherstonhaugh, R.C., *A Short History of the Royal Canadian Dragoons*. Southam Press, Toronto, 1932.
Greenhous, Brereton, *Dragoon: The Centennial History of the Royal Canadian Dragoons, 1883-1983*. RCD, 1983.
Landell, K.E., ed., *Royal Canadian Dragoons 1939-1945*. RCD, 1946.
Worthington, Larry, *The Spur and the Sprocket*. RCD, 1968.

LdSH
Williams, S.H., *Stand to Your Horses*. Friesen and Son, 1961.
McAvity, J.M., *Lord Strathcona's Horse (Royal Canadians): A Record of Achievement*. Brigdens, Toronto, 1947.
Fraser, W.B., *Always a Strathcona*. Comprint Publishing, 1976.
Cunliffe, R., *The Story of a Regiment*. LdSH, 1995.

GGHG
Chambers, E., *The Governor-General's Body Guard*. Ruddy, Toronto, 1902.
——, *The Governor General's Horse Guards, 1939-1945*. Canadian Military Journal, 1954.
Marteinson, John, *The Governor General's Horse Guards: An Illustrated History*. Forthcoming.

1H
Conron, A.B., *A History of the First Hussars Regiment*. n.p., republished 1980.

4 PLDG
Jackson, H.M., *The Princess Louise Dragoon Guards: A History*. n.p., Ottawa, 1952.

8th Hussars
How, Douglas, *The 8th Hussars*. Maritime Publishing, 1964.
Crook, E.D. and J.K. Marteinson, *An Illustrated History of the 8th Canadian Hussars*. 8CH Regt Assn, 1973.

17 DYRCH
Steele, Harwood, *The Long Ride*. N.p., 1934.
Pavey, Walter G.H., *7th Canadian Reconnaissance Regiment in World War II*. 7 Recce Regt, Montreal, 1948.

14th Hussars (8th Recce)
Green, R.F., *A Short History of the 8th Canadian Reconnaissance Regiment (14th Canadian Hussars)*. n.p., n.d..
Alway, B.M., *Battle History of the Regiment*. n.p., n.d..

BCD

Roy, R.H., *Sinews of Steel*. Whizzbang Association, 1965.

FGH

McMahon, J.S., *Deeds Not Words: A Short History of The Fort Garry Horse*. Unpublished manuscript, 1938.

Davidson, F., *Vanguard*. Holland, 1945

Service, G.T. and J.K. Marteinson, *The Gate: A History of The Fort Garry Horse*. Commercial Printers, Calgary, 1971.

Ont R

Schragg, L., *History of the Ontario Regiment, 1866-1951*. Regimental Association, n.p., n.d.

Sullivan, C.M., *3 Troop*. Centennial Print, Saint John, 1998.

TRR

Prieur, Charles, *Chronicles of the Three Rivers Regiment (Tank) 1939-1945*. Unpublished manuscript, n.d.

Gravel, J-Y.and Michel Grondin, *Histoire du Régiment de Trois-Rivières (1871-1968)*. Trois Rivières, 1981.

Jones, G., *To the Green Fields Beyond: A Soldier's Story*. General Store Publishing, Burnstown, 1993.

Calg R

Maltby, R., *Onward*. Unpublished manuscript, 1990.

Maltby, R., *Onward II*. Unpublished manuscript, 1991.

A Short History of the 14th Canadian Armoured Regiment. Holland, n.p. 1945.

12 D

Tascona, B., *XII Manitoba Dragoons: A Tribute*. Friesen Printers, Altona, 1991.

Roberts, J.A., *The Canadian Summer*. University of Toronto Press, 1981.

Henry, C., *Regimental History of the 18th Armoured Car Regiment*. Holland, 1945.

GGFG

Baylay, G.T., *The Regimental History of the Governor General's Foot Guards*. Ottawa, 1948

Harris, S., *Governor General's Foot Guards 125th Anniversary History: The Second World War*. Forthcoming.

CGG

Duguid, A.F., *History of the Canadian Grenadier Guards 1760-1964*. Gazette Printing, Montreal, 1965.

Halifax Rifles

Quigley, J.G., *The Halifax Rifles 1860-1960*. Macnab and Son, Halifax, 1960.

Elgin Regt

Curchin, L.A. and B.D. Sim, *The Elgins: The Story of the Elgin Regiment (RCAC) and its Predecessors*. St. Thomas, 1977.

Grey and Simcoe Foresters

Rutherford, T.J., *An Unofficial History of The Grey and Simcoe Foresters Regiment 1866-1973*. N.p, n.d.

Brown, B. *Foresters*. Boston Mills Press, Erin, Ont., 1991.

Sher Fus R

Jackson, H.M., *The Sherbrooke Regiment (12th Armoured Regiment)*. n.p., 1958.

BCR

Harker, D.E., *The Story of the British Columbia Regiment 1939-1945*. n.p., Vancouver, 1950.

Harker, D.E., *The Dukes: The Story of the Men who have Served in Peace and War with the British Columbia Regiment (D.C.O.) 1883-1973*. n.p., Vancouver, 1974.

SAR

MacDougall, Major G.L., *A Short History of the 29 Cdn Armd Regt (South Alberta Regiment)*. Amsterdam, 1945.

Graves, Donald, *South Albertas: A Canadian Regiment at War*. Robin Brass Studio, Toronto, 1998.

RMR

Fetherstonhaugh, R.C., *The Royal Montreal Regiment 1925-1945*. Gazette Printing, Montreal, 1949.

1st APC Regt

Ramsden, K., *The Canadian Kangaroos in World War II*. Ramsden-Cavan Publishing, Peterborough, 1997.

QYR

Bull, Stewart, *The Queen's York Rangers*.

R de Hull

Programme Souvenir Le Régiment de Hull. 1989.

Windsor Regt

McNorgan, M.R. and D.A. Lock, *The Black Beret*. Unpublished manuscript, 1991.

Algonquin Regiment

Cassidy, Major G.L., *Warpath: The Story of the Algonquin Regiment 1939-1945*. Ryerson, Toronto, 1948

RCEME

Johnston, M., *Canada's Craftsmen at 50: The Story of Electrical and Mechanical Engineering in the Canadian Forces*. N.p., Ottawa, 1997.

Unpublished Theses

Cessford, M.P., *Warriors for a Working Day: The 5th Canadian Armoured Division in Italy, 1943-1945*. M.A. Thesis, University of New Brunswick, 1989.

Henry, H.G., *The Tanks at Dieppe: The 14th Canadian Army Tank Regiment (The Calgary Regiment [Tank]), 1939-19 August 1942*. M.A. Thesis University of Victoria, *1991*.

Hutchinson, W.E.J., *Test of a Corps Commander: Lieutenant-General Guy Granville Simonds, Normandy – 1944*. M.A. Thesis, University of Victoria, 1982.

Other Important Sources

Annual Reports of the Canadian Cavalry Association, 1913 to 1939.

Annual Reports of The Royal Canadian Armoured Corps Association (Cavalry), 1946 to 1999.

The Regiments and Corps of the Canadian Army. Queen's Printer, 1964.

The Armour Bulletin. RCAC (School) 1973-1999.

Burns, E.L.M., *General Mud*. Clarke, Irwin, Toronto, 1970.

English, J., *The Canadian Army and the Normandy Campaign: A Study of Failure in High Command*. Praeger, New York, 1991.

Gardam, J., *Korea Volunteer*. General Store Publishing, Burnstown, 1994.

Greenhous, B., *Dieppe, Dieppe*. Art Global (for DND), Montreal, 1992.

Granatstein, J.L. and R. Bothwell, *Pirouette*. University of Toronto Press, 1990.

Grodzinski, J.R., *Operational Handbook for the First Canadian Army: Formation Organization, Staff Technique and Administration*. Halifax, privately published, 1998.

Harris, S.J., *Canadian Brass*. University of Toronto Press, 1988.

Maloney, S.M., *War Without Battles: Canada's NATO Brigade in Germany 1951-1993*. McGraw-Hill Ryerson, Toronto, 1997.

Marteinson, J., *We Stand on Guard: An Illustrated History of the Canadian Army*. Ovale, Montreal, 1992.

McAndrew, W., Donald Graves and Michael Whitby, *Normandy 1944: The Canadian Summer*. Art Global (for DND), Montreal, 1944.

McAndrew, W., *Canadians and the Italian Campaign 1943-1945*. Art Global (for DND), Montreal, 1996

McAndrew, W., Bill Rawling and Michael Whitby, *Liberation: The Canadians in Europe*. Art Global (for DND), Montreal, 1995.

Morton, D., *A Military History of Canada*. Hurtig, Edmonton, 1990.

Portugal, Jean E., *We Were There: A Record for Canada* (7 volumes). Royal Canadian Military Institute, Toronto, 1998.

Reid, B.A., *Our Little Army in the Field*. Vanwell, St. Catharines, Ont., 1996.

Reynolds, M., *Steel Inferno: 1st SS Panzer Corps in Normandy*. Spellmount, Staplehurst (UK), 1997.

Roy, R., *1944: The Canadians in Normandy*. Macmillan, Toronto, 1984.

Seely, J.E.B., *Adventure*. Heinemann, London, 1930.

Snowie, Captain J. Allan, *Bloody Buron: The Battle of Buron, Normandy, 8 July 1944*, Boston Mills Press, Erin, Ont., 1984.

Vokes, C., *My Story*. Gallery Books, 1984.

Whitaker, W.D. and S. Whitaker, *Rhineland*. Stoddart, Toronto, 1989.

Williams, J., *The Long Left Flank: The Hard Fought Way to the Reich, 1944-1945*. Stoddart, Toronto, 1988.

The Royal Canadian Armoured Corps Association
acknowledges the generous support provided
for publication of this book by

Grateful appreciation is extended to

In appreciation of the financial support of

Grateful appreciation is extended to

THE
QUEEN'S OWN RIFLES
OF CANADA

whose generous support helped to make this publication possible

The Royal Canadian Armoured Corps Association
extends grateful thanks for the generous support of

31 COMBAT ENGINEER REGIMENT (THE ELGINS)

who served loyally in the Armoured Corps from 1942 to 1999

In appreciation of the financial support of

DOMGROUP

The Royal Canadian Armoured Corps Association
acknowledges the generosity of

POWER CORPORATION of CANADA

in support of the Millennium projects.

To acknowledge the generosity of

DETROIT DIESEL-ALLISON CANADA

With grateful thanks
to

CIBC Charitable Foundation

Donors

Publication of this commemorative history of the Royal Canadian Armoured Corps has been made possible by the generous financial support of members and friends of the Corps. The Royal Canadian Armoured Corps Association would like to acknowledge the contributions of the donors, who are listed in categories according to the amount provided.

ARMOURED DIVISION COMMANDERS

MGen F.F. Worthington, CB, MC & Bar, MM & Bar, CD, 1890-1967. WWI: RHC, CMMG Corps; Post-War I: PPCLI; Tasked to raise AFV School in London, ON, 1936, CO CAFVS Camp Borden 38; WWII: Comdt CAFV Trg Centre 1939, **Formed Cdn Armd Corps 1940**, Comd 1st Armd Bde 1940, lead designer of the Ram Tk, Brigadier 1940, MGen Comd 4th Cdn Armd Div 1942, converted Div to Armour 43; and took it to the UK, Comd Camp Borden 1944, Comd Pacific Command 1945; Post-War: Comd Western Comd 1946-47; civilian career: Civil Defence Coordinator 1948-57; **First Col Comdt** RCAC 1948-67.

Mrs L.D. "Larry" Worthington, 1902-92; loyal and dedicated partner from 1924 till Worthy died in 1967; author of Worthy's life in the biography titled "Worthy", Larry continued to attend RCAC functions and presenting his Sword till failing health precluded her participation.

MGen Bertram M.Hoffmeister, OC, CB, CBE, DSO, ED, CD. Seaforth Highlanders 1927 to 1943, CO 42-43 incl Sicily; Comd 2 Cdn Inf Bde 1943; Comd 5 Cdn Armd Div 43-45 (Italy & NWE); Comd 6 Cdn Div (Pacific Force) 1945; Post War: Comd 15 Inf Bde (Res) 1946; MacMillan-Bloedell 1949, Chrmn 1956-59; HCol Seaforths 57-/96.

MGen George Kitching, CBE, DSO, CD. RMC Sandhurst; WWII: RCR 39-40, HQ I Cdn Div 40, HQ I Cdn Corps 42, CO Loyal Eddies 42, GSOI 1 Cdn Div 43, Comd 11 Cdn Inf Bde 43-44, GOC 4 Cdn Armd Div 44, COS I Cdn Corps 44-45; Post War: Vice QMG AHQ, Comdt CASC, Comd BC Area, VCGS, Chair Cdn Joint Staff, London England, Comd Central Comd, Col of the Regt RCR, Col Comdt RCIC 74-78.

ARMOURED BRIGADE COMMANDERS

BGen G.G. Bell, OC, MBE, CD, PhD. QYR 40; WWI I: TRR (I2CAR); RCD 50-65, QYR: HLCol 74-84; Col of the Regt RCD 84-90; Col Comdt RCAC 90-93, Hon Pres RCAC Association (Cavalry) 1996-99.

Colonel A. Brandon Conron, DSO, CdeG, CD. WW II: 1H (6CAR); CO 1H 1950-52, Honorary Col 69-78 (in memoriam).

LCol J.J. Dorfman, OMM, CD, AdeC. GGHG 1962, RSM 1974-79, Dist RSM 79-80, CO 1988-91; Bde DCOS Ops 91-95, DCOS Sp 95-97; LFCA G1 Res Advisor 97-99, ACOS 99- , President RCACA (Cavalry) 1998-00; Co-Chair RCACA Heritage Appeal 1996-2000.

Col The Hon H.N.R. "Hal" Jackman, OC, KStJ, CD, BA, LLB, LLD. Governor General's Horse Guards: HLCol 83-92, Hon Col 1992-.

LCol Ian Golding, CD. Elgin R 58-66, The Ontario Regiment (RCAC) 66-93, Tp Ldr, Sqn Comd, CO 1983-86, SSO Armd LFCA 91-93.

BGen P.V.B. Grieve, CD. WWII: HalR & CGG; GGHG 46; RCD: CO 63-65, Col of the Regt 78-81; Comd 4 CMBG 72-74.

MGen J.P.R. LaRose, CD. WW II; Post-War :LdSH(RC) 49- Korea 53-54; FGH (NATO) 62-65; I2eRBC: CO 68-69, Col du Régt 1979-87; HLCol GGFG (WWII 21CAR) 90-96; Col Comdt RCAC 1996-99, Chairman RCACA Heritage Appeal 1996-2000.

MGen B.F. Macdonald, DSO, CdeG, CD. WW II: FGH, Col of the Regt 1968-70, Comdt RCACS 1946-49; DArmd 1955-57, Comd 1 CIBG 62-65; Col Comdt RCAC 73-77 (in memoriam).

Colonel David Macdonald-Stewart, OC, KStJ, CD. Honorary Colonel Queen's York Rangers (1st Americans) 1968-84 (in memoriam).

Colonel Liliane Macdonald-Stewart, CStJ, CD. Honorary Colonel Queen's York Rangers (1st Americans) 1984- .

Brigadier W.C. Murphy (1905-61), CBE, DSO, ED, CD, QC. BCR 1927; WWII: CO BCD/Comd 1CAB; Post War: Comd 22 Armd Bde 46-50; Pres RCACA (Cavalry) 51-52; Pres CDA 54; HCol BCD 54-61 (in memoriam).

MGen A.C. Spencer, CBE, ED, CD. IH: WWI Tp/Sqn Ldr, WWII, C0 39-41; Comd: 2CAB 41-42, Borden 42-45; AHQ-Vice AG 45 (in memoriam).

Colonel J. Gordon Thompson, CD. WWI: RCASC, HQ Cars 1914-18; 6th Armd Regt/1st Hussars (RCAC); HCol 1950-1969 (in memoriam).

Colonel James G. Thompson, CD. RC Naval College 1944-46; RCN(R) 1946-49; 1st Hussars: HLCoI 1975-78, HCol 1978-99.

BGen G. de S. "Swatty" Wotherspoon, DSO, ED, CD, AdeC, QC. RMC 26-30; PreWar: GGHG; WWII: CO SAR(29 Recce), HQ 4 Armd Bde; PostWar: CO GGHG 46-48, Comd 19 Armd Bde 49-51, Pres RCACA (Cavalry) 53-54, Col Comdt RCAC 68-73 (in memoriam).

REGIMENTAL COMMANDING OFFICERS

MGen Clive J. Addy, OMM, CD. 4 PLDG; FGH; 12eRBC; RCD: CO 1980-82, Comd 4CMBG 91-92; Comd LFWA 93-96; National Chairman FMUSIC 1997- .

Col The Hon Justice Geo. Addy, ED, CD. RdeHull 36; WWII: RdeHull 46, C0 56-9, HCoI 73-88; Pres RCACA (Cavalry) 63 (in memoriam).

LGen Paul G. Addy, CMM, CD. 8CH; 12eRBC CO 1977-79, Comd 5GBMC 1983-85; ADM Per 1992-95; CNMR NATO 1995-98.

BGen E.A.C. Amy, DSO, OBE, MC, CD. RMC 1938-40, WWII Italy: Calg R, Ont R; NWE: CO CGG; Post War: Comdt RCACS 49-51; CO RCD 53-56, Col of the Regt 70-74; DArmd 61-64; Comd 1CMBG 65-66, Comd 4CMBG 66-68; Col Comdt RCAC 77-78.

LCol Robert A. Attersley. Honorary Lieutenant Colonel The Ontario Regiment (RCAC) 1998- .

Colonel Ian D. Barnes, CD, BSc. LdSH(RC) 1963; Comdt RCAC/Arrnour School 1984-86; DS CFCSC 1986; Attaché Ankara 1991-93.

Colonel Eric L. Barry, KStJ, CD. 17 DYRCH 1949-57; Royal Canadian Hussars (Mtl) 1958-64, CO 1960-64; HQ 10 Militia Group 1965.

LCol E.F. Bastedo. COTC Osgoode Hall 39-41; OntR 41; 12 Manitoba Dragoons (18 CAR) 42-46(UK, NWE); OntR 46-51, CO 48-51.

Col M.H. Bateman, CD. WWII: Sher Fus Regt; RCD 46 ; Comdt RCACS 1958; RCD: CO 61-63, Colonel of the Regt 74-78.

Colonel Georges A. Bordet, CD. RMC 64; CIntC 64-68; 8CH 68-69; 12eRBC 1969-95, CO 1985-87.

LCol N.A. Buckingham, CD. WWII: RMR(32 Recce Regt), Int 0ffr GGFG (21CAR) & 4 Cdn Armd Bde; 0C D Sqn LdSH (RC) (NATO) 53-55; D Ceremonial 1960/1985.

LCol Douglas J.Burke, MC. WWII: 4PLDG; CO 14CH 47-54 & 55-60; Pres RCACA (Cavalry) 1960 (in memoriam).

Colonel G. Allan Burton, OC, DSO, ED. GGHG from 1933, WWII: OC 'C' Sqn/Regt 2IC; Post War: CO 48-50, HLCol 62-71.

LGen Michael Caines, CMM, CD. RMC 71; 12eRBC71, CO 87-89; Comd CTC 94-96; Comd CFRETS 96-99; ADM Per 99-00.

LCol W. Campbell, CD. 3R22eR – MG Pl Comd Korea 53-54; 8CH-Adjt 1961-62; CO 12eRBC 1971-73.

LCol George Campbell, CD. WWII: 40 Tpr RMR(MG), 41 COTC McGill, 42-45: 12 Man. Dragoons; Post War: 1H 48-65, CO 59-63, Adv.18 Mil Gp.

BGen P.H.C. Carew, CD. BCD 48-51, HLCol 87-90; LdSH(RC)1951-65, Korea 52-532-53, Cyprus 66, CO 70; FGH 65-70; RCD: CO 70-72, Col of Regt 90-93; Comdt CLFCSC 79-82.

LCol S.L. Caseley, MC, ED, CD. WWII: PEI Lt Horse 41; CAC41, SAR(29 Recce)42-45; Post War: PEIR OC B Sqn, HLCol 87-00.

Colonel A.K. Casselman, CD. OC A Sqn RCD Cyprus 65; CO Army Air Tac Trg School 61-68; CO 403 Hel Sqn 68-71; Armd Directorate 71-73.

Col R.J. Chapman, MMM, OStJ, CD, AdeC. RCAPC 70-73; OntR (RCAC) 73, RSM 82-87, CO 94-97; DComd 32 CBG 97-99; Comd 33 CBG 99- .

BGen A.G. Chubb, DSO, CD. RMC 36; WWII: BM 4CAB; CO BCR (28CAR) 44-45; Post War: CO LdSH 47-51, Comd CALE 62-65 (in memoriam).

LCol Bernie Ciarroni, CD. RCH1967, SSM B Sqn 74-77, RSM 77-80, RSM Area Battle Sch.78-79, OC A Sqn 88-91, CO 97-00.

Colonel W.L. Claggett, CD; RMC 60; LdSH(RC) 60; Ist Hussars: CO 86-8; Comd London Dist 89/91; Pres RCACA (Cavalry) 93-94.

LCol Iver Clifton, CD, AdeC: Army Cdts 1945-47; 14th Cdn Hussars: 67-68, CO 65-68; President Army Cdt League of Cda 88-91.

Lieutenant Colonel Stewart G. Cober, CD, PhD: Queen's York Rangers (1st Americans) (RCAC) 1980, CO 1995-99.

LCol John S. Cochrane, CD: SherH 71-77; RCH (Montreal) 77, OC B Sqn 80-83, CO 84-87; Comd Mtl Dist 88-91.

LCol C.S. Coles, CD: Ont Rs: Recce/Tpt/QM/Recce BC/OpsO/OC Recce & HQ Sqn, G3 MilDist Toronto, 2IC, CO 97/2000.

Colonel Chris J. Corrigan, CD, MA: 8th Canadian Hussars (PL) 1972, CO 89-91; Commander LFCA 1999- .

LCol W. Coupland, OMM, CD; Army Cdts.51-3; 19 Med Regt RCA(M) 53-5; SALH 55-7; 8CH 57-93; Comdt RCAC(S) 79-81.

Lcol Pierre Couture; Cadets de l'Armée 55/56, Régt de Mais (Milice) 56/7; Lcol hon 12e Régt blindé du Canada (Milice) 97- .

LCol J. Doug Crashley, CM, CD, AdeC; COTC 39; GGHG: WW II 1940-45 & from 1946, CO 52/54; Pres RCACA (Cavalry) 1961.

M. Roland O. Cyrenne, 12e Régiment blindé du Canada (Milice) à Trois-Rivières, Co-Président Les Amis du 12eRBC(M) 1999- .

LGen. J.K. Dangerfield, CMM, MSC, CD; BCR; LdSH(RC) 1959; 8CH; DArmd 70-73; NATO: Comd 4CMBG 84-86; Comd 1 Cdn Div 89-91; RCD: CO in NATO 74-76, Col of the Regt 1998- .

Capt Frank P. Davidson. RCAC 40-45, Tpr/Cpl/Sgt/OCdt/2Lt/Lt; Fort Garry Horse (10 CAR) NWE: Tp Ldr/IO/Historian 44/45.

Colonel Christopher J.R. Davis, CD; RCD 76-81; 8CH 82-present; Comdt RCAC/Armour School 93-95; Dir Land Requirements 98- .

LCol Terry A. Davis, CD; I 2eRBC 1980-99, OC D 91-92, CO 1997-99; CO 92nd Tpt Coy Cambodia '92; COS 36 CBG 96-97.

Colonel Des Deane-Freeman, CD; RMC 1936; LdSH(RC) 1936, Guides Cup 1939, CO 1951-54; WWII – Italy and NWE.

LCol John C. Drake, BA, LLB :President Drake Goodwin Corporation; Honorary LCol 1st Hussars 1999- .

LCol H.R.S. Ellis.DSO. PreWar: 15 Med Bty, St John Fus, NB Hussars; WWII: 8PL(NB)H (5CAR) (sqn comd); HLCol 8CH 1992-95.

LCol W.T.E. Finan, CD; WWII 1940-45:4PLDG, TRR (12CAR); RCD 1946, UNEF:OC Recce Sqn RCD 59-60; CO RCD 65-67.

Col Bernard Finestone, CD. COTC'37; WWII 41-45: BCD(9 CAR), IO 5 Armd Bde & 5Armd Div; BCD: HLCoI 90-97; HCol 97- .

LGen J.A. Fox, CMM, CD. 8CH 57-65; LdSH CO 71-73, D Armd 74-77; Comd 4CMBG 78-80; Comd FMC 86-89; Col of the Regt LdSH 1992-2000.

Col W.G. Fulton, MSC, CD. RMC '72 , 8CH; RCD; UNEF 78-79; Comdt RCACS 91-93; COS UNM in Haiti 94-96; DArmd 96- .

MGen J.C. Gardner, CD. RMC 40; RTR 1940-44 West Desert/Eritrea/Italy/ Escaped POW; LdSH 46-58; FGH CO 58-61; Comd 4CMBG 68-70; Dep Dir Intl Military Staff (NATO) 72-75; Dir Gen Land Ops & Doctrine 75-78.

LGen James C. Gervais, CMM, CD. RMC 1962; RCD 62-70; 12eRBC: 1971, CO 73-75; Comd 5 GBMC 85-87; Comd FMC.

Col J.W. Gibson, CD. Windsor R:58 Tpr/Sgt/Lt, CO 73-77, HCol 93-97; Comd Windsor Mil Dist 77-80; Pres RCACA (Cavalry) 80-81.

Lieut David H. Gilmour. Governor General's Horse Guards.

LCol I.T. Goodine, CD. ROTP 52-56; RCE, RCA 56-59, 8CH 59-62; 65-67 OC 21 Ind Fd Sqn RCE; 8CH CO 1967-68.

LCol Edwin A. Goodman, PC, OC, QC. WWII 40/45: FGH(10 CAR) m.i.d.; HLCol Queen's York Rangers (1st Americans) 1995-00.

Capt D.H. Gould, BA, MD, CM, CD: McGill COTC (RCACS & RCD) 51-53; RCH (Mtl) 53-58; Med Offr 59th Fd Regt 67-73.

Colonel J.W. Graham, ED, QC; PreWar: Governor General's Horse Guards; WW II: 1st Hussars; HLCoI GGHG 1970-75.

Colonel W.F. Bill Grainger, CD; WWII: 1939-45: SherFusRegt (27CAR); Post War -G&SF: 1950-68, HLCol 92-97; HCol 97- .

LCol Ian MacD. Grant, DSO, CD: WWII: BCR(DCO) 40-3, TRR (12 CAR) 43-6; LdSH(RC) 46-71, OC Recce NATO 57, CO 61-64.

LGen J.A. René Gutknecht, CMM, OStJ, CD.LdSH(RC):CO 68-70; Col of Regt 86-92; Comd 5GBMC 75-76; Col Comdt RCAC 93-96.

Col I.M. Haldane, CD:Army Cdts, 56 Fd Bty; WW II 56 Bty 40; 8CH 43-6 UK, Italy; NWE, HLCol 8CH 79-83; HCol 22 Svc Bn 85-88.

BGen The Hon Justice D.J. Halikowski, OMM, CD, AdeC. OntR:67, CO 86-90; Comd TD 91-4; HQ LFCA:A/C0S 94-9, DComd 99- .

Colonel W.F. Hayball, CD; WWII: OntR 1940/42; RCNVR – Defensively Equipped Merchant Ship 42/47; HCol The Ont R 94- .

LCol Donald G. Hearn: Pres & CEO Hearn Group: Army Cdts at W.D.Lowe; Honorary LCol The Windsor Regiment (RCAC) 1999- .

MGen W.A. Howard, CMM, CM, CD, QC.WWII; Post War: KOCR: CO 54-57, HCol 73-87; Chief of Res; Col Comdt RCAC 87-90.

Col Frank J. Hull, CD; 6th Armd Regt (1st H) 1948; 1st H (RCAC) CO 63/66; Comd London Dist 73/77; Pres RCACA (Cavalry) '68.

LCol Peter W. Hunter CD. GGHG from 1953, CO 1965-67, HLCol 1992 to present; Co-Chair Reserves 2000.

LCol Robert A. Karn, CD; Army Cdts 55-6; Elgin R (RCAC) 56-75; Windsor R O/Cdt 59-60; London MD 69-70; Elgin R CO 71/75

Col David F.B. Kinloch, CD; cotc 1934; BCD 1939, WWII (9 CAR), CO 47-51, Comd 27 Mil Gp 63-64; BCD Hon Col 1973-97.

MGen C.G. Kitchen, CD. COTC 50-52; LdSH(RC) 53-58; FGH 59-67 (OC Recce Cyprus); RCD CO 67-69; Comdt CFCSC 78-81; Defence Attaché Pakistan, Iran, Washington, DC; DCORAE 82; External Affairs 82-85.

LCol Karl H. Kramell, CD; 8CH(PL) 1958/72; RCD 72/77; l2eRBC 77/84; RCH(Mtl) 85/97, CO 94/97; President Friends RCH.

Col J.P.P.J. Lacroix, CD:12eRBC 78-81, Cyprus 90-91, CO 95-97; RCD (NATO) 81-84; RCACS 85-87; FMC HQ 92-93; RMC DCdts 99- .

Lcol Daniel Lafleur, CD, OStJ. CIL Offr 73-87; Régt de Hull 87, CO 93-96; SO 34 Bde 97-98; ACOS 33 Bde 99- ; VP East RCACA 1996- .

LCol Grant B. Larkin, CD: British Columbia Regiment (DCO) 1948-73, CO 70-73; President RCACA (Cavalry) 1973.

CWO Clarence Layne, CD: CIBC "Employees as Ambassadors Program"; RCAC/RCH 65-84, RSM RCH 82-84.

Colonel Gordon H.Lennard BA, MBA, FICB. King's Own Calgary Regiment: HLCol 1998-99, Honorary Colonel 1999- .

LCol W.D. Little, MC, CD. WWII: FGH (10CAR); Post War: RCACS, RCD, 2IC FGH; Military Attaché Cyprus 1966-71.

LCol W.R.C. Little, CD. WWII:1H (6CAR); Post War: 2IC LdSH58-59; CO FGH 62-65; HLCol G&SF 81-91, Honorary President RCAC Association (Cavalry)1999- .

Col Arthur F. Lungley, CD. BCR(DCO) 1939, WW II-BCR (28CAR), Sqn OC & Regtl 2IC; Post War: BCR Regtl 2IC & CO 55-58.

LCol Herb Locke, CD. A&SH of C 44-45; 17th DYRCH 55-58, RCH 58-71, CO 67/71; RCACA (Cavalry): Pres 72, Sec-Treas 80-92, Asst S/T 93- .

BGen Owen W. Lockyer, OMM, CD. WWII: 42-46 Algonquin R; 8 CH: CO 68-70, Col of the Regt 86-90; Dist Comd NB 70-72; Comd LFAA 74-77.

Col The Hon Justice A.G. Lynch-Staunton, CD. PreWar 15 Light Horse; WWII: 14 Fd & 13 Fd RCA; PostWar: 19 Alta Dragoons 50-64; CO 20 Fd 65-69, HLCol & HCol 20 Fd 76-92; HLCol 5 Fd Regt 1993- .

Colonel Gerald J. Maier, CD, FCAE; King's Own Calgary Regiment (RCAC) Honorary LCol 1984-87, Honorary Colonel 1987-99.

LCol John Marteinson, CD, MA: COTC 56-58; Reg Force 58-87 (FGH-8CH); Militia 87-91; Editor *Canadian Defence Quarterly* 87-95.

LCol The Hon Justice J. Fraser Martin, CD. COTC Sir GWU 56-59, Contingent 2IC 61-67; RCAC/8CH/RCH 59-61; HLCol RCH 1998- .

Major Paul Mast, CD. Army Cadets 1960-63; South Alberta Light Horse 1963-2000 (Trooper to 2IC).

LCol G. Irvine Mathieson, CD. BCR:1962, CO73-74; QYR:75, CO 76-79; Pres RCACA (Cavalry) 82-83, Pres CDA 1986.

LCol F.W. McAndless, CD. 9 Sigs Regt 58-65; 1H 65-67 & 71-72; 9 Sigs Sqn 67-71; London Svc Bn 72, CO 76-79; Elgin Regt CO 81-84, HLCol Elgin R (RCAC) and 31 CER 1996- .

Col James M. McAvity, DSO, MBE, CD. RMC 31; WWII: AFVS/Meaford/UK 39-42; LdSH(RC) 43 CO 44-45, Col of the Regt 66-71.

LCol Alex. F. McIntosh, ED, CD. Calgary R 1928, RSM 38; WWII 39-45: RCAC, SherH; PostWar: KOCR 46, CO 57-60, HLCol 73-84.

LCol Donald G.A. McKenzie, MBA, CD; Queen's York Rangers (1st Americans) (RCAC) 1974, CO 1992-95.

LCol J.W. McNeil, CD. Elgin R 36 – Bugler, Sgt; WWII: RMC 40-2; 4PLDG 42-46 (Italy/NWE); PostWar: Elgin R 1946, CO 58-62.

LCol Charles Meagher, CD: Lieut RCAC 55-57; South Alberta Light Horse 1972-1982, CO 1975-1982.

Col W.K. Megill, CD. RMC 62; LdSH(RC)62-5; FGH 66-9, OC A; 12eRBC 69-77, OC A, HQ, D (Op Essai); LdSH(RC) CO 77-9; CFE 87-92.

BGen R.S. Millar, OMM, CD. 8CH 69-71; RCD 71-73; LdSH(RC) 78-80; KOCR 82, CO 82-86, Comd SAMD 87-90, AB Mil Dist 94-96; DComd LFWA 97-00; Pres RCACA (Cavalry) 87-88; Chairman CDA 1990.

Major Francis H. Milledge, CD. WWII: Sherbrooke Fusilier Regiment (27CAR) 1944-46; Post War: Royal Canadian Dragoons.

MGen Clive Milner, OMM, MSC, CD. LdSH(RC) 58; RCD: CO 76-78; DArmd 80-83; Comd 1 CMBG 85-87; Comdt CLFCSC 87-89; Comd UNFICYP 89-92; National Chairman FMUSIC 1993-97; Col of the Regt RCD 1995-98, ; Col Comdt RCAC 1999- .

LGen W.A. Milroy, DSO, CM, CD, DMilS. LdSH(RC):WWII 2IC, CoI of' the Regt 71-78; Comdt RCACS 60-61 & CLFCSC 66-6; Comd FMC 72-73; ADM (Per) 73-75.

LCol Leo Morin, CD. C.I.L.(N) 63-6; OntR (RCAC) 66, CO 80-83; Pres RCACA (Cavalry) 84-85; DComd TMD 88-94; SSO Armd LFCA 94-97.

LCol J.H. Joe Murray, CD. First Hussars: Cadet Corps London #9 1968-70, Regt 1970, CO 1996-2000, HQ 31 Bde 00- .

Col W.J. Natynczyk, CD. RCD 79-98 CO 96-98; 8CH 86-7; UNPROFOR (Bosnia) 94-95; Comd CCSFOR Bosnia 98-99; J3 Ops NDHQ 99- .

LCol W. Robert Newman, OStJ, CD. 4 Colm RCASC 56-65, 32 Tpt Coy 65-69; 1H:1969, CO 75-79; Comd London Mil Dist 80-83.

LCol Ronald E. Newton, CD, BSc(Mil). WWII: Three Rivers Regiment (12CAR); Post War: RCD 1946, LdSH(RC) 1951; Comds & NDHQ Staff.

Col E.R. Nurse, CD, MA. RHLI 60-63, 8th Canadian Hussars (Princess Louise's) 63-71, RCD 71-76, 8th CH(PL) 76-96, CO 81-83.

BGen Gordon J. O'Connor, OMM, CD. RCD; Commandant RCAC/Armour School 1976/78; CO Royal Canadian Dragoons 1978/80.

Lieutenant Colonel Charles G. Phipps, CD. 6th Armoured Regiment (1st Hussars):1951-68, Commanding Officer 1H 1967-68.

BGen S.V. Radley-Walters, CMM, DSO, MC, CD. WWII: Sherbrooke Fusilier Regiment; PostWar: RCD; 8CH(PL):CO 64-65, Col of the Regt 71-73; Comdt RCAC School 64-65; Comd 2 Bde 69-71; Comd CTC 71-73; Col Comdt RCAC 80-87.

LCol W. Martin Raine, CD: Army Cdts 54/56; RCAF 2405 AC&W Sqn 57/61; Hal Rifles 63/65; 1ST Fd Regt 65/75; KOCR 82/89, CO 86/89.

Lcol Guy Reny, CD. RCD, 12e Régiment blindé du Canada 1968, CO 1979-78; HQ NATO 1990-2002.

F/L Howard B. Ripstein, CEM, MBA, CA. 6th DCRCH 1939-42; RCAF 1942-45, Air Res 1948-58.

LCol Dick Roach, CD. 14 Cdn Hussars Cadets 47-51; 14 CH 1952; King's Own Calgary Regiment 1953-71, CO 1968/71, Museum Curator 96- .

Col George Routley, CD. 17th Dukes 1939; WWII: 7th Recce Regt (17H) 15CAR; 17th DYRCH:1946/50, HLCol RCH(Mtl) 80/91; HCol 91- .

Major Bruce Rutherford CD. WWII: NWE- RCD; Post War: LdSH(RC) from 1949; RCAC School/Combat Arms School.

Col The Hon R.C. Rutherford, MBE, CD, QC. WWII: G&SF 40-43, 7/11H 43/5; PostWar: GGHG 46-61, CO 56-61, HLCol 76-80; HCol G&SF 80-97.

Brigadier T.J. "Old Tom" Rutherford, CBE, ED. G&SF:WWI, CO 1925-9; WWII C0 1940-41, Comd 1CAB 41-43, Comd CACRUs in UK and Senior Advisor Canadian Armoured Corps 43-45; Honorary Colonel G&SF 60-76 (in memoriam).

LCol Jack Sader, CD. WWII 1940-5: 14CH (8th Recce); Post War: Adjt 10 Field 55-7; Adjt 20th Armd 57-62; HLCol Sask Dragoons 1994- .

Lcol Gilles Séguin, 12eRBC (Milice); Major honoraire 85-90, Lcol hon 1990-7, Président Les Amis du 12eRBC (M) à Trois-Rivières 1999- .

Colonel George T. Service, CD. FGH 1960-72; 12eRBC 72-83, CO 81-83 (Valcartier and Cyprus); DComdt CLFCSC 83-85.

LCol J.P. Seymour, CD. Air Cdts 66-69; CIL 69-71; QY Rangers 71-79; British Columbia Regiment (DCO) 80-96, CO 1991-95.

LCol David A. Sproule, CD. RCD 1960-72; LdSH(RC) 72-77; SSO Ops NRHQ 74-77; Militia: BCR(DCO) 1959-60 & 1987-93, CO 89-92.

Colonel Robert W. Stanley, CD, AdeC; FGH 1960-74; BCR(DCO) 74-85, CO 82-85; Comd BC Dist 91-94; Pres RCACA (Cavalry) 89/90.

MGen A. James Tedlie, DSO, CD. WWII: RMR(32 Recce), BCR (28CAR); Post War: Comdt RCAC School 1958-60; DArmd 60-61; Comd 2CIBG 63, & 4CMBG 1964-66; DCDS 1968-70.

Col H.E. Theobald, MC, CD. Argyles(Tk) 1936-41; WWII: FGH (10 CAR) 41-45; RCH (7th Recce)45-46; Post War: 8CH, LdSH, CO FGH 64-65 in Germany & 65-66 in Calgary, DComd CTC Gagetown 1967-71.

Colonel J.W. Toogood, EM, CD. BCR(DCO) 1939, WWII Sqn OC, 21C, CO 45-46 & Post War CO 46-50, HLCol 63-92, HCol 92-96 (in memoriam).

Lcol Lucien R. Villeneuve, CD: Régt de Hull 1956-79, CO 1976-79; CFHQ (Supp Ready Reserve) 1989-95.

LCol George B. Walker, CD; Windsor Regiment (RCAC): CO 1990-93

BGen G.J.H. Wattsford, CD. RMC 33; LdSH(RC): 33, WWII: 2IC Italy; PostWar: CO RCD 49-51; Comdt RCACS 51-54; Comd Sask Area 62-65.

Captain Ralph "Cowboy" Willis, m.i.d. 14th Cdn Lighthorse 1934-39; WWII 39-46:14th Cdn Hussars (8thRecce), 12 CAR (TRR) Italy & NWE.

LCol Tom A. Wolf, CD. King's Own Calgary Regiment CO 1991-93; Commander 41 Canadian Brigade Group 1996-97.

Lieutenant Douglas G. Wotherspoon, a Friend of the Governor General's Horse Guards and son of BGen G.de S. Wotherspoon.

Mr Michael Wotherspoon, a Friend of the Governor General's Horse Guards and son of BGen G.de S. Wotherspoon.

Ms M.D. Wotherspoon, a Friend of the Governor General's Horse Guards and daughter of BGen G.de S. Wotherspoon.

Mr Richard H. "Swatty" Wotherspoon, a Friend of the Governor General's Horse Guards and son of BGen G.de S. Wotherspoon.

LCol D.W. Wright, CD, AdeC: CO 1st H 82-6; SSO Ops/Trg London Dist; SSO Cdts Cent Reg HQ 88-97; Secy-Treas RCACA (Cavalry) 93- .

LCol Larry J. Zaporzan, CD; 8CH 81-92; RCD 92-98; CI RCAC/Armour School 97-99; CO 8th Canadian Hussars (Princess Louise's) 1999- .

Directorate of Armour

The Royal Canadian Dragoons
Lord Strathcona's Horse [Royal Canadians]
12e Régiment blindé du Canada
The Governor General's Horse Guards
8th Canadian Hussars [Princess Louise's]
The Ontario Regiment (RCAC)
The Queen's York Rangers [1st American Regiment] (RCAC)
12e Régiment blindé du Canada [Milice]
1st Hussars
The British Columbia Regiment [Duke of Connaught's Own] (RCAC)
The South Alberta Light Horse
The British Columbia Dragoons
The Fort Garry Horse
Le Régiment de Hull (RCAC)
The Armoured School

REGIMENTAL SERGEANT MAJORS

CWO D. Anderson, CD. CWO/RSM OntR 2000- .
CWO A. Arelis, CD, CWO/RSM SALH 1968-74.
CWO D.A. Bentley, CD. MWO-CWO/RSM BCR(DCO) 1999- .
CWO E.A. Brown, MMM, CD. CWO/RSM RCD 1968-70 and 1971-73.
CWO J.G. Brown, CD. CWO/RSM Armour Battle School 94-96, RCAC & Armour School 1996-2000.
Capt R.M. Brown, CD. CWO/RSM OntR 96-2000.
Capt J.J. Drygala, MMM, CD, AdeC. CWO/RSM OntR 76-80, Toronto Dist 80-85, CMA 85/87.
CWO J.P. Gilmartin, CD. CWO/RSM BCR(DCO) 1994-96.
CWO D.J. Green, CD. CWO/RSM RCA 1991-92 and RCH(Mtl) 1994-99.
Major C. Levesque, CD. WO1/RSM 8CH(PL) Regular 1965-66.
Captain K.H. Maybee, OMM, CD. RSM/12eRBC Regular 1984-87.

CWO B.N. McLean, CD. CWO/RSM Windsor R (RCAC) 1992-95.
Major D.T. Mezzabotta, CD. CWO/RSM GGHG 1979-82.
Major D.W. Parry, CD. CWO/RSM OntR 1989-90.
CWO T. Smith, CD. CWO/RSM SALH 1999- .
CWO J. Stecyk, CD. CWO/RSM BCD 1995- .
Major R.D. Trottier, CD. CWO/RSM Windsor R (RCAC)1989-92.
CWO J.G. Tuffin, CD. CWO/RSM 1st Hussars 1972-77, London Dist 77-87, LFCA 87-89.
CWO T.E. Urbanowski, CD. CWO/RSM RCAC/Armour School 1987-9, CFB Gagetown 89-90 and CTC 90-2.
Captain J. M. Vanthournout, CD. CWO/RSM Windsor R(RCAC)1995-99.
CWO J.D. Vienneau, CD. CWO/RSM RCAC/Armour School 1993-94.

SQUADRON COMMANDERS

LCol J.R. Aubry	Maj F.N. Clifford	Col A.S. Henry	LCol W.R.F. McKee	LCol C.D. Thomas
Maj H.A. Barcelo	Col K.T. Eddy	MGen N.B. Jeffries	MGen P.A. Neatby	Capt C.M. Williams
Maj J.A. Beament	Mr R.G. Ewing	LCol C.O. Judd	Maj W.M. Prince MD	Capt P.J. Worthington
Maj A.C. Beckingham	Maj R.D. Grant	Maj E.C.H. Latham	HLCol P.L. Reid	
LCol J. Benbow	LCol D.E. Green	Maj J.R. MacDougall	Mr D. Shaver	
Maj D.J. Charron	LCol D.A. Henderson	Maj J.L.C. Machabee	LCol S.J. Skea	

TROOP LEADERS

Dr L.L. Allen	Guards Club of Ottawa	LCol R.S. McLeod	Lt J.M. O'Dell (in	Mr L. Struzik
Col J.C. Bond	BGen J.I. Hanson	LCol B. Moore	memoriam)	Mr E.W. Wilson
Maj G.V. Clark	Mr J.D. Knowles	LCol E.M. Moore	Ontario Regiment	LCol F.S. Wotton
LCol J.D. Conyers	Mr J.A. MacMillan	Lt A.P. Morin	Association	
Capt R.H. Dunn	BGen J.A. McGinnis	Col L.J. Noiles	Mr R.E. Royles	
Capt P.B. Edwards	LCol J.R. McLaughlin	Mr E.M. O'Connell	LCol C.J.N. Sproule	

CREW COMMANDERS

LCol K.C. Booth
Mr A. Brown
WO H.K. Brown
WO J.F. Brown
LCol D. Calfas
Mr P.J. Ceasrine
Capt C.E.G. Chance
Capt D.I. Chant
LCol J.V. Davies
Mr L.B.R. deCotret
LCol G.deV. Domville
Mr B.A. Flemming
LCol H.K. Forbes

HLCol J.R. Garneau
Maj E.H.P. Garneau
GGFG Association
LCol C.H. Graham
Mr R.D. Grant
Mr J.L. Harris
Sgt G.W. Headley
Mr E.V. Heesaker
LCol J.D. Heine
LCol M.S. Holder
LCol E.M. Irwin (in
    memoriam)
LCol F.W. Johnson

Mr J.M. Jolley
Mr G. Jones
Mr S. Jourard
MGen G.S. Kells
Mrs C.E. Keys
Mr G. Lamy
Col R.J. LeBlanc
Mr J.A. Lowry
Sgt E. Mabee
Maj J.E. Malone
Mr D. McDonald
Mr R. Mead
Mr G.H. Meyers

CWO C.D. Mullins
Mr H.G. Perry
Mrs A.G. Regan
Col D.E. Rive
Col M.W. Robinson
Col H.D. Ross
Mr C.B. Rycroft
Mr A.E. Schnarr
Mr J.D. Scythes
Mr B. Senecal
Col B. Smith
Col G.C. Solar
Mr H.W. Stack

Mr F. Sundborg
Mr E.O. Sutley
Terminal & Cable TC Inc.
Three Rivers Veterans
    Association
Maj B.J. Walsh CD
Capt G.W. Woollard
Mr D. Wotherspoon
Mr G.S. Wotherspoon
Mr R. Wotherspoon
Capt A. Van Rooyen

CREWMEN

Mr L. Albers
Mr M.L. Atkinson
Mr D.C. Baillie
Maj G.W.G. Barling
Mr H.G. Barnes
Mr D.G. Barrow
Lt H.D. Beach
Mr G. Beecroft
Mr R.T. Belliveau
Col J.R. Beveridge
Mr A.G. Blackwell
Mr. M.J. Blanchet
Mrs P.L. Blanchet
Mr B. Blandford
Sgt K. Bracewell
Mr F. Brown
Mr J. Bunting
Maj A.M. Burka
Mr L.J. Burns
Mr S. Campbell
Mr A.S. Canavan
Capt C. Chadderton
LCol R.S. Chamberlain
LCol R.L. Chantler (in
    memoriam)
Mr R.B. Cayford
Maj H.A. Chestnut
Maj W. Clarke
LCol A.F. Coffin
Mr W. Colpitts
Mr J.E. Coombs
Capt B.J. Corbiere
Col A.G. Coulter

Mr R.A. Cunning
Capt M.A.U. Damour
LCol M.B.W. David
Mr. J.R. Davies
Mr E.A. Desjardins
Lt J.A. Despaties
Maj P. Donnelly
Lt E. Doyle
Mr W.E. Falls
LCol J.R. Ferron
Mr M. Fitzpatrick
Capt J.J. Flannery
Mr J.S. Fowler
CWO T.A. Fox
Mr D. Friesen
Maj I.M. Galbraith
Lt K. Gale
Mr J.A. Galipeau
Col J.A. Gardam
LCol R.A. Gauthier
Mr G.J. Groleau
LCol B. Hasiuk
Mr A.A. Hayes
Mr R.A. Hayes
Capt N.S. Hill
Cpl H. Hochgeschurz
Lt R.J. Hodger
Mr N.W. Holbrook
HLCol J.T.F. Horn
LCol R.F. Hubley
Mr A. Hulberg
Mr W. Hunnisett
Capt G.E. Irving

Mr D.K. Jamieson
LCol R.J. Jarymowycz
Mr R.J. Keddie
Mrs L.M. Keslick
Dr R.J. Kimmerly
Mr G. Lancia
Mrs M. Landers-Stoddart
Mr D.E. Larkin
Mr D.G. Latter
Tpr J.R. Leduc
Maj G.P. Long
Mr N.C. MacDougall
Mr G.A. MacKay
Mr A. McCourt
LCol J.J.L. Petit
Lt M.J. McDonald
Mr J.T. McGoey
Tpr N.K. McLeod
Maj M.R. McNorgan
Mr L. Menard
Mr K.P. Merkley
Mr J.C. Mills
Mr E.T. Moore
Mr J.H. Morrison
LCol J.K. Moyer
Col K.A. Munn
Mr D.C. Munro
Mr L. Murphy
LCol P. Nichita
Mr A.F. Nisbet
Mr R.A. O'Neil
LCol J.W. Ostiguy
Mr J.H. Owen

Mr P.E. Paradis
Phoenix Research
    Foundation
LCol W.H. Porter
Capt B.R. Power
LCol J.H. Quarton
Capt K.R. Ramsden
LCol A.J.K. Rasmussen
Mr E.H. Reardon
Mr E. Roberts
Maj J.B.S. Rose
LCol A. Rousseau
Mr W.J. Royer
Sgt W.F. Sandeson
Maj W.J. Schneider
LCol R.G. Sear
Maj W.L. Seasons
Maj Rev R.A. Sharp
Mr M. Shimkoff
Mr L.W. Smith
Mr P.F. Smith
Mr J. Southern
Mr W.A. Spence
Col Hon M. Starr
LCol C.D. Stef
Capt E.A. Stoakley
LCol M.A. Stevenson
Mr R.D. Stoddart
Mr C. Stowe
Capt C.M. Sullivan
Mr D.W. Suttie
Capt P.Thibault
LCol W.J.P. Thomas

Maj R.P. Torpe
Tpr A. Trenton
LCol J.D. Trueman
LCol Dr R.W. Turnell
Capt W.B. Wadds
Lt J.F. Wallace
Mr G. Wallace
Col M.J. Ward
LCol H.R. Warren
Lt L. Weatherhead
Mr E. Wellington
Mr J.C. Wells
HCol R.D. West
LCol E.J. Wesson
Mr E. Whalen
Mr D. White
LCol C.D. Williams
WO D.W. Winterburn
Mr V.N. Wood
Mr W.B. Wyville
Mr G. Yorgan

The King's Own Calgary
    Regiment
The Prince Edward Island
    Regiment
The Royal Canadian
    Hussars
The Sherbrooke Hussars
The Windsor Regiment
The Saskatchewan
    Dragoons

Index